"buy where the dealers buy"

ALFIES
ANTIQUE MARKET
London's biggest & busiest antique market

ALFIES

vintage fashion
20th C design
antique jewellery
clocks & watches
ceramics & glass
posters, pictures, prints
old dolls, toys & games
art deco, art nouveau
textiles, linen & lace
scientific instruments
silver & collectables
antique furniture
old advertising
arts & crafts
kitchenalia

...not forgetting the Rooftop Restaurant!

OPEN 10am-6pm Tuesday to Saturday
13 Church Street Marylebone NW8
Tel 020 7723 6066 www.alfiesantiques.com

MILLER'S

collectables

collectables

MADELEINE MARSH *GENERAL EDITOR*

2004/5
VOLUME XVI

MILLER'S COLLECTABLES PRICE GUIDE 2004/5

Created and designed by
Miller's
The Cellars, High Street
Tenterden, Kent, TN30 6BN
Tel: 01580 766411
Fax: 01580 766100

General Editor: Madeleine Marsh
Managing Editor: Valerie Lewis
Production Co-ordinator: Kari Reeves
Editorial Co-ordinator: Deborah Wanstall
Editorial Assistants: Melissa Hall, Joanna Hill
Production Assistants: June Barling, Gillian Charles, Ethne Tragett
Advertising Executive: Jill Jackson
Advertising Co-ordinator & Administrator: Melinda Williams
Advertising Assistant: Emma Gillingham
Designer: Philip Hannath
Advertisement Designer: Simon Cook
Indexer: Hilary Bird
Jacket Design: Victoria Bevan
Production Controller: Sarah Rogers
Additional Photographers: Emma Gillingham, Gareth Gooch, David Mereweather, Dennis O'Reilly, Robin Saker
North American Consultants: Marilynn and Sheila Brass

First published in Great Britain in 2004
by Miller's, a division of Mitchell Beazley,
imprint of Octopus Publishing Group Ltd,
2–4 Heron Quays, London E14 4JP

© 2004 Octopus Publishing Group Ltd

A CIP catalogue record for this book is
available from the British Library

ISBN 1-84000-863-6

Illustrations by 1.13, Whitstable, Kent, England
Printed and bound by Rotolito Lombarda, Italy

Front Cover Illustrations:
A Carnival glass vase, by Fenton, American, 1910–15, 10in (25.5cm) high. **£40–45 / €55–65 / $65–75 ⊞ CAL**
A coffee grinder, with wood painted base, 1920s–30s, French. **£40–45 / €55–65 / $65–75 ⊞ CEMB**
Jean de Brunhoff, *Babar's Travels,* 1936.

Contents

Acknowledgments

We would like to acknowledge the great assistance given by our consultants who are listed below. We would also like to extend our thanks to all the auction houses, their press offices, dealers and collectors who have assisted us in the production of this book.

BEVERLEY/BETH
30 Church Street
Alfie's Antique Market
Marylebone
London NW8 8EP
(Ceramics)

ALAN BLAKEMAN
BBR Elsecar Heritage Centre
Wath Road, Elsecar, Barnsley
Yorks S74 8AF
(Advertising, Packaging, Bottles, Breweriana)

GLEN CHAPMAN
Unique Collections
52 Greenwich Church Street
London SE10 9BL
(Toys)

COLIN COX
The Camera House
Oakworth Hall, Colne Road
Oakworth, Keighley
Yorkshire BD22 7HZ
(Cameras)

ANDREW HILTON
Special Auction Services
The Coach House, Midgham Park
Reading, Berks RG7 5UG
(Commemorative Ware)

STEVE HUNT
Antique Amusement Company
Mill Lane, Swaffham Bulbeck
Cambridgeshire CB5 0NF
(Amusement & Slot Machines)

DAVID HUXTABLE
S03/05 Alfie's Antique Market
13–25 Church Street
London NW8 8DT
(Advertising & Packaging)

DAVID NATHAN
Vectis Auctions Ltd
Fleck Way, Thornaby
Stockton-on-Tees TS17 9JZ
(Toys)

MALCOLM PHILLIPS
Comic Book Postal Auctions
40–42 Osnaburgh Street
London NW1 3ND
(Comics)

JOHN PYM
Hope & Glory
131a Kensington Church Street
London W8 7LP
(Royal Commemorative)

T. VENNETT-SMITH
11 Nottingham Road
Gotham, Nottinghamshire NG11 0HE
(Autographs)

LESLIE VERRINDER
Tin Tin Collectables
G38–42 Alfie's Antique Market
13–15 Church Street
London NW8 8DT
(Textiles & Fashion)

DOMINIC WINTER BOOK AUCTIONS
The Old School
Maxwell Street
Swindon
Wiltshire SN1 5DR
(Books)

JAMIE WOOLLARD
Offworld
142 Market Halls
Arndale Center
Luton, Bedfordshire
LU1 2TP
(Sci-Fi)

How To Use This Book

It is our aim to make this guide easy to use. In order to find a particular item, turn to the contents list on page 7 to find the main heading, for example, Ceramics. Having located your area of interest, you will see that larger sections may be sub-divided by subject or maker. If you are looking for a particular factory, maker, or object, consult the index, which starts on page 453.

Caption
provides a brief description of the item including the maker's name, medium, date, measurements and in some instances condition.

Cross Reference
directs the reader to where other related items may be found.

Information Box
covers relevant collecting information on factories, makers, care, restoration, fakes and alterations.

Price Guide
these are based on actual prices realized at auction or offered for sale by a dealer, shown in £sterling, Euros and $US. Remember that Miller's is a PRICE GUIDE not a PRICE LIST and prices are affected by many variables such as location, condition, desirability and so on. Don't forget that if you are selling, it is quite likely you will be offered less than the price range. Price ranges for items sold at auction tend to include the buyer's premium and VAT if applicable. The exchange rate used in this edition is 1.6 for $ and 1.42 for €.

Further Reading
directs the reader towards additional sources of information.

Source Code
refers to the 'Key to Illustrations' on page 443 that lists the details of where the item was sourced. The 🔨 icon indicates the item was sold at auction. The ⊞ icon indicates the item originated from a dealer.

Introduction

There are many factors that make an object collectable, such as design, maker, medium, age and rarity. Perhaps most important is a quality that doesn't belong to the item at all – the passion of the purchaser.

This passion can be the major element in determining an object's value. In terms of materials and craftsmanship, the 1912 football programme illustrated in Record Breakers (page 429) has very little intrinsic merit, but its value to the football fan who purchased it was clearly immense, since he was prepared to pay the highest price ever achieved at auction for a single football programme: £14,400 / €20,500 / $23,000. Like many of the items illustrated, this programme was not originally thought of as being valuable. One of the ways objects can become collectable is by being so ordinary that most people simply don't bother to keep them. Our sections devoted to Bottles and to Comics (subjects also featured on the Record Breakers page) provide a perfect illustration of this.

Something else that people tend not to keep is packaging, particularly when it comes to children and toys. This year we devote an expanded section to toys, reflecting the fact that the market is currently extremely buoyant, with objects such as space toys and diecast vehicles making top prices.

This is another area that is clearly driven by passion as grown men buy back the favourite toys of their childhood. However, in this instance at least, love is not blind but extremely discriminating. The examples that make the highest prices are those where the object and its packaging are in the best possible condition. Paradoxically, this can be even rarer with more recent toys, which being carded rather than boxed, the packaging has to be ripped open in order for the toy to be played with. Perfect examples command a huge premium, such as the Star Wars action figures shown on pages 405–406.

Another aspect of the market that is currently very strong is vintage fashion which, over the past couple of years, has become far more mainstream. Film stars wear vintage designer gowns at awards ceremonies, some department stores now have vintage sections, and antique clothing is regularly featured in modern fashion magazines. This year we look at the history of the handbag (undoubtedly one of the most collectable accessories), ladies' fashion from underwear to outerwear and men's dress from 19th-century top hats to 1950s American jackets.

American costume jewellery features strongly in our Jewellery section. We also look at the charm bracelet, a favourite accessory in the 1950s and '60s and now undergoing a revival in popularity after a period in the doldrums.

It is fascinating to witness how an object progresses from being a state-of-the-art modern creation to an out-moded chuck-out, and finally to a collectable antique. A case in point is cine cameras, to which we devote a special section in this year's guide. Although one might imagine that new technology would have rendered these items entirely redundant, they are sought after today not just by collectors but by young film-makers wanting to make animated films. Vintage technology is covered in sections of the guide devoted to Radios and Televisions, Science, Telephones and Amusement Machines, where computer and video games are a developing area of the market.

For those who don't want to sit there pushing buttons, vintage or otherwise, the guide offers many more traditional and decorative collectables. Our Ceramics section looks at a host of different factories; features in Glass include Scandinavian glass, pressed glass and humble Pyrex; our expanded Silver section explores the history of cutlery and the silver spoon. The great joy of Miller's Collectables Price Guide is its infinite variety. There are pages dedicated to the collectable pig, desirable dog collars, bicycles and medical implements. Objects range in value from under £5 / €7 / $8 (see Pocket Money Collectables pages 426–427) to collectables worth thousands. The oldest items in the guide are small antiquities dating from the 2nd millennium BC and we end with Collectables of the Future, which this year includes Concorde material, a Harry Potter train set, a beer bottle decorated by Tracey Emin and a programme for the 2003 Rugby World Cup Final.

If you have any suggestions for subjects that you would like to see covered in this guide, please let us know. Collecting is a huge joy, and one that we want to share with you. Thank you for your support and good luck.

Madeleine Marsh

Advertising & Packaging

◀ **Two Colman's Mustard booklets of children's stories,** 'The Old Village Green' and 'All Over the World', c1890, 5 x 4in (12.5 x 10cm).
£25–30
€35–40
$40–50 ⊞ J&J

A James Keiller & Son's Marmalade ceramic shop display jar, c1890, 10in (25.5cm) high.
£160–200 / €230–290
$260–320 ⊞ SMI

A Cadbury's 'Welfare' Chocolates wrapper, mounted, c1890, 3 x 11in (7.5 x 28cm), framed and glazed.
£70–75 / €95–105
$110–120 ⊞ AAA

A Keen's Mustard glove button hook, 1900, 2½in (6.5cm) long.
£25–30 / €35–40
$40–50 ⊞ HUX

A Joseph Cawston & Sons ceramic inkwell, c1900, 2¾in (7cm) high.
£80–90 / €115–125
$130–145 ⌁ G(L)

A Schweppes boot bottle opener, 1900, 3in (7.5cm) high.
£25–30 / €35–40
$40–50 ⊞ HUX

A Grimwades ceramic rolling pin, with wooden handles, decorated with pictures and descriptions of other Grimwades products, some restoration, c1900, 19in (48.5cm) long.
£570–680 / €800–970
$910–1,100 ⌁ BBR

A Carters of Poole ceramic paperweight, modelled as a lion, 1900–10, 6in (15cm) wide.
£165–185 / €230–260
$260–290 ⊞ MURR

A Chocolat Lombart tin-covered jotter pad, 1905, 4in (10cm) high.
£80–90 / €115–125
$130–145 ⊞ HUX

A Fry's give away tin folding ruler, 1905, 12in (30.5cm) long.
£125–140 / € 175–200
$200–220 ⊞ HUX

Items in the Advertising & Packaging section have been arranged in date order within each sub-section.

An Onoto pen mahogany counter display case, with bevelled glazing, the rear door enclosing three sloping shelves fitted for pens, c1905, 21in (53.5cm) high.
£300–360 / € 430–510
$480–580 ✗ PF
Onoto pens were made by the English company De la Rue, and first appeared in 1905.

A Hill, Evans & Co Pure Malt Vinegar tin sign, c1910, 12in (30.5cm) high.
£130–145 / € 185–200
$210–230 ⊞ SMI

A Yorkshire Pride Cigars tin spinner, c1910, 2¾in (7cm) high.
£35–40 / € 50–55
$55–65 ⊞ HUX

A Viyella Knitting Yarn package and contents, 1920s, 4in (10cm) high.
£10–14 / € 14–20
$16–24 ⊞ Do

A Sodax Ltd wooden crate, with 12 bottles, c1920, 12in (30.5cm) wide.
£55–60 / € 80–85
$90–95 ⊞ AL

◀ **A Vimto tin clicker,** 1920s, 2in (5cm) high.
£35–40 / € 50–55
$55–65 ⊞ HUX

A John cigarette packet, 1920s, 2½in (6.5cm) high.
£10–14 / € 14–20
$16–24 ⊞ Do

A CWS Pelaw Polish tin advertising yo-yo, 1920s, 2in (5cm) diam.
£40–45 / € 55–65
$65–70 ⊞ HUX

A Gill's Pork Sausage ceramic stand, 1920s, 17in (43cm) diam.
£225–250 / €320–350
$360–400 ⊞ SMI

A Holbrook's Worcestershire Sauce shop display package, to contain glass bottles, 1920s, 10in (25.5cm) high.
£180–200 / €250–280
$290–320 ⊞ AAA

A Marshalls' Semolina shop display dummy, 1920s, 15in (38cm) high.
£180–200 / €250–280
$290–320 ⊞ AAA

◄ An Atlee's Special Bird Seed Mixture cardboard package, 1920s, 3½in (9cm) high.
£8–12 / €11–17
$13–19 ⊞ Do

Two Card Seed Co seed packets, for Bush Beans and Sweet Corn, 1930s, 4in (10cm) high.
£6–9 / €9–13
$10–15 ⊞ Do

A Favarger Cacao packet, 1930s, 4½in (11.5cm) high.
£10–14 / €14–20
$16–24 ⊞ **Do**

A Good Luck Jar Rubbers packet, 1930s, 3½in (9cm) wide.
£10–14 / €14–20
$16–24 ⊞ **Do**

A Boots the Chemist carved wooden shop sign, 1930s, 48in (122cm) wide.
£900–1,000 / €1,300–1,400
$1,450–1,600 ⊞ **AAA**

Jesse Boot (1850–1931) was the son of a Methodist farm labourer-turned-herbalist and the family had a small shop in Nottinghamshire selling soaps and simple homeopathic remedies. In 1877, Jesse took over a chemist's shop, introducing lines at reduced prices in order to attract a new, working-class clientele. Special offers were advertised by a bell-ringer patrolling the streets of Nottingham. The company began to make doctors' prescriptions, undercutting other druggists by half, and created their own brand products identified by the distinctive Boots logo.

Under the influence of his wife Florence, Jesse also introduced other merchandise such as stationery and the hugely successful Boots Library, where books could be borrowed for 2d a volume. On reaching the age of 70, Jesse sold what was now a chain of 600 shops to a US businessman but, in 1933, his son John lead a group of British financiers to buy back Boots, and that same year saw the opening of the 1,000th Boots store. This store sign dates from this period.

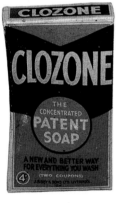

A Clozone soap packet, 1930s, 6in (15cm) high.
£8–12 / €11–17
$13–19 ⊞ **HUX**

A Dunhill The White Spot rubberoid gloved hand counter display, on a base, lighter missing, 1950–60, 10½in (26.5cm) high.
£200–240 / €285–340
$320–390 ⚒ **BBR**

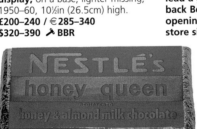

A Nestlé's Honey Queen dummy display chocolate bar, c1955, 4in (10cm) wide.
£8–12 / €11–17
$13–19 ⊞ **HUX**

A Renée Pavy cardboard hat box, 1950s, 13in (33cm) diam.
£7–10 / €10–14
$11–16 ⊞ **HSt**

A Clarks shoe box, 1950–60, 7in (18cm) wide.
£3–6 / €4–8
$5–10 ⊞ **RTT**

◄ **A Royal Doulton model of HMV 'Nipper',** by Millennium Collectables Ltd, limited edition of 2,000 but only 1,000 were actually made, to celebrate the centenary of the use of Nipper in the company's advertising, 2000, 6¼in (16cm) high.
£315–350 / €450–500
$500–560 ⊞ **MCL**

Gollies

The golly first appeared in a series of American children's books written and illustrated by Florence and Bertha Upton from 1895, and featuring two wooden Dutch dolls and a 'golly', inspired by a minstrel-type toy that Florence had played with as a child. Toy manufacturers began to produce gollies and shortly before WWI, one of James Robertson's sons returned from the USA with one of these fashionable toys.

The company began using the golly as a promotional image for their famous jams and marmalades. In 1928 they introduced golly paper labels on the jar, which could eventually be exchanged for enamel badges, thus creating one of the longest running collecting schemes in the UK. Over the decades an estimated 20 million badges were produced until 2002 when, bowing to changing tastes and political correctness, Robertson's retired the golly in favour of Roald Dahl characters.

As well as badges, a host of other golly memorabilia was produced ranging from advertising figures to ceramics. Golly material is still popular with collectors today, hence the value of these items.

◀ A Robertson's Mincemeat cut-out showcard, 1950s, 18in (45.5cm) high.
£135–150
€190–210
$220–240
⊞ MURR

▶ A Robertson's Golly wrist-watch, 1970s.
£55–60
€80–95
$90–95 ⚲ BBR

A Robertson's Golden Shred plaster Golly figure, wired and fitted with a bulb for illuminating the jar, 1950s, 27½in (70cm) high.
£600–720 / €850–1,000
$950–1,150 ⚲ BBR

A Robertson's Golden Shred plaster Golly shop display figure, minor repairs to base, 1950s, 18½in (47cm) high.
£350–420 / €500–600
$560–670 ⚲ BBR

Prices

The price ranges quoted in this book reflect the average price a purchaser might expect to pay for a similar item from a similar source. The price will vary according to the condition, rarity, size, popularity, provenance, colour and restoration of the item, and this must be taken into account when assessing values. Don't forget that if you are selling it is quite likely that you will be offered less than the price range.

▶ A Robertson's Golly teapot, designed by J. & G. Morten, some repair, c1985, 8¾in (22cm) high.
£240–290 / €340–410
$385–465 ⚲ BBR

Posters

A Fry's Milk Chocolate poster, in the original frame, 1903, 21 x 13in (53.5 x 33cm).
£790–880 / €1,100–1,250
$1,250–1,400 ⊞ AAA

A National Savings Association poster, 1930s, 30 x 20in (76 x 51cm).
£135–150 / €190–210
$220–240 ⊞ Do

Cross Reference
See Posters
(pages 294–300)

▶ A Cadbury Bourn-Vita poster, 1930s, 15 x 21in (38 x 53.5cm).
£90–100 / €125–140
$145–160 ⊞ Do

A Turmac Cigarettes poster, by Iwan E. Hugentobler (1886–1972), c1915, 36½ x 25in (93 x 63.5cm).
£300–360 / €430–510
$480–580 ✦ VSP

A Canadian Tinned Soups poster, 1930s, 20 x 15in (51 x 38cm).
£60–70 / €85–100
$95–110 ⊞ Do

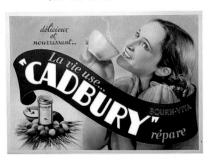

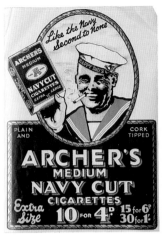

An Archer's Medium Navy Cut Cigarettes poster, 1920s, 12½ x 8½in (32 x 21.5cm).
£40–45 / €55–65
$65–70 ⊞ Do

A Remy's Voedsels poster, 1930s, 20 x 26in (51 x 66cm).
£150–180 / €210–250
$240–290 ⊞ Do

A du Maurier Cigarettes poster, 1930s, 30 x 19½in (76 x 49.5cm).
£140–155 / €200–220
$220–250 ⊞ Do

Advertisement Cards & Showcards

A Mellin's Food cut-out stand-up card, depicting a baby kneeling on a sheepskin rug, 1870–80, 19 x 15in (48.5 x 38cm).
£70–90 / €100–125
$110–145 ➤ BBR

A Morning Glory Cigarettes showcard, depicting an Eastern lady within borders of floral-embossed pillars and a Turkish skyline, c1900, 14 x 9¾in (35.5 x 25cm).
£300–350 / €430–500
$480–560 ➤ VS

◀ **A Komo Metal Paste stone lithograph hanging showcard,** 1920s, framed and glazed, 11 x 8in (28 x 20.5cm).
£220–250
€310–350
$360–400
⊞ AAA

A Mazawattee Tea stone lithograph showcard, c1910, framed and glazed, 10 x 16in (25.5 x 40.5cm).
£120–150 / €170–210
$200–240 ⊞ AAA

A 'Bermaline' Bread showcard, 1910–18, 10 x 12in (25.5 x 30.5cm).
£120–145 / €170–200
$200–230 ⊞ MURR

A Zebo Liquid Grate Polish stone lithograph cut-out showcard, 1920s, framed and glazed, 13 x 9in (33 x 23cm).
£150–175 / €210–250
$240–280 ⊞ AAA

A State Express 333 Cigarettes showcard, 1920s, 14 x 9in (35.5 x 23cm).
£85–95 / €120–135
$135–150 ⊞ Do

A Betta Biscuits stone lithograph
showcard, 1920s, framed and
glazed, 10 x 13½in (25.5 x 34.5cm).
£270–300 / €380–430
$430–480 ⊞ AAA

An Anis del Táup showcard, 1930s,
20 x 13in (51 x 33cm).
£85–95 / €120–135
$135–150 ⊞ Do

A Wye Valley Preserves showcard,
1930s, 14½ x 9½in (37 x 24cm).
£270–300 / €380–430
$430–480 ⊞ AAA

An OXO stone lithograph
hanging showcard, 1920s, framed
and glazed, 14 x 9in (35.5 x 23cm).
£270–300 / €380–430
$430–480 ⊞ AAA

A Canadian Club showcard,
1930s, 16 x 11in (40.5 x 28cm).
£65–75 / €90–105
$105–120 ⊞ Do

A Ski showcard, 1950s,
10in (25.5cm) square.
£12–16 / €17–23
$20–26 ⊞ Do

A Cadbury's die-cut stone
lithograph printer's proof for a
showcard, 1920s, framed and
glazed, 17 x 13in (43 x 33cm).
£250–275 / €355–390
$400–440 ⊞ AAA

A Siscolin Powdered Distemper
showcard, c1935, 21in (53.5cm) high.
£100–120 / €140–170
$160–190 ⊞ Do

A Pierrot Gourmand cut-out showcard, 1950s, 25in (63.5cm) high.
£85–95 / €120–135
$135–150 ⊞ Do

Enamel Signs

A Venus Soap enamel sign, set into a shop chair, c1880.
£400–450 / €570–640
$640–720 ⊞ SMI

A Hudson's Soap enamel advertising sign, c1890, 18 x 10½in (45.5 x 26.5cm).
£500–600 / €710–850
$800–960 ⅃ BBR

An Eye-Gene enamel sign, c1910, 9 x 8in (23 x 20.5cm).
£75–100 / €105–140
$120–160 ⊞ MURR

A Burnard & Alger's enamel sign, 1910–20, 20 x 12in (51 x 30.5cm).
£800–900 / €1,150–1,300
$1,250–1,450 ⅃ BBR

A 1d Monsters double-sided enamel sign, 1910–20, 22in (56cm) long.
£160–180 / €230–260
$260–290 ⅃ BBR

Items in the Advertising & Packaging section have been arranged in date order within each sub-section.

A Nectar Tea enamel sign, c1900, 4½ x 18in (11.5 x 45.5cm).
£65–75 / €90–105
$105–120 ⊞ AAA

◀ **A Sunlight Soap cut-out enamel sign,** c1910, 30½in (77.5cm) high.
£4,500–5,000
€6,400–7,100
$7,200–8,000 ⊞ AAA

Tins

A Palmer Bros biscuit tin, modelled as a work basket, c1898, 8in (20.5cm) wide.
£85–115 / €120–165
$135–185 ⊞ MURR

A Huntley & Palmer's biscuit tin, modelled as a set of eight books, c1900, 6¼in (16cm) wide.
£140–170 / €200–240
$220–270 ↗ BBR

A Callard & Bowser's Butter-Scotch tin, 'The Children's Box', c1900, 4in (10cm) wide.
£180–200 / €260–280
$290–320 ⊞ AAA

Three Rowntree's miniature tins, in the shape of butterflies, c1910, 2in (5cm) wide.
£80–90 / €115–125
$130–145 ⊞ HUX

◄ **A Gallaher's Cut Golden Bar tobacco tin,** c1910, 4in (10cm) long.
£270–300 / €380–430
$430–480 ⊞ HUX
The early portrayal of a female golfer adds interest and value to this tin.

A Lambert & Butler's Gold Leaf Cigarettes tin, 1920s, 3½in (9cm) long.
£45–55 / €65–80
$70–90 ⊞ HUX

A Stolwerck Chocolate tin, modelled as a vending machine, with illustrations of shadowgraphs, c1900, 6½in (16.5cm) high.
£160–180 / €230–260
$260–290 ⊞ HUX

A Hemosine Gaufrettes tin, 1910, 6½in (16.5cm) long.
£40–45 / €55–65
$65–70 ⊞ HUX
The contents are described as regenerating the blood and providing a tonic for the nerves.

LOCATE THE SOURCE

The source of each illustration in Miller's can be found by checking the code letters below each caption with the Key to Illustrations, pages 443–451.

A His Master's Voice gramophone needles tin, c1920, 1½in (4cm) wide.
£16–20 / €23–28
$26–32 ⊞ AAA
Nipper, a mongrel with a touch of bull terrier, belonged to artist François Barraud (1856–1924). When not nipping the backs of visitors' legs (hence his name), Nipper enjoyed looking down the phonograph in the studio. Barraud painted him in this pose, calling the picture 'His Master's Voice'. The Gramophone Company, London, agreed to buy it, on condition that Barraud changed the Edison-Bell phonograph for their own new disc gramophone. Barraud was paid £50 / €70 / $80 for the picture and the same amount for the copyright.

Nipper first appeared in advertisements in 1900 and the Gramophone Company eventually adopted the name His Master's Voice or HMV. In the USA, Nipper appeared on advertisements for the Victor Company and RCA.

Two Mackintosh's toffee tins and a Cadbury's Dairy Milk Chocolate tin, modelled as milk churns, 1925, largest 6in (15cm) high.
£70–90 / €100–125
$110–145 each ⊞ HUX

A Crawford's biscuit tin, in the shape of an aeroplane, 1925, 16½in (42cm) long.
£1,800–2,000 / €2,550–2,850
$2,900–3,200 ⊞ HUX
Early tins shaped as planes, boats, cars and other vehicles are among the most desirable of all biscuit tins. Because children played with them, surviving examples are very rare. As with all tins, condition is crucial to value.

A pencil tin, depicting Charlie Chaplin, c1925, 8in (20.5cm) long.
£60–70 / €85–100
$95–110 ⊞ HUX

A Sutton's Seeds tin, 1920s, 10in (25.5cm) wide.
£75–85 / €105–120
$120–135 ⊞ MURR

A Dawsonia Toffee tin, 1920s, 10in (25.5cm) high.
£250–280 / €360–400
$400–450 ⊞ MURR

A Lyon's Toffee tin, depicting Greta Garbo, 1920s, 7in (18cm) long.
£40–50 / €55–70
$65–80 ⊞ TMa

▶ A Songster gramophone needles tin, 1920–30, 1½in (4cm) wide.
£12–15 / €17–21
$19–24 ⊞ AAA

A Salmon's Toffees tin, 1920s,
12in (30.5cm) diam.
£50–75 / €70–105
$80–120 ⊞ MURR

A Riley's Bunny-Bons toffee tin,
c1930, 9in (23cm) wide.
£20–25 / €28–35
$32–40 ⊞ YR

A Victory V counter display
tin, with a glass front, c1930,
10in (25.5cm) diam.
£45–55 / €65–80
$70–90 ⊞ TMa

A McVitie & Price's biscuit tin,
1930s, 3¾in (9.5cm) diam.
£14–16 / €20–23
$22–25 ⊞ Do

A ReMaCo Typewriter Ribbon
tin, c1935, 2½in (6.5cm) diam.
£9–10 / €12–14
$14–16 ⊞ HUX

A Mickey Mouse lunch tin,
modelled as a basket, French,
c1935, 7½in (19cm) long.
£220–250 / €310–350
$350–400 ⊞ HUX

A Rowntree's tin, 1930s,
7in (18cm) diam.
£18–20 / €25–28
$28–32 ⊞ RTT

A Thorns toffee tin, c1950,
6in (15cm) long.
£10–15 / €14–20
$16–25 ⊞ TMa

▶ A Lyle's Golden Syrup tin,
1950s, 12in (30.5cm) high.
£8–9 / €10–12
$12–14 ⊞ AL

A Huntley & Palmer's biscuit tin,
decorated with the Black & White
Minstrels, 1963, 9in (23cm) square.
£30–35 / €40–50
$50–55 ⊞ HUX

Aeronautica

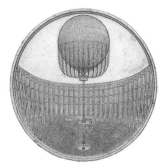

Four cachou tins, each depicting
an aeronautical subject, c1910,
2½in (6.5cm) wide.
**£90–100 / € 125–140
$145–160 each ⊞ HUX**

A gilt-white metal medal, by
Labouche, depicting a balloon
tethered in an enclosure, 1868,
2in (5cm) diam.
**£350–390 / € 500–550
$560–620 ⊞ TML**
This enterprise was the brainchild
of a Frenchman named Henry
Giffard, who brought the balloon
to London from Paris where it
had been exhibited at the
International Exhibition of 1867.
The British venture proved a
financial disaster since few
people were willing to risk their
lives by going up in the basket.

**A pair of Edwardian rosewood
photograph frames,** made from
aircraft propellers, 11in (28cm) high.
**£130–150 / € 185–210
$210–240 ⊞ BSA**

Wreckage from Zeppelin L.31,
shot down during a raid over Potter's
Bar, 1 October 1916, framed and
glazed, 16 x 18in (40.5 x 45.5cm).
**£800–900 / € 1,150–1,300
$1,300–1,450 ⊞ Cas**

**A Schneider Trophy Contest
souvenir programme,** 1929,
11 x 9in (28 x 23cm).
**£50–60 / € 70–85
$80–95 ⊞ MURR**

**A 'Victory' wooden jigsaw
puzzle,** depicting the Imperial Flying
Boat, 1930s, 10 x 9in (25.5 x 23cm).
**£50–60 / € 70–85
$80–95 ⊞ MURR**

◄ **A silver-plated Schneider
trophy,** 1935, 4in (10cm) high.
**£100–120 / € 140–170
$160–190 ⊞ HarC**

► **A gilt-bronze presentation
ballooning medal,** by M. Betannoy,
1936, 3in (7.5cm) diam, in original
fitted leather case, lid marked
'Ministère de l'Air'.
**£250–300 / € 350–420
$400–480 ↗ DNW**

◄ **A photographic
album,** 'Zeppelin-
Weltfahrten', 1932,
14in (35.5cm) wide.
**£130–150 / € 185–210
$210–240 ⊞ ABCM**

A brass model of a bi-plane, 1930s, 8in (20.5cm) long.
£130–150 / €185–210
$210–240 ⊞ HarC

Five issues of *The Aeroplane* **magazine,** 1937, 12 x 9in (30.5 x 23cm).
£5–6 / €7–8
$8–9 each ⊞ COB

An aviation pocket watch, 1930s, 2½in (6.5cm) diam.
£45–50 / €65–70
$70–80 ⊞ COB

A Lakehurst pennant, featuring the Hindenburg, 1937, 24in (61cm) long.
£450–550 / €640–780
$720–880 ⊞ COB

◄ **A Bronze cigarette lighter,** modelled as a pilot holding up a two-bladed propeller, the pilot's head tilts back to reveal the lighter, on a wooden plinth handwritten 'Won by W. Halsall at Moss Bank June 24th 1940', 9½in (24cm) high.
£220–250 / €310–350
$350–400 ➶ H&H

A pair of Luftwaffe flying goggles, German, 1939–45, 3in (7.5cm) high.
£85–95 / €120–135
$135–150 ⊞ OLD

► **A Luftwaffe fur-lined leather flying helmet,** German, 1940s.
£100–120 / €140–170
$160–190 ⊞ COB

A flying outfit, consisting of a C-type helmet, Mk VIII goggles, oxygen mask, flying suit, 1941 pattern boots and gloves.
£450–500 / €640–710
$720–800 ➶ RTo

A Jagger eight-day aircraft clock, 1942, 2½in (6.5cm) square.
£85–95 / €120–135
$135–150 ⊞ TIC

A three-bladed variable pitch propeller and cylinders, from a Wright Cyclone radial engine, corroded, 1943–44.
£80–100 / €115–140
$130–160 ➶ RTo
This type of radial engine was used in B17 Flying Fortress bombers.

Items in the Aeronautica section have been arranged in date order within each sub-section.

A gilt-brass Berlin Air-Lift cigarette case, the front with engraved polychrome map, the reverse machined, 1948–49, 4¾ x 3½in (12 x 9cm).
£180–220 / €250–310 $290–350 ⚒ B(Kn)

A leather flying jacket, American, c1948.
£75–90 / €100–130 $120–145 ⊞ COB

A BEA badge, with gilt thread, 1950s, 2in (5cm) wide.
£25–30 / €35–40 $40–50 ⊞ COB

A Princess Flying Boat calendar, unused, 1951, 10 x 8in (25.5 x 20.5cm).
£12–15 / €17–21 $20–24 ⊞ COB

A BEA magazine advertisement, 1951, 10 x 8in (25.5 x 20.5cm).
£8–10 / €11–14 $12–16 ⊞ RTT

A BOAC ashtray, by Wade, c1960, 6in (15cm) square.
£12–15 / €17–21 $20–24 ⊞ ABCM

A wooden propeller, 1960s, 44in (112cm) long.
£115–135 / €165–190 $185–215 ⊞ TRA

A BOAC Centenary 'Echo' Tour itinerary, 1964, 9 x 4in (23 x 10cm).
£7–10 / €10–14 $11–16 ⊞ COB

A mahogany generator propeller, c1970, 36in (91.5cm) diam.
£180–200 / €250–280 $290–320 ⊞ JUN

◄ **A Concorde leather folder and brochure,** 1990s, 13in (33cm) wide.
£10–15 / €15–20 $16–24 ⊞ COB

Posters

◀ **A Coventry Air Training Club Dance Cabaret poster,** 1938, 30 x 20in (76 x 51cm).
£250–300 / €350–420 $400–480 ⊞ Do

An air crew training poster, 1945, 18 x 24in (45.5 x 61cm).
£75–90 / €100–130 $120–145 ⊞ COB

◀ **An American Airlines/Sabena Belgian World Airlines lithographic poster,** by Edward McKnight Kauffer, signed and dated 1948, 45¼ x 30in (115 x 76cm).
£1,000–1,300 / €1,500–1,800 $1,700–2,000 ➢ BERN

A Sabena Belgian World Airlines lithographic poster, mounted on cardboard, 1950–55, 39¼ x 25¼in (99.5 x 64cm).
£280–310 / €400–440 $450–500 ➢ BERN

▶ **An Air France poster,** by Bernard Villemot, 1952, 39¼ x 24¼in (99.5 x 61.5cm).
£340–410 / €480–580 $540–650 ➢ VSP

A Sabena Belgian World Airlines lithographic poster, mounted on cardboard, 1952, 39½ x 25½in (100.5 x 65cm).
£250–300 / €350–420 $400–480 ➢ BERN

A Sabena Belgian World Airlines lithographic poster, by O. Derycker, mounted on cardboard, 1950s, 39 x 25in (99 x 63.5cm).
£2,300–2,700 €3,200–3,800 $3,700–4,300 ➢ BERN

◀ **A KLM poster,** by Frans Mettes, 1954, 39¾ x 25in (101 x 63.5cm).
£320–380 / €450–540 $510–610 ➢ VSP

An Air-India poster, c1965, 39¾ x 25¼in (101 x 64cm).
£160–200 / €230–280 $260–310 ➢ VSP

LOCATE THE SOURCE
The source of each illustration in Miller's can be found by checking the code letters below each caption with the Key to Illustrations, pages 443–451.

Amusement & Slot Machines

The collecting of slot machines, hugely popular in the USA, took off in the UK with the advent of decimalization in 1971. At that time, old mechanical machines were being discarded in favour of all new electrical machines, with their flashing lights and exciting sounds. The mechanical examples, many of which were still in everyday use 50 or more years after they had been built, rapidly became very old fashioned. Thousands were literally dumped, burned, even thrown off the end of seaside piers – the traditional venue for amusement machines. All this has led to their rarity.

Today there is a strong collectors' market for old machines with prices rising steadily both in the USA and the UK year after year. Just five years ago, machines were only collectable if they dated from the 1950s or earlier, but now certain examples from the 1960s and '70s are sought-after. In the past couple of years interest has also surged in early video games dating from the late 1970s and early '80s, as collectors return to the space-age pleasures of their youth. However, for many enthusiasts the 'beep beep' of video games is simply no match for the whizz of ball bearings and the whirr and clank of traditional mechanical machines. Remember, however, that if you want to play on a vintage slot machine you will also need old-fashioned money: pounds, shillings and pence.

▶ **A J. Meurice & Co Is Marriage a Failure? fortune card dispenser,** London, c1900, 30in (76cm) high.
£400–480 / €570–680 $640–770 ⊞ HAK

An Electra Shooter C slot machine, with original enamel, German, 1899, 27in (68.5cm) high, with a quantity of pfennigs.
£2,000–2,400 €2,800–3,500 $3,200–4,000 ⚲ AMc

An Allwin De Luxe slot machine, restored, 1920–30, 26in (66cm) high.
£600–700 / €850–1,000 $950–1,100 ⚲ AMc
One of the most popular games was the Allwin, which originated in Leipzig. A ball is sent round a metal spiral, falling into a line of winning or losing cups. As with all machines, the structure ensured that winning odds were in favour of the machine and its owner rather than the player.

An Allwin De Luxe slot machine, 1914, 31½in (80cm) high.
£900–1,000 €1,300–1,400 $1,400–1,600 ⊞ AAA

A Jennings Peacock one-armed bandit, c1932, 28in (71cm) high.
£850–950 / €1,200–1,400 $1,350–1,500 ⚲ AMc
The term 'one-armed bandit' reflected both the design of the machine with its single pull-down lever and its unfailing ability to extract money from the player.

A Hooper Automatic Co Electric Volta machine, c1918, 22in (56cm) high.
£450–550 / €640–780 $720–880 ⊞ HAK

A Mills Extraordinary one-armed bandit, built for the Chicago World's Fair, 1933, 27in (68.5cm) high.
£350–400 / €500–570 $550–650 ⚲ AMc

A penny-in-the-slot amusement
machine, in a glazed oak case, 1930s,
14in (35.5cm) long.
£130–150 / €185–210
$210–240   ✗ G(L)

A Daval 'Tit-Tat-Toe' machine,
restored, 1930s, 9in (23cm) wide.
£200–240 / €280–340
$320–380   ✗ AMc

◄ A Mills Black Cherry
one-armed bandit, with
jackpot and escalator,
1945, 28in (71cm) high.
£400–480 / €570–680
$640–770   ✗ AMc

An Ahrens viewing
machine, 1930s,
68in (172.5cm) high.
£700–800
€1,000–1,100
$1,100–1,300   ✗ AMc

A Jennings Sun Chief
one-armed bandit,
1949, 26in (66cm) high.
£1,100–1,300
€1,550–1,850
$1,750–2,100   ✗ AMc

A Brenner ball-past-the-
arrow machine, 1950s,
27in (68.5cm) high.
£360–420 / €510–600
$580–680   ✗ AMc

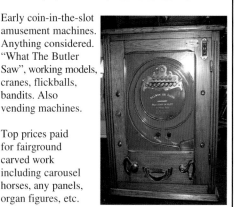

A Mills Golden Nugget
machine, restored,
c1950, 26in (66cm) high.
£700–800
€1,000–1,100
$1,100–1,300   ✗ AMc

A gum ball machine,
American, 1950s,
16in (40.5cm) high.
£100–120 / €140–170
$160–190   ⊞ TRA

◄ A Watling Rol-A-Top one-armed bandit, the case cast with Roman coinage, requires restoration, 1950s, 16in (40.5cm) wide.
£1,300–1,500
€1,850–2,150
$2,100–2,400 ➹ B(WM)

A Bryan's Pilwin Clown Face pinball machine, by Pilwin, 1956, 25in (63.5cm) high.
£700–800 / €1,000–1,150
$1,100–1,300 ⊞ AAA

An Aristocrat Clubmaster one-armed bandit, with playing card reels, Australian, 1960s, 28in (71cm) high.
£150–180 / €210–250
$240–290 ➹ AMc

◄ A Jennings Governor chrome one-armed bandit, 1960s, 28in (71cm) high.
£1,000–1,200
€1,400–1,700
$1,600–1,900 ➹ AMc

A Sega Bell one-armed bandit, with jackpot and escalator, 1960s, 28in (71cm) high.
£250–300 / €350–420
$400–480 ➹ AMc

A Gottlieb's Central Park pinball machine, 1962, 52in (132cm) long.
£450–500 / €640–710
$720–800 ⊞ AAA

◄ A Taito Space Invaders Part II video game, Japanese, 1970s, 68in (172.5cm) high.
£220–280 / €310–400
$350–450 ⚡ AMc

An Aristocrat Nevada Mardi Gras one-armed bandit, 1970s, 28in (71cm) high.
£150–180 / €210–250
$240–290 ⚡ AMc

A Gottlieb's World Fair pinball machine, 1964, 52in (132cm) long.
£450–500 / €640–710
$720–800 ⊞ AAA

▶ A Taito Phoenix arcade table-top game, Japanese, 1980, 34in (86.5cm) wide.
£1,100–1,300 / €1,550–1,850
$1,700–2,100 ⊞ WAm

A Sega Star Wars Trilogy arcade computer game, 1998, 78in (198cm) high.
£1,400–1,600
€2,000–2,300
$2,250–2,550 ⊞ WAm

Antiquities

A cuneiform fired clay tablet, inscribed on both sides with 14 lines of text, repaired cracks and chips, Old Babylonian, c1655 BC, 2½in (6.5cm) high.
£250–300 / €350–420
$400–480 ⋏ B(Kn)
This is accompanied by a full translation, which includes the following explanatory notes: 'The document comes from a large estate such as that of the palace, a temple or a big private estate and records outgoings of barley, and barley products during one calendar month. A sila was about .85 of a litre, and a gur consisted of 300 sila.'

Two carved steatite scarabs, with decorated bases, Egyptian, mid-2nd millennium BC, 1in (2.5cm) wide.
£80–90 / €115–125
$130–145 each ⊞ HEL
Steatite is a form of soapstone.

A bronze Apis bull, wearing a solar disc with frontal uraeus, with suspension loop, engraved details, on an integral plinth, Egyptian, c600 BC, 1½in (4cm) high.
£300–350 / €420–500
$470–560 ⋏ B(Kn)

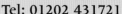
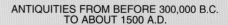

◀ **A socketed and looped bronze axe head,** slightly uneven, c900–600 BC, 3¾in (9.5cm) long.
£155–185
€220–260
$250–300
⊞ A&O

A faïence, calcite and amber eye inlay, some pitting and bitumen residue, mounted, Egyptian, after 600 BC, 3¼in (8.5cm) long.
£650–780 / €920–1,100
$1,050–1,250 ⋏ B(Kn)

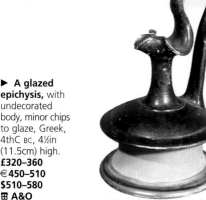

▶ **A glazed epichysis,** with undecorated body, minor chips to glaze, Greek, 4thC BC, 4½in (11.5cm) high.
£320–360
€450–510
$510–580
⊞ A&O

A silver tetradrachma, Greek, Thossos, 3rdC BC, 1½in (3cm) diam.
£200–220 / €285–310
$320–350 ⊞ HEL

◀ **A terracotta figure,** modelled on a contemporary sculpture representing a nature goddess, probably Demester, vent hole to rear, original pigments and slip, Tanagran, c380 BC, 8¼in (21cm) high.
£650–750 / €920–1,050
$1,050–1,200 ⊞ A&O

A bronze openwork fitting, comprising four horse-head protomes issuing from a central embossed point, each mane with two engraved recesses, Scythian, c3rd–2ndC BC, 1¼in (3cm) wide.
£140–160 / €200–230
$225–255 ✦ B(Kn)

A zoomorphic buckle plate, modelled as an animal head with recessed eyes at the top, with three loops, early Anglo-Saxon, 1½in (4cm) long.
£65–75 / €90–100
$100–120 ⊞ ANG

A glass dish, with deep sides and everted rim, the central rondo raised and set on a ring base, light encrustations, c2ndC AD, 7in (18cm) diam.
£350–400 / €500–570
$560–640 ✦ B(Kn)

A bronze spiral bracelet, the shaft with a raised central ridge, a scroll at each end, Celtic, c3rd–1stC BC, 2¾in (7cm) long.
£400–450 / €570–640
$640–720 ✦ B(Kn)

▶ **An agate intaglio ring,** in original gold mount, Roman, 2nd–3rdC AD.
£2,000–2,200
€2,800–3,100
$3,200–3,500 ⊞ NBL

A cruciform brooch, with head plate and zoomorphic foot, the animal head with prominent eyes and enlarged nostrils, linear decoration, hinge lug and long catch plate, top knob and iron pin missing, 5th–6thC AD, 3¼in (8.5cm) long.
£85–95 / €120–135
$135–150 ⊞ ANG

An amber glass juglet, the body with pinched ribs, the indented base with pontil mark, some iridescence, Roman, 4th–5thC AD, 4½in (11.5cm) high.
£200–250 / €280–350
$320–400 ✦ B(Kn)

Architectural Salvage

An iron and steel trivet, c1770, 14in (35.5cm) high.
£520–580 / €740–820
$830–930 ⊞ SEA

A pair of wrought-iron fire dogs, French, c1780, 15in (38cm) high.
£410–450 / €580–640
$660–720 ⊞ SEA

A brass sundial, c1800, 6in (15cm) high.
£320–350 / €450–500
$510–560 ⊞ RGe
Specialist advice should be sought when purchasing sundials as they have been widely copied from Victorian to modern times.

◄ **A pair of York stone ball pillar caps,** 19thC, 18in (45.5cm) high.
£230–250 / €330–360
$370–400 ⊞ WRe

A cast-iron boot scraper, in the form of two winged beasts, 19thC, 10¾in (27.5cm) high.
£250–300 / €360–430
$400–480 ↗ SWO

A Victorian cast-iron boot scraper, 16in (40.5cm) wide.
£100–110 / €140–160
$160–180 ⊞ WRe

◄ **A ceramic bell pull,** c1870, 4½in (11.5cm) diam.
£90–100 / €130–140
$145–160 ⊞ Penn

Cast iron

Antique cast-iron pieces often have diamond registration marks and pattern numbers as well as a maker's name. They tend to be well finished – scar marks or casting bubbles are rare, and any rust will be hard and brown.

A Victorian lavatory pull and chain, 5in (12.5cm) high.
£90–100 / €130–140
$145–160 ⊞ SAT

A cherrywood *faux* bamboo hook, 1900, 14in (35.5cm) high.
£105–115 / €150–165
$170–185 ⊞ MLL

A cast-iron fire surround, with stylized floral decoration and ceramic tiles, c1900.
£420–500 / €600–720
$670–820 ⚹ RTo

A brass handle, c1900, 4in (10cm) long.
£15–20 / €20–25
$25–30 ⊞ Penn

A pine window mirror, glass replaced, c1900, 32in (81.5cm) high.
£105–115 / €150–165
$170–185 ⊞ AL

◀ **A servant's electric bell,** with a wooden surround and a brass bell, c1920, 17in (43cm) wide.
£80–90 / €120–130
$130–145 ⊞ JUN

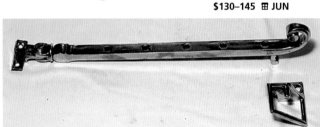

A set of four copper coat hooks, c1920, 6in (15cm) high.
£130–145 / €185–200
$210–230 ⊞ SAT

A brass window casement stay, c1930, 26in (66cm) long.
£35–40 / €50–60
$55–65 ⊞ WRe

A pair of Bakelite and metal drawer tassels, 1930s, 7in (18cm) long.
£60–65 / €85–90
$95–105 ⊞ LBe

A walnut-veneered fire surround, with crossbanding, brushed aluminium grille and three bar electric fire, inoperative, 1930s.
£200–240 / €280–340
$320–380 ⚹ BIG

A Shanks ceramic basin, on a chrome stand, with chrome taps, 1940–50, 35in (89cm) high.
£270–300 / €380–430
$430–480 ⊞ WRe

Door Furniture

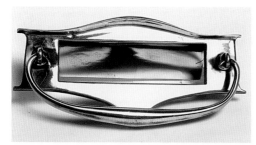

A Regency brass letter plate and door knocker,
9in (23cm) wide.
£180–200 / €260–280
$290–320 ⊞ SAT

A brass hand-shaped knocker and strike,
c1820, 7in (18cm) high.
£360–400 / €510–570
$580–640 ⊞ SAT

A cast-iron door
knocker, in the form of a
Pharoah's head, c1850,
8in (20.5cm) high.
£115–125 / €165–180
$185–200 ⊞ SAT

◄ A Victorian brass
door knocker, in the
form of a lion's mask,
8in (20.5cm) high.
£175–195 / €260–280
$280–310 ⊞ SAT

Four pairs of brass door handles, with floral-
embossed decoration, c1850, 3in (7.5cm) wide.
£320–350 / €450–500
$510–560 ⊞ SAT

**A set of six brass finger
plates,** with floral
decoration, c1900,
12in (30.5cm) high.
£115–125 / €165–180
$185–200 ⊞ SAT

A brass door knocker,
c1860, 7in (18cm) high.
£210–230 / €300–330
$340–370 ⊞ Penn

A bronze door knocker,
in the form of a bear's
head, on a wooden shield,
19thC, 11in (28cm) high.
£700–840
€1,000–1,200
$1,100–1,350 ↗ G(L)

**A pair of brass finger
plates,** c1885,
12in (30.5cm) high.
£90–100 / €130–145
$140–160 ⊞ Penn

An Edwardian brass letter plate, 6in (15cm) wide.
£35–40 / €50–60
$55–65 ⊞ WRe

An Art Nouveau copper door knocker,
9in (23cm) high.
£85–95 / €120–135
$135–150 ⊞ SAT

An Edwardian cast-iron door knocker, by Kenrick & Sons, 9in (23cm) high.
£145–160 / €210–230
$230–260 ⊞ OLA

A brass letter plate, c1910, 7in (18cm) wide.
£35–40 / €50–60
$55–65 ⊞ WRe

Door Stops

A Victorian cast-iron door stop, modelled as a coat-of-arms, 7in (18cm) high.
£250–280 / €360–400
$400–450 ⊞ WAA

▶ **A cast-iron door porter,** in the form of Mr Punch, 1860, 14in (35.5cm) high.
£130–145
€185–210
$210–230
⊞ GBr

Cast-iron door porters

Cast-iron door porters were made in large quantities during the late 19th and early 20th centuries, and came in a wide range of designs. They were robustly constructed so many have survived to the present day, making them relatively inexpensive – only the rarest and most decorative examples command high prices. Some models, such as Mr Punch, have been reproduced, so it is advisable to purchase from a reputable dealer.

A Victorian brass door stop, in the form of a fox's head and a whip, on an iron base, 18in (45.5cm) high.
£150–180 / €200–260
$240–290 ⚒ G(L)

◀ **A cast-iron door stop,** in the form of a cockerel, French, 1930s, 9in (23cm) high.
£60–65 / €85–90
$95–105 ⊞ BET

Art Deco
Glass

An Art Deco Bagley glass vase, c1930s, 9in (23cm) high.
£80–90 / €115–130 $130–145 ⊞ SAT

An engraved decanter, with a silvered stopper and four matching drinking glasses with silvered bases, engraved, 1920–35.
£410–450 / €580–640 $660–720 ⊞ JAS

A Le Verre Français cameo glass vase, by Charles Schneider, acid-etched with three birds, engraved mark, c1925, 7in (18cm) high.
£190–230 / €270–330 $300–370 ⚒ G(L)

A cut-glass cocktail shaker, 1930s, 9in (23cm) high.
£65–70 / €90–100 $105–110 ⊞ GRo

Further reading

Miller's Art Nouveau & Art Deco Buyer's Guide, Miller's Publications, 2001

▶ **A Lalique Ormeaux vase,** decorated with press-moulded leaves, moulded mark 'R. Lalique', c1930, 6½in (16.5cm) high.
£580–640 / €820–910 $930–1,000 ⚒ G(L)

A Lalique Coquilles bowl, engraved mark 'R. Lalique, France', c1930, 9½in (24cm) wide.
£220–260 / €310–370 $350–430 ⚒ G(L)
René Lalique (1860–1945) was the leading glass designer of the Art Deco period and produced a wide range of items for the mass market, most of which were machine-made.

▶ **A glass liqueur set,** comprising a decanter and five glasses, possibly Hungarian, 1930s, 9¾in (25cm) high.
£260–310 / €370–440 $420–500 ⚒ SWO

A glass cocktail shaker, hand-painted, 1930s, 9in (23cm) high.
£65–70 / €90–100 $105–110 ⊞ GRo

Metalware

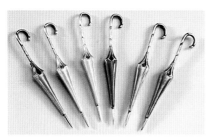

A set of six silver and enamel cocktail sticks, in the form of rolled umbrellas, Birmingham 1922, 2¼in (5.5cm) long.
£120–145 / €170–210
$190–230 TMA

A marble clock garniture, the eight-day movement striking on a bell, inscribed, the top surmounted by a jester playing a mandolin, with side garnitures of tapered design, c1930, 17½in (44cm) high.
£240–290 / €340–410
$380–460 TRM

▶ **An Art Deco chrome picture frame,** 14½in (37cm) high.
£170–190 / €240–270
$270–300 GRo

A pewter Sunray four-piece tea service, by Hutton, Sheffield, with matching tray, 1930s, teapot 5½in (14cm) high.
£100–120 / €140–170
$160–190 SWO

▶ **A chrome ice bucket,** with black Bakelite handles, by Thermos, 1940, 6in (15cm) high.
£40–45 / €55–65
$65–70 JAZZ

A pair of silvered spelter book ends, in the form of squirrels, on marble bases, signed 'Franjou', French, 1920s, 6in (15cm) high.
£175–195 / €250–280
$280–310 SAT

A bronze figure of a lady, by Guerbe after M. Le Verrier, on a marble base, French, c1930, 16¾in (42.5cm) high.
£580–700 / €820–990
$930–1,100 SWO

◀ **A spelter and bronze centrepiece,** in the form of two birds, signed 'Trebig', French, c1930, 23in (58.5cm) wide.
£810–900
€1,150–1,300
$1,300–1,450 SAT

A patinated-spelter figure of a waitress, in the style of Lorenzl, on an onyx base, 1930s–40s, 9½in (24cm) high.
£190–230 / €270–330
$300–370 G(L)

Ceramics

A Thomas Forester Phoenix
ware Ronda bowl, c1920s,
12in (30.5cm) diam.
£110–120 / €155–170
$175–190 ⊞ SAT

◄ A Katzhütte earthenware
figure, in the form of a dancer, on
an oval base, printed mark, 1920s,
12½in (32cm) high.
£360–430 / €510–610
$580–690 ↗ G(L)

A Wade figure, entitled 'Dawn',
some minor restoration, printed marks,
early 20thC, 8½in (21.5cm) high.
£230–280 / €330–400
$370–450 ↗ SWO

A lustre pincushion
doll, German, c1920s,
6in (15cm) high.
£110–120 / €155–170
$175–190 ⊞ MURR

A pair of Hancock & Sons Corona
ware candlesticks, decorated
with Corea pattern, c1922,
8in (20.5cm) high.
£150–165 / €210–230
$240–260 ⊞ PIC

A Hancock & Sons Corona ware bowl,
decorated with Daffodil pattern, c1925,
7in (18cm) diam.
£250–280 / €360–400
$400–450 ⊞ PIC

An earthenware figure, in the form of a lady with a
lamb, glazed in bronze with green patination, c1930,
27½in (70cm) wide.
£220–260 / €310–370
$350–420 ↗ G(L)

◄ A Royal Dux group, in the form of two lovers,
c1925, 13in (33cm) high.
£350–420 / €500–600
$560–670 ↗ EH

A porcelain figure of a
women, by Hutschenreuther,
German, c1930,
10in (25.5cm) high.
£230–250 / €330–360
$370–400 ⊞ ASP

A Torquay pottery lemon squeezer, in the form of a boat, 1930, 6½in (16.5cm) wide.
£30–35 / €45–50
$50–55 ⊞ BET

A Kensington ware wall pocket, 1930, 8in (20.5cm) high.
£45–50 / €65–70
$70–80 ⊞ BET

A Wade figure, entitled 'Conchita', printed marks, c1930, 8¾in (22cm) high.
£260–310 / €370–440
$420–500 ⚲ SWO

A lemon squeezer, with painted decoration, c1930, 2in (5cm) high.
£60–65 / €85–90
$95–105 ⊞ BET

A novelty candlestick, in the form of a lion, c1930, 3in (7.5cm) high.
£65–70 / €90–100
$105–110 ⊞ BET

A Mintons pottery vase, with signature mark, c1930, 6½in (16.5cm) high.
£45–55 / €65–80
$70–90 ⚲ SWO

▶ **A Beswick model of a fawn,** c1930, 6in (15cm) high.
£85–95 / €120–135
$135–150 ⊞ SAT

A Mabel Lucie Attwell string holder and cutter, in the form of two children, c1930, 2in (5cm) high.
£160–175 / €230–250
$260–280 ⊞ MEM

A Keeling Losol ware jug, c1930, 7in (18cm) high.
£75–85 / €105–120
$120–135 ⊞ HarC

A John Shaw & Sons Burlington ware vase, with hand-painted decoration, c1931, 7in (18cm) high.
£60–65 / €85–90
$95–105 ⊞ CoCo

A Tuscan Decoro pottery basket, 1933, 8in (20.5cm) wide.
£40–45 / €55–65
$65–70 ⊞ HO

A Hollinshead & Kirkham pottery bowl, decorated with Autumn pattern, 1933–42, 9in (23cm) diam.
£70–80 / €100–115
$110–130 ⊞ HO

A novelty box and cover, German, 1930s, 5in (12.5cm) high.
£40–45 / €55–65
$65–70 ⊞ BET

A novelty cruet set, German, 1930s, 3½in (9cm) high.
£40–45 / €55–65
$65–70 ⊞ BET

A novelty box and cover, 1930s, 5in (12.5cm) high.
£85–95 / €120–135
$135–150 ⊞ LBe

A Radford jug, decorated with a floral design, 1935–45, 3in (7.5cm) high.
£40–45 / €55–65
$65–70 ⊞ RH

A Delphine ceramic trio, 1930s, plate 6in (15cm) square.
£30–35 / €40–50
$50–55 ⊞ HarC

A Burslem sugar sifter, 1930s, 6in (15cm) high.
£25–30 / €35–40
$40–50 ⊞ BrL

A Fryer Tunstall cake stand, 1930s, plate 8½in (21.5cm) diam.
£25–30 / €35–40
$40–50 ⊞ TAC

A Maling lustre dish, 1930s, 11in (28cm) wide.
£90–100 / €130–140
$145–160 ⊞ TAC

▶ **A Maling lustre jug,** c1930s, 7½in (19cm) high.
£100–110 / €140–155
$160–175 ⊞ TAC

Art Nouveau

A pair of copper finger plates, c1890, 12in (30.5cm) high.
£100–110 / € 140–155 $160–175 ⊞ Penn

A silver dish, by A. J., London 1891, 6in (15cm) wide.
£80–90 / € 115–130 $130–145 ⊞ WAC

A painted wood photograph frame, c1900, 9in (23cm) high.
£145–160 / € 210–230 $230–260 ⊞ HaH

◀ **A Minton Secessionist vase,** decorated with stylized flowerheads, minor damage, impressed mark, c1900, 19in (48.5cm) high.
£510–570 / € 720–800 $820–910 ↗ WW

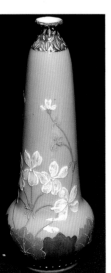

◀ **A pâte-sur-pâte vase,** with floral decoration, Continental, c1900, 7¼in (18.5cm) high.
£310–350 / € 440–500 $500–560 ⊞ ANO

A silver casket, with iris and scroll decoration, Chester 1902, 6in (15cm) wide.
£150–180 / € 210–260 $240–290 ↗ G(L)

A jardinière, by Eichwald, Bohemian, c1900, 8in (20.5cm) high.
£160–180 / € 230–260 $260–290 ⊞ ASP

A 9ct gold pendant necklace, set with peridot and seed pearls, on a fine link chain, c1900, 18in (45.5cm) long.
£200–240 / € 280–340 $320–380 ⊞ DA

A silver and enamel frame, by William Hutton & Sons, 1903, 3in (7.5cm) high.
£300–360 / € 430–510 $480–580 ↗ G(L)

A Liberty Tudric two-handled tankard, decorated with stylized trees and a motto 'For Old Times Sake', stamped 'Tudric 010', 1902–10, 7¾in (19.5cm) high.
£340–410 / €480–580
$540–660 ➶ SWO

A Liberty Tudric pewter charger, the rim applied with seven mother-of-pearl hearts in leafy frames, impressed 'Tudric 0113', early 20thC, 13in (33cm) diam.
£220–260 / €310–370
$350–420 ➶ G(L)

A WMF pewter-mounted glass decanter, with pierced stylized foliate handle and stopper, the base with maidens and water lily feet, early 20thC, 15in (38cm) high.
£650–780 / €920–1,100
$1,050–1,250 ➶ L&E
Württembergische Metallwarenfabrik (WMF) was one of the principal German producers of Art Nouveau silver and silver-plated items during the early 20th century.

A Wileman faïence washbasin and ewer, with printed foliate motif, printed and painted marks, c1905, ewer 16¼in (41.5cm) high.
£180–220 / €260–310
$290–350 ➶ WW

A pewter and earthenware fruit bowl, moulded in stylized ribbonwork, hair cracks, impressed mark 'Osiris 791', early 20thC, 14in (35.5cm) wide.
£460–550 / €650–780
$740–880 ➶ BWL

▶ **An Omar Ramsden silver spoon,** London 1919, 6in (15cm) long.
£500–550 / €710–780
$800–880 ⊞ SHa

A Handel-style spelter table lamp, with carved stiff-leaf decoration, shade damaged, c1910, 22in (56cm) high.
£110–130 / €160–180
$180–210 ➶ EH

An inlaid mahogany mantel clock, with an eight-day movement, c1910, 10¼in (26cm) high.
£320–380 / €450–540
$510–610 ➶ AMB

A scent flask, by Cussons, London, c1910, 2in (5cm) wide, in original box.
£135–150 / €190–220
$210–240 ⊞ LBr

Arts & Crafts

A pair of velvet Cherwell curtains, by John Henry Dearle for Morris & Co, worn, 1887, 64¾ x 93in (164 x 236cm), together with another similar curtain and a tieback.
£860–1,000 / €1,200–1,400
$1,400–1,600 ⚒ WW

A Burmantofts faïence Persian-style vase, painted with stylized flowers, impressed mark and painted numbers, 1891–1904, 6¾in (17cm) high.
£240–290 / €340–410
$380–460 ⚒ SWO

A pair of Bretby pottery vases, with streaky glaze, impressed 'Bretby/England 01260', late 19thC, 9in (23cm) high.
£120–145 / €170–200
$190–230 ⚒ SWO

A Murrle Bennett enamel bracelet, composed of a series of lozenge links with a central plaque of enamel decoration, maker's mark, c1900, 7½in (19cm) long.
£240–290 / €340–410
$380–460 ⚒ S(O)

A Martin Brothers stoneware jug, incised with a foliate motif and 'Martin London & Southall', c1900, 6in (15cm) high.
£260–310 / €370–440
$420–500 ⚒ WW

◄ **A Liberty pewter vase,** designed by Archibald Knox, with stylized foliate decoration, stamped 'Tudric Solkets made in England', early 20thC, 7¼in (18.5cm) high.
£240–290 / €340–410
$380–460 ⚒ SWO

A copper vase, design attributed to John Williams, c1900, 12in (30.5cm) high.
£290–320 / €410–450
$460–500 ⊞ C&W

A Glasgow School copper tray, repoussé-decorated with peacocks and pear trees, c1900, 16in (40.5cm) wide.
£160–190 / €230–270
$260–300 ⚒ SWO

◄ **An oak umbrella stand,** c1900, 27in (68.5cm) high.
£165–185 / €235–260
$265–295 ⊞ SAT

Autographs

Louise Brooks, a signed card, in red crayon, mid-20thC.
£210–250 / €300–360
$340–400 🖋 VS
Actress Louise Brooks (1906–85) appeared in 24 silent films between 1925–38 and was a dancer and a writer.

Douglas Bader, a signed photographic illustration from *Reach for the Sky* by Paul Bracknell, 1954, 8 x 5in (20.5 x 12.5cm).
£55–60 / €80–85
$90–95 ⊞ ES

Arthur James Balfour, a signed letter, 1918, 8 x 5in (20.5 x 12.5cm).
£90–100 / €130–140
$145–160 ⊞ AEL

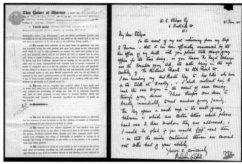

Malcolm Campbell, a signed two-page letter to his solicitor, Stilgoe, requesting that he take charge of his affairs in the event of his death, together with one other related typed letter, 1945, 2°.
£800–960 / €1,150–1,350
$1,250–1,550 🖋 VS

SYLVIE AND BRUNO

BY
LEWIS CARROLL.

WITH FORTY-SIX ILLUSTRATIONS
BY
HARRY FURNISS

PRICE THREE HALFCROWNS

London
MACMILLAN AND CO.
AND NEW YORK
1889

The Right of Translation and Reproduction is Reserved

Nigel Bruce, a signed and inscribed caricature, 1946, 6 x 4in (15 x 10cm).
£100–120 / €140–170
$160–190 🖋 VS
The actor Nigel Bruce (1895–1953) appeared in many films including *The Hound of the Baskervilles, Treasure Island, The Scarlet Pimpernel* and *Lassie Come Home.*

Charles Lutwidge Dodgson (Lewis Carroll), a signed and inscribed first edition of *Sylvie and Bruno*, together with a first edition of *Sylvie and Bruno Concluded*, both contained in cloth slipcase, minor damage, 1889, 8°.
£460–550 / €650–780
$740–880 🖋 DW

► **Queen Elizabeth II and Prince Philip,** a signed photograph, framed and glazed in original blue leather frame, 1961, 10 x 13in (25.5 x 33cm).
£600–720 / €850–1,000
$960–1,150 🖋 VS

Erté, a signed copy of *Costumes and Sets for Der Rosenkavalier*, in full colour, 1980, 13 x 9½in (33 x 24cm).
£45–50 / €65–70
$70–80 BIB

Marianne Faithfull, a signed black and white photograph from the film *Girl on a Motorcycle*, 1968, 10 x 8in (25.5 x 20.5cm).
£170–200 / €240–280
$270–320 CO

Jacqueline Kennedy, a signed typed letter of appreciation to Mrs John J. McCann for help with the processing of mail after the death of the President, with matching envelope, 8°, and a printed John F. Kennedy memorial card with black and white photograph and prayer, 1964, 4¾ x 3½in (12 x 9cm).
£600–720 / €850–1,000
$960–1,150 DW

Duke and Duchess of York, a photograph, signed and dated 'Albert & Elizabeth 1927', in a silver frame by H. H. Plante, with applied crowned monogram 'E.A', London 1926–27, 13 x 10in (33 x 25.5cm).
£500–600 / €710–850
$800–960 G(L)

Matt Groening, signed and inscribed pen and ink sketch of Bart Simpson, 1995, 10 x 8in (25.5 x 20.5cm).
£120–140 / €170–210
$190–230 VS

Jairzinho, a signed colour photograph, 1970, 10 x 8in (25.5 x 20.5cm).
£110–130 / €155–185
$175–210 VS

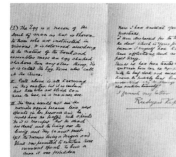

Rudyard Kipling, a signed three-page letter, addressed to 'White Man at Kassala', and an associated envelope with manuscript address panel also signed by Kipling, 1906, 59 x 38¼in (150 x 97cm).
£460–550 / €650–780
$740–880 RTo

Laurel and Hardy, a signed and inscribed album page, in blue ballpoint pen, 1950–51, 3½ x 6in (9 x 15cm).
£190–230 / €270–330
$300–370 B(Kn)

▶ **John Lennon,** a signed copy of *The Penguin John Lennon*, with original wrappers, 1965, 8°.
£490–590 / €700–840
$780–940 BBA

Arthur Lowe, as Captain Mainwaring in *Dad's Army*, a signed card with reproduction photograph, 1970s, 10 x 8in (25.5 x 20.5cm).
£80–95 / €115–135 $130–150 ✗ **VS**

Liberace, a signed and inscribed photograph, 1981, 10 x 8in (25.5 x 20.5cm).
£55–65 / €80–90 $90–105 ✗ **VS**

Harpo Marx, a signed and inscribed photograph, 7 x 5in (18 x 12.5cm).
£200–240 / €280–340 $320–380 ✗ **VS**

Tenzing Norgay, a signed and dated copy of his autobiography, published by George Allen & Unwin Ltd, original cloth, 1977, 8°.
£210–250 / €300–360 $340–400 ✗ **BBA**

◄ **Piers Paul Read,** a signed copy of *The Train Robbers*, published by W. H. Allen & Co, signed by Read and three of the robbers, Roy James, Buster Edwards and Tommy Wisbey, 1978, 10 x 6in (25.5 x 15cm).
£180–200 / €260–280 $290–320 ⊞ **ADD**

Richard Rodgers and Oscar Hammerstein, a menu for a tribute dinner, signed by Rodgers and Hammerstein, 1960.
£340–410 / €480–580 $540–660 ✗ **VS**

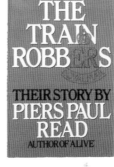

I Paderewski, a signed sepia cabinet photograph, c1900, 6 x 4in (15 x 10cm).
£150–180 / €220–260 $240–290 ✗ **VS**
A famous pianist and composer, Ignacy Paderewski (1860–1941) also became Prime Minister of Poland.

► **Margaret Thatcher,** a signed and inscribed photograph, 1959, 10 x 8in (25.5 x 20.5cm).
£145–175 / €210–250 $230–280 ✗ **VS**

The Duke of Wellington, Arthur Wellesley, an autographed letter to a Mr Barclay dated Woodford 25 Aug 1824, on watermarked paper, 9 x 7in (23 x 18cm).
£200–240 / €280–340 $320–380 ✗ **SWO**

◄ **Elijah Wood,** as Frodo in *The Lord Of The Rings*, signed colour photograph, 2002, 10 x 8in (25.5 x 20.5cm).
£70–85 / €100–120 $110–140 ✗ **VS**

Charlie Webber, as Ben in *Buffy*, signed Inkworks card, 2001, 2½ x 3½in (6.5 x 9cm).
£45–50 / €65–70 $70–80 ⊞ **NOS**

Automobilia

A brass matchbox cover, c1905, 1¾ x 3in (4.5 x 7.5cm).
£40–45 / €55–65
$65–70 ⊞ JUN

A set of four silver place settings, in the form of motor vehicles, Chester 1907, in original box, 2 x 6in (5 x 15cm).
£770–850 / €1,100–1,200
$1,250–1,350 ⊞ SSM

A Royal Doulton ceramic Toby jug, in the form of a veteran motorist, c1910, 8½in (21.5cm) high.
£100–125 / €150–175
$170–200 ↗ BB(S)

A white metal inkwell, in the form of a car, c1910, 5in (12.5cm) long.
£70–80 / €100–115
$110–130 ⊞ JUN

A pair of polished brass Model F electric headlamps, by C. A. Vandervill & Co, with fork mounting points and bevelled clear glass lenses, c1910, 9in (23cm) diam.
£400–480 / €570–680
$640–770 ↗ B(Kn)

A traction engine rear lamp, by Dependence, c1910, 9in (23cm) high.
£70–80 / €100–115
$110–130 ⊞ JUN

A Rushmore Lamps Ltd catalogue, with brown covers, together with a Salsbury No. 112 catalogue, November 1912.
£140–170 / €200–240
$220–270 ↗ B(Kn)

A Morris Commercial Trucks brass vesta case, c1920, 3in (9cm) wide.
£35–40 / €50–55
$55–60 ⊞ JUN

A chrome and leather bus ticket punch, 1919–48, 4 x 6in (10 x 15cm).
£25–30 / €35–40
$40–50 ⊞ GAC

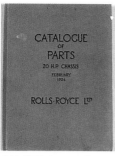

A Rolls Royce catalogue of parts for the 20hp chassis, hardbound, 241pp, 1924.
£160–190 / €230–270
$260–300 ✗ B(Kn)

▶ An AA membership card, with leather holder, 1925, 3in (7.5cm) wide.
£10–15 / €14–20
$16–25 ⊞ COB

A Chad Valley The Autocar Meteors of Road and Track jigsaw puzzle, illustrated by F. Gordon-Crosby, c1927, 8 x 12in (20.5cm x 30.5cm).
£135–150 / €190–210
$220–240 ⊞ MURR

Cross Reference
See Games (pages 206–208)

▶ A Brooklands membership badge and guest brooches, in vitreous enamels, in presentation box with instruction label, 1935, largest 1½in (4cm) wide.
£230–250 / €330–360
$370–400 ⊞ BARCC

A Gamages one gallon motor oil tin, 1930, 11in (28cm) high.
£230–250 / €330–360
$370–400 ⊞ JUN

A Wakefield Patent Castrol motor oil can, 1930s, 10¼in (26cm) high.
£70–80 / €100–115
$110–130 ⊞ HUX

A BP Super petrol pump, with reproduction globe, 1930s, 120in (305cm) high.
£810–900 / €1,150–1,300
$1,300–1,450 ⊞ JUN

◄ **A Southern National Coach Tours enamel sign,** c1930, 42 x 24in (106.5 x 61cm).
£340–380 / €480–540
$540–610 ⊞ MURR

A Listroil oil tin, 1930s, 9in (23cm) wide.
£75–85 / €105–120
$120–140 ⊞ MURR

An RAC Rally flag, 1930s, 13in (33cm) wide.
£65–70 / €90–100
$105–110 ⊞ BiR

A Corgi Mark IV motorcycle handbook, 1948, 8 x 5in (20.5 x 12.5cm).
£15–20 / €20–28
$25–32 ⊞ COB

A printer's proof of a car tax disc, printed for HMSO by Bradbury Wilkinson & Co, 1948, 3 x 12in (7.5 x 30.5cm).
£25–30 / €35–40
$40–50 ⊞ WP

A Shell oil tin, c1950, 9in (23cm) high.
£25–30 / €35–40
$40–50 ⊞ JUN

A Brown Brothers motor accessories catalogue, c1956, 11 x 9in (27.5 x 23cm).
£20–25 / €28–35
$32–40 ⊞ JUN

► **A Castrol enamel forecourt spinning sign,** 1970, 41in (105cm) high.
£110–120 / €155–170
$175–190 ⊞ JUN

A metal roadworks sign, with reflectors, c1960, 49in (124.5cm) wide.
£70–80 / €100–110
$115–130 ⊞ COB

Badges & Mascots

Early motorists decorated cars with personalized mascots, and motor manufacturers soon followed their lead by creating factory mascots for their company's vehicles. Vulcan Motors, Lancashire, was one of the pioneering firms in this field. Their bronze portrayal of Vulcan the Blacksmith, God of Industry, appeared on automobiles from c1903. The same mascot was often produced in different sizes to suit different vehicles, and over the decades a design was sometimes modified to suit changing fashions and new products. Mascots were made out of a wide range of metals including bronze, and less expensively, brass, zinc, pewter and polished aluminium. Among the most expensive mascots are those made from glass. René Lalique, who exhibited alongside Citroën at the famous *Exposition des Arts Décoratifs et Industriels Modernes* in 1925, produced the first glass mascot for Citroën that same year, and went on to design another 28 models. As the example illustrated below shows, his mascots can command exceptionally high prices.

Badges were another decorative favourite with drivers. The Royal Automobile Club (RAC) was started in 1897 by Frederick Richard Simms and the Automobile Association (AA) was established in 1905. Both clubs sought to protect their members from over-zealous police traps, which could restrict drivers to a crawling pace of four miles per hour. The AA introduced the first motoring club badge in 1906. The RAC followed suit in 1907 when Edward VII became their patron (hence the royal in their title). Early badges can be highly collectable.

A bronze mascot, in the form of a bulldog, on a glass plinth, c1920, 3in (7.5cm) high.
£135–150 / € 190–210
$220–240 ⊞ BrL

A Lalique glass mascot, in the form of a falcon, marked 'R. Lalique', French, 1925, 7in (18cm) high.
£2,000–2,400
€ 2,850–3,400
$3,200–3,850 ⚹ B(SF)
This is one of Lalique's most famous mascots.

An RAC full member's badge, by Elkington & Co, first edition with enamel union badge and King Edward VII profile to verso, Birmingham, c1910.
£1,000–1,200
€ 1,400–1,700
$1,600–1,900 ⚹ B(SF)

▶ **A brass mascot,** by Vulcan Motor Manufacturing & Engineering Co, entitled 'God of Industry', mounted on a radiator top, 1920s, 7in (18cm) high.
£115–125 / € 165–180
$185–200 ⊞ JUN

A bronze mascot, in the form of a chained bulldog, with nickel patina, French, 1920s.
£180–220 / € 260–310
$290–350 ⚹ BB(S)

A chrome mascot, 1920s, 6in (15cm) high.
£180–200 / €260–280
$290–320 ⊞ JUN

A Brooklands membership badge, decorated in vitreous enamels, stamped 'Spencer, London', 1930s, 8in (20.5cm) high.
£500–550 / €710–780
$800–880 ⊞ BARCC

A Fleet Air Arm chrome car badge, 1950s, 4in (10cm) high.
£20–25 / €28–35
$32–40 ⊞ COB

A bronze mascot, in the form of a kingfisher, marketed by Finnigan, London, 1920s–30s, 4in (10cm) high.
£220–260 / €310–370
$350–420 ⚒ H&H

▶ **A bronze Schneider mascot,** in the form of an aeroplane, 1931, 7in (18cm) long.
£380–420 / €540–600
$610–670 ⊞ COB

An aluminium Empire State building car badge, 1930s, 6in (15cm) high.
£45–50 / €65–70
$70–80 ⊞ COB

A Monte Carlo Rallye plaque, 1955, 4in (10cm) high.
£150–165 / €210–230
$240–260 ⊞ BiR

A chrome-plated brass Delage greyhound mascot, by Casimir Brau, display mounted, signed, 1929, 4in (10cm) high.
£580–690 / €820–980
$920–1,100 ⚒ B(SF)

A chrome-plated brass rear mounting mascot, by A.E.L., in the form of a Devil cocking-a-snook, 1950s, 3½in (9cm) wide.
£135–150 / €190–210
$220–240 ⊞ CARS

Two enamelled-chrome automobile club badges, one British Automobile Racing Club, and one British Racing & Sports Car Club, c1960.
£65–80 / €92–110
$105–130 ⚒ G(L)

Bicycles

◄ **A 'boneshaker',** possibly by Pickering, with blacksmith-made forged iron frame, spring steel backbone saddle mount, bronze steering head with unusual split forged handlebars, sheet metal saddle pan, 1860s, rear wheel 35in (89cm) diam.
£2,600–2,900
€3,700–4,100
$4,200–4,600 ⚒ COPA

An Ordinary bicycle, saddle and brake missing, right pedal replaced, handles bent, minor dents to one fork, c1882, front wheel 54in (137cm) diam.
£650–750 / €920–1,060
$1,050–1,200 ⚒ B(Kn)

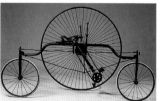

A Rudge rotary tricycle, later saddle, brake gear and pedal rubbers missing, c1885, central driving wheel 48in (122cm) diam.
£10,000–12,000
€14,000–17,000
$16,000–19,000 ⚒ B(Kn)

A Crypto Bantam, c1894, rear wheel 20in (51cm) diam.
£800–950 / €1,150–1,350
$1,300–1,500 ⚒ B(Kn)

LOCATE THE SOURCE
The source of each illustration in Miller's can be found by checking the code letters below each caption with the Key to Illustrations, pages 443–451.

An Eagle tandem, by The Eagle Bicycle Manufacturing Co, American, c1900, frame 24in (61cm) high.
£900–1,100 / €1,300–1,500
$1,450–1,750 ⚒ B(Kn)

A Roadmaster Supreme, by the Cleveland Welding Co, restored, American, c1937.
£4,900–5,800 / €7,000–8,200
$7,800–9,300 ⚒ COPA
This model is extremely rare. Having been produced in limited quantities in 1937 it was to change to a different tank and tack for 1938. This example has been completely restored in an original colour scheme and is correct in every respect.

A Schwinn American Flyer Louisville autocycle, restored, painted red, minor chips and scrapes, 1948, white-wall tyres 26in (66cm) diam.
£250–300 / €350–420
$400–480 ⚒ COPA

► **A Hetchins Super Special Racing Bicycle,** with all original components, 1949.
£600–700
€850–990
$950–1,100
⊞ AVT

A BSA paratrooper's folding cycle, with original brake callipers, saddle, wheels and chainset replaced, 1940s.
£340–400 / €480–570
$540–640 ⚒ RTo

A Shelby Donald Duck boy's balloon-tyre bicycle, c1951, wheels 24in (61cm) diam.
£2,600–2,900 / €3,700–4,100
$4,200–4,600 ⚒ COPA

A Claud Butler Avant Coureur special model racing bicycle, with original finish, 1954.
£320–400 / €450–550
$510–640 ⊞ AVT

A Victorian-style fairground galloper, mounted on a tricycle, made from delivery and roadster components with early motorcycle handlebars, with original scroll and leaf paintwork, built for cavalcades and processions, 1950s, 64in (162.5cm) long.
£850–1,000 / €1,200–1,400
$1,350–1,600 ⚒ B(Kn)

Bicycle Memorabilia

A spelter photograph frame, modelled as an Ordinary, with ribbon and wreath motif, one handlebar missing, 1880–90, 6½in (16.5cm) high.
£110–130 / €160–185
$175–210 ⚒ COPA

◄ **A Lucas adjustable wrench,** 'King No. 1', for solid-tyred machines, c1890.
£40–50 / €55–70
$65–80 ⚒ B(Kn)

A Starley Bros Stevengraph advertising bookmark, embroidered in silk, with tassel, c1890, 4¾in (12cm) long.
£300–350 / €420–500
$470–560 ⚒ B(Kn)

A carbide bicycle lamp, 'Electro', with mounting hardware, convex lens cracked, patented 1897, 24in (61cm) high.
£65–80 / €95–115
$105–125 ↗ COPA

A silver souvenir spoon, with a wheelman on a safety bicycle, marked 'Asberry Park, NJ, July 8–15, 1895', 5in (12.5cm) long.
£120–135
€170–190
$190–220
↗ COPA

A nickel-plated cast-iron toy velocipede rider, 19thC, 4in (10cm) long.
£250–300 / €350–400
$400–480 ↗ COPA

A nickel-plated Road Clearer horn, by Abercrombie & Fitch, with mouthpiece, flat bell and two belt rings, signed, 19thC, 11½in (29cm) long.
£50–55 / €70–80
$80–90 ↗ COPA

◄ **A nickel-plated carbide bicycle lamp,** 'Columbia Model C Automatic', by Hine-Watt Manufacturing Co, American, patented 1900.
£35–40 / €50–55
$55–60 ↗ COPA

▶ **A photographic postcard of a lady cyclist,** 1912, 6 x 4in (15 x 10cm).
£6–8 / €8–10
$10–12 ⊞ S&D

A nickel-plated bicycle bell, with cast decoration, thumb activator and mounting bracket, signed 'Sterling', plate worn, c1898.
£140–170 / €200–240
$220–270 ↗ COPA

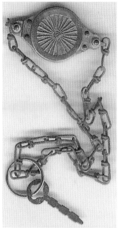

A cast nickel-plated bicycle lock, with key, modelled as a spoked wheel with chain, 19thC, 2in (5cm) wide.
£80–85 / €115–120
$125–135 ↗ COPA

A lithographed music sheet, 'I Won the Bicycle', depicting a crash between a cyclist and a horse and buggy, 19thC, 12 x 8½in (30.5 x 21.5cm), framed.
£65–85 / €90–120
$105–135 ↗ COPA

A nickel-plated bicycle oil lamp, 'Fire Ball', by The Cycle Danger Signal Co, with one clear and three red jewelled lenses, original sprung mounting bracket, dents to base, American, 19thC.
£700–810 / €990–1,150
$1,100–1,300 ↗ COPA

A 9ct gold Cambridge Town & Country CC pin badge, with two shields set below a winged wheel with scroll, the whole on a further pierced scroll, assay mark, Birmingham 1913.
£280–330 / €400–470
$450–530 ↗ B(Kn)

A leather saddle, for a Pneumatic Safety bicycle, c1915.
£45–55 / €65–80
$70–85 COPA

A metal Northern Cycle Club cycling trophy, on a marble base, 1933, 12in (30.5cm) wide.
£320–400 / €450–550
$510–640 ⊞ MURR

Thirty issues of *The C.T.C. Gazette,* c1933, 11in (28cm) high.
£40–50 / €55–70
$65–80 ⊞ AVT

◄ **Two BSA quill-type racing pedals,** 1935–55, 5in (12.5cm) wide.
£35–45
€50–65
$55–70 ⊞ AVT

A pair of Dunlop racing cycle handlebar grips, 1935–55, 7in (18cm) long, boxed.
£10–12 / €14–17
$16–19 ⊞ AVT

Two Airlite racing tandem wheel hubs, 1935–60, 7in (18cm) long.
£75–90 / €100–130
$120–145 ⊞ AVT

◄ **A pair of Resillion cantilever bicycle brakes,** unused, 1930–50.
£70–90 / €100–130
$110–145 ⊞ AVT

A Lobdell saddle, 'Emery', with side-rails and seat post, probably from a Monark bicycle, spring rails with surface rust, cover worn, 1940s.
£35–45 / €50–65
$55–70 COPA

A Bluemel's cycle inflator, unused, c1948, 16in (40.5cm) long.
£25–30 / €35–40
$40–50 ⊞ AVT

▶ **A Miller's bicycle bell,** c1950, 3in (7.5cm) wide.
£7–9 / €9–12
$11–14 ⊞ AVT

A Carradice canvas saddle bag, c1955, 21in (53.5cm) wide.
£10–15 / €14–20
$16–25 ⊞ AVT

Posters

A Dürkopp poster, mounted on cardboard, c1925, 17 x 13¼in (43 x 33.5cm).
£85–100 / € 120–145 $135–160 ♪ VSP

A Hillman, Herbert Cooper Ltd lithographed advertising poster, depicting a lady and a gentleman on pre-pneumatic tricycles and hard tyre safeties, attributed to George Moore, printed by Frederick Dangerfield for the French market, mounted on linen, minor loss and restoration, c1888, 14½ x 9½in (37 x 24cm).
£1,300–1,450 € 1,850–2,050 $2,100–2,300 ♪ COPA

A Cycles Rochet advertising poster, mounted on linen, French, c1895, 51 x 36½in (129.5 x 92.5cm).
£1,000–1,100 € 1,400–1,550 $1,600–1,750 ♪ COPA

A Cycles Lea et Norma advertising poster, mounted on linen, French, c1910, 38½ x 25½in (98 x 65cm).
£500–600 / € 700–780 $800–950 ♪ COPA

A J. B. Louvet advertising poster, by 'Mich', mounted on linen, French, c1930, 44 x 31½in (119 x 80cm).
£780–950 / € 1,100–1,350 $1,250–1,500 ♪ COPA

A La Française Diamant advertising poster, French, 1930s, 23 x 15in (58.5 x 38cm).
£160–200 / € 230–285 $255–320 ⊞ Do

A Singer chromolitho-graphed advertising poster, 'Best of All', rolled, repaired, French, 1920s, 57½ x 39½in (146 x 100.5cm).
£350–420 / € 500–600 $560–670 ♪ B(Kn)

A Cycles et Motos De Dion-Bouton chromo-lithographed advertising poster, after C. Fournery, laid on linen, French, 1927, 63 x 47¼in (160 x 120cm), framed and glazed.
£700–840 / € 1,000–1,200 $1,100–1,350 ♪ B(Kn)

▶ **A Raleigh advertising poster,** 1950, 18 x 30in (45.5 x 76cm).
£240–300 / € 340–430 $380–480 ⊞ AVT

A British Cycling Federation poster, 1950s, 30 x 19in (76 x 48.5cm).
£45–50 / € 65–70 $70–80 ⊞ Do

Books

The following section opens with a general selection of works available on the market, after which the books are divided into categories including Children's; Cookery; Fashion & Beauty; Gardening & Natural History; Illustrations; Modern First Editions and Religious & Esoteric. With the exception of the final category, Religious & Esoteric, in which books are organized by date, in every other section works are arranged in alphabetical order by author, illustrator or publisher. The price ranges shown reflect not just the rarity and desirability of a certain title, but the condition and quality of the specific volume illustrated. In this opening section, for example, there are several works whose value lies not so much in their literary content as in their elaborately tooled and decorated 19th-century bindings, thus disproving the adage that a book cannot be judged by its cover.

Condition, binding and dust jacket are all critical features when it comes to assessing the value of a book. Our section devoted to Modern First Editions features a copy of Conan Doyle's *The Hound of the Baskervilles* (1902), with a price range of £2,000–2,250 / €2,800–3,200 / $3,200–3,600. Only three copies of this book are known to exist with original dust jacket, and when one of these came up for auction (as featured in *Miller's Collectables Price Guide 1999/2000*) it fetched over £80,000 / €113,000 / $128,000. First editions command a premium and the author's signature will add value, a factor to remember when buying new books. Many bookshops will sell signed copies of recent publications and, as this section shows, works by modern authors can command surprisingly large sums in the collector's market.

John Bunyan, *Pilgrim's Progress*, published by Religious Tract Society, cloth, c1880, 9in (23cm) high.
£22–25 / €30–35
$35–40 ⊞ TDG

John Bunyan, *Select Works*, bound in tooled and gilt leather, 1869, 11in (28cm) high.
£220–240 / €315–340
$350–380 ⊞ TDG

► **John Fairfax,** *Adrift on the Star Brow of Taliesin*, first edition, 500 copies, published by The Phoenix Press, with woodcut plates from drawings by Anthony Horrocks, bound in hand-made paper covers by Cramp Printers, Cornwall, 1974, 8¼ x 4in (21 x 10cm).
£35–40 / €50–55
$55–65 ⊞ ES

Edwin Foley, *The Book of Decorative Furniture, its Form, Colour, & History*, published by T. C. & E. C. Jack, 2 volumes, 100 mounted colour plates, one black and white folding 'Family Tree', original cloth binding, light spotting, cloth scuffed, c1925, 4°.
£55–65 / €80–90
$90–100 ✗ RTo

► **Jean Ingelow,** *Poems*, published by Longman, illustrated by George Pinwell, A. B. Houghton and Dalziel, 1867, 9½in (24cm) high.
£190–220 / €270–310
$300–350 ⊞ TDG

Omar Khayyam, *The Rubaiyat of Omar Khayyam*, 300 copies, with 75 quatrains, woodcut frontispiece, printed privately at the Carolon Press, bound with boards, 1908, 10¾ x 6½in (27.5 x 16.5cm).
£80–100 / €115–145 $130–160 ⊞ ES

W. L. F. Wastell and P. G. R. Wright, *The 'Ensign' Handbook of Photography*, published by Ensign, 160 pages, c1900, 4 x 5½in (10 x 14cm).
£22–25 / €30–35 $35–40 ⊞ CaH

◄ **Archibald Williams,** *How It Works*, published by Nelson, 1910, 8in (20.5cm) high.
£12–15 / €17–21 $19–24 ⊞ JUN

Omar Khayyam, *The Rubaiyat of Omar Khayyam*, The Rose Garden Series, published by T. N. Foulis, with stuck-in colour photographs, gilt cloth, 1913, 8 x 5in (20.5 x 12.5cm).
£60–75 / €85–105 $95–120 ⚲ SWO

▶ **Henry Wadsworth Longfellow,** *Longfellow's Poetical Works*, published by Gall & Inglis, illustrated and gilt cloth, c1880, 8in (20.5cm) high.
£55–65 / €80–90 $90–95 ⊞ TDG

Kirk White, *Kirk White's Poems and Prose Works*, published by Gall & Inglis, gilt and decorated cloth cover, steel engravings, c1885, 8in (20.5cm) high.
£40–45 / €55–65 $65–70 ⊞ TDG

◄ **Henry Wadsworth Longfellow,** *Moxon's Poets*, published by E. Moxon, Son & Co, illustrated by T. Seccombe, white glazed boards with gilt decoration, c1860, 7¼in (18.5cm) high.
£160–175 / €230–250 $260–280 ⊞ TDG

Patrick Moore and David Hardy, *The New Challenge of the Stars*, foreword by Arthur C. Clarke, first edition, published by Mitchell Beazley, 39 original illustrations by David A. Hardy, 1977, 2°.
£12–15 / €17–21 $19–24 ⊞ ES

Children's

Children's books are an area of growing interest. The massive success of the Harry Potter series has not only introduced a new generation of children to the delights of reading, but has also reawakened in many grown-ups a passion for children's literature; reminding them of the joys of a good plot, strong characters, and the dramatic conflict between good and evil, qualities all too often missing from adult fiction.

The popularity of contemporary children's writing has also affected the collector's market. The selection of Harry Potter books shown here illustrates with what seemingly magical speed a recent work can become valuable. J. K. Rowling is not the only author to demonstrate this. In *Miller's Collectables Price Guide 2001/2* we featured Philip Pullman's newly-published *The Amber Spyglass* (the concluding volume in his Dark Materials trilogy) on our Collectables of the Future page. This year we have found a signed copy of that same title at a leading dealer and it now appears in this edition with a price range of £112–125 / €160–175 / $180–200. *The Subtle Knife* (Vol. 2 in Pullman's trilogy) is also shown with a price range of £575–650 / €820–920 / $920–1,050. Children's hardbacks tend to be printed in comparatively small numbers and many copies end up in libraries. Therefore, when authors such as Pullman and Rowling become successful, there is both a strong demand for, and a limited supply of, first editions of earlier works.

Enid Blyton, *House-at-the-Corner*, first edition, illustrated by Elsie Walker, published by Lutterworth Press, 1947, 7 x 5in (18 x 12.5cm).
£23–25 / €30–35 $35–40 ⊞ **J&J**

Herbie Brennan, *Faerie Wars*, published by Bloomsbury, signed by the author, 2003, 8 x 5¼in (20.5 x 13.5cm).
£45–50 / €65–70 $70–80 ⊞ **BIB**

Thomas Dalziel (illus), *The Arabian Nights*, published by Ward, Lock & Tyler, with 150 illustrations, 1890, 8½in (21.5cm) high.
£75–85 / €105–120 $125–135 ⊞ **TDG**

Charles Lutwidge Dodgson (Lewis Carroll), *The Hunting of the Snark, An Agony in Eight Fits*, first edition, published by Macmillan, half-title and black and white illustrations by Henry Holiday, original pictorial cloth, minor wear, 1876, slim 8°.
£270–320 / €380–450 $430–510 ⚒ **DW**

◄ **Michael Hoeye,** *Time Stops for No Mouse. A Hermux Tantamaq Adventure*, signed by the author, published by Puffin Books, 1999, 9½ x 5½in (24 x 14cm).
£25–30 / €35–40 $40–50 ⊞ **BIB**

Elizabeth Gould, *Farm Holidays*, illustrated by Eileen Soper, published by Blackie & Son, 1953, 10 x 8in (25.5 x 20.5cm).
£6–8 / €7–12 $8–15 ⊞ **J&J**

▶ **W. E. Johns,** *Biggles in the Terai*, first edition, published by Brockhampton Press, gilt spine, dust jacket, 1966, 8°.
£300–350 / €430–500 $480–560 ⚒ **BBA**

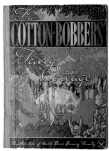

Uncle Ben Kirby, *The Cotton-Bobbers' Fairy Cottage*, published by L. R. Davis, 1944, 10 x 8in (25.5 x 20.5cm).
£10–12 / €14–17 $16–19 ⊞ J&J

Andrew Lang, *The Book of Saints & Heroes*, first edition, illustrated by Henry Ford, published by Longman, 1912, 8½in (21.5cm) high.
£140–155 / €200–220 $220–250 ⊞ TDG

◄ **Elsie J. Oxenham,** *Rosamund's Tuck-Shop,* first edition, published by Girl's Own Paper, colour frontispiece, original cloth, dust jacket, 1937, 8°.
£350–400 / €500–570 $560–640 ♪ DW

George Macdonald, *At the Back of the North Wind*, first edition, published by Strahan & Co, half-title, numbered black and white wood engraved illustrations by Arthur Hughes, original gilt cloth with design, damaged, endpapers replaced, 1871, 8°.
£290–320 / €410–450 $460–510 ♪ DW
This is a first edition of George Macdonald's most famous fairy story, in the second binding.

A. A. Milne, *The House at Pooh Corner*, first edition, published by Methuen, illustrated by E. H. Shepard, black and white illustrations, in a later full gilt vellum exhibition binding with colour illustration of Winnie-The-Pooh and Christopher Robin, 1928, 8°.
£500–550 / €710–780 $800–880 ♪ DW

Items in the Books section have been arranged in alphabetical order by author.

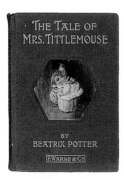

◀ **Beatrix Potter,** *The Tale of Mrs Tittlemouse*, first edition, published by F. Warne, half-title, frontispiece, 26 colour illustrations, black and white illustrations to text, old Hamley's sticker to rear endpaper, owner's inscription to half-title, original boards with colour pictorial panel, 1910, small 4°.
£140–160 / €200–230 $220–250 ⤢ **DW**

Terry Pratchett, *Equal Rites*, first edition, published by Gollancz, original cloth, dust jacket, 1987, 8°.
£300–350 / €430–500 $480–560 ⤢ **DW**

Philip Pullman, *The Subtle Knife*, first edition, published by Scholastic Children's Books, original boards, gilt, dust jacket, 1997, 8°.
£575–650 / €820–920 $920–1,050 ⤢ **BBA**

Philip Pullman, *The Amber Spyglass*, first edition, signed by the author, published by Scholastic Children's Books, 2000, 9 x 5½in (23 x 14cm).
£112–125 / €160–175 $180–200 ⊞ **BIB**

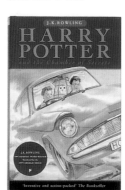

J. K. Rowling, *Harry Potter and the Chamber of Secrets*, first edition, published by Bloomsbury, original pictorial boards, dust jacket, 1998, 8°.
£840–1,000 €1,200–1,400 $1,300–1,600 ⤢ **DW**

J. K. Rowling, *Harry Potter and the Philosopher's Stone*, 1999, *Harry Potter and the Chamber of Secrets*, 1999, *Harry Potter and the Prisoner of Azkaban*, 1999, *Harry Potter and the Goblet of Fire*, 2000, all first deluxe editions, published by Bloomsbury, original pictorial cloth gilt with facsimile author signature, 8°.
£1,000–1,200 / €1,400–1,700 $1,600–1,900 ⤢ **DW**

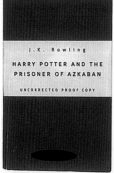

J. K. Rowling, *Harry Potter and the Prisoner of Azkaban*, first state, uncorrected proof copy, by Bloomsbury, one of 50 copies, two extra pages of text, original wrappers, 1999, 8°.
£880–1,050 €1,200–1,450 $1,400–1,650 ⤢ **BBA**

Dodie Smith, *The Hundred and One Dalmatians*, first edition, illustrated by Janet and Anne Grahame-Johnstone, original cloth, dust jacket, 1956, 8°.
£260–290 / €370–410 $410–460 ⤢ **BBA**

Louis Wain, *Louis Wain's Annual for 1902*, published by A. Treherne & Co, black and white illustrations by the author, original printed wrappers, spine worn, 4°.
£155–185 / €220–260 $250–300 ⤢ **DW**

Meg Wohlberg, *Jody's Wonderful Day*, with animated pictures, c1950, 10 x 8in (25.5 x 20.5cm).
£18–20 / €25–28 $29–32 ⊞ **J&J**

Cookery

◀ **Mrs Isabella Beeton,** *Beeton's Book of Household Management*, first edition, published by Bouverie, 12 full-page colour plates, losses and wear, 1861, 8°.
£550–600 / €780–850
$880–960 ⚒ DW

M. L. Doods, *Practical Cookery*, with silver cover, 1906, 2½in (6.5cm) high.
£90–100 / €125–140
$145–160 ⊞ SMI

Mrs Isabella Beeton, *Mrs Beeton's All About Cookery*, published by Ward Lock, 1907, 8¼ x 5½in (21 x 14cm).
£80–90 / €115–125
$130–145 ⊞ OPB

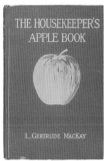

Escoffier, *Escoffiers Stora Kokbok*, published by Husmoderns Bok, Vol II, 1928, 9½ x 7in (24 x 18cm).
£25–30 / €35–40
$40–50 ⊞ MSB

▶ **H. H. Tuxford,** *Miss Tuxford's Modern Cookery for the Middle Classes*, published by Simkin Marshall, 1920s, 7 x 5in (18 x 12.5cm).
£5–10 / €7–14
$8–16 ⊞ COB

L. Gertrude MacKay, *The Housekeeper's Apple Book*, published by Little, Brown & Co, 1918, 7½ x 5¼in (19 x 12.5cm).
£25–30 / €35–40
$40–50 ⊞ MSB

Many Reasons for Jell-O, Genese Pure Food Company pamphlet, 1920, 6¼ x 4¼in (16 x 11cm).
£20–23 / €28–32
$32–37 ⊞ MSB

Fashion & Beauty

La Coupe d'Or, fashion design book, printed in Germany, 1930s, 8in (20.5cm) high.
£25–30 / €35–40
$40–50 ⊞ LBe

◀ **Elizabeth Arden,** *The Quest of the Beautiful*, 1933, 6 x 4in (15 x 10cm).
£5–6 / €7–9
$8–10 ⊞ RTT

Pedro Silmon, *The Bikini*, first edition, published by Diadem, 1986, 12½ x 10in (32 x 26.5cm).
£22–25 / €30–35
$35–40 ⊞ BIB

Gardening & Natural History

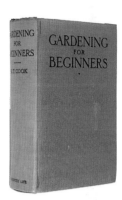

David Attenborough, *Zoo Quest to Guiana*, first edition, signed by the author, published by Lutterworth Press, London, 1956, 8°.
£35–40 / €50–55
$55–65 ⊞ ES

David Austin, *The Heritage of the Rose*, first edition, published by the Antique Collector's Club, 1988, 12½ x 7½in (32 x 19cm).
£30–35 / €42–50
$50–55 ⊞ BIB

E. T. Cook, *Gardening for Beginners*, eighth edition, published by Country Life, London, 1934, 9 x 6in (23 x 15cm).
£8–10 / €10–14
$12–16 ⊞ BIB

W. Cooper Ltd, *The Gardeners' and Poultry Keepers' Guide*, 1920, 7in (18cm) high.
£12–15 / €17–21
$19–24 ⊞ COB

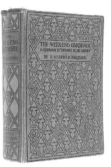

Laurence Fleming and Alan Gore, *The English Garden*, second impression, published by Michael Joseph, 1980, 10 x 7¾in (25.5 x 19.5cm).
£22–25 / €30–35
$35–40 ⊞ BIB

Geoffrey Grigson, *Thornton's Temple of Flora*, published by Collins, 1951, 17 x 12in (43 x 30.5cm).
£270–300 / €380–420
$430–480 ⊞ BAY

F. Hadfield Farthing, *The Weekend Gardener*, published by Grant Richards, 1914, 8½ x 6in (21.5 x 15cm).
£12–15 / €17–21
$19–24 ⊞ BIB

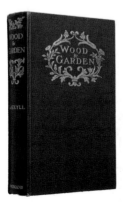

Shirley Hibberd, *Familiar Garden Flowers*, published by Cassell & Co, five volumes, with coloured plates by F. E. Hulme, c1905, 8 x 6in (20.5 x 15cm).
£85–95 / €120–135
$135–150 ⊞ BAY

◄ **Gertrude Jekyll,** *Wood & Garden*, 13th edition, published by Longman's, Green & Co, 1926, 9 x 6in (23 x 15cm).
£40–45 / €55–65
$65–70 ⊞ BAY

John Lindley, *Ladies' Botany: or A Familiar Introduction to the Study of the Natural System of Botany*, 2nd edition, published by James Ridgeway & Sons, London, coloured plates, c1840, 8 x 6in (20.5 x 15cm).
£160–180 / €230–250
$260–290 ⊞ BAY

Mrs Loudon, *The Ladies' Companion to the Flower Garden*, published by Bradbury & Evans, 1865, 7 x 5in (18 x 12.5cm).
£55–60 / €80–85
$90–95 ⊞ BAY

Richard Lydekker (ed), *The Royal Natural History*, published by Frederick Warne, six volumes, 71 chromolithographed plates, wood engraved illustrations, one plate missing, half-calf binding, 1893–96, large 8°.
£80–90 / €115–125
$130–145 ⋗ RTo

A. J. Macself, *Hardy Perennials*, first edition, published by Collingridge, 1950, 9½ x 6½in (24 x 16.5cm).
£8–10 / €10–14
$12–16 ⊞ BIB

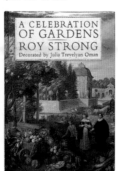

◄ **Routledge (pub),** *The Young Angler, Naturalist, and Pigeon and Rabbit Fancier*, inscription to front free endpaper, original gilt cloth, 1860, small 8°.
£190–230 / €270–330
$300–370 ⋗ BBA

William Paul, *The Rose Garden*, 10th edition, published by Simpkin, Marshall, Hamilton Kent & Co, 21 chromolithographed plates, black and white illustrations, original gilt cloth, 1903, 4°.
£380–450 / €540–640
$610–720 ⋗ DW

Frances Perry, *Beautiful Leaved Plants*, first edition, published by Scholar Press, 1979, 10 x 7¾in (25.5 x 19.5cm).
£16–18 / €22–25
$25–28 ⊞ BIB

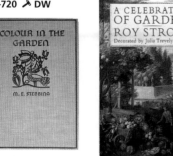

M. E. Stebbing, *Colour in the Garden*, revised edition, published by Thomas Nelson & Sons, 1947, 10½ x 8in (26.5 x 20.5cm).
£15–18 / €21–25
$25–30 ⊞ BIB

Roy Strong, *A Celebration of Gardens*, published by Harper Collins, 1991, 11 x 8in (28 x 20.5cm).
£22–25 / €30–35
$35–40 ⊞ BIB

Illustrations

◄ **John Gould,** *Campylopterus Roberti/ Helianthea Bonapartei*, two hand-coloured lithographs, 1870s, 2°, framed and glazed.
£115–140 / €165–200 $180–220 ⚒ **DW**

Edward Mortlemans, full page illustration, *Love and Sir Lancelot*, from a book by P. G. Wodehouse, c1950, 14 x 10in (35.5 x 25.5cm).
£980–1,150 €1,400–1,650 $1,550–1,850 ⊞ **BRG**

George Study, watercolour illustration for *Bonzo and the Caravan*, 1948, 10½ x 7½in (26.5 x 19cm).
£880–980 / €1,250–1,400 $1,400–1,550 ⊞ **BRG**

Donald Myall, a watercolour illustration from *The Book of the Rose*, by Michael Gibson, 20 x 15in (51 x 38cm).
£880–980 / €1,250–1,400 $1,400–1,550 ⊞ **BRG**

La Mode Illustrée, 152 hand-colourated plates, bound in quarter morocco, 1872–85, 2°.
£460–550 / €650–780 $740–880 ⚒ **DW**

► **John Ryan,** three signed pen and ink sketches of Captain Pugwash, Cut Throat Jake and Tom The Cabin Boy, 2002, 6 x 4in (15 x 10cm).
£80–95 / €115–135 $130–150 ⚒ **VS**

Margaret Tempest, 'Hedgehogs at Tea', watercolour on paper, original artwork for *Little Grey Rabbit*, by Alison Uttley, c1940, 4in (10cm) diam.
£4,500–5,000 / €6,400–7,100 $7,200–8,000 ⊞ **BRG**
Margaret Tempest (1892–1982) was born in Ipswich. She studied at Ipswich and Westminster Schools of Art and taught at Chelsea, her pupils including the naturalist and bird painter Peter Scott. She illustrated 66 books, most famously the *Little Grey Rabbit* series conceived by Alison Uttley and published from 1929. Tempest also wrote some of the stories herself, many of which remain in print. Her works are also familiar to many from having been transformed into wrapping paper and greetings cards by the Medici Society.

Timothy Marwood, quarter page illustration from *Thomas The Tank Engine and Friends*, by Rev W. Awdry, 1980s.
£500–600 / €710–850 $800–950 ⊞ **BRG**

Value

The earliest printed form of the text is usually the most sought-after, hence the value of the first edition or impression. Dust jackets were not commonly used in the US and UK until the early 1900s and were often discarded. Today they are crucial to the value of a book, as is overall condition.

Jenny Tylden-Wright, by Agatha Christie, coloured pencil.
£900–1,000 / €1,300–1,400 $1,450–1,600 ⊞ **BRG**

Modern First Editions

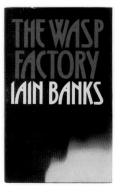

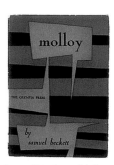

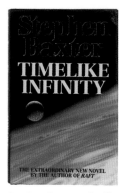

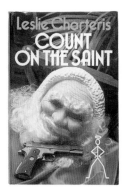

Iain Banks, *The Wasp Factory*, first edition, published by Macmillan, title page signed by author, original cloth, price-clipped dust jacket, 1984, 8°.
£200–230 / €280–320
$320–370 ↗ DW

Stephen Baxter, *Timelike Infinity*, first edition, published by Harper Collins, original boards, dust jacket, 1992, 8°.
£150–180 / €210–250
$240–290 ↗ BBA

▶ **Arthur C. Clarke,** *2010 Odyssey Two*, first edition, published by Granada Books, 1982, 8°.
£10–12 / €14–17
$16–19 ⊞ ES

Samuel Beckett, *Molloy*, first UK edition, published by Olympia Press, original boards, dust jacket, 1955, 8°.
£190–220 / €270–310
$300–350 ↗ BBA

Leslie Charteris, *Count on the Saint*, first edition, published by Hodder & Stoughton, 1980, 8 x 5in (20.5 x 12.5cm).
£25–30 / €35–40
$40–50 ⊞ ADD

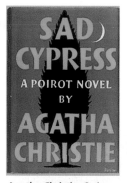

Agatha Christie, *Sad Cypress*, first edition, published by Collins, original cloth, pictorial dust jacket, 1940, 8°.
£2,250–2,500
€3,200–3,550
$3,600–4,300 ⊞ JON

Michael Crichton, *Jurassic Park*, first edition, published by Century, 1991, 9 x 6½in (23 x 16.5cm).
£40–48 / €56–68
$64–76 ⊞ BIB

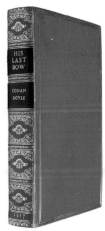

Sir Arthur Conan Doyle, *His Last Bow*, first edition, published by John Murray, rebound, 1917, 7½ x 5in (19 x 12.5cm).
£480–530 / €680–750
$770–850 ⊞ NW

Alex Garland, *The Beach*, first edition, published by Viking, 1996, 8¼ x 5½in (21 x 14cm).
£40–48 / €56–68
$64–76 ⊞ BIB

Sue Grafton, *'J' is for Judgment*, first edition, published by Henry Holt, 1993, 8°.
£40–48 / €56–68
$64–76 ⊞ ES

◀ **Michael Gilbert,** *Sky High*, first UK edition, published by Hodder & Stoughton, 1955, 7½ x 5¼in (19 x 13.5cm).
£65–75 / €90–110
$100–120 ⊞ BIB

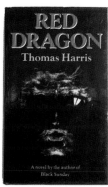

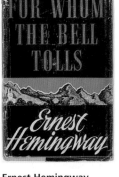

Thomas Harris, *Red Dragon*, first edition, published by The Bodley Head, 1981, 9½ x 6¼in (24 x 16cm).
£30–35 / €40–48 $48–55 ⊞ BIB

L. P. Hartley, *The Go-Between*, first edition, published by Hamish Hamilton, original gilt cloth, dust jacket, wrap-around, 1953, 8°.
£120–140 / €170–200 $190–220 ↗ DW

Seamus Heaney, *Door Into The Dark*, first edition, published by Oxford University Press, original cloth, dust jacket, 1969, 8°.
£240–280 / €340–400 $380–450 ↗ BBA

Ernest Hemingway, *For Whom the Bell Tolls*, first edition, published by Scribern's, 'A' on copyright page, photographer uncredited on rear panel of dust jacket, 1940, 8°.
£320–350 / €450–500 $510–560 ↗ DW

◄ **Nick Hornby,** *Fever Pitch*, first edition, published by Victor Gollancz, original boards, dust jacket, 1992, 8°.
£400–450 / €570–640 $640–720 ↗ BBA

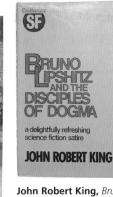

John Robert King, *Bruno Lipshiz and the Disciples of Dogma*, first edition, author's first book, published by Victor Gollancz, 1976, 8°.
£18–20 / €25–28 $28–32 ⊞ ES

P. D. James, *The Black Tower*, first edition, published by Faber & Faber, 1975, 8 x 5½in (20.5 x 14cm).
£300–350 / €430–500 $480–560 ⊞ BIB

Michael Jecks, *A Moorland Hanging*, first edition, published by Headline, 1996, 8¾ x 5½in (22 x 14cm).
£60–75 / €85–100 $95–120 ⊞ BIB

◄ **Charles Lewis,** *The Cain Factor*, first edition, published by Harwood-Smart, 1975, 8°.
£10–15 / €14–20 $16–25 ⊞ ES

► **Jonathan Lunn,** *Killigrew R.N.*, first edition, signed by the author, published by Headline, 2000, 9½ x 6½in (24 x 16.5cm).
£150–180 / €210–250 $240–290 ⊞ BIB

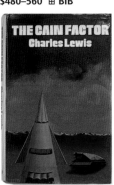

Matthew Kneale, *English Passengers*, first edition, published by Hamish Hamilton, 2000, 9½ x 6½in (24 x 6.5cm).
£50–60 / €70–85 $80–95 ⊞ BIB

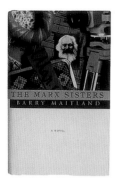

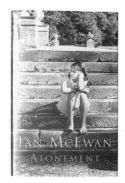

Barry Maitland, *The Marx Sisters*, first edition, published by Hamish Hamilton, original cloth, dust jacket, 1994, 8°.
£240–270 / €340–380 $380–430 ✒ **BBA**

Ian McEwan, *Atonement*, first edition, signed by the author, published by Jonathan Cape, 2001, 9¼ x 6½in (24 x 16.5cm).
£120–135 / €170–190 $190–210 ⊞ **BIB**

J. T. McIntosh, *One in Three Hundred*, first edition, prizewinner for the 1955 International Fantasy Award, published by the Museum Press, dust jacket, 1956, 8°.
£25–30 / €35–40 $40–50 ⊞ **ES**

Michael Ondaatje, *The English Patient*, first edition, published by Bloomsbury, 1992, 9½ x 6¼in (24 x 16cm).
£80–90 / €115–125 $130–145 ⊞ **BIB**

Ellis Peters, *Death Mask*, first edition, published by Crime Club, original boards, dust jacket, 1959, 8°.
£140–165 / €200–240 $220–260 ✒ **BBA**

Ian Rankin, *Black & Blue*, first edition, published by Orion, 1979, 9 x 6¼in (23 x 16cm).
£250–300 / €350–420 $400–480 ⊞ **BIB**

Ruth Rendell, *The Best Man To Die*, first edition, published by John Long, 1968, 8 x 5in (20.5 x 12.5cm).
£480–530 / €680–750 $770–850 ⊞ **NW**

Salman Rushdie, *Grimus*, first edition, published by Victor Gollancz, original cloth, dust jacket, 1975, 8°.
£180–210 / €250–290 $290–330 ✒ **DW**

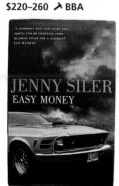

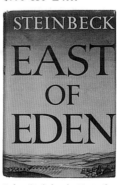

Jenny Siler, *Easy Money*, first edition, author's first novel, published by Orion, foreword by Ian Rankin, 1999, 8°.
£40–50 / €55–70 $65–80 ⊞ **ES**

Karin Slaughter, *Blindsighted*, first edition, published by Random House, 2001, 9 x 6¼in (23 x 16cm).
£45–55 / €65–75 $70–85 ⊞ **BIB**

John Steinbeck, *East of Eden*, first edition, published by Viking, original cloth, dust jacket, 1952, 8°.
£380–430 / €540–610 $610–690 ✒ **BBA**

Graham Swift, *Waterland*, first edition, signed presentation copy from the author, published by Heinemann, later endpapers, original boards, dust jacket, 1983, 8°.
£220–240 / €310–340 $350–380 ✒ **BBA**

Paul Theroux, *Waldo,* first edition, published by The Bodley Head, 1967, 8 x 6in (20.5 x 15cm).
£100–120 / €140–165 $160–190 ⊞ ADD

Jules Verne, *The Chase of the Golden Meteor,* first UK edition, published by Grant Richards, 22 plates, original pictorial cloth, 1909, 8°.
£260–300 / €370–430 $410–480 ⋏ BBA

P. G. Wodehouse, *Laughing Gas,* first edition, published by Jenkins, original cloth, dust jacket, 1936, 8°.
£260–300 / €370–430 $410–480 ⋏ DW

Irvine Welsh, *Porno,* first edition, signed by the author, published by Jonathan Cape, 2002, 8¾ x 5¾in (22 x 14.5cm).
£90–110 / €125–155 $145–175 ⊞ BIB

Religious & Esoteric

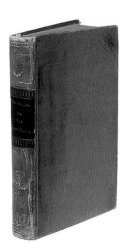

◄ *Histoire Obligations et Statuts...des Francs-Maçons,* five engraved plates of music, signed leaf of authentication, spine with gilt Masonic symbols, 1742, 8°.
£230–260 / €320–370 $370–410 ⋏ BBA

Church Services, gilt leather, 1860, 5in (12.5cm) high.
£125–140 / €175–200 $200–220 ⊞ TDG

◄ **The Book of Common Prayer,** wood engraved borders throughout by Mary Byfield after Holbein, Durer and others, 1863, 7½in (19cm) high.
£120–140 / €170–200 $190–220 ⊞ TDG

The Holy Bible, with five illustrations, original gilt tooled leather, 1864, 15 x 11in (35.5 x 28cm).
£90–110 / €125–155 $145–175 ⊞ PaA

► **Francis Barrett,** *The Magus, or Celestial Intelligencer; Being a Complete System of Occult Philosophy,* with five hand-coloured plates, 17 black and white plates, engraved portrait, modern marbled boards with original pictorial gilt morocco spine, new endpapers, c1875, 4°.
£360–400 / €510–570 $570–640 ⋏ BBA

Bottles

If an antique can be described as a fine objet d'art, hand-crafted for a person of some wealth or standing, then a collectable can perhaps be defined as an everyday object mass-produced for everyday use by ordinary people. Bottles fit perfectly into this category. Created as purely functional and ultimately disposable items, much of their potential value is derived from the fact that they were simply thrown away. The 19th century saw the taking out of many patents and the production of a huge variety of different designs of bottle. Some models were highly successful and were produced in vast numbers, others were less so and it is these rare variants that are particularly sought-after by collectors today.

The bottles illustrated in this section range from miniature sample bottles through to large shop display pieces – many are unusual, hence their often high values. Price ranges depend on factors such as shape, size, colour, company name, decoration and label and, of course, condition. Some bottles can fetch three- or even five-figure sums. One of the great joys of bottles is that you can begin collecting for literally nothing if, like many diggers, you excavate a Victorian rubbish dump. Even the most ordinary 19th-century bottles, worth no more than a pound or two can still seem like an exciting discovery when you pull them out of the ground. There is always the tantalizing possibility of coming across a fabulous find – a piece of discarded old rubbish that, to a serious bottle collector, could be worth a small fortune.

◄ **A glass bladder wine bottle,** embossed 'RH 1733', 7¾in (17cm) high.
£7,500–9,000
€ 10,500–12,500
$12,000–14,500 ➹ BBR
Sealed bladders are rarer than sealed onion bottles. The shape was only produced for a short period and very few have survived.

A glass wine bottle, with Welman seal, minor damage, dated 1723, 6¾in (17cm) high.
£700–840 / € 1,000–1,200
$1,150–1,350 ➹ G(L)

> Items in the Bottles section have been arranged in date order within each sub-section.

A Victorian glass ale bottle, embossed 'Robinson's Brighton Brewery', 11in (28cm) high.
£7–10 / € 10–14
$11–16 ⊞ TASV

A glass hamilton flat-bottomed bottle, embossed 'J Schweppe & Co, Genuine Superior Aerated Waters, 79 Margaret Street', 1860–70, 7½in (19cm) high.
£700–840 / € 1,000–1,200
$1,150–1,350 ➹ BBR

◄ **A slab flask,** embossed 'Old No. 12', minor damage, 1860–70, 7½in (19cm) high.
£65–75
€ 90–105
$105–120 ➹ BBR

Fire grenades

Glass fire grenades were so-called because they were designed to be thrown in the same way as military grenades. They were found in hotels, railway carriages and factories, as well as schools and homes, and contained water, carbolic acid, chalk and sulphur. They were available as singles or in racks of two, three or more.

A glass fire grenade, embossed 'Preyoy-Ante/Extingteur/Grenade', 1880–90, 5¾in (14.5cm) high.
£160–190 / €230–270
$260–300 BBR

A stoneware gin bottle, Dutch, c1890, 14in (35.5cm) high.
£15–18 / €21–25
$25–30 YT

◄ **A glass bottle,** with printed label 'Warner's Safe Compound', 1890–1900, 5½in (14cm) high, with contents, box and promotional leaflet.
£850–1,000 / €1,200–1,400
$1,350–1,600 BBR
This bottle was found in a chemist's shop in Malton, North Yorkshire.

A glass bulb-neck codd bottle, embossed 'Duncan Flockhart & Co, Chemists to the Queen, Edinburgh', 1890–1900, 7½in (19cm) high.
£2,200–2,600
€3,100–3,700
$3,500–4,200 BBR
This item is, to date, the only complete Scottish coloured-glass dumpy bulb-neck codd bottle to have been recorded. It is also only the second green bulb-neck example in the world.

▶ **A glass bottle,** embossed 'Roses Lime Juice', c1895, 14in (35.5cm) high.
£18–20 / €25–28
$28–32 JAM

A full bottle of Bass & Co Royal Brew Ale, bottled by Plowman & Co, London, 1911, 11in (28cm) high.
£110–120
€160–170
$180–190
ABBC

A bed-warmer, in the form of a penguin, the beak as the stopper, minor damage, stamped on base, 1920–30, 10¾in (27.5cm) high.
£180–210
€260–300
$290–340 BBR

A bottle of Black Bowmore single malt whisky, limited edition 101, distilled 1964, bottled 1994, in a wooden presentation case.
£1,000–1,200
€1,400–1,700
$1,600–1,900 TRM

Ginger Beer Bottles & Flagons

A stoneware ginger beer bottle, transfer-printed 'Geo. Jeff & Co, Hull', restored, 1890–1900, 8in (20.5cm) high.
£360–430
€510–610
$570–680 ➤ BBR

A Denby stoneware miniature ginger beer bottle, transfer-printed 'J. Bourne & Son, near Derby', 1900, 2in (5cm) high.
£480–580 / €680–820
£770–930 ➤ BBR

A stoneware flagon, transfer-printed 'Pentiman's Direct Supply Co. Ltd', c1900, 12in (30.5cm) high.
£40–45 / €55–65
$65–70 ⊞ QW

A stoneware ginger beer bottle, transfer-printed 'H. Sanderson & Co, Birmingham', c1920, 7in (18cm) high.
£14–16 / €20–22
$23–25 ⊞ JAM

Syphons

A mesh-covered glass syphon, French, c1890, 19in (48.5cm) high.
£110–130 / €160–180
$180–210 ⊞ JAM

A glass syphon, c1930, 13in (33cm) high.
£50–55 / €70–80
$80–90 ⊞ JAM

Boxes

A walnut snuff shoe, c1790, 4in (10cm) wide.
£430–480 / €610–680
$690–770 ⊞ SEA

A George III mahogany-veneered tea chest, the interior with three lidded zinc canisters and a spoon tray, 9¾in (25cm) wide.
£160–190 / €230–270
$260–300 ↗ WW

A mahogany and ebony writing slope, c1820, 12in (30.5cm) wide.
£220–240 / €310–340
$350–380 ⊞ MB

An oak snuff box, in the shape of a house, c1896, 4in (10cm) wide.
£115–125 / €165–175
$185–200 ⊞ MB
This snuff box was made of oak that came from Winchester Cathedral.

An oak and bell-metal table snuff box, 19thC, 5½in (14cm) diam.
£135–150 / €190–210
$210–240 ⊞ MB

A mahogany snuff box, in the shape of a book, 19thC, 3in (7.5cm) high.
£55–60 / €80–85
$90–95 ⊞ MB

A carved birch box, Swedish, 19thC, 8in (20.5cm) wide.
£135–150 / € 190–210
$210–240 ⊞ MB

A Mauchline ware sycamore box, depicting Dunkeld
Cathedral, 19thC, 4in (10cm) wide.
£65–70 / € 90–100
$100–110 ⊞ MB

A painted birch snuff box, French, 19thC,
4in (10cm) wide.
£250–280 / € 350–400
$400–450 ⊞ SEA

► **A Tunbridge
ware box,**
the cover
with tumbling
block design,
19thC, 2½in
(6.5cm) square.
£80–90
€ 115–125
$130–145
⊞ MB

◄ **A glass casket,** 19thC,
5in (12.5cm) wide.
£65–70 / € 90–100
$100–110 ⊞ MB

A steel-bound wooden box,
with brass fittings, c1880,
27in (68.5cm) wide.
£450–500 / € 640–710
$720–800 ⊞ MLL

A Victorian walnut writing box,
with mother-of-pearl inlay,
11¾in (30cm) wide.
£75–90 / € 105–130
$120–145 ✗ SWO

**A walnut and brass-bound tea
caddy,** with bone overlay, and
two lidded canisters, c1880,
7in (18cm) wide.
£100–120 / € 140–170
$160–190 ✗ WL

**An ebony, quill and bone-inlaid
box,** c1900, 7in (18cm) wide.
£40–45 / € 55–65
$65–70 ⊞ MB

► **A pine butter box,** early 20thC,
14½in (37cm) wide.
£115–125 / € 165–175
$185–200 ⊞ B&R
This box was used by the Royal
Arsenal Co-Operative Society for
sending butter by post or rail.

Breweriana

Three enamel labels, probably Bilston, late c1800, 2in (5cm) wide.
£150–165 / €220–230
$240–260 ⊞ JAS

An Usher's Pale Ale bar mirror, 19thC, 33½in (85cm) wide, with later frame.
£170–200 / €240–280
$270–320 ✗ TRM

A Victorian pottery sherry keg, with gilt label and banding, printed and painted with a kingfisher, 12½in (32cm) high.
£40–50 / €55–70
$65–80 ✗ PFK

A Copeland pottery Golden Jubilee jug, with a central medallion inscribed 'Bass & Co's Pale Ale', c1897, 7in (18cm) high.
£380–460 / €540–650
$610–740 ✗ SAS

▶ **A Mettlach pewter-mounted beer stein,** decorated with a tavern scene and verse, impressed marks, early 20thC, 9¾in (25cm) high.
£210–250 / €300–350
$340–400 ✗ SWO

A brass spigot, for a wine keg, c1900, 6in (15cm) long.
£7–10 / €10–14
$11–16 ⊞ GAC

An Edwardian oak tantalus, with three decanters, a games compendium compartment, the lock marked 'Daniel and Arter, Birmingham', 15in (38cm) wide.
£320–380 / €450–540
$510–610 ✗ WilP

Four advertising spinners, for Red Tape The Whisky, John Drummond & Sons, Félix Pernod and Roger's Price Medal Ales, c1910, largest 2¾in (7cm) high.
£35–40 / €50–55
$55–65 ⊞ HUX
Advertising spinners were used to select the next person to buy a drink or cigar.

Items in the Breweriana section have been arranged in date order within each sub-section.

A Bass advertising mirror, c1910, 12 x 10in (30.5 x 25.5cm).
£180–200 / €250–280
$290–320 ⊞ MURR

A Dorchester Crystal Ale glass
jug, 1910–20, 10in (25.5cm) high.
£90–100 / €125–140
$145–160 ⊞ MURR

◀ A Watson's No. 10
Scotch water jug,
printed mark to base,
some wear, 1910–20,
6¾in (17cm) high.
£240–290 / €340–410
$380–460 ⚒ BBR

▶ A carved
wooden bottle
stopper, Italian,
c1920, 5in
(12.5cm) high.
£28–32
€40–46
$45–52 ⊞ Dall

A Stewart's Scotch Whisky
ceramic water jug, some rim
restoration, 1920s, 4in (10cm) high.
£170–200 / €240–280
$270–320 ⚒ BBR

A Walker's Falstaff Ales ceramic
ashtray, 1920s, 7½in (19cm) diam.
£65–75 / €90–105
$105–120 ⊞ MURR

A pair of Fremlins' Ales advertising
signs, transfer on wooden board,
left and right facing, 1920s, 18 x 22in
(45.5 x 56cm), framed and glazed.
£230–250 / €330–350
$370–400 ⊞ AAA

◀ A Johnnie Walker metal menu
holder, 1925–35, 3in (7.5cm) high.
£55–60 / €80–85
$90–95 ⊞ HUX

A D. C. L. Whisky stone lithograph showcard, illustrated by
Lawson Wood, 1920s, 19 x 14in
(48.5 x 35.5cm), framed.
£320–350 / €450–500
$500–560 ⊞ AAA

▶ A Leney's enamel four-quart
crate sign, restored, c1930,
19 x 13in (48.5 x 33cm), framed.
£450–500 / €640–710
$720–800 ⊞ AAA

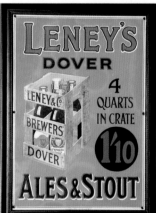

A Fremlin's pressed tin four-
quart crate sign, c1930,
29 x 27in (73.5 x 68.5cm),
in original oak frame.
£450–500 / €640–710
$720–800 ⊞ AAA

A Lemon Hart Rum plaster
advertising figure, 1930,
10½in (26.5cm) high.
£230–250 / €330–350
$370–400 ⊞ HUX

A Courage glass sign, minor
damage, 1930, 18in (45.5cm) high,
with hanging chain.
£75–90 / €105–125
$120–145 ↗ BBR

A Wills's Gold Flake ceramic water
jug, 1930s, 8in (20.5cm) high.
£65–75 / €90–105
$105–120 ⊞ MURR

▶ A Trumans
Beer rubber
advertising
figure, on a
plastic base,
c1960, 8in
(20.5cm) high.
£50–55
€70–80
$80–90 ⊞ PrB

An Amstel Bier poster,
by Jan Wijga, margins cut
away, c1935, 30¾ x 21½in
(78 x 54.5cm).
£125–150 / €175–210
$200–240 ↗ VSP

A Heineken poster,
by Frans Mettes,
c1957, 45¾ x 32½in
(116 x 82.5cm).
£340–410 / €480–580
$540–650 ↗ VSP

A Carlton Ware
advertising figure, for
Pick Flowers Keg Bitter,
1960s, 10in (25.5cm) high.
£160–175 / €230–250
$260–280 ⊞ MURR

A Babycham party pack,
consisting of six glasses
and two plastic Babycham
models, 1960s, models
7½in (19cm) high.
£38–44 / €54–62
$60–70 ↗ BBR

Guinness

In 1759, Arthur Guinness (1725–1803) took over a small run-down Dublin brewery and began brewing a drink called porter. This popular 18th-century drink was a mixture of beer and stout, and was so-called because it was popular with the porters of London where it was originally devised. He named his drink Guinness, and it became hugely successful. The business stayed in family ownership and when Arthur's grandson, Benjamin, died in 1868, the Guinness Brewery was the largest in the world.

It was not until 1928, however, that the firm began their famous publicity campaign. Advertising agency S. H. Benson came up with the famous slogan 'Guinness is good for you'. The artist John Gilroy (1898–1985) produced a series of classic images, including the famous 'Guinness for Strength' man-with-a-girder poster, and a range of advertisements using animal themes, initially inspired by a visit to Bertram Mills' Circus. The most famous Guinness creature is undoubtedly the toucan, introduced in 1936. Gilroy had initially used a pelican, but copywriter and crime novelist Dorothy L. Sayers changed the bird, provided the slogan 'How grand to be a Toucan/Just think what Toucan do', and masterminded a symbol that was to be part of Guinness's corporate image for decades.

In the 1950s, Guinness commissioned Carlton Ware to produce promotional items, resulting in toucan lamps, flying toucan wall plaques and a host of other material. Guinness memorabilia is popular with collectors today but high prices, particularly when it comes to ceramics, have helped stimulate a market for fake items and Guinness enthusiasts should always buy with a clear head and a sober perspicacious eye!

A Guinness advestisement, 'A Guinness a Day', 1920, 8¾ x 13in (22 x 33cm).
£100–120 / €140–170
$160–190 ⚲ BBR

> **Cross Reference**
> See Advertising & Packaging
> (pages 11–22)

A Guinness celluloid sign, by John Gilroy, 1930s, 18 x 10in (45.5 x 25.5cm).
£175–190 / €250–270
$280–300 ⊞ MURR

A T. G. Green Guinness ceramic basin, decorated with a zookeeper and animals, 1950s, 6in (15cm) diam.
£45–55 / €65–78
$75–90 ⚲ BBR

A set of three Guinness toucan wall plaques, 1950–60, 10in (25.5cm) wide.
£320–380 / €450–540
$520–610 ⚲ BBR

A Carlton Ware Guinness water jug, c1957, 12in (30.5cm) high.
£750–825 / €1,050–1,150
$1,200–1,300 ⊞ MURR
This jug is particularly rare.

A Guinness tin tray, 'Have a round of Guinness', 1950–60, 10½in (26.5cm) diam.
£10–12 / €14–17
$16–19 ⚲ BBR

◄ **A Guinness card,** 'Guinness for Strength', 1950s, 6 x 8in (15 x 20.5cm).
£6–8 / €8–12
$10–14 ⊞ Do

A Guinness celluloid sign, by R. Pepé, 'Goodness! I need a Guinness', c1962, 9 x 12in (23 x 30.5cm).
£175–190 / €250–270 $280–300 ⊞ MURR
This sign won the London Transport Sign of the Year competition.

◄ **A Guinness poster,** 'See the Guinness animals at Edinburgh Zoo', 1960s, 30 x 20in (76 x 51cm).
£310–350 €430–470 $480–530 ⊞ Do

► **A Guinness ceramic lamp,** with a revolving shade, 1960s, 15in (38cm) high.
£180–220 €260–310 $290–350 ⚒ BBR

A Guinness watch, 1960s, 3½in (9cm) diam.
£250–275 / €350–390 $400–440 ⊞ MURR

Brian Sibley, *The Guinness Book of Advertising,* 239pp, paperback, 1985, 12 x 8¾in (30.5 x 22cm).
£25–30 / €35–40 $40–50 ⊞ BIB

◄ **A Royal Doulton ceramic Guinness toucan,** limited edition of 2,000, 2000, 6in (15cm) high.
£300–330 / €430–470 $480–530 ⊞ MCL
This promotional toucan was manufactured exclusively for Millennium Collectables Ltd as part of their 20th Century Advertising Classics range.

Buttons & Buckles

Nine batchelor's solitaires,
eight chased metal, one abalone,
with various backs, 19thC,
largest ¾in (2cm) diam.
£8–10 / €10–15
$11–16 each ⊞ EV

◄ **A pair of brass shoe buckles,**
stamped 'L.W. Paris', 1850–1910,
2½in (6.5cm) high.
£45–50 / €65–70
$70–80 ⊞ EV

A set of six inlaid horn buttons,
c1870, 1in (2.5cm) diam.
£175–195 / €250–280
$280–310 ⊞ JBB

A brass and enamel button,
painted with a head of Columbine,
with a paste border, 1870–75,
1¼in (3cm) diam.
£250–280 / €350–400
$400–450 ⊞ TB

A brass button, stamped with a
figure of a woman with a parasol,
in a gated border, 1880–90,
1½in (4cm) diam.
£20–25 / €28–35
$32–40 ⊞ TB

A Satsuma pottery button,
painted with two noblewomen,
highlighted in gold, Japanese,
late 19thC, 1in (2.5cm) diam.
£165–185 / €230–260
$260–300 ⊞ TB

A brass button, with stamped
and painted design, late 19thC,
1½in (4cm) diam.
£25–30 / €35–40
$40–50 ⊞ TB

An enamel and silver button,
decorated with an iris on a textured
foil ground, Japanese, late 19thC,
1¼in (3cm) diam.
£340–380 / €480–540
$540–610 ⊞ TB

A brass button, stamped with the
head of a pierrot, late 19thC,
1½in (4cm) diam.
£40–45 / €55–65
$65–70 ⊞ TB

A mother-of-pearl button, carved with a sheaf of wheat, with a cut-steel scythe, late 19thC, 1½in (4cm) diam.
£230–250 / €330–350
$370–400 ⊞ TB

A shell cameo button, carved with a woman's head, set in a brass border, c1900, 1in (2.5cm) diam.
£140–155 / €200–220
$230–250 ⊞ TB

A set of six pearl waistcoat buttons, with a red stone centre and metal rims, early 20thC, ½in (1.5cm) diam.
£40–45 / €55–70
$65–70 ⊞ EV

A set of six Edwardian mother-of-pearl waistcoat buttons, ½in (1.5cm) diam.
£35–40 / €50–55
$55–65 ⊞ OH

A diamanté and brass buckle, c1900, 2½in (6.5cm) wide.
£25–30 / €35–40
$40–50 ⊞ EV

A set of six Edwardian glass waistcoat buttons, ½in (1.5cm) diam.
£35–40 / €50–55
$55–65 ⊞ OH

A set of six chromolithographed waistcoat buttons, depicting playing cards, c1920, ½in (1.5cm) diam.
£65–70 / €90–100
$100–115 ⊞ EV

A brass clasp, decorated with multicoloured enamel, c1920, 4in (10cm) wide.
£30–35 / €40–50
$50–55 ⊞ EV

▶ A Bakelite button, by Martha Sleeper, c1930, 1¼in (3cm) diam.
£230–250 / €330–350
$370–400 ⊞ TB
This design of button was made in various colours, the red and green having the highest values.

A pair of diamanté shoe button-covers, 1920s, 1in (2.5cm) diam.
£10–12 / €14–17
$16–20 ⊞ EV

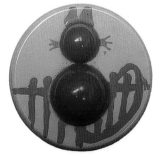

A set of four celluloid daisy buttons, 1930s, 2in (5cm) diam.
£18–20 / €25–30
$28–32 田 EV

An Art Deco 18ct gold and platinum-mounted dress set, comprising a pair of cufflinks, two studs and four buttons, cased, case damaged, c1930, 2½ x 4in (6.5 x 10cm).
£320–380 / €450–540
$510–610 🔨 G(L)

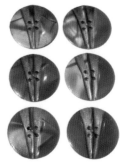

A pair of diamanté shoe buckles, in the form of bows, c1930, 1½in (4cm) wide.
£25–30 / €35–40
$40–50 田 EV

A set of six celluloid buttons, 1930s, 1in (2.5cm) diam.
£15–18 / €20–25
$25–30 田 EV

A set of five multicoloured cold-painted enamel buttons, Czechoslovakian, 1930s, 1in (2.5cm) diam.
£22–25 / €30–35
$35–40 田 EV

A wooden button, moulded and painted with Bashful, from *Snow White and the Seven Dwarfs*, Czechoslovakian, late 1930s, 1in (2.5cm) diam.
£30–35 / €40–50
$50–55 田 TB

A Bakelite mah-jong game-piece button, incised and painted, c1940, 1in (2.5cm) high.
£25–30 / €35–40
$40–50 田 TB

A celluloid button, in the form of peas in a pod, 1940s, ½in (1.5cm) wide.
£115–125 / €165–175
$185–200 田 TB

◀ **An Arita porcelain button,** in the form of a glazed and gilded penguin, Japanese, mid-20thC, 1in (2.5cm) high.
£140–155 / €200–220
$220–250 田 TB

▶ **A set of eight astrological glass buttons,** 1950s, ½in (1.5cm) diam.
£30–35 / €40–50
$50–55 田 EV

Cameras

This year's camera section includes a large selection of domestic cine cameras. Traditionally, the professional film industry had used 35mm film which was cumbersome, expensive and dangerously flammable. Amateur cinematography took off in the 1920s, and in 1924 Kodak came up with a 16mm camera. The Cine Kodak camera introduced the possibility of high-quality home movies. It weighed in at 7lbs (3kg) and cost a whopping £210 / €300 / $335. With the subsequent introduction of 8mm film, cameras became easier to use and more affordable and, by the 1950s and '60s, 8mm cine cameras were a common sight at family parties, holidays and other social occasions.

Although superseded by camcorders and other contemporary equipment, there is still a demand for these vintage pieces. Collecting cine equipment is a recent phenomenon and part of the interest of 'old technology'. There is no such thing as a typical collector. Some people buy to use, hence demand for the more modern high-specification models with reflex or through-the-lens viewing/metering. Cameras with single shot

facility for animation are also sought, mainly by students. Others collect old cameras as design 'icons', as examples of technological history or simply for reasons of nostalgia.

Collectors usually narrow their field of collecting to a theme based on a particular maker or gauge of film. Some cameras are more desirable than others, such as the rarer Bolex Paillard cameras illustrated in the following section.

Even when bought for display, as is often the case, the camera or projector is preferred in working order and in excellent cosmetic condition. It should have no rust or missing parts and show only signs of light use. An original case, box, copy of instructions, accessories and traditional lenses, in the case of interchangeable lens equipment, will also enhance value.

There are antiques fairs, dealers, newspaper advertisements and car boot sales where this equipment can be found so this is a good field for the new collector. There are also books dedicated to cine camera collecting and specialist cine clubs.

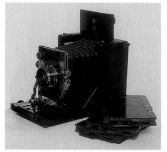

A Gandolfi Universal Patent hand camera, with 3¼in lens, in original case, together with three matching double dark slides and two lens boards with flanges, c1900, plates 5in (12.5cm) wide.
£200–240 / €280–340
$320–380 ↗ B(WM)

A Lizar's Challenge stereoscopic hand camera, for 7in (18cm) plates, with Bausch & Lomb rapid rectilinear lenses, in original case, c1905, with three double dark slides and a Brewster viewer.
£220–260 / €310–370
$350–420 ↗ B(WM)

A Kodak No. 2 folding pocket Brownie camera, with black bellows and metal lens board, 1907–15, 7in (18cm) wide.
£25–30 / €35–40
$40–50 ⊞ HEG
With red bellows this camera would be worth £30–35 / €40–50 / $50–55.

◀ **An Ernemann rollfilm K box camera,** c1920, 5in (12.5cm) square.
£50–55 / €70–80
$80–90 ⊞ ARP

▶ **An Eastman Kodak Eight Model 60 8mm cine camera,** with f1.9/13mm lens, c1927, 7in (18cm) wide, with case.
£90–100 / €130–140
$145–160 ⊞ CaH

A Pathéscope Pat Gold 9.5mm cine camera, clockwork, with two-hole slide bar lens, c1930, 5in (13cm) wide, with case.
£35–40 / €50–55
$55–65 ⊞ CaH

A Kodak Standard 8 Model 20 cine camera, with f3.5 lens, 1932–47, 7in (18cm) long, with case.
£30–35 / €45–50
$50–55 ⊞ CaH

A Balda Baldi 35mm camera, with Trioplan Uctd, cable release, c1930s, 4in (10cm) wide, with original box.
£40–45 / €55–65
$65–75 ⊞ CaH

▶ **A Leica IIIc camera,** engraved 'Luftwaffen eigentum', 1941, 6in (15cm) wide, together with original matching grey leather case.
£2,800–3,100 / €4,000–4,400
$4,500–4,950 ⊞ ARP
This camera was made especially for the Luftwaffe in Luftwaffe grey, and is engraved 'Luftwaffen eigentum' (made for the Luftwaffe). There are fakes on the market, but genuine ones such as this command high prices.

A Specto 9.5mm cine projector, with Dallmeyer lens, c1930, 15in (38cm) high.
£55–60 / €75–85
$85–95 ⊞ CaH

A Rollei Rolleicord 1 camera, c1933, 6in (15cm) high.
£150–165 / €210–230
$240–260 ⊞ ARP

A Gic 16 16mm cine camera, with Dallmeyer Anastigmat f3.5/1in lens, clockwork, c1930–37, 6in (15cm) high.
£60–65 / €85–95
$95–105 ⊞ CaH

A Wirgin Wirginex Bakelite camera, c1935, 6in (15cm) wide.
£45–50 / €65–70
$70–80 ⊞ ARP

◀ **A Bolex Paillard H16 Triple Turret 16mm cine camera,** Gorlitz Trioplan f2.9/50mm lens, with lens hood, Triofocal Viewfinder with levers, rewind handles and two body caps, c1938, 12in (30.5cm) high, with instructions and fitted case.
£155–175 / €220–250
$250–280 ⊞ CaH

▶ **A Kodak Brownie Flash B camera,** c1950, 4in (10cm) high.
£30–35
€40–50
$50–55 ⊞ CaH

A Bolex Paillard L8 8mm cine camera, with single turret Yvar f2.8/12.5mm AR lens, c1942, 5in (12.5cm) high, with leather case and box.
£22–25 / €30–35
$35–40 ⊞ CaH

A Bolex Paillard H16 Deluxe Triple Turret 16mm cine camera, with rewind handle and critical visual focuser, c1950, with Bolex case, 11 x 9in (28 x 23cm).
£260–290 / €370–410
$420–470 ⊞ CaH

A Newman and Guardia Special Pattern B camera, c1950, 9in (23cm) wide.
£330–370 / €470–530
$530–590 ⊞ ARP

◀ **A Bolex Paillard H16 Reflex Triple Turret 16mm cine camera,** with Pizar and Yvar lenses, rewind handle, RX fader, eye level focus, Octameter, rewind handle, set of five filters and three body caps, c1950, with case, 10 x 12in (25.5 x 30.5cm).
£630–700 / €890–1,000
$1,000–1,100 ⊞ CaH

◀ **A Bell & Howard 605 Double Run Eight 8mm cine camera,** Kaligar WA f2.5/7mm lens, c1950, 6in (15cm) high, with case.
£55–60
€75–85
$85–95 ⊞ CaH

▶ **A Durst Automatica 35mm camera,** c1956, 5¾in (14.5cm) wide.
£85–95 / €120–135
$135–150 ⊞ ARP

Items in the cameras section have been arranged in date order.

A Rolleiflex 3.5E camera, f3.5 planar lens, c1956, 6in (15cm) high.
£250–280 / €350–400
$400–450 ⊞ ARP

A Bolex Paillard B8L Twin Turret 8mm cine camera, with Yvar lenses and winding handle, c1958, 6in (15cm) high, with case.
£60–70 / €85–100
$95–110 ⊞ CaH

A Voigtlander Bessa I camera, with f3.5/105mm Scopar lens, 1950s, 6in (15cm) high.
£35–40 / €50–55
$55–65 ⊞ HEG

A Bolex Paillard H8 standard 8mm cine camera, c1950s, 10in (25.5cm) high.
£160–180 / €230–260 $260–290 ⊞ ARP

A Rollei Universal P11.0 35mm projector, c1960–65, 11in (28cm) high, with two slide magazines and case.
£540–600 / €770–850 $860–960 ⊞ CaH

► **A Bolex Paillard 155 Super 8mm cine camera,** with f1.9/8.5–30mm Macrozoom lens, viewfinder eyepiece with eyecup stop, c1965–75, 8in (20.5cm) long, with instructions and case.
£100–110 / €140–155 $160–180 ⊞ ARP

A Sekonic Dualmatic 50 camera, with rotating back, c1963, 8in (20.5cm) wide.
£27–30 / €38–42 $42–50 ⊞ ARP

A Minolta 16MG camera, with flash gun, c1966, 7in (18cm) wide.
£22–25 / €30–35 $35–40 ⊞ ARP

◄ **A Leitz Leicina 8S standard cine camera,** with Dygon lenses, lens hoods, Leica UVA filter, 22502Q battery holder and BYVOO charger, c1960, 8in (20.5cm) long, with case and box.
£65–70 / €90–100 $105–120 ⊞ CaH

A Leica Leitz M3 Single-Stroke 35mm camera, No. 114, with 35mm Simmicron 50/f2 lens rigid mount lens, c1960, 5½in (14cm) wide, with case.
£1,050–1,150 / €1,400–1,600 $1,600–1,800 ⊞ CaH

► **A Bolex Paillard P3 8mm cine camera,** with power zoom, c1963, 9in (23cm) wide.
£75–85 €105–120 $120–135 ⊞ ARP

A Eumig Mark S Silent & Sound 8mm cine projector, c1966, 12in (30.5cm) wide.
£45–50 / €65–70 $70–80 ⊞ CaH

► **A Fujica Single 8 P300 8mm cine camera,** with f1.8/10.5–27 zoom lens, c1968, 7in (18cm) high.
£18–21 €25–30 $30–35 ⊞ CaH

A Rolleiflex SL26 cartridge loading SLR camera, c1968, 4in (10cm) wide.
£90–100 / €125–140
$145–160 ⊞ ARP

A Kodak Super 8 XL55 cine camera, c1970, 9in (23cm) wide.
£14–16 / €20–22
$22–26 ⊞ ARP

A Kodak Pocket Instamatic 60 camera, c1972, 5½in (14cm) wide.
£18–20 / €25–28
$28–32 ⊞ CaH

▶ A Leitz Leica R3 MOT Electronic 35mm camera, with Summicron-R 50/f2 lens and cap, c1977, 6in (15cm) wide.
£450–500 / €640–710
$720–800 ⊞ CaH

An Elmo Super 8 Sound 600 SD 8mm cine camera, with Elmo f1.8/8–50mm zoom and manual lens and cap, c1970, 9in (23cm) wide, with two microphones, accessories and case.
£160–180 / €230–260
$260–290 ⊞ CaH

A Gaf Super SS 250 SL Sound 8mm cine camera, with f1.1/9–22.5mm zoom lens, cap and eye cup, 1970–75, 8in (20.5cm) wide.
£55–65 / €80–90
$90–105 ⊞ CaH

A half-plate wooden tailboard camera, with nickel fittings, Russian, c1975, 10½in (26.5cm) high.
£135–150 / €190–210
$210–240 ⊞ HEG

A Polaroid Polavision Land camera, with instant film, c1977, 10in (25.5cm) high.
£40–45 / €60–65
$65–70 ⊞ ARP

▶ A Minolta 110 Zoom MKII SLR camera, c1979, 5in (12.5cm) long.
£100–110
€140–155
$160–175
⊞ ARP

Ceramics

Animals

A Paris porcelain flask,
modelled as a seated
monkey wearing women's
clothes, with stopper,
initials for Jacob Petit
on base, 19thC,
9¼in (23.5cm) high.
£300–360 / €430–510
$480–580 ⚹ SJH

**A Meissen model of a Bologna
Hound,** marked, 19thC,
9¼in (23.5cm) high.
£520–620 / €740–880
$830–990 ⚹ SJH

A bone china stirrup cup, in the form
of a dog's head, minor damage, c1830,
5¼in (13.5cm) long.
£400–480 / €570–680
$640–770 ⚹ G(L)

**A pair of bisque miniature models of
daschunds,** 1920s, 1in (2.5cm) long.
£30–35 / €45–50
$50–55 ⊞ CCs

◀ **A pottery plate,** hand-painted with a
portrait of a cat, 1960s, 9in (23cm) diam.
£18–20 / €25–28
$38–32 ⊞ LBe

A ceramic plate, painted with a
portrait of a poodle, 1950,
5in (12.5cm) diam.
£20–25 / €30–35
$35–40 ⊞ LBe

A Goebel model of a horse, c1960,
4in (10cm) high.
£20–25 / €30–35
$35–40 ⊞ PrB

**A Wade Disney Blow Up
model of Am,** 1961–65,
5¾in (14.5cm) high.
£120–145 / €170–200
$190–230 ⚹ BBR

**A Wade Disney Blow Up
model of Bambi,** 1961–65,
4½in (11.5cm) high.
£65–75 / €90–105
$105–120 ⚹ BBR

◄ A Royal Albert model of Beatrix Potter's Goodie and Timmy Tiptoes, 1986–96, 4in (10cm) high.
£65–75 / €90–105
$105–120 ⊞ BAC

A Royal Albert model of Beatrix Potter's Mittens and Moppet, 1990–94, 4in (10cm) high.
£110–125 / €155–175
$175–200 ⊞ BAC

A Royal Albert model of Beatrix Potter's Little Black Rabbit, 1977–97, 4in (10cm) high.
£35–40 / €50–55
$55–60 ⊞ BAC

A Royal Albert model of Beatrix Potter's Mother Ladybird, 1989–96, 3in (7.5cm) high.
£45–50 / €65–70
$70–80 ⊞ BAC

A Royal Albert model of Beatrix Potter's Jemima Puddleduck and Foxy Whiskered Gentleman, 1990–99, 5in (12.5cm) high.
£45–55 / €65–70
$70–80 ⊞ BAC

A Royal Albert model of Beatrix Potter's Christmas Stocking, 1991–94, 4in (10cm) high.
£160–180 / €230–260
$260–290 ⊞ BAC

A Wade model of a Library bear, limited edition of 500, 1998, stamped, 6in (15cm) high.
£40–50 / €55–70
$65–80 ⊞ BBR

► A Winstanley pottery millennium cat, limited edition of 200, 2000, 11in (28cm) high.
£180–200 / €260–280
$290–320 ⊞ CP

◄ A Winstanley pottery model of a cat, 2001, 6in (15cm) high.
£25–30
€35–40
$40–50 ⊞ CP

Belleek

Based in County Fermanagh, Northern Ireland, Belleek Pottery was established in 1863 and was noted for its high-quality, cream-coloured porcelain with an iridescent glaze, developed with the assistance of William Bromley, who had worked at the W. H. Goss factory. In 1883, Bromley travelled to the USA where he supervised the development of American Belleek. Typical products were extravagantly modelled, often inspired by nautical, floral and Irish themes and included basket work, fine piercing and moulding. Eggshell-thin clays were used as well as lustrous glazes and gilding. Popular with Queen Victoria, Belleek was displayed at the great 19th-century exhibitions, enjoyed a huge export market throughout the 20th century and remains in production today. Vintage pieces are highly collectable, although owing to the delicacy of the designs condition should always be carefully checked.

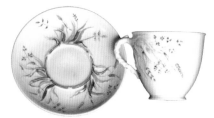

A Belleek Grass pattern breakfast cup and saucer, First Period, 1863–96, cup 4in (10cm) high.
£190–210 / €270–300
$300–340 ⊞ WAA

Belleek marks

Most Belleek pieces can be marked in two ways, either impressed or by use of a transfer/decal backstamp. Early baskets had impressed Parian strips applied to the base, while later baskets carry a Parian pad with a backstamp transfer/decal.

The traditional transfer/decal backstamp consists of the Irish Wolfhound, Round Tower and Harp above the word Belleek encased in a ribbon edged with sprigs of shamrocks.

A Belleek Neptune teapot, on shell feet, c1910, 5½in (14cm) high.
£160–190 / €230–270
$260–300 ➶ JAd
This design is named after Neptune, Lord of the Seas, as it incorporates several sea shells. The Neptune teapot was made in three sizes and came with green or pink colouring.

A Belleek Handbag vase, with floral decoration, black mark, minor damage, Second Period, 1891–1926, 7in (18cm) wide.
£250–300 / €360–430
$400–480 ➶ BWL

Baskets without handles should be carefully examined to ensure that the handles have not been removed as a means of disguising damage.

◄ **A Belleek basket,** four strand, with Henshall's Twig Pattern, marked, mid-20thC, 7¾in (19.5cm) diam.
£420–500 / €600–710
$670–800 ➶ SWO

A Belleek flower pot, Second Period, 1891–1926, 4in (10cm) diam.
£90–100 / €125–140
$145–160 ⊞ WAA

A Belleek covered pot, Third Green Period, 1965–81, 5in (12.5cm) high.
£60–70 / €85–100
$95–110 ⊞ TAC

Beswick

◀ A Beswick model of a polar bear, designed by Mr Owen, No. 417, 1936–54, 7in (18cm) high.
£75–90
€105–125
$120–140
↗ BBR

A Beswick model of Beatrix Potter's Timmy Willie, by Arthur Gredington, stamped, 1949–93, 2¾in (9.5cm) high.
£30–35 / €45–50
$50–60 ↗ BBR

A Beswick model of Beatrix Potter's Squirrel Nutkin, by Arthur Gredington, stamped, 1948–80, 3¾in (9.5cm) high.
£60–70 / €85–100
$95–110 ↗ BBR

▶ A Beswick model of Beatrix Potter's Auntie Pettitoes, 1970–93, 4in (10cm) high.
£55–65 / €80–90
$90–100 ⊞ BAC

A Beswick model of a rabbit, by Albert Hallam and Graham Tongue, No. 2131, 1967–73, 2½in (6.5cm) high.
£50–60 / €70–85
$80–95 ↗ BBR

A Beswick model of a song thrush, by Albert Hallam, No. 2308, impressed mark, 1970–89, 5¾in (14.5cm) high.
£70–80 / €100–115
$110–130 ↗ BBR

A Beswick model of Beatrix Potter's Old Mr Bouncer, 1986–95, 3in (7.5cm) high.
£55–65 / €80–90
$90–100 ⊞ BAC

A Beswick model of Beatrix Potter's Chippy Hackee, 1979–93, 4in (10cm) high.
£60–70 / €85–100
$95–110 ⊞ BAC

▶ A Beswick model of Beatrix Potter's Mr Jeremy Fisher, 1987–92, 3in (7.5cm) high.
£115–130 / €165–185
$185–210 ⊞ BAC

Blue & White

A Delft pottery charger, painted with a flowering vase, on a moulded foot, Dutch, 18thC, 17½in (44.5cm) diam.
£200–240 / €280–340
$320–380 ♪ EH

A delft plate, painted with a gentleman in a garden, 18thC, 7¾in (19.5cm) diam.
£190–230 / €270–330
$300–370 ♪ G(L)

A tin-glazed earthenware dish, painted with Oriental figures in a landscape, with a lobed rim, reeded border and raised central boss, cracked, Dutch, early 18thC, 13½in (34.5cm) diam.
£130–160 / €180–230
$210–370 ♪ G(L)

A pearlware coffee pot, painted with Oriental landscape panels, late 18thC, 10in (25.5cm) high.
£100–120 / €140–170
$160–190 ♪ G(L)

A Delft blue and white wall pocket, modelled as a violin, painted with river scenes and foliage, restored, Dutch, 19thC, 18½in (47cm) wide.
£150–180 / €210–250
$240–290 ♪ G(L)

A Staffordshire half-pint mug, 19thC, 4in (10cm) high.
£30–35 / €40–50
$50–55 ⊞ MCC

◀ **A Don Pottery teapot,** decorated with Vermicelli pattern, the cover with a loop knop, restoration and hair crack, 1820–30, 11¼in (28.5cm) wide.
£220–260 / €310–370
$350–420 ♪ DN

Transfer printing

The Chinese were the first to decorate ceramics with blue and white patterns in the 17th century – an expensive process, as the decoration was hand-painted on to porcelain. However, the more cost-effective method of transfer-printing decorations was introduced in the 18th century, making these patterned ceramics more affordable.

A coffee pot, decorated with Tendril pattern, the domed cover with a button knop, with ochre lining to the rim, spout and handle, restored, 1805–20, 8¼in (21cm) high.
£70–85 / €100–120
$110–135 ♪ DN

A spittoon, transfer-printed with fruit and flowers with a border of fruiting vines, restoration and crack, 1835–50, 5in (12.5cm) diam.
£80–100 / €110–140
$130–160 ♪ DN

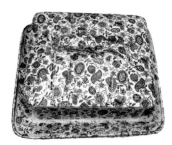

A Victorian sardine dish,
7¼in (18.5cm) wide.
£90–100 / €130–140
$140–160 ⊞ TASV

A plate, decorated with Vintage
pattern, damaged, c1860,
10in (25.5cm) diam.
£13–17 / €18–24
$21–27 ⊞ FOX

◀ **A Copeland pottery plaque,**
painted with a waterfall beside a
mill, signed and inscribed, impressed
marks, c1880, 12¼in (31cm) diam.
£90–110 / €130–160
$140–180 ↗ WW

▶ **A George Jones plate,**
decorated with Crescent pattern,
1930s, 8in (20.5cm) diam.
£14–18 / €20–26
$23–29 ⊞ FOX

A Delft wall plaque, hand-painted
with a rural scene, signed Louis
Apal, c1910, 21½in (55cm) wide.
£140–170 / €200–240
$220–270 ↗ SWO

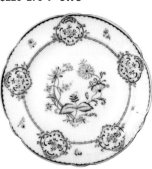

Brannam

Brannam was founded in 1879 when Charles
Herbert Brannam took over his father's
pottery in Barnstaple, Devon. In the 1880s,
Brannam introduced Barum ware, named after
Barnstaple's Roman name. Art pottery was
decorated with carved and sgraffito patterns
that revealed the red body of the ware. Blue
and green were favourite glazes, and curving
forms and marine-inspired imagery (fish and
trailing seaweed) reflected the influence of
Art Nouveau. Children's teasets became
another popular line. C. H. Brannam retired
in 1914 and the pottery was taken over by
his sons. It remains active today, producing
terracotta vases and flower pots, as well as
tableware. Pieces tend to be marked, so check
the bases for the name of the pottery, date
and the initials of the individual designer.

◀ **A C. H.
Brannam Barum
ware water jug,**
decorated with
a bird design
and foliate
bands, dated
1881, 10in
(25.5cm) high.
£70–85
€100–120
$110–140
↗ G(L)

**A pair of C. H. Brannam pottery
vases,** by James Dewdney, with
dragon handles, the bodies incised
with fish panels, repaired, incised
marks 'JD 1903', 16½in (42cm) high.
£340–410 / €480–580
$540–660 ↗ WW

**A C. H. Brannam
pottery pot,** 1920–30,
9in (23cm) high.
£150–180 / €210–250
$240–290 ⊞ LBe

Candle Extinguishers

A Worcester blush porcelain candle extinguisher, entitled 'French Cook', 1901, 2½in (6.5cm) high.
£250–270 / €350–380 $400–430 ⊞ TH

A Volkstedt porcelain candle extinguisher, German, c1900, 3½in (9cm) high.
£200–220 / €280–310 $320–350 ⊞ TH

A Minton candle extinguisher, c1880, 3½in (9cm) high.
£170–190 / €240–270 $270–300 ⊞ TH

A Royal Worcester candle extinguisher, modelled as a young lady, repaired, green printed marks, 19thC, 3¾in (9.5cm) high.
£270–320 / €380–450 $430–510 ➹ WW

Candle extinguishers became decorative items from 1840 when the new 'snuffless' candle, which could be blown out easily, was introduced. Many 19th-century extinguishers caricatured popular figures of the time.

▶ **A Volkstedt candle extinguisher,** modelled as a dog, German, c1900, 3½in (9cm) high.
£120–130 / €170–180 $190–210 ⊞ TH

Carlton Ware

A Victorian Carlton Ware cheese dish, with hand-painted and flow blue decoration, 9in (23cm) wide.
£100–110 / €140–160
$160–180 ⊞ TASV

A Carlton Ware trio, decorated with Buttercup pattern, 1930s, plate 7in (18cm) diam.
£60–65 / €85–90
$95–105 ⊞ TAC

A Carlton Ware Rouge Royale ashtray, 1930, 4in (10cm) wide.
£40–45 / €55–65
$65–70 ⊞ BET

A Carlton Ware butter dish, decorated with bees, 1930s, 6in (15cm) diam.
£240–270 / €340–380
$380–430 ⊞ CCs

A Carlton Ware cup and saucer, decorated with a polka dot pattern, with a gilded interior and handle, 1930s, saucer 4½in (11.5cm) diam.
£30–35 / €40–50
$50–55 ⊞ BET

A Carlton Ware Art Deco cream-ware coffee set, comprising 15 pieces, printed and painted marks, 1930s, coffee pot 7¾in (19.5cm) high.
£320–380 / €450–540
$510–610 ✦ SWO

A Carlton Ware bowl, decorated with Apple Blossom pattern, 1930s, 9in (23cm) wide.
£55–65 / €80–90
$90–100 ⊞ CoCo

A Carlton Ware dish, decorated with Flowers and Basket pattern, 1940, 11¾in (30cm) wide.
£65–75 / €90–110
$100–120 ⊞ StC

A Carlton Ware mug, decorated with embossed cherries, 1948–50, 4in (10cm) high.
£70–80 / €100–110
$110–130 ⊞ StC

◀ **A Carlton Ware jug,** with hand-painted decoration, 1950s, 3½in (9cm) high.
£16–20 / €23–28
$26–32 ⊞ GRo

Successfully established in the market-place since the early 1930s, the Carlton name became synonymous with lavishly decorated vases and coffee sets with rich gilding and enamel relief work. It was also well-known for its lustres and ornamental tableware designed by Violet Elmer. The Carlton works continued production throughout WWII and an impressive list of modellers and designers worked for the firm into the 1960s, their work reflecting the design advances of the period.

A Carlton Ware coffee set, 1960s, pot 13in (33cm) high.
£40–45 / €55–65
$65–70 ⊞ CCO

A Carlton Ware money box, 1970, 7in (18cm) wide.
£35–40 / €50–55
$55–65 ⊞ LUNA

A Carlton Ware Walking Ware plate, 1970s, 10in (25.5cm) high.
£24–27 / €34–38
$38–43 ⊞ BAC
Tea ware on legs was designed by husband and wife team Roger Mitchell and Danka Napiorkowska. They developed the idea in their own Lustre Pottery before linking up with Carlton Ware to mass-produce Walking Ware from 1973. This new range was very successful and expanded to include Running, Jumping and Standing Still services.

A Carlton Ware Red Baron teapot, 1980s, 9in (23cm) wide.
£75–85 / €110–120
$120–140 ⊞ TOP

A Carlton Ware Walking Ware Oxo cruet set, 1990s, 5in (12.5cm) high.
£35–40 / €50–55
$55–65 ⊞ BAC

Chinese Cargo Ware

The Chinese porcelain in this section is all cargo ware rescued from sunken ships. The Vung Tau cargo was excavated from the wreck of a Chinese junk which foundered off the coast of Vietnam, south of Vung Tau in about 1690. Some 60 years later a Dutch export vessel sank in the South China Seas. An expedition led by Englishman Mike Hatcher in 1985 resulted in a haul of 18th-century Chinese porcelain that was sold at auction under the collective name of Nanking cargo. The huge success of this sale encouraged the search for other vessels. In 1995, Christie's auctioned

porcelain salvaged from the *Diana*, a trading ship lost in about 1816 while working the India to China route. Some 24,000 objects were recovered but even this astonishing number was exceeded by the *Tek Sing* cargo, recovered in 1999. When she sank in the South China Seas in 1822, the *Tek Sing* (True Star) was carrying approximately 350,000 pieces of porcelain, making this by far the largest cargo of Chinese ceramics to be rescued from the sea and providing a fascinating insight into an early 19th-century shipment. Condition is crucial to the value of all the objects illustrated here.

Items in the Ceramics section have been arranged in date order within each sub-section.

◄ **A Vung Tao cargo miniature vase,** c1690, 2in (5cm) high.
£80–90 / €110–130
$130–145 ⊞ RBA

A Vung Tao cargo tea bowl and saucer, 1690–1700, tea bowl 1½in (4cm) high.
£130–145 / €180–200
$210–230 ⊞ McP

A Vung Tao cargo covered cup and saucer, 1690–1700, 5in (12.5cm) high.
£165–185 / €230–250
$260–290 ⊞ McP

A Nanking cargo soup dish, decorated with a Pavilion, c1750, 9in (23cm) diam.
£360–400 / €510–570
$580–640 ⊞ RBA

A Nanking cargo tea bowl and saucer, decorated with Vatavian bamboo and peonies, c1750, saucer 5in (12.5cm) diam.
£270–300 / €380–430
$430–480 ⊞ RBA
Currently known as Nanjing, Nanking was the port on the Yangtze River from where porcelain was shipped. It was not made in Nanjing, but in Jingdezhen. Nanking refers to a particular type of export porcelain, and is the type that was found on the *Geldermalsen* cargo ship which sank in 1751.

A *Diana* cargo longevity dish, 1817, 11in (28cm) diam.
£360–400 / €510–570
$580–640 ⊞ RBA

A *Tek Sing* cargo saucer, decorated with an aster flower, c1822, 5in (12.5cm) diam.
£55–60 / €80–85
$90–100 ⊞ RBA

Further reading

Miller's Chinese & Japanese Antiques Buyer's Guide, Miller's Publications, 2004

Clarice Cliff

A Clarice Cliff Bizarre Biarritz plate, c1930, 9in (23cm) wide.
**£70–85 / €100–110
$110–130** ✗ SWO

A Clarice Cliff coffee set, comprising 15 pieces, c1930.
**£220–260 / €310–370
$350–420** ✗ G(L)

A Clarice Cliff Bon Jour preserve pot and cover, decorated with Rhodanthe Aurea pattern, c1930, 4in (10cm) high.
**£180–220 / €250–310
$290–350** ✗ G(L)

A Clarice Cliff preserve pot and cover, decorated with Autumn Crocus pattern, c1930, 3½in (9cm) high.
**£150–180 / €210–250
$240–290** ✗ SWO

A Clarice Cliff bowl, moulded and painted with parrots and foliage, c1930, 8¼in (21cm) diam.
**£150–170 / €210–240
$240–270** ✗ G(L)

A Clarice Cliff bread plate, decorated with Woodland pattern, printed and inscribed marks, c1930, 8¾in (22.5cm) diam.
**£140–170 / €200–240
$220–270** ✗ SWO

A Clarice Cliff Fantasque bowl, decorated with Floreat pattern, slight wear, printed marks, c1930, 8¾in (22cm) diam.
**£100–120 / €140–170
$160–190** ✗ SWO

During the 1930s Clarice Cliff became a household name and her wares were exported around the British Empire. The secret of her success was that she was able to both model her own shapes (which by 1935 totalled over 600) and control the patterns put on them. The result was a vast choice of wares in abstract, fruit, floral and landscape designs.

A Clarice Cliff vase, decorated with Crocus pattern, c1930, 6in (15cm) high.
**£280–330 / €400–470
$450–510** ✗ L&E

A Clarice Cliff Fantasque Bizarre Athens jug, decorated with Orange Tree and House pattern, printed marks, c1930, 7in (18cm) high.
**£300–330 / €430–470
$480–530** ✗ SWO

A Clarice Cliff tureen, decorated with Solomon's Seal pattern, 1931, 6in (15cm) diam.
**£300–340 / €430–480
$480–540 ⊞ TAC**

A Clarice Cliff Bizarre sandwich plate, decorated with Idyll pattern, 1930s, 7in (18cm) wide.
**£300–360 / €430–510
$480–580 ✿ E**

A Clarice Cliff Bizarre bowl, decorated with My Garden pattern, the handles modelled as flowers, 1930s, 8in (20.5cm) high.
**£200–240 / €280–340
$320–380 ✿ DA**

Values for Clarice Cliff depend largely on pattern. Rare patterns can command thousands of pounds. In 2003 an 18in (45.5cm) May Avenue charger sold at Christie's for a world record hammer price of £34,000 / €48,300 / $54,400. The previous record was held by an Applique Windmill plaque, sold by Bonhams for £18,000 / €25,600 / $28,800.

A pair of Clarice Cliff Bizzare plates, decorated with Blue Chintz pattern, printed and impressed marks, c1933, 7½in (19cm) diam.
**£300–360 / €430–510
$480–580 ✿ Bea(E)**

A Clarice Cliff match striker and candlestick, decorated with Rhodanthe pattern, 1935, 3½in (9cm) diam.
**£95–115 / €130–160
$150–180 ⊞ BET**

A pair of Clarice Cliff Fantasque Bizarre dishes, decorated with Solitaire pattern, 1930s, 3¾in (9.5cm) wide.
**£300–350 / €430–510
$500–570 ✿ SWO**

A Clarice Cliff Bizarre salad bowl, with printed marks, 1930s, 8¼in (21cm) diam.
**£200–240 / €280–340
$320–380 ✿ L&E**

Susie Cooper

A Susie Cooper part dinner service, pattern No. E214, comprising 23 pieces, minor damage, 1930s.
£110–130 / €160–185
$175–210 ⚘ SWO

A Susie Cooper teapot, decorated with Pink Patricia Rose pattern, c1930, 5in (12.5cm) high.
£175–195 / €250–280
$280–310 ⊞ BD

A Susie Cooper coffee cup and saucer, decorated with Feather pattern, c1930, 2¼in (5.5cm) high.
£45–50 / €65–70
$70–80 ⊞ RH

Susie Cooper (1902–95) was one of the leading British ceramic designers of the 20th century. The appeal of her work lies largely in the attractive yet functional range of shapes and in the understated charm of her floral patterns with their attention to detail and muted colours.

A Susie Cooper tea cup and saucer, decorated with Talisman pattern, c1958, 3in (7.5cm) high.
£45–50 / €65–70
$70–80 ⊞ CHI

◀ **A Susie Cooper plate,** decorated with Venetia pattern, 1950s, 6½in (16.5cm) diam.
£7–11 / €10–16
$12–18 ⊞ FOX

Crown Devon

◀ **A Crown Devon charger,** with tube-lined tree, flower and leaf decoration, printed and painted mark, c1930, 11¾in (30cm) diam.
£120–140
€170–200
$190–220
⚘ SWO

A Crown Devon jug, 1950, 5in (12.5cm) high.
£11–15 / €16–20
$18–24 ⊞ BET

Crown Devon was the trade name used by the family firm of S. Fielding & Co, founded in Stoke-on-Trent in 1873 by Simon Fielding and rescued from bankruptcy five years later by Fielding's son, Abraham. Under the directorship of the latter the company prospered and expanded, developing a prolific, highly collectable range of moulded earthenware tableware, salad ware, novelties and figures. Vases, dishes and wall plaques in innovative shapes with hand-painted decoration ranging from florals to fantasy landscapes are all highly sought after by collectors. The business eventually closed in 1982.

A Crown Devon sugar shaker, hand-painted, 1930s, 4½in (11.5cm) high.
£45–50 / €65–70
$70–80 ⊞ TAC

Cups, Saucers & Mugs

◀ **A Rocking-ham cup and saucer,** pattern No. 643, crack to saucer, red printed mark, c1839.
£160–190
€**230–270**
$260–300
⚹ **WW**

A Lowestoft-style porcelain coffee cup, hand-painted, with an internal drape-and-dart border, damaged, 18thC, 2½in (6.5cm) high.
£90–110 / €**130–160**
$140–180 ⚹ **DMC**

A Coalport mug, decorated with Cossacks being addressed by Count Platov, with a gilt rim, c1812, 5½in (14cm) high.
£110–130 / €**160–180**
$180–210 ⚹ **SAS**

▶ **A salt-glazed loving cup,** with greyhound handles, depicting George and the Dragon, c1860, 5¼in (13.5cm) high.
£130–140 / €**180–200**
$210–220 ⊞ **KES**

A Victorian pottery loving cup, transfer-printed 'God Speed the Plough' and 'To My Mother 1871', 5¼in (13.5cm) high.
£70–85 / €100–120
$110–140 ⚒ PF

A George Jones trio, c1900, plate 6in (15cm) diam.
£30–35 / €40–50
$50–55 ⊞ FOX

An Aynsley silver-mounted bone china coffee set, comprising 12 pieces, the stands hallmarked Birmingham 1918.
£180–220 / €250–310
$290–350 ⚒ G(L)

◄ **A Wilkinson Romany fortune-telling tea cup and saucer,** 1930s, saucer 6in (15cm) diam.
£30–35 / €40–50
$50–55 ⊞ BET

A Crown Staffordshire cup and saucer, decorated with a golf scene, 1950s, saucer 5in (12.5cm) diam.
£40–45 / €55–65
$65–70 ⊞ CHI

◄ **An Adams cup and saucer,** decorated with Daisy pattern, 1960s, cup 3in (7.5cm) high.
£16–20 / €24–28
$26–32 ⊞ CHI

► **A Royal Albert TV cup and saucer,** decorated with Queen's Messenger pattern, 1960s, saucer 9in (23cm) wide.
£35–40 / €50–55
$55–65 ⊞ CHI

◄ **A Meissen cup and saucer,** painted with birds and chrysanthemum sprigs, crossed swords mark, late 19thC.
£180–220 / €250–310
$290–350 ⚒ G(L)

A Radford trio, with transfer-printed decoration, 1900–15, plate 5in (12.5cm) diam.
£45–50 / €65–70
$70–80 ⊞ BET

A Palissy cup and saucer, from the Game Series, 1950s, cup 4in (10cm) high.
£14–18 / €20–26
$23–29 ⊞ CHI

A Cauldon Grindley Passover trio, 1950s, cup 3in (7.5cm) high.
£30–35 / €40–50
$50–55 ⊞ CHI

A Royal Albert Gossamer cup and saucer, 1950s, cup 3in (7.5cm) high.
£20–25 / €30–35
$35–40 ⊞ CHI

The ORIGINAL Golliwogg Company™ present:

Free Newsletter for each Millers reader. The Original Golliwogg is very 'PC' - and he's back.

Learn all about him and his fabulous creator, Florence Upton, in 'The Original Golly Times' - FREE.

Badges, Dolls, Pottery. Limited Editions. 'Read all about it!'

Telephone for your free copy - 0208 3189580.

Golly in his Auto Cart: Blue Edition 250 only - Made by Carlton Ware. £55 inc. p&p.

FREE

New Golly Book:

The Golliwogg's Circus.

Limited Edition 1000. Hardback A4.

Signed and numbered

First Issue: 1903

Reissued: 2003 Price £25

By the Original Golliwogg

Company: 020 8318 9580

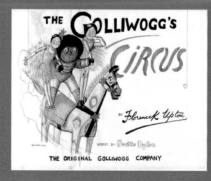

THE ORIGINAL GOLLIWOGG COMPANY

Denby

◀ **A Denby Pastel Blue vase,** designed by Donald Gilbert, moulded with an owl, early 1930s, 4in (10cm) high.
£175–195 / €250–280 $280–310 ⊞ KES

A Denby tankard, designed by Glyn Colledge, hand-decorated with scenes of jousting knights, signed, c1949, 6in (15cm) high.
£110–120 / €155–170 $175–190 ⊞ KES

A Denby jug, designed by Glyn Colledge, decorator's mark, early 1950s, 9in (23cm) high.
£110–120 / €155–170 $175–190 ⊞ KES

▶ **A Denby Falstaff plate,** c1971, 8in (20.5cm) diam.
£18–22 / €26–30 $28–35 ⊞ CHI

A Denby Ode water jug, c1963, 10in (25.5cm) high.
£20–25 / €28–35 $32–40 ⊞ CHI

A Denby Canterbury coffee pot, c1965, 9in (23cm) high.
£25–30 / €35–40 $40–50 ⊞ CHI

Denby Pottery is famous for its leadless salt-glazed stoneware in subdued colours. It was founded in Denby, Derbyshire, by William Bourne in 1809. By the 1920s many lines had become outmoded, but in 1931 Norman Wood joined the company and modernized production. He was joined in 1934 by designer and modeller Donald Gilbert. Denby's potential for making decorative wares moved up another gear, with the post-WWII range being much enhanced by the work of the designer Glyn Colledge. After nearly 200 years the company is still going strong.

◀ **A Denby Romany cup and saucer,** 1970s, cup 2½in (6.5cm) high.
£14–16 €19–22 $23–26 ⊞ CHI

▶ **A Denby Falling Leaves cup and saucer,** c1984, cup 2½in (6.5cm) high.
£12–14 €17–20 $19–24 ⊞ CHI

Doulton

A Doulton Lambeth Slaters Patent lemonade jug and two beakers, with silver collars and raised floral gilt decoration, late 19thC, jug 8in (20.5cm) high.
£80–100 / €110–140
$130–160 ⚒ DMC

A Royal Doulton Natural Foliage ware vase, decorated with impressed leaves and enamels, c1910, 6¾in (17cm) high.
£110–130 / €155–185
$175–200 ⚒ G(L)

A Doulton Lambeth candlestick, by Emily Partington, with stylized floral and foliate decoration, 19thC, 11¾in (30cm) high.
£160–190 / €230–270
$250–300 ⚒ WilP

◄ **A Royal Doulton stoneware fruit bowl,** impressed marks and inscription, 1927, 9¾in (25cm) diam.
£100–120 / €140–170
$160–190 ⚒ SWO

A Royal Doulton cake tray, 1920s, 13in (33cm) long.
£65–75 / €90–105
$105–120 ⊞ BET

Doulton pottery dates from 1815 when a factory was founded by the partnership of John Doulton, Martha Jones and John Watts at Vauxhall Walk, Lambeth, London. It produced a range of wares from decorative bottles to salt-glazed sewer pipes. By 1853 John Doulton and his son, Henry, had established themselves as makers of fine English stoneware and the company assumed the Doulton name. In the early years of the reign of Queen Victoria there was a great revolution in personal sanitation, and Doulton was at the forefront of domestic and industrial stoneware. This enabled Doulton to become Britain's leading manufacturer of sanitary ware and a major influence and producer of artistic pottery and commemorative, ornamental and tableware products. In 1901 the factory was granted both the Royal Warrant and the right to use 'Royal' on the company name. Production at this world-famous factory continues today.

A Royal Doulton figure, entitled 'The Cobbler', designed by C. J. Noke, HN1705, restored, maker's marks, 1935–49, 8¼in (21cm) high.
£190–230 / €270–330
$300–370 ➚ BBR

A Royal Doulton Robin Hood loving cup, designed by C. J. Noke and H. Fenton, No. 230 of 600, hair crack, 1938, 8¾in (22cm) high.
£220–260 / €310–370
$350–420 ➚ TRM

◀ A Royal Doulton tea cup and saucer, decorated with Gleneagles pattern, 1950s, 3in (7.5cm) high.
£27–30
€38–42
$42–50 ⊞ CHI

A Royal Doulton figure, entitled 'The Mask Seller', designed by Lesley Harradine, HN2103, c1960, 9in (23cm) high.
£120–145 / €170–200
$190–230 ➚ DA

A Royal Doulton Chatcull model of a monkey, HN2657, 1960–69, 4in (10cm) high.
£110–130 / €155–185
$175–210 ➚ SWO

▶ A Royal Doulton trio, decorated with Tapestry pattern, 1960s, cup 3in (7.5cm) high.
£35–40 / €50–60
$55–65 ⊞ CHI

A Royal Doulton figure, entitled 'Southern Belle', designed by M. Davies, HN2229, maker's marks, c1960, 8in (20.5cm) high.
£65–75 / €90–105
$105–120 ➚ BBR

A Royal Doulton coffee pot, decorated with Parquet pattern, 1960s, 8in (20.5cm) high.
£35–40 / €50–60
$55–65 ⊞ CHI

◀ **A Royal Doulton coffee pot,** decorated with Caprice pattern, 1960s, 9½in (24cm) high.
£35–40 / €50–60
$55–65 ⊞ CHI

A Royal Doulton jug, decorated with Larchmont pattern, 1960s, 3in (7.5cm) high.
£18–20 / €25–28
$28–32 ⊞ CHI

A Royal Doulton Nightwatchman character jug, designed by Max Henk, No. D6569, maker's mark, c1970, 7¼in (18.5cm) high.
£50–60 / €70–85
$80–95 ♦ BBR

A Royal Doulton teapot, decorated with Summer Days pattern, 1970s, 7in (18cm) high.
£40–45 / €60–65
$65–70 ⊞ CHI

▶ **A Royal Doulton Wyatt Earp character jug,** designed by Stanley J. Taylor, No. D6711, maker's mark, 1985–89, 5¼in (13.5cm) high.
£45–55 / €65–80
$70–90 ♦ BBR

A Royal Doulton Beefeater character jug, designed by Harry Fenton, No. D6251, 1987–91, 2½in (6.5cm) high.
£22–26 / €30–36
$35–42 ♦ BBR

A Royal Doulton model of Bride Bunnykins, designed by Graham Tongue, DB101, maker's mark, 1991, 4¼in (11cm) high, with box.
£25–30 / €35–40
$45–50 ♦ BBR

◀ **A Royal Doulton Winston Churchill character jug,** by Stanley James Taylor, special edition, 1992, 7in (18cm) high, with certificate.
£95–115 / €135–165
$150–185 ♦ WAL

Dunmore Pottery

The art pottery of Dunmore demonstrates many influences stretching from the celebration of natural form and mythical creatures of the Arts and Crafts Movement to the international eclecticism and extravagance of the Aesthetic Movement. The work of this small estate pottery (1834–1902) near Airth in Stirlingshire is now known for its distinctive rich and deep-coloured lead glazes. The local master potter, Peter Gardner, was particularly inventive in creating both form and glazes. Queen Victoria was a patron and in 1876 Glasgow Museum and Art Gallery purchased over 100 pieces from the pottery. After Gardner's death in 1902 the pottery was sold and it finally closed down during WWI.

A Dunmore jug, c1880,
6in (15cm) high.
£130–145 / €185–210
$210–230 ⊞ GLB

A Dunmore vase, c1885,
5½in (14cm) high.
£115–130 / €165–185
$185–210 ⊞ GLB

A Dunmore cauldron, c1890,
6in (15cm) high.
£260–290 / €370–420
$420–460 ⊞ GLB

▶ **A Dunmore tea tray,**
by Peter Gardner, c1890,
18in (45.5cm) wide.
£300–340 / €420–480
$480–540 ⊞ SAAC

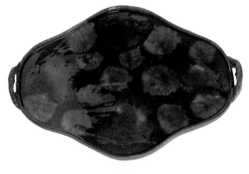

**A Dunmore double gourd
vase,** decorated with *sang
de boeuf* glaze, 1890–1900,
9in (23cm) high.
£260–290 / €370–420
$420–460 ⊞ SAAC

A Dunmore vase, c1890,
11in (28cm) high.
£170–190 / €240–270
$270–300 ⊞ GLB

◀ **A Dunmore majolica
bread plate,** 1890–1900,
12in (30.5cm) diam.
£230–260 / €320–370
$370–420 ⊞ SAAC

Egg Cups

A Royal Crown Derby egg cup, c1897, 2in (5cm) high.
£100–110 / €140–155 $160–175 ⊞ AMH

An egg cup, decorated with Willow pattern, c1840, 2½in (6.5cm) high.
£45–50 / €65–70 $70–80 ⊞ AMH

A Minton egg cup, c1891, 2¼in (6.5cm) high.
£75–85 / €105–120 $120–135 ⊞ AMH

A Royal Worcester egg cup, 1901, 2¼in (5.5cm) high.
£55–60 / €80–85 $90–95 ⊞ AMH

A Grainger's Worcester egg cup, 1902, 2in (5cm) high.
£45–50 / €65–70 $70–80 ⊞ AMH

A Crown Staffordshire egg cup, c1906, 2¼in (5.5cm) high.
£35–40 / €50–55 $55–65 ⊞ AMH

A Copeland Spode egg cup, transfer-printed with Tower pattern, c1910, 2¼in (5.5cm) high.
£35–40 / €50–55 $55–65 ⊞ AMH

A Rifle Society egg cup, 1910, 2½in (6.5cm) high.
£18–20 / €25–28 $28–32 ⊞ HUX

A Minton egg cup, decorated with Blue Copenhagen pattern, c1912, 2in (5cm) high.
£55–60 / €80–85 $90–100 ⊞ AMH

▶ **A pair of Quimper goose egg cups,** c1940, 3in (7.5cm) high.
£35–40 / €50–55 $55–65 ⊞ SER

◀ **Two lustre egg cups,** Japanese, 1920s, 3in (7.5cm) high.
£25–30 / €35–40 $40–50 each ⊞ CoCo

A Worcester egg cup, in the shape of a hen, 1960s, 4in (10cm) high.
£25–30 / €35–40 $40–50 ⊞ AMH

Figures & Fairings

A Derby figure of Mars,
c1780, 7in (18cm) high.
£220–250 / €310–350
$350–400 ⊞ SER

**A Sampson figure of a
gentleman,** wearing
18thC dress, 19thC,
5in (12.5cm) high.
£165–185 / €230–260
$260–300 ⊞ SER

**A Prattware figure
of Apollo,** c1790,
5in (12.5cm) high.
£135–150 / €190–210
$210–240 ⊞ SER

▶ **A Meissen
figural group,**
of a gentleman
and a lady with
a child on her
knee, German,
19thC, 9in
(23cm) high.
£300–360
€420–500
$480–580 ✦ AH

**A Prattware figure
of a lady,** c1780,
5in (12.5cm) high.
£155–175 / €220–250
$250–280 ⊞ SER

LOCATE THE SOURCE
The source of each illustration in Miller's can be
found by checking the code letters below each
caption with the Key to Illustrations, pages 443–451.

A porcelain figural group,
of a Scotsman and a boy
seated on rockwork with
moulded thistles, inscribed
'Ye Maunna Tramp on
the Scotch Thistle Laddie',
Continental, 19thC,
7½in (19cm) wide.
£200–240 / €280–340
$320–380 ✦ SWO

**A Derby figure
of a child,** c1810,
4½in (11.5cm) high.
£115–130 / €165–185
$185–200 ⊞ SER

A fairing, entitled
'Trespassing', c1870,
5½in (14cm) high.
£150–180 / €210–260
$240–290 ✦ SAS

A fairing, entitled 'Attack',
c1870, 5½in (14cm) high.
£180–210 / €260–300
$290–330 ✦ SAS

▶ **A Royal Dux porcelain
compote,** modelled as a girl
and two putti supporting
a bowl, 1890–1910,
19½in (49.5cm) high.
£340–400 / €480–570
$540–640 ✦ BAu

A bisque figure of a putto, German, 1910, 1½in (4cm) high.
£55–60 / €80–85
$90–95 ⊞ CCs

A bisque figure of a boy, symbolizing faith, hope and charity, German, 1910, 1½in (4cm) high.
£40–45 / €60–65
$65–70 ⊞ CCs

A bisque piano baby, c1910, 4in (10cm) long.
£90–100 / €130–140
$145–160 ⊞ JOA

Founded by Miklos Zsolnay in 1853, the Zsolnay pottery of Pecs in southwest Hungary was known for stoneware, earthenware, art pottery and architectural ceramics. They pioneered new materials and glazes, including an outdoor ceramic that was resistant to weather and pollution. Chemist Vinsce Wartha (1844–1914) developed a distinctive red glaze much sought-after by collectors. Highly successful in the 19th and first half of the 20th century, the company suffered from the advance of communism during WWII. The Zsolnay family were seen as catering to borgeois taste and were ousted and persecuted. In the 1950s, however, the factory regained its creativity and it remains in operation today.

A Zsolnay figure of a female nude, Hungarian, 1914, 14in (35.5cm) high.
£450–500 / €640–710
$720–800 ⊞ KA

▶ **An Ipsen figure of a girl,** designed by M. Kursten, c1925, 8½in (21.5cm) high.
£220–250 / €310–350
$350–400 ⊞ DSG
Ipsens Enke pottery was founded in Copenhagen in 1843 by Peter Ipsen (1815–60). After his death, his widow continued the business until his son Bertel (1846–1917) took over in 1865. The company was associated with many internationally known artists including Kay Nielson and Georg Jensen, and won countless awards from all over the world.

A bisque figure of a girl, c1920, 4in (10cm) high.
£35–40 / €50–55
$55–65 ⊞ YC

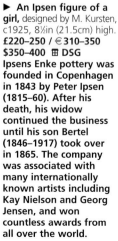

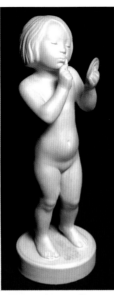

A porcelain figural perfume burner, 1950, 8½in (21.5cm) high.
£60–70 / €85–100
$95–110 ⚑ GK

A Wade Pex Nylons figure of a fairy, c1952, 2½in (6.5cm) high.
£200–240 / €290–340
$320–380 ⚑ BBR

A porcelain figure, modelled as Galina Vishnevskaya as Marfa, printed mark, Russian, c1920s, 15in (38cm) high.
£360–430 / €500–600
$580–690 ⚑ SJH
The soprano Galina Vishnevskaya (b. c1928) was a leading diva at the Bolshoi Theatre, and sung in major opera houses of the world. In this piece she is modelled as Marfa in Rimsky-Korsakoff's opera *The Tsar's Bride*.

An Ipsen bisque figure of a girl, signed, c1925, 8in (20.5cm) high.
£220–250 / €310–350
$350–400 ⊞ DSG

Hummels were the result of a collaboration between W. Goebel porcelain factory, established in 1871 in West Germany, and a young nun, Sister Maria Innocentia Hummel. Born Berta Hummel in 1909, she trained as an artist before entering the Franciscan Convent of Siessen in 1931. Nevertheless, she continued to draw and her pictures of country children were published in the form of postcards. Franz Goebel obtained the rights to turn her creations into ceramic figures which were launched to immediate acclaim at the Leipzig Spring Fair in 1935. Sister Hummel died from tuberculosis in 1946 at the age of only 37. Production of the figures continued, based on her original drawings and approved by an artistic board established at her convent to continue the Hummel tradition. As well as figures, in 1971 the company introduced the first annual M. I. Hummel plate and 1977 saw the introduction of the Goebel Collectors' Club.

A Hummel figure of a goat herder, by Goebel, 1960–72, 4½in (11.5cm) high.
£150–165 / €210–240
$240–270 ⊞ TAC

Three bisque 'Memories of Yesterday' Mabel Lucie Attwell figures, 1988–99, 6in (15cm) high.
£40–45 / €55–65
$60–70 each ⊞ MEM

A Hummel figure of a boy, by Goebel, 1970, 4in (10cm) high.
£75–85 / €105–120
$120–135 ⊞ PrB

◀ **Two Shelley figures,** Lilbet and Lil Bill, made for the Shelley China Club USA, 1997, 5¾in (14.5cm) high, with box and certificates.
£120–140 / €170–200
$190–220 ⚑ BBR

Gaudy Welsh

Gaudy Welsh or Gaudy ware is the name given to 19th-century earthenware that was 'gaudily' painted with stylized flower patterns. It was first produced in Staffordshire in the 1820s and favourite colours included orange, green and cobalt blue. Pink, yellow and turquoise were also used and wares were accented with gold and pink lustre. Competing with Staffordshire, Welsh potteries including Swansea, Llanelly and Cambrian soon began to produce their own Gaudy Welsh. In Wales, however, the cheap and cheerful pottery which decorated many country cottages and farmhouse dressers was popularly known as 'Swansea Cottage'. Much Gaudy Welsh was exported to the USA, where it is very collectable today, and production continued into the early 20th century. While early pieces are generally speaking unmarked, later examples of Gaudy Welsh are often stamped with the manufacturer's name.

A Gaudy Welsh jug, decorated with Grape pattern, c1840, 4in (10cm) high.
£45–50 / €65–70
$70–80 ⊞ **TOP**

A Gaudy Welsh child's mug, c1840, 3in (7.5cm) high.
£60–65 / €85–95
$95–105 ⊞ **TOP**

A Gaudy Welsh mug, decorated with Conway pattern, c1845, 3in (7.5cm) high.
£80–90 / €115–130
$130–145 ⊞ **TOP**

◀ **A Gaudy Welsh plate,** decorated with Vine pattern, c1845, 10in (25.5cm) diam.
£120–135 / €170–190
$190–210 ⊞ **TOP**

▶ **A Gaudy Welsh vase,** with lion's head handles, c1845, 7in (18cm) high.
£120–135 / €170–190
$190–210 ⊞ **TOP**

A Gaudy Welsh teapot, decorated with Venus pattern, c1850, 10in (25.5cm) wide.
£200–220 / €280–310
$320–350 ⊞ **FOX**

▶ **A Gaudy Welsh cup and saucer,** decorated with Columbine pattern cup damaged, c1850, saucer 6in (15cm) diam.
£25–30 / €35–40
$40–50 ⊞ **FOX**

A Gaudy Welsh jug, 19thC, 5in (12.5cm) high.
£55–60 / €75–85
$85–95 ⊞ **WAC**

Goss & Crested China

A model of a steam locomotive, with Hythe crest, marked, German, c1920s, 1¼in (3cm) high.
£110–125 / €155–175
$175–200 ⊞ JMC

A model of Felix the Cat, c1920s, 5in (12.5cm) high.
£110–125 / €155–170
$175–195 ⊞ MURR

A lustre model of a donkey, with Hastings crest, German, c1910–24, 3½in (9cm) high.
£45–50 / €60–70
$70–80 ⊞ TWO

An Arcadian ashtray, with Bognor crest, early 20thC, 3½in (9cm) wide.
£14–16 / €19–22
$23–26 ⊞ G&CC

An Arcadian model of a fireplace, inscribed 'We've Kept the Home Fires Burning', c1915, 5in (12.5cm) high.
£35–40 / €50–55
$55–60 ⊞ JUN

A model of a Cheddar cheese, with Cheddar crest, possibly 1930s, 2½in (6.5cm) diam.
£22–25 / €32–35
$35–40 ⊞ JMC

◀ **An Arcadian model of a mortar-board,** with Wembley crest, 1924, 2¾in (7cm) wide.
£25–30 / €35–40
$40–45 ⊞ JMC

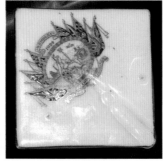

An Arcadian model of a Tommy and his machine gun, with arms of Taunton, 1914–18, 3in (7.5cm) high.
£65–75 / €95–105
$105–120 ⊞ TWO
Tommy was the traditional name for British soldiers in WWI. The expression was made popular by Rudyard Kipling in his poem about Tommy Atkins called 'Tommy'.

An Arcadian model of Tower Bridge, with Wembley Exhibition crest, c1925, 4in (10cm) high.
£60–65 / €85–95
$95–105 ⊞ JMC

An Arcadian model of a cat on a jug, No.1 of a series of 24, with Grange over Sands crest, 1924–33, 2½in (6.5cm) high.
£60–70 / €85–100
$95–110 ⊞ G&CC

An Arcadian model of a petrol can, with arms of Melrose, 1920s–30s, 2¼in (5.5cm) high.
£20–25 / €28–35
$32–40 ⊞ JMC

An Arcadian cigarette holder, with Worcester crest, 1925–33, 4in (10cm) high.
£140–160 / €210–230
$230–260 ⊞ G&CC

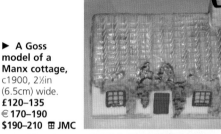

An Arcadian model of a wicker basket and six milk bottles, with Derby crest, 1920s–30s, 2½in (6.5cm) high.
£25–30 / €35–40
$40–45 ⊞ JMC

A Carlton vase, inscribed 'Lucky White Heather from Eastbourne', 1920s–30s, 3¼in (8.5cm) high.
£12–15 / €17–21
$19–24 ⊞ JMC

A Carlton model of a cabinet gramophone, inscribed 'Music Hath Charms', c1920s, 4in (10cm) high.
£90–100 / €125–140
$145–160 ⊞ MURR

A Carlton lustre model of the World Cup, with Brighton crest, c1920s, 4½in (11.5cm) high.
£85–95 / €120–135
$135–150 ⊞ MURR

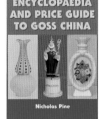

▶ **A Goss model of a Manx cottage,** c1900, 2½in (6.5cm) wide.
£120–135
€170–190
$190–210 ⊞ JMC

A Goss club vase, with Merchants Mark of John Halle crest, c1900, 2¼in (5.5cm) high.
£16–18 / €22–25
$25–28 ⊞ G&CC

A Goss Bath Roman jug, with the arms of five London boroughs, c1900, 6in (15cm) high.
£25–30 / €35–40
$40–45 ⊞ G&CC

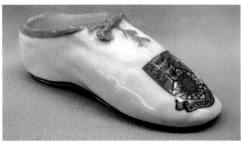

A Goss model of Queen Victoria's first shoe, with Westgate-on-Sea crest, c1900, 4in (10cm) long.
£30–35 / €45–50
$50–55 ⊞ G&CC

A Goss model of Isaac Walton's birthplace at Shallowford, c1900, 3½in (9cm) wide.
£360–400 / €510–570
$580–640 ⊞ G&CC

A Goss model of a Rufus stone, with Lyndhurst, New Forest crest, c1900, 3¾in (9.5cm) high.
£20–25 / €30–35
$35–40 ⊞ G&CC

A Goss model of an Elizabethan jug, with Stamford and Queen Elizabeth crests, c1900, 3½in (9cm) high.
£35–40 / €50–55
$55–60 ⊞ G&CC

A Goss loving cup, with Goss crests of Stoke and Staffordshire, c1900, 2in (5cm) high.
£35–40 / €50–55
$55–60 ⊞ G&CC

Goss china

Goss china was first produced at the Stoke-on-Trent pottery owned by William Henry Goss. It became a craze in Victorian and Edwardian times, when day trippers bought small ivory-coloured porcelain ornaments decorated with the coat-of-arms of the locality to take home as a memento.

When storing your crested china be sure not to wrap it in newspaper – the ink can oxidize the paint, resulting in faded colours.

A Goss model of St Nicholas Chapel, Ilfracombe, c1910, 3in (7.5cm) wide.
£180–200 / €260–290
$290–320 ⊞ G&CC

Items in the Goss & Crested China section have been arranged in alphabetical order by factory, with non-specific pieces appearing first.

A Goss model of a Welsh picyn, c1910, 2¼in (6cm) diam.
£35–40 / €50–55
$55–60 ⊞ CCC
Picyn is the Welsh name for a porridge bowl.

◄ A Goss nightlight, modelled in the form of Robert Burns' cottage, 1920–29, 6in (15cm) wide.
£150–170 / €210–240
$240–270 ⊞ TWO

A Goss cream jug, in the form of a Welsh lady, c1920s, 4in (10cm) high.
£45–50 / €60–70
$70–80 ⊞ TWO

A Goss bagware cream jug, decorated with seagulls, c1920s, 3in (7.5cm) high.
£65–75 / €90–100
$105–120 ⊞ TWO

A Goss model of the First and Last house, 1920–29, 2½in (6.5cm) wide.
£110–125 / €160–180
$180–200 ⊞ TWO

A Goss bell, in the form of a lady, with clapper, 1929–39, 3¾in (9.5cm) high.
£130–145 / €185–210
$210–230 ⊞ G&CC

A Goss Toby jug, 1929–39, 6¼in (16cm) high.
£150–170 / €210–240
$240–270 ⊞ G&CC

▶ **A Goss pin dish,** decorated with plums, c1920s, 4in (10cm) diam.
£75–85
€105–120
$120–135
⊞ TWO

A Goss model of a cheddar cheese, 1930s, 2in (5cm) high.
£50–55 / €70–80
$80–90 ⊞ JMC

A Goss beaker, with arms of Burns crest, 1930s, 4½in (11.5cm) high.
£50–55 / €70–80
$80–90 ⊞ JMC

A Grafton model of a calf, with Goudhurst crest and Isle of Wight verse, 1920s, 2in (5cm) high.
£40–45 / €50–60
$65–75 ⊞ G&CC

A Grafton model of a boat, with Weston-Super-mare crest, early 20thC, 4½in (11.5cm) wide.
£35–40 / €50–55
$55–60 ⊞ G&CC

A Grafton figure of a golfer, inscribed 'The Colonel', with crest, early 20thC, 3½in (9cm) high.
£55–65 / €80–90
$90–100 ⊞ G&CC

◄ **A Willow Art model of a bottle,** with Gretna Green crest, early 20thC, 4in (10cm) high.
£16–18 / €22–25
$25–28 ⊞ JMC

► **A Willow Art model of a chair,** inscribed 'The Old Priest's Chair Gretna Green', with crest, early 20thC, 3¼in (8.5cm) high.
£22–25 / €32–35
$35–40 ⊞ G&CC

► **A Willow Art model of a sundial,** decorated with a picture of Felix the Cat, c1920s, 6in (15cm) high.
£180–200 / €250–280
$290–320 ⊞ MURR

◄ **A Wilton model of a coal truck,** with City of Manchester crest, 1920s, 2¼in (5.5cm) wide.
£50–55 / €70–80
$80–90 ⊞ JMC

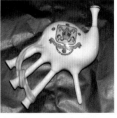

A Wilton model of a radio operator, with arms of Margate, 1920–27, 3¼in (8.5cm) high.
£110–125 / €155–175
$175–200 ⊞ G&CC

A Wilton model of a set of bagpipes, with Glastonbury crest, early 1920s, 4¾in (9.5cm) wide.
£55–60 / €75–85
$85–95 ⊞ JMC

T. G. Green

A T. G. Green Grassmere hors d'oeuvres dish and sauce boat, 1930s, dish 9¼in (23.5cm) diam.
£35–40 / €50–56
$56–64 ⊞ RET

A T. G. Green bulb bowl, 1927–30, 7in (18cm) diam.
£80–90 / €115–130
$130–145 ⊞ CAL

A T. G. Green jug, 1900–10, 6½in (16.5cm) high.
£130–140 / €185–200
$210–220 ⊞ CAL

Two T. G. Green Cornish Ware storage jars, c1930, 3½in (9cm) high.
£100–110 / €140–155
$160–175 each ⊞ CHI

A T. G. Green mug, c1930s, 4½in (10.5cm) high.
£50–55 / €70–80
$80–90 ⊞ CAL

A T. G. Green Eclipse trio, c1930, cup 3in (7.5cm) high.
£20–25 / €28–35
$32–42 ⊞ CAL

▶ A T. G. Green Cornish Ware mug, 1930s–50s, 4in (10cm) high.
£60–70
€85–100
$95–110 ⊞ CAL

Cornish Ware

Blue-banded Cornish Ware is made from white earthenware which is dipped in blue slip. The bands are then cut through the slip, using a lathe, revealing the white body underneath. Other colours of Cornish Ware were introduced after the 1960s. These include yellow, black, gold and red, which was a test range that never went into production and is therefore very rare. Green has been introduced more recently.

A T. G. Green Blue Domino teapot,
1930s–50s, 5in (12.5cm) high.
£145–160 / €210–230
$230–260 ⊞ CHI

A T. G. Green coffee cup and saucer, 1950s,
cup 2½in (6.5cm) high.
£16–18 / €22–25
$25–28 ⊞ CAL

A T. G. Green Cornish Ware cruet set, with two salts, 1960,
tray 6in (15cm) diam.
£115–130 / €165–185
$185–210 ⊞ CAL

A T. G. Green Cornish Ware teapot, designed by Judith Onions,
1966, 5in (12.5cm) high.
£50–55 / €70–80
$80–90 ⊞ CAL

A T. G. Green Blue Domino cruet set, 1950,
tray 6in (15cm) diam.
£55–65 / €80–90
$90–100 ⊞ CAL

▶ **A T. G. Green Patio sandwich plate and cup,** decorated with
Safari pattern, 1956, plate 9in (23cm) wide.
£35–40 / €50–55
$55–60 ⊞ CAL

Further reading

Miller's Ceramics of the '50s & '60s: A Collector's Guide,
Miller's Publications, 2001

A T. G. Green tea set, 1956,
teapot 5in (12.5cm) high.
£35–40 / €50–55
$55–60 ⊞ RET

◀ **A T. G. Green black Cornish Ware storage jar,** 1960,
5in (12.5cm) high.
£100–110 / €140–155
$160–175 ⊞ CAL
Black Cornish Ware was not mass produced and is therefore rare.

Judith Onions

In the 1960s, a young designer named Judith Onions worked with T. G. Green. Her work involved a major restyle of the Cornish Ware using clean and modern shapes. She also designed the target backstamp that was based on the Cornish bands and used throughout the 1970s.

A T. G. Green Channel Isles coffee pot,
designed by Judith Onions and Martin Hunt, 1968,
8in (20.5cm) high.
£60–70 / €85–100
$95–110 ⊞ CAL

A T. G. Green Cornish Ware collector's plate, 1996, 9in (23cm) diam.
£22–25 / €30–35
$35–40 ⊞ CAL
This plate is from a limited edition that was produced exclusively for the Cornish Collectors' Club.

Honey Pots

A porcelain honey pot and cover, with transfer-printed floral decoration and gilt borders, 19thC, 4¼in (11cm) high.
£65–75 / €90–105
$105–120 ↗ JAd

A Clarice Cliff Fantasque Bizarre honey pot, decorated with Red Roof pattern, minor damage, printed marks, 1920s, 2½in (6.5cm) high.
£200–240 / €280–340
$320–380 ↗ L&E

A Carter, Stabler & Adams honey box, 1930, 5in (12.5cm) square.
£340–380 / €480–540
$540–610 ⊞ CCs

A Shorter & Sons honey box, c1930, 5in (12.5cm) square.
£240–270 / €340–380
$380–430 ⊞ CCs

A Carlton Ware honey box, 1930s, 7in (18cm) square.
£360–400 / €510–570
$580–640 ⊞ CCs

A ceramic honey pot, commemorating the Coronation of George VI, 1937, 5in (12.5cm) high.
£70–80 / €100–110
$110–130 ⊞ BAC

A lustre honey pot, inscribed 'A Present from Margate', 1930s, 5in (12.5cm) high.
£13–15 / €18–20
$20–24 ⊞ CCs

A pottery honey pot, 1930s, 5in (12.5cm) high.
£60–70 / €85–100
$95–110 ⊞ CCs

▶ **A Marutomo ware honey pot,** Japanese, 1940s, 4in (10cm) wide.
£40–45 / €55–60
$65–75 ⊞ BAC

A Marutomo ware honey box, Japanese, 1930s, 4in (10cm) square.
£45–50 / €65–70
$70–80 ⊞ BAC

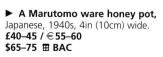

A Crown Devon honey box,
1940, 5in (12.5cm) square.
**£150–165 / €210–230
$240–260 ⊞ CCs**

Cross Reference
See Figures & Fairings
(pages 112–114)

A Goebel honey pot, in the
form of a bee, German, 1940s,
4¾in (12cm) high.
**£65–75 / €90–105
$105–120 ⊞ BET**

◄ **A cottage ware honey pot,**
1950s, 5in (12.5cm) high.
**£25–30 / €35–40
$40–45 ⊞ BAC**

A ceramic honey pot, with floral
decoration, 1990s, 6in (15cm) high.
**£6–8 / €9–11
$10–12 ⊞ BAC**

Honiton

◄ **A Honiton vase,** with stylized floral
decoration, 1900s, 10in (25.5cm) high.
**£75–85 / €105–120
$120–135 ⊞ HPCS**

A Honiton dish, with sgraffito Jacobean
pattern, 1920s, 10in (25.5cm) wide.
**£55–65 / €80–90
$90–105 ⊞ HPCS**

◄ **A Honiton ashtray,** 1940,
3½in (9cm) diam.
**£10–12 / €14–17
$16–19 ⊞ BrL**

A Honiton posy vase,
1950, 3¾in (9.5cm) high.
**£12–15 / €17–20
$20–24 ⊞ BrL**

A Honiton dish, 1950,
4¾in (12cm) high.
**£8–10 / €12–14
$14–16 ⊞ BrL**

A Honiton jug, 1950, 3¼in (8.5cm) high.
**£12–15 / €17–20
$20–24 ⊞ BrL**

Hornsea

Hornsea Pottery was established in 1949 by two brothers, Desmond and Colin Rawson. They first produced gift ware and 'fancies' aimed at the souvenir trade. Items such as Toby jugs, boots, posy vases and other novelties that were produced in the early 1950s are now highly prized by collectors. The Rawsons moved to larger premises on the outskirts of Hornsea in 1954, which gave room for expansion, development and larger kilns. This enabled the production of large vases and contemporary-style pieces that are now sought after by enthusiasts of post-WWII pottery.

One of the strengths of Hornsea was the willingness of its owners to invest in new design and designers. This resulted in stylized animal figures by Marion Campbell, vases, lamps and wall plaques by John Clappison and tableware by Martin Hunt.

In the late 1960s and '70s the factory achieved great success with patterns such as Saffron and Heirloom. These brown pots and storage jars with a handmade look fitted perfectly into the country-style kitchens fashionable at that time.

Hornsea Pottery closed in 2000 but there is a strong Collectors' Club and one of its satelite companies, Park Rose, is still producing pottery in nearby Bridlington.

A Hornsea model of a black panther, designed by Marion Campbell, 1956, 9in (23cm) long.
£80–90 / €115–125
$130–145 ⊞ HOR

A Hornsea Bull at a Gate posy vase, 1954, 6in (15cm) long.
£40–45 / €55–65
$65–70 ⊞ HOR

▶ **A Hornsea stylized flower holder,** designed by John Clappison, 1957, 4in (10cm) high.
£80–90 / €115–125
$130–145 ⊞ HOR

A Hornsea Lamb posy holder, 1958, 4½in (11.5cm) high.
£30–35 / €40–50
$50–55 ⊞ HOR

◀ **A Hornsea Heirloom coffee storage jar,** 1960s, 4in (10cm) high.
£8–10 / €10–14
$12–16 ⊞ CHI
These storage jars are still easily found in boot fairs and charity shops, but they are also attracting attention from dealers and collectors interested in post-war pottery.

A Hornsea Studiocraft vase, 1959, 5¼in (13.5cm) high.
£60–70 / €85–100
$95–110 ⊞ PrB

A Hornsea Heirloom coffee
storage jar, 1960s, 6in (15cm) high.
£10–12 / €14–17
$16–20 ⊞ CHI

A Hornsea pottery vase, c1970,
6in (15cm) high.
£22–25 / €30–35
$35–40 ⊞ LUNA

A Hornsea Saffron coffee pot,
1970–92, 10in (25.5cm) high.
£25–30 / €35–40
$40–50 ⊞ CHI

A Hornsea wall plaque, designed
by John Clappison, 1972,
7¾in (19.5cm) diam.
£22–25 / €30–35
$35–40 ⊞ HOR

A Hornsea Coral coffee pot,
1970s, 7in (18cm) high.
£35–40 / €50–55
$55–65 ⊞ CHI

A Hornsea Cinnamon teapot and
coffee pot, 1980, 6½in (16.5cm) high.
£35–40 / €50–55
$55–65 each ⊞ CHI

A Hornsea Pebble flower vase,
designed by Colin Rawson, 1982,
6¾in (17cm) high.
£65–75 / €90–105
$105–120 ⊞ HOR

A Hornsea Image cream jug,
1980, 3in (7.5cm) high.
£20–22 / €30–32
$32–35 ⊞ CHI
Designed for special occasions,
the Hornsea Image range was
introduced at the Birmingham
International Spring Fair in 1980.
Also launched at the fair were
the Cinnamon and Cirrus ranges.

A Hornsea Cirrus oil jug,
1980s, 4in (10cm) high.
£25–30 / €35–40
$40–50 ⊞ CHI

▶ Two Hornsea Swan
Lake cups and saucers,
1983–92, 3in (7.5cm) high.
£14–16 / €21–23
$23–25 each ⊞ CHI

Japanese Pottery & Porcelain

An Imari charger, decorated with a boatman on a river, signed, late Edo period, 1615–1868, 14in (35.5cm) diam.
£450–500 / €640–710
$720–800 ⊞ BAC

▶ **A pair of Imari dishes,** decorated with a landscape, Meiji period, 1868–1912, 6in (15cm) wide.
£45–50 / €65–70
$70–80 ⊞ BAC

An Imari bowl, marked 'Maru-fuku', 1825–75, 5in (12.5cm) diam.
£140–160 / €200–230
$220–260 ⊞ BAC

◀ **An Imari dish,** decorated with a fan design, Meiji period, 1868–1912, 4½in (11.5cm) diam.
£25–30
€35–40
$40–50 ⊞ BAC

A Kutani gourd vase, by Onokiln, decorated with a geometric design, 1850–60, 8in (20.5cm) high.
£135–150 / €190–220
$220–240 ⊞ BAC

An Imari plate, decorated with a bird and fan design, signed, Meiji period, 1868–1912, 9in (23cm) diam.
£145–160 / €200–220
$230–240 ⊞ BAC

◀ **A pair of Satsuma vases,** decorated with wisteria, signed, Meiji period, 1868–1912, 6in (15cm) high.
£115–125 / €165–175
$185–200 ⊞ BAC

An Imari plate, decorated with plum, pine and bamboo design, Meiji period, 1868–1912, 9in (23cm) diam.
£80–90 / €115–130
$130–145 ⊞ BAC

A part tea service, comprising five pieces, hand-painted with violets, sun mark, c1900.
£160–180 / €230–250
$260–290 ⊞ DgC

▶ **An Imari figure of a *bijin*,** late 19thC, 9in (23cm) high.
£210–230 / €300–330
$340–370 ⊞ BAC
A *bijin* is a beautiful Japanese woman.

A Satsuma dish, decorated with figures, signed, early 20thC, 4in (10cm) diam.
£25–30 / €35–40
$40–50 ⊞ BAC

▶ **A Noritake vase,** 1910–20, 14in (35.5cm) high.
£180–200 / €250–280
$290–320 ⊞ MURR

A Kutani pail, decorated with men in robes, signed, late 19thC, 6in (15cm) high.
£85–95 / €120–135
$135–150 ⊞ BAC

A pair of Imari boat dishes, late 19thC, 7in (18cm) wide.
£70–80 / €100–115
$110–130 ⊞ BAC

A pair of Satsuma vases, decorated with birds and flowers, 19th–20thC, 4in (10cm) high.
£75–85 / €105–120
$120–140 ⊞ BAC

A pair of vases, hand-painted, Kinjo Nippon mark, c1900, 9½in (24cm) high.
£270–300 / €380–430
$430–480 ⊞ DgC

Noritake

In 1891 it was declared that all Japanese wares imported into the USA were to be marked with the word 'Nippon'. One of the most important factories to produce Nippon wares was the Noritake Company. Established in 1904 in Nagoya by Icizaemon Morimura, the company specialized in the production of hand-painted porcelain in competition with industrially-printed ceramics. After 1921 the Nippon mark was changed to 'Japan' or 'Made in Japan'.

A Noritake coffee can and saucer, c1912, cup 2in (5cm) high.
£45–50 / €65–70
$70–80 ⊞ BAC

A coffee can and saucer, decorated with flowers and gold, 1915–20, 2in (5cm) high.
£55–60 / €80–85
$90–95 ⊞ BAC

A cruet set, modelled as clowns, c1930, 3in (7.5cm) high.
£25–30 / €35–40
$40–50 ⊞ CoCo

A cruet set, modelled as birds, c1930, 2in (5cm) high.
£16–20 / €22–28
$26–32 ⊞ CoCo

A Happy Hounds cruet set, c1930, 2in (5cm) high.
£35–40 / €50–55
$55–65 ⊞ CoCo

A Maruhon ware candlestick, hand-painted, 1930s, 4in (10cm) diam.
£30–34 / €42–48
$48–54 ⊞ TAC

A cruet set, hand-painted, 1930s, 2½in (6.5cm) high.
£12–16 / €17–23
$20–26 ⊞ TAC

A Marutomo ware jam pot, hand-painted, 1930s, 3½in (9cm) high.
£35–40 / €50–55
$55–65 ⊞ BET

A Maruhon ware dish, hand-painted, 1930s, 6in (15cm) diam.
£30–34 / €42–48
$48–54 ⊞ TAC

A Marutomo ware jam pot, modelled as a cottage, 1930s, 4in (10cm) high.
£30–34 / €42–48
$48–54 ⊞ TAC

A Bonzo cruet set and mustard pot, 1930s, 3½in (9cm) high.
£75–85 / €105–120
$120–135 ⊞ MURR

A Maruhon ware chamberstick, 1930s, 3½in (9cm) high.
£32–36 / €45–50
$50–58 ⊞ TAC

Jugs

A Derby jug, painted with flowers, monogrammed in gilt, pink painted mark, c1800, 8¼in (21cm) high.
£200–240 / €280–340
$320–380 ⚲ WW

A bone china goat and bee jug, small chips, 19thC, 4¼in (11cm) high.
£160–190 / €230–270
$260–300 ⚲ WW

An Ironstone jug, decorated with an Imari design, moulded dragon handle, hair crack, 19thC, 8½in (21.5cm) high.
£190–230 / €270–330
$300–360 ⚲ BWL

A set of three silver-mounted stoneware jugs, with embossed decoration, 19thC, largest 6½in (16.5cm) high.
£220–250 / €310–350
$350–400 ⊞ SER

◀ **An earthenware jug,** printed and enamelled with scenes and verse 'Industry Produceth Wealth', mid-19thC, 7½in (19cm) high.
£140–170
€200–240
$220–270 ⚲ G(L)

◀ **A Castle Hedingham pottery jug,** with applied floral decoration, damaged, raised castle mark, 19thC, 4¼in (11cm) high.
£70–85 / €100–120
$110–135 ⚲ SWO

Toby & character jugs

Earthenware jugs in the form of a corpulent seated man wearing 18th-century dress and a tricorn hat were made by Ralph Wood and his son from around 1760 at their Staffordshire pottery, and were widely copied by other makers. The original Toby was probably Toby Philpot, about whom the song *The Brown Jug* was published in 1761. Many other jugs were made depicting contemporary celebrities and literary characters. In the 20th century Royal Doulton became perhaps the best-known British manufacturer of character jugs.

A pottery character jug, modelled as a gentleman taking snuff, with a loop handle, mid-19thC, 9½in (24cm) high.
£75–90 / €105–130
$120–145 ⚲ AH

▶ **A Victorian Emery one pint measuring jug,** transfer-printed with the Government stamp, inscribed 'Pint Imperial Measure' to the underside of coloured line and 'Submitted to the Standard Department of the Board of Trade', damaged, 4½in (11cm) high.
£50–60 / €70–85
$80–95 ⚲ TMA

A pottery character jug, modelled as a toper, with a loop handle, mid-19thC, 11in (28cm) high.
£320–380 / €450–540
$510–610 ⚲ AH

A Staffordshire ale jug, mid-19thC, 5½in (14cm) high.
£16–20 / €23–28
$26–32 ⊞ FOX

An Aller Vale Pottery watering jug, modelled as a Roman oil lamp, c1900, 9in (23cm) high.
£110–120 / €160–170
$175–190 ⊞ DPC

▶ **A Bernard Leach slipware pottery jug,** with impressed BL seal mark, c1960, 7in (18cm) high.
£165–185 / €230–260
$260–300 ⊞ RUSK

A Cinque Ports pottery jug, 1960s, 4½in (11.5cm) high.
£25–30 / €35–40
$40–45 ⊞ TAC

▶ **A Tintagel Pottery jug,** c1970, 4¼in (11cm) high.
£6–8 / €8–10
$9–12 ⊞ PrB

Two Mocha ware jugs, c1880, larger 8in (20.5cm) high.
£230–250 / €330–350
$370–400 ⊞ SMI

Aller Vale Pottery

Founded c1887 in Devon, Aller Vale Pottery used local clays to produce terracotta and slip-decorated ware. The company merged with Watcombe Terracotta Co c1900 and, by 1904 was advertising a wide range of richly coloured and glazed grotesque and mottoed ware. The company continued to make slipware for the tourist market until its closure in 1962.

Mocha ware

The mossy decoration on Mocha ware was made by dabbing the wet pot with a liquid pigment known as tea, said to contain tobacco juice, urine and manganese, which then fanned out into frond-like patterns when fired. Mocha ware was cheap and utilitarian – in the 19th century most pieces cost less than a shilling. Today it is very popular in the US market.

Three pottery water jugs, 1920s, largest 7in (18cm) high.
£14–18 / €20–25
$23–28 each ⊞ AL

Three Jersey Pottery jugs, 1960–70, largest 8in (20.5cm) high.
£12–15 / €17–21
$20–24 each ⊞ RET

A Colclough Royale jug, 1980s, 4in (10cm) high.
£18–22 / €25–32
$28–36 ⊞ CHI

Lustre Ware

A Clews Staffordshire charger, with a lustre border, early 19thC, 14½in (37cm) diam.
£140–170 / €200–240
$220–270 ➶ G(L)

A Sunderland lustre plaque, entitled 'The Duke of Wellington – 131 Guns', 1845–60, 9½in (24cm) wide.
£150–180 / €210–250
$240–290 ➶ DN

A Victorian Ironstone jug, with raised copper lustre decoration of leafy branches, 7½in (19cm) high.
£75–85 / €105–120
$120–135 ➶ DA

A pair of Sunderland lustre wall plates, with copper lustre edges, the centre with a verse 'May Peace and Plenty on our Nation Smile and Trade with Commerce Bless the British Isle', 19thC, 8¼in (21cm) diam.
£380–460 / €540–650
$610–740 ➶ SWO

Lustre

Lustre ware is pottery with an iridescent metallic surface. The glazed body is painted with metallic oxides mixed with fine ochre and then refired at a low temperature. Varying shades of pink, purple, dark red and pale yellow can be achieved by using silver, gold, copper or platinum. Large quantities of popular items were produced during the 19th century by Wedgwood and potteries in Leeds, Staffordshire, Sunderland, Swansea and Tyneside.

A Sunderland lustre bowl, painted inside and out with tall ships among panels of proverbs, mid-19thC, 10¾in (27.5cm) diam.
£190–210 / €270–300
$300–340 ➶ G(L)

A pearlware lustre jug, inscribed 'Protestant Ascendancy', and 'Let Brotherly Love Continue', dated 1826, 5½in (14cm) high.
£170–190 / €240–270
$270–300 ➶ SAS

A pair of lustre plaques, printed with religious verse, mid-19thC, 8½in (21.5cm) wide.
£140–170 / €200–240
$220–270 ➶ G(L)

A Sunderland lustre jug, commemorating the Crimean War, restoration and star crack, 1854–56, 7¼in (18.5cm) high.
£360–430 / €510–610
$580–690 ➶ DN

◀ **A Wedgwood lustre spoon,** impressed marks, c1885, 5in (12.5cm) long.
£60–70 / €85–100
$95–110 ➶ WW

Majolica

▶ **A majolica basket,** with floral decoration, 1870, 10in (25.5cm) high.
£160–180 / €230–250
$260–290 ⊞ CoCo

A majolica teapot, possibly by Foresters, modelled as an elephant, some damage and repair, 19thC, 5½in (14cm) high.
£460–550 / €650–780
$740–880 ⋗ SWO

Victorian majolica, inspired by 16th-century Italian maiolica, is a type of earthenware moulded in relief and painted with colourful translucent glazes. Bold shapes predominate, such as jugs modelled as fish and plates as shells. Jardinières, umbrella stands, fountains and tiles were also popular. Manufacturers included Minton, George Jones, Wedgwood and many smaller factories.

◀ **A Victorian majolica planter,** moulded with leaves and flowers, 17in (43cm) wide.
£320–380 / €450–540
$510–610 ⋗ SWO

A pair of majolica asparagus plates, by Luneville, 1880, 9in (23cm) diam.
£160–180 / €230–250
$260–290 ⊞ MLL

Measham Ware

Bargeware

Measham ware is also known as bargeware and is the name given to earthenware with a treacly-brown glaze. The items were decorated with applied clay that had been moulded into various shapes including flowers, fruit, animals and birds.

Bargeware is said to have been used by the people who worked the barges along the inland waterways and was produced from the mid-19th century until c1939.

A Measham ware teapot, decorated with sprigged foliage and an inscription, the cover with an acorn finial, dated 1881.
£80–95 / €115–130
$130–150 ⋗ G(L)

A Measham ware jug, with an inscription, chipped, dated 1881, 7in (18cm) high.
£220–250 / €310–350
$350–390 ⊞ KES

◀ **A Measham ware teapot,** with a miniature teapot finial, the body with an inscription, handle and finial restored, c1890, 12in (30.5cm) high.
£300–330
€420–470
$480–530
⊞ KES

A Measham ware cream jug, with a sparrow-beak lip, c1890, 4in (10cm) high.
£70–80 / €100–115
$110–130 ⊞ JBL

A Measham ware cream jug, c1890, 5in (12.5cm) high.
£80–90 / €115–130
$130–145 ⊞ JBL

Midwinter

A Midwinter Stylecraft jug,
designed by Hugh Casson,
decorated with Riviera pattern,
c1954, 6in (15cm) high.
£55–60 / €80–85
$90–95 ⊞ CHI
Lively sketches of the South of France were used for the two Hugh Casson patterns Riviera and Cannes.

A Midwinter Fashion trio and plate, designed by Jessie Tait,
decorated with Zambezi pattern,
1956, plate 10in (25.5cm) wide.
£75–85 / €105–120
$120–135 ⊞ CHI

A Midwinter Stylecraft plate,
decorated with Melody pattern,
c1958, 6in (15cm) diam.
£6–8 / €8–10
$9–12 ⊞ FLD

A Midwinter meat plate, designed
by Jessie Tait, decorated with Bolero
pattern, 1955, 14in (35.5cm) wide.
£80–90 / €115–125
$130–145 ⊞ RET

A Midwinter Stylecraft plate,
designed by Terence Conran,
decorated with Salad Ware pattern,
1955, 8in (20.5cm) wide.
£60–65 / €85–90
$95–105 ⊞ CHI

**A Midwinter Stylecraft celery
vase,** designed by Terence Conran,
decorated with Salad Ware pattern,
1950s, 7in (18cm) high.
£180–200 / €250–280
$290–320 ⊞ BET

A Midwinter meat plate, designed
by Terence Conran, decorated
with Nature Study pattern, 1955,
14in (35.5cm) wide.
£90–100 / €130–140
$145–160 ⊞ RET

A Midwinter plate, designed
by Jessie Tait, decorated with
Toadstools pattern, c1956,
6in (15cm) wide.
£35–40 / €50–55
$55–65 ⊞ CHI

Further reading

*Miller's Ceramics of the '50s
& '60s: A Collector's Guide,*
Miller's Publications, 2001

A Midwinter jug, designed by
Charles Cobelle, decorated with
Fishing Boats pattern, 1950s,
3½in (9cm) high.
£30–35 / €42–50
$50–55 ⊞ CHI

A Midwinter Stylecraft trio,
c1960, plate 6½in (16.5cm) wide.
£18–20 / €25–28
$28–32 ⊞ PrB

A Midwinter coffee pot, cup and saucer, designed by Nigel Wilde, decorated with Cherry Tree pattern, 1962–66, coffee pot 9in (23cm) high.
£55–60 / €80–85
$90–95 ⊞ CHI

A Midwinter dish, designed by Jessie Tait, decorated with Flower Song pattern, c1972, 12in (30.5cm) wide.
£16–18 / €22–25
$24–28 ⊞ CHI

A Midwinter Stonehenge cruet set, designed by Jessie Tait, decorated with Nasturtium pattern, 1974–82, 4in (10cm) high.
£12–14 / €17–20
$19–22 ⊞ CHI

A Midwinter Stonehenge teapot, designed by Eve Midwinter, decorated with Invitation pattern, 1970s, 7in (18cm) high.
£40–45 / €56–64
$64–72 ⊞ CHI

A Midwinter Stonehenge bowl, designed by Eve Midwinter, decorated with Moon pattern, 1973–82, 9in (23cm) diam.
£14–16 / €20–22
$23–25 ⊞ CHI

Minton

A Minton jam pot, moulded with flowers, hand-painted, c1930, 5in (12.5cm) high.
£80–90 / €115–130
$130–145 ⊞ BET

A Minton sugar shaker, in the form of a flower, hand-painted, 1920s, 5in (12.5cm) high.
£70–80 / €100–110
$115–130 ⊞ TAC

▶ **A Minton Consort coffee pot,** 1980s, 9in (23cm) high.
£120–135 / €170–190
$190–210 ⊞ CHI

Moorcroft

A Moorcroft Flamminian ware vase, decorated with three foliate roundels, Liberty mark, early 20thC, 8in (20.5cm) high.
£200–240 / €280–340
$320–380 🏹 BWL

A Moorcroft vase, decorated with Pomegranate pattern, early 20thC, 8in (20.5cm) high.
£310–370 / €440–520
$500–590 🏹 DuM

▶ **A Moorcroft dish,** decorated with Hibiscus pattern, c1940s, 3¾in (9.5cm) diam.
£125–140
€180–200
$200–225 ⊞ PGO

▶ **A Moorcroft Macintyre salt dish,** c1920s, 2½in (6.5cm) high.
£60–70
€85–95
$100–110
⊞ MRW

A Moorcroft vase, decorated with Anemone pattern, c1940, 3¼in (8.5cm) high.
£250–275 / €350–390
$400–440 ⊞ PGO

A Moorcroft vase, decorated with Anemone pattern, 1940–50, 5½in (14cm) high.
£265–295 / €380–420
$430–475 ⊞ PGO

▶ **A Moorcroft powder bowl and cover,** decorated with Hibiscus pattern, c1960, 4½in (11.5cm) diam.
£150–180
€210–250
$240–290 🏹 G(L)

A Moorcroft vase, decorated with Magnolia pattern, c1975, impressed marks, 9½in (24cm) high.
£260–310 / €370–440
$420–500 🏹 G(L)

▶ **Two Moorcroft vases,** decorated with Swan pattern, signed 'Beverley Wilkes', 1990, 7in (18cm) high.
£340–380 / €480–540
$540–600 each ⊞ MPC

Two Moorcroft vases, decorated with Tamarin monkey pattern, 1990, 7in (18cm) high.
£260–290 / €370–410
$420–470 each ⊞ MPC

Nursery Ware

A Yorkshire pottery child's plate, relief-moulded, early 19thC, 5½in (14cm) diam.
£35–40 / €50–55
$55–60 ⊞ CoCo

A nursery plate, printed with a portrait entitled 'Miss F. Kemble as Belvidera', c1829, 5½in (14cm) diam.
£260–310 / €370–440
$420–500 ⋟ SAS

A nursery plate, printed with a scene entitled 'The Great Performer of the Adelphi', c1829, 6¾in (17cm) diam.
£140–165 / €200–230
$220–260 ⋟ SAS

A nursery plate, printed with a portrait, entitled 'Earl Grey, First Lord of the Treasury', c1832, 6in (15cm) diam.
£120–145 / €170–200
$190–230 ⋟ SAS

A Victorian child's tureen, decorated with Persia pattern, 6in (15cm) wide.
£25–30 / €35–42
$40–48 ⊞ BAC

A Wilkinsons child's jug, designed by Joan Shorter, c1928, 4in (10cm) high.
£220–240 / €310–340
$350–390 ⊞ BDA
Joan Shorter was the daughter of Colley Shorter, director of Wilkinsons who, after the death of his wife, married Clarice Cliff in 1940.

A Torquay ware child's mug, decorated with a Cornish lucky piskie, c1920s, 4½in (11.5cm) wide.
£75–85 / €100–120
$120–135 ⊞ MURR

A lamp base, moulded with rabbits, c1938, 5½in (14cm) high.
£175–195 / €250–275
$280–310 ⊞ KES

A Staffordshire Pinky and Perky cup, c1960, 3in (7.5cm) high.
£12–15 / €17–20
$20–24 ⊞ CTO

A Staffordshire Pinky and Perky plate, c1960, 7in (18cm) diam.
£12–15 / €17–20
$20–24 ⊞ CTO

Pilkington

Pilkington's Tile and Pottery Company was established in 1891, near Manchester. Initially the firm made bricks and tiles but they soon started producing decorative pottery under the leadership of William and Joseph Burton. New glazes were developed, particularly lustre, for which Pilkington became famous. In 1903 the pottery launched their Lancastrian range which, following the award of a Royal Warrant from George V in 1913, became known as Royal Lancastrian. Shapes were inspired by ancient Greek, Roman and Asian prototypes, and Pilkington employed a range of important artists and designers including Walter Crane, Gordon Forsyth and William S. Mycock.

A Pilkington's Lancastrian plate, 1903–04, 10in (25.5cm) diam.
£195–220 / €280–310
$310–350 ⊞ **C&W**

A Pilkington's Royal Lancastrian Lapis Ware bowl, incised 'E. T. R.' for Edward Thomas Radford, 1920s, 8¾in (22cm) high.
£100–120 / €140–170
$160–190 ⚒ **PFK**

A Pilkington's Royal Lancastrian vase, c1920, 5in (12.5cm) high.
£85–95 / €120–135
$135–150 ⊞ **RUSK**

A Pilkington's Royal Lancastrian vase, 1930–38, 10½in (26.5cm) high.
£240–270 / €340–380
$380–430 ⊞ **C&W**

A Pilkington's Royal Lancastrian vase, by William S. Mycock, impressed marks, 1931, 6¾in (17cm) high.
£300–360 / €430–510
$480–580 ⚒ **WW**

A Pilkington's Royal Lancastrian lustre vase, by Gladys Rodgers, 1930s, 4½in (11.5cm) high.
£500–550 / €710–780
$800–880 ⊞ **ASA**

A Pilkington's Royal Lancastrian vase, by William S. Mycock, 1932, 12in (30.5cm) high.
£450–500 / €640–710
$720–800 ⊞ **C&W**

▶ **A Pilkington's Royal Lancastrian bowl,** by William S. Mycock, impressed marks, 1935, 5in (13cm) diam.
£250–300 / €360–430
$400–480 ⚒ **WW**

▶ **A Pilkington's Royal Lancastrian Curd and Feather vase,** 1948–57, 9½in (24cm) high.
£160–175
€220–250
$250–280 ⊞ **C&W**

Poole Pottery

A Carter, Stabler & Adams bowl,
c1922, 5in (12.5cm) diam.
£55–65 / €80–90
$90–105 ⊞ BAC

A Carter, Stabler & Adams bowl, 1920s,
9in (23cm) diam.
£130–150 / €185–210
$210–250 ⊞ BAC

**A Carter, Stabler &
Adams preserve pot,**
designed by Truda Carter,
painted by Phyllis Allen,
1934–35, 5in (12.5cm) high.
£90–100 / €130–140
$145–160 ⊞ PGO

◄ **A Poole Pottery two-handled
vase,** decorated with Bluebird
pattern, incised No. 462, painted
initials 'H.E.', 1930s, 7in (18cm) high.
£170–200 / €240–280
$270–320 ⊞ AMB

► **A Carter, Stabler & Adams
vase,** c1930, 6in (15cm) high.
£130–150 / €185–210
$210–250 ⋆ SWO

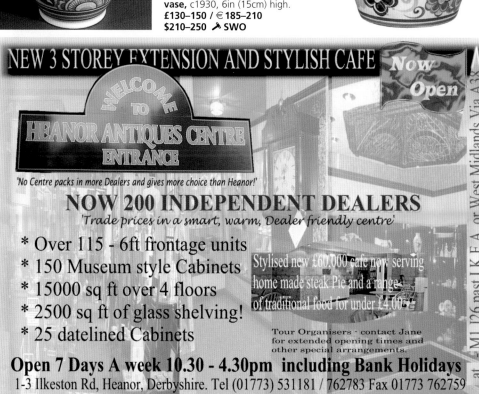

A Poole Pottery plate, decorated with a fish, c1950, 9in (23cm) diam.
£55–60 / €75–85
$90–100 ⊞ BAC

A Poole Pottery vase, decorated with Totem pattern, moulded No. 542, 1950s, 7¼in (18.5cm) high.
£180–210 / €250–300
$290–340 ⚒ SWO

A Poole Pottery vegetable dish, 1950s, 10in (25.5cm) diam.
£25–30 / €35–40
$40–50 ⊞ CHI

Three Poole Pottery teacups and saucers, designed by Robert Jefferson, c1965, 3in (7.5cm) high.
£12–14 / €17–20
$19–23 each ⊞ CHI

A Poole Pottery Delphis bowl, 1960s, 10in (25.5cm) diam.
£75–85 / €105–120
$120–135 ⊞ CHI

A Poole Pottery Delphis vase, 1960s, 6in (15cm) high.
£60–70 / €85–100
$95–110 ⊞ CHI

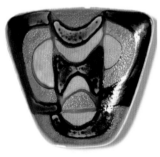

A Poole Pottery Delphis dish, 1960s, 6in (15cm) wide.
£55–60 / €75–85
$90–100 ⊞ CHI

A Poole Pottery Delphis plate, early 1970s, 8in (20.5cm) diam.
£30–35 / €42–50
$50–55 ⊞ WAC

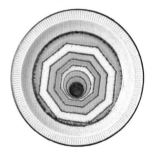

A Poole Pottery Vortex plate, c1975, 7in (18cm) diam.
£8–10 / €10–14
$12–16 ⊞ CHI

◀ **A Poole Pottery Aegean bowl,** 1976, 10in (25.5cm) diam.
£55–60 / €75–85
$90–100 ⊞ GRo

▶ **A Poole Pottery Atlantis vase,** monogram for Hazel Jones, No. A 191, 1970s, 9¾in (25cm) high.
£360–430 / €510–610
$580–690 ⚒ SWO

Portmeirion

A Portmeirion butter dish, decorated with Totem pattern, c1963, 8in (20.5cm) wide.
£60–70 / €85–100
$95–110 ⊞ CHI

Two Portmeirion storage jars, decorated with Greek Key pattern, c1963, 6in (15cm) high.
£60–70 / €85–100
$95–110 ⊞ CHI

A Portmeirion teapot, decorated with Totem pattern, 1960s, 6in (15cm) high.
£30–35 / €40–50
$50–55 ⊞ LUNA
Designed by Susan Williams-Ellis in 1963, the Totem design was inspired by historical ceramics including an embossed 18th-century Prattware teapot and Victorian tiles. An instant success, Totem was the mainstay of Portmeirion during the 1960s.

▶ **A Portmeirion coffee pot,** decorated with Variations pattern, 1964, 12in (30.5cm) high.
£90–100 / €125–140
$145–160 ⊞ CHI

A Portmeirion mug, decorated with Totem pattern, c1963, 4½in (11.5cm) high.
£35–40 / €50–55
$55–65 ⊞ CHI

A Portmeirion mug, decorated with Greek Key pattern, 1960s, 4½in (11.5cm) high.
£22–26 / €32–36
$36–42 ⊞ CHI

A Portmeirion storage jar, decorated with Greek Key pattern, c1963, 8in (20.5cm) high.
£90–100 / €125–140
$145–160 ⊞ CHI

A Portmeirion storage jar, decorated with Stoke pattern, c1964, 7in (18cm) high.
£85–95 / €120–135
$135–150 ⊞ CHI

A Portmeirion salad bowl, decorated with Peony pattern, 1980s, 10in (25.5cm) diam.
£55–60 / €75–85
$90–100 ⊞ CHI

Pot Lids

'Arctic Expedition in Search of Sir John Franklin', c1850, 2¾in (7cm) diam.
£360–430 / €510–610
$580–690 ⤴ SAS

'Garibaldi', by F. & R. Pratt, c1840, 4¼in (11cm) diam.
£75–85 / €105–120
$120–135 ⊞ TASV

'All Feeding Chickens', by F. & R. Pratt, c1845, 4in (10cm) diam.
£75–85 / €105–120
$120–135 ⊞ TASV

▶ **'St Paul's Cathedral',** c1850, 3¾in (9.5cm) diam.
£150–180 / €210–250
$240–290 ⤴ SAS

'Napirima, Trinidad', No. 2987, c1854, 3¾in (9.5cm) diam.
£180–210 / €250–300
$290–340 ⤴ SAS

◀ **'The Swallow',** with registration mark to the reverse, c1860, 3¼in (8.5cm) diam.
£260–310 / €370–440
$420–500 ⤴ SAS

'The Bear Pit', by F. & R. Pratt, c1850, 3¼in (8.5cm) diam.
£30–35 / €40–50
$50–55 ⤴ BBR

Pot lids are covers made for shallow pots that contained potted meats, savouries, toothpaste or bear's grease for dressing men's hair. They were transfer-printed with pictures of buildings, landscapes, portraits and bears. Although many companies made these pots, F. & R. Pratt specialized in their manufacture between 1846 and 1880. Early lids are flat and often in black only, while later examples are more colourful and slightly domed in shape.

'Walmer Castle with Sentry', by Tatnell & Son, c1860, 3¼in (8.5cm) diam.
£460–550 / €650–780
$740–880 ⤴ SAS

◀ **'A Letter from the Diggings',** by F. & R. Pratt, c1870, 4in (10cm) diam.
£75–85 / €105–120
$120–135 ⊞ TASV

'Master of the Hounds', by F. & R. Pratt, c1870, 4¼in (11cm) diam.
£75–85 / €105–120
$120–135 ⊞ TASV

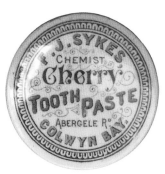

'F. J. Sykes Chemist Cherry Toothpaste', 19thC, 2¾in (7cm) diam.
£150–180 / €210–260
$240–290 ⚒ BBR

'Genuine Bear's Grease For Strengthening & Thickening the Hair', 19thC, 3½in (9cm) diam.
£2,800–3,300 / €4,000–4,700
$4,500–5,300 ⚒ BBR
This large size pot lid was a previously unrecorded example and in very good condition, hence its high price range.

'Oriental Rose Toothpaste prepared by J. Brierley Dental Surgeon', 19thC, 3¾in (9.5cm) diam.
£1,800–2,100 / €2,500–3,000
$2,900–3,300 ⚒ BBR
This is another example of a rare and attractive pot lid in good condition.

'Piesse & Lubin 28 South Molton St London', 19thC, 3¼in (8.5cm) diam.
£140–170 / €200–240
$220–270 ⚒ BBR

'Woods Dandruff Pomade', 19thC, 1½in (4cm) diam.
£220–260 / €310–370
$350–410 ⚒ BBR

▶ 'Williams' Swiss Violet Shaving Cream', 19thC, 3½in (9cm) diam.
£240–290 / €340–410
$380–460 ⚒ BBR

A cold cream pot, 1900–10, 3in (7.5cm) diam.
£40–45 / €55–65
$65–70 ⊞ YT

An Oriental Toothpaste pot, 1900–05, 3in (7.5cm) diam.
£40–45 / €55–65
$65–70 ⊞ YT

◀ An Anchovy Paste pot, 1900–14, 4in (10cm) diam.
£35–40 / €50–55
$55–65 ⊞ YT

Quimper

Quimper in Brittany, north-west France, has been a pottery town since Roman times. Four nearby rivers provided abundant clay and the means to transport wares, while local forests supplied fuel for the kilns. In 1690, Jean-Baptiste Bousquet established a pottery in Quimper, later known as the HB Factory, which specialized in faïence. Other factories were founded in the 18th century including the Porquier and the Henriot factories. In the late 19th century, with the development of tourism encouraged by the expansion of the railway system, the Quimper factories began producing faïence pieces reflecting local imagery and depicting peasants in the traditional costumes of Brittany, known as 'Le Petit Breton'. Production continued throughout the 20th century, and hand-decorated pottery inspired by native folklore is still produced at Quimper today. The most collectable pieces date from before WWII, and values depend on age, object and artist.

A Quimper stand, 1920, 10in (25.5cm) diam.
£130–145 / €185–200
$210–230 ⊞ MLL

A Quimper plate, 1920, 12in (30.5cm) diam.
£175–195 / €250–280
$260–310 ⊞ MLL

A Quimper vase, by M. Fouiller, c1930, 6½in (16.5cm) high.
£110–120 / €155–170
$175–190 ⊞ SER

▶ **A Quimper handled pot with two spouts,** c1940, 5in (12.5cm) high.
£50–55 / €70–80
$80–90 ⊞ SER

A pair of Quimper sauce pots, c1940, 2in (5cm) diam.
£18–22 / €25–30
$28–35 ⊞ SER

A Quimper vase, c1940, 5in (12.5cm) high.
£40–45 / €55–65
$65–70 ⊞ SER

▶ **A Quimper plate,** c1940, 8in (20.5cm) square.
£55–60 / €75–85
$90–100 ⊞ SER

A Quimper footed bowl, c1940, 9in (23cm) wide.
£130–145 / €185–210
$210–230 ⊞ SER

Charlotte Rhead

▶ **A Charlotte Rhead vase,** by Crown Ducal, decorated with Golden Leaves pattern, printed and facsimile signature, c1930, 5in (12.5cm) high.
**£100–120 / €140–170
$160–190 ✗ SWO**

A Charlotte Rhead vase, by Crown Ducal, decorated with Persian Rose pattern, printed mark, facsimile signature, c1930, 12¼in (31cm) high.
**£280–330 / €400–470
$450–530 ✗ WW**

A Charlotte Rhead Bursley ware jug, by Burgess & Leigh, printed marks, c1930, 8¾in (22cm) high.
**£150–180 / €210–250
$240–290 ✗ SWO**

A Charlotte Rhead plate, decorated with Byzantine pattern, printed mark, facsimile signature, c1930, 10½in (26.5cm) diam.
**£170–200 / €240–280
$270–320 ✗ WW**

▶ **A Charlotte Rhead charger,** by Crown Ducal, decorated with Rhodian pattern, printed mark and facsimile signature, c1930, 14¼in (36cm) diam.
**£280–340
€400–480
$450–540 ✗ WW**

A Charlotte Rhead bowl, by Burgess & Leigh, artist and beehive mark to base, c1930, 10¼in (26cm) diam.
**£230–270 / €330–380
$370–430 ✗ G(L)**

Royal Winton

A Royal Winton milk jug,
decorated with Marguerite pattern,
1928, 3in (7.5cm) high.
£80–90 / €115–130
$130–145 ⊞ CoCo

A Royal Winton Olde Inne hot
water pot, c1930, 6in (15cm) high.
£60–70 / €90–100
$95–110 ⊞ RH

A Royal Winton Old Mill biscuit
barrel, c1930, 8in (20.5cm) high.
£60–70 / €90–100
$95–110 ⊞ RH

A Royal Winton breakfast set, comprising
seven pieces, decorated with English Rose
pattern, 1930s.
£280–330 / €400–470
$450–530 ⚘ MEA

▶ **A Royal Winton sifter,** hand-painted
with Gera pattern, 1930, 5½in (14cm) high.
£30–35 / €42–50
$48–55 ⊞ BET

A Royal Winton quart jug,
decorated with June Roses pattern,
1935, 5in (12.5cm) high.
£220–240 / €310–340
$350–380 ⊞ CoCo

A Royal Winton lustre bowl, 1938,
12½in (32cm) diam.
£60–75 / €85–105
$95–120 ⊞ BET

A Royal Winton tazza, decorated
with Sweet Pea pattern, c1940,
7in (18cm) diam.
£130–140 / €185–200
$210–220 ⊞ RH

◀ **A Royal Winton flower bowl,**
with frog, 1940s, 7½in (19cm) high.
£75–85 / €105–120
$120–135 ⊞ BET

A Royal Winton vase,
decorated with Cottage
Chintz pattern, 1950,
6in (15cm) high.
£45–50 / €65–70
$70–80 ⊞ BET

Scandinavian Ceramics

Scandinavian decorative arts were widely exported in the 20th century, particularly after WWII, when Scandinavian Modernism became fashionable both in Europe and the USA. What distinguishes many Scandinavian potteries is the fact that they manufactured both mass-produced tableware and studio pottery, the same designers often working in both areas.

The following section includes works from a number of major Nordic companies. Gustavsberg, established 1825, was the leading ceramics factory in Sweden, where designers Wilhelm Kåge (1889–1960) and Stig Lindberg (1916–82), pioneered the organic, soft-form shapes that came to epitomize the 'New Look' of the 1950s. Rörstrand, established in 1726, was another major Swedish factory, and

important designers of the period include Carl-Harry Ståhlane, born in 1920, and Gunnar Nylund, born in 1904. In Finland, Arabia, established in 1873, produced highly influential industrial and studio pottery under Kaj Franck, born in 1911, another seminal figure in the creation of post-war Scandinavian style.

However, the story of Scandinavian ceramics is not just restricted to producing stylish modern tableware and studio pottery. In the 19th century Royal Copenhagen, established 1755, and Bing & Grøndahl, established 1853, both began making porcelain figures. These traditional-style models were hugely successful throughout the 20th century for both Danish companies, and they eventually merged in 1987.

A Royal Copenhagen figure of a dancer, entitled 'Colombine', Danish, c1915, 7in (18cm) high.
£360–400 / €510–570
$580–640 ⊞ PSA

A Royal Copenhagen figure of a milkmaid, Danish, c1915, 8½in (21.5cm) high.
£350–390 / €500–560
$560–620 ⊞ PSA

▶ **A Bing & Grøndahl figure of a horsewoman,** Danish, c1948, 8in (20.5cm) high.
£150–170 / €210–240
$240–270 ⊞ PSA

◀ **A Royal Copenhagen figure of Pan playing with a bear,** Danish, c1944, 7½in (19cm) high.
£320–360 / €450–510
$510–580 ⊞ PSA
This figure is no longer in production, making this piece highly collectable.

A Gustavsberg pottery vase, designed by Josef Ekberg, with hand-painted gold detailing, Swedish, c1930s, 5½in (14cm) high.
£270–300 / €390–430
$430–480 ⊞ MARK

A Bing & Grøndahl model of a bull, Danish, c1948, 14in (35.5cm) wide.
£470–520 / €570–740
$750–830 ⊞ PSA
This figure is no longer in production, making this piece highly collectable.

A Bing & Grøndahl figure of a girl with a cat, Danish, c1948, 4½in (11.5cm) high.
£125–140 / €180–200
$200–220 ⊞ PSA

▶ **A Bing & Grøndahl model of a polar bear,** Danish, c1952, 9in (23cm) high.
£330–370 / €470–520
$530–590 ⊞ PSA

A Royal Copenhagen model of a partridge, Danish, c1950, 8in (20.5cm) wide.
£170–190 / €240–270
$270–300 ⊞ PSA

A Bing & Grøndahl figure group, entitled 'Fisherman's Friend', Danish, c1952, 12½in (32cm) high.
£520–580 / €740–820
$830–930 ⊞ PSA
This figure is no longer in production, making this piece highly collectable.

A Royal Copenhagen model of a pair of geese, Danish, c1958, 9in (23cm) high.
£350–390 / €500–550
$560–620 ⊞ PSA
This figure is no longer in production, making this piece highly collectable.

A Royal Copenhagen faïence Tenera dish, designed by Inge Lise Koefoed, Danish, c1959, 10½in (26.5cm) wide.
£70–80 / €100–110
$115–130 ⊞ ORI

A Nymolle plaque, designed by Bjorn Wiinblad, decorated with a couple in a garden, Danish, c1950s, 6in (15cm) diam.
£10–14 / €14–20
$16–22 ⊞ GRo

A Rörstrand footed bowl, designed by Carl-Harry Ståhlane, Swedish, c1950s, 3½in (9cm) high.
£40–45 / €55–60
$65–75 ⊞ MARK

A Gustavsberg Våga bowl, designed by Wilhelm Kåge, Swedish, c1950s, 8in (20.5cm) diam.
£65–75 / €90–105
$105–120 ⊞ MARK

A Gustavsberg dish, designed by Stig Lindberg, Swedish, c1950s, 7½in (19cm) wide.
£55–60 / €75–85
$85–95 ⊞ MARK

A Rörstrand bowl, designed by
Carl-Harry Ståhlane, Swedish,
c1950s, 5in (12.5cm) diam.
£50–55 / €70–80
$80–90 ⊞ MARK

A Rörstrand bowl, designed by
Gunnar Nylund, Swedish, c1950s,
5in (12.5cm) diam.
£85–95 / €120–135
$135–150 ⊞ MARK

An Alumina vase, decorated with
peacock pattern, Danish, c1950s,
5in (12.5cm) high.
£75–85 / €105–120
$120–135 ⊞ MARK

**A Royal Copenhagen model of a
boy with two calves,** Danish,
c1968, 9in (23cm) high.
£360–400 / €510–570
$580–640 ⊞ PSA

A Royal Copenhagen faïence bowl,
Danish, 1960s, 3in (7.5cm) diam.
£30–35 / €45–50
$50–55 ⊞ MARK

An Arabia stoneware teapot,
Finnish, 1960s, 7in (18cm) high.
£40–45 / €55–60
$65–75 ⊞ GRo

◄ **A stoneware bowl,** by Britt-
Louise Sundell, Swedish, 1960s,
4½in (11.5cm) diam.
£45–50 / €60–70
$70–80 ⊞ MARK

**An Arabia stoneware cup
and saucer,** Finnish, 1960s,
2½in (6.5cm) high.
£13–17 / €18–24
$21–27 ⊞ GRo

A vase, Danish, 1960s,
8in (20.5cm) high.
£45–50 / €60–70
$70–80 ⊞ MARK

◄ **A Rörstrand goblet,** Swedish,
c1975, 4in (10cm) high.
£20–25 / €30–35
$35–40 ⊞ MARK

Shelley

A set of six Shelley coffee cans and saucers, with silver holders, Birmingham 1923.
£110–130 / €155–185
$175–210 ⚒ G(L)

A Shelley jug, with banded decoration, c1920s, 10in (25.5cm) high.
£90–100 / €125–140
$145–160 ⊞ SAT

A Shelley ginger jar, with banded decoration, c1925, 6½in (16.5cm) high.
£70–85 / €100–120
$115–135 ⚒ SWO

A Shelley Boo-Boo Mushroom House teapot, designed by Mabel Lucie Attwell, c1926, 4½in (11.5cm) high.
£130–155 / €185–220
$210–250 ⚒ G(L)

▶ **A Shelley Mode trio,** decorated with Red Block pattern, c1930, plate 7in (18cm) diam.
£180–200 / €250–280
$290–320 ⊞ RH

A Shelley Queen Anne trio, decorated with Sunset pattern, c1930, plate 7in (18cm) square.
£110–120 / €155–170
$175–195 ⊞ RH

Shelley shapes

The solid triangular handles on the Mode tea cup, while fashionably Art Deco, made the cup hard to hold. Mode was not a popular shape and was only produced from 1930 to 1931. The rarity of this design makes it very collectable. The Eve shape, with its pierced triangular handle was manufactured from 1932 to 1939 and Queen Anne, another successful shape, was first registered in 1926 and remained in continuous production because it was comparatively practical and the panels provided a good surface for decoration.

A Shelley vase, with banded decoration, c1930, 4½in (11.5cm) high.
£35–40 / €50–55
$55–60 ⊞ PrB

A Shelley Eve lustre tea service, with banded decoration, 1930.
£340–410 / €480–580
$540–650 ⚒ L&E

A Shelley Vincent trio, 1930s, cup 3in (7.5cm) high.
£45–50 / €60–70
$70–80 ⊞ CoCo

A Shelley Eve trio, decorated with Iris pattern, 1932, plate 7in (18cm) square.
£90–100 / €125–140
$145–160 ⊞ RH

A Shelley vase, with banded decoration, c1930s, 9in (23cm) high.
£90–100 / €125–140
$145–160 ⊞ SAT

A Shelley Regent breakfast set, comprising 55 pieces, with floral decoration, maker's marks, c1935.
£500–600 / €710–850
$800–960 ⋏ Bea(E)

A Shelley Harmony ginger jar, cover missing, c1930s, 9in (23cm) high.
£115–130 / €165–185
$185–210 ⊞ SAT

A Shelley egg cup set, 1930s, 4½in (11.5cm) high.
£100–110 / €140–155
$160–175 ⊞ TAC

A Shelley bowl, 1930s, 5¾in (14.5cm) diam.
£35–40 / €50–55
$55–60 ⊞ TAC

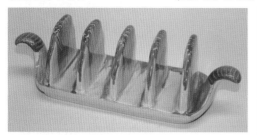

A Shelley toast rack, 1930s, 7in (18cm) wide.
£55–60 / €75–85
$90–100 ⊞ TAC

A Shelley jug, with floral decoration, 1930s, 4½in (11.5cm) high.
£10–14 / €14–20
$16–22 ⊞ FOX

A Shelley preserve pot, with hand-painted decoration, 1930s, 4½in (11.5cm) high.
£40–45 / €55–65
$60–70 ⊞ TAC

Staffordshire

A Staffordshire figure of a girl riding a zebra, c1850, 7in (18cm) high.
£360–400 / €510–570 $580–640 ⊞ ML

A pair of Staffordshire porcellaneous figures of a boy and girl, c1835, 6in (15cm) high.
£160–190 / €230–270 $250–300 ⋟ SJH

A Staffordshire pastille burner, modelled as a cottage, c1850, 5½in (14cm) high.
£130–150 / €185–210 $210–240 ⊞ SER

▶ **A Staffordshire quill holder,** modelled as a huntsman and a dog, c1850, 6in (15cm) high.
£240–270 / €340–380 $380–430 ⊞ DAN

A Staffordshire spill vase, modelled as huntsmen wearing kilts, c1850, 13½in (34.5cm) high.
£200–240 / €280–340 $320–380 ⋟ SJH

A Staffordshire figure of a Scots guard, entitled 'War', c1854, 15½in (40cm) high.
£180–210 / €260–300 $290–340 ⋟ SJH

A Staffordshire figure of Uncle Tom, c1852, 9in (23cm) high.
£210–250 / €300–350 $340–400 ⋟ SJH
Uncle Tom was a character from the novel *Uncle Tom's Cabin* by Harriet Beecher Stowe, which was first published in 1852.

A Staffordshire figure of a sailor, c1855, 13½in (34.5cm) high.
£300–360 / €430–510 $480–580 ⋟ SJH

A pair of Staffordshire models of pug dogs, c1880, 12in (30.5cm) high.
£540–600 / €770–850 $860–960 ⊞ ML

A pair of Victorian Staffordshire
models of spaniels, 8¾in (22cm) high.
£250–300 / €360–430
$400–480 ✗ BR

A Staffordshire figure of a girl
and a St Bernard dog, 19thC,
9in (23cm) high.
£340–410 / €480–580
$540–650 ✗ DA

A Staffordshire model of a
pointer, 19thC, 5¼in (13.5cm) high.
£170–200 / €240–280
$270–320 ✗ WW

A Victorian Staffordshire inkwell,
modelled as a seated greyhound,
restored, 6¾in (17cm) high.
£300–360 / €430–510
$480–580 ✗ EH

A pair of Victorian Staffordshire figures of
Dick Turpin and Tom King, 11¾in (30cm) high.
£120–145 / €170–200
$190–230 ✗ G(L)

A pair of Staffordshire spill vases,
modelled as a doe and faun, restored,
19thC, 6¾in (17cm) high.
£240–290 / €340–410
$390–460 ✗ SWO

A pair of Staffordshire models of St Bernard
dogs, late 19thC, 10in (25.5cm) high.
£280–330 / €400–470
$450–530 ✗ BWL

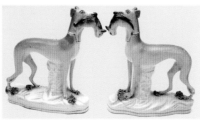

A pair of Staffordshire models of
whippets, late 19thC, 7½in (19cm) high.
£130–150 / €185–215
$210–240 ✗ G(L)

A Staffordshire figure
of Garibaldi, 19thC,
19¾in (50cm) high.
£200–240 / €280–340
$320–380 ✗ AH

A pair of Staffordshire
models of Dalmations,
19thC, 6in (15cm) high.
£300–360 / €430–510
$480–580 ✗ AH

A Staffordshire Toby
jug, modelled as Mr
Pickwick, late 19thC,
8in (20.5cm) high.
£55–65 / €80–95
$90–105 ✗ G(L)

Studio Pottery

An Upchurch Pottery vase, c1925,
6in (15cm) high.
£300–340 / €430–480
$480–540 ⊞ HUN

A studio pottery two-handled bowl,
1930s, 10in (25.5cm) diam.
£20–25 / €30–35
$35–40 ⊞ HSt

**A pair of Devon Tors
Art Pottery vases,**
1930s, 7in (18cm) high.
£70–80 / €100–110
$110–125 ⊞ DPC

A Celtic Pottery coffee set, 1960s–70s, coffee pot
10in (25.5cm) high.
£260–310 / €370–440
$420–500 ↗ SWO

An Iden Pottery vase,
c1960, 3½in (9cm) high.
£10–14 / €14–20
$16–22 ⊞ PrB

**A Priddoes Pottery
lamp base,** c1960,
12in (30.5cm) high.
£30–35 / €45–50
$50–55 ⊞ DPC

**An Isle of Wight
Pottery plate,** c1970,
4½in (11.5cm) diam.
£8–12 / €12–17
$13–19 ⊞ PrB

**A Gambone Pottery
bottle vase,** Italian,
1970s, 5in (12.5cm) high.
£110–130 / €155–185
$175–210 ↗ SWO

A Cobridge Pottery vase,
1970s, 6½in (16.5cm) high.
£90–100 / €125–140
$145–160 ⊞ DSG

A Briglin Pottery vase,
1970s, 7in (18cm) high.
£40–45 / €55–60
$65–75 ⊞ GRo

Tiles

A Delft tile, depicting a figure holding a jug of ale, Dutch, 17thC, 5in (12.5cm) square.
£85–95 / €120–135 $135–150 ⊞ JHo

A London delft tile, depicting a woman in a landscape, c1750, 5in (12.5cm) square.
£85–95 / €120–135 $135–150 ⊞ JHo

A Bristol delft tile, depicting houses in a landscape, c1760, 5in (12.5cm) square.
£50–55 / €70–80 $80–90 ⊞ JHo

LOCATE THE SOURCE
The source of each illustration in Miller's can be found by checking the code letters below each caption with the Key to Illustrations, pages 443–451.

A Liverpool delft tile, depicting a fisherman on a bank, c1770, 5in (12.5cm) square.
£85–95 / €120–135 $135–150 ⊞ JHo

A Delft tile, depicting a religious scene, Dutch, 18thC, 5in (12.5cm) square.
£40–45 / €55–60 $65–75 ⊞ JHo

A Minton tile, designed by William Wise, from the Animals of the Farm series, c1879, 6in (15cm) square.
£105–115 / €150–165 $165–185 ⊞ C&W
A fine artist and craftsman, William Wise was born in London in 1847. He trained at art school and in the 1870s began designing for Minton's Kensington Art Pottery studio. Following the death of his first wife, Wise moved to the Minton factory in Stoke-on-Trent. His tile designs were produced from 1879 and Wise was responsible for every part of the process, from supplying the original sketches to engraving the copper plate from which the highly detailed image was printed. Wise died in 1889 at the age of 42 leaving his second wife with eight children.

A Maw & Co tile, c1875, 6in (15cm) square.
£250–280 / €360–400 $400–450 ⊞ KMG
The decoration on this tile is based on the poem *The Hanging of the Crane,* by Henry Wadsworth Longfellow.

A Minton tile, designed by J. Moyr Smith, from the Husbandry series of tiles, c1876, 6in (15cm) square.
£80–90 / €115–130 $130–145 ⊞ C&W
There were 12 in this series, each one depicting a figure in medieval dress involved in a country pursuit.

A set of seven Minton tiles, based on drawings by Helen Houghton, from the Days of the Week series, and another, c1880, 6in (15cm) square.
£390–470 / €550–660
$620–750 ↗ BWL

A Maw & Co tile, with raised decoration, c1880, 6in (15cm) square.
£90–100 / €125–140
$145–160 ⊞ C&W

A Minton tile, c1885, 6in (15cm) square.
£4–8 / €6–11
$7–13 ⊞ SAT

A Minton, Hollins & Co tile, from the Bird series, c1885, 6in (15cm) square.
£60–70 / €85–100
$95–110 ⊞ C&W

A Sherwin & Cotton tile, c1885, 6in (15cm) square.
£11–15 / €16–21
$18–24 ⊞ SAT

A tile, with raised decoration of a heron, c1890, 6in (15cm) square.
£70–80 / €100–115
$110–130 ⊞ C&W

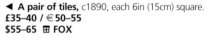

◄ **A pair of tiles,** c1890, each 6in (15cm) square.
£35–40 / €50–55
$55–65 ⊞ FOX

◄ **A Minton tile,** by Leonard Thomas Swetnam, depicting Cardinal Beaton's house, Edinburgh, c1890, 6in (15cm) square.
£80–90
€115–130
$130–145
⊞ C&W

A Sherwin & Cotton tile, with raised floral decoration, c1890, 6in (15cm) square.
£6–10 / €8–14
$10–16 ⊞ SAT

◄ **A Victorian tile,** designed by William Morris, 8in (20.5cm) square.
£35–40 / €50–55
$55–65 ↗ G(L)

► **A walnut jardinère with inset tiles,** in the style of William De Morgan, with moulded marks, late 19thC, 11in (28cm) square.
£180–210 / €260–300
$290–340 ↗ G(L)

A Wedgwood tile, entitled 'May', c1890, 6in (15cm) square.
£120–135 / €170–190
$190–220 ⊞ SaH

A tile, by William De Morgan, decorated with BBB pattern, minor damage, impressed mark, late 19thC, 6¼in (15.5cm) square.
£180–210 / €260–300
$290–340 ⚹ WW

A Sherwin & Cotton tile, with raised decoration, c1905, 6in (15cm) square.
£45–50 / €60–70
$70–80 ⊞ C&W

A tile, with Art Nouveau decoration, c1905, 6in (15cm) square.
£40–45 / €55–65
$65–75 ⊞ C&W

A tile, commemorating the coronation of George V, 1911, 6in (15cm) square.
£55–65 / €80–90
$90–100 ⊞ TASV

A Minton, Hollins & Co tile, c1920, 6in (15cm) square.
£40–45 / €55–65
$65–75 ⊞ C&W

A Flint Faïence Tile Co tile, American, c1925, 3in (7.5cm) square.
£155–175 / €220–250
$250–280 ⊞ KMG

A tile, by Ernest A. Batchelder, American, c1925, 6in (15cm) square.
£170–190 / €240–270
$270–300 ⊞ KMG

◄ **A Solon & Schemmel corner tile,** American, c1930, 6in (15cm) square.
£105–115 / €150–165
$165–185 ⊞ KMG

► **A Porceleyne Fles tile,** Dutch, c1925, 4in (10cm) square.
£55–60 / €75–85
$85–100 ⊞ KMG

A Wheatley Pottery tile, American, c1925, 6in (15cm) square.
£280–310 / €400–440
$450–500 ⊞ KMG

Wedgwood

◄ **A Wedgwood jasper ware plaque,** impressed marks, 18thC, 4½in (11.5cm) high.
£200–220 / €280–340
$320–380 ✗ SJH
Wedgwood's famous blue jasper ware was made at his second factory at Etruria – a name derived from the Greek classical pottery excavated at Pompeii and Herculaneum, that was at the time thought to be Etruscan.

A Wedgwood coffee can, c1815, 2½in (6.5cm) high.
£70–80 / €100–110
$115–130 ⊞ JAY

A pair of Wedgwood redware jugs, enamelled with flower and leaf sprays, one with small chip, impressed marks, 19thC, 8¼in (21cm) high.
£260–310 / €370–440
$420–500 ✗ WW

Five Wedgwood Moonstone coffee cans and 9 saucers, by Keith Murray, some damage, 1930s, cup 3in (7.5cm) high.
£120–140 / €170–200
$190–220 ✗ CAu

Keith Murray

Keith Murray (1892–1981) trained as an architect and his background is evident in the design of his ceramic wares during the 1930s and '40s. His work is recognizable for its simple geometric forms and lack of surface embellishment, he specialized in vases which are often ribbed or fluted.

From 1932 to 1948 Murray worked for Wedgwood as an outside designer. He then returned to architecture, but Wedgwood continued to use his shapes for several years. His work was shown at many national and international exhibitions and in 1936 he became one of Britain's first Royal Designers for Industry.

A Wedgwood wall pocket, by Keith Murray, signature mark, c1930, 8½in (21.5cm) high.
£150–180 / €210–250
$240–280 ✗ G(L)

A Wedgwood tea cup and saucer, decorated with Florentine pattern, c1959, cup 3½in (9cm) high.
£50–60 / €75–85
$85–95 ⊞ CHI

A Wedgwood Sterling coffee pot, 1960s, 6in (15cm) high.
£40–45 / €55–65
$65–75 ⊞ CHI

► **A Wedgwood cup, saucer and sideplate,** decorated with Black Eyed Susan pattern, 1960s, cup 3in (7.5cm) high.
£40–45
€55–65
$65–75 ⊞ CHI

A Wedgwood coffee pot, decorated with Runnymede pattern, c1972, 8in (20.5cm) high.
£110–125 / €155–175
$175–200 ⊞ CHI

A Wedgwood Peter Rabbit cup and saucer, early 1970s, cup 1¼in (3cm) high, boxed.
£50–60 / €70–85
$80–95 ⊞ CCH

A Wedgwood Peter Rabbit Christmas dish, 1970s, 4¼in (11cm) diam.
£45–50 / €65–70
$75–80 ⊞ CCH

A Wedgwood Peter Rabbit cream jug, 1970s, 5½in (14cm) high.
£18–22 / €26–30
$30–35 ⊞ CCH

◄ **A Wedgwood Peter Rabbit plate,** 1980s, 8in (20.5cm) diam.
£16–20
€23–28
$26–32 ⊞ CCH

A Wedgwood Peter Rabbit tea cup and saucer, 1980s, cup 3½in (9cm) high.
£18–22 / €26–30
$30–35 ⊞ CCH

A Wedgwood Peter Rabbit mug, made for the Japanese market, 1993, 3in (7.5cm) high.
£13–17 / €18–24
$21–27 ⊞ CCH

► **A Wedgwood Peter Rabbit 'Happy Birthday' plate,** 1995, 8in (20.5cm) diam.
£12–16 / €17–23
$20–26 ⊞ CCH

A Wedgwood Peter Rabbit calendar plate, 1994, 8in (20.5cm) diam.
£18–22 / €26–30
$30–35 ⊞ CCH

► **A Wedgwood figure,** by Jenny Oliver, entitled 'Inspiration', 1997, 12¼in (31cm) high.
£40–45 / €55–65
$65–75 ⋗ L&E

Worcester

A Chamberlain's Worcester jug, chipped, c1800, 3½in (9cm) high.
£80–95 / €115–135
$130–150 ⚲ BWL

A Royal Worcester spill holder, with two lovebirds perched on bamboo, small chip, impressed marks, 1860–70, 7in (18cm) high.
£250–300 / €350–430
$400–480 ⚲ WW

A Royal Worcester ewer, design registered 1884, 12½in (32cm) high.
£240–290 / €340–410
$380–460 ⚲ G(L)

A Royal Worcester figure, mould No. 1250, modelled as a water carrier, date code for 1888, 9½in (24cm) high.
£240–290 / €340–410
$380–460 ⚲ G(L)

◀ **A Royal Worcester flatback jug,** shape No. 1094, puce printed marks, c1897, 6¼in (16cm) high.
£110–130 / €155–185
$175–210 ⚲ WW

A Royal Worcester ewer, shape No. 1136, c1888, 8in (20.5cm) high.
£200–240 / €280–340
$320–380 ⚲ WW

A pair of Royal Worcester vases, with hand-painted vignettes, one with hairline crack, raised moulded mark, c1900, 9in (23cm) high.
£200–240 / €280–340
$320–380 ⚲ SWO

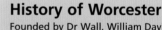

A pair of Grainger's Worcester plates, painted with views of 'Corralynn on the Clyde' and 'The Roman Bridge over the Moose', painted and impressed marks, c1900, 9½in (24cm) diam.
£150–180 / €210–250
$240–290 ⚲ WW

▶ **A pair of Royal Worcester coffee cups and _trembleuse_ saucers,** date code 1904, saucers 4in (10cm) diam.
£65–75 / €90–105
$105–120 ⚲ G(L)

History of Worcester

Founded by Dr Wall, William Davis and others in 1751, the factory has continued at Worcester to the present day. Early Worcester porcelain was the finest in England and consisted mainly of tea and coffee sets and dinner ware. Transfer-printing was introduced in 1756, at first in black with designs of buildings and celebrities. From the 1760s, Oriental and European subjects became popular decoration in a wide range of colours. In 1783, the factory was bought by Thomas Flight who, with Martin Barr, formed Flight & Barr. Owing to changes in partnership, the company became Barr, Flight & Barr (1804–13), Flight, Barr & Barr (1813–40) and from 1862, the Royal Worcester Porcelain Company.

A Royal Worcester coffee set,
comprising ten pieces, printed marks,
1918, coffee pot 7in (18cm) high.
£100–120 / €140–170
$160–190 ⚒ SWO

A Royal Worcester jug, with
applied lizard decoration, puce
printed mark, early 20thC,
6in (15cm) high.
£150–180 / €210–250
$240–290 ⚒ DMC

A Royal Worcester vase, hand-
painted with roses, signed E. M.
Fildes, puce painted mark, early
20thC, 3¼in (8.5cm) high.
£100–120 / €140–170
$160–190 ⚒ DMC

◄ **A Royal Worcester dish,** signed
'Powell', printed marks, c1936,
3¼in (8.5cm) diam.
£100–120 / €140–170
$160–190 ⚒ WW

A Royal Worcester cup and saucer, 1933,
saucer 3¼in (8.5cm) diam.
£70–75 / €100–105
$110–120 ⊞ BET

A Royal Worcester cup and saucer,
hand-painted by H. Price, date code
for 1941, saucer 3½in (9cm) diam.
£260–310 / €370–440
$420–500 ⚒ G(L)

► **A Royal Worcester figure,** entitled 'Joan',
modelled by D. Doughty, date code for 1951,
4½in (11.5cm) high.
£90–105 / €130–150
$145–170 ⚒ G(L)

A Royal Worcester trio, decorated with
Fiesta pattern, 1950s, plate 6in (15cm) diam.
£40–48 / €56–68
$64–76 ⊞ BET

A Royal Worcester plate, painted
with flowers, with a raised gilt border,
black printed mark, signed 'Freeman',
c1952, 10½in (26.5cm) diam.
£250–300 / €350–430
$400–480 ⚒ WW

**A Royal Worcester soup bowl, stand and
plate,** decorated with Bernina pattern, 1960s,
plate 8in (20.5cm) diam.
£60–68 / €85–95
$95–108 ⊞ CHI

◄ **A Royal Worcester coffee pot,**
decorated with Balmoral pattern,
1960s, 9in (23cm) high.
£180–200 / €250–280
$290–320 ⊞ CHI

Christmas

A bisque Christmas
cake decoration, 1920s,
3½in (9cm) high.
£45–50 / €65–70
$70–80 ⊞ MURR

A bisque Christmas cake decoration,
c1930, 2½in (6.5cm) high.
£35–40 / €50–55
$55–65 ⊞ YC

◄ A Christmas toffee tin, 1930s,
5½ x 4in (14 x 10cm).
£26–30 / €37–43
$42–48 ⊞ HUX

A cabinet card, by A. Holborn,
c1880, 6½ x 4½in (16.5 x 11.5cm).
£6–10 / €8–14
$10–16 ⊞ J&S

A Christmas card from the *Queen
Mary*, 1936, 5in (12.5cm) square.
£25–30 / €35–40
$40–45 ⊞ COB

A box of Tom Smith
Noddy Christmas crackers,
1950s, 11 x 9in (28 x 23cm).
£60–65 / €85–90
$95–105 ⊞ UD

A Huntley & Palmer's Christmas biscuit tin,
1950s, 10in (25.5cm) diam.
£45–50 / €65–70
$70–80 ⊞ MURR

A James Brown LP record 'Christmas
Songs', by Pye Records, 1966.
£90–100 / €125–140
$145–160 ⊞ BNO

A Price Kensington Christmas pudding
teapot, early 1960s, 7in (18cm) high.
£32–36 / €45–50
$50–57 ⊞ TWI

An Avon Christmas
stocking glass scent bottle,
1960–70, 3in (7.5cm) high.
£16–20 / €23–28
$26–32 ⊞ CoCo

Cigarette & Trade Cards

Cigarette cards were introduced in the USA as packet stiffeners, to prevent cigarettes crushing in their paper containers. Initially, cards carried only the name of the company but the late 1870s saw the introduction of the pictorial card.

Britain began producing cigarette cards in the 1880s. Manufacturers took advantage of new techniques of colour litho printing and photography. The trade war (1901–02) between the American Tobacco Company and the British-based Imperial Tobacco Company stimulated a host of attractive designs as companies fought for a share of the market.

Since most smokers were men, the subjects reflected male interests such as sport, war and female beauties. Many of the most prized examples come from the Edwardian period, as reflected in the price ranges of the early sets illustrated below. During WWI, certain sets were withdrawn for political reasons. W. D. & H. O. Wills removed the German figures from their Musical Celebrities set and pulped their 1915 Waterloo set which it was

thought, might embarrass the French, thus making any surviving examples from these series highly collectable.

Wartime paper shortages brought an end to cigarette cards in 1917, but manufacture resumed in the 1920s. By this time women were smoking and themes expanded to include more female interests ranging from flowers to film stars, but typically male-orientated subjects such as football, cricket and transport predominated – in 1936 Wills's Railway Engines had an initial printing of 600 million cards.

Cigarette card collecting was at its heyday in the 1930s with the introduction of clubs, dedicated shops and a monthly collector's magazine. While WWII initially inspired a host of military and emergency themes (including the Air Raid Precautions series), once again production was suspended due to paper shortages. Very few cigarette cards were produced after WWII, although trade cards available with sweets, tea, cereals and other comestible products, remained popular with children.

W. D. & H. O. Wills, Cricketers, set of 50, 1896.
£2,900–3,500 / €4,100–4,600
$4,600–5,200 ⊞ MUR

Turkish Lady

Taddy & Co, Natives of the World, set of 25, 1899.
£540–650 / €770–920
$860–1,050 ⚹ B

FAMOUS ACTORS.
No. 7.

Mr. W. S. Penley
in "Charley's Aunt."

Taddy & Co, Famous Actors/ Actresses, set of 25, 1903.
£270–320 / €380–450
$430–510 ⚹ B

MR. H. D. G.
LEVESON-GOWER,
SURREY.

Taddy & Co, County
Cricketers, set of 23, 1907.
£370–450 / € 520–640
$600–720 ⚔ B

Order of St Michael & St George

▶ **Taddy & Co,** British
Medals & Decorations,
series 2, set of 50, 1912.
£370–450 / € 520–640
$600–720 ⚔ B

◀ **Véritable Extrait de Viande Liebig,** Flowers &
Dragonflies, set of 6, 1907.
£18–22 / € 25–30
$28–35 ⊞ LENA

W. D. & H. O. Wills, Celebrity series, set of 50, 1912.
£105–115 / € 150–165
$170–185 ⊞ MUR

W. A. & A. C. Churchman, Footballers, set of 50, 1914.
£320–380 / € 450–540
$510–610 ⚔ B

Typhoo Tea, Common Objects Highly Magnified,
set of 25, 1925.
£20–25 / € 30–35
$35–40 ⊞ MUR

▶ **W. D. & H. O.
Wills,** Flower
Culture in Pots,
set of 50, 1925.
£20–25
€ 30–35
$35–40 ⊞ SOR

Carreras Ltd, The Nose Game, set of 50, 1927.
£18–22 / €**25–30**
$28–35 ⊞ SOR

John Player & Sons, Flags of the League of Nations, set of 50, 1928.
£18–22 / €**25–30**
$28–35 ⊞ SOR

The reply to a Turkish question should be in Turkish.

W. A. & A. C. Churchman, Eastern Proverbs, set of six, c1930, framed.
£22–26 / €**30–36**
$35–42 ⊞ ES

Carreras Ltd, Alice in Wonderland, set of 48, 1930.
£65–75 / €**90–105**
$105–120 ⊞ MUR

THE VEIL-TAILED GOLDFISH

John Player & Sons, Aquarium Studies, set of 25, 1932.
£35–40 / €**50–55**
$55–65 ⊞ SOR

◀ **W. A. & A. C. Churchman,** Prominent Golfers, set of 50, 1931.
£420–500 / €**600–710**
$670–800 🪛 B

Carreras Ltd, Film Stars, set of 72, 1934.
£85–95 / €120–135
$135–150 ⊞ MUR

Kensitas, Silk Flowers, second series, 1933–34.
£4–8 / €6–10
$7–12 each ⊞ SOR
Silk cards were both embroidered and printed and came in a paper envelope containing information about the subject represented (often flowers, flags or badges). Sometimes collectors stitched these silks into patchworks.

John Player & Sons, Motor Cars, set of 50, 1937.
£45–50 / €65–70
$70–80 ⊞ LCC

John Player & Sons, Coronation Ceremonial Dress, set of 50, 1937.
£8–12 / €10–16
$12–18 ⊞ MUR

▶ **John Player & Sons,** Golf, set of 25, 1939.
£170–190 / €240–270
$270–300 ⊞ MUR

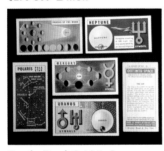

Brooke Bond, Out into Space, set of 50, 1958.
£32–36 / €45–50
$50–58 ⊞ MUR

W. D. & H. O. Wills, Air Raid Precautions, set of 50, 1938.
£35–40 / €50–55
$55–65 ⊞ SOR

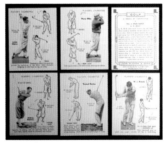

John Player & Sons, Tennis, set of 50, 1936.
£40–45 / €55–65
$65–75 ⊞ SOR

Gallagher Ltd, The Navy, set of 48, 1937.
£32–36 / €45–50
$50–58 ⊞ SOR

Godfrey Phillips Ltd, Famous Love Scenes, set of 36, 1939.
£12–16 / €17–22
$18–26 ⊞ SOR

Barratt & Co, The Wild West, set of 25, 1963.
£4–8 / €6–10
$7–12 ⊞ MUR

◀ **Barratt & Co,** Stingray, set of 50, 1964.
£60–70 / €85–100
$95–110 ⊞ SSF

Clocks

A walnut and Tunbridge ware-style drop-dial clock, with eight-day movement, American, late 19thC, 29½in (75cm) high.
£240–290 / €340–410
$380–460 ✠ BIG

A carved walnut wall clock, by Fredrick Mauthe, early 20thC, 41in (104cm) high.
£270–330 / €380–470
$430–530 ✠ BAu

◄ **A brass mantel timepiece,** modelled as a firescreen, late 19thC, 14in (35.5cm) high.
£100–120 / €140–170
$160–190 ✠ EH

A mahogany mantel clock, by Ansonia, with eight-day movement, American, late 19thC, 18½in (47cm) high.
£100–120 / €140–170
$160–190 ✠ BIG

◄ **An Oswald novelty clock,** German, early 20thC, 7¾in (20cm) high.
£85–95 / €120–135
$135–150 ✠ AMB

A chrome and glass clock, by Fortnum & Mason, 1930s, 5½in (14cm) high.
£135–150 / €190–210
$210–240 ⊞ TIC

◄ **An Art Nouveau mahogany clock,** by W. A. Perry & Co, with French eight-day movement, 12in (30.5cm) high.
£210–230 / €300–330
$340–370 ⊞ SAT

► **A brass alarm clock,** with eight-day movement, Swiss, c1960, 3½in (9cm) high.
£60–70 / €90–100
$105–110 ⊞ PTh

A mahogany mantel timepiece, with later platform escapement, c1900, 7in (18cm) high.
£85–100 / €120–140
$135–160 ✠ WW

A Bulle electric dome clock, 1920s, 16½in (42cm) high.
£240–290 / €340–410
$380–460 ✠ SWO

Comics & Annuals

In December 2002, Comic Book Postal Auctions sold *The Beano* No. 1 for £7,650 / €10,860 / $12,240, a world record auction price for a British comic. 'The market is very strong for rare material but condition is crucial,' explains auctioneer Malcolm Phillips. 'Take Rupert, for example. A *Daily Express Rupert Annual* No. 1 recently fetched over £6,000 / €8,500 / $9,500 at auction. I'd never seen one of such fine grade. It was pristine, in a very nice dust jacket and even had its original mailing box. The same book without its dust wrapper would only be worth £200–300 / €285–425 / $320–480. Condition makes all the difference!' The same maxim applies to the 1960s *Rupert* annuals that came complete with 'magic painting' pages, which most children painted in with water to reveal the hidden colours. 'With coloured-in pages a 1960s annual might sell for £20–40 / €28–57 / $32–64,' says Phillips.

'But if they weren't painted in, the same book could be worth £100–120 / €140–170 / $160–190.'

Condition is not the only important factor with comics. The recent *Hulk*, *Spiderman* and *X-Men* films have helped stimulate demand for US comics and included below is *The Amazing Spider-Man* No. 1. First issues of comics are always desirable but the price range also reflects the fact that this is a 'cents' copy sold in the USA as opposed to a 'pence' copy, produced for the UK. 'It might be exactly the same basic comic, but American collectors are not interested in 'pence' copies and so these are worth far less than 'cents' comics,' advises Phillips. 'Many comic price guides only list the prices for 'cents' comics and don't make this distinction clear, so people often think their comics are worth far more than they actually are.'

Adventure Comics,
No. 310, 1963.
£10–14 / €14–20
$16–22 ⊞ CoC

Adventures in 3D comic,
No. 1, published by
Harvey Comics, 1959.
£30–35 / €42–50
$48–55 ⊞ SSF

Amazing Fantasy comic,
No. 15, 1962.
£740–880
€1,050–1,250
$1,200–1,400 ⚒ CBP

The Amazing Spider-
Man comic, No. 1,
cents copy.
£1,300–1,550
€1,850–2,200
$2,100–2,500 ⚒ CBP

The Amazing Spider-Man
comic, No. 4, published
by Marvel Comics, 1963.
£550–600 / €780–860
$880–960 ⊞ NOS

The Amazing Spider-Man
comic, No. 6, published
by Marvel Comics, 1963.
£110–130 / €155–185
$175–210 ⚒ CBP

The Avengers comic,
No. 2, 1963.
£55–65 / €80–95
$90–105 ⚒ CBP

Insurance values

Always insure your valuable collectables for the cost of replacing them with similar items, regardless of the original price paid. Both dealers and auctioneers can provide a valuation service for a fee.

The Beano comic, No. 2, worn, 1938.
£1,000–1,200
€1,400–1,700
$1,600–1,900 ✎ CBP
Very few copies of this issue are known to exist.

The Beano comic, No. 59, 1939.
£145–175 / €205–250
$230–280 ✎ CBP
The first issue of The Beano was published on 30 July 1938.

The Beano comic, No. 61, c1939.
£100–120 / €140–170
$160–190 ✎ CBP

Captain America comic, No. 32, damaged, 1943.
£160–190 / €230–270
$250–300 ✎ CBP

► **The Dandy comic,** Nos. 258–282, complete year in bound volume, 1944.
£900–1,050
€1,300–1,500
$1,450–1,700 ✎ CBP
The Dandy was first released on 4 December 1937.

◄ **The Dandy comic,** No. 12, 1938.
£120–145 / €170–200
$190–230 ✎ CBP

The Dandy comic, Nos. 309–334, complete year in bound volume, 1946.
£500–600 / €710–850
$800–950 ✎ CBP

► **The Dandy Monster Comic,** No. 2, restored, 1940.
£1,000–1,200
€1,400–1,700
$1,600–1,900 ✎ DW

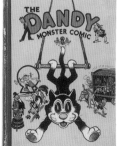

Daredevil comic, No. 1,
published by Marvel
Comics, 1964.
£370–440 / €520–620
$590–700 ✗ CBP

Detective Comic,
No. 415, published by
DC Comics, 1971.
£8–12 / €10–16
$12–18 ⊞ CoC

Fantastic Four comic,
No. 48, published by
Marvel Comics, 1966.
£190–220 / €270–310
$300–350 ✗ CBP

The Hotspur comic, Nos.
561–597, 20 issues, 1947.
£70–80 / €100–115
$110–130 ✗ CBP

The Incredible Hulk
comic, No. 1, 1962.
£880–1,050
€1,250–1,500
$1,400–1,700 ✗ CBP

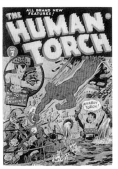

The Human Torch comic,
No. 7, restored, 1942.
£220–260 / €310–370
$350–420 ✗ CBP

Justice League of
America comic, No. 10,
published by DC Comics,
1950–60.
£155–175 / €220–250
$250–280 ⊞ PICC

The Magic-Beano
Book, 1948.
£670–800 / €950–1,150
$1,100–1,300 ✗ CBP
It is rare to find a copy
of this book in such
good condition.

▶ Mickey Mouse Annual,
published by Dean, 1936.
£55–65 / €80–90
$90–105 ✗ CBP

Mickey Mouse Annual,
No. 1, worn, 1930.
£240–280 / €340–400
$380–450 ✗ CBP

Radio Fun Annual,
No. 1, 1940.
£120–145 / €170–200
$190–230 ✗ CBP

More Adventures of
Rupert annual, No. 2,
published by The Daily
Express, 1937.
£170–200 / €240–290
$270–320 ✗ CBP

◀ Rupert in More Adventures annual, published by
The Daily Express, 1944.
£240–280 / €340–400
$380–450 ✗ CBP

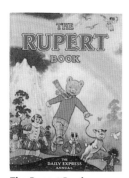

The Rupert Book annual, published by *The Daily Express*, 1948.
£65–75 / €90–105
$105–120 ↗ CBP

Rupert annual, published by *The Daily Express*, 1949.
£45–55 / €65–80
$70–85 ↗ CBP

The Sandman, No. 50, published by DC Comics, 1993.
£18–22 / €26–30
$28–35 ⊞ NOS

The Silver Surfer comic, No. 2, published by Marvel Comics, 1968.
£35–40 / €55–60
$55–65 ⊞ CoC

Strange Adventures comic, No. 3, published by DC Comics, 1950–60.
£450–500 / €640–710
$720–800 ⊞ PICC

Strange Adventures comic, No. 15, published by DC Comics, 1950–60.
£155–175 / €220–250
$250–280 ⊞ PICC

Superman comic, No. 4, worn, 1940.
£400–480 / €570–680
$640–770 ↗ CBP

Superman vs The Amazing Spider-Man, The Battle of the Century, published by Marvel Comics and DC Comics, 1976.
£45–50 / €65–70
$75–80 ⊞ NOS

Items in the Comics & Annuals section have been arranged in alphabetical order.

Superman comic, No. 1, reprinted by Chronological Books, 1999.
£30–35 / €45–50
$50–55 ⊞ NOS
An original 1939 copy of this comic would be worth £10,000–15,000 / €14,200–21,300 / $16,000–24,000.

Warrior Summer Special, published by Quality Communications, 1982.
£8–12 / €10–16
$12–18 ⊞ NOS

Zago, No. 4, Matt Baker cover, 1949.
£75–85 / €105–120
$120–135 ↗ CBP

Commemorative Ware

A pottery jug, commemorating Richard Reynolds, transfer-printed with a portrait, c1820, 6¾in (17cm) high.
£55–65 / €80–95
$90–105 SAS
Richard Reynolds, a Bristol iron merchant, was a philanthropist who founded the Bristol Samaritan Society Orphan Asylum Infirmary and Almshouses. The Reynolds Commemoration Society was established after his death in 1816.

A mug, commemorating 'The Miners' New Offices, Barnsley', by Robinson & Hollinshead, transfer-printed, c1874, 5in (13cm) high.
£140–165 / €200–240
$220–260 DN

Condition

The condition is absolutely vital when assessing the value of a collectable. Damaged pieces on the whole appreciate much less than perfect examples. However a rare desirable piece may command a high price even when damaged.

A wall plaque, commemorating John Wesley, possibly by Dixon & Co, transfer-printed with a portrait, slight damage, 1820–30, 6¼in (16cm) diam.
£220–260 / €310–370
$350–420 DN

A pottery plate, commemorating the Swaithe Main Pit Disaster in 1875, by J. Wardle & Co, transfer-printed, 8¾in (22.5cm) diam.
£200–240 / €280–340
$320–380 SAS

A jug, commemorating Thomas Carlyle, 1795–1881, 8in (20.5cm) high.
£210–230 / €300–330
$330–370 POL

LOCATE THE SOURCE

The source of each illustration in Miller's can be found by checking the code letters below each caption with the Key to Illustrations, pages 443–451.

A glass plate, commemorating the Tichborne Claimant, with moulded inscription and portrait, c1874, 5in (12.5cm) diam.
£70–80 / €100–115
$115–130 SAS
The Tichborne Claimant was the name given to the man who, in 1865, claimed to be Roger Tichborne, heir to a large Hampshire estate and who had been missing at sea since 1854. After two marathon trials which attracted huge public interest across the world, the claimant was revealed to be Arthur Orton, son of a butcher from Wapping. He was imprisoned for perjury and died in poverty in London in 1898.

A Montereau pottery plate, commemorating the Horticultural Exhibition in 1890, with raised decoration, 15¾in (40cm) diam.
£50–60 / €70–85
$80–95 SAS

Military & Naval

A set of three sash window rests, in the form of the bust of The Duke of Wellington, early 19thC, 4in (10cm) high.
£650–780 / €920–1,100
$1,050–1,250 ↗ G(L)

A pearlware jug, commemorating Lord Wellington and General Hill, with silver lustre, slight damage, 1810–15, 5¼in (13.5cm) high.
£130–155 / €185–220
$210–250 ↗ DN

A Doulton Lambeth stoneware jug, commemorating General Gordon, c1884, 7½in (19cm) high.
£340–380 / €480–540
$540–610 ↗ SAS

A stoneware jug, commemorating the relief of Mafeking, by Elliot of London, with incised inscriptions, c1900, 9½in (24.5cm) high.
£340–380 / €480–540
$540–610 ↗ SAS
Robert Baden Powell became a national hero for his 217-day defence of Mafeking in the Boer War of 1899–1902; he later became famous as founder of the Boy Scouts and Girl Guides.

► **A Prattware jug,** commemorating Admiral Nelson and Captain Berry, slight damage, early 19thC, 6in (15cm) high.
£600–720
€850–1,000
$960–1,150
↗ G(L)

► **A Copeland & Garrett feldspar bust of the Duke of Wellington,** c1835, 8in (20.5cm) high.
£340–380 / €480–540
$540–610 ⊞ H&G

◄ **A creamware mug,** commemorating Marquis Wellington, restored, c1812, 4½in (11.5cm) high.
£340–380 / €480–540
$540–610 ↗ SAS

A plate, commemorating the Boer War, transfer-printed with named portraits of Buller, White and MacDonald, c1900, 9½in (24.5cm) diam.
£100–120 / € 140–170
$160–190 ⚒ SAS

A ceramic teapot stand, with a portrait of Robert Baden Powell, c1901, 10in (25.5cm) diam.
£80–90 / € 115–130
$130–145 ⊞ MURR

A Doulton Lambeth plaque, commemorating Heihachiro Togo, with impressed mark, minor damage, 1905, 7¼in (18.5cm) diam.
£80–90 / € 115–130
$130–145 ⊞ MURR
Heihachiro Togo, (1846–1934), was Japan's greatest naval hero. He studied naval science in England, gained international recognition for his service in the First Sino-Japanese War, and contributed greatly to the development of Japanese sea power. He defeated the Russian fleet at Port Arthur in 1904 and destroyed the Russian Baltic fleet in 1905 at the battle of Tsushima. Later he was chief of the naval general staff and a member of the supreme war council.

A Grimwades plate, with transfer-printed illustration of Old Bill the WWI soldier created by Bruce Bairnsfather, 1914–18, 9in (23cm) diam.
£75–85 / € 105–120
$120–135 ⊞ MURR
During WWI, Bairnsfather was a cartoonist with the US forces in Europe.

A plate, decorated with the portraits of four allies, George V, Czar of Russia, King Albert of Belgium and President Poincare, 1914–18, 10in (25.5cm) diam.
£60–70 / € 85–100
$95–110 ⊞ RCo

A Royal Doulton tankard, commemorating victory and peace after WWI, 1919, 3in (7.5cm) high.
£70–80 / € 100–115
$110–130 ⊞ H&G

A ceramic plate, commemorating the liberation of Maastricht, 1944, 9in (23cm) diam.
£45–50 / € 65–70
$75–80 ⊞ MGC

A framed tile, commemorating Admiral Jellicoe, c1915, 13½ x 10¼in (34 x 26cm).
£75–90 / € 105–130
$120–145 ⚒ SAS

◀ **A bronze medallion,** commemorating the French liberation, c1945, 2¾in (7cm) diam.
£55–65 / € 80–90
$90–105 ⚒ SAS

Politics

A Doulton Lambeth stoneware flask, modelled as Lord John Russell, c1845, 7½in (19cm) high.
£320–380 / €450–540
$510–610 ⋋ SJH

A plaque, by Craven Dunhill, commemorating Joseph Chamberlain, c1895, 4½in (11.5cm) high.
£75–85 / €105–120
$120–140 ⋋ SAS

Items in the Commemorative Ware section have been arranged in date order within each sub-section.

A Wedgwood jug, commemorating the death of Benjamin Disraeli, with transfer-printed portrait, impressed mark, 1881, 6½in (16.5cm) high.
£100–120 / €140–170
$160–190 ⋋ DN

A Parian bust of Lenin, Russian, c1935, 10in (25.5cm) high.
£240–270 / €340–380
$380–430 ⊞ H&G

A Beswick Toby jug, in the form of Winston Churchill, with printed mark, c1943, 8in (20cm) high.
£300–360 / €430–510
$480–580 ⋋ SAS

A pottery plate, by Wallis Grimson, commemorating Randolph Churchill, with transfer-printed portrait, c1886, 10in (25.5cm) high.
£75–90 / €105–130
$120–145 ⋋ SAS

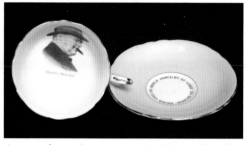

A cup and saucer, commemorating Winston Churchill, c1940, saucer 4in (10cm) diam.
£190–210 / €270–300
$300–340 ⊞ H&G

A Copeland Spode jug, commemorating Winston Churchill, c1942, 7½in (19cm) high.
£260–290 / €370–410
$420–460 ⊞ H&G

▶ **A silver page marker,** in the form of Winston Churchill, hall-marked, c1965, 4¼in (11cm) high.
£120–145 / €170–200
$190–230 ⋋ SAS

A **Crown mug,** celebrating the New Labour victory, 1997, 3½in (9cm) high.
£40–45 / € 55–65
$65–75 ⊞ H&G

◀ A **pottery bust of Winston Churchill,** c1965, 5½in (14cm) high.
£320–380 / € 450–540
$510–610 ⚒ SAS

A **ceramic teapot,** in the form of William Hague, with finial in the form of Margaret Thatcher, 2000, 8in (20.5cm) high.
£80–90 / € 115–130
$130–145 ⊞ POL

◀ **Twelve Bairstow Manor Toby jugs,** in the form of British Prime Ministers, with handles, 2001, 4in (10cm) high.
£25–30 / € 35–40
$40–50 each ⊞ POL

Royalty

A **tea caddy,** commemorating William of Orange, 1780, 4in (10cm) high.
£370–410 / € 520–580
$590–660 ⊞ WAA

A **plate,** commemorating the coronation of Queen Victoria, 1838, 6in (15cm) diam.
£450–500 / € 640–710
$720–800 ⊞ WAA

▶ A **plate,** commemorating the Diamond Jubilee of Queen Victoria, 1897, 10in (25.5cm) diam.
£85–95 / € 120–135
$135–150 ⊞ WAA

A **Royal Doulton mug,** commemorating the Diamond Jubilee of Queen Victoria, 1897, 3½in (9cm) high.
£125–140 / € 180–200
$200–220 ⊞ H&G

A photograph of the Duke of York and Princess Mary of Tech, 1897, 15 x 11in (38 x 28cm).
£11–15 / €16–21
$18–24 ⊞ J&S

A lithophane mug, commemorating King Edward VII, 1902, 3in (7.5cm) high.
£28–32 / €40–45
$45–50 ⊞ ATK
Invented by Baron de Bourgoing in 1827, a lithophane is a transluscent porcelain plaque with a moulded or impressed design that can be viewed when the object is held to the light. Lithophanes were often inserted into the bases of cups.

A Royal Doulton loving cup, commemorating the coronation of King George V and Queen Mary, 1911, 3½in (9cm) high.
£115–130 / €165–185
$185–210 ⊞ H&G

◄ **A pair of dishes,** commemorating the wedding of HRH the Duke and Duchess of York, c1923, 4in (10cm) diam.
£105–125
€150–175
$175–200 ⋟ SAS

A photograph of the Duke of York, signed and stamped, c1923, 8½ x 5in (21.5 x 12.5cm).
£50–60 / €70–85
$80–95 ⋟ BWL
The Duke of York became King George VI in 1936.

A photograph of the Duke and Duchess of York with Princesses Elizabeth and Margaret, signed and inscribed, c1934, 6in (15cm) square.
£1,550–1,750 / €2,200–2,500
$2,500–2,800 ⊞ AEL

A T. G. Green & Co mug, commemorating the silver jubilee of King George V and Queen Mary, 1935, 3in (7.5cm) high.
£20–25 / €32–35
$35–40 ⊞ CAL

▶ *The Illustrated London News,* Silver Jubilee Record Number, c1935, 14 x 11in (35.5 x 28cm).
£35–40 / €50–55
$55–60 ⊞ J&S

◄ **A stamp box,** commemorating the coronation of King George VI, 1937, 3½in (9cm) wide.
£180–200 / €250–280
$290–320 ⊞ VB

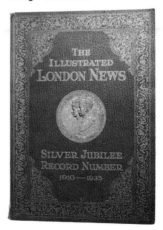

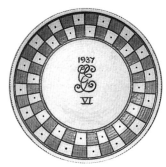

A Crown Ducal plaque,
commemorating the coronation
of King George VI and Queen
Elizabeth, 1937, 12¼in (31cm) diam.
**£140–170 / €200–240
$220–290 ✗ PF**

A handkerchief, with printed
portrait of Queen Elizabeth, 1930s,
8in (20.5cm) square.
**£14–18 / €20–26
$22–28 ⊞ ATK**

A Foley bone china mug,
commemorating the coronation
of Queen Elizabeth II, 1953,
3½in (9cm) high.
**£40–45 / €55–65
$65–75 ⊞ JMC**

A Spode bone china tankard,
commemorating the Silver Jubilee
of Queen Elizabeth II, 1977,
4in (10cm) high.
**£55–60 / €75–85
$85–95 ⊞ H&G**

A bone china mug, commemorating the divorce of Princess
Margaret and the Earl of Snowdon,
1978, 4in (10cm) high.
**£120–135 / €170–190
$190–210 ⊞ H&G**

A Wedgwood mug, commemorating the investiture of Prince
Charles as Prince of Wales, 1969,
5in (12.5cm) high.
**£45–50 / €65–70
$75–80 ⊞ H&G**

**A Royal Crown Derby bone
china loving cup,** commemorating
the birth of Prince Henry, 1984,
1½in (4cm) high.
**£65–75 / €95–105
$105–120 ⊞ H&G**

A Coalport bone china goblet,
commemorating the wedding of
Prince Charles and Lady Diana
Spencer, limited edition of 2,000,
1981, 5in (12.5cm) high.
**£90–100 / €125–140
$145–160 ⊞ H&G**

A Coalport bone china plate,
commemorating the 90th birthday
of the Queen Mother, limited edition
of 5,000, 1990, 11in (28cm) diam.
**£85–95 / €120–135
$135–150 ⊞ H&G**

◀ **A Crown loving cup,**
commemorating Diana Princess of
Wales, limited edition of 400, 1997,
3in (7.5cm) high.
**£55–60 / €75–85
$85–95 ⊞ H&G**

Corkscrews

A steel corkscrew, with bone handle and brush, late 18thC, 6in (15cm) long.
£165–185 / €230–260
$260–300 ⊞ SAT

A steel folding pocket bow corkscrew, 19thC, 3in (7.5cm) long.
£45–50 / €60–70
$70–80 ⊞ JOL

A steel penknife with corkscrew, with mother-of-pearl handle, 19thC, 1in (2.5cm) long folded.
£25–30 / €35–40
$40–45 ⊞ JOL

A medicine bottle corkscrew, with mother-of-pearl handle, 19thC, 1½in (4cm) long.
£65–75 / €95–105
$105–120 ⊞ JOL

A corkscrew, with wooden handle and brush, 19thC, 6in (15cm) long.
£55–65 / €80–90
$90–105 ⊞ SAT

There are two main types of corkscrew, straight pull and mechanical. The most desirable are those with unusual mechanisms, those made from precious materials and those with popular makers' names. When collecting corkscrews, make sure that the item is clean, works smoothly and is complete. The screw on a corkscrew can also be known as the worm or helix. Damage to the worm and repairs will devalue a corkscrew.

◄ **A steel corkscrew,** by Lund, c1855, 8in (20.5cm) long.
£130–145 / €185–210
$210–230 ⊞ SAT

A corkscrew, with wooden handle, 19thC, 4in (10cm) long.
£45–50 / €60–70
$70–80 ⊞ JOL
The wooden plunger in the handle was designed to push down the marble in codd bottles.

A brass corkscrew, by Jarrow & Jackson, with wing nut handle, 19thC, 6in (15cm) long.
£140–165 / €200–230
$220–260 ➷ G(L)

A steel corkscrew, with bone handle and brush, 1820, 8in (20.5cm) long.
£310–350 / €440–500
$500–560 ⊞ CS

A sprung corkscrew,
German, 19thC,
6in (15cm) long.
£45–50 / €60–70
$70–80 ⊞ JOL

A bow corkscrew, 1880,
1½in (4cm) long.
£45–50 / €60–70
$70–80 ⊞ Dall

**A spring barrel
corkscrew,** German,
c1900, 6in (15cm) long.
£30–35 / €45–50
$50–55 ⊞ Dall

**◄ A Victorian
steel corkscrew,**
in the form
of a key, 8in
(20cm) long.
£85–100
€120–140
$135–160 ↗ BR
The handle
unscrews to
reveal the helix.

A Willets corkscrew,
marked 'The Surprise',
1884, 5½in (14cm) long.
£45–50 / €60–70
$70–80 ⊞ Dall

A corkscrew, with
wooden handle and
brush, German, c1890,
7in (18cm) long.
£75–85 / €105–120
$120–135 ⊞ Dall

A Peerage corkscrew,
modelled as a dog, c1925,
3in (7.5cm) long.
£30–35 / €45–50
$50–55 ⊞ Dall

**◄ A carved wood
corkscrew,** modelled as
a St Bernard, c1900,
4in (10cm) long.
£60–70 / €85–100
$95–110 ⊞ TOP

**◄ A folding
seven-tool bow
corkscrew,**
c1930, 6½in
(16.5cm) long.
£175–195
€250–280
$280–310
⊞ Dall

A Holborn corkscrew,
probably by Edwin
Wolverson, c1876,
6in (15cm) long.
£55–65 / €80–90
$90–105 ⊞ SAT

**A steel double-lever
corkscrew,** marked 'Magic
Lever Cork Drawer', c1900,
5½in (14cm) long.
£30–35 / €45–50
$50–55 ⊞ CS

A bell corkscrew, with
green painted handle,
slight damage, German,
c1930, 7in (18cm) long.
£20–25 / €30–35
$35–40 ⊞ BSA

Cosmetics & Hairdressing

A silver-mounted jar, by WW/FD, London, 1890, 3in (7.5cm) high.
£35–40 / €50–55
$55–60 ⊞ WAC

A silver-backed moustache brush, 1900, 2in (5cm) long.
£55–65 / €80–90
$90–100 ⊞ LBe

A Bakelite comb, modelled as a crocodile, 1920, 11½in (30cm) long.
£30–35 / €45–50
$50–55 ⊞ LBe

A porcelain dressing table set, comprising five pieces, with foral decoration, c1900, tray 12in (30.5cm) wide.
£70–80 / €100–110
$110–130 ⊞ FOX

An enamel compact, in the form of a pendant, 1925–30, 1½in (4cm) diam.
£155–175 / €220–250
$250–280 ⊞ SUW

A silver and enamel minaudiére, with black silk tassle, 1920s, 4in (10cm) long.
£500–550 / €710–780
$800–880 ⊞ LBe
Popular in the 1920s, a minaudiére was a vanity case with compartments for powder, rouge and cigarettes.

A tortoiseshell powder box, with original swan's down powder puff, c1925, 3½in (9cm) diam.
£270–300 / €380–430
$430–480 ⊞ JTS

A double-sided cigarette and compact vanity case, 1930s, 4½in (11.5cm) long.
£85–95 / €120–135
$135–150 ⊞ LBe

◀ **A compact,** by Richard Hudnut, c1930, 2¼in (65.5cm) diam, with original box.
£220–250 / €310–350
$350–400 ⊞ SUW

▶ **A silver and enamel dressing table set,** by Finnigans Ltd, comprising six pieces, London 1930.
£280–330 / €400–470
$450–530 ⚲ EH

A butterfly wing compact, 1930s, 2in (5cm) diam.
£75–85 / €105–120
$120–135 ⊞ LU

◄ **A compact, atomizer and lipstick,** with mother-of-pearl overlay, French, c1930, 4in (10cm) wide.
£135–150 / €190–210
$220–240 ⊞ SUW

A chrome and Bakelite manicure set, 1930, box 6 x 9in (15 x 23cm).
£20–25 / €30–35
$35–40 ⊞ LBe

A compact and perfume atomizer, decorated with a picture of a flapper girl, 1930, 2½in (6.5cm) long.
£135–150 / €190–210
$220–240 ⊞ LBe
A flapper was the term for a young girl in the 1920s flaunting her unconventional dress and behaviour.

A 9ct gold backed and engine-turned dressing table set, by William Neale & Sons, comprising five pieces, Birmingham 1931.
£500–600 / €710–850
$800–960 ⚒ WL

A Nina Hanky Puff advertising shop display, 1920–30, 16in (40.5cm) high.
£40–45 / €55–65
$65–75 ⊞ LBe

A white metal 'carry all' vanity case, with compartments for rouge, powder and cigarettes, 1930s, 3¼in (8.5cm) long, with chain.
£45–50 / €65–70
$75–80 ⊞ CCO

A dressing table set, by Regent of London, with gilt floral decoration, 1930s–40s, mirror 13in (33cm) long.
£25–30 / €35–40
$40–48 ⊞ CRT

A tin of shaving soap, 1925–35, 3½in (9cm) high.
£16–20 / €23–28
$26–32 ⊞ HUX

► **A bottle of 'Saturday Night' lotion,** 1930s, 5in (12.5cm) high.
£12–16 / €17–23
$20–26 ⊞ HUX

A lady's razor, 1930s, metal box 2in (5cm) square.
£13–17 / €18–24
$21–27 ⊞ RTT

A tin of Eau de Cologne Talculm Powder, 1935, 6½in (16.5cm) high.
£12–16 / €17–23
$20–26 ⊞ HUX

A Park Lane 'carry all' compact, 1950s, 5in (12.5cm) long, with metal strap.
£50–55 / €70–80
$80–90 ⊞ CCO

◄ A white metal lipstick case with mirror, Italian, c1940s, 2¼in (5.5cm) high.
£25–30 / €35–40
$40–48 ⊞ SUW

A souvenir compact, c1950s, 2½in (6.5cm) diam.
£14–18 / €20–26
$22–28 ⊞ CCO

A metal lipstick and fan mirror, 1950–60, 2in (5cm) high.
£22–26 / €31–37
$35–42 ⊞ LBe

A gilt-metal and marcasite compact, 1950–60, 3¼in (8.5cm) wide.
£40–45 / €55–65
$65–75 ⊞ LBe

A gilt metal compact, in the form of a basket, 1950s, 2¼in (5.5cm) diam.
£75–85 / €105–120
$120–135 ⊞ SUW

◄ An enamel mirror, 1950s, 9in (23cm) long.
£55–65 / €80–90
$90–105 ⊞ CCO

A Coalport enamel compact, 1950s, 3½in (9cm) diam.
£12–16 / €17–23
$20–26 ⊞ CCO

A tin of Lemaire's Olde English Lavender Brilliantine, c1955, 3½in (9cm) diam.
£10–14 / €14–20
$16–22 ⊞ HUX

◄ A Pond's Mancatcher 001 lipstick, early 1960s, 4 x 3½in (10.5 x 9cm).
£11–15 / €16–21
$18–24 ⊞ TWI

► A Bon Voyage manicure set, c1965, 3in (7.5cm) high.
£20–25 / €30–35
$35–40 ⊞ TWI

Dog Collars

A leather dog collar, Dutch, late 16thC, 5in (12.5cm) diam.
£340–380 / €480–540
$540–610 ⊞ GGv

▶ **A steel dog collar,** Belgian, 18thC, 2½in (6.5cm) diam.
£340–380
€480–540
$540–610
⊞ GGv

A leather and brass dog collar, French, 19thC, 4¾in (12cm) diam.
£160–175 / €220–250
$250–280 ⊞ GGv

A metal dog collar, German, late 18thC, 14in (35.5cm) long.
£300–330 / €430–470
$480–530 ⊞ GGv
During the 15th and 16th centuries, dog collars were often made with spikes. This was to protect the hunting dogs from attacks by wolves and boars.

A brass dog collar, inscribed 'Willm Dicker Hask 1814', with padlock, restored, early 19thC.
£190–230 / €270–320
$300–360 ⚒ WW

A metal dog collar, 1870, 3in (7.5cm) diam.
£250–280 / €350–400
$400–450 ⊞ GGv

A leather and brass dog collar, French, c1880, 5in (12.5cm) diam.
£180–200 / €250–280
$290–320 ⊞ GGv

A leather and steel dog collar, French, c1880, 6¼in (16cm) diam.
£250–280 / €350–400
$400–450 ⊞ GGv

▶ **A leather dog collar,** with metal studs, French, c1880, 5¾in (14.5cm) diam.
£180–200 / €250–280
$290–320 ⊞ GGv

A metal dog collar, c1890, 4in (10cm) diam.
£155–175 / €220–250
$250–280 ⊞ GGv

A leather and metal dog collar, marked 'S. Lieutenant', French, late 19thC, 5in (12.5cm) diam.
£210–230 / €300–330
$330–370 ⊞ GGv

A leather dog collar, with metal studs, c1930, 5in (12.5cm) diam.
£50–55 / €70–80
$80–90 ⊞ GGv

Dolls

A wooden doll, with gesso face, glass eyes, nailed wig and jointed limbs, arms replaced, 1800, 12¼in (31cm) high.
£600–720 / €850–1,000
$960–1,100 ⚖ B(Kn)

A wax shoulder-headed doll, with glass eyes, turned head, cloth body and wax lower arms and legs, with original satin bridal dress, c1880, 15in (38cm) high.
£250–300 / €350–430
$400–480 ⚖ B(Kn)

A porcelain half-doll, 1920s, 2in (5cm) high.
£75–90 / €105–125
$120–145 ⚖ FHF

▶ **A Berlin glazed china shoulder-headed doll,** with a cloth body and china lower arms and legs, damaged and repaired, c1850, 23¼in (59cm) high.
£620–740
€880–1,050
$1,000–1,200
⚖ B(Kn)

A Lucy Peck wax shoulder-headed doll, with glass eyes, wig and cloth body with wax lower arms and legs, damaged and repaired, c1900, 29½in (75cm) high.
£280–330 / €400–470
$450–530 ⚖ B(Kn)

A pair of porcelain half-dolls, modelled as a Dutch boy and girl, 1930s, 1in (2.5cm) high.
£40–50 / €55–65
$65–70 ⚖ FHF

▶ **A porcelain half-doll,** incised mark '10039', 1930s, 3in (7.5cm) high.
£180–210 / €250–300
$290–340 ⚖ FHF

A carved wood pedlar doll, with painted features, metal glasses and a peg-jointed body, her wicker basket laden with wares, c1880, 11in (28cm) high, under a glass dome.
£400–480 / €570–680
$640–770 ⚖ B(Kn)

A Chinaman doll, with original embroidered silk clothes, 1915, 9in (23cm) high.
£65–75 / €90–105
$105–120 ⊞ POLL

Barbie

The following section is devoted to Barbie dolls and Barbie-related merchandise. Ruth and Elliot Handler, who ran the US company Mattel, established in 1945, launched the famous doll in 1959. She was named after their daughter Barbara and was inspired both by Barbara's love for playing with cut-out paper dolls and by the emerging popularity of adult fashion dolls such as Bild Lili, based on a sexy cartoon character in a German newspaper.

Although stores were initially reluctant to stock a doll with breasts, little girls were instantly seduced by the glamorous all-American teenager. Ruth Handler deliberately did not give the doll a specific personality, so that children could create their own character

for her, as they dressed up Barbie (and her family and friends) in an ever-expanding wardrobe of clothes.

For collectors, the most desirable Barbie products come from the vintage period 1959–72. Dolls are marked on the right buttock. While the date might simply refer to the copyright year, look out for the word 'Japan', where 'vintage period' dolls were manufactured. Condition is crucial to value. The price ranges in this section for dolls, outfits and merchandise represent not only the rarity of early items, but the fact that many of them have never been removed from their box or packaging (often referred to as NRFB), which hugely enhances their value to grown-up Barbie fans.

A Mattel Barbie Luncheon Embroidery Set, c1962, 12 x 18in (30.5 x 45.5cm).
£270–300 / €380–430
$430–480 ⊞ T&D

A Mattel Barbie doll, slight damage, c1960, 11in (28cm) high.
£65–75 / €90–105
$105–120 ⊞ POLL

A Mattel Barbie knitting tin, with contents, c1961, 11in (28cm) high.
£65–75 / €90–105
$105–120 ⊞ T&D

▶ A Mattel Midge doll, wearing an 'Its Cold Outside' outfit, c1963, 6in (15cm) high.
£140–155 / €200–220
$220–250 ⊞ T&D
Midge, a freckle-faced redhead, was introduced in 1963 and is Barbie's oldest friend.

◀ A Webster's Barbie dictionary, in original unopened packaging, c1962, 6in (15cm) square.
£450–500 / €640–710
$720–800 ⊞ T&D

A Mattel Skipper straight leg doll, c1963, 9in (23cm) high, with original box.
£135–150 / €190–210
$215–240 ⊞ T&D

Two Mattel dolls, Scooter and Ricky, with original outfits, c1964, 9in (23cm) high.
£90–100 / € 130–140 $145–160 ⊞ T&D
Scooter and Ricky were designed as friends for Barbie's little sister, Skipper.

A Skipper carrying case, c1964, 10 x 7in (25.5 x 18cm).
£40–45 / € 55–65 $65–75 ⊞ T&D

A Mattel American Girl Barbie, wearing a bathing outfit, c1965, 13in (33cm) high, boxed.
£900–1,000 € 1,300–1,400 $1,400–1,600 ⊞ T&D
Released in 1965 American Girl, also known as Bendable Leg Barbie, is one of the most popular models with collectors of vintage Barbie dolls. Her 'Dutch Boy' hairdo came in several colours including blonde, titian (red) and brunette. Lip colours also varied, although pink and coral were favourite shades. A new line of clothing known as '1600s' (because stock numbers all start with 16) was introduced with the doll. The elegant and elaborate outfits were inspired by the wardrobe of the former First Lady, Jacqueline Kennedy.

A Mattel Bendable Leg Midge doll, c1966, box 13in (33cm) high.
£360–400 / € 510–570 $580–640 ⊞ T&D

A Mattel Busy Barbie, with holding hands, c1971, 11in (28cm) high.
£110–125 / € 155–175 $175–200 ⊞ T&D

A Mattel No Bangs Francie doll, c1966, 6in (15cm) high.
£450–500 / € 640–710 $720–800 ⊞ T&D
Mattel issued Barbie's cousin Francie in 1966. The doll was designed to wear all the latest mod fashions and came with various hairstyles. This model with swept-back hair and Alice band is known as 'No Bangs' Francie. It is very hard to find and is popular with collectors today.

A Mattel Bubblecut Barbie doll, wearing a 'Brides Dream' outfit, c1967, 9in (23cm) high.
£220–250 / € 310–350 $350–400 ⊞ T&D

A Mattel Hair Happenings Francie doll, with accessories, c1971, 6in (15cm) high.
£270–300 / € 380–430 $430–480 ⊞ T&D

◀ **A Mattel Francie doll,** c1974, in original packaging, 13in (33cm) high.
£270–300 / € 380–430 $430–480 ⊞ T&D

A Malibu Skipper doll, on a sledge, c1975, 9in (23cm) high.
£155–175 / € 220–250 $260–290 ⊞ T&D

Bisque

◀ **A Jumeau bisque-headed bébé doll,** with glass eyes, feather brows, pierced ears and a fully-jointed composition body, wearing a dress, bonnet, underclothes and leather shoes, together with an extra dress and bag, hands replaced, French, c1895, 25¼in (64cm) high.
£950–1,100 / €1,300–1,500
$1,500–1,700 ⚒ B(Kn)
Jumeau produced dolls from 1842–99 and the first bébé dolls were made in 1885.

Armand Marseille

Armand Marseille was one of Germany's most prolific doll makers, making bisque dolls from 1885 onwards. From 1900 to 1930 they also supplied dolls to other makers.

An Armand Marseille bisque-headed baby doll, with sleeping eyes, moulded hair, composition hands and padded jointed legs, with a crying voice box, c1900, 12½in (32cm) high.
£200–240 / €280–340
$320–380 ⚒ DMC

▶ **A pair of bisque miniature dolls,** with glass eyes, bodies jointed at the shoulders and hips, with original clothes and painted shoes, German, c1910, 3½in (9cm) high.
£150–180 / €210–250
$240–290 ⚒ B(Kn)

A Porzellanfabrik Burggrub bisque-headed doll, with weighted glass eyes, moving tongue and five-piece composition body, impressed marks, 1915–20, 23in (58.5cm) high.
£140–170 / €200–240
$220–260 ⚒ FHF

▶ **A Simon & Halbig Arundel museum doll,** with original clothes and wig, 1920, 15in (38cm) high.
£330–370 / €470–520
$520–590 ⊞ POLL

Simon & Halbig

Simon & Halbig made dolls from c1869 to 1930, not only for themselves but for other companies such as Jumeau and Kämmer & Reinhart. All their dolls have a mould number and the 'SH' letter mark.

A Gerbrüder Heubach ceramic piano baby, with side-glancing eyes, c1920, 10¼in (26cm) high.
£630–700 / €890–990
$1,000–1,100 ⊞ YC

▶ **An Armand Marseille bisque-headed baby doll,** with glass eyes, rag body and composition arms, impressed marks, No. 341, 1920s, 10in (25.5cm) high.
£110–130 / €155–185
$175–210 ⚹ FHF

◀ **An Armand Marseille bisque-headed doll,** with bent limbs and vintage clothes, No. 990, 1925, 17in (43cm) high.
£340–380 / €480–540
$540–610 ⊞ POLL

▶ **An Armand Marseille bisque-headed doll,** with sleeping eyes, original wig and vintage clothes, c1925, 22in (56cm) high.
£380–420 / €540–600
$610–670 ⊞ POLL

◀ **An Armand Marseille bisque-headed doll,** with weighted glass eyes, moving tongue and five-piece composition body, impressed marks, No. 996, 1930s, 16in (40.5cm) high.
£150–180 / €210–250
$240–280 ⚹ FHF

Celluloid

A Celluloid Doll Co Mabel Lucie Attwell Diddums doll, c1930, 9in (23cm) high.
£160–180 / €230–250
$260–290 ⊞ MEM

▶ **A celluloid ventrilo-quist's doll,** c1940, 29in (73.5cm) high.
£85–95 / €120–135
$135–150 ⊞ UD

A celluloid doll, with moulded hair, French, 1930s, 21in (53.5cm) high.
£135–150 / €190–210
$210–240 ⊞ POLL

Cloth

A Raggedy Anne cloth doll, attributed to P. F. Volland & Co, with hand-painted features, cardboard heart and shoe-button eyes, c1918, 16in (40.5cm) high.
£1,100–1,300
€1,500–1,800
$1,800–2,100 ⚹ HAYS
Raggedy Anne was a character doll created by American illustrator John Barton Gruelle (1880–1938). He registered Raggedy Anne as a trademark in 1915, producing dolls and story books. In c1918 he also introduced the Raggedy Andy character. Over the years Raggedy Anne dolls have been produced by numerous manufacturers as well as being home made. P. F. Volland made Raggedy Anne c1920–34, their dolls coming with an edible red candy heart attached to the chest. Early examples of this famous doll are very collectable.

A Dean's Betty Oxo cloth doll, c1930, 17in (43cm) high.
£120–135 / €170–190
$190–210 ⊞ UD

A Dean's Rag Book Lupino Lane cloth doll, c1939, 10in (25.5cm) high.
£40–45 / €55–65
$65–75 ⊞ COB
Lupino Lane (1892–1959), cousin of actress Ida Lupino, was a British director and comic actor on stage and screen. He starred in the 1937 musical *Me and My Girl* and its film version *The Lambeth Walk*, 1939.

◀ **A Schuco Apache Samson Jr plush doll,** 1950s, 10½in (26.5cm) high, with box.
£40–50 / €55–70
$65–80 ⚹ TQA

A Käthe Kruse cloth child doll, with painted eyes and cloth body, No. 7534, marked on foot, German, c1930, 20in (51cm) high, in original box, together with additional clothes and shoes.
£700–840 / €1,000–1,200
$1,100–1,300 ⚹ B(Kn)
Käthe Kruse made a small range of cloth dolls 1911–56. Her early dolls are most sought-after and can be recognized by three hand-stitched seams on the doll's head.

▶ **A Lancastria sailor cloth doll,** 1930s, 8in (20.5cm) high.
£65–75 / €95–105
$105–120 ⊞ COB

A cloth sailor doll, 1960, 8in (20.5cm) high.
£40–45 / €55–65
$65–75 ⊞ COB

A Lenci felt doll, with a swivel head, jointed at the shoulders and hips, Italian, 1930, 11¾in (30cm) high, in original box.
£450–540 / €640–770
$720–860 ⚹ B(Kn)

A Ronald McDonald rag doll, c1985, 12in (30.5cm) high.
£35–40 / €50–55
$60–65 ⊞ McD
Versions of this doll dating from the early 1970s can be worth approximately double this price range to a McDonald's collector.

Composition

A Horseman Campbell Kid doll, with composition head and hands, jointed arms and legs, the body stuffed with straw, 1910, 13in (33cm) high.
£250–280 / €360–400
$400–450 ⊞ SaB

▶ **An Armand Marseille bent-limbed baby doll,** German, 1920s, 15in (38cm) high.
£75–85 / €105–120
$120–135 ⊞ POLL

An Effanbee composition baby doll, with painted eyes and a soft body, American, 1930s, 24in (61cm) high.
£110–125 / €155–175
$175–200 ⊞ POLL

◀ **A composition doll,** with original wig, marked 'IDL', 1930s, 18in (45.5cm) high.
£210–230 / €300–330
$340–370 ⊞ POLL

An Ideal Novelty & Toy Co composition Shirley Temple doll, shoes missing, American, c1934, 13in (33cm) high.
£310–370 / €440–520
$500–590 ↗ HAYS

A Pedigree bent-limbed composition baby doll, some wear, 1930s, 12in (30.5cm) high.
£75–85 / €105–120
$120–135 ⊞ POLL

A Topsy composition doll, American, c1940, 11in (28cm) high.
£85–95 / €120–135
$135–150 ⊞ UD

Plastic & Vinyl

A Terri Lee Sales Corporation Terri Lee hard plastic doll, with painted eyes, American, c1946, 16in (40.5cm) high.
£240–280 / €340–400
$380–450 ↗ HAYS

A Tudor Rose hard plastic doll, wearing knitted clothes, c1950, 9in (23cm) high.
£40–45 / €55–65
$65–75 ⊞ POLL

A Rosebud hard plastic doll, 1950s, 13in (33cm) high.
£45–50 / €65–70
$75–80 ⊞ UD

A Palitoy walking talking hard plastic doll, c1950, 21in (53.5cm) high.
£65–75 / €95–105
$105–120 ⊞ UD

A Rosebud hard plastic doll, c1950, 16in (40.5cm) high, in original box.
**£150–165 / €215–235
$240–265 ⊞ UD**

The Rosebud Twins dolls and knitting pattern book, from *Woman's Weekly,* 1950s, dolls 6in (15cm) high.
**£11–15 / €16–21
$18–24 each ⊞ POLL**

A Rosebud bent-limbed hard plastic doll, 1950s, 13in (33cm) high.
**£130–145 / €185–205
$210–230 ⊞ POLL**

A Chiltern vinyl doll, with original clothes, 1958–67, 12in (30.5cm) high.
**£20–25 / €30–35
$35–40 ⊞ POLL**

A Pedigree vinyl doll, 1962, 27in (68.5cm) high.
**£85–95 / €120–135
$135–150 ⊞ UD**

A Pedigree bent-limbed plastic doll, with a mohair wig, 1950s, 10in (25.5cm) high.
**£55–60 / €75–85
$85–95 ⊞ POLL**

A Palitoy Tiny Tears vinyl doll, 1960s, 16in (40.5cm) high.
**£40–45 / €55–65
$65–75 ⊞ UD**

A Roddy vinyl doll, 1950–60, 21in (53.5cm) high.
**£45–50 / €65–70
$75–80 ⊞ POLL**

An Amanda Jane doll, with original Flower Power trouser suit, 1960s, 7in (18cm) high.
**£60–70 / €85–100
$95–110 ⊞ POLL**

► **A Pedigree Sindy doll,** 1984, 11in (28cm) high, with original box.
**£100–120 / €145–170
$160–190 ⋟ AH
This model never appeared on the retail market. Only 400 were made for a special awards dinner in 1984.**

A Remco Sweet April plastic doll, in a plastic carry case/swing, 1972, 10in (25.5cm) high.
**£25–30 / €35–40
$40–48 ⊞ UD**

A Palitoy Action Man Combat Division soldier, with original box, 1981, 13in (33cm) high.
**£100–110 / €140–160
$160–175 ⊞ GTM**

Prams & Accessories

A child's wooden fold-up pushchair, with metal spoked wheels and solid rubber tyres, late 19thC, 34½in (87.5cm) high.
£130–145 / €180–200
$210–230 ⊞ CHAC
Doll collectors often buy children's prams, push-chairs and high chairs to display their dolls.

A tinplate toy pram with a bisque doll, doll German, 1910, pram 6in (15cm) long.
£270–300 / €380–430
$430–480 ⊞ Beb

A doll's pram, with new lining, hood and apron, 1930s, 33in (84cm) wide.
£350–390 / €500–550
$550–620 ⊞ POLL

A doll's trunk, 1930–40, 15½in (39.5cm) high.
£85–95 / €120–135
$135–150 ⊞ MCa

► A Royal doll's pram, with a loose bottom section and padded interior, 1940s, 43in (109cm) long.
£500–550
€710–780
$820–880
⊞ POLL

◄ A Tri-ang doll's high chair, with original padded seat, 1940s, 23in (58.5cm) high.
£60–70 / €90–100
$100–110 ⊞ POLL

A Tri-ang doll's high chair, 1950s, 20in (51cm) high.
£30–35 / €45–50
$50–55 ⊞ UD

A Palitoy Carrie carrycot and doll, with original clothes, 1970, 7in (18cm) wide.
£40–45 / €55–65
$65–75 ⊞ POLL

Doll's House Accessories

◄ **A child's painted wooden toy grocer's shop,** with counters and goods, probably German, late 19thC, 18½in (47cm) high.
£220–250 / €310–370
$350–420 ✗ PFK

A set of ten bisque doll's house dolls, with glass eyes, plaited wigs, jointed bodies, wearing dresses and painted shoes, German, c1920, 3in (7.5cm) high, boxed.
£125–150 / €175–210
$200–240 ✗ AH

A bisque doll's house doll, with jointed limbs, c1900, 4in (10cm) high.
£220–250 / €310–350
$350–400 ⊞ YC

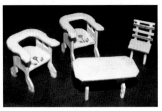

A set of wooden doll's house furniture, hand-painted, 1940s, 1in (2.5cm) high.
£45–50 / €65–70
$75–80 ⊞ JMC

A set of doll's house furniture, covered in silk, 1940s, chair 3½in (9cm) high.
£55–65 / €80–90
$90–105 ⊞ JMC

A doll's house, modelled as a front-opening thatched cottage, with six rooms and some original furniture, 1950s, 30in (76cm) wide.
£220–260 / €310–370
$350–420 ✗ L&E

A Tudor-style doll's house, with some contents and a stand, 1950s, 48in (122cm) wide.
£190–220 / €270–310
$300–350 ✗ BR

A set of soft metal doll's house furniture, German, c1990, chairs 3in (7.5cm) high.
£190–220 / €270–310
$300–350 ✗ B(Kn)

▶ **A doll's house wooden tool chest,** by Terry McAllister, 2002, 3in (7.5cm) wide.
£125–140 / €175–200
$200–220 ⊞ CNM

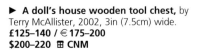

A doll's house Japanese-style half-tester bed, by Judith Dunger, 2002, 8in (20.5cm) long.
£150–170 / €210–240
$240–270 ⊞ CNM

Eighties

A Karl Lagerfeld Kelly-style plastic handbag, with authenticity badge, c1980, 8in (20.5cm) wide.
£90–100 / €130–145
$145–160 ⊞ HIP

A Memphis lacquered-metal Oceanic Lamp, by Michele De Lucchi, Italian, 1981, 31in (78.5cm) high.
£300–400 / €470–570
$530–640 ➤ BB(L)

An Allied Stars poster, *Breaking Glass,* c1982, 30 x 40in (76 x 101.5cm).
£16–20 / €23–28
$26–32 ⊞ CTO

Star Wars, pilot figure, from *Return of the Jedi,* 1983, 4in (10cm) high.
£145–160 / €210–230
$230–260 ⊞ SSF

A Vivienne Westwood gauze T-shirt, from the Witches collection, c1983, 28in (71cm) long.
£270–300 / €380–430
$430–480 ⊞ ID

◀ **A Donald Campbell silk dress,** printed with a balloon pattern, 1980s.
£135–150 / €190–210
$210–240 ⊞ Ci

Masters of the Universe, plastic He-man action figure, Italian, 1983, 5in (12.5cm) high.
£75–85 / €105–120
$120–135 ⊞ OW

A Hornsea Swan Lake teapot, 1983–92, 5½in (14cm) high.
£45–50 / €65–70
$75–80 ⊞ CHI

A Saporiti Butterfly chair, Italian, 1985, 38in (96.5cm) high.
£370–440 / €530–620
$590–700 ➤ BB(L)

Kiss, oil painting, 1989, 36 x 20in (91.5 x 51cm).
£130–150 / €180–210
$210–240 ➤ CO

Ephemera

A parchment land indenture, 1793,
12 x 20in (30.5 x 51cm).
£16–20 / €23–28
$26–32 ⊞ J&S

**A handwritten receipt for the hire of a
slave,** American, Mississippi, signed and
dated 1847, 8in (20.5cm) wide.
£90–100 / €125–140
$140–160 ⊞ COB

Two Champagne Delbeck menus, c1895,
12½ x 8½in (32 x 21.5cm).
£140–155 / €200–220
$220–250 ⚒ VSP

► **An official
guide to
the funeral
procession
of King
Edward VII,**
1910, 6 x 4in
(15 x 10cm).
£11–15
€16–21
$18–24 ⊞ COB

**A Solent Sea Baths advertising
card,** 1843, 3 x 5in (7.5 x 12.5cm).
£11–15 / €16–21
$18–24 ⊞ COB

◄ **A London & Edinburgh Steam
Packet Co advertising broadsheet,**
1830s, 9 x 5in (23 x 12.5cm).
£70–75 / €100–120
$110–120 ⊞ COB

A calendar, with Saints days,
German, 1889, 16 x 13in
(40.5 x 33cm).
£16–20 / €23–28
$26–32 ⊞ J&S

Two hotel restaurant menus,
French, 1920s, 8 x 6in (20.5 x 15cm).
£6–10 / €8–14
$10–16 each ⊞ COB

> **Cross Reference**
> See Automobilia (pages 48–52)

► **A** *Daily Mail* **road map of
London,** and ten miles around,
c1930, 11 x 6in (28 x 15cm).
£5–9 / €7–13
$8–14 ⊞ JUN

A Gun licence, 1909,
11 x 7in (28 x 18cm).
£16–20 / €23–28
$26–32 ⊞ J&S

A *Men of Action* booklet, on School of Accountancy, 1940s, 9¾ x 7in (25 x 18cm).
£1–5 / €2–7
$3–8 ⊞ RTT

▶ **An SS *Empress of England* Gala Night programme,** 1961, 11 x 9in (28 x 23in).
£11–15 / €16–20
$18–24 ⊞ COB

A *Mame* flier, starring Ginger Rogers, 1969, 8½ x 5in (21.5 x 12.5cm).
£1–5 / €2–7
$3–8 ⊞ CAST

A theatre programme, for *London Laughs*, 1952, 5 x 7¼in (18.5 x 12.5cm).
£6–10 / €8–14
$10–16 ⊞ CAST

A theatre programme, for *Joseph and the Amazing Technicolor Dreamcoat*, 1973, 9 x 5¼in (23 x 13.5cm).
£10–14 / €14–20
$16–22 ⊞ CAST

◀ **An SS *Canberra* menu,** 1976, 12 x 8in (30.5 x 20.5cm).
£6–10 / €8–14
$10–16 ⊞ COB

A mail order fashion catalogue, 1955, 8½ x 5in (21.5 x 12.5cm).
£3–7 / €4–9
$5–10 ⊞ RTT

An Economy Designs catalogue, 1961, 15 x 12in (38 x 30.5in).
£26–30 / €38–42
$42–48 ⊞ COB

A Rawson calendar, 1963, 19 x 14in (48.5 x 35.5cm).
£1–5 / €2–7
$3–8 ⊞ JUN

Erotica

A silver and enamel cigarette case,
with a picture of a can-can dancer, c1900,
5½ x 3½in (14 x 9cm)
**£1,650–1,850 / €2,300–2,600
$2,600–2,900 ⊞ SHa**

Two bisque porcelain figures,
entitled 'Bathing Belles', German,
early 20thC, 3½in (9cm) high.
**£650–780 / €920–1,100
$1,000–1,200 ⚒ G(L)**

**Two bisque porcelain
figures,** entitled 'Bathing
Belles', German, early
20thC, 2½in (6.5cm) high.
**£700–840 / €1,000–1,200
$1,100–1,300 ⚒ G(L)**

Razzle magazine, 1930s,
12 x 9½in (30.5 x 24cm).
**£2–6 / €3–8
$4–10 ⊞ RTT**

**A pack of glamour
playing cards,**
Belgian, 1930s.
**£35–40 / €50–55
$55–65 ⚒ VS**

**The New 1951 Folies
Bergere Revue
programme,** 7¼ x 5in
(18 x 12.5cm).
**£2–6 / €3–8
$4–10 ⊞ CAST**

C'est Paris magazine,
September 1951,
10½ x 8½in (26.5 x 21.5cm).
**£2–6 / €3–8
$4–10 ⊞ RTT**

**A Marilyn Monroe
'Golden Dreams'
calender,** 1955,
21¾ x 11¾in (55 x 30cm).
**£380–450 / €540–640
$600–720 ⚒ GK**

Liliput magazine, 1956,
10 x 8in (25.5 x 20.5cm).
**£2–6 / €3–8
$4–10 ⊞ RTT**

Esquire magazine,
March 1957, 13¼ x 10in
(33.5 x 25.5cm).
**£6–10 / €8–14
$10–16 ⊞ RTT**

▶ **A peek-a-boo cowgirl tie,** 1950s.
**£105–115 / €150–165
$165–180 ⊞ CAD**

◄ **Reginald Heade (illus),** five paperbacks, *Desert Fury, One man in his Time, Torment for Trixy, Vengeance, Whiplash,* 1950s.
£175–195 / €230–280
$260–310 ⊞ CBP

Reginald Heade

Reginald Heade (1903–57) was one of the finest pulp fiction cover artists of the day. His glamorous portrayal of hard-boiled gun molls and femmes fatales are acclaimed in both the UK and the USA. In his heyday he produced many cover paintings for Archer Press and latterly Gaywood Press, who distributed the hugely successful Hank Janson paperbacks. They became a publishing sensation in the 1940s and '50s with their risqué story lines and erotic pin-up covers. Heade's book covers and his original artwork are becoming increasingly collectable.

Reginald Heade (illus), five paperbacks, *Dame in my Bed, Plaything of Passion, Vice rackets of Soho, Sin-Stained, Flame,* 1950s.
£110–130 / €160–190
$180–210 ⊞ CBP

A Combex hot water bottle, modelled as Jayne Mansfield, c1950s, 21in (53.5cm) high.
£115–130 / €165–185
$185–210 ⊞ MARG
Jayne Mansfield was an American actress and sexual icon of the 1950s and '60s.

Glamour **magazine,** Vol 5, 1950s, 8 x 5in (20.5 x 12.5cm).
£6–10 / €8–14
$10–16 ⊞ RTT

Parade **magazine,** with pin-up supplement, 1963, 11 x 8½in (28 x 21.5cm).
£1–5 / €2–7
$3–8 ⊞ RTT

A pen and ink sketch, by Neiman Leroy, signed, 1964, 4½ x 3½in (10 x 9cm).
£95–115 / €135–160
$150–180 ⚒ VS

Playboy Club, memorabilia, 1969.
£55–60 / €75–85
$85–95 ⊞ CTO

◄ **Timothy Lea,** *Confessions from a Holiday Camp,* hardback, 1974, 7 x 4½in (18 x 11.5cm).
£2–6 / €3–8
$4–10 ⊞ RTT

Terence Donovan, a gelatin silver photograph, entitled 'Glance', signed and dated, numbered 1/5, 1983, image 10¾ x 9½in (27.5 x 24cm).
£190–230 / €270–320
$300–360 ⚒ BBA

Fans

A **lithographic fan,** hand-coloured, with pierced and gilded bone sticks, Italian, c1840, 10½in (26.5cm) wide.
£270–300 / €380–420
$430–480 ⊞ VK

An **Albert Smith paper-leaf fan,** with wooden sticks and lithograph illustrations, caption 'Programme of Mr Albert Smith's Ascent of Mont Blanc, August 12th and 13th 1851', c1853.
£1,150–1,350 / €1,650–1,900
$1,850–2,150 ≱ BBA
This fan was sold at the Egyptian Hall during the course of Albert Smith's immensely popular entertainment *The Ascent of Mont Blanc*. The show lasted for over 2,000 performances and the success of the merchandising operation spread the popularity of the new sport of mountaineering far and wide.

◄ A **pair of felt and lace screens,** with beaded handles, c1870, 18in (45.5cm) high.
£310–350 / €440–500
$500–560 ⊞ JPr

A **fan,** with bone sticks and 18thC-style decoration, French, 19thC, 9in (23cm) wide.
£125–140 / €180–200
$200–220 ⊞ LaF

A **fan,** hand-painted with carved sticks, French, c1900, 13in (33cm) wide.
£65–75 / €90–105
$105–120 ⊞ SAT

A **paper and bamboo fan,** hand-painted, Chinese, 20thC, 9in (23cm) wide.
£55–60 / €75–85
$85–95 ⊞ MARG

◄ A **paper fan,** advertising Amer Picon, 1930s, 9in (23cm) high.
£20–25 / €30–35
$35–40 ⊞ JUJ

Buying tips

Early hand-painted and lithographic fans with particularly unusual motifs, such as the mountaineering fan above, are very desirable. With changing fashions in the 20th century, the fan survived largely as an advertising medium.

Look out for splits, broken sticks and staining. Try not to handle them and do not have them framed for display as light and heat can cause damage. With all fans, condition is crucial to value.

A **paper fan,** advertising Cognac, French, 1930s, 7½in (19cm) wide.
£35–40 / €50–55
$55–65 ⊞ JUJ

Fifties

This section is devoted to furnishing, fashion and decorative arts from the 1950s. It opens, however, with an object from the 1940s, which is surely one of the most curious items to have become an icon of modern design. In 1941, the American designers Charles and Ray Eames married and moved to California where they experimented with the manufacture of curved and moulded plywood. This resulted in the development of leg splints, which were produced for the US Navy from 1942. The pair illustrated here includes one splint still in its original brown paper packaging with label designed by Ray

Eames. In the post-war period, the couple went on to become arguably the most famous modern furniture designers of their day. Their work in plywood was innovative and highly influential, hence the value of these legs splints to collectors of post-war furniture and design.

This section includes other works by the Eames, including the 'Giant House of Cards' designed in 1953. Decorated with various images inspired by art, science and 'the world around us', cards came with slots so that they could literally be built up into a house or a free-standing sculpture.

A pair of moulded plywood leg splints, designed by Charles and Ray Eames for Evans Products, stamped, one in original wrapping, American, 1941, 43in (109cm) high.
£350–420 / €500–600
$560–670 BB(L)

A fibre and steel bubble lamp, by George Nelson for Howard Miller, c1950, 18in (45.5cm) diam.
£160–190 / €230–270
$260–300 BB(L)

Items in the Fifties section have been arranged in date order.

'The Coloring Toy', designed by Charles and Ray Eames for Tigrett Enterprises, 1953.
£720–860
€1,000–1,200
$1,150–1,350 BB(L)
This is the rarest item designed by the Eames Office for Tigrett Enterprises.

◄ **A Cone chair,** by Verner Panton, 1956.
£590–650 / €840–920
$940–1,050 MARK

A lacquered metal and brass Sputnik chandelier, by Arteluce, c1950, 45in (114.5cm) high.
£880–1,050
€1,250–1,500
$1,400–1,700 BB(L)

A 'Giant House of Cards', designed by Charles and Ray Eames for Tigrett Enterprises, 1953.
£660–790 / €940–1,100
$1,050–1,250 BB(L)

A plastic tray, by George Nelson, American, c1956, 13¾in (35cm) wide.
£125–150 / €175–210
$200–240 BB(L)

◄ **A Triennale floor lamp,** Italian, c1957, 58½in (148.5cm) high.
£1,350–1,600
€1,900–2,250
$2,200–2,550 BB(L)

A pair of matching spinner lamps, by Moss Lamps Co, revolving ceramic figures by Hedi Schoop, American, c1957, 32in (81.5cm) high.
£1,100–1,250
€ 1,550–1,750
$1,750–2,000 ⊞ MARK

▶ **A plastic cruet set,** with polka dot pattern, 1950s, 3½in (9cm) high.
£35–40 / € 50–55
$55–60 ⊞ BET

A pair of low lounge chairs, Swedish, 1950s.
£250–280 / € 360–400
$400–450 ⊞ MARK

A wicker chair, by Sir Terence Conran, on metal hairpin legs, 1950s, 26½in (67.5cm) high.
£90–100 / € 125–140
$145–160 ⊞ MARK

A cane chair, on metal legs, 1950s.
£55–60 / € 80–85
$90–95 ⊞ MARK

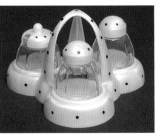

▶ **An Imhof clock,** Swiss, 1950s, 6in (15cm) high.
£60–70
€ 85–100
$95–110 ⊞ GRo

Ceramics & Glass

◀ **A dinner service,** by Raymond Loewy, c1958, dinner plates 10½in (26.5cm) diam.
£310–370 / € 440–530
$500–600 ⤳ BB(L)

A Palissy coffee set, 1950s, coffee pot 9in (23cm) high, with original box.
£45–50 / € 65–70
$75–80 ⊞ CCO

A Rörstrand Chamotte vase, by Gunnar Nylund, Swedish, 1950s, 6in (15cm) high.
£70–80 / € 100–110
$115–130 ⊞ MARK

A Foley vase, designed by James Kent, c1950s, 5½in (14cm) high.
£45–50 / € 65–70
$75–80 ⊞ BET

A jug, German, 1958, 14in (35.5cm) high.
£55–65 / € 80–90
$90–105 ⊞ GRo

A Carlton Ware mustard pot, 1950s, 2½in (6.5cm) high.
£6–10 / € 8–14
$10–16 ⊞ GRo

An Alfred Meakin plate, decorated with a cowboy and girl in an orchard, 1950s, 6¾in (17cm) diam.
£2–6 / €3–8
$4–10 ⊞ CHI
Meakin's designs were often inspired by popular films and stage shows and this pattern recalls the musical *Oklahoma*, produced as a movie in 1955.

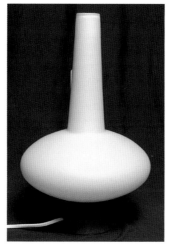

A wood and glass table lamp, Scandinavian, 1950s, 13½in (34.5cm) high.
£50–55 / €70–80
$80–90 ⊞ CHI

◄ **A Spode gravy boat and saucer,** decorated with Summer Days pattern, 1950s, 6in (15cm) wide.
£45–50 / €65–70
$75–80 ⊞ CHI

A bubble glass ashtray, 1950s, 7in (18cm) wide.
£15–20 / €20–25
$25–30 ⊞ MARK

Cross Reference
See Glass (pages 211–225)

A heart-shaped glass dish, with applied clear glass decoration, Italian, 1950s, 7½in (19cm) wide.
£6–10 / €8–14
$10–16 ⊞ MARK

Fashion

A tie, entitled 'Dance Pretty Lady!', 1949–52.
£85–95 / €120–135
$135–150 ⊞ CAD

Cross Reference
See Erotica
(pages 198–199)

An HBarC gabardine Western shirt, with embroidered decoration, 1950s.
£210–230 / €300–380
$340–380 ⊞ CAD
Vintage Western-style clothes, particularly with elaborate decoration, are very sought after by collectors.

A printed cotton dress, 1950.
£145–160 / €210–230
$230–260 ⊞ RER

► **A hostess apron,** printed with a poodle pattern, 1950s, 20in (50.5cm) wide.
£25–30 / €35–45
$40–50 ⊞ SpM

A printed cotton dress, by Heathgate, 1950s.
£15–20 / €20–25
$25–30 ⊞ REPS

A chiffon dress, by Frank Usher, with ruched bodice and embroidered skirt, 1950s.
£45–50 / €65–70
$75–80 ⊞ CCO

A printed cotton dress, 1950s.
£85–95 / €120–135
$135–150 ⊞ RER

A silk scarf, with printed decoration of handbags and valises, 1950s, 34in (86.5cm) square.
£55–65 / €80–90
$90–105 ⊞ LBe

A basket bag, with velvet and 'jewelled' decoration and plastic lining, c1950, 13in (33cm) wide.
£60–70 / €85–100
$95–110 ⊞ HIP

A Hoop-la underskirt, in original box, 1950s, 12in (30.5cm) square.
£55–65 / €80–90
$90–105 ⊞ SpM

A handbag, with floral decoupage decoration, American, c1950, 10in (25.5cm) high.
£250–280 / €360–400
$400–450 ⊞ TIN

A Park & Tilford Party Time lipstick, in the form of a cocktail shaker, 1950s, 2¼in (6.5cm) high, in original box.
£135–150 / €190–210
$220–240 ⊞ SpM

A needlepoint bag, with embroidered decoration of a cowboy, c1950s, 8in (20.5cm) wide.
£270–300 / €380–430
$430–480 ⊞ TIN

▶ A cotton mesh two-piece, by Mel Warshaw, late 1950s.
£150–165 / €210–230
$240–270 ⊞ SpM

Festival of Britain

This section is devoted to memorabilia from the Festival of Britain in 1951. Planned from 1947, the festival was designed to mark the centenary of the Great Exhibition of 1851, to showcase modern developments in arts and science, and to signal the end of the austerity of the 1940s with huge celebration. It would provide a 'tonic to the nation,' claimed Director General Gerald Barry. 'The motives which inspire the festival are common to us all,' declared George VI. 'Pride in our past and all that it has meant, confidence in the future which holds so many opportunities for us to continue our contribution to the wellbeing of mankind, and thanksgiving that we have begun to surmount our trials.'

A bomb site on the South Bank of the Thames was transformed by a team of architects and designers who created a series of pavilions and buildings including the Royal Festival Hall, the Dome of Discovery and the Skylon. Battersea Park was turned into a giant funfair, complete with miniature railway designed by Rowland Emmett. In five months, nearly 8.5 million visitors came to the South Bank Exhibition. The festival stimulated a wealth of memorabilia, bearing the distinctive symbol designed by Abram Games, and half a century on this material is still very sought after.

A Webb's glass ashtray, 1951, 6in (15cm) diam.
£30–35 / €40–45
$50–55 ⊞ MURR

A Paragon bone china bowl, 1951, 6in (15cm) diam.
£105–120 / €150–170
$165–190 ⊞ MURR

A pair of cufflinks, 1951, in original box, 3 x 4½in (7.5 x 11cm).
£45–50 / €65–70
$75–80 ⊞ MURR

◀ **An Emett Railway cardboard jigsaw puzzle,** 1951, 9 x 10in (23 x 25.5cm).
£70–80 / €100–115
$115–130 ⊞ MURR

Welcome to London, map and transport information, 1951, 5¾ x 3in (14.5 x 7.5cm).
£6–10 / €8–14
$10–16 ⊞ RTT

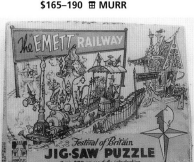

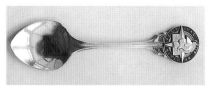

A silver-plated teaspoon, with enamel decoration, 1951, 6in (15cm) long.
£30–35 / €40–45
$50–55 ⊞ MURR

A wood and brass weather vane and compass, 1951, 4in (10cm) high.
£55–65 / €80–90
$90–105 ⊞ MURR

Games

A mahogany solitaire board, with original marbles, c1830, 10in (25.5cm) diam.
£55–65 / €80–90
$90–105 ⊞ F&F

A mahogany solitaire board, with original clay marbles, c1840, 7½in (19cm) diam.
£55–65 / €80–90
$90–105 ⊞ F&F

A Victorian mahagony solitaire board, with 39 marbles, 9¼in (23.5cm) diam.
£145–175 / €210–250
$230–280 ⋏ DMC

A Victorian mahogany, rosewood and satinwood-inlaid games box, 18½in (47cm) wide.
£130–155 / €185–220
$210–250 ⋏ SWO

A bone barley-corn chess set, c1850, king 2¾in (7cm) high, in original wooden box.
£40–45 / €55–65
$65–75 ⋏ G(L)

A wooden box of magic tricks, French, c1880, 7 x 11in (18 x 28cm).
£680–750 / €970–1,100
$1,100–1,200 ⊞ AUTO
Sets such as this, complete and in good condition, are very rare and much sought after by enthusiasts of early games and magical equipment.

A Staunton ebony and boxwood weighted chess set, with impressed stamps, slight damage, late 19thC, king 3½in (9cm) high, with chessboard and original wooden box with paper label.
£75–90 / €100–130
$120–145 ⋏ G(L)
Howard Staunton was regarded as the world's leading chess player in the 1840s. In 1849 he designed a chess set that was adopted as the standard type to be used in chess tournaments and matches.

A Snip card game, depicting caricatures of Charles Darwin, Benjamin Disraeli and Alfred Lord Tennyson, c1880, 4½ x 3½in (11.5 x 9cm).
£135–150 / €190–210
$220–240 ⊞ MURR

▶ **A Tunbridge ware cribbage board,** late 19thC, 9¼in (23.5cm) long.
£55–65 / €80–90
$90–105 ⊞ SDA

A Staunton ebonized and boxwood weighted chess set, late 19thC, king 4in (10cm) high, in original wooden box.
£75–90 / €100–130
$120–145 ⋏ G(L)

A pack of **Worshipful playing cards,** depicting the Prince of Wales, 1920, 4½ x 3in (11.5 x 7.5cm).
£65–75 / €90–105
$105–120 ⊞ MURR

A pack of **Dewar's playing cards,** 1920s, 3¾in (9.5cm) high.
£20–25 / €30–35
$35–40 ⊞ HUX

A pack of **Great Western Railway playing cards,** depicting Lands End in Cornwall, c1920s, 4½ x 2½in (11.5 x 5cm).
£45–50 / €65–70
$75–80 ⊞ MURR

A **Mabel Lucie Attwell jigsaw puzzle,** c1920s, 9 x 6in (23 x 15cm).
£155–175 / €220–250
$250–280 ⊞ MEM

A **Hiking board game,** with lead figures, c1930, 10 x 9in (25.5 x 23cm).
£40–45 / €55–65
$65–75 ⊞ J&J

◄ A **Delft chess set,** Dutch, 1930s, king 4in (10cm) high.
£550–660
€780–940
$880–1,050
↗ G(L)

Further reading

Miller's American Insider's Guide to Toys & Games, Miller's Publications, 2002

► A pack of **playing cards,** advertising Morelands matches, 1930s, 3½ x 2½in (9 x 6.5cm).
£14–18 / €20–25
$22–28 ⊞ BOB

◄ A pack of **P&O playing cards,** 1930s, 3½ x 2½in (9 x 6.5cm).
£30–35 / €40–45
$50–55 ⊞ BOB

A pack of Guinness playing
cards, 1950s, 3½ x 2½in (9 x 6.5cm).
£15–20 / €20–25
$25–30 ⊞ BOB
With the original box this pack
would be worth about £20–25 /
€30–35 / $35–40.

Two Monkees jigsaw puzzles,
by Topsail Productions, 1966,
8 x 11in (20.5 x 28cm).
£45–50 / €65–70
$75–80 each ⊞ CTO

◀ **A Kargo golfing game,** c1940s,
3¼in (8.5cm) high.
£20–25 / €30–35
$35–40 ⊞ HUX

A wooden chess set, 1940s,
box 7½in (19cm) wide.
£65–75 / €90–105
$105–120 ⊞ HUX

A *Man from U.N.C.L.E* card game,
by Milton Bradley Co, American,
1965, 10in (25.5) wide.
£35–40 / €50–55
$55–60 ⊞ HAL

A Yogi Bear Pin Ball game,
American, c1970, 7in (18cm) wide.
£15–20 / €20–25
$25–30 ⊞ HarC

A Merit Grand Prix game, 1950s,
16 x 20in (41.5 x 51cm).
£20–25 / €30–35
$35–40 ⊞ GTM

**A James Bond 007 Secret Service
board game,** by Spears Games,
1966, 15in (38cm) wide.
£35–40 / €50–55
$55–60 ⊞ HAL

A Popeye bagatelle game, by Lido,
American, c1970, 13in (33cm) high.
£15–20 / €20–25
$25–30 ⊞ HarC

Garden & Farm Collectables

A staddle stone, 19thC,
32in (81.5cm) high.
£270–300 / €380–420
$430–480 ⊞ WRe
Staddle stones were used to
raise haystacks or ricks from the
ground, in order to protect them
from rodents.

▶ **A carved sandstone
trough,** 19thC,
64in (162.5cm) long.
£340–410 / €480–580
$540–650 ⋏ AH

**A pair of ash and elm wagon
wheels,** 19thC, 68in (172.5cm) diam.
£290–320 / €410–450
$460–510 ⊞ HiA

A painted watering can, 19thC,
16½in (42cm) high.
£45–50 / €65–70
$75–80 ⊞ FOX

▶ **A pair of garden shears,**
19thC, 22in (56cm) long.
£60–70 / €85–100
$95–110 ⊞ FOX

**A cast-iron rustic-style garden
seat,** 19thC, 36in (91.5cm) wide.
£480–570 / €680–810
$770–910 ⋏ AH

▶ **A dibber,** with wooden handle,
c1880, 37in (94cm) long.
£55–60 / €75–85
$85–95 ⊞ YT

**A pair of cast-iron agricultural
wheels,** c1900, 40in (101.5cm) high.
£55–60 / €75–85
$85–95 ⊞ WRe

A pair of steel sheep shears, c1910, 14in (35.5cm) long.
£24–28 / €35–40
$40–45 ⊞ YT

A garden trowel, with wooden handle, c1910,
13in (33cm) long.
£24–28 / €35–40
$40–45 ⊞ YT

A five pronged garden hoe, c1910, 56in (142cm) long.
£50–55 / €70–80
$80–90 ⊞ YT

A garden rake, with wooden handle, c1910,
54in (137cm) long.
£35–40 / €50–55
$55–60 ⊞ YT

A Barrows metal twin-lever pruner, c1913,
9in (23cm) long.
£35–40 / €50–55
$55–65 ⊞ WiB

A galvanized watering can, with
copper rose, c1920, 15in (38cm) high.
£45–50 / €65–70
$75–80 ⊞ FOX

◀ A wooden dibber, c1920,
14in (35.5cm) long.
£14–18 / €20–25
$22–28 ⊞ YT

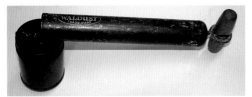

A Waldust garden sprayer, c1920, 14in (35.5cm) long.
£6–10 / €8–14
$10–16 ⊞ AL

▶ A painted
wooden
wheelbarrow,
1920s, 40in
(101.5cm) long.
£110–120
€155–170
$175–195 ⊞ SMI

A grain scoop, with wooden
handle, c1920, 9in (23cm) diam.
£11–15 / €16–21
$18–24 ⊞ YT

▶ A wooden malt shovel, c1920,
39in (99cm) long.
£30–35 / €45–50
$50–55 ⊞ AL

A long-nosed watering can, with brass rose, c1930,
32in (81.5cm) long.
£45–50 / €65–70
$75–80 ⊞ YT

Glass

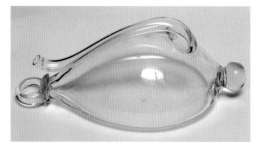

A Dunbar brandy warmer, 18thC, 8in (20.5cm) long.
£300–330 / €420–470
$480–530 ⊞ JAS

A glass pipe, early 19thC, 8in (20.5cm) long.
£55–65 / €80–90
$90–105 ⊞ JAS

A glass ice-cream lick, 19thC, 3in (7.5cm) high.
£75–85 / €105–120
$120–135 ⊞ JAS
This bowl was used to hold 4d worth of ice-cream.

A cranberry glass vase, on a clear foot, 19thC, 15¾in (40cm) high.
£220–260 / €310–370
$350–420 ➶ SWO

◀ **A set of six glass finger bowls,** 1830, 7in (18cm) diam.
£470–520
€670–740
$750–830
⊞ JAS

A Nailsea glass bottle, with banded decoration, 19thC, 6¾in (17cm) high.
£100–120 / €140–170
$160–190 ➶ WilP
Robert John Lucas set up a glass-house at Nailsea, near Bristol, in 1788. As tax on bottle glass was much less than on flint glass, Nailsea and other glass works specialized in domestic ware using dark brown, dark green and smoky-green bottle glass. To make them more attractive, pieces were decorated with fused-on enamel flecks or splashed in various colours, or threads, loops and stripes in white enamels.

A glass wine funnel, c1830, 9in (23cm) high.
£65–75 / €90–105
$105–120 ⊞ JAS

An opaline glass biscuit barrel, with silver-plated mounts and enamel decoration of two storks, 19thC, 7in (18cm) high.
£100–120 / €140–170
$160–190 ➶ SWO

A glass one gill measure, 1810–20, 4¾in (12cm) high.
£220–250 / €310–350
$350–400 ⊞ JAS

A pair of Whitefriars ruby glass fruit plates, 1855, 8¾in (22cm) diam.
£115–130 / €165–185
$185–210 ⊞ JAS

A glass fly trap, c1860,
7in (18cm) high.
£65–75 / €90–105
$105–120 ⊞ YT

A glass sweetmeat dish, c1860,
5½in (14cm) diam.
£120–135 / €170–190
$190–210 ⊞ JAS

A glass vinaigrette, with silver-gilt
top, c1860, 2½in (6.5cm) high.
£210–240 / €300–340
$340–380 ⊞ VK

A glass spirit jug, c1860,
7in (18cm) high.
£200–230 / €290–330
$320–370 ⊞ JAS

◀ **A glass
spirit decanter,**
1860, 10in
(25.5cm) high.
£300–330
€420–470
$480–530 ⊞ JAS
The shaft-
and-globe
form was a
favourite shape
for decanters.
Necks could be
smooth, such
as this one, or
decorated with
rings to stop
the fingers
from slipping.

A Bristol glass bowl, c1860,
5in (12.5cm) diam.
£160–180 / €230–260
$260–290 ⊞ JAS

A Bristol glass finger bowl,
c1860, 4¾in (12.5cm) diam.
£230–260 / €330–370
$370–420 ⊞ JAS

An amethyst glass plate, c1860,
8¼in (21cm) diam.
£150–165 / €210–240
$240–270 ⊞ JAS

**A pair of Victorian opaque and
flecked glass ewers,** with clear
glass handles, 10in (25cm) high.
£70–85 / €100–120
$115–135 ➚ L&E

**A Victorian pressed Vaseline glass
jug and matching bowl,** with clear
glass handles, 10in (25cm) high.
£115–130 / €165–185
$185–210 ⊞ TOP

◀ **A pair of cranberry glass finger
bowls,** c1860, 5¼in (13.5cm) diam.
£260–290 / €370–410
$420–460 ⊞ JAS

A pair of John Derbyshire pressed glass models of lions, c1974, 7in (18cm) wide.
£230–270 / €330–380
$370–430 ➢ G(L)

A pair of enamelled glass bottle vases, late 19thC, 14½in (37cm) high.
£220–260 / €310–370
$350–420 ➢ G(L)

A silver-mounted cranberry glass match tidy, late 19thC, 2¼in (5.5cm) high.
£100–120 / €140–170
$160–190 ➢ G(L)

A pair of encased glass vases, Bohemian, late 19thC, 12½in (32cm) high.
£200–240 / €280–340
$320–380 ➢ SWO

A hand-blown glass float, c1890, 8in (20.5cm) diam.
£65–75 / €90–105
$105–120 ⊞ YT

▶ **A glass claret jug,** engraved with flowers, c1895, 11in (28cm) high.
£430–480 / €610–680
$690–770 ⊞ JAS

A cut-glass and silver decanter stopper, London 1897, 4in (10cm) high.
£80–90 / €115–130
$130–145 ⊞ EXC

Items in the Glass section have been arranged in date order within each sub-section.

A cranberry glass sugar sifter, with original silver-plated top, c1910, 6in (15cm) high.
£110–125 / €155–175
$175–200 ⊞ GRI

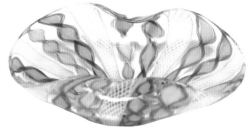

A latticino glass dish, 1920s, 4in (10cm) high.
£50–55 / €70–80
$80–90 ⊞ BET

▶ **A glass travelling bottle,** with silver-gilt and enamel top, Birmingham 1924, 4in (10cm) high.
£75–85 / €105–120
$120–135 ⊞ TOP

A Gray-Stan glass vase, signed, 1926–36, 5¾in (14.5cm) high.
£310–350 / €440–500
$500–560 ⊞ RW
Founded by Elizabeth Graydon-Stannus, Gray-Stan was a small London glassworks operating 1926–36. It is best known for its opaque, mottled, multicoloured art glass, made by rolling a gather of clean glass in white enamel and then adding coloured powders. The wares are similar in style to Monart glass, which was produced by John Moncrieff in Perth from 1924.

A Gray-Stan glass vase, signed, 1926–36, 7in (18cm) high.
£300–330 / €430–470
$480–530 ⊞ RW

A Monart glass bowl, 1930s, 2in (5cm) high.
£140–155 / €200–220
$220–250 ⊞ SAAC

A Monart glass powder bowl and cover, 1930s, 4½in (11.5cm) high.
£270–300 / €380–430
$430–480 ⊞ SAAC

A Monart glass pin tray, 1930s, 3½in (9cm) diam.
£80–90 / €115–130
$130–145 ⊞ SAAC

▶ **A Sabino glass ashtray,** depicting a female nude blowing bubbles, 1930s, 4½in (11.5cm) long.
£75–85 / €105–120
$120–135 ⊞ LBe

A Monart glass vase, 1930s, 6in (15cm) high.
£270–300 / €380–430
$430–480 ⊞ SAAC

A pair of pressed glass bonbon dishes, c1930, 3½in (9cm) high.
£2–6 / €4–8
$5–10 ⊞ BAC

A Monart glass vase, 1930s, 6in (12.5cm) high.
£175–195 / €250–280
$280–310 ⊞ SAAC

A Thomas Webb Rich Cameo glass vase, 1930s, 8in (20.5cm) high.
£300–330 / €430–470
$480–530 ⊞ RW
Vases and bowls in the Rich Cameo range were produced in green, blue, yellow, amethyst and, rarest of all, red.

An Art Deco pressed glass dish,
10in (25.5cm) diam.
£8–12 / €**12–17**
$13–19 ⊞ BAC

A uranium pressed glass jug,
1930s, 3¾in (9.5cm) high.
£11–15 / €**16–20**
$18–24 ⊞ GRo

**A Bagley pressed glass butter
dish,** 1930s, 7in (18cm) wide.
£11–15 / €**16–20**
$18–24 ⊞ BAC

**A Depression glass cup and
saucer,** American, 1930s,
saucer 6in (15cm) diam.
£6–10 / €**8–12**
$10–15 ⊞ GRo

Pressed glass

Pressed glass, produced by pouring molten glass into a mould and pressing it with a plunger, became extremely popular in the 1930s. The technique had been developed a hundred years earlier in the USA as a way of producing affordable copies of expensive cut glass. It was revived in the interwar years to produce a wide range of colourful glass from decorative vases to dressing table sets. Major British glass companies include Jobling & Co, George Davidson & Co and the Bagley Crystal Company. In the USA, glass from this period is known as Depression glass, styles ranging from so-called 'Elegant Glass' (pressed glass that was finely produced and hand-finished) to basic, everyday glassware that was literally distributed free with cereal packets. Major US manufacturers include Federal, Hocking, Jeanette, Macbeth Evans, along with many other glass companies.

Although pressed glass is often unmarked, attribution can be made through period catalogues and pattern books. In terms of value, however, the design and appeal of a particular piece is often more important than the name of the maker. Patterns could be extremely inventive. Companies produced ware inspired by Lalique and designs reflected the latest Art Deco fashions. They came in clear and frosted glass and in a wide range of colours, the most popular being green, amber, blue and pink. Although more elaborate figures are now sought after, much pressed glass is still very reasonably priced and attractive, providing an affordable way to collect Art Deco items.

**A Chippendale pressed glass
bowl,** 1930s, 5in (12.5cm) diam.
£5–9 / €**7–13**
$8–14 ⊞ BAC

**A Depression glass cup and
saucer,** American, 1930s,
saucer 5½in (14cm) diam.
£6–10 / €**8–12**
$10–15 ⊞ GRo

A pressed glass vase, with
Art Deco decoration, 1930s,
5in (12.5cm) high.
£5–9 / €**7–13**
$8–14 ⊞ BAC

◀ **A pair of uranium pressed glass
vases,** 1930s, 8in (21cm) high.
£25–30 / €**35–40**
$40–50 each ⊞ GRo

A pressed glass tray and matching covered bowl, 1930s, tray 14in (35.5cm) wide.
£8–12 / €12–17
$13–19 ⊞ BAC

A Vasart glass vase, signed, 1947–54, 7in (18cm) high.
£110–120 / €155–170
$175–195 ⊞ RW

A studio glass bowl, Italian, 1950, 14in (35.5cm) diam.
£130–145 / €185–210
$200–230 ⊞ TOP

A Whitefriars bubble glass bowl, 1950s, 9½in (24cm) diam.
£60–70 / €85–100
$95–110 ⊞ GRo

A pressed glass vase, with Art Deco geometric decoration, 1930s, 7in (18cm) wide.
£8–12 / €12–17
$13–19 ⊞ BAC

A set of four pressed glass pin trays, in original box, c1940s, box 7in (18cm) square.
£2–6 / €4–8
$5–10 ⊞ BAC

A pressed glass posy vase, c1950, 6in (15cm) high.
£1–5 / €2–7
$3–8 ⊞ BAC

Two pressed glass salts, with plastic stand, French, 1930s, stand 5in (12.5cm) wide.
£45–50 / €65–70
$75–80 ⊞ GRo

A Whitefriars glass bowl, designed by James Hogan, c1940s, 12in (30.5cm) wide.
£50–55 / €70–80
$80–90 ⊞ SAT

A moulded glass hors d'oeuvre dish, c1950, 9in (23cm) diam.
£2–6 / €4–8
$5–10 ⊞ BAC

A Keith Murray-style glass water jug and four glasses, c1950, jug 7in (18cm) high.
£6–10 / €8–14
$10–16 BAC

A Venini glass pitcher, with etched signature, Italian, 1950s, 8in (20.5cm) high.
£65–75 / €90–105
$105–120 ⊞ MARK

Pyrex

In the early 20th century, the Corning Glass Company in America experimented with the heat-resistant glass pioneered by German technologist Dr Otto Schott. In 1912, they came up with 'Nonex' (the name for non-expansion glass) which was used for batteries and lantern globes. Three years later they developed a heat-resistant glass suitable for kitchen ware, which they registered under the name Pyrex. Pyrex dishes were extremely popular in the 1920s and '30s and the post-war period saw the successful introduction of coloured and decorated Pyrex. In 1921, the British Jobling factory purchased the rights to manufacture Pyrex in the British Empire with the exception of Canada.

A glass dish, with iridescent centre, probably Italian, c1960s, 12½in (32cm) wide.
£50–55 / €70–80
$80–90 ⊞ MARK

A glass vase, 1950s, 6in (15cm) high.
£30–35 / €45–50
$50–55 ⊞ MCC

A Pyrex glass casserole dish, 1950s, 5½in (14cm) diam.
£2–6 / €4–8
$5–10 ⊞ GRo

A pressed glass cake stand, on a chrome base, 1950s, 11in (28cm) diam.
£8–12 / €12–17
$13–19 ⊞ BAC

A bubble glass ashtray, Italian, 1960s, 7in (18cm) wide.
£6–10 / €8–14
$10–16 ⊞ MARK

A Pyrex glass bowl, 1950s, 3½in (9cm) diam.
£2–6 / €4–8
$5–10 ⊞ BAC

A Pheonix glass casserole dish, 1950s, 5in (12.5cm) diam.
£1–5 / €2–7
$3–8 ⊞ GRo

A Whitefriars glass vase, 1950s, 5in (12.5cm) high.
£30–35 / €45–50
$50–55 ⊞ LUNA

A cased glass ashtray, 1960s, 4¾in (12cm) diam.
£15–20 / €20–25
$25–30 ⊞ MARK

A glass bowl, c1960s,
9in (23cm) diam.
£8–12 / €12–17
$13–19 ⊞ BAC

A faceted glass cigarette lighter,
1960s, 3¾in (9.5cm) high.
£24–28 / €34–40
$38–45 ⊞ GRo

A glass ashtray, Italian, 1960s,
5in (12.5cm) wide.
£1–5 / €2–7
$3–8 ⊞ MARK

**A Whitefriars Knobbly
glass vase,** streaky
brown lead crystal, 1960s,
7in (18cm) high.
£50–55 / €70–80
$80–90 ⊞ LUNA
The Knobbly range of
lumpy glass vessels was
designed by William
Wilson and Harry
Dyer and launched by
Whitefriars in 1964. It was
produced in two main
forms: cased coloured
soda glass in single
colours such as kingfisher
blue and meadow green;
and streaked lead crystal.

**A Whitefriars smoked
glass vase,** 1960s,
10in (25.5cm) high.
£135–150 / €190–210
$220–240 ⊞ GRo

**A textured glass
cigarette lighter,** 1960s,
3½in (9cm) high.
£24–28 / €34–40
$38–45 ⊞ GRo

A glass vase, probably
Czechoslovakian, 1960s,
8in (20.5cm) high.
£8–12 / €12–17
$13–19 ⊞ MARK

A smoked glass vase,
1970, 8in (20.5cm) high.
£8–12 / €12–17
$13–19 ⊞ BAC

A Mdina glass vase,
Maltese, signed, c1970,
8in (20.5cm) high.
£35–40 / €50–55
$55–60 ⊞ MARK

**A Murano cased glass
vase,** Italian, c1970,
12in (30.5cm) high.
£165–185 / €230–260
$260–300 ⊞ GRo

**A Siddy Langley
iridescent glass bottle,**
with stopper, 2001–02,
5in (12.5cm) high.
£55–65 / €80–95
$90–105 ⊞ RW

Drinking Glasses

A glass, engraved with a clipper under Sunderland bridge, early 19thC, 5¾in (14.5cm) high.
£350–390 / €500–550
$560–620 ⊞ JAS

▶ A Bristol wine glass, 1850–60, 10¼in (26cm) high.
£390–430 / €550–610
$620–690 ⊞ JAS

A slice-cut deceptive wine/spirit glass, 1830–40, 4½in (11.5cm) high.
£30–35 / €45–50
$50–55 ⊞ JHa
Deceptive glasses had bowls with thick bases and sides, and so held less liquid than the size of the glass would suggest.

▶ A Whitefriars glass, engraved 'ER', 1950s, 8in (20.5cm) high.
£165–185 / €230–260
$260–300 ⊞ JAS

A Bristol high drop wine glass, 1830, 5in (12.5cm) high.
£130–145 / €185–210
$210–230 ⊞ JAS

▶ A pair of glass punch cups, 1835, 2¼in (5.5cm) high.
£130–145
€185–210
$210–230 ⊞ JAS

A glass goblet, engraved with a huntsman shooting geese, late 19thC, 5¼in (13.5cm) high.
£145–160 / €210–230
$230–260 ⊞ JAS

Two pressed glass champagne sampling glasses, 1920, 6in (15cm) high.
£16–19 / €22–27
$25–30 each ⊞ MLL

A harlequin set of six Royal Brierley cut-glass hock glasses, c1930, 7¾in (19.5cm) high.
£270–300 / €380–430
$430–480 ⊞ GRI

▶ Four Smoke glasses, designed by Joe Colombo, 1964, 5½in (14cm) high.
£310–350 / €440–500
$500–560 ⊞ MARK
Created by the celebrated Italian designer Joe Colombo (1930–71), Smoke glasses were designed so that you could hold a glass and a cigarette in the same hand.

Paperweights & Dumps

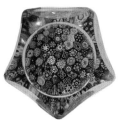

A Baccarat glass paper-weight, enclosing a pansy, 1845–60, 2¾in (7cm) diam.
£630–700 / € 900–1,000 $1,000–1,100 ⊞ SWB

A Clichy nosegay glass paperweight, with three cane flowers, 1845–60, 2in (5cm) diam.
£300–340 / € 430–480 $480–540 ⊞ SWB

A Baccarat faceted millefiori glass paper-weight, 1845–60, 2½in (6.5cm) diam.
£710–790 / € 1,000–1,100 $1,150–1,300 ⊞ SWB
The Italian word 'millefiori' means 'a thousand flowers'.

A Baccarat millefiori glass paperweight, with silhouettes on an upset muslin ground, slight damage, 1848, 2¼in (5.5cm) diam.
£420–500 / € 600–710 $670–800 ➤ B

A St Louis glass paper-weight, with a pink jasper ground, 1845–60, 2¾in (7cm) diam.
£380–430 / € 540–610 $610–690 ⊞ SWB

A Clichy open concentric glass paperweight, with pastry moulds and moss canes, 1845–60, 1¾in (4.5cm) diam.
£270–300 / € 380–430 $430–480 ⊞ SWB

► **A Baccarat glass paperweight,** enclosing a primrose, c1850, 2½in (6.5cm) diam.
£360–430 / € 510–610 $580–690 ➤ B

◄ **A Clichy glass paper-weight,** with pastry mould canes, minor damage, c1850, 3¼in (8.5cm) diam.
£300–360 € 430–510 $480–580 ➤ B

► **A Clichy faceted glass paperweight,** with garlands, minor damage, c1850, 2½in (6.5cm) diam.
£280–330 € 400–470 $450–530 ➤ B

A Clichy concentric millefiori glass paperweight, c1850, 2½in (6.5cm) diam.
£190–230 / €270–320
$310–370 ♨ B
Clichy was one of three great French glass and paperweight-making factories of the mid-19th century, situated on the outskirts of Paris. Clichy paperweights are probably the most popular with today's collectors, follwed by Baccarat and St Louis.

A St Louis scrambled glass paperweight, with a silhouette of a dancing devil, c1850, 3¼in (8.5cm) diam.
£580–690 / €830–980
$930–1,100 ♨ S(O)

A Whitefriars bubble glass paperweight, 1950s, 2½in (6.5cm) high.
£30–35 / €45–50
$50–55 ⊞ GRo

A glass dump, enclosing a pagoda, late 19thC, 3½in (9cm) diam.
£105–120 / €150–170
$170–190 ⊞ RWA
Dumps were made from waste glass that would otherwise have been dumped, hence their name. They were used as doorstops.

A Paul Ysart scrambled glass paperweight, with paper label, c1975, 2½in (6.5cm) diam.
£200–230 / €280–330
$320–370 ⊞ PCC

A Paul Ysart paperweight, signed, c1930, 3in (7.5cm) high.
£400–440 / €570–630
$640–700 ⊞ SWB

A Caithness glass paperweight, with silver frog, No. 6 of 10, 1984, 3in (7.5cm) diam.
£590–650 / €840–920
$940–1,050 ⊞ SWB

◀ **A Paul Ysart glass paperweight,** c1975, 2½in (6.5cm) diam.
£310–350 / €440–500
$500–560 ⊞ PCC

A millefiori glass paperweight, by Jim Brown, signed, American, 2001, 3¼in (8.5cm) diam.
£400–440 / €570–630
$640–700 ⊞ SWB

Scandinavian Glass

Scandinavian glass from before WWII has become increasingly collectable. The Nordic landscape was a major influence – the glass was blown or moulded into organic shapes and the colours reflected the textures of snow and ice. 'We believe that nature is the true source of lasting beauty,' explained Finnish designer Kaj Frank (1918–89). Scandinavian designers sought to reconcile traditional craftsmanship with modern industry. 'We need human design, sensitivity and the power of machines,' declared Timo Sarpaneva (b. 1926) who, working at Iittala in Finland, won major awards for both his glass sculptures and his functional 'i-line' tableware. Tapio Wirkkala (1915–85) was another famous Iittala designer who created both art glass and affordable everyday glassware.

Iittala produced about 50 per cent of the glass in Finland, the other major Finnish factories including Nuutajärvi and Riihimäki. In Denmark, glass production was dominated by the Holmegaard factory where designer Per Lütken (1916–98) was known for his subtle colours and fluid organic forms, imbuing even humble domestic items with a sense of sculptural

beauty. Also popular with 1960s enthusiasts are the colourful bottle-shaped Gulvases produced for Holmegaard by Otto Brauer.

In Sweden the major glassworks was Orrefors, where designers Edward Hald (1883–1980), Sven Palmqvist (1906–84) and Ingeborg Lundin (1921–92) continued the inventive tradition that had made Orrefors a design leader in the 1920s and '30s. Another major factory was Kosta, where Vicke Lindstrand (1904–83) produced an astonishing range of designs. It is also worth looking out for lesser-known companies such as Flygsfors which produced high quality cased glass but, until recently, was overlooked by many collectors.

There is a huge variety of Scandinavian glass to choose from with a wide range of prices. While one-off, hand-made works of art by leading names in the field can fetch three-figure sums and more, the fact that many great designers also made simple domestic pieces provides a more affordable starting point. High-quality works by lesser-known factories could be a good investment, while mass-produced wares such as Lassi vases and Gulvases are visually striking and still reasonably priced.

► **A Kosta glass vase,** designed by Vicke Lindstrand, Swedish, 1955, 9in (23cm) high.
£75–85
€ **105–120**
$120–135
⊞ **MARK**

A pair of Kosta glass vases, designed by Vicke Lindstrand, Swedish, 1950–54, 4½in (11.5cm) high.
£85–95 / € 120–135
$135–150 ⊞ **MARK**

A Kastrup glass vase, designed by Jacob Bang, Danish, 1955, 10in (25.5cm) high.
£60–70 / € 85–100
$95–110 ⊞ **GRo**

Marks

Much post-WWII glass is marked, particularly hand-made pieces. Check the base of the piece for the name of the factory, the monogram of a designer and any dates or serial numbers. If the mark is hard to read, hold it up to the light or place it against a piece of black paper or cloth which can help to highlight a softly etched signature. Machine-made pieces, while they might not be marked on the base, could be identified by a sticky paper label. If you find one of these, do not remove it from the glass. On many pieces, however, the label will have already been removed.

A Kosta glass vase,
Swedish, 1955,
3¾in (9.5cm) high.
£40–45 / €55–65
$65–75 ⊞ GRo

An Ekenas glass vase,
by John Orwar Lake,
signed, Swedish, c1950s,
8in (20.5cm) high.
£40–45 / €55–65
$65–75 ⊞ JMM

A Kosta glass vase,
designed by Vicke
Lindstrand, Swedish,
1959, 5in (12.5cm) high.
£55–60 / €80–85
$90–95 ⊞ MARK

**A Holmegaard glass
vase,** designed by Per
Lütken, Danish, 1950s–60s,
7½in (19cm) high.
£60–70 / €85–100
$95–110 ⊞ ORI

An Orrefors glass vase,
designed by Ingeborg
Lundin, Swedish, 1960,
6in (15cm) high.
£35–40 / €50–55
$55–65 ⊞ MARK

**An Orrefors glass
vase,** designed by Sven
Palmqvist, Swedish, 1960,
8in (20.5cm) high.
£75–85 / €105–120
$120–135 ⊞ MARK

A Flygsfors glass vase,
signed, Swedish, 1963,
13in (33cm) high.
£165–185 / €230–260
$260–300 ⊞ PLB

◄ **A waisted glass
vase,** Swedish, c1960s,
8in (20.5cm) high.
£18–22 / €25–30
$30–35 ⊞ JMM

► **An Orrefors glass
vase,** Swedish, 1960s,
8in (20.5cm) high.
£40–45 / €55–65
$65–75 ⊞ JMM

**A littala textured glass
vase,** designed by Tapio
Wirkkala, Finnish, 1960s,
7in (18cm) high.
£60–70 / €85–100
$95–110 ⊞ MARK

**A littala textured glass
goblet,** Finnish, 1960s,
4¾in (12cm) high.
£8–12 / €12–17
$13–19 ⊞ GRo

A Riihimäki Lassi vase, Finnish, 1960s, 7in (18cm) high.
£24–28 / €35–40 $40–45 ⊞ **JMM**
Lassi is the Finnish word for glass and Lassi vases, produced by Riihimäki in the 1960s–70s, are popular with collectors today.

A Holmegaard glass decanter, with paper label, Danish, 1960s, 12in (30.5cm) high.
£55–60 / €80–85 $90–95 ⊞ **MARK**

A Holmegaard Gulvase, designed by Otto Brauer, Danish, 1960s, 10in (25.5cm) high.
£55–65 / €80–90 $90–105 ⊞ **JMM**

A Skruf glass vase, Swedish, 1960s, 12in (30.5cm) high.
£40–45 / €55–65 $65–75 ⊞ **GRo**

▶ **An Orrefors glass bowl,** Swedish, c1970s, 5in (12.5cm) diam.
£45–50 / €65–70 $75–80 ⊞ **PIL**

A Kosta Boda glass vase, with crackle finish, signed, Swedish, c1970s, 5in (12.5cm) high.
£20–25 / €30–35 $35–40 ⊞ **JMM**

A Kosta Boda Atoll votive glass bowl, designed by Anna Ehrner, Swedish, c1990s, 4in (10cm) diam.
£35–40 / €50–55 $55–65 ⊞ **JMM**

A Riihimäki Lassi vase, Finnish, c1970, 11in (28cm) high.
£55–65 / €80–90 $90–105 ⊞ **PLB**

▶ **A Kosta Boda Seaside glass vase,** designed by Göran Wärff, Swedish, 1999, 11in (28cm) high.
£160–180 / €230–260 $260–290 ⊞ **HaG**

▶ **A Kosta Boda Cesare Brains glass sculpture,** designed by Bertil Vallien, Swedish, 1999, 3in (7.5cm) high.
£35–40 / €50–55 $55–65 ⊞ **HaG**

Handbags

The handbag as we know it appeared in the 1800s when tight-fitting, empire-line dresses made bulging pockets a sartorial impossibility and ladies took to carrying small draw-string bags. Beaded pouches remained popular in the Victorian and Edwardian periods.

After WWI, wearing cosmetics and smoking cigarettes in public became increasingly acceptable for women, so the handbag became even more important. Dangling mesh, beaded and needlepoint bags complemented 1920s flapper dresses. New materials such as Bakelite provided colourful clasps and frames and the 1930s saw the growth in popularity of the clutch bag. While the 1940s was a period of austerity, the 1950s was a golden age for handbag design. Frivolity was all the rage and America led the way. Lucite bags were studded with rhinestones and baskets and boxes were

in any shape from animals to houses. For the more formal in taste, there were purses in leather, crocodile and other exotic skins. In 1955, Hermès named their Kelly bag after Grace Kelly, on the occasion of her marriage to Prince Rainier of Monaco, thus creating one of the most desirable handbags of all time.

The swinging shoulder bag became fashionable in the freedom-loving '60s and Paco Rabanne's experiments with metal discs inspired a host of clanking high street imitations. Ethnic designs and natural materials came to the fore in the 1970s and the 1980s saw the development of the handbag as a status symbol and the rise of the big name designer. Vintage bags are sought-after today both as collectors' pieces and chic wearable fashion items. Values depend on age, shape, material, maker and condition, both inside and out.

A steel bead miser's purse, early 19thC, 13in (33cm) long.
£55–60 / €80–85
$90–95 ⊞ JPr

Beads

Beadwork was popular in the 19th and 20th centuries, but was used originally in the 17th century for decorating frames and cabinets. The nature of glass beads means that they never fade, thus retaining their vibrancy to the present day. Condition should be checked carefully, as repair is difficult and expensive.

A beaded purse, 1880, 6in (15cm) long.
£70–75
€100–105
$110–120 ⊞ L&L

An 18ct gold evening bag, with 9ct gold frame, the clasp decorated with sapphires, early 20thC, 7in (18cm) high.
£900–1,000
€1,250–1,400
$1,450–1,600 ⊞ LaF

An Edwardian crocodile skin wallet, with Art Nouveau silver mounts, Birmingham 1901, 6in (15cm) wide.
£55–65 / €80–95
$90–105 ⊞ BrL

◄ A petit point bag, with engraved 14ct gold frame and rose quartz clasp, c1910, 6in (15cm) wide.
£590–650
€840–920
$950–1,050
⊞ VK

A devoré velvet bag, with gilt and paste frame, and chain handle, 1920s, 7in (18cm) wide.
£220–245 / €310–350
$350–390 ⊞ TIN

A woollen bag, embroidered with raffia flowers, c1920, 8in (20.5cm) wide.
£75–85 / €110–120
$120–135 ⊞ TIN

A silk evening bag, the Bakelite frame decorated with swans, 1920s, 8in (20.5cm) wide.
£110–120 / €155–170
$175–190 ⊞ LBe

Three raffia and fabric souvenir handbags, in the form of dolls with painted faces, Italian, Florence, c1930, largest 10in (25.5cm) high.
£200–220 / €280–310
$320–350 ⊞ TIN

A metal mesh purse, with abstract pattern, 1930s, 8in (20.5cm) long.
£70–75 / €100–105
$110–120 ⊞ LBe

A satin bag, with sequin and bead motif, pearl and gilt frame, original labels, French, 1930s, 6in (15cm) wide.
£200–220 / €280–310
$320–350 ⊞ LaF

A plastic handbag, with Bakelite frame, 1930s, 15in (38cm) wide.
£85–95 / €120–135
$135–150 ⊞ LBe

A fabric handbag, the frame set with amber stones, 1930s, 9in (23cm) wide.
£135–150 / €190–210
$220–240 ⊞ LBe

◄ **A Perspex handbag,** with plastic handle, 1930s, 8in (20.5cm) wide.
£230–250 / €320–350
$360–400 ⊞ LBe

A crocodile skin handbag, by Gucci, Italian, 1930s, 12in (30.5cm) wide.
£180–200 / €250–280
$290–320 ⊞ RGA

A petit point bag, 1930–40, 8in (20.5cm) wide.
£60–65 / €85–95
$95–105 ⊞ L&L

A leather handbag, by Milch, inset with a Louis pocket watch on a chain, 1956, 11in (28cm) high.
£270–300 / €380–430
$430–480 ⊞ SpM

A basket bag, decorated with coral, shells, seahorse and starfish, 1950s, 11in (28cm) wide.
£90–100 / €125–140
$145–160 ⊞ SpM

A leather and Bakelite accordion-style bag, 1940s, 7in (18cm) wide.
£760–840 / €1,100–1,200
$1,200–1,350 ⊞ TIN

A plastic-covered bag, by SAKS, Fifth Avenue, inset with lace, flowers and pearls, American, 1950s, 13in (33cm) wide.
£75–85 / €110–120
$120–130 ⊞ Ci

A vinyl-covered wire handbag, in the form of a fish, 1950s, 15in (38cm) wide.
£430–480 / €610–680
$690–770 ⊞ TIN

A beaded bag, with gilt frame, 1950s, 8in (20.5cm) wide.
£55–65 / €80–95
$90–100 ⊞ DE

A crocodile skin handbag, by Martin, with matching inside pouch, 1940s, 13½in (34.5cm) wide.
£150–165 / €210–230
$240–260 ⊞ MCa

A vinyl bag, American, 1950s, 15in (38cm) wide.
£65–70 / €90–100
$100–110 ⊞ LaF

Novelty handbags were very popular in the 1950s. They were highly decorative, using many unusual materials including shells, ribbons, sequins, brocade, straw, raffia, metal and plastic.

A wooden box bag, painted with a tennis scene, American, 1957–67, 10in (25.5cm) wide.
£90–100 / €130–145
$145–160 ⊞ LaF

◀ **A Perspex bag,** studded with rhinestones, 1950–60, 9in (23cm) wide.
£55–65 / €80–95 $90–105 ⊞ LBe

A plastic box bag, in the shape of a house, American, c1960, 9in (23cm) wide.
£125–140 / €180–200 $200–220 ⊞ LBe

A leather Kelly bag, by Hermès, with brass lock and key, French, c1960, 11½in (29cm) wide.
£1,200–1,400 / €1,700–2,000 $1,900–2,200 ➹ S(O)
Classic bags made by famous 20th-century designers are very sought after.

A tapestry handbag, with wooden bead handles, 1960s, 11in (28cm) high.
£110–120 / €155–170 $175–195 ⊞ LBe

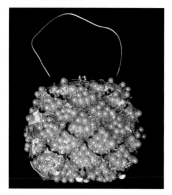

A *faux* pearl and sequin evening bag, c1970, 7in (18cm) wide.
£30–35 / €45–50 $50–55 ⊞ SBL

A crocodile skin Kelly handbag, by Hermès, 1970–80, 12in (30.5cm) wide.
£5,000–5,500 / €7,100–7,800 $8,000–8,800 ⊞ OH

A leather shoulder bag, by Gucci, the flap modelled as a saddle with stirrups, and a matching belt, 1980s, bag 6in (15cm) wide.
£160–180 / €230–250 $260–290 ⊞ OH

A quilted leather handbag, by Chanel, 1980s, 7in (18cm) wide.
£180–200 / €250–280 $290–320 ⊞ OH
Coco Chanel was in her 70s when in February 1955 she launched her famous quilted handbag. She named it the 2:55 after the date of its conception and the bag had a distinctive chain and leather braided strap. Variations of this design have been produced by Chanel ever since. The linked C monogram on the front was a later addition. This bag has frequently been copied, so always check for a Chanel stamp on the frame and the lining.

A sequined satin bag, by Gianni Versace, 1980s, 8in (20.5cm) high.
£45–50 / €65–70 $75–80 ⊞ HIP

A patent leather shoulder bag, by Celine, with gilt insignia, 1980s, 8in (20.5cm) wide.
£160–180 / €230–250 $260–290 ⊞ OH

Jewellery
Belts

An Edwardian silver-plated belt, 32in (81.5cm) long.
£40–45 / €55–65
$65–75 ⊞ Ech

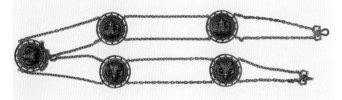

A chain belt, with owl's head roundels, 1940s, 34in (86.5cm) long.
£40–45 / €55–65
$65–75 ⊞ LBe

A metal and enamel belt, by Billy Boy, 1980, 28in (71cm) long.
£55–65 / €80–95
$90–100 ⊞ LBe

Bracelets

◀ **A gilt bracelet,** inset with a micro-mosaic panel, 19thC, panel 1in (2.5cm) square.
£160–190
€230–270
$260–300
⚡ BWL

A gold metal bracelet, 1940s, 1¼in (3cm) wide.
£85–95 / €120–135
$135–150 ⊞ LBe

A paste bracelet, by Weiss, American, 1950s, 7½in (19cm) long.
£115–130 / €165–185
$185–205 ⊞ LaF

A Victorian gold hinged bracelet, set with garnets.
£160–190 / €230–270
$260–300 ⚡ G(L)

A gold metal bracelet, with paste clasp, set with *faux* rubies and diamonds, 1940s, 1¼in (3cm) wide.
£55–65 / €80–90
$90–105 ⊞ LBe

◀ **A glass and paste bracelet,** by Hattie Carnegie, American, c1960, 8in (20.5cm) long.
£80–90 / €115–125
$130–145 ⊞ SBL

A gilt and enamel bracelet, by Kenneth J. Lane, American, c1970.
£45–50 / €65–70
$75–80 ⊞ SBL

Brooches

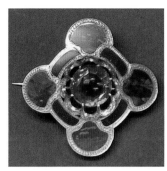

A silver brooch, with inlaid hardstone plaques and claw-set cairngorm, 19thC.
£130–150 / €185–210
$210–240 ➤ BWL

A Victorian shell cameo brooch, in a gold rub-over frame with beaded decoration, 2in (5cm) wide.
£180–210 / €260–300
$290–340 ➤ G(L)

Cameos

Cameos became extremely popular from the beginning of the 19th century. During the Victorian period cameos were produced for every level of the market, ranging from finely-carved precious stones to more affordable examples made from shell or lava stone, produced in Italy from the lava of Mount Vesuvius. Whatever the medium, however, classical subjects were a favourite theme.

A vulcanite brooch, in the form of apples on a branch, 19thC, 3in (7.5cm) wide.
£65–70 / €90–100
$100–110 ⊞ FMN
Vulcanite, a form of vulcanized or hardened rubber developed by the scientist and tyre manufacturer Charles Goodyear in 1846, provided an alternative to jet. Sometimes called ebonite, vulcanite was moulded rather than carved so even complex designs could be mass-produced. When exposed to sunlight the colour of vulcanite can fade.

A Victorian gold and silver butterfly brooch, set with diamonds, rubies, sapphires and split pearls.
£420–500 / €600–710
$670–800 ➤ G(L)

A silver *Mizpah* brooch and a name brooch, 'Minnie', 1891, 1in (2.5cm) wide.
£60–65 / €85–90
$95–105 each ⊞ FMN

▶ **A Ruskin-style silver-mounted cabochon brooch,** slight damage, early 20thC, 2in (5cm) wide.
£40–45 / €55–65
$65–75 ⊞ GLB

Two Victorian coloured glass butterfly brooches, 1½in (4cm) wide.
£25–30 / €35–40
$45–50 each ⊞ VB

A Victorian 15ct gold bar brooch, with bead and wirework decoration, set with three synthetic rubies.
£90–105 / €130–150
$145–170 ➤ G(L)

A silver name brooch, 'Maggie', 1887, 2in (5cm) wide.
£65–75 / €90–105
$105–120 ⊞ FMN

A silver and fossil brooch, Chester 1895, 1½in (4cm) wide.
£80–90 / €115–125
$130–145 ⊞ FMN
The fossil in this brooch was found at Lyme Regis, Dorset.

A fretwork and engraved mother-of-pearl brooch, c1900, 3in (7.5cm) wide.
£30–35 / €45–50
$50–55 ⊞ FMN

A carved mother-of-pearl brooch, c1900, 3in (7.5cm) wide.
£35–40 / €50–55
$55–65 ⊞ FMN

A carved ivory horse brooch, c1910, 4in (10cm) wide.
£35–40 / €50–55
$55–65 ⊞ FMN

An Iona Celtic revival silver brooch, marked 'AR' & 'ICA', Birmingham 1934, 1¾in (4.5cm) diam.
£160–180 / €230–260
$260–290 ⊞ AFD

▶ **An Edwardian gold bar brooch,** millegrain set with a peridot flanked by pairs of leaves and set seed pearls.
£50–60 / €70–85
$80–95 ⚒ G(L)

An Edwardian gold bar brooch, set with seed pearl heart motif and beaded decoration.
£65–75 / €95–110
$105–120 ⚒ G(L)

A carved and fretwork ivory brooch, decorated with a rose, c1920, 2in (5cm) diam.
£20–25 / €30–35
$35–40 ⊞ FMN

◀ **A 9ct gold fox tie pin,** with ruby eyes, 1920s, 2¼in (5.5cm) wide.
£55–65 / €80–90
$90–105 ⊞ CUF

A metal and enamel flower brooch, 1930, 2in (5cm) diam.
£40–45 / €55–65
$65–75 ⊞ LBe

▶ **A silver brooch,** modelled as a spider and web, 1930s, 3in (7.5cm) diam.
£50–55 / €70–80
$80–90 ⊞ LBe

Two silver, garnet and amethyst name brooches, 'Tina' and 'Agnes', 1900–04, 1½in (4cm) wide.
£70–80 / €100–115
$115–130 each ⊞ FMN

A silver and paste basket brooch, French, 1920s, 2in (5cm) wide.
£180–200 / €250–280
$290–320 ⊞ RGA

A gilt-metal brooch, set with turquoise pastes in an Art Deco design, c1930.
£55–65 / €80–90
$90–105 ⚒ G(L)

A pierced metal brooch, set with Bohemian glass, Czechoslovakian, 1930s, 2in (5cm) diam.
£12–16 / €18–22
$20–25 ⊞ CCO

A sterling silver, paste and *faux* pearl brooch, by Reja, American, 1940s, 3½in (9cm) wide.
£160–180 / €230–250
$260–290 ⊞ RGA

A monkey brooch, by Trifari, American, 1950s, 1¼in (3cm) wide.
£50–55 / €70–80
$80–90 ⊞ CRIS

A paste butterfly brooch, by Weiss, American, c1970, 2in (5cm) wide.
£70–80 / €100–110
$115–130 ⊞ SBL

A silver brooch, in the form of birds in flight, possibly by Anton Rosen, 1940s, 2in (5cm) wide.
£220–240 / €310–340
$350–380 ⊞ ANO

A hand-made leather brooch, with a bag and umbrella hanging from a bow, 1940s, 3in (7.5cm) high.
£30–35 / €45–50
$50–55 ⊞ SpM

A silver brooch, modelled as two tennis racquets with a pearl ball, 1950s, 1¾in (4.5cm) wide.
£30–35 / €45–50
$50–55 ⊞ CUF

Items in the Jewellery section have been arranged in date order within each sub-section.

A sterling silver and enamel butterfly brooch, by Nettie Rosenstein, American, 1940s, 4in (10cm) wide.
£220–250 / €320–350
$360–400 ⊞ RGA

A glass sunflower brooch, 1940s, 4in (10cm) diam.
£85–95 / €120–135
$135–150 ⊞ LBe

Charms

A charm was originally an amulet or small object worn to ward off evil and bring good luck, but the magic of charm bracelets is principally decorative. Charms became popular in the late Victorian period, but it was in the 20th century that the charm bracelet became a massive craze, both in the USA and Europe. Soldiers brought charms back from overseas as gifts to their loved ones and young girls were often given a charm bracelet in childhood. Charms would be added to bracelets over the years to commemorate holidays, birthdays and other important dates, the bracelet eventually becoming a chronicle of the life of its owner.

Charms have been produced in a vast number of forms such as animals, buildings, sporting equipment, transport, musical instruments – in fact, almost every subject imaginable. Among the most popular with serious collectors are vintage mechanical charms with moving parts or those that open up to reveal a miniature scene.

A typical example is a church, its roof lifting off to display a wedding party – many charms were produced to celebrate weddings, anniversaries, birthdays and christenings. With the post-war expansion of travel, famous buildings were another favourite subject. Many landmarks such as the Eiffel Tower have been manufactured in vast quantities. Others, however, are rarer such as the Post Office Tower in London, an icon of 1960s' architecture that was only produced as a charm when the building – now known as the BT Tower – was a newly fashionable landmark.

Charm bracelets fell from grace in the 1970s but since the 1990s they have again become popular, particularly in the USA. Values of vintage charms depend on material and design, and collectors often focus upon a specific theme: animals, moveable charms, fashion, transport etc. Modern charm bracelets are also being produced by contemporary fashion designers and costume jewellers.

◄ **A Victorian 9ct gold Masonic ball,** opening to reveal a cross, with chain and T-bar, 4in (10cm) long.
£175–195
€250–270
$280–310 ⊞ SPE

A 9ct gold donkey charm, 1940–50, 1in (2.5cm) high.
£85–95 / €120–135
$135–150 ⊞ NEG

A 9ct gold wedding cake charm, opening to reveal a pram, 1940–50, 1in (2.5cm) high.
£30–35 / €45–50
$50–55 ⊞ NEG

A 9ct gold teddy bear charm, with ruby eyes, 1940–50, 1in (2.5cm) high.
£80–90 / €115–125
$130–145 ⊞ NEG

A 9ct gold squirrel and nut charm, 1940–50, ¾in (2cm) high.
£45–50 / €65–70
$75–80 ⊞ NEG

► **A 9ct gold grand piano charm,** 1940–50, 1in (2.5cm) high.
£150–165 / €210–230
$240–260 ⊞ NEG

A 9ct gold cowboy hat and gun charm, 1940–50, 1in (2.5cm) wide.
£50–55 / €70–80
$80–90 ⊞ NEG

Two 9ct gold fawn charms, 1940–50, 1in (2.5cm) high.
£55–65 / €80–90
$90–105 each ⊞ NEG

A 9ct gold shopping basket charm, 1950, 1in (2.5cm) high.
£45–50 / €65–70
$75–80 ⊞ SPE

A 9ct gold Buddha charm, 1940–50, 1in (2.5cm) high.
£115–125 / €160–175
$180–200 ⊞ NEG

A 9ct gold golf clubs and bag charm, 1940–50, 1in (2.5cm) high.
£90–100 / €125–140
$145–160 ⊞ NEG

◀ **A 9ct gold devil charm,** 1940–50, 1in (2.5cm) high.
£50–60
€70–85
$80–95 ⊞ NEG

▶ **A 9ct gold Donald Duck charm,** 1940–50, 1in (2.5cm) high.
£75–85
€105–120
$120–135 ⊞ NEG

A 9ct gold charm, containing a ten Shilling note, 1950s, ¾in (2cm) high.
£20–25 / €30–35
$35–40 ⊞ SPE

A 9ct gold whistle charm, 1940–50, 1in (2.5cm) wide.
£30–35 / €45–50
$50–55 ⊞ NEG

A 9ct gold first aid box charm, 1940–50, 1in (2.5cm) high.
£115–125 / €160–175
$180–200 ⊞ NEG

A 9ct gold football charm, opening to reveal a footballer, 1940–50, 1in (2.5cm) high.
£85–95 / €120–135
$135–150 ⊞ NEG

A 9ct gold koala bear charm, inset with an opal, 1950–60, 1in (2.5cm) high.
£55–65 / €80–90
$90–105 ⊞ NEG

A 9ct gold charm bracelet, with 25 charms, 1950–60, 4in (10cm) long.
£850–950 / € 1,200–1,300
$1,300–1,500 ⊞ NEG

A 9ct gold cannon charm,
1950–60, 1in (2.5cm) high.
£55–65 / € 80–90
$90–105 ⊞ NEG

A 9ct gold boot and mice charm,
1950–60, 1in (2.5cm) high.
£40–45 / € 55–65
$65–75 ⊞ NEG

◄ **A 9ct gold Rolls Royce mascot charm,** 1950–60, 1½in (4cm) high.
£135–150 / € 190–210
$210–240 ⊞ NEG

A 9ct gold windmill charm,
1950–60, 1in (2.5cm) high.
£40–45 / € 55–65
$65–75 ⊞ NEG

A 9ct gold piano charm, 1950–60,
1in (2.5cm) high.
£20–25 / € 30–35
$35–40 ⊞ NEG

▶ **A gilt-metal charm bracelet,**
with key charms,
1950–60,
7in (28cm) long.
£75–85
€ 105–120
$120–135
⊞ NEG

A 9ct gold paddle steamer charm, 1960, 1in (2.5cm) high.
£45–50 / € 65–70
$75–80 ⊞ SPE

◄ **A 9ct gold owl charm,**
1960s, 1in
(2.5cm) high.
£16–20
€ 22–28
$26–32 ⊞ SPE

A 9ct gold charm bracelet,
with six charms, safety chain and padlock, 1960, 7in (18cm) long.
£90–100 / € 145–170
$160–190 ⋟ SWO

▶ **A 9ct gold World Cup trophy charm,** 1966,
1¼in (3cm) high.
£42–48
€ 58–65
$65–72 ⊞ SPE

Cross Reference
See Sixties & Seventies
(pages 337–339)

A 9ct gold charm, modelled as a the Old Woman Who Lived in a Shoe, opening to reveal enamel family inside, 1960s, 1½in (4cm) high.
£85–95 / €120–135
$135–150 ⊞ SPE

A 9ct gold church charm, opening to reveal a wedding couple, 1960s, ½in (1cm) high.
£42–48 / €58–65
$65–72 ⊞ SPE

A 9ct gold ice skating boot charm, 1960s, ¾in (2cm) high.
£24–28 / €35–40
$40–45 ⊞ SPE

A 9ct gold veteran car charm, 1960s, 1in (2.5cm) high.
£50–55 / €70–80
$80–90 ⊞ SPE

A 9ct gold Viking longship charm, 1960s, 1in (2.5cm) high.
£24–28 / €35–40
$40–45 ⊞ SPE

◄ **A 9ct gold space rocket charm,** 1960s, 1in (2.5cm) high.
£45–50
€65–70
$75–80 ⊞ NEG

A gold charm bracelet, with 30 charms and a padlock, 1960s.
£420–500 / €600–710
$670–800 ➶ TRM

A 9ct gold articulated doll charm, inset with coloured stones, 1960s, 1¾in (4.5cm) high.
£75–85 / €105–120
$120–135 ⊞ SPE

A 9ct gold ship's wheel and bell charm, 1960s, 1½in (4cm) high.
£85–95 / €120–135
$135–150 ⊞ SPE

Auction or dealer?

All the pictures in our price guides originate from auction houses ➶ and dealers ⊞. When buying at auction, prices can be lower than those of a dealer, but a buyer's premium and VAT will be added to the hammer price. Equally, when selling at auction, commission, tax and photography charges must be taken into account. Dealers will often restore pieces before putting them back on the market. Both dealers and auctioneers can provide professional advice, so it is worth researching both sources before buying or selling your antiques.

Cufflinks

Cufflinks are a relatively recent addition to the male wardrobe. In the early 1600s, sleeves were tied with cord or ribbon but the late 17th century saw the introduction of the sleeve button – the ancestor of the cufflink. Matching pairs of buttons were attached by a small chain and richly decorated with jewels and precious metals, an extravagance restricted to the wealthy. Cufflinks became more available in the second half of the 19th century owing to the combination of an expanding middle class, cheaper production methods and the evolution of the modern shirt cuff as opposed to the ruffle.

Although Victorian gentlemen were not encouraged to wear jewellery, under the influence of the fun-loving and fashion-conscious Prince of Wales (later Edward VII) men became more colourful. Edward loved jewellery – he shopped at Fabergé and distributed gifts of jewelled tie pins and cufflinks on Royal visits. The turn-of-the-century cufflinks illustrated below reflect the taste for coloured stones alongside more simple designs.

After WWI, and under the influence of yet another fun-loving and fashion-conscious Edward, Prince of Wales (later Edward VIII), cufflinks became more decorative still. Dress sets (links and studs) were produced in Art Deco-style enamels and mother-of-pearl, cufflinks were decorated with animals, gambling and sporting scenes. The post-WWII period, particularly in the USA, saw a taste for mass-produced novelty designs, often large in size, marketed as fashion items and targeted at the lower end of the market. Cufflinks fell from grace somewhat in the 1960s but returned to popularity (and to large size) in the 1970s, along with the vogue for big jewellery.

Some cufflinks are linked by chains or loops, others have a solid baton designed for pushing through the shirt cuff with one hand. The condition of both sides should be checked when buying. Although works by famous designers will always carry a premium, generally value depends on medium and style.

► **A set of gold and ruby dress studs,** 1895–1905, in a box.
£220–250
€310–350
$350–400 ⊞ CUF

A pair of Victorian 18ct gold cufflinks, inset with turquoise stones.
£400–440 / €570–630
$640–710 ⊞ SPE

A pair of silver and enamel cufflinks, by Charles Horner, c1900.
£100–115 / €140–165
$160–185 ⊞ SPE

A pair of pearl and enamel cufflinks, c1905, in a box.
£370–420 / €520–600
$590–670 ⊞ CUF

◄ **A pair of 18ct gold cufflinks,** engraved, 1899.
£220–250 / €310–350
$350–400 ⊞ SPE

A pair 14ct gold cufflinks, inset with diamonds and emeralds, c1915.
£140–165 / €200–230
$230–270 ↗ LCM

A pair of gilt cufflinks, set with imitation rubies, 1910–20.
£40–45 / €55–65
$65–75 ⊞ CUF

A pair of 14ct gold cufflinks, c1920.
£55–65 / €80–90
$90–105 ⚹ LCM

A pair of silver and enamel cufflinks, c1920.
£50–60 / €70–85
$80–95 ⚹ LCM

◀ A platinum and 18ct gold dress set, c1920, in a box.
£250–280
€360–400
$400–450 ⊞ CUF

A pair of 14ct gold cufflinks, inset with rubies, Hungarian, c1920, in a box.
£450–500 / €640–710
$720–800 ⊞ CUF

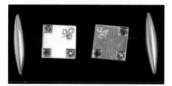

A pair of 18ct gold cufflinks, inset with diamonds and rubies, c1925.
£400–450 / €570–640
$640–720 ⊞ CUF

A pair of mother-of-pearl cufflinks, inset with seed pearls, 1920s.
£20–25 / €30–35
$35–40 ⊞ EV

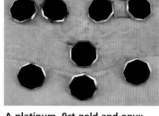

A platinum, 9ct gold and onyx dress set, 1920s, in original box.
£315–350 / €450–500
$500–560 ⊞ SPE

A pair of gilt-metal cufflinks, with celluloid and mother-of-pearl centres, 1920s.
£15–20 / €20–30
$25–35 ⊞ EV

A pair of gilt and metal cufflinks, 1920s.
£30–35 / €45–50
$50–55 ⊞ CUF

A pair of sterling silver and enamel cufflinks, 1925–30, in a box.
£110–125 / €155–175
$175–200 ⊞ CUF

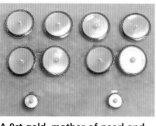

A 9ct gold, mother-of-pearl and enamel dress set, 1930s, in a box.
£580–650 / €820–920
$930–1,050 ⊞ EV

A pair of gilt-metal and crystal cufflinks, decorated with a fox terrier, 1930s.
£20–25 / €30–35
$35–40 ⊞ EV

A pair of gilt-metal cufflinks, late 1930s.
£45–50 / €65–70
$75–80 ⊞ CUF

A pair of silver and moonstone cufflinks, in the style of Georg Jensen, Danish, 1930s–40s.
£65–75 / €95–105
$110–120 ⊞ CUF

A pair of silver and lapis cufflinks, by Georg Jensen, 1940s.
£160–175 / €230–250
$250–280 ⊞ CUF

A pair of mother-of-pearl cufflinks, modelled as dice, French, late 1940s.
£55–65 / €80–90
$90–105 ⊞ CAD

A pair of gilt cufflinks, decorated with Scottie dogs, early 1950s.
£15–20 / €20–30
$25–35 ⊞ CUF

A set of Guinness dress buttons, decorated with Guinness advertising characters, 1950s, with box.
£70–75 / €95–105
$110–120 ⊞ CUF

▶ **A pair of white metal cufflinks,** modelled as guns in leather holsters, 1950s.
£55–65 / €80–90
$90–105 ⊞ CAD

LOCATE THE SOURCE
The source of each illustration in Miller's can be found by checking the code letters below each caption with the Key to Illustrations, pages 443–451.

A pair of gilt-metal cufflinks, decorated with musical notes and keys, 1950s.
£40–45 / €55–65
$65–75 ⊞ CAD

A Scripto trout fisherman's lighter, cufflinks and tie pin set, decorated with leaping trout, 1950s, with box.
£45–50 / €65–70
$75–80 ⊞ CAD

▶ **A pair of Lucite cufflinks,** by Anson, 1950s, with box.
£54–58 / €76–82
$86–92 ⊞ CAD

◀ **A pair of 18ct gold cufflinks,** modelled as cigars, French, 1960s.
£350–390
€500–550
$560–620
⊞ CUF

A pair of agate and gold-plated cufflinks, by Guy la Roche, early 1970s.
£30–35 / €45–50
$50–55 ⊞ CUF

Earrings

A pair of carved Whitby jet earrings, with silver hooks, c1880.
£175–195 / €250–270 $280–310 ⊞ EXC

A pair of silver drop earrings, set with turquoises, on leaf suspensions, late 19thC.
£130–150 / €185–220 $210–250 ⚒ G(L)

A pair of Lucite earrings, with applied gilt and paste flowers, American, c1950.
£28–32 / €40–45 $45–50 ⊞ LaF

A pair of drop earrings, by Trifari, American, 1950–60.
£40–45 / €55–65 $65–75 ⊞ LBe

▶ **A pair of paste and glass earrings,** American, 1960.
£65–75 / €95–105 $105–120 ⊞ LBe

A pair of glass earrings, 1930s.
£60–65 / €85–95 $95–105 ⊞ LBe

A pair of flower earrings, by Kramer, American, c1950.
£45–50 / €65–75 $75–80 ⊞ LaF

A pair of paste and *faux* pearl earrings, by Christian Dior, 1960.
£60–65 / €85–95 $95–105 ⊞ LBe

Hatpins

A Bakelite butterfly hat-pin, c1900, 3in (7.5cm) wide.
£240–270 / €340–380 $380–430 ⊞ LaF

A gilded hatpin, possibly blonde tortoiseshell, French, c1890, 1½in (6.5cm) diam.
£135–150 / €190–210 $210–240 ⊞ VK

An Art Nouveau silver and enamel hatpin, c1900, 1in (2.5cm) wide.
£85–95 / €120–135 $135–150 ⊞ VK

A pair of silver hatpins, by Pearson Thomson, Birmingham 1911, 11in (28cm) long.
£60–65 / €85–95 $95–105 each ⊞ VB

▶ **A pair of silver hat-pins,** by Charles Horner, modelled as golf clubs, 1923, 11in (28cm) long.
£450–500 / €640–710 $720–800 ⊞ LaF

Hatpins were an essential part of a lady's wardrobe from the late 19th century until WWI. They came in many different designs and materials, and value depends on medium and style. Prominent makers include Charles Horner.

Necklaces & Pendants

A Victorian gold pendant, set
with split pearls, turquoises and
a diamond.
£360–400 / €510–570
$580–640 ✈ G(L)

An Edwardian gold pendant,
set with seed pearls and emeralds.
£180–220 / €250–300
$290–350 ✈ G(L)

A 15ct gold hinged locket,
decorated with enamel and set with
natural pearls, c1885, 2in (5cm) high.
£320–350 / €440–500
$500–560 ⊞ EXC

An Edwardian 15ct gold pendant,
set with seed pearls, 2¼in (6cm) high.
£150–180 / €210–250
$240–290 ✈ SWO

**A carved and fretwork ivory
pendant,** c1920, 1½in (4cm) wide.
£25–30 / €35–40
$45–50 ⊞ FMN

A faceted glass bead necklace,
with gold plated wires, 1930s,
14in (35.5cm) long.
£14–18 / €20–25
$24–28 ⊞ CCO

A silver and enamel necklace, by
Bernard Instone, set with marble,
1920s, 16in (40.5cm) long.
£500–550 / €710–780
$800–880 ⊞ RGA

◄ **A Bakelite necklace,** French,
c1930, 16in (40.5cm) long.
£35–40 / €50–55
$55–65 ⊞ LaF

A chrome and glass necklace, 1930s,
14in (35.5cm) long.
£14–18 / €20–25
$24–28 ⊞ CCO

A Bakelite and brass collar,
French, c1930, 2in (5cm) wide.
£220–240 / $310–340
$350–390 ⊞ LaF

**A paste and glass
bead necklace,** 1930s,
14in (35.5cm) long.
£125–140 / €180–200
$200–220 ⊞ LBe

A paste and baguette-cut stone necklace,
by Norman Hartnell, c1950, 15in (38cm) long.
£225–250 / €320–360
$360–400 ⊞ LaF

**A pearl and amber Cleopatra
necklace,** by Miriam
Haskell, American, c1955,
14in (35.5cm) long.
£320–350 / €450–500
$510–560 ⊞ LaF

A *faux* pearl and jet choker, by Miriam
Haskell, with a paste inset, American, 1960s,
12in (30.5cm) long.
£110–120 / €155–170
$170–190 ⊞ SBL

A pearl and gilt necklace,
by Miriam Haskell, with
a paste centrepiece,
American, c1956,
14in (35.5cm) long.
£120–135 / €170–190
$190–210 ⊞ LaF

▶ **A glass necklace,**
with a paste clasp, 1970s,
14in (35.5cm) long.
£35–40 / €50–55
$55–60 ⊞ SBL

**A coral and gilt five-row rope
necklace,** 1970s, 2in (5cm) wide.
£45–50 / €65–70
$75–80 ⊞ SBL

Jewellery Sets

A gilded brass and *faux* pearl
necklace, bracelet and earrings
set, by Miriam Haskell, American,
1940s, earrings 2½in (6.5cm) long.
£270–300 / €380–430
$430–480 ⊞ RGA

▶ A Lucite earrings
and bracelet set, late
1940s–50s, earrings
1in (2.5cm) diam.
£115–125 / €155–175
$175–200 ⊞ SpM

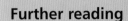

A lavender and amethyst crystal parure, by Mitchell Mayer, for Christian
Dior, 1951–54, in original box, 2in (5cm) square.
£1,300–1,500 / €1,800–2,000
$2,100–2,400 ⊞ LaF
A parure is the name for a jewellery set or suite comprising matching
bracelet, necklace, brooch and earrings. A demi-parure is the term for
a less than full set. A complete parure will command a premium and,
where possible, matching sets should be preserved in the original box.

An Austrian crystal and blue
lustre stone necklace and
earrings set, by Stanley Hagler,
American, c1950, necklace
19in (48.5cm) long.
£630–700 / €890–990
$1,000–1,100 ⊞ LaF

A copper set, decorated with musical
notes, 1950s, brooch 2in (5cm) high.
£70–78 / €100–110
$110–125 ⊞ SpM

A *faux* ruby and diamond
necklace and earrings set,
designed by Alfred Philippe for
Trifari, as a copy of Cartier's
invisible set gems, American,
1950s, earrings 1½in (4cm) long.
£360–400 / €500–570
$570–640 ⊞ RGA

▶ A glass and
paste brooch
and earrings set,
by Christian Dior,
1960s, brooch
2in (5cm) diam.
£135–150
€190–210
$210–240 ⊞ RGA

Further reading

*Miller's Costume Jewellery:
A Collector's Guide,*
Miller's Publications, 2001

A glass bracelet, brooch and earrings
set, designed by Elsa Schiaparelli, Italian,
1950s, brooch 3in (7.5cm) wide.
£270–300 / €380–430
$430–480 ⊞ RGA

Tiaras

An Edwardian paste tiara, 4in (10cm) high.
£90–100 / €125–140
$145–160 ⊞ MARG

A Victorian paste tiara, 3in (7.5cm) high.
£135–150 / €190–210
$210–240 ⊞ MARG

▶ A ballerina's
white metal
and paste
tiara, 1930s,
4in (10cm) high.
£75–85
€105–120
$120–135 ⊞ JBB

◀ A coated metal and paste tiara, 1920s,
3in (7.5cm) high.
£720–800 / €1,000–1,100
$1,100–1,200 ⊞ JBB
This tiara is a replica of a Russian crown jewels
tiara displayed and sold by Christie's in the 1920s.

Kitchenware

A wrought-iron game hanger,
18thC, 10in (25.5cm) high.
£130–145 / €185–210
$210–230 ⊞ TOP

A set of A. K. & Sons iron imperial weights, 1880, largest 5¼in (13.5cm) diam.
£85–95 / €120–135
$135–150 ⊞ SMI

A maid's painted metal bucket,
1890–1900, 14½in (37cm) high.
£30–35 / €45–50
$50–55 ⊞ CHAC

◄ **A painted flour tin,** c1890,
9in (23cm) high.
£50–55 / €70–80
$80–90 ⊞ AL

A Bryant & May metal spice box, with internal nutmeg grater, c1890, 4½in (11.5cm) diam.
£50–55 / €70–80
$80–90 ⊞ AL

A metal herb chopper, with a wooden handle, c1900, 6in (15cm) high.
£20–25 / €30–35
$35–40 ⊞ AL

A bread knife, with a carved wooden handle, c1900, 12¾in (32.5cm) long.
£35–40 / €50–55
$55–60 ⊞ CHAC

A lignum vitae pestle,
c1900, 19in
(48.5cm) long.
£60–70
€85–100
$95–110 ⊞ AL

► **A carved wood bread board,** c1900,
11½in (29cm) diam.
£20–25 / €30–35
$35–40 ⊞ CHAC

A wooden biscuit barrel,
painted with farmyard and hunting scenes, early 20thC, 7in (18cm) high.
£70–85 / €100–120
$115–135 ➚ WilP

An oak cutlery rack, early 20thC, 20in (51cm) high.
£110–120 / €155–170
$175–195 ⊞ B&R

A tin herb chopper, c1910, 7in (18cm) wide.
£11–15 / €14–20
$16–24 ⊞ AL

A tin jug, c1910,
20in (51cm) high.
£38–42 / €54–60
$60–66 ⊞ YC

A meat press, c1920,
10in (25.5cm) high.
£13–18 / €18–21
$21–24 ⊞ AL

◀ **A pine knife tray,**
c1920, 16in (42cm) long.
£25–30 / €35–40
$40–48 ⊞ AL

A wicker cutlery basket, c1920,
16in (40.5cm) long.
£15–20 / €20–30
$25–30 ⊞ AL

A pine bread shovel, eastern European, c1920, 59in (150cm) long.
£15–20 / €20–30
$25–30 ⊞ HRQ

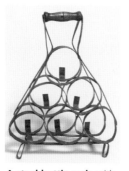

A steel bottle rack, with
a wooden handle, French,
c1920, 18in (45.5cm) high.
£55–65 / €80–90
$90–105 ⊞ SMI

A wire egg basket, c1920,
12in (30.5cm) high.
£25–30 / €35–40
$40–48 ⊞ AL
Eggs were traditionally
stored in open wire or
willow baskets and
hung from the ceiling
of the larder to keep
them away from rats
and mice.

▶ **A set of cast-iron scales,**
with enamel face, 1920s.
£35–40 / €50–55
$55–60 ⊞ SMI

An iron 'bull' can opener, c1930,
6in (15cm) long.
£18–22 / €**25–30**
$28–34 ⊞ **TOP**

A Bonzo trivet, 1930s,
6in (15cm) diam.
£20–25 / €**30–35**
$35–40 ⊞ **HYP**

A pack of jam pot covers, 1940s,
5 x 6in (12.5 x 15cm).
£6–10 / €**8–14**
$10–16 ⊞ **NFR**

A Tala icing set, c1950, 4½ x 6¼in (11.5 x 16cm).
£4–8 / €**6–10**
$8–12 ⊞ **AL**

Three potato mashers,
with wooden handles,
c1950, 10in (25.5cm) long.
£4–8 / €**6–10**
$8–12 each ⊞ **AL**

**A Tupperware Wonderlier plastic
pudding bowl,** with a lid for
steaming, 1960, 7½in (19cm) diam.
£6–10 / €**8–14**
$10–16 ⊞ **Mo**

Ceramics

A stoneware flagon,
1880, 14in (35.5cm) high.
£30–35 / €**45–50**
$50–55 ⊞ **AL**

A Mochaware jug, with
banded decoration,
c1880, 8in (20.5cm) high.
£220–250 / €**310–360**
$350–400 ⊞ **SMI**

▶ **A salt-
glazed tureen,**
French, c1900,
7in (18cm) diam.
£30–35
€**45–50**
$50–55 ⊞ **AL**

▶ **A Burleigh
milk jug,** 1920,
7in (18cm) high.
£50–60
€**70–80**
$80–95 ⊞ **YT**

A ceramic salt box,
c1900, 9in (23cm) high.
£50–55 / €**70–80**
$80–90 ⊞ **CHAC**

A Nutbrown pie funnel,
c1920, 2in (5cm) high.
£12–16 / €**18–22**
$20–26 ⊞ **B&R**

A shop display margarine crock, with wooden lid, c1920, 12½in (32cm) high.
£220–250 / €310–360
$350–400 ⊞ B&R

A ceramic butter dish, the moulded basketware with floral decoration, c1920, 8in (20.5cm) diam.
£90–100 / €125–140
$145–160 ⊞ SMI

Two Borden's Malted Milk ceramic beakers, c1920, 4in (10cm) high.
£30–35 / €45–50
$50–55 ⊞ SMI

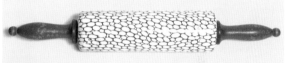

A Maling rolling pin, with cobblestone pattern, c1920.
£145–160 / €200–230
$230–260 ⊞ SMI

◄ **Two Maling storage jars,** with cobblestone pattern, c1920.
£70–80 / €100–115
$115–130 ⊞ SMI

Items in the Kitchenware section have been arranged in date order within each sub-section.

A gilded porcelain wedding cake decoration, modelled as a dove on a horseshoe, 1920–40, 1in (2.5cm) wide.
£10–15 / €14–20
$16–24 ⊞ FMN

◄ A Price's ceramic storage jar, c1950, 6in (15cm) high.
£10–15 / €14–20
$16–24 ⊞ TAC

A bisque cake decoration, in the form of a musician, c1930, 2½in (6.5cm) high.
£50–60 / €70–80
$80–95 ⊞ YC

A ceramic storage jar and cover, 1930s, 6in (15cm) high.
£45–50 / €60–70
$70–80 ⊞ YT

A ceramic Ovaltine mixer, 1930s, 8in (20.5cm) high.
£35–40 / €50–55
$55–65 ⊞ SMI

◄ Six T. G. Green storage jars, 1970s, largest 6in (15cm) high.
£10–15
€14–20
$16–24 each
⊞ RET

Copper & Brass

A brass and wrought-iron chafing dish, c1720, 8in (20.5cm) diam.
£300–330 / €430–470
$480–530 ⊞ RGe
A chafing dish has a heat source beneath it to keep food warm at the table.

A Georgian copper chocolate pot, 9in (23cm) high.
£85–95 / €120–135
$135–150 ⊞ TOP

◄ A copper jug, c1850, 5in (12.5cm) high.
£110–125 / €155–175
$175–200 ⊞ YT

► A copper cooking pot, initialled 'R. & B.', c1880, 8in (20.5cm) diam.
£150–165 / €210–230
$240–270 ⊞ YT

A copper kettle, c1820, 12in (30.5cm) high.
£220–250 / €310–360
$350–400 ⊞ YT

A copper cooking pot, c1880,
8in (20.5cm) diam.
£130–145 / € 185–210
$200–230 ⊞ YT

A copper picnic kettle, c1910,
6in (15cm) high.
£35–40 / € 50–60
$55–65 ⊞ AL

◀ **A maid's hot water can,**
1920s, 10in (25.5cm) high.
£50–60 / € 70–80
$80–95 ⊞ YT
These items are often wrongly
described as plant watering cans.

A copper electric water heater,
c1915, 20in (51cm) high.
£110–125 / € 155–175
$175–200 ⊞ YT

Dairying

A sycamore butter smoother,
19thC, 8in (20.5cm) diam.
£18–22 / € 26–30
$28–34 ⊞ MFB
This item was used to smooth
the top of the butter before it
was taken to market.

**A shop display porcelain milk
churn,** c1860, 18in (45.5cm) high.
£2,250–2,500 / € 3,200–3,550
$3,600–4,000 ⊞ SMI
Decorative dairying pieces such
as this churn are rare and very
sought after by collectors.

A butter marker, c1870,
2in (5cm) diam.
£50–60 / € 70–80
$80–95 ⊞ WeA

◀ **A ceramic butter dish,**
with wooden surround, c1920,
6in (15cm) diam.
£30–35 / € 45–50
$50–55 ⊞ AL

▶ **A sycamore butter hand,**
c1920, 14in (35.5cm) long.
£15–20 / € 20–28
$24–32 ⊞ AL

A cream carton, 1930–50,
4in (10cm) high.
£1–5 / € 2–7
$3–8 ⊞ AL

Enamel Ware

From the Victorian period to the 1930s, enamel ware was a household favourite. Called granite ware in the USA, it was made from sheets of metal coated with powdered glass which was fused to the metal in a hot oven.

Enamel ware was mass-produced from the second half of the 19th century, and became extremely popular for use in kitchens because it was durable, affordable, easy to clean and permitted the use of bright colours. Main centres of production in Europe include England, the former Yugoslavia, Poland, France, Germany and Holland. Typical pieces include storage jars, bread and flour bins and jugs. White and single-colour pieces are the most easily found but patterned enamel ware was also produced, often in spattered or mottled glazes. France specialized in elaborately decorated and stencilled pieces and French kitchen canisters, often colourfully enamelled with Art Deco-style designs, are now highly sought after. Although some enamel ware was produced after WWII, to a large extent it was replaced by new materials such as aluminium and plastic.

The most collectable enamel ware includes 19th-century pieces, patterned or unusually coloured examples and complete sets of matching storage jars. Although hard to break, enamel ware is prone to chipping and rust and comparatively few pieces survive in perfect condition. Values depend on colour, lettering and any unusual features, such as a domed lid.

Two enamel storage jars, with ceramic knobs, Continental, c1890, 8½in (21.5cm) high.
£40–45 / €55–65
$65–75 ⊞ B&R

An enamel bread bin, 1900–20, 14¼in (36cm) high.
£40–45 / €55–65
$65–75 ⊞ B&R

An enamel flour bin, c1900, 9½in (24cm) high.
£24–28 / €34–40
$38–45 ⊞ CHAC

An enamel bread bin, 1900–10, 12in (30.5cm) high.
£35–40 / €50–55
$55–65 ⊞ CHAC

▶ **An enamel jug,** 1900–10, 14¾in (37.5cm) high.
£28–32 / €40–44
$45–50 ⊞ CHAC

Further reading
Miller's Buying Affordable Antiques Price Guide, Miller's Publications, 2004

An enamel chamberstick, c1910, 6in (15cm) diam.
£6–10 / €8–14
$10–16 ⊞ AL

◀ **A set of six enamel storage jars,** French, c1920, largest 6½in (16.5cm) high.
£220–240 / €310–340
$340–380 ⊞ AL

An enamel coffee pot, c1930, 7in (18cm) high.
£20–25 / €30–35
$35–40 ⊞ AL

An enamel mug, c1950, 3in (7.5cm) high.
£2–6 / €3–7
$4–8 ⊞ AL

An enamel food safe, c1930, 17in (43cm) wide.
£35–40 / €50–56
$55–65 ⊞ AL

▶ **An enamel colander,** c1960, 11in (28cm) diam.
£18–22 / €26–32
$30–35 ⊞ AL

An enamel kettle, c1960, 8in (20.5cm) high.
£11–15 / €16–20
$18–24 ⊞ AL

Irons

◀ **A Victorian cast-iron lace iron,** by Kenrick, with wooden handle, 5in (12.5cm) wide.
£70–80
€100–110
$110–125 ⊞ HL

A set of three Mrs Potts irons, handle restored, American, c1885, 6½in (16.5cm) long.
£65–75 / €90–100
$105–120 ⊞ AL
In 1871, Mary Florence Potts patented her famous iron in the USA. Known as 'Mrs Potts Patent' or 'Mrs Potts Cold-handled Sad Iron', this was a set of three irons that came with a detachable wooden handle that could be removed while the iron was being heated, so that it was always cold to the touch. In their 1902 mail order catalogue, Sears Roebuck advertised a set of these irons (complete with iron stand) for 67 cents or 73 cents if you wanted them nickel-plated.

▶ **An Omega spirit iron,** with wooden handle and brass fittings, German, c1900, 6½in (16.5cm) long.
£40–45
€55–65
$65–75 ⊞ AL

Moulds

A Victorian copper mould, 2¾in (7cm) wide.
£14–18 / €20–25
$22–28 ⊞ WiB

A copper mould, with a lid, c1900, 6in (15cm) high.
£45–50 / €65–70
$75–80 ⊞ YT

A Victorian ceramic jelly mould, 8in (20.5cm) wide.
£20–24 / €28–34
$32–38 ⊞ TOP

A metal cheese mould, French, c1900, 4in (10cm) wide.
£24–28 / €35–40
$40–45 ⊞ B&R

A tin chocolate mould, in the form of a boot, c1900, 7in (18cm) high.
£115–125 / €160–175
$180–200 ⊞ YT

A metal chocolate mould, in the form of a rabbit in a car, 1900–20, 7in (18cm) high.
£35–40 / €50–55
$55–65 ⊞ CHAC

A glass mould, in the form of a rabbit, c1930, 8½in (21.5cm) wide.
£10–14 / €15–20
$16–22 ⊞ AL

A glass mould, in the form of a tortoise, c1930, 7½in (19cm) wide.
£15–20 / €20–28
$24–32 ⊞ AL

A Shelley ceramic jelly mould, 1920s, 4½in (11.5cm) high.
£32–38 / €45–50
$50–60 ⊞ WiB

Cross Reference
See Glass (pages 211–225)

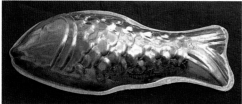

◀ **A set of five aluminium moulds,** in the form of fish, c1950, largest 5in (12.5cm) long.
£1–5 / €2–7
$3–8 each ⊞ AL

A plastic jelly mould, in the form of a space shuttle, 1980s, 10in (25.5cm) wide.
£4–8 / €5–10
$7–13 ⊞ TWI

Toasters

An iron toaster/spit, 19thC, 15in (38cm) long.
£75–85 / €110–120
$120–135 ⊞ TOP

A wire toaster, French, c1920, 12in (30.5cm) wide.
£35–40 / €50–55
$55–65 ⊞ AL

A Calor aluminium electric toaster, French, 1930s, 8in (20.5cm) wide.
£30–35 / €45–50
$50–55 ⊞ TRA

A Toastmaster chrome automatic electric toaster, American, 1930s, 10in (25.5cm) wide.
£35–40 / €50–55
$55–65 ⊞ TRA

A Son Chef chrome electric toaster, American, 1960s, 8in (20.5cm) high.
£15–20 / €20–28
$24–32 ⊞ TRA

Lighting

A brass lantern,
Dutch, late 18thC,
14in (35.5cm) high.
£100–110 / €145–160
$160–175 ⊞ WAA

**A rushlight and candle
holder,** on a pine base,
18thC, 11in (28cm) high.
£600–670 / €850–950
$960–1,000 ⊞ SEA

An iron lantern, c1800,
10in (25.5cm) high.
£220–250 / €310–360
$350–400 ⊞ SEA

An iron Cruisie lamp,
Continental, 19thC,
10in (25.5cm) high.
£115–125 / €160–180
$180–200 ⊞ SEA

A brass chamberstick,
with a scroll handle,
19thC, 5in (12.5cm) diam,
with snuffer.
£55–65 / €80–95
$90–105 ⚒ EH

A brass chamberstick, with side
ejector, 19thC, 7in (18cm) diam.
£65–75 / €95–105
$105–120 ⊞ TOP

A Victorian brass chamberstick,
7in (18cm) wide.
£55–60 / €75–80
$90–95 ⊞ TOP

**A Victorian etched
cranberry glass shade,**
6¾in (17cm) high.
£45–50 / €65–75
$75–80 ⊞ BrL

Always check that electric
lighting conforms to the
current safety regulations.

► **A Victorian
glass oil
lamp,** with
relief decoration,
on a pressed
brass socle,
21in (53cm) high.
£340–400
€480–570
$540–640
⚒ AMB

◄ **A Victorian
cranberry
glass shade,**
6in (15cm) high.
£60–70
€85–100
$95–110 ⊞ BrL

A pair of Victorian copper and brass candle-sticks, 4in (10cm) high.
£60–70 / €85–100
$95–110 ⊞ TOP

A pair of gilded bronze ecclesiastical candelabras, c1890, 12in (30.5cm) diam.
£400–450 / €570–640
$640–720 ⊞ TOP

Items in the Lighting section have been arranged in date order.

A gilded bronze pendant lamp, with glass beads, French, c1900, 11in (28cm) diam.
£200–220 / €280–310
$320–350 ⊞ EAL

A Victorian etched glass oil lamp, with a cranberry glass reservoir, brass column and pottery plinth, 26¾in (68cm) high.
£145–175 / €210–250
$230–280 ⚒ TRM

A bronze chamberstick, with a serpent coiled around the base, late 19thC, 3in (8cm) high.
£40–50 / €55–70
$65–80 ⊞ SWO

A brass two-branch gas lamp, with original cranberry glass shades, c1900, 24in (61cm) high.
£340–400 / €480–570
$540–640 ⊞ EAL

A copper and brass gas lamp, 1870–80, 31in (78.5cm) wide.
£290–320 / €410–450
$460–510 ⊞ EAL

A metal and brass Cornish miner's lamp, late 19thC, 12in (30.5cm) high.
£430–480 / €610–680
$690–770 ⊞ SEA

◀ **A pendant lamp,** with vaseline glass shade, 1900–10, 9in (23cm) diam.
£210–240 / €300–340
$340–380 ⊞ EAL

A brass lantern, with stained glass panels, originally for gas, c1890, 24in (61cm) high.
£320–350 / €450–500
$510–560 ⊞ EAL

A polished brass Corinthian column table lamp, c1900, 16in (40.5cm) high.
£210–230 / €300–330
$340–370 ⊞ EAL

A cut-glass pendant lamp, with brass fittings, 1900–10, 14in (35.5cm) diam.
£200–220 / €280–310 $320–350 ⊞ EAL

A brass desk lamp, with swing frame and stepped plinth, stamped 'Mordan & Co', c1910, 14in (35.5cm) high.
£90–110 / €130–155 $145–175 🔧 G(L)

A cut-glass pineapple pendant lamp, 1910–20, 9in (23cm) high.
£80–90 / €115–125 $130–145 ⊞ EAL

A milk glass portable lamp, c1920, 12in (30.5cm) high.
£40–45 / €55–65 $65–75 ⊞ JAM

A brass-carbide lamp, c1920, 13in (33cm) high.
£110–120 / €155–170 $170–190 ⊞ GAC

A holophane pendant lamp, with original brass fittings, c1920, 8in (20.5cm) diam.
£55–60 / €80–85 $90–95 ⊞ EAL

A pair of alabaster pendant lamps, with oxidized copper fittings, 1920s, 12in (30.5cm) diam.
£400–450 / €570–640 $640–720 ⊞ EAL

An anglepoise lamp, c1950, 17in (43cm) high.
£45–50 / €65–75 $75–80 ⊞ JUN

An Art Deco five-light chandelier, with nickel-plated brass fittings, French, c1930, 23in (58.5cm) diam.
£290–320 / €410–450 $460–510 ⊞ EAL

▶ **A chrome and glass Spring table lamp,** 1960s, 14in (35.5cm) high.
£110–125 / €155–175 $175–200 ⊞ MARK

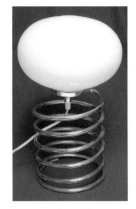

An Art Deco spelter lamp, in the form of a nude woman standing by a column, c1930, 19in (48.5cm) high.
£190–230 / €270–320 $300–360 🔧 G(L)

Spelter

Spelter, a zinc-based alloy, provided a cheaper alternative to bronze and was much used for figures and lamps in the Art Deco period. It is lighter than bronze and fractured more easily.

◄ A pearl shell, metal and wood Fun 3DM lamp, designed by Verner Panton for J. Luber AG, Swiss, c1964, 84in (213.5cm) high.
£7,000–8,400
€9,950–11,900
$11,200–13,400 ➶ BB(L)
Danish architect Verner Panton (b. 1926) was one of the most influential designers of the post-war period. In the 1960s and '70s he created a number of highly innovative lights for the Luber company, playing on the traditional notion of the grand chandelier and transforming it into a space-age item. This famous light (rare in this tripartite form) made from polished shell disks, launched a host of clanking, cheaper imitations. Post-war lighting is currently attracting much interest, and seminal designs by major names can command large sums.

► A chrome Flower Pot table lamp, designed by Verner Panton for Louis Poulsen, 1969, 12in (30.5cm) high.
£1,300–1,550
€1,850–2,200
$2,100–2,500
➶ BB(L)

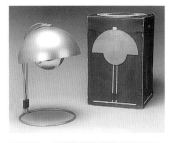

A plastic table light, 1960s, 9in (23cm) high.
£10–15 / €14–20
$16–22 ⊞ MARK

An aluminium and smoked glass table lamp, 1970s, 15in (38cm) high.
£75–85 / €105–120
$120–135 ⊞ MARK

Further reading
Miller's 20th-Century Design Buyer's Guide, Miller's Publications, 2003

A chrome ceiling light, 1970, 16in (40.5cm) wide.
£110–125 / €155–175
$175–200 ⊞ MARK
This clever sputnik-style lamp uses reflection to make it look twice the size, but allowing it to be hung from a low ceiling.

Two lacquered metal Daphine-Terra floor lamps, designed by Tomasso Cimini for Lumina, designed 1976, 28½in (98cm) high.
£650–780 / €920–1,100
$1,000–1,200 ➶ S(O)

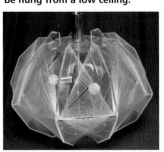

◄ A Perspex and nylon filament ceiling lamp, 1970s, 26in (66cm) diam.
£75–85 / €105–120
$120–135 ⊞ MARK

An aluminium lamp, 1970s, 17in (43cm) high.
£65–75 / €95–105
$105–120 ⊞ MARK

Luggage

A sealskin travelling trunk,
early 18thC, 36in (91.5cm) long.
£500–550 / €710–780
$800–880 ⊞ SWN

A leather and wood box, from
Thos Christy Saddlery and Military
Cap Store, with brass handle and
studwork, label on underside of the
lid, c1800, 10in (25.5cm) wide.
£110–125 / €155–175
$175–200 ⊞ ChC

A leather hatbox, c1830,
8in (20.5cm) high.
£170–190 / €240–270
$270–300 ⊞ TOP

A hatbox, with original lining and
key, mid-19thC, 17in (43cm) wide.
£240–270 / €340–380
$380–430 ⊞ MCa

Two Victorian brass handle locks,
5¾in (14.5cm) wide.
£25–30 / €35–40
$40–50 each ⊞ ChC
The purpose of these locks was
to hold two handles of a bag
such as a Kit or Gladstone
together. Although the bag
could be opened slightly it
would be enough to deter any
thief. The shape of these brass
locks meant that they could also
be used as an additional handle
to carry the bag.

▶ **A rosewood toilet box,** with
silver-mounted bottles, removable
tray and base drawer, 1870s,
11¾in (30cm) wide.
£150–180 / €210–250
$240–290 ⋏ SWO

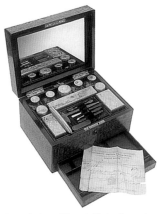

An ash travelling toiletry box, by
William Neal, London, with hinged
lid and removable tray, enclosing
silver-mounted jars and scent
bottles, 1864, 12¼in (31cm) wide,
together with original bill of sale.
£390–470 / €550–670
$620–750 ⋏ Bea(E)

**A Victorian lady's tooled leather
companion,** by Baxter, enclosing
sewing tools with mother-of-pearl
handles, 4½in (11.5cm) wide.
£100–120 / €140–170
$160–190 ⋏ G(L)

A double hatbox, for top hats,
c1880, 13in (33cm) high.
£310–350 / €440–500
$500–560 ⊞ MCa
A travelling essential for the
gentleman, hatboxes came in
different shapes and materials
and were often designed to
hold several hats at once, for
example two top hats for day
and evening wear and a flat cap
for shooting engagements.

A lady's crocodile skin Gladstone bag, c1880s, 12in (30.5cm) wide.
£260–290 / €370–410
$420–460 ⊞ MCa

A leather overnight case, c1880s, 14in (35.5cm) wide.
£100–110 / €140–155
$160–175 ⊞ MCa

A brass-banded wood and leather linen trunk, c1900–10, 12in (30.5cm) wide.
£155–175 / €220–250
$250–280 ⊞ MCa

A crocodile skin dressing case, with enamel backed silver items, some pieces missing, initialled exterior, 1927, 19¾in (50cm) wide.
£460–550 / €650–780
$740–880 ⤻ SWO

► **A leather glove box,** c1900, 10½in (26.5cm) long.
£40–45 / €55–65
$65–75 ⊞ MCa

A Louis Vuitton canvas and leather-bound hatbox, c1900s, 15in (38cm) high.
£800–880 / €1,100–1,250
$1,250–1,400 ⊞ MARK

A hide leather case, with brass locks, c1910, 25in (63.5cm) wide.
£80–90 / €115–130
$130–145 ⊞ HO

A crocodile skin suitcase, relined, 1920s, 14in (35.5cm) wide.
£260–290 / €370–410
$415–465 ⊞ HIP

A Christy's hatbox, 1920s, 13in (33cm) wide.
£16–20 / €22–28
$26–32 ⊞ OH

An Edwardian leather Gladstone travel bag, with leather lining, 18in (45.5cm) wide.
£165–185 / €230–260
$260–300 ⊞ MCa
There was a vogue in the 19th century for naming bags after well-known politicians and in addition to the Gladstone bag, there was also a Rosebery and Hartington bag, both named after celebrated statesmen. W. E. Gladstone (1809–98) also gave his name to a cheap claret when, as Chancellor of the Exchequer, he reduced the duty on French wines in his famous 1860 budget.

A car case, with replacement leather handle, c1920, 36in (91.5cm) wide.
£180–200 / €250–280
$290–320 ⊞ HIP
This case slopes at the front and was designed to sit on the exterior of a period automobile.

A canvas and leather bucket hatbox, 1920s, 10in (25.5cm) high.
£220–250 / €310–350
$350–400 ⊞ OH

A gentleman's travelling case, by Drew & Sons of Piccadilly, containing ivory brush set and removable tray, 1920s, 14in (35.5cm) wide.
£220–250 / €310–350
$350–400 ⊞ OH

A leather hatbox, 1930s, 18in (45.5cm) diam.
£200–220 / €280–310
$320–350 ⊞ MCa

An imitation shagreen lady's dressing case, 1930s, 14in (35.5cm) wide, together with canvas cover.
£70–80 / €100–110
$110–125 ⊞ MCa

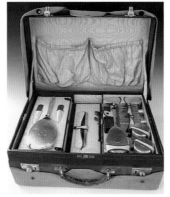

A lady's travelling vanity case, with silver-backed brushes and accessories by Mappin & Webb, London, with removable tray, c1941, 15¾in (40cm) wide.
£130–155 / €185–220
$210–250 ⚒ SWO

A gentleman's leather and Bakelite travelling toiletry case, 1930s.
£75–85 / €105–120
$120–135 ⊞ SAT

A Harrods cardboard box, 1950s, 11in (28cm) square.
£14–18 / €20–25
$22–28 ⊞ HSt

Picnic Sets

A picnic set, with replaced cups and saucers, c1910, 13in (33cm) wide.
£220–250 / €310–350
$350–400 ⊞ MCa

A Brexton picnic set, 1950s, 13in (33cm) square.
£55–65 / €80–90
$90–105 ⊞ LUNA

A Brexton picnic set, 1950s, 16in (40.5cm) wide.
£155–175 / €220–250
$250–280 ⊞ PPH
In the 1950s motor travel was beginning to develop more widely and the idea of a day out in the car for a family picnic was very appealing. Sirram and Brexton were the most popular mass manufacturers of these picnic sets and complete examples in good useable condition are sought after today.

Medals
Commemorative

A silver prize medal, for the Society for the Improvement of Agriculture, Cheshire, minor damage, 1767, 2in (5cm) diam.
£210–230 / €300–330
$330–370 ⊞ TML

A silver prize medal, for Mr Whichelo's Academy, in the form of an artist's palette, 1820, 2½in (6.5cm) diam.
£580–650 / €820–920
$930–1,050 ⊞ TML

A white metal medal, commemorating the abolition of slavery, engraved 'Liberty Proclaimed to the Captives', 1834, 1¾in (4.5cm) diam.
£440–490 / €620–700
$700–780 ⊞ TML

A silver ticket, commemorating the Pantheon, Oxford St, London, 1790–91, 1¼in (3.5cm) diam.
£14–18 / €20–25
$22–28 ⊞ TML
This ticket belonged to Thomas Coutts (1735–1822), founder, with his brother James, of the banking house of Coutts & Co in the Strand, London. On the death of his brother in 1778, he remained sole partner and became banker to George III and a large number of the aristocracy.

A silver prize medal, by W. J. Taylor, commemorating the Thames Regatta, 1843, 1¾in (4.5cm) diam.
£135–150 / €190–210
$220–240 ⊞ TML

A white metal medal, by J. Taylor, commemorating Nelson's Column, 1843, 1¾in (4.5cm) diam.
£165–185 / €230–260
$260–300 ⊞ TML

A silver-gilt prize medal, for the Lancashire Bowmen, 1791, 2in (5cm) diam.
£670–750 / €950–1,050
$1,050–1,200 ⊞ TML

▶ **A silver-gilt medal,** by J. Henning Sr, commemorating the Duke of Clarence's appointment as Lord High Admiral, 1827, 2½in (6.5cm) diam.
£150–180 / €210–250
$240–290 ⋗ DNW

A white metal medal, by T. Halliday, commemorating the Battle of Waterloo, 1815, 3in (7.5cm) diam.
£220–250 / €310–350
$350–400 ⊞ TML

A Bois Durci portrait plaque, commemorating Lord Byron, c1860, 4½in (11.5cm) diam.
£220–250 / €310–350
$350–400 ⊞ TML

A bronze medal, by T. Ottley, commemorating Yorkshire Fine Art and Industrial Exhibition, 1879, 3in (7.5cm) diam, in original case.
£110–125 / €155–175
$175–200 ⊞ TML

A silver prize medal, by J. Restall, for the Workman's Industrial Exhibition, People's Palace, 1888, 2in (5cm) diam.
£670–750
€950–1,050
$1,050–1,200 ⊞ TML

A bronze prize medal, by T. Ottley, for the Birmingham and Midland Counties Bulldog Club, 1895, 1¾in (4.5cm) diam, in original case.
£55–65 / €80–90
$90–105 ⊞ TML

A silver-gilt medal, by F. Bowcher, for the College of Science, 1895, 2½in (6.5cm) diam, in original case.
£200–230 / €280–330
$320–370 ⊞ TML

◄ **A silver-gilt prize medal,** for Loch Leven Curling Province, in the form of two crossed brooms with a curling stone beneath, c1900, 1in (2cm) diam.
£75–85
€105–120
$120–135
⊞ TML

Two enamelled 9ct gold medals, by Vaughton, for Aston Villa Football Club, in original boxes, c1900, larger 23.37g.
£560–670 / €800–950
$900–1,050 ➣ DNW

◄ **An enamelled pass,** by A. Wylie, for the Empire Theatre, Leicester Square, 1907, 1in (2.5cm) diam.
£55–65 / €80–90
$90–105 ⊞ TML
Originally named the Royal London Panorama in 1881, Thomas Verity converted the building into the Empire Theatre in 1884. It then became a music hall, and in 1905 staged its first revue.

Further reading

Miller's Antiques Price Guide,
Miller's Publications, 2004

A silver prize medal, for the Eastbourne Canine Club, 1910, 1½in (4cm) diam.
£90–100 / €125–140
$145–160 ⊞ TML

A gold medal, for the London Boxing Wrestling and Weightlifting Club, engraved '300lbs Pullover & Push World's Record', 1913, 1½in 3.5cm) high.
£90–100 / €125–140
$145–160 ⊞ TML
World record medals of any type are rarely seen for sale.

A silver prize medal, by H. Maryon, for the National Pig Breeders Association, 1926, 2in (5cm) diam.
£65–75 / €90–105
$105–120 ⊞ TML

Military

◄ **A Naval General Service medal,** with four clasps, St Sebastian, Martinique, Trafalgar, Copenhagen 1801, 1793–1840.
£600–720 / €850–1,000 $960–1,150 ⚒ **BAL**

Two Commissariat Zulu War medals, including Campaign Services and Long Service, 1879.
£240–270 / €340–380 $380–430 ⊞ **ABCM**

A Battle of the Nile gilt-bronze medal, awarded to John Cork, c1798.
£700–840 / €1,000–1,200 $1,150–1,350 ⚒ **BAL**
Lord Nelson employed a prize agent, Mr Alexander Davison, to handle the disposal of the ships and other booty captured at the Battle of the Nile. Mr Davison presented a medal to every officer and seaman of Nelson's fleet; gold to Captains and Lieutenants, silver to Warrant officers, gilt-bronze to Petty Officers, and bronze to seamen and mariners.

A group of dress medals, by Hunt & Roskell, awarded to Colonel J. H. King of the Grenadier Guards late 48th Regiment, including Order of the Bath, Military Division Medal, minor damage, mid-19thC, in fitted leather case.
£800–960 / €1,150–1,350 $1,300–1,550 ⚒ **DNW**

> Medals are often impressed on the edge with the name, rank and service number of the recipient.

A Franco-Prussian War Iron Cross medal, 1870.
£270–300 / €380–430 $430–480 ⊞ **ChM**
The Iron Cross originated not in Germany but in Prussia, where it was instituted in 1813 for the war against Napoleon. It was discontinued until the Franco-Prussian War of 1870 and then revived for a third time in 1914. In 1939, Adolf Hitler brought back the Prussian Iron Cross as a German order.

An Egypt Medal and Khedives Star, awarded to Private J. Butcher of the Shropshire Light Infantry, 1885.
£180–200 / €250–280 $290–320 ⊞ **JBM**

A group of four medals, including Egypt Medal, China Medal, Royal Victorian Medal and Khedives Star, awarded to P. O. R. Gale of the Royal Navy, 1880–1900.
£590–650 / €840–920 $950–1,050 ⊞ **JBM**

▶ **A group of four dress medals,** including the Victoria Cross, Afghanistan with one clasp, Meritorious Service Medal and Army Medal, awarded to Sergeant P. Mullane of the Royal Horse Artillery, 1880s.
£1,500–1,800 / €2,150–2,550
$2,400–2,900 ✗ DNW

A group of South Africa medals, awarded to Sergeant R. H. Millis of the Scots Guards, c1900.
£340–410 / €480–580
$540–650 ✗ G(L)

A Royal Field Artillery Battery medals, including trio and long service conduct medals, awarded to Major W. Calmer, 1914–15.
£110–125 / €155–175
$175–200 ⊞ GBM

▶ **A war medal,** by René Lalique, 1915.
£270–300 / €380–430
$430–480 ⊞ ANO

A group of medals, including George V, British War and Victory Medals, awarded to Sergeant F. D. Williams of the Royal Field Artillery, 1918.
£380–420 / €540–600
$610–670 ⊞ JBM

A Spanish Civil War bronze medal, German, 1936–39.
£310–350 / €440–500
$500–560 ⊞ ChM

A WWII Purple Heart, American, 1945.
£20–25 / €30–35
$35–40 ⊞ GBM
The Purple Heart is awarded to members of the American armed forces who are wounded by an instrument of war in the hands of the enemy and to the next of kin in the name of those who are killed in action or die of wounds received in action. It is specifically a combat decoration.

A Campaign Services medal, with one bar, Kenya, 1956.
£40–45 / €55–65
$65–75 ⊞ ABCM

A group of three dress medals, including Queen's South Africa, Shanghai Municipal Council Emergency and Shanghai Volunteer Corps, awarded to Lieutenant R. P. Tilley of Shanghai Volunteer Corps, late Norfolk Regiment, 1937.
£200–240 / €280–340
$320–380 ✗ DNW

▶ **A group of three medals,** including Gulf War, UN Protectorate and Campaign Service medal, awarded to Trooper Horrocks of the Life Guards, 1991.
£500–550 / €710–780
$800–880 ⊞ GBM

Mickey Mouse

In the 1920s, the young Walt Disney (1901–66) created a successful cartoon character called 'Oswald the Lucky Rabbit'. With his white face and black body, he provided the inspiration for Disney's subsequent cartoon character – in more ways than one.

When Disney discovered that, through a clause in his contract, Universal Pictures owned the rights to Oswald, he responded by coming up with 'Mortimer Mouse'. It was his wife who changed the name to Mickey. The 'talkie' cartoon *Steamboat Willie* was premiered in New York on 18 November 1928 and Mickey Mouse became an instant star, rivalling the popularity of Charlie Chaplin. The first merchandising deal was struck in 1929 when a businessman offered Disney £190 / €270 / $300 for the rights to produce Mickey Mouse on a school notebook, thus opening the doors to an avalanche of 'Mickeyana', which appeared in every conceivable form.

A painted wood rocking Mickey Mouse, c1930, 35in (89cm) long.
£280–330 / €400–470
$450–530 ✎ AH

A Mickey Mouse metal jelly mould, 1934, 7in (18cm) wide.
£35–40 / €50–55
$55–65 ⊞ HYP

A Mickey Mouse Post Office money box, depicting Mickey, Minnie and baby mouse, 1935, 6in (15cm) high.
£80–90 / €115–130
$130–145 ⊞ HUX

Mickey Mouse Movie Stories Book 2, published by Dean & Son, 1935.
£100–120 / €140–170
$160–190 ✎ CBP

A Mickey Mouse cast-iron trivet, 1930s, 6in (15cm) diam.
£45–50 / €65–70
$75–80 ⊞ HYP

A Mickey Mouse Bakelite box camera, by Ettelson Corp, American, c1956.
£125–145 / €180–210
$200–230 ⊞ TNS

A tinplate Disney Dipsy Car, by Louis Marx & Co, 1950s, 6in (15cm) long.
£480–530 / €680–750
$770–850 ⊞ CBB

A Disneyland tinplate ferris wheel, by J. Chein & Co, American, 1950s, 17in (43cm) high.
£510–560 / €720–800
$810–900 ⊞ OSF

Militaria

A copper powder flask, by A. M. Flask & Cap Co, decorated with game, slight damage, c1850, 9in (23cm) long.
£150–165 / €210–240
$240–270 ⊞ MDL

A horn powder flask, with steel-mounted ends, c1800, 13in (33cm) long.
£260–310 / €370–440
$420–500 ⚒ AH

A horn powder flask, Scottish, c1780, 7in (18cm) long.
£220–250 / €310–360
$350–400 ⊞ SEA

A Frazier's patent leather ammunition pouch, with brass hinges and embossed badge 'NG', stamped, 1878, 7in (18cm) long.
£75–90 / €110–130
$120–145 ⚒ WAL

A brass box, containing tobacco, cigarettes, card and a photograph of Princess Mary, 1914, 3¼ x 5¼in (8.5 x 13.5cm).
£80–90 / €115–130
$130–145 ⊞ HUX
A fund created by Princess Mary, the 17-year old daughter of King George V and Queen Mary, enabled gift boxes to be issued to everyone who would be wearing the King's uniform on Christmas Day 1914. The contents varied considerably – officers and men on active service afloat or at the front received a box containing a combination of pipe, lighter, 1oz of tobacco and 20 cigarettes in distinctive yellow monogrammed wrappers. Non-smokers and boys received a bullet pencil and a packet of sweets instead. Indian troops often got sweets and spices, and nurses were treated to chocolate.

A memorial card for Field Marshall the Rt Hon H. H. Lord Kitchener of Khartoum, 1916, 3 x 5in (7.5 x 12.5cm).
£15–20 / €20–28
$24–32 ⊞ COB
Lord Kitchener drowned off the coast of Scotland when HMS *Hampshire* was sunk on 5 June 1916.

A civilian gas mask, 1939–45, in original box, 5 x 7in (12.5 x 18cm).
£11–15 / €16–20
$18–24 ⊞ J&S

LOCATE THE SOURCE
The source of each illustration in Miller's can be found by checking the code letters below each caption with the Key to Illustrations, pages 443–451.

◄ **A Royal Air Force Benevolent Fund bell,** with raised portrait of Sir Winston Churchill, 1939–45, 6in (15cm) high.
£24–28
€34–40
$38–44 ⊞ HUX

A Huntley & Palmer's biscuit tin, depicting the Horse Guards, 1950s, 10 x 8in (25.5 x 20.5cm).
£11–15 / €16–20
$18–24 ⊞ RGa

Arms & Armour

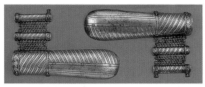

A pair of steel armguards, decorated with chiselled scrolls, with original buckles, Russian or Caucasian, early 19thC.
**£420–500 / €600–710
$670–800 ⚒ DNW**

A pair of Light Infantry officer's wings, decorated with copper-gilt scales and silver-plated bugles, early 19thC, 7in (18cm) wide.
**£190–230 / €270–320
$300–360 ⚒ WAL**

A steel cabasset, with scale cheek pieces, decorated with brass rosettes, restored, Italian.
**£1,100–1,200
€1,550–1,850
$1,750–2,100 ⚒ JDJ**
The cabasset is an open-faced helmet characterized by its almond-shaped top (often called pear-shaped) and the curious little point projecting from the apex of the helmet. The cabasset was most popular among infantry soldiers and pikemen in Europe during the 16th and 17th centuries.

A Victorian Prince of Wales's Own Bengal Lancers officer's belt, with silver flap pouch, 30in (76cm) long.
**£240–290 / €340–410
$380–460 ⚒ WAL**

▶ **A Hyderabad Contingent 5th Battalion Field Officer's full dress tunic,** with gold lace sash and cloth cap, inscribed 'J. Woodcock', 1868.
**£580–700
€820–990
$930–1,100
⚒ DNW**

A Victorian Queen's Own Oxfordshire Hussars silver badge, 2in (5cm) high.
**£135–150 / €190–210
$220–240 ⊞ ABCM**

A Victorian 3rd Dragoon Guard's helmet.
**£630–700 / €900–1,000
$1,000–1,100 ⊞ GBM**

▶ **A 6th Dragoon Guards (Carabiniers) officer's shoulder belt,** with silver decoration and buckle, initialled 'MC', losses, c1879.
**£60–70 / €85–100
$95–110 ⚒ WAL**

A Home Service Army Service Corps helmet, 1901–10.
**£500–550 / €710–780
$800–880 ⊞ GBM**

▶ **A pair of Royal Naval Armoured Services brass badges,** 1914–18, larger 1¾in (4.5cm) wide.
**£110–125 / €155–175
$175–200 ⊞ ABCM**

A Victorian Royal Artillery Private's dress tunic.
**£90–100 / €125–140
$145–160 ⊞ ChM**

A German Imperial Army camouflage helmet, 1914–18.
£220–250 / €310–350
$350–400 ⊞ ChM

A Prussian Artillery *Pickelhaube*, 1914–18.
£390–430 / €550–610
$620–690 ⊞ GBM

◀ A Royal Flying Corps Cadet's cap, 1914–18.
£290–320
€410–450
$460–510
⊞ ABCM

A US Army Aero Squadron tunic and breeches, 1914–18.
£310–350 / €440–500
$500–560 ⊞ ChM

A Royal Marines jacket, 1910–36.
£75–85 / €105–120
$120–135 ⊞ ABCM

A pair of British army officer's leather riding boots, 1930s.
£90–100 / €125–140
$145–160 ⊞ ChM

An 11th Hussars dress uniform, 1914–18.
£135–150 / €190–210
$210–240 ⊞ ChM

◀ A German Air Force officer's flight blouse, 1939–45.
£400–450 / €570–640
$640–720 ⊞ ChM

Items in the Militaria section have been arranged in date order within each sub-section.

A military jacket, 1940s.
£45–50 / €65–70
$75–80 ⊞ NFR

A paratrooper's denison smock and matching helmet, 1944.
£780–930 / €1,100–1,300
$1,250–1,500 ⚒ B(O)

◀ A Royal Air Force double-breasted overcoat, c1940s.
£55–65 / €80–90
$90–105 ⊞ NFR

An Intelligence Corps officer's service dress, c1955.
£135–150 / €190–210
$210–240 ⊞ ABCM

Edged Weapons

A Starr Cavalry sabre, damaged and repaired, American, 1821, 31¾in (80.5cm) long, with iron scabbard.
£320–380 / €450–540
$510–600 ↗ JDJ
History records that towards the end of 1818, the US government signed a contract with Nathan Starr for the production of 10,000 cavalry sabres for the arming of state militias. The swords were manufactured between 1820 and 1822. Some of them were stamped on the guard with the year of manufacture.

A Model 1841 naval cutlass, with brass hilt, inscribed, slight damage, American, 1842, 21¼in (54cm) long.
£560–670 / €800–950
$950–1,050 ↗ JDJ

A double-edged dagger, with stylized bird's head pommel, Indian, 19thC, 9¼in (23.5cm) long.
£300–360 / €430–510
$480–580 ↗ WAL

An Argyll and Sutherland Highlanders officer's field service sword, by Sanderson Bros and Newbould, with nickel-plated crosspiece and pommel, wire-bound fishskin-covered grip, inscribed, 1918, 33in (84cm) long, with leather scabbard.
£400–480 / €570–680
$640–770 ↗ WAL

A Royal Naval officer's dress sword, 1914–18, 37in (94cm) long.
£340–380 / €480–540
$540–610 ⊞ ChM

A Scottish Infantry sword, by C. Boyton & Son, 1910–36, 41in (104cm) long.
£165–185 / €230–260
$260–290 ⊞ ABCM

A German Airforce officer's dress sword, 1939–45, 36in (91.5cm) long.
£430–480 / €610–680
$690–770 ⊞ ChM

A German Third Reich 'Radman's' dagger, by R. J. Solinger, with chrome-plated handle and antler horn grip, the Roman-style blade inscribed 'Arbeit adelt', c1940, 15½in (39.5cm) long, with chromed-metal sheath.
£360–430 / €510–610
$580–690 ↗ G(L)

A fighting knife, by Sykes Fairburn, pattern 2, 1942, 12in (30.5cm) long, with leather sheath.
£200–220 / €280–310
$320–350 ⊞ ABCM

Firearms

A single barrel flintlock sporting gun, by Walker of Darlington, the walnut halfstock with crosshatched neck grip, fitted with a ramrod, steel lock with maker's name, c1775, barrel 28in (71cm) long.
£450–540 / €640–770
$720–860 ✗ PF

A flintlock duelling pistol, by Fowler, Dublin, the walnut halfstock with inlaid silver label, wooden ramrod, Irish, late 18thC, 14in (35.5cm) long.
£500–600 / €710–850
$800–960 ✗ PF

▶ **An inlaid flintlock pistol,** Continental, c1800, 10in (25.5cm) long.
£260–290 / €370–410
$420–460 ⊞ ABCM

A flintlock boxlock brass-framed *éprouvette*, by Jones of Wrexham, with calibrated brass wheel and walnut slab side butt, 1832–50, 6in (15cm) long.
£280–330 / €400–470
$450–530 ✗ PF

A .577 Volunteer two band Enfield percussion rifle, with walnut fullstock and steel mounts, sling swivels, steel ramrod, the lock stamped 'Reeves, London & Toledo Works, Birmm', 1855, 48¾in (124cm) long.
£500–600 / €710–850
$800–960 ✗ WAL

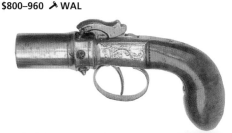

A six-shot .28 self-cocking percussion pepperbox revolver, with projecting nipples, engraved frame and walnut butt, 1855, 7¼in (18.5cm) long.
£180–210 / €260–300
$290–340 ✗ WAL

A Robert's Patent single-shot breech-loading military rifle, with walnut fullstock, two folding leaf rearsights, steel mounts, sling swivels, stamped, American, 1860s, 56in (142cm) long.
£500–600 / €710–850
$800–960 ✗ WAL

Trench Art

Trench Art is the name given to objects predominantly associated with World War I (1914–18) and manufactured by both soldiers and civilians from bullets, shrapnel and miscellaneous battlefield debris. In addition to metal items such as cigarette cases, lighters, ashtrays and decorated shell cases, another softer form of Trench Art is embroidered and painted textiles. Also produced by civilians and soldiers (needlework was considered good therapy for those convalescing in nursing homes), these textiles range from silk postcards to large pictures and wall hangings, often featuring regimental crests.

Trench Art was also made from other materials including wood and bone. Created by a whole range of people from front line fighters to grieving widows and prisoners of war – not forgetting a thriving local industry manufacturing souvenirs for visiting soldiers to take back to their loved ones – Trench Art provides a fascinating and intimate insight into the Great War.

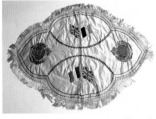

A copper box, made from bullets from the Busaco battlefield, Portuguese, c1910, 5in (13cm) wide.
£110–125 / €155–175 $175–200 ⊞ MB
This is an example of pre-WWI Trench Art using bullets from an early 19th-century battle to create a piece of early 20th-century memorabilia.

A Royal Engineer's embroidered silk tray cloth, 1914–18, 18 x 25in (45.5 x 63.5cm).
£30–35 / €45–50 $50–55 ⊞ J&S

A Royal Berkshire woolwork crest, framed, 1914–18, 10 x 12in (25.5 x 30.5cm).
£40–45 / €55–65 $65–75 ⊞ COB

◄ **A brass and copper lighter,** in the form of a lady's boot, 1915, 3¼in (8.5cm) high.
£55–65 / €80–95 $90–105 ⊞ NLS

> Items in the Trench Art section have been arranged in date order.

► **A copper and steel lighter,** in the form of a lady's leg, 1915, 4in (10cm) high.
£150–165 / €210–230 $240–270 ⊞ NLS

A copper lighter, in the form of a face, engraved 'Nach Paris', 1915, 2½in (6.5cm) high.
£130–145 / €185–210 $200–230 ⊞ NLS
The face on this lighter is sad on one side and smiling on the other.

► **A Royal Fleet Auxillary embroidered silk postcard,** 1916.
£10–15 / €14–20 $16–24 ⊞ JMC

A Royal Army Medical Corps embroidered silk souvenir of Palestine, framed, 1939–45, 16 x 13in (40.5 x 33cm).
£12–16 / €17–23 $20–26 ⊞ J&S

Money Boxes

Known as money banks in the USA, pottery money boxes have been produced since ancient times, when coins were often hidden in sealed terracotta jars that could be buried in the ground. Decorative money boxes, such as the piggy bank, were manufactured in Europe from the 17th century, the fat pig being a traditional symbol of wealth. Money boxes were also made from other materials, including metal and wood and the Victorian period saw the development of the cast-iron money bank. This was a favourite material in America where 'still' (non-animated) and 'mechanical' banks of huge ingenuity were produced in large numbers from the 1870s to the 1920s. Leading manufacturers included the J. & E. Stevens Co of Cromwell, Connecticut and the Shepard Hardware Co. Designs were often humorous and subjects ranged from sporting to military scenes, from animals to black characters and political figures. Mechanisms worked either by the weight of a coin or the pulling of a lever and a popular subject was a soldier shooting a coin into a slot.

In the UK, cast-iron banks were made by the firm of John Harper & Co, and bank buildings were a popular design for 'still' money boxes. During the interwar period, tinplate was a much used material. Germany produced some particularly fine examples including the mechanical sailor shown in this section, which salutes when the coin is dropped in. More commonplace designs include the red pillar box money bank, which was manufactured in Britain from the Victorian period onwards, the cipher on the front changing along with the ruling monarch.

Mechanical cast-iron banks from the 19th and 20th centuries can fetch large sums, but buyers should beware of reproductions. Animated tinplate banks from the 1920s and '30s are also very collectable, depending on condition. Collectors should also look out for more recent novelty and battery-operated designs such as Mr Money, the plastic robot produced by Tomy in 1987. Still to be found at boot fairs and garage sales, objects such as these are becoming increasingly sought after.

A Staffordshire money box, in the form of a man's head, early 19thC.
£60–70 / €85–100
$95–110 ↗ BWL

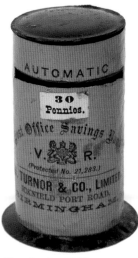

A Victorian Post Office Savings paper and tinplate money box.
£65–75 / €90–105
$105–120 ⊞ HUX

A Mauchline ware money box, decorated with a clock and the church of Llanbadarn Fawr, nr Aberystwyth, 19thC, 4in (10cm) high.
£20–25 / €30–35
$35–40 ⊞ VBo

A cast-iron money box, by J. & E. Stevens, American, 1879, 10in (25.5cm) wide.
£320–350 / €450–500
$510–560 ⊞ HAL

▶ **A cast-iron Wimbledon money box,** by John Harper, 1892, 12in (30.5cm) wide.
£1,600–1,800
€2,250–2,550
$2,550–2,900 ⊞ HAL

A cast-iron Creedmore mechanical money bank, by J. & E. Stevens, American, late 19thC, 10in (25.5cm) wide.
£300–350 / €430–490
$480–560 ⊞ HAL
Possibly the first example of a man shooting at a target, the Creedmore money bank was devised in 1877 for J. & E. Stevens by James H. Bowen, one of the most talented designers of mechanical banks.

A cast-iron mechanical money bank, by J. & E. Stevens, 'Paddy and the Pig', American, 1892, 8in (20.5cm) high.
£630–700 / €890–990
$1,000–1,100 ⊞ HAL

A majolica money box, in the form of a child's head, Austrian, c1900, 4in (10cm) high.
£45–50 / €65–70
$75–80 ⊞ HAL

A mechanical money box, in the form of Jonah and the whale, coin trap missing, late 19thC, 10¼in (25.5cm) wide.
£2,200–2,650 / €3,100–3,750
$3,500–4,250 ⚒ JDJ

◀ **A spelter money box,** in the form of a dog with a pipe, German, c1905, 4in (10cm) high.
£270–300 / €380–420
$430–480 ⊞ HAL

▶ **A spelter money box,** in the form of a dog, cat and kennel, German, c1920, 3in (7.5cm) high.
£300–350 / €430–500
$480–560 ⊞ HAL

A cast-iron money box, by John Harper, 'Transvaal', c1895, 6¼in (16cm) high.
£320–380 / €450–540
$510–610 ⚒ G(L)

A cast-iron money box, by John Harper, 'County Bank', 1892, 5in (112.5cm) wide.
£100–120 / €140–170
$160–190 ⊞ HAL

A ceramic money box, in the form of a student pig, Austrian, c1900, 4in (10cm) wide.
£45–50 / €65–70
$75–80 ⊞ HAL

A mechanical money box, in the form of a magician, late 19thC, 8¼in (21cm) high.
£2,700–3,250 / €3,850–4,600
$4,300–5,200 ⚒ JDJ

A cast-iron money box, in the form of a bank building, c1910, 7in (18cm) high.
£140–160 / €200–230
$230–260 ⊞ MFB

A tinplate money box, in the form of a post box, 1915, 3in (7.5cm) high.
£50–60 / €70–85
$80–95 ⊞ HUX

An Elastolin money box, in the form of a camel, German, c1920, 4in (10cm) high.
£60–70 / €85–100
$95–110 ⊞ HAL

A mechanical money box, in the form of Uncle Sam, American, 1920s, 11½in (29cm) high.
£1,050–1,250
€1,500–1,800
$1,700–2,000 ⚒ JDJ

▶ **A Wemyss money box,** by Jan Plichta, in the form of a pig, decorated with thistles, signed, c1930, 6in (15cm) high.
£540–600
€770–850
$860–960 ⊞ CCs

◀ **A tinplate money box,** in the form of a saluting sailor, German, c1920, 7in (28cm) high.
£450–500 / €640–710
$720–800 ⊞ HAL

A Royal Arsenal Co-Operative Society tinplate money box, 1925, 4⅞in (12cm) high.
£35–40 / €50–55
$55–65 ⊞ HUX

A Post Office tinplate money box, 1950s, 5in (12.5cm) high.
£8–12 / €11–17
$12–18 ⊞ RTT

◀ **A plastic money box,** by Tomy, 'Mr Money', 1987.
£30–35
€45–50
$50–55 ⊞ HUX

Newspapers & Magazines

Bristol Times and Felix Farley's Bristol Journal, 16 April 1958, 25 x 18in (63.5 x 45.5cm).
£25–30 / €35–40
$40–50 ⊞ J&S

The Westminster Journal and Old British Spy, 22–29 January 1803, 18 x 14in (45.5 x 35.5cm).
£20–25 / €28–35
$32–40 ⊞ HaR

The Times, 17 December 1812, 16in (40.5cm) wide.
£11–15 / €16–20
$18–24 ⊞ TOP

▶ **Union Jack,** No. 1343, July 1929, 11 x 7in (28 x 18cm).
£8–12 / €11–17
$12–18 ⊞ ADD

The Daily Mirror, Lord Kitchener Memorial Number, 1916, 21 x 15in (53.5 x 38cm).
£11–15 / €16–20
$18–24 ⊞ COB

Les Modes de la Femme en France, 1923, 12½ x 9½in (32 x 24cm).
£6–10 / €8–14
$10–16 ⊞ RTT

Vogue, ten issues including Paris Fashion and Pattern Book, 1932, 11½ x 8¾in (29 x 22cm).
£180–200 / €260–280
$290–320 ⚘ ONS

◀ **Detective Weekly,** No. 371, March 1940, 12 x 10in (30.5 x 25.5cm).
£4–8 / €6–11
$6–12 ⊞ ADD

The New Yorker, 1942, 12 x 9in (30.5 x 23cm).
£3–7 / €4–10
$5–11 ⊞ RTT

Gourmet, 1950, 11½ x 8½in (29 x 21.5cm).
£3–7 / €4–10
$5–11 ⊞ RTT

Vogue, 1953, 11½ x 8¾in (29 x 22cm).
£15–20/ €20–25
$25–30 ⊞ RTT

Woman's Day, 27 June 1959, 13 x 10in (33 x 25.5cm).
£1–5 / €2–7
$3–8 ⊞ RTT

Noddy

Noddy was created by Enid Mary Blyton (1897–1968), one of the most successful children's authors of the 20th century. Her first book appeared in 1922 and by the time of her death she had produced over 400 titles – she could famously complete a book in a five-day working week.

Noddy goes to Toyland was published in 1949, with text by Blyton and illustrations by the Dutch artist Harmsen van der Beek. The stories of little Noddy and his friends Big Ears, Mr Plod, the golly and all the other inhabitants of Toyland were a huge success and the *Evening Standard* newspaper commissioned a Noddy cartoon strip. In 1954 Enid produced a Noddy Christmas Pantomime, written with her usual speed in just two weeks and, in 1955, the Noddy puppet show appeared on television.

Harmsen van der Beek died of a heart attack in 1953, and other illustrators took over the stories. Over 150 Noddy books were produced, along with a vast amount of merchandise. Noddy survived accusations of racism, prejudice and political incorrectness and remains a children's favourite. In 1998 he appeared in a 40-part series on US television and, in 2002, Channel 5 launched a new Noddy series.

Harmsen van der Beek, an illustration from *Noddy and Naughty Gobby*, 1948–53, 3in (9.5cm) square.
£315–350 / €450–500
$500–480 ⊞ BRG

A Noddy and Big Ears composition salt and pepper, on a wooden base, 1950s, 5in (12.5cm) high.
£115–125 / €165–175
$185–200 ⊞ HYP

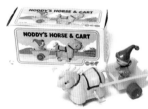

A Noddy figure, by Marx Toys, 1950s–60s, 6in (15cm) high, in original box.
£90–100 / €125–140
$145–160 ⊞ BBe

◀ **A plastic clockwork Noddy Horse and Cart,** by Marx Toys, 1976, 7in (18cm) long.
£55–65 / €80–90
$90–105 ⊞ UD

A Noddy plastic pinball game, Spanish, c1970, in original packaging, 17 x 10in (43 x 25.5cm).
£25–30 / €35–40
$40–50 ⊞ HarC

A plastic clockwork Noddy car, by Dekkertoys, 1990s, 8in (20.5cm) long.
£20–25 / €28–35
$32–40 ⊞ CBB

◀ **Enid Blyton,** *Noddy*, the contents of a Sotheby's Catalogue, London, 1997, 10½ x 8½in (26.5 x 21.5cm).
£30–35 / €40–50
$50–55 ⊞ PICC

Paper Money

A Bank of Wellington Salop branch £1 note, 1815.
£170–200 / €240–280
$270–320 ✦ DNW

A Yeovil Old Bank £1 note, 1820.
£100–120 / €140–170
$160–190 ⊞ NAR

A Rhode Island 20 shillings note, 1786.
£70–80 / €100–115
$115–130 ⊞ NAR

▶ A Jersey Bank £1 note, 1843.
£1,350–1,500
€1,900–2,150
$2,150–2,400 ⊞ WP

A Siege of Mafeking £1 note, 1900.
£550–600 / €780–850
$880–960 ⊞ NAR
On several occasions during times of siege, paper money was produced as a replacement for coins. A famous example was in Africa when the town of Mafeking was besieged by the Boers from 16 October 1899 to 17 May 1900. Brevet-Colonel Robert Baden-Powell (later founder of the Boy Scouts movement) was a commander of the small British garrison defending the town. As coins ran out at the Standard Bank, Baden-Powell issued paper notes which, the printed legend stated, could be exchanged for cash at the Standard Bank 'on the resumption of Civil Law'. Baden-Powell himself provided the designs for the 10 shillings and £1 notes which featured soldiers manning guns. The 10 shillings note, he recalled, was printed by cutting a croquet head in half and using it to make a woodcut. Only 638 of these £1 notes were printed and Mafeking notes are sought after by collectors today.

A Bank of England Portsmouth branch £5 note, payable to Mr Matthew Marshall, 1849.
£1,800–2,000 / €2,550–2,850
$2,800–3,200 ✦ B
This note is believed to be the earliest Portsmouth branch note to be offered to the collectors' market, and only the second from the 19th century.

A Siege of Khartoum note, signed by General Gordon, 1884.
£290–320 / €400–450
$460–510 ⊞ NAR

A Banque de Syrie 50 piastres note, specimen with handwritten numbers and date, 1919.
£130–150 / €185–210
$210–240 ✦ DNW

A 10 shillings Treasury note, signed by John Bradbury, 1914.
£90–100 / €130–140
$145–160 ⊞ NAR

▶ A £1 Treasury note, signed by Fisher, 1920s.
£25–30 / €35–40
$40–50 ⊞ NAR

A United States of America gold $10 note, 1922.
£100–120 / €140–170
$160–190 ⊞ NAR

A Reichsbank 1 billion marks note, German, 1923.
£20–25 / €28–35
$32–40 ⊞ NAR
After WWI, Germany was plunged into economic crisis and by 1921 the reichsmark had fallen to one thousandth of its 1918 value. Inflation and financial chaos reigned. A loaf of bread or a box of matches cost millions of marks and workmen had to carry their daily wages home in suitcases and laundry baskets. The Reichsbank printed notes of larger and larger denominations and in January 1922 they introduced a 10,000 mark note. In 1923 notes were being produced in millions and even billions, culminating with the production of a 100 billion mark note on 15 February 1924. That same year Germany repudiated its national debt and introduced a new system of money, 'renten-marks', which were guaranteed by mortgage bonds and brought the extreme financial crisis to an end.

A Bank of England Manchester branch £5 note, signed by Harvey, 1923.
£270–300 / €380–420
$430–480 ⊞ NAR

A Bank of England 10 shillings note, signed by Mahon, 1928.
£170–200 / €240–270
$280–320 ⊞ NAR

▶ A Bank of Ireland Belfast branch £1 note, 1933.
£24–28 / €34–40
$38–45 ⊞ WP

A Bank of England £1 note, signed by Mahon, 1928.
£100–120 / €140–170
$160–190 ⊞ NAR

A National Bank Dublin branch £5 note, 1929.
£350–420 / €500–600
$560–670 ✗ JAd

A Government of Barbados $1 note, 1939.
£65–75 / €90–105
$105–120 ✗ DNW

A Bank of England blue wartime £1 note, signed by Peppiatt, 1940–48.
£8–12 / €11–17
$12–18 ⊞ NAR

A Reichsbank 5 marks note, 1942.
£1–5 / €2–7
$3–8 ⊞ NAR

A British Military Authority 1 shilling note, 1943.
£11–15 / €16–20
$18–24 ⊞ NAR

A British Armed Forces 5 shillings note, 2nd series,
1950–60.
£8–12 / €11–17
$12–18 ⊞ NAR

**A Central Bank of Ireland 10
shillings note,** 1960s.
£11–15 / €16–20
$18–24 ⊞ NAR

A Bank of England £5 note,
signed by O'Brien, 1960.
£45–50 / €60–70
$70–80 ⊞ NAR

**A Belfast Banking Co £100
note,** 1963.
£160–180 / €230–260
$260–290 ⊞ NAR

A Bank of England £10 note,
signed by Hollom, 1960s.
£20–25 / €28–35
$32–40 ⊞ NAR

**A Government of Seychelles 50
rupees note,** 1972.
£310–350 / €440–500
$500–560 ⊞ NAR

**A Central Bank of Ireland 1 punt
note,** 1979.
£16–20 / €22–28
$26–32 ⊞ WP

**▶ A Bank of England
£5 note,** Somerset
signature missing, 1980s.
£90–100 / €125–140
$145–160 ⊞ NAR
Error notes are
worthless as legal
tender but are valued
by collectors.

A Bank of England £20 note,
signed by Somerset, 1984.
£360–400 / €510–570
$580–640 ⊞ NAR
This bank note is particularly
desirable to collectors because
of its low serial number – OIA
000099.

Penknives

Although the term penknife is now applied to folding and pocket knives of every variety, the name originates from the knives used by scribes in the 18th century to sharpen the points of quill nibs and scratch out mistakes from the vellum or thick grade paper used at that time.

Folding knives have a long history. They were used by the Romans who produced knives with decorative metal handles made from bone, ivory and bronze. The 1600s saw the invention of puzzle knives, with curious mechanisms for closing the blade, and in the late 17th century folding knives and forks were made for well-to-do travellers. Silver blades were traditionally favoured for fruit knives, since the metal is resistant to fruit acids and many decorative examples were produced in the 18th and 19th centuries, often with mother-of-pearl handles. The fad for multi-bladed knives took off in the 19th century. In 1822, the firm of Rodgers celebrated their Royal Appointment to George IV by creating a knife with 1822 blades, one for each Christian year.

The folding knives shown here date from the late 18th century onwards and reflect some of the different types available. Values depend on age, design and condition. Complex mechanisms and the number of blades will affect prices and so will a decorative haft, featuring, for example, a good advertising or sporting subject.

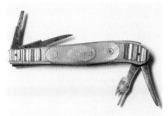

A mother-of-pearl and brass quill cutter, c1790, 4in (10cm) long.
£400–450 / €570–640
$640–720 ⊞ ANGE

A Rodgers ivory and nickel quill cutter with knife, 19thC, 4in (10cm) long.
£200–220 / €280–310
$320–350 ⊞ PPL

A white metal penknife, with advertising haft, German, c1880, 3in (7.5cm) long.
£100–110 / €140–155
$160–175 ⊞ NEG

A bone-handled penknife, with gardening tools, French, c1800, 5in (12.5cm) long.
£150–165 / €210–230
$240–270 ⊞ ANGE

A mother-of-pearl and silver folding fruit knife, c1882, 3½in (9cm) long.
£45–50 / €65–75
$75–85 ⊞ NEG

A Bakelite penknife, advertising Beehive Brandy, 1930, 2in (5cm) long.
£40–45 / €55–65
$65–75 ⊞ NLS

A tortoiseshell penknife, with 50 blades, c1870, 4½in (11.5cm) long.
£4,500–5,000 / €6,400–7,100
$7,200–8,000 ⊞ ANGE

An ivoreen folding knife, German, c1880, 3in (7.5cm) long.
£11–15 / €16–20
$18–24 ⊞ NEG

A brass penknife, the haft decorated with cats, 1930, 3in (7.5cm) long.
£75–85 / €105–120
$120–135 ⊞ NLS

Photography

A quarter plate daguerrotype,
c1850, 3½ x 4¾in (9 x 12cm).
£900–1,000 / €1,250–1,400
$1,450–1,600 ⊞ APC

A photograph album, containing
50 photographs of Italy, c1880,
11¾ x 15¾in (30 x 40cm).
£270–300 / €380–420
$430–480 ⊞ APC

**A Victorian leather-bound
photograph album,** embossed,
11 x 9in (30 x 23cm).
£60–70 / €85–100
$95–110 ⊞ TOP

A Victorian cabinet portrait,
showing a group dressed in 18thC
costume, 7 x 10in (18 x 25.5cm).
£4–8 / €5–11
$7–13 ⊞ J&S

◀ **A photograph of the Royal
Navy at Chatham,** 1914–18,
8 x 10in (20.5 x 25.5cm).
£6–10 / €8–14
$10–16 ⊞ J&S

**A photograph of a girl with a
pram and china doll,** late 19thC,
6 x 4in (15 x 10cm).
£12–16 / €17–22
$18–26 ⊞ RUSS

A photograph album, published
by H. F. & Ph. F. Reemtsma,
containing 113 photographs of
the Japanese participation of the XI
Olympiad in Berlin, with printed text,
1936, 14¼ x 18in (36 x 45.5cm).
£920–1,100 / €1,300–1,550
$1,500–1,750 ➶ F&C

◀ **Terence Donovan,** a gelatin
silver photograph, inscribed 'Ritz
1/5', signed, 1985, 15 x 12¼in
(38 x 31cm).
£170–200 / €240–280
$270–320 ➶ BBA

Henry Clarke, a gelatin silver
photograph of a woman on a street,
signed, minor damage, American,
c1950s, 14½ x 11½in (36.5 x 29cm).
£600–720 / €850–1,000
$960–1,150 ➶ BBA

Condition

The condition is absolutely
vital when assessing the
value of a collectable.
Damaged pieces on the
whole appreciate much less
than perfect examples.
However a rare desirable
piece may command a high
price even when damaged.

David Bailey, a gelatin silver photograph, inscribed 'Flower London', one of 11, signed, 1987, 11¾ x 7¼in (30 x 19.5cm).
£260–310 / €370–440
$420–500 ↗ BBA

Edward Maxey, a gelatin silver photograph, entitled 'Melody', numbered 1/10, signed and dated, 1988, 23¾ x 19¼in (60 x 50cm).
£400–480 / €570–680
$640–770 ↗ BBA

Karl Lagerfeld, a gelatin silver photograph, frontispiece for the Lagerfeld Collection Spring/Summer, signed, 1990, 20½ x 17in (52 x 43cm).
£400–480 / €570–680
$640–770 ↗ BBA

Photograph Frames

A Victorian silver-plated photograph frame, inset with coloured stones, 4in (10cm) high.
£155–175 / €220–250
$250–280 ⊞ HaH

A Victorian ormolu easel photograph frame, decorated with birds and foliage, 7in (18cm) high.
£90–105 / €125–150
$145–170 ↗ DA

A gutta-percha photograph frame, French, c1860–70, 11in (28cm) high.
£300–340 / €430–480
$480–540 ⊞ HaH
Gutta-percha is a type of rubber obtained from the gutta-percha tree, native to Malaysia.

◄ **A Victorian diamanté and silver photograph frame,** 3in (7.5cm) high.
£200–230 / €280–320
$320–370 ⊞ HaH

► **A Tunbridge ware photograph frame,** c1880, 6 x 5in (15 x 12.5cm).
£80–90 / €115–130
$130–145 ⊞ MB

An Islamic-style brass photograph frame, in the form of a gate, c1880, 10in (25.5cm) high.
**£850–950 / € 1,200–1,350
$1,350–1,550 ⊞ HaH**

A Victorian velvet and brass photograph frame, 12in (30.5cm) high.
**£60–70 / € 85–100
$95–110 ⊞ HaH**

An inlaid wood photograph frame, Italian, c1900, 10in (25.5cm) high.
**£180–200 / € 250–280
$290–320 ⊞ HaH**

A carved mahogany photograph frame, c1900, 12 x 10in (30.5 x 25.5cm).
**£60–70 / € 85–100
$95–110 ⊞ AMR**

A tooled leather photograph frame, c1910–20, 13 x 10in (33 x 25.5cm).
**£85–95 / € 120–135
$135–150 ⊞ MCa**

A silver and wirework photograph frame, with a wooden back, 1918, 5in (12.5cm) high.
**£160–180 / € 230–260
$260–290 ⊞ EXC**

◀ **A silver photograph frame,** Birmingham 1919, 7in (18cm) high.
**£65–75 / € 90–105
$105–120 ⚒ G(L)**

A mirrored-glass photograph frame, with Art Deco decoration, 1930s, 4½in (11.5cm) high.
**£100–115 / € 140–160
$160–185 ⊞ HaH**

A chrome photograph frame, 1930s, 10in (25.5cm) high.
**£80–90 / € 115–130
$130–145 ⊞ BEV**

Pigs

Many people collect objects based on a favourite animal and this year we devote a section to the pig. The pig has a chequered history in terms of symbolism. It was held sacred by the ancient Cretans because Jupiter was suckled by a sow, but was also a sacrificial animal in many cultures. Pork is considered unclean by Jews and Muslims but was a favourite food at Christian festivals. The custom of fattening up pigs for a feast is one of the origins given for the development of the piggy bank, which you stuff with money. Pigs have been used as symbols of wealth, and in medieval art they often represented lust and gluttony. The word pig is still a term of abuse for the greedy, the slovenly, for male chauvinists, and for the police (the description originating in Victorian England, but popularized in 20th-century America).

Pigs appear in many nursery rhymes and famous pigs in film and literature include *Babe*, Wilbur in *Charlotte's Web*, Beatrix Potter's Pigling Bland and Napoleon from George Orwell's *Animal Farm*. This section also includes objects relating to Pinky and Perky, Britain's most famous pig puppets, created in 1956 by Czech couple Jan and Vlasta Dalibor, who were granted political asylum in the UK at the height of the Cold War. Pinky and Perky's TV series ran from 1957 to 1972 in the UK and was transmitted around the world. They released some 16 albums, appeared live (as much as puppets can) at the London Palladium and in Las Vegas, and guests on their show ranged from Frank Sinatra to the Beatles. But no star, porcine or human, can hold top position for ever. In 1969, Jim Henson's Muppets first appeared on *Sesame Street*, subsequently graduating to their own show and the glamorous Miss Piggy became the most famous pig in the world.

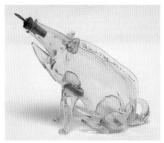

A glass wild boar gin flask,
19thC, 11in (28cm) long.
£580–640 / €820–910
$930–1,000 ⊞ JAS
This is a rare piece, hence its value. Pairs are rarer still.

A Belleek porcelain pig, Second Period, 1891–1926, 3in (7.5cm) long.
£200–220 / €280–310
$320–350 ⊞ WAA

A Bristol glass pig gin jug, c1900, 9in (23cm) long.
£400–440 / €570–620
$640–700 ⊞ JAS
Pigs and pig jugs were made as friggars – fanciful items produced by a glassmaker in his own time – generally with the left-over molten glass remaining in the pot at the end of the working day. In the USA, these friggars are also known as 'off-hand glass'.

A Royal Dux porcelain pig, 20thC, 4in (10cm) long.
£40–45 / €55–65
$65–75 ⊞ TAC

A Swan pig, with Newcastle-on-Tyne crest, 1900–25, 2½in (6.5cm) high.
£25–30 / €35–40
$40–50 ⊞ JMC

▶ **A silver pig pincushion,**
Birmingham 1913, 2in (5cm) long.
£175–195 / €250–280
$280–310 ⊞ VK

An Arcadian pig, with Newquay crest, 1900–30, 2½in (6.5cm) high.
£22–26 / €30–36
$36–42 ⊞ JMC

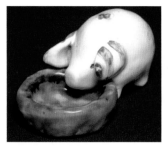

A Denby pottery pig ashtray,
c1936, 2in (5cm) high.
£220–250 / €310–350
$350–400 ⊞ KES

A Wemyss pig, by Jan Plichta,
1938, 9½in (24cm) long.
£410–450 / €580–640
$650–720 ⊞ CCs

A Wemyss pig hat pin holder, by
Jan Plichta, 1930s, 4in (10cm) long.
£110–120 / €155–170
$175–190 ⊞ CCs

A 9ct gold pig charm, c1940,
1in (2.5cm) long.
£65–75 / €95–105
$105–120 ⊞ NEG

▶ **Enid Blyton,** *Polly Piglet,*
illustrated by Eileen Soper,
published by Brockhampton Press,
c1955, 5in (12.5cm) square.
£12–16 / €17–23
$18–26 ⊞ J&J

Two silver pig charms, c1960,
larger 1in (2.5cm) long.
£11–15 / €16–20
$18–24 each ⊞ NEG

**Three Schuco felt-covered
mechanical pig musicians,**
playing the flute, drum and violin,
maker's stamp on feet, 1950s,
4¼in (11cm) high.
£340–410 / €480–580
$540–650 ⋟ BR

Two Beswick models of pigs,
designed by Arthur Gredington,
model Nos. 1452A and 1453A,
1956–98, 2¾in (7cm) high.
£60–70 / €85–100
$95–110 ⋟ BBR

Helen Haywood, *Peter Tiggywig
Goes Camping,* by Helen Haywood,
published by Nelson, c1950,
6 x 5in (15 x 12.5cm).
£2–6 / €3–8
$4–10 ⊞ J&J

▶ **A pair of Pinky and Perky
puppets,** by Pelham Puppets,
1960s, 10in (25.5cm) high.
£65–70 / €90–100
$100–110 ⊞ J&J

**Four Pinky and Perky handker-
chiefs,** 1964, 9 x 8in (23 x 20.5cm).
£6–10 / €8–14
$10–16 ⊞ J&J

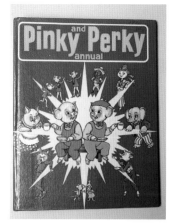

Pinky and Perky Annual, published by Purnell, 1974, 11 x 9in (28 x 23cm).
£3–7 / €4–10
$5–11 ⊞ J&J

Four National Westminster Bank ceramic pigs, Sir Nathaniel Westminster, Maxwell, Annabel and Baby Woody, c1983, Sir Nathaniel 8in (20.5cm) high.
£85–100 / €120–140
$135–160 ⚲ L&E

A *Muppet Show* jigsaw puzzle, by Hope Hestair products, 1997, 6 x 10in (15 x 25.5cm).
£1–5 / €2–7
$3–8 ⊞ J&J

National Westminster Bank pigs

In 1983, the National Westminster Bank in the UK devised a family of ceramic pigs made by Wade to encourage children to invest. If an account was opened with £3 / €4 / $5, Baby Woody was awarded. After six months, if the account contained £25 / €35 / $40, Annabel was received. After one year, and if there was £50 / €70 / $80 in the account, Maxwell appeared; after 18 months and with £75 / €105 / $120, Lady Hilary, and finally, after two years and if at least £100 / €140 / $160 had been saved, Sir Nathaniel Westminster. The offer ended in 1988. Comparatively few children collected the full set and so Sir Nathaniel is the rarest figure.

Maxwell was rather unfortunately named after tycoon Sir Robert Maxwell. Following his death and disgrace, National Westminster Bank produced fewer of these pigs, thus making them more collectable today. In 1999, Wade produced a further pig for the series, Cousin Wesley, designed to promote a £1,000 / €1,400 / $1,600 childrens' savings bond. This was not very successful, making these pigs much sought-after by collectors (beware of fakes). Twenty-five gold Woodys were also produced for National Westminster directors, but these very rarely come on the market.

Some National Westminster pigs were made by another pottery company but it is the Wade examples that are the most desirable, so look out for the incised Wade logo on the base.

A Beswick model of Beatrix Potter's Yock-Yock in the Tub, designed by David Lyttleton, c1986, 3in (7.5cm) high.
£50–60 / €70–85
$80–95 ⚲ BBR

A porcelain pig cruet set, 20thC, 3in (7.5cm) high.
£4–8 / €6–11
$7–12 ⊞ BAC

◄ **A Wemyss model of a pig,** tail damaged, 20thC, 6¼in (16cm) wide.
£200–240 / €280–340
$320–380 ⚲ EH

A porcelain pig teapot, by Otagiri, 1980s, 8in (20.5cm) high.
£6–10 / €8–14
$10–16 ⊞ BAC

A Wade model of Truffles the Pig, from the Pocket Pals series, 2000, 2½in (6.5cm) long.
£2–6 / €3–8
$4–10 ⊞ JMC

Police

A police iron shackle, mid-18thC, 4in (10cm) diam.
£30–35 / €40–50
$50–55 ⊞ KEY

A pair of policeman's iron hand-cuffs, mid-18thC, 5in (12.5cm) wide.
£45–50 / €65–70
$75–80 ⊞ KEY

A miner's-style policeman's brass tobacco box, inscribed 'P.C. Dan Davies, Police Station, Pennal, N.W.', 1880, 3in (7.5cm) wide.
£80–90 / €110–125
$130–145 ⊞ MB

A policeman's painted truncheon, c1835, 26in (66cm) long.
£130–150 / €185–210
$210–240 ⊞ HUM

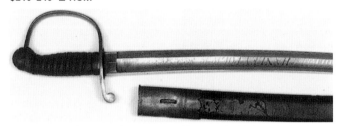

A Victorian police sword, by Parker Field & Son, the blade etched with foliage, a coat-of-arms and 'Borough of Hanley Police', in a steel-mounted leather scabbard, grip wire damaged, blade 22in (56cm) long.
£420–500 / €600–710
$670–800 ⚔ WAL

A Special Constabulary truncheon, 1860, 18in (45.5cm) long.
£65–75 / €90–105
$105–120 ⊞ MDL

A police lamp, by Smith & Sons, 'The Wooden Lantern', 1930s, 6in (15cm) high.
£55–65 / €80–95
$90–105 ⊞ GAC

◄ **A policeman's leather-on-cork motorcycle helmet,** 1948.
£55–65 / €80–95
$90–105 ⊞ UCO

► **An Isle of Man Police helmet,** mounted on a wooden plaque, c1950, 9in (23cm) wide.
£70–80 / €100–115
$115–130 ⊞ Q&C

A police helmet, 1939–45.
£110–125 / €155–175
$175–200 ⊞ GBM

Postcards

The first British postcard was mailed on 1 October 1870. The plain buff card came ready-printed with a halfpenny stamp (half the price of a letter). Initially, the Post Office stipulated that illustrations could only appear on the message side of the card, not on the address side but once regulations were lifted in 1902, the picture postcard became an instant craze and a favourite Edwardian collectable.

Produced in vast numbers, vintage postcards are still very affordable today with a huge range of material available for well under £5 / €7 / $8. For many collectors, the Edwardian period is still the golden age of the postcard – look out for Art Nouveau-style illustrations, interesting topographical views, transport scenes and photographic images of disasters, train crashes, shipwrecks etc. Postcards depicting anything connected with the *Titanic* make high prices. Comic postcards were another favourite throughout the 20th century, featuring famous artists such as cat painter Louis Wain (1860–1939), Donald McGill (1875–1962), master of the saucy seaside picture and Mabel Lucie Attwell (1879–1964), whose chubby-cheeked infants appeared on literally millions of cards from 1911 onwards.

A souvenir postcard, printed in Germany, c1897.
£15–20 / €22–28
$24–32 ⊞ JMC

A souvenir postcard, published by Raphael Tuck & Sons, Atlantic City, from the Views of US Cities series, No. 5077, 1900–05.
£4–8 / €5–11
$6–12 ⊞ JMC

A Royal Navy postcard, c1900.
£8–12 / €11–17
$12–18 ⊞ JMC

A souvenir postcard, by Florence Robinson, published by Raphael Tuck & Sons, New York, from the Views of US Cities series, No. 5055, 1900–05.
£4–8 / €5–11
$6–12 ⊞ JMC

▶ **A Cupid's Alphabet 'M' postcard,** from the Tuck Art series, No. 6114, c1906.
£6–10 / €8–14
$10–16 ⊞ JMC

A photographic postcard, depicting the village blacksmith, 1906–10.
£10–14 / €14–20
$16–22 ⚚ DAL

A photographic postcard, depicting suffragettes Mrs Pankhurst and her daughter Christabel, early 20thC.
£40–50 / €55–70
$65–80 ⚚ VS

A postcard, depicting the Cornish Riviera Express, Dawlish, Devon, 1909.
£2–6 / €3–8
$4–10 ⊞ S&D

A photographic postcard, depicting the Liverpool Strike of 1911.
£40–50 / €55–70
$65–80 ⚚ VS

A photographic postcard, depicting a charabanc, 1914.
£1–5 / €2–7
$3–8 ⊞ S&D

A photographic postcard, depicting the German Empress, c1908.
£1–5 / €2–7
$3–8 ⊞ S&D

A Milkmaid Condensed Milk advertising postcard, published by Raphael Tuck & Sons, from the Collectors Postcard series, No. 1510, 1910.
£11–15 / €16–20
$18–24 ⊞ S&D

A photographic postcard, featuring movie stars Ellaline Thorne and Jack Leopold, 1920.
£1–5 / €2–7
$3–8 ⊞ S&D

A photographic postcard, published by L. & N. W. R., depicting a single-horse family omnibus, c1908.
£11–15 / €16–20
$18–24 ⊞ S&D

A Maidstone Horse Repository postcard, depicting a polo pony, the reverse advertising an auction of '65 Valuable Horses' on 7 March 1911.
£8–12 / €11–17
$12–18 ⊞ JMC

▶ A photographic postcard, depicting 'The Wrecked Titanic', posted from Portsmouth 23 April 1912.
£200–250
€290–350
$340–400 ⚚ SJH

A P. G. Lewin postcard, 'At last we am alone Dinah', 1921.
£16–20 / €22–28
$28–32 ⊞ CWO

◄ **A Donald McGill postcard,** 'May you wake up to a Merry Christmas', from the Comique series, c1929.
£1–5 / €2–7
$3–8 ⊞ **JMC**

A Mabel Lucie Attwell postcard, 'I'm coming along – if I have to swim for it!', published by Valentine, c1926.
£4–8 / €5–11
$6–12 ⊞ **JMC**

► **Two photographic postcards,** depicting ships, 1920 and 1950.
£2–6 / €3–8
$4–10 each
⊞ **COB**

A photographic postcard, depicting Queen Elizabeth, 1936.
£1–5 / €2–7
$3–8 ⊞ **S&D**

A postcard, 'Best Wishes for A Happy Birthday', from an original painting by Madeleine Renaud, 1943.
£1–5 / €2–7
$3–8 ⊞ **JMC**

A Vera Paterson postcard, 'Forgotten', from the Regent Series, c1933.
£1–5 / €2–7
$3–8 ⊞ **JMC**

A photographic postcard, depicting Elvis Presley in *Jailhouse Rock*, 1957.
£2–6 / €3–9
$3–10 ⊞ **CTO**

◄ **A photographic postcard,** depicting Elvis Presley in *GI Blues*, 1960.
£2–6 / €3–8
$4–10 ⊞ **CTO**

Posters

The colourful advertising poster emerged in the second half of the 19th century, coinciding with Art Nouveau and resulting from advances in lithography and printing techniques. France pioneered the development of the poster, notable figures ranging from Toulouse-Lautrec, who produced only 31 posters, to commercial artist Jules Cheret, who founded l'Imprimerie Chaix in 1866 and created over 1,000 different designs. Among the first clients for this bright new form of advertising were theatres and food and drink manufacturers, but whatever the product, an attractive woman was a favourite decorative feature.

With the explosion of travel in the 20th century, railways, shipping lines, automobile manufacturers and airlines also embraced the poster. In the interwar years, Art Deco, streamlined and modern, provided the perfect style for capturing the speed and glamour of transport. French artist Cassandre created classic images both for the railways and the *Normandie* ocean liner, while in the UK the Shell Oil Company and London Transport

(under the design management of Frank Pick) commissioned an influential series of posters. WWII inspired a host of powerful propaganda posters using well-known artists including Fougasse and Abram Games.

Cinema was another 20th-century phenomenon that relied on posters for publicity. Today these are collectable, not just for the films and stars they were promoting but also in certain instances for the designer or illustrator of the image.

While rock and pop initially inspired fairly mundane posters that simply advertised dates and venues of gigs, the advent of psychedelia spawned a renaissance of poster art both in the USA and Europe. Reflecting the tastes of a teenage throw-away society, posters – instant art – became popular for home decoration as well as public information. Values of posters depend on a range of factors including subject, artist and size – the same image could be printed with different dimensions. Although mass-produced, many posters were simply thrown away after use, hence their rarity. Condition is also crucial to value.

A Cacao van Houten poster, by Piote, c1900, 26¼ x 20¼in (66.5 x 51.5cm).
£270–320 / €380–450
$430–510 ⚦ VSP

A Chocolat Lyon des 3 Frères poster, by Pièrre Bonnard, with metal strips, 1901, 25¼ x 18¼in (64 x 46.5cm).
£380–460 / €540–650
$610–730 ⚦ VSP

► A Brasserie Schneider poster, French, c1910, 23 x 32in (61 x 81.5cm).
£180–200
€250–280
$290–320 ⊞ RTT

◄ A Salus Acqua Minerale poster, printed by G. Fedetto & C. Torino, on cardboard, c1910, 19¼ x 13½in (49 x 34.5cm).
£70–85 / €100–120
$110–135 ⚦ VSP

An EOS Gold-füllfeder poster, by Buhe, printed by J. C. König & Ebhardt, German, c1915, 27¾ x 18½in (70.5 x 47cm).
£220–260 / €310–370
$350–410 ⚦ VSP

A Norwich Union Insurance Societies poster, 1920s, 30 x 20in (76 x 51cm).
£200–240 / €280–340
$320–380 ⊞ Do

◀ **A poster,** 'Next Week', by Robert Beebey, printed by Mather & Co, American, 28 x 41½in (71 x 105.5cm).
£250–300
€360–430
$400–480 ➚ VSP

A poster, 'A Leak in the Tank!', by Willard F. Elmes, printed by Mather & Co, American, 1929, 44 x 36¼in (111.5 x 92cm).
£510–610 / €720–860
$820–980 ➚ VSP

A Philips Miniwatt advertising poster, c1935, 25½ x 19¼in (65 x 49cm).
£340–410 / €480–580
$540–660 ➚ VSP

An Olimpic poster, by Paolo F. Garretto, Italian, 1937, 13 x 9¼in (33 x 23.5cm).
£75–90 / €105–125
$120–145 ➚ VSP

A National Savings Committee poster, printed by Alf Cooke Ltd, 1940s, 14½ x 9½in (37 x 24cm).
£300–360 / €430–510
$480–570 ➚ ONS

An ATS at the Wheel poster, by Beverley Pick, printed for HMSO by Field Sons & Co, folds, 1940s, 29½ x 19¼in (75 x 49cm).
£300–360 / €430–510
$480–570 ➚ ONS

A propaganda poster, 'Plan Before you Buy', by Beverley Pick, printed for HMSO by Fosh and Cross, 1940s, 30 x 20in (76 x 51cm).
£50–60 / €75–85
$80–95 ➚ ONS

A propaganda poster, 'Electricity, 100 tons of coal to build a Spitfire', printed for HMSO by Multi Machines Plates Ltd, 1940s, 19¼ x 29½in (49 x 75cm).
£150–180 / €210–250
$240–280 ➚ ONS

Items in the Posters section have been arranged in date order within each sub-section.

▶ **An Agfa poster,** by Herbert Leupin, printed by Art Institut Orell Füssli, Swiss, 1956, 50½ x 35½in (128.5 x 90cm).
£350–420 / €500–600
$560–670 ➚ VSP

A Levi's poster, 'The Original Jeans', by René van Rossen, printed by Wassermann AG, Swiss, 1975, 50½ x 35½in (128.5 x 90cm).
£170–200 / €240–280
$270–320 ➚ VSP

A Bally poster, by Roger Bezombes, printed by Imprimerie a Karcher, c1985, 68½ x 46½in (174 x 118cm).
£270–320 / €380–450
$430–510 ➚ VSP

Entertainment

An *Airs and Graces* poster, by William H. Barribal, printed by David Allen, small tears, early 20thC, 30 x 20in (76 x 51cm).
£40–50 / €55–70
$65–80 ⚒ ONS

A *Pirates of Penzance* poster, 1920s, 30 x 20in (76 x 51cm).
£55–60 / €80–85
$90–95 ⊞ Do

A Billy Smart's Circus poster, 1950s, 30 x 20in (76 x 51cm).
£135–150 / €190–210
$220–240 ⊞ Do

A Holland Festival poster, by Dick Elffers, printed by Steendrukkerij De Jong & Co, Dutch, 1956, 39½ x 27½in (100.5 x 70cm).
£200–240 / €280–340
$320–380 ⚒ VSP

A Pink Floyd and Jimmy Hendrix silkscreen poster, advertising two concerts at the Saville Theatre, published by Osiris Visions, 1967, 55 x 49in (139.5 x 124.5cm).
£600–720 / €850–1,000
$950–1,150 ⚒ CO

An Isle of Wight Festival poster, designed by David Roe, c1969, 30 x 20in (76 x 51cm).
£150–180 / €210–250
$240–280 ⚒ CO

An Elton John silkscreen advertising poster, for a concert at Leeds University Union, 1973, 28 x 19in (71 x 48.5cm).
£100–120 / €145–170
$160–190 ⚒ CO

> **Cross Reference**
> See Rock & Pop
> (pages 309–315)

▶ A Cotton Club poster, by Jean-Luc Kerchervé, 1975, 47 x 31¼in (119.5 x 79.5cm).
£240–290 / €340–410
$380–460 ⚒ VSP

An Open Air Love & Peace Festival poster, 1970, 43 x 16in (109 x 40.5cm).
£520–620 / €740–870
$830–990 ⚒ CO
Held in Insel Fehmarn in Germany, this three-day festival featured Jimi Hendrix's final performance. The coloured print is more desirable than the monochrome version.

A Malvern Festival Theatre poster, advertising Dave Swarbrick in concert, 1978, 30 x 20in (76 x 51cm).
£60–70 / €85–100
$95–110 ⚒ CO

Film

◄ A film poster, *Earth Versus the Flying Saucers,* starring Hugh Marlowe and Joan Taylor, c1956, 30 x 40in (76 x 102cm).
£1,000–1,200
€1,400–1,700
$1,600–1,900
⊞ CTO

A film poster, *Les Degourdis de la M.P.,* Belgian, c1953, 18 x 14in (45.5 x 35.5cm).
£55–60 / €80–85
$90–95 ⊞ RTT

A Hammer film poster, *La Revancha de Frankenstein,* starring Peter Cushing and Francis Matthews, Argentinian, 1958, 41 x 29in (104 x 73.5cm).
£20–25 / €28–35
$32–40 ⚒ B(Kn)

► A foyer poster, *Liasons Sécrètes,* starring Kirk Douglas, Walter Matthau and Kim Novak, 1960, 15 x 23in (38 x 58.5cm).
£110–125 / €160–175
$180–200 ⊞ MARK

An Amicus Productions poster, *Le Cinque Chivai del Terrore of Terror,* Italian, 1965, 55 x 38in (139.5 x 96.5cm).
£145–160 / €210–230
$230–250 ⊞ SDP

A film poster, *Dalla Russia con Amore,* starring Sean Connery, mounted on linen, Italian, 1964, 18¼ x 26¾in (46.5 x 68cm).
£190–230 / €270–320
$300–370 ⚒ ONS

An ABC Cinemas poster, *Girl Happy,* starring Elvis Presley and *Sandokan the Great,* 1965, 30 x 40in (76 x 101.5cm).
£190–230 / €270–320
$300–370 ⊞ CTO

Cross Reference
See Toys (pages 388–389)

A film poster, *La Tente Rouge,* starring Sean Connery, 1969, 15 x 23in (38 x 58.5cm).
£110–125 / €160–175
$180–200 ⊞ MARK

A Warner Brothers poster, *Clockwork Orange,* framed, 1971, 30 x 40in (76 x 101.5cm).
£65–75 / €90–105
$105–120 ⚒ StDA

◄ A Clifton Cinema screen and bill poster, c1969, 12 x 10in (30.5 x 25.5cm).
£16–20 / €23–28
$26–32 ⊞ CTO

▶ **A film poster,** *Jaws,* 1975, 30 x 40in (76 x 101.5cm).
£70–85 / €100–120
$110–130 ⚲ **StDA**

A Palace Pictures poster, *Merry Christmas Mr Lawrence,* starring David Bowie, c1980, 30 x 40in (76 x 101.5cm).
£45–50 / €65–75
$75–80 ⊞ **CTO**

A Warner Brothers poster, *The Exorcist* and *Exorcist II The Heretic,* c1980, 30 x 40in (76 x 101.5cm).
£35–40 / €50–55
$55–65 ⊞ **CTO**

◀ **A film poster,** *The Empire Strikes Back,* 1980, 30 x 40in (76 x 101.5cm).
£95–115 / €135–160
$150–180 ⚲ **StDA**

John Hassall

British artist and illustrator John Hassall (1868–1948) was a famous poster designer. Working under contract to the printers David Allen, he designed hundreds of trade, theatre and travel posters. His broad, brightly-coloured humorous style is epitomized by his famous 'Skegness is so Bracing' poster, which was produced for the Great Northern Railway in 1908 and is still being used nearly a century later by Skegness hoteliers.

Hassall worked for the *Daily Sketch* from 1893 to 1912 and designed approximately 800 book covers, including the adventure stories of G. A. Henty, producing a huge range of work from serious paintings to comic illustrations. He was famous for never throwing anything interesting away. When he died his studio had not been cleaned for around 40 years and contained a remarkable miscellany of objects including an Elizabethan four-poster bed, a Native American feathered headdress and Napoleon's death mask. As writer John Jenkins recalled: 'The dust that lay on the Indian gods and the ammonites was like grey sugar more than an inch thick'.

A *Weekly Telegraph* **poster,** by John Hassall, printed by Sir W. C. Leng & Co, London, early 20thC, 25¼ x 20in (64 x 51cm).
£100–120 / €145–170
$160–190 ⚲ **ONS**

> **Cross Reference**
> See Advertising & Packaging (page 16)

A Royal Naval & Military Tournament poster, by John Hassall, printed by Dobson Molle Ltd, minor damage, early 20thC, 40¼ x 25¼in (102 x 64cm).
£50–60 / €70–85
$80–95 ⚲ **ONS**

A Drury Lane Pantomime poster, by John Hassall, advertising 'Bluebeard', printed by Waterlow, minor damage, early 20thC, 30 x 20in (76 x 51cm).
£80–95 / €115–135
$130–150 ⚲ **ONS**

A *Love & A Cottage* **poster,** by John Hassall, advertising the book by Keble Howard, printed by Thos Storer, early 20thC, 30 x 20in (76 x 51cm).
£320–380 / €450–540
$510–610 ⚲ **ONS**

Travel

An Electric Railway House poster, 'Edgware by Tram', by E. A. Cox, printed by Avenue Press, on linen, 1916, 30 x 20in (76 x 51cm).
£250–300 / €360–430 $400–480 ⚒ ONS

A Netherlands Railway poster, 'Visit Picturesque Holland', by Joseph Rovers, printed by Emrik & Binger, on linen, Dutch, c1930, 39¼ x 27½in (100 x 70cm).
£400–480 / €570–680 $640–770 ⚒ VSP

◄ **A travel poster,** 'Holland Centre of Europe' by Jan Lavies, printed by N. V. J. Smulders & Co, on linen, Dutch, c1937, 34 x 25½in (86 x 65cm).
£135–160 / €190–230 $220–260 ⚒ VSP

A Southern Railway poster, 'Healthy Herne Bay on the Kentish Coast', printed by Simpson & Turner, c1920, 40¼ x 25in (102 x 63.5cm).
£550–650 / €780–920 $880–1,050 ⚒ VSP

A Compagnie de Navigation Paquet poster, 'Sénégal', printed by Moullot, French, c1930, 39¼ x 24¼in (99.5 x 61.5cm).
£110–130 / €155–185 $175–210 ⚒ VSP

► **An LB&SC Railway poster,** 'Selsey on Sea', printed by Iris, 1922, 40 x 25in (101.5 x 63.5cm).
£510–610 / €720–870 $820–980 ⚒ VSP

A promotional poster, 'Visit Ribe in Denmark', 1929, 30 x 21in (76 x 53.5cm).
£135–150 / €190–210 $220–240 ⊞ Do

A Münchener Festsommer poster, by Ludwig Hohlwein, printed by Kunstanstalt A. G., German, 1935, 47¾ x 33¼in (121 x 84.5cm).
£380–460 / €540–650 $610–740 ⚒ VSP

◄ **A travel poster,** 'Bologna', by Severino Trematore, printed by Barabino & Gaeve, Swiss, c1930, 40¼ x 25½in (102.5 x 65cm).
£270–320 / €380–450 $430–510 ⚒ VSP

Auction or dealer?

All the pictures in our price guides originate from auction houses ⚒ and dealers ⊞. When buying at auction, prices can be lower than those of a dealer, but a buyer's premium and VAT will be added to the hammer price. Equally, when selling at auction, commission, tax and photography charges must be taken into account. Dealers will often restore pieces before putting them back on the market. Both dealers and auctioneers can provide professional advice, so it is worth researching both sources before buying or selling your antiques.

A Frederiksberg poster, 'Svomme Hal', Danish, 1938, 35 x 26in (89 x 66cm).
£400–450 / €570–640
$640–720 ⊞ Do

LOCATE THE SOURCE
The source of each illustration in Miller's can be found by checking the code letters below each caption with the Key to Illustrations, pages 443–451.

A Nelson Steam Navigation Company poster, 1930s, 40 x 25in (101.5 x 63.5cm).
£550–600 / €780–850
$880–960 ⊞ Do

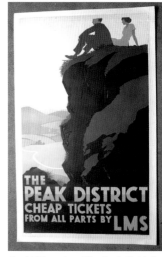

An LMS poster, 'The Peak District', by Ralph Mott, printed by S. C. Allen, 1930s, 40 x 24in (101.5 x 61cm).
£500–550 / €710–780
$800–880 ⊞ Do

A promotional poster, for Hans Anderson's House, Odense, Denmark, printed by Hagen & Sorensen, Danish, 1947, 38¼ x 24½in (97 x 62cm).
£85–100 / €120–140
$135–160 ⚲ VSP

▶ **A Royal Interocean Lines poster,** by Reyn Dirksen, Dutch, c1955, 36 x 24½in (91.5 x 62cm).
£760–910 / €1,100–1,300
$1,200–1,400 ⚲ VSP

A promotional poster, 'Salzburger Land', by Karl Schwetz, Austrian, c1950, 35½ x 24¾in (90 x 63cm).
£300–360 / €430–510
$480–580 ⚲ VSP

A promotional poster, 'Sevilla', printed by Jose Ma. Ventura Hita, on japan paper, Spanish, 1952, 19¼ x 13in (49 x 33cm).
£120–145 / €170–200
$190–230 ⚲ VSP

A promotional poster, 'Samana Sant Sevilla', by F. Mariscal, printed by Orla-Jerez, Spanish, 1955, 39¼ x 24¼in (99.5 x 61.5cm).
£120–145 / €170–200
$190–230 ⚲ VSP

◀ **A promotional poster,** 'Visit Britain', by Bromfield, printed by Charles & Read, 1960, 40¼ x 25in (102 x 63.5cm).
£210–250 / €300–350
$340–400 ⚲ VSP

Puppets

A Pelham Mrs Macboozle string puppet, c1947–52, 12in (30.5cm) high, with box.
£220–240 / €310–340 $350–380 ⊞ ARo

A plush cat hand puppet, 1950–60, 11in (28cm) high.
£30–35 / €40–50 $50–55 ⊞ LBe

A Pelham Poodle string puppet, 1960s, 10in (25.5cm) high, with box.
£65–75 / €95–105 $110–120 ⊞ UD

A Pelham Pinocchio string puppet, c1947–52, 12in (30.5cm) high.
£200–220 / €280–310 $320–350 ⊞ ARo
This puppet was produced before the appearance of Walt Disney's Pinocchio, and is therefore scarce.

A Pelham Guitarist string puppet, with instructions, 1967, 12in (30.5cm) high, with box.
£145–175 / €210–250 $230–280 ✗ CO
This puppet was dressed in similar clothes to those worn by George Harrison.

A Pelham Witch string puppet, late 1960s, in original box.
£32–38 / €45–55 $50–60 ✗ FHF

▶ **A Pelham Fido string puppet,** 1960s, 26in (66cm) high.
£85–95 / €120–130 $135–150 ⊞ POLL

Radios, Televisions & Sound Equipment

Gramophones & Tape Recorders

A Columbia table gramophone, with an oak base, c1924, 15in (38cm) square.
**£155–175 / €220–250
$250–280 ⊞ OIA**

An Edison Standard Model D gramophone, for two- and four-minute cylinders, with oak case, brass horn and stand, 1910, 43¼in (110cm) long, with additional horn and four cylinders.
**£850–1,000
€1,200–1,400
$1,350–1,600 ⚒ GK**

A painted tin horn gramophone, in an oak case, replaced Garrard spring motor, 1915, case 13in (33cm) square.
**£200–240 / €290–350
$320–380 ⚒ GK**

An S. G. Brown horn speaker, with a mahogany base and screw adjustment for armature, 1923, 21in (53.5cm) high.
**£115–130 / €165–185
$185–210 ⊞ GM**

An HMV Lumière 460 gramophone, with a mahogany case, brass fittings and automatic stop function, 1925, case 17¼in (44cm) wide.
**£1,950–2,300
€2,750–3,300
$3,100–3,700 ⚒ GK**

A Parlaphone Carl Lindström table gramophone, in an oak case with pierced woodwork, marked, German, 1925, case 17¾in (45cm) square.
**£155–185 / €220–260
$250–300 ⚒ GK**

LOCATE THE SOURCE

The source of each illustration in Miller's can be found by checking the code letters below each caption with the Key to Illustrations, pages 443–451.

An HMV Model 1 gramophone, c1928, 42½in (108cm) high.
**£500–600 / €710–850
$800–960 ⚒ TMA**

A Columbia copper-plated record cleaner, c1930s, 4in (10cm) diam.
£18–22 / €25–30
$30–35 ⊞ CBGR

Mario Bellini

Italian designer Mario Bellini (b. 1935) created furniture, ceramics and lighting as well as designing electronic equipment for firms including Olivetti, Brionvega and Yamaha. This wedge-shaped tape deck was designed to display all the functions clearly and make them easier to use. Rather than being specifically styled for the home, it looks like a deck from a recording studio, pioneering the taste for black-cased, professional-looking equipment that became a feature of Japanese technology and domestic living-rooms from the 1970s onwards.

◀ An Antoria portable gramophone, c1940, 11in (28cm) wide.
£80–90 / €115–130
$130–145 ⊞ OIA

▶ An Elizabethan Major tape recorder, four-track, with three-speed Collero tape deck, 1963, 16in (40.5cm) wide.
£35–40 / €50–55
$55–65 ⊞ GM

A Revox A77 tape recorder, by Willi Studer, 1974, 16in (40.5cm) wide.
£180–200 / €250–280
$290–320 ⊞ GM
This is a two-speed, quarter-track stereo capable of taking 10½in tape spools.

A Yamaha cassette deck, designed by Mario Bellini, 1974, 12in (30.5cm) wide.
£155–175 / €220–250
$250–280 ⊞ MARK

Radios

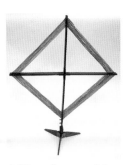

A Climax frame aerial, minor damage, 1927, 38in (96.5cm) high.
£60–70 / €85–100
$95–110 ⊞ GM

A Pye Twintriple radio, with sunrise fret and walnut wings, 1930, 18in (45.5cm) wide.
£220–250 / €310–350
$350–400 ⊞ GM

▶ An Ekco M23 radio, in a Bakelite case, c1933, 16in (40.5cm) high.
£150–180 / €210–250
$240–290 ✦ GK

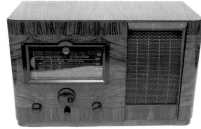

◀ **An HMV 656 radio,**
in a walnut-veneered case,
1938, 23in (58.5cm) high.
**£90–100 / €125–140
$145–160** ⊞ **GM**

A Philco K268T car radio, 1938,
9in (23cm) high.
**£135–150 / €190–210
$220–240** ⊞ **GM**
As radio historian Jonathan Hill
notes, in the 1930s there was
considerable concern about the
idea of introducing a radio into a
car. Worries were expressed that
the driver would take his eyes off
the road while tuning the dial, or
become distracted if listening to
a debate or lively piece of music.
Practical Wireless Magazine
suggested the broadcasting of
special motorist's programmes
consisting largely of slow foxtrots.
It was rumoured that the Ministry
of Transport wanted to ban radios,
but by 1938 the radio had become
a standard automobile accessory.

An Ace A50 radio, 1945, 19in (48.5cm) wide.
**£45–50 / €65–75
$75–80** ⊞ **GM**

Items in the Radios, Televisions
& Sound Equipment section
have been arranged in date
order within each sub-section.

**A Pennine Ranger
Console radio,** restored,
1947, 30in (76cm) high.
**£160–180 / €230–260
$260–290** ⊞ **GM**
This is a coventional
receiver but with
bandspread on the
short-wave bands.

▶ **A GEC BC
4855 radio,** in
a Bakelite case,
1948, 16in
(40.5cm) wide.
**£90–100
€125–140
$145–160** ⊞ **GM**

◀ **A Bush DAC
90 radio,** in an
ivory Bakelite
case, long and
medium wave,
1949, 12in
(30.cm) wide.
**£100–110
€140–155
$160–175** ⊞ **GM**

▶ **A Bush DAC
10 radio,** in a
Bakelite case,
c1950, 12½in
(32cm) wide.
**£80–95
€115–135
$130–150**
⚒ **SWO**

A Kriesler radio, in a Bakelite case, Australian, c1950, 10in (25.5cm) wide.
£70–80 / €100–110
$110–125 ⊞ GM

An Ekco U159 radio, in a plastic case, 1950, 11in (28cm) wide.
£50–60 / €70–85
$80–95 ⊞ GM
This model was also available in grey, green and burgundy. Coloured examples are more valuable.

A Pye extension speaker, in a Bakelite case, 1950, 10in (25.5cm) high.
£20–25 / €28–35
$32–40 ⊞ GM

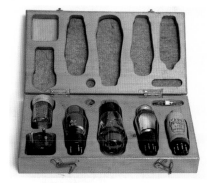

◀ **A set of spare valves for a Marconi Crystal Calibrator No. 6,** 1950, box 11in (30cm) wide.
£15–20 / €20–28
$24–32 ⊞ GM

▶ **A Dynatron Ether Conqueror radio,** with an audio amplifier, restored, 1950, 35in (89cm) high.
£450–500 / €640–710
$720–800 ⊞ GM

A Murphy 188 radio, with a baffle board receiver, 1950, 33in (84cm) wide.
£70–80 / €100–110
$110–125 ⊞ GM

A KB FB10 radio, in a Bakelite case, 1951, 10in (25.5cm) wide.
£90–100 / €125–140
$145–160 ⊞ OTA
This model was known as the 'Toaster' radio and was also available in red and green.

A type 813 transmitter valve, 1955, 7in (18cm) long.
£8–12 / €11–17
$12–18 ⊞ GM

A UNIC radio, in a chrome case, French, c1955, 12in (30.5cm) high.
£540–600 / €770–850
$860–960 ⊞ MARK

A Cossor Melody Maker 524 radio, in a Bakelite case, 1955, 18in (45.5cm) wide.
£50–60 / €70–80
$80–95 ⊞ GM

A Bush Long Play transistor radio, in a plastic case, 1960, 6in (15cm) wide.
£35–40 / €50–55
$55–65 ⊞ GM
Long Play refers to the larger than usual battery fitted to this small receiver.

A Ferguson 354U radio, in a Bakelite case, 1961, 14in (35.5cm) wide.
£45–50 / €65–70
$75–80 ⊞ GM

◄ **A Roberts R200 radio,** 1962, 10in (25.5cm) wide, with original travel case.
£65–75 / €90–105
$105–120 ⊞ GM

Televisions

A Grundig Aphelion television, damaged, 1970s, 36in (91.5cm) high.
£720–800 / €1,000–1,100
$1,150–1,300 ⊞ MARK

A Bush Bakelite TV22 television, c1950, 16in (40.5cm) high.
£150–180 / €210–250
$240–290 ⊞ OTA
In 1950 this television would have cost £35.10s / €50 / $57.

A Sharp plastic bedside television, c1970, 9in (23cm) high.
£110–125 / €155–175
$175–200 ⊞ LUNA

Cross Reference
See Sixties & Seventies (pages 337–339)

▶ **A Sinclair TV80 pocket television,** 1984, 6in (15cm) wide.
£50–60 / €70–80
$80–95 ⊞ LUNA

As early as the 1960s, Clive Sinclair was fascinated with the idea of producing a miniature television. This was a difficult project. Liquid-crystal displays were not invented until the 1970s forcing Sinclair to use miniaturized versions of the cathode-ray tubes used on full-size televisions. These were hard to find and needed considerable power. In 1966 he designed the prototype 'Microvision', which was never put into production. Eighteen years later he produced the TV80, a slim, flat-screen pocket television, with the CRT (cathode-ray tube) set into the side of the machine. The TV80 (so called after its £80 / €114 / $128 selling price), cost £4,000,000 / €5,700,000 / $6,400,000 to produce and only approximately 15,000 examples were sold. The screen had a very narrow viewing angle and Sinclair's ingenious technology was soon made redundant by the development of LCD by Casio and other Japanese electronics companies.

Railwayana

An ivory disc, inscribed 'Free Pass, All Stations on the Eastern Counties and Norfolk Lines', valid for one year, 1849–50, 1½in (4cm) diam.
£700–800
€1,000–1,150
$1,100–1,300 ♣ BWL

A Midland Railway wall drinking fountain, from Rowsley Station. Derbyshire, 1873, 64in (162.5cm) high, together with an illustration of a similar fountain at Burton-on-Trent.
£580–680 / €820–970
$930–1,100 ♣ SRA

Cross Reference
See Toys (pages 411–414)

► A Caledonian Railway oak wall clock, by Alex Gill, Aberdeen, with fusee movement, pendulum and key, 1910, dial 12in (30.5cm) diam.
£1,000–1,200
€1,400–1,700
$1,600–1,900 ♣ SRA

A GER wall lantern, 'West Mill', with vessel, burner, glass funnel and enamelled reflector, minor damage, 1863, 19½in (49.5cm) high.
£880–1,050
€1,250–1,500
$1,400–1,700 ♣ SRA

► A BR(E) station totem, 'Darfield', repaired, 1901, 36in (91.5cm) wide.
£1,000–1,200
€1,400–1,700
$1,600–1,900 ♣ SRA

A Prussian Railway brass plaque, 1910, 10in (25.5cm) diam.
£310–350 / €440–500
$500–560 ⊞ COB

A Southern Railway glass lamp tablet, 'Bideford', in original wooden frame, 1872, 18in (45.5cm) wide.
£1,800–2,150 / €2,550–3,050
$2,900–3,450 ♣ SRA

A LNER enamel lamp tablet, 'Cullercoats', 1882, minor damage, 16in (40.5cm) wide.
£200–240 / €280–340
$320–380 ♣ SRA

A South Western Railway cream jug, pewter cover missing, c1910, 4½in (11.5cm) high.
£65–75 / €90–105
$105–120 ⊞ MURR

A cast-brass worksplate, for the Saxon State Railways, German, 1913, 14in (35.5cm) wide.
£650–750 / €920–1,100
$1,050–1,200 ⚒ SRA

A GWR brass cabside numberplate, '4985', face restored, 1937, 25in (63.5cm) wide.
£3,700–4,400 / €5,200–6,200
$5,900–7,000 ⚒ SRA

◄ **A North Eastern Railway pot lamp,** inscribed 'LNER Malton No. 6', with a Bullpitts metal badge, 1919, 17in (43cm) high.
£200–240 / €280–340
$320–380 ⚒ SRA

A cast-brass worksplate, 'Andrew Barclay Sons & Co Limited No. 1590. 1918 Caledonia Works Kilmarnock', carried by 'Glynteg', 1918, 16¾in (42.5cm) wide.
£450–540 / €640–770
$720–860 ⚒ SRA

A Southern Railway brass ashtray, c1930s, 7in (18cm) diam.
£75–85 / €105–120
$120–135 ⊞ MURR

◄ **A BR Southern Region hanging sign,** 'Waiting and Ladies Rooms', with original hooks and brackets, 1950s, 16in (40.5cm) wide.
£160–190 / €230–270
$250–300 ⚒ VEC

A BR London Midland Region station totem, 'Hatch End', edges repainted, damaged, 1950s, 36in (91.5cm) wide.
£440–520 / €620–740
$700–830 ⚒ VEC

A British Railways cast-aluminium nameplate, 'The Royal Alex', 1965, 59in (150cm) wide, together with the official EWS Certificate of Authenticity.
£2,200–2,600 / €3,100–3,700
$3,500–4,150 ⚒ SRA

Rock & Pop

◄ **Count Basie,** a concert
programme, 1959,
10 x 8in (25.5 x 20.5cm).
**£15–20 / €20–28
$24–32** ⊞ **CTO**

**AC/DC World Tour
poster,** a reproduction of
their 'Ball Breaker' world
tour poster, with printed
autographs, 1995,
24 x 18in (61 x 45.5cm).
**£50–60 / €70–85
$80–95** 🪓 **CO**

The Animals, a mounted
photograph and a card
signed by Hilton Valentine,
Eric Burdon, John Steel,
Alan Price and their road
manager Tappy Wright,
c1964, 16 x 11in
(40.5 x 28cm).
**£100–120 / €140–170
$160–190** 🪓 **CO**

The Clash, a mounted
colour photograph and
autographs of Mick Jones,
Joe Strummer, Paul
Simonon and Topper
Headon, framed and
glazed, 2001, 21 x 17in
(53.5 x 43cm).
**£100–120 / €140–170
$160–190** 🪓 **CO**

▶ **The Eagles,** world tour programme, signed by Don
Henley, Glenn Frey, Don Felder, Joe Walsh and Timothy
B. Schmit, 1994.
**£150–180 / €210–250
$240–290** 🪓 **CO**

John Entwistle

Following the death of
John Entwistle (b.1946)
on the eve of The Who's
2002 American tour,
the possessions of the
world famous bass
player were auctioned
by Sotheby's in 2003.
It was the guitars that
attracted the greatest
interest, most notably
Entwistle's much-loved
'Frankenstein' Fender
bass, so-called because
Entwistle put it together
himself from the remains
of five smashed guitars.
While The Who became
famous for smashing
their equipment on
stage (an act that started
accidentally when Pete
Townshend broke the
neck of his guitar in a
low-ceilinged club),
Entwistle built up a
huge collection of
guitars in his hunt for
the perfect bass.

John Entwistle,
a Fender Precision
bass guitar, 'Franken-
stein', stamped
'13081', 1967,
in worn rigid case.
**£62,400–74,800
€88,600–106,200
$100,000–120,000**
🪓 **S(O)**

▶ **John Entwistle,** a Gibson Moderne guitar, with gold-plated hardware, impressed 82282021, 1982, in a Gibson case.
£1,800–2,200
€2,550–3,100
$2,900–3,500 ⚲ S(O)

John Entwistle, a tie-dyed suede suit, with safari-style jacket and flared trousers, 1970s.
£1,200–1,400
€1,700–2,000
$1,900–2,250 ⚲ S(O)

John Entwistle, a zebra-wood Warwick Buzzard eight-string bass guitar, neck inlaid 'Custom-Made for John E.' and 'D–011–89', 1989, with spare bridge, machine heads and a flight case with transit labels.
£5,300–6,300 / €7,500–9,000
$8,500–10,000 ⚲ S(O)

John Entwistle, an ink and felt pen drawing of Eric Clapton, signed and dated 2000, mounted and framed, 30 x 21½in (76 x 54.5cm).
£950–1,150
€1,350–1,600
$1,500–1,800 ⚲ S(O)

Fleetwood Mac, a Marshall MKII amplifier, 1969, 9in (23cm) high, together with a letter from Bob Brunning and a signed copy of his Fleetwood Mac biography.
£2,600–3,100 / €3,700–4,400
$4,200–5,000 ⚲ CO
This amplifier was given to Bob Brunning by John McVie when his own equipment had been stolen from Broadcasting House prior to recording a spot for Alexis Korner's BBC *World Service* radio show in 1969.

Billy Fury, a signed promotional photograph from the film *Play It Cool*, 1962, 8 x 10in (20.5 x 25.5cm).
£90–100 / €130–140
$145–160 ⚲ CO

▶ **Buddy Holly and the Crickets,** a mounted black and white photograph and autographs of Buddy Holly, Jerry Allison and Joe Maudlin, framed and glazed, 1950s, 17 x 12in (43 x 30.5cm).
£450–540 / €640–770
$720–860 ⚲ CO

Jimi Hendrix, New York address book, worn, 1967–70.
£1,700–2,000 / €2,400–2,850
$2,700–3,200 ⚲ CO
This address book contains many of Jimi's personal and industry contacts and entries for doctors, dentists and dry cleaners.

BB King, a signed Gibson 'Lucille' custom guitar, with laminated maple body, c1980s, with hard case.
£3,200–3,800 / €4,550–5,400
$5,100–6,100 ⚲ CO

◄ **The Love Affair,** an original song sheet for 'Everlasting Love', 1967.
£30–35 / €40–50
$50–55 ♪ CO

Elvis Presley, a 20th Century-Fox poster for *Love Me Tender*, 1956, 30 x 20in (76 x 51cm).
£180–210 / €260–300
$290–340 ♪ B(Kn)

Elvis Presley, a souvenir photograph, 1957, 8 x 6in (20.5 x 15cm).
£4–8 / €6–11
$7–12 ⊞ CTO

▶ **Sex Pistols,** a signed limited edition screenprint, 'Never Mind the Bollocks', signed by Jamie Reid, 1997, 40 x 29in (101.5 x 73.5cm).
£450–500 / €640–710
$720–800 ⊞ PLB

Madonna, a signed poster, 1990s, 38 x 27in (96.5 x 68.5cm).
£150–180 / €210–260
$240–290 ♪ CO

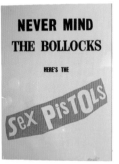

Sex Pistols, a signed limited edition screenprint, 'Never Mind the Bollocks'

Simon and Garfunkel, a signed album sleeve, 'The Concert in Central Park', c1982, vinyl not included.
£90–100 / €130–140
$145–160 ♪ CO

◄ **Soft Machine,** a silkscreen poster for a concert at the Guildhall, Portsmouth, 1970, 30 x 20in (76 x 51cm).
£80–95 / €115–135
$130–150 ♪ CO

Oasis, a signed concert poster, some creasing, 2000, 54 x 39in (137 x 99cm).
£200–240 / €280–340
$320–380 ♪ CO

The Shadows, a photocard, by Valex of Blackpool, 1960s, 8 x 6in (20.5 x 15cm).
£2–6 / €3–8
$4–10 ⊞ CTO

Wham, a signed colour photograph, 1980s.
£50–60 / €70–85
$80–95 ♪ CO

The Beatles

A gas light fitting, 1957, 8in (20.5cm) high, together with guarantee of authenticity.
£450–500 / €640–710
$720–800 ⊞ CTO
This light fitting was taken from the left side of the stage in St Peter's Parish Church, where John Lennon played with The Quarry Men and first met Paul McCartney.

Paul McCartney, a typed and signed letter, mounted with envelope and plaque, 8 March 1963, letter 9 x 8in (23 x 20.5cm).
£1,400–1,600 / €2,000–2,300
$2,250–2,600 ⊁ B(Kn)

In the 1960s Beatles' signatures were reproduced by members of their team and there have also been modern fakes. A good provenance is important when buying autographs.

The Beatles, autographs, 21 November 1963, 5in (12.5cm) square, together with a ticket for their performance at ABC Carlisle on 26 October and a cutting from the *Cumberland Evening News* 22 November 1963.
£900–1,000 / €1,300–1,400
$1,450–1,600 ⊁ TRM
These were collected at the Crown and Mitre hotel in Carlisle when The Beatles were top of the bill at the ABC.

▶ **John Lennon,** a black and white postcard, c1963, 5 x 3in (12.5 x 7.5cm).
£2–6 / €3–8
$4–10 ⊞ CTO

The Beatles, a tour programme, 1964, 11¾ x 8¼in (29.7 x 21cm).
£35–40 / €50–55
$55–65 ⊞ BTC

▶ **A Beatles comb,** by Lido Toys, 1960s, 15in (38cm) long, together with a Beatles scrapbook, by NEMS Enterprises.
£120–140 / €170–200
$190–230 ⊁ CO

The Beatles, a fan club Christmas flexi disc, with original sleeve signed 'Best wishes Anne Collingham', and newsletter, 1964.
£50–60 / €70–85
$80–95 ♪ CO
Anne Collingham was the fictitious head of the Beatles' Fan Club in Britain, created by the press officer Tony Barrow. 'Anne' also wrote a regular column in the Beatles' monthly magazine.

A gouache on celluloid picture of 'Your Blueness', from *Yellow Submarine*, with full production notes, 1968, 15¾ x 11¾in (40 x 30cm).
£500–600 / €710–850
$800–960 ♪ B(Kn)

A Beatles jigsaw puzzle, some wear, 1960s, in original box, 17 x 11in (43 x 28cm).
£90–105 / €125–150
$145–170 ♪ CO

Jukeboxes

▶ **A Rock-Ola 1478 Tempo II jukebox,** with 120 selections, 1950s, 61in (155cm) high.
£4,000–4,500 / €5,700–6,400
$6,400–7,200 ⊞ WAm

A Rock-Ola 120 jukebox, with 120 selections, American, 1958, 55in (139.5cm) high.
£2,700–3,000 / €3,800–4,250
$4,300–4,800 ⊞ AAA

Wurlitzer, established 1856, is a famous name in jukeboxes. The US company designed their first coin-operated phonograph in 1933 and produced their final jukebox in 1973.

A Wurlitzer 2310 stereo jukebox, takes American coins, restored, 1961, 51in (129.5cm) high.
£3,100–3,500 / €4,400–5,000
$5,000–5,600 ⊞ WAm

▶ **A Wurlitzer Nostalgia 1050 jukebox,** with 100 selections, plays 45rpm records, c1973, 60in (152.5cm) high.
£3,800–4,500 / €5,400–6,400
$6,100–7,300 ♪ S(O)
This jukebox formed part of the John Entwistle collection. This was Wurlitzer's last model.

Records

Lionel Bart, *'Fings Ain't Wot They Used T'be',* LP record, by HMV, 1960.
£20–25 / €28–35
$32–40 ⊞ TOT

▶ **Richard Hell and The Voidoids (Part II),** 'Don't Die Time', EP record, 1980.
£8–12 / €11–17
$12–18 ⊞ BNO

Jack Kerouac, 'Poetry For The Beat Generation', LP record, with Steve Allen, by Hanover Records, original pressing, American, 1959.
£150–180 / €210–250
$240–290 ⊞ BNO
An earlier issue, released by Dot Records, was quickly banned when the company's president announced that parts of the record were 'in bad taste', 'off colour', and 'not clean family entertainment'. Before production was halted 130 copies were pressed. Hanover then decided to release recordings unedited. Allen Ginsberg's response to the LP was: 'The record has a kind of mellow Frank Sinatra beauty, but openly philosophical, and would bring children to a religious sense of life.'

Fats Domino, 'Blues for Love Vol 2', EP record, by London Records, 1957.
£35–40 / €50–55
$55–65 ⊞ BNO

▶ **Michael Jackson,** 'Got To Be There', LP record, by Tamla Motown, American, 1972.
£4–8 / €5–11
$6–12 ⊞ BNO

Madonna, 'Music', CD, by Warner Brothers, limited edition in book form, 2000, 5in (12.5cm) square.
£25–30 / €35–40
$40–50 ⊞ BNO

▶ **Travelling Wilburys,** 'The Travelling Wilburys', CD, by Wilbury Records, 1990.
£45–50 / €65–70
$75–80 ⊞ BNO

Bob Dylan, 'Another Side of Bob Dylan', LP record, by CBS, 1964.
£65–75 / €90–105
$105–120 ⊞ BNO

Buddy Holly, 'The Late Great Buddy Holly', EP record, by Coral, 1960.
£20–25 / €28–35
$32–40 ⊞ BNO

Scent Bottles

There are two types of scent bottle – those designed for personal use into which you decanted the scent of your choice, and the commercial variety where both bottle and box were created to market a named fragrance. The majority of 19th-century bottles fall into the first category. Examples shown here range from coloured glass dressing table flasks to the double-ended portable bottle, designed to hold perfume in one end and smelling salts in the other – an essential aid for tightly-laced ladies who were prone to fits of the vapours.

After WWI, when ladies cast off their corsets, smelling salts were no longer so necessary, and scent (along with wearing cosmetics in public) became increasingly popular. Fashion houses began to produce their own fragrance lines

(Chanel No. 5, launched in 1921, was the first scent to bear the name of a designer) and as couturiers competed with perfume companies, bottle and package design became ever more inventive. One of the most successful perfumes of the interwar years, particularly in the USA, was Evening in Paris, launched by Bourjois in 1928. The small blue bottle with a silver label was designed by French artist Jean Helleu. The bottle came inside a variety of blue Bakelite boxes, each one depicting a night time theme and ranging from the owl shown here to a miniature hotel door with his 'n' hers shoes left outside. In the case of commercial perfume bottles, the more complete the presentation the better. Bottles still with their boxes will command a higher premium, and any remaining perfume should not be decanted.

An Oxford Lavender scent bottle, with contents, c1830, 8½in (21.5cm) long.
£135–150 / €190–210 $220–240 ⊞ JAS
Oxford Lavenders were purchased ready-filled with perfume and designed to be thrown away when empty.

A silver-gilt and ruby glass scent bottle and vinaigrette, by Sampson Mordan & Co, London 1872, 3¼in (8.5cm) long.
£600–650 / €850–920 $960–1,050 ⊞ VK

A silver-mounted double-ended glass scent bottle, c1890, 4in (10cm) long.
£150–165 / €210–240 $240–270 ⊞ EXC

A hand-painted ruby glass scent bottle, c1850, 4½in (11.5cm) high.
£125–140 / €175–200 $200–220 ⊞ TASV

A silver-mounted cut-glass scent bottle, c1860, 3½in (9cm) high.
£230–260 / €330–370 $370–410 ⊞ VK

◄ **A silver-mounted cut-glass scent bottle,** by John Grinsell, 1896, 5in (12.5cm) high.
£190–230 / €270–320 $310–370 ⋏ G(L)

► **A glass scent bottle,** minor damage, c1890, 4in (10cm) high.
£100–110 / €140–155 $160–175 ⊞ TASV

A silver-mounted Worcester ceramic scent bottle, by Sampson Mordan & Co, in the form of a Willow pattern plate, 1902, 2¼in (5.5cm) diam.
**£300–340 / €430–480
$480–540 ⊞ VK**

Two Crown Perfumery glass scent bottles, the stoppers in the form of crowns, c1900, larger 4in (10cm) high.
**£15–20 / €20–28
$24–32 ⚲ BBR**

A Victorian silver scent flask, by Sampson Mordan & Co, engraved with ivy, 2in (5cm) high.
**£140–165 / €200–240
$230–270 ⚲ G(L)**

► **An amethyst glass scent bottle,** the stopper in the form of a star, 1920s, 5in (12.5cm) high.
**£40–45 / €55–65
$65–75 ⊞ TASV**

A ceramic scent bottle, modelled as a girl and a parrot, the stopper in the form of a crown, Continental, c1910, 3¼in (8.5cm) high.
**£150–170 / €210–240
$240–270 ⊞ VK**

An L. T. Piver Astris glass scent bottle, by Baccarat, with bronze overlay, c1910, 4in (10cm) high.
**£270–300 / €380–430
$430–480 ⊞ LaF**
Bottles by major glass-makers such as Lalique or Baccarat command a premium.

► **A Potter & Moore scent bottle,** in the form of Ooloo the Cat, 1920s, 3in (7.5cm) high.
**£110–125 / €155–175
$175–200 ⊞ HYP**
Created for the *Sketch* newspaper in the 1920s by cartoonist George Studdy, Ooloo the Cat was designed as a feline counterpart to Studdy's most famous comic creation, Bonzo the Dog.

A Le Golli scent bottle,
1920s, 3½in (9cm) high.
£220–250
€310–360
$350–400 ⊞ LBe

▶ **A Bourjois Evening in Paris scent bottle,** in an owl-shaped case, 1930s, 3¾in (9.5cm) high, with original box.
£65–75
€90–105
$105–120 ⚒ G(L)

A Mury Le Narcisse Bleu scent bottle, with painted decoration, French, 1920–30, 3in (7.5cm) high.
£85–90 / €120–135
$135–150 ⊞ LBe

A Limoges porcelain atomizer, in the form of a rose, with a butterfly sprayer, French, 1930, 5in (12.5cm) high.
£55–65 / €80–90
$90–105 ⊞ BET

A glass perfume bottle, Czechoslovakian, 1930s, 6in (15cm) high.
£135–150 / €190–210
$220–240 ⊞ LBe

A His aftershave glass bottle, with a Bakelite stopper, 1930s, 6½in (16.5cm) high.
£200–220 / €280–310
$320–350 ⊞ LaF

A frosted glass perfume bottle, with a coloured glass stopper, 1930s, 4½in (11.5cm) high.
£20–25 / €28–35
$32–40 ⊞ TASV

A Lilly Dache Dashing perfume bottle, American, 1930–40, 7in (18cm) high, in original quilted silk presentation box.
£270–300 / €380–430
$430–480 ⊞ LBe

A glass atomizer, by Viard, with a tassel, 1930s, 7in (18cm) high.
£110–120 / €155–170
$175–195 ⊞ LBe

◀ **A Goya scent bottle,**
1950–60, 1½in (4cm) high.
£20–25 / €28–35
$32–40 ⊞ LBe

A Whitefire scent bottle,
1950s, 1½in (4cm) high.
£20–25 / €28–35
$32–40 ⊞ LBe

A Yardley Lavender Water bottle, with contents, c1950, 4in (10cm) high.
£8–12 / €11–17
$12–18 ⊞ LaF

Science & Technology

A pair of silver 'Solomons Improv'd' spectacles, by Joseph Millard, with two folding auxillary lenses, London 1835, 4½in (11.5cm) wide.
£210–250 / €300–350
$340–400 ✗ WW

Spectacles first appeared in Europe in the late 13th century and were initially balanced on the nose. Not until the 18th century were side pieces introduced, terminating in flat rings that gripped the temples on either side. In 1866, London scientific instrument makers R. & J. Beck included spectacles with side pieces in their catalogue. These curled round the ear and were particularly recommended for sportsmen.

An oil prospector's blowpipe set, comprising 40 pieces, 1880, 10½in (25.5cm) wide.
£300–330 / €430–470
$480–530 ⊞ WO
This item was designed for field use in metallic ore exploration.

A microscope, by Leitz, 1890–95, 14¼in (36cm) high, with original wooden box.
£550–650 / €780–920
$880–1,050 ✗ GK

◀ **A lacquered-brass telescope,** by Negretti & Zambra, 19thC, 39¼in (100cm) long, with fitted mahogany case.
£1,500–1,800
€2,150–2,550
$2,400–2,900 ✗ SWO

A pair of opera glasses, covered with crocodile skin, c1900, 4in (10cm) wide, with case.
£70–80 / €100–115
$110–125 ⊞ MCa

A pair of compasses, by Napier, 19thC, 3in (7.5cm) long, in original box.
£55–65 / €80–90
$90–105 ⊞ WO

A pair of mother-of-pearl and gilt opera glasses, by Gibson, French, late 19thC, 4in (10cm) wide, with case.
£85–95 / €120–135
$135–150 ⊞ SAT

◀ **A Victorian globe,** with engraved brass ring, on a turned wood stand, 24in (61cm) high.
£110–130 / €155–185
$175–210 ⋏ G(L)

A pair of spectacles, possibly Chester, dated 1908, 10in (25.5cm) wide, with metal case.
£180–200 / €250–280
$290–320 ⊞ CRT

A wooden typewriting exercise keyboard, by Jamet-Bufferau, French, c1910, 10¼in (26cm) wide.
£170–200 / €240–290
$270–320 ⋏ GK
As typewriters were expensive 100 years ago, typing schools used exercise keyboards instead as they were cheaper. These keyboards are rarely found today.

A brass safe time lock, American, 1911, 6 x 8in (10.5 x 15cm).
£400–450 / €570–640
$640–720 ⊞ MB

A brass compass, 1918, 3in (7.5cm) diam, with a leather case.
£55–65 / €80–90
$90–105 ⊞ ABCM

A slide rule, c1920, 12in (30.5cm) long, in original case.
£16–20 / €22–28
$25–32 ⊞ ETO

▶ **A bone or celluloid Clark's Computer calculating disc,** by H. D. Clark, 1913, 4in (10cm) diam, with original cardboard box.
£250–300 / €360–430
$400–480 ⋏ GK
Clarke's Computers were used for converting decimal parts of an acre into rods and perches and into square yards or vice versa.

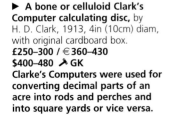

A C. F. Casella & Co Meteorological Instruments catalogue, c1920, 10 x 6in (25.5 x 15cm).
£160–180 / €230–260
$260–290 ⊞ RTW

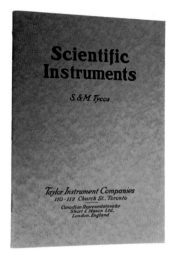

A Taylor Instrument Companies Scientific Instruments catalogue, 1926, 10 x 8in (25.5 x 20.5cm).
£90–100 / €125–140
$135–160 ⊞ RTW

A Walkers harpoon depth gauge, with instructions, early 20thC, 6¾in (17cm) high, in original box.
£220–250 / €310–350
$350–400 ⊞ SPA

A cast-iron adding machine, American, 1920s, 9in (23cm) high.
£220–250 / €310–350
$350–400 ⊞ MARK

► **A Bakelite desktop barometer,** 1930s, 4in (10cm) high.
£14–18 / €20–26
$22–28 ⊞ DHAR

A Philip's terrestrial globe, with chrome-metal mounts, on a wooden stand containing a copy of *Philip's Record Atlas*, c1930, 9in (23cm) diam.
£120–145 / €170–200
$190–230 ↗ RTo

A laboratory microscope, by Sass, Wolfe & Co, with two eyepieces, German, c1940, 14½in (37cm) high, with accessories and original wooden box.
£140–170 / €200–240
$230–270 ↗ GK

◄ **A Universal sun compass,** on a turned wood display mount, 1940, 1in (28cm) diam.
£230–260
€330–370
$370–420 ⊞ OLD
This compass was used during WWII by the long range Desert Group to navigate.

Medical

Collecting medical instruments is particularly popular with members of the medical profession. Surgery has been practised since Neolithic times, and Neolithic skulls have been discovered with marks of trepanning – holes drilled in the skull to relieve pressure. Blood-letting also has a long history. It was recommended from the Ancient Greek period onwards, using traditional methods such as leeches, cupping and scalpels. In Europe, surgery was practised as a secondary trade by barbers (hence their red and white striped pole, symbolic of blood and bandages) and in 1540 Henry VIII founded the Company of Barber Surgeons. Not until 1745 did the surgeons break away from the barbers to form

their own company and the Royal College of Surgeons was established in London in 1880.

Early surgery was a fairly primitive craft. Until the discovery of anaesthetics in the mid-19th century speed was of the essence – the Scottish surgeon Robert Liston (1794–1847), on one occasion amputated a leg in under two minutes, also slicing off his assistant's fingers and the coat tails of a spectator who got too close.

The gory aspect certainly appeals to collectors today, hence the demand for amputation saws, bleeding knives and other curious pieces of period equipment. Ceramic and glass drug jars and bottles are also popular and leech jars (in which leeches could be kept alive for blood-letting) can also command higher prices.

A brass scarificator, c1840, 2in (5cm) square, in orginal case.
£240–270 / €340–380
$380–430 ⊞ CuS
Scarificators were used for blood-letting.

A boxwood pill roller, 19thC, 3in (7.5cm) diam.
£55–65 / €80–90
$90–105 ⊞ WO

A brass and steel bleeding knife, French, 18thC, 4in (10cm) long.
£350–390 / €500–550
$560–620 ⊞ ANGE

A mahogany apothecary's box, fitted with ten glass bottles, scales and a pestle and mortar, 19thC, 6½in (16.5cm) high.
£420–500 / €600–710
$670–800 ↗ SWO

A rubber model of a bisected head, 1950, 10in (25.5cm) high.
£200–230 / €280–330
$320–370 ⊞ CuS

A chemist's jar, with a gilt cover, decorated with a royal coat-of-arms and inscribed 'Magnesia', 19thC, 27½in (70cm) high.
£480–580 / €680–820
$770–930 ↗ TRM

A Dr Nelson's Improved Inhaler, by Boots, c1910, 10in (25.5cm) high.
£45–50 / €65–75
$75–80 ⊞ YT

A urethral dilator, 1900, 11½in (29cm) long.
£135–150 / €190–210
$220–240 ⊞ CuS

Sewing

An embroidered pincushion, 1783, 3½in (9cm) high.
£200–240 / €280–340
$320–380 ✎ BWL

◀ **An ivory sewing bobbin,** inscribed 'Mary', dated 1824, 4in (10cm) long.
£155–175 / €220–250
$250–280 ⊞ SEA

A bone lace bobbin, with beaded decoration, inscribed 'Saly', c1850, 4½in (11.5cm) long.
£20–25 / €28–35
$32–40 ⊞ HL

A wooden Honiton lace bobbin, c1850, 4in (10cm) long.
£55–65 / €80–90
$90–105 ⊞ HL

A coquilla nut pincushion, in the form of a basket, c1860, 3in (7.5cm) high.
£40–45 / €55–65
$65–75 ⊞ HTE
The nut of the Brazillian coquilla palm tree was often used by wood turners to produce decorative items.

A vegetable ivory Stanhope tape measure, showing views of Bournemouth, 19thC, 2in (5cm) high.
£60–70 / €85–100
$95–110 ⊞ HTE

A Wheeler & Wilson sewing machine, with mahogany table, American, 1878, 30in (76cm) high.
£135–150 / €190–210
$220–240 ⊞ JUN

◀ **A Wilcox & Gibbs sewing machine,** American, 1880, with original box, 12in (30.5cm) high.
£70–80 / €100–115
$110–130 ⊞ JUN

A silver thimble, by Charles Horner, Chester 1907, 1in (2.5cm) high.
£65–75 / €90–105
$105–120 ⊞ LaF

▶ **A silver thimble,** commemorating the coronation of Queen Elizabeth II, 1953, 1in (2.5cm) high.
£80–90 / €115–130
$130–145 ⊞ DHA

A silver duck pincushion, marked C&N, Birmingham 1907, 2¼in (5.5cm) long.
£160–190 / €230–270
$260–300 ✎ DMC

Shipping

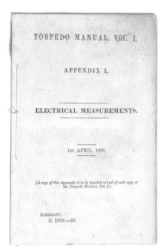

A wooden lifebelt, inset with a clock, 1890, 7½in (19cm) diam.
£500–550 / €700–780
$800–880 ⊞ REG

A wood and iron ship's block,
19thc, 15in (38cm) high.
£35–40 / €50–55
$55–65 ⊞ OLD

> Items in the Shipping section have been arranged in date order.

An Admiralty Torpedo Manual,
Vol 1, 1886, 8 x 5in (20.5 x 12.5cm).
£25–30 / €35–40
$40–50 ⊞ COB
This was one of the first Naval torpedo manuals.

A shipwright's masting knife, by R. Sorby, 19thC, 26in (66cm) long.
£110–125 / €155–175
$175–200 ⊞ WO

A shipping company ledger,
French, c1900, 20 x 15in (51 x 38cm).
£80–90 / €115–130
$130–145 ⊞ COB

A wooden ship's wheel, inset with a barometer, early 20thC, 8in (20.5cm) high.
£165–185 / €230–260
$260–300 ⊞ SAT

A Copeland tea cup, from the Royal yacht *Victoria & Albert*, c1910, 6in (15cm) diam.
£180–200 / €250–280
$290–320 ⊞ MURR

A Captain's standing orders book, from the Royal yacht *Victoria & Albert*, 1920s, 9 x 8in (23 x 20.5cm).
£135–150 / €190–210
$220–240 ⊞ COB

A White Star Line envelope, c1911.
£115–140 / €165–200
$185–220 ↗ DW

A Cadbury's Bourneville sample tin, depicting an ocean liner, 1915, 1½ x 2in (4 x 5cm).
£220–250 / €310–360
$350–400 ⊞ HUX

A General Steam Navigation Co cast-iron plaque, German, 1920s, 23in (58.5cm) diam.
£600–650 / €850–920
$960–1,050 ⊞ COB

A zig zag puzzle, by Intalok, featuring RMS *Majestic*, c1930s, 9 x 10in (23 x 25.5cm).
£110–120 / €155–175
$175–195 ⊞ MURR

A sailor's hatband ribbon, from the Royal yacht *Victoria & Albert*, 1920s, 32in (81.5cm) long.
£70–80 / €100–115
$115–130 ⊞ COB

A lifeboat station brass badge, 1920s, 2in (5cm) high.
£11–15 / €16–20
$18–24 ⊞ COB

◄ **An HMS *Duke of York* souvenir penant,** 1930s, 25in (63.5cm) long.
£50–55 / €70–80
$80–90 ⊞ COB

The Story of RMS Queen Mary, a souvenir magazine, 1936, 12 x 9in (30.5 x 23cm).
£20–25 / €28–35
$32–40 ⊞ COB

A tin model of RMS *Queen Mary*, 1930s, 30in (76cm) long.
£1,300–1,500 / €1,850–2,150
$2,100–2,400 ⊞ GBM

A silver-plated and enamel ashtray, from RMMV *Stirling Castle*, 1940, 5in (12.5cm) diam.
£100–110 / €140–155
$160–175 ⊞ REG

A Smith's astral ship's clock, 1940, 10in (25.5cm) diam.
£125–140 / €180–200
$200–220 ⊞ OLD

The Queen Mary

Commissioned by the Cunard Steamship Co, the *Queen Mary*, launched in 1934, was one of the most famous ocean liners of her day. Measuring 1,019.5ft (310.74m) long and weighing in at 81.237 tonnes, she was able to carry 1,957 passengers and 1,174 crew, most of whom were there to serve the guests. Seductive advertisements suggested that passengers could 'live like a king' when travelling by liner. The *Queen Mary's* dining room could seat 800 at one sitting and supply lists for a single voyage included 106 tons of beef, 4.5 tons of lamb and 500lbs of smoked salmon. All this was washed down with some 2,500 bottles of whisky, 3,000 bottles of wine accompanied by 15,000 cigars and 1,500,000 cigarettes.

If luxurious living was one attraction, another was speed. In the 1930s, the *Queen Mary* held the record for the fastest Atlantic crossing (three days, 11 hours and 40 minutes) but, perhaps most importantly, the *Queen Mary* was known by passengers and crew alike as a 'happy ship'. This happiness was brought to an end by WWII. The *Queen Mary* and her sister liner the *Queen Elizabeth* operated as troopships, carrying between them over 1,500,000 military personnel and, according to Winston Churchill (a regular wartime passenger), hastening the end of the war by at least a year. After the war the *Queen Mary* returned to peacetime service. She made a total of 1,001 Atlantic crossings before being retired in 1967 and sold for £2,156,000 / €3,062,000 / $3,450,000 to the City Council of Long Beach, California, where she still serves as a hotel, conference centre and maritime museum.

A wooden jigsaw puzzle, by Victory, featuring the Royal Mail Lines TS *Andes*, 1949, 6 x 8in (15 x 20.5cm).
£35–40 / €50–55
$55–65 ⊞ MRW

A souvenir handkerchief, from HMS *Hermes*, 1940s, 10in (25.5cm) square.
£11–15 / €16–20
$18–24 ⊞ COB

The Royal Tour, by Neil Ferrier, a photographic record of the 1953–54 Royal tour of Australasia aboard SS *Gothic*, 1954, 11 x 9in (28 x 23cm).
£15–20 / €20–28
$24–32 ⊞ COB

A Union-Castle Line passenger list for SS *Dunluce Castle*, 1957, 35½ x 8¼in (14 x 21cm).
£1–5 / €2–7
$3–8 ⊞ RTT

A P&O bar list, 1957, 6 x 4in (15 x 10cm).
£1–5 / €2–7
$3–8 ⊞ RTT

A Holland America Line polyester scarf, featuring SS *Nieuw Amsterdam*, 1950, 34¾in (88.5cm) square.
£135–160 / €190–230
$220–260 ⚲ VSP

Two Cunard Line baggage stickers, 1950s, 6in (15cm) wide.
£6–10 / €8–14
$10–16 each ⊞ COB

A Cunard Line tin, depicting RMS *Queen Elizabeth*, 1950s, 5½ x 9in (14 x 23cm).
£20–25 / €28–35
$32–40 ⊞ HUX

A ship's badge, from SS *Uganda*, 1960s, 1in (2.5cm) diam.
£6–10 / €8–14
$10–16 ⊞ COB

A model of the Clyde tug boat *Joffre*, with fibreglass hull, 1980s, 30in (76cm) long.
£50–60 / €70–85
$80–95 ⚒ FHF

A Royal Copenhagen ceramic ashtray, depicting RMS *Queen Mary*, c1950s, 4½ x 8in (11.5 x 20.5cm).
£55–60 / €80–85
$90–95 ⊞ MURR

An Admiral diver's depth gauge, 1950s, 2in (5cm) diam.
£15–20 / €20–28
$24–32 ⊞ TIC

A set of four silk panels, for the World Restaurant tables of the *QE2*, 1970s, 37 x 40in (94 x 101.5cm).
£270–300 / €380–420
$430–480 ⊞ COB

A promotional model of RMS *Titanic*, 1997, 11in (28cm) long.
£30–35 / €40–50
$50–55 ⊞ COB
This model was used to promote the film *Titanic*.

A wooden boat station sign, 1950s, 34in (86.5cm) wide.
£135–150 / €190–210
$220–240 ⊞ COB

An 8mm film, *Mersey & Humber Ferries*, distributed by Meteor Film Services, 1963, 4in (10cm) square.
£11–15 / €16–20
$18–24 ⊞ COB

A Zippo lighter, from HMY *Britannia*, 1980s, 3in (7.5cm) high.
£40–45 / €55–65
$65–75 ⊞ COB

A brass badge, of RMS *Lusitania*, 1990s, 2in (5cm) long.
£1–5 / €2–7
$3–8 ⊞ COB

Silver & Metalware

This opening section is devoted to silver and silver plate. Once upon a time a silver teapot was a favourite wedding gift, and a certain amount of family silver was a prerequisite to gracious living. Tastes, however, have changed. Servants have been replaced by dishwashers, entertaining tends to be more informal and home cooking is increasingly international – modern homes are more likely to have a wok and a pizza cutter than a silver teapot. Small wonder that demand for much functional silver tableware has dropped. One auctioneer recently described tea and coffee services as, quite simply, a liability, as we live in a world where many of us have neither the time nor the inclination to care for silver. Nevertheless, if the market for mainstream silverware is less than shining, bright sparks are certainly provided by niche collecting areas, such as wine-related antiques, vesta cases, sewing accessories, and the smaller and novelty items.

Another popular subject is flatware (to which we have devoted a special feature), particularly spoons – for which there is a strong collectors' market. Early spoons tend to command the highest prices and the oldest example here is a Roman spoon with a coiled handle, inspired by ancient Egyptian spoons used for mixing cosmetics. The medieval period saw the development of the large-bowled tablespoon with a decorative top or 'knop'. Silver spoons were often given as presents at weddings and christenings, hence the expression 'born with a silver spoon in your mouth'. Apostle spoons, decorated with the figure of the child's patron saint, were a popular gift; seal-topped spoons could be pricked with the initials of the owner. During the Commonwealth period, (1653–60), after the English Civil War, spoon design became simpler but with the restoration of the monarchy in the later 17th century, fancy patterns came back into vogue and spoons could be lavishly engraved. New shapes and sizes were gradually introduced; the dessert spoon, the teaspoon, and a host of specific designs for spices, condiments and other fashionable luxuries, such as the mote spoon for sifting impurities from tea, caddy spoons and marrow spoons for extracting bone marrow, a favourite delicacy.

With the general introduction of the table fork in the late 1600s, cutlery began to be produced in sets. The range of flatware expanded in the 18th and 19th centuries, along with the rise of mass-production and the middle-classes, culminating in the late Victorian period with the introduction of the soup spoon and the fish knife and fork. Queen Victoria regarded the latter as a vulgar innovation, and at the Royal table fish was eaten with two forks. With prices starting at very affordable levels, flatware in general can provide a very interesting area, whether for a collector focusing on a specific subject or for a home owner who simply wishes to use a bit of silver cutlery.

◄ **A silver pap boat,** c1820, 5in (12.5cm) wide.
£320–350 / €450–500
$510–560 ⊞ CuS

A silver wool or silk holder, Austrian, 1820–40, 7½in (19cm) high.
£340–380 / €480–540
$540–600 ⊞ ANGE

◄ **A silver-plated honey pot,** by G. R. Collis & Co, modelled as a bee skep, c1850, 3¾in (9.5cm) high.
£270–300 / €380–430
$430–480 ⊞ GRe

A child's silver mug, London 1837, 2¾in (7cm) high.
£200–220 / €280–310
$320–350 ⊞ LaF

Items in the Silver & Metalware section have been arranged in date order within each sub-section.

A silver mustard pot, by Robert Hennell, the engraved hinged lid with shell finial, pierced body, liner damaged, London 1857, 2½in (6.5cm) high.
£170–200 / €240–280
$270–320 ⚲ BR

A pair of Sheffield plate wine coasters, 19thC, 6in (15cm) diam.
£200–220 / €280–310
$320–360 ⊞ JAS

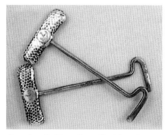

A pair of silver-handled boot pulls, by Messrs Drew, London 1904, 7¼in (18.5cm) long.
£80–100 / €115–140
$130–160 ⚲ WW

A silver pincushion, modelled as a fish, maker's mark S. M. & Co, Chester 1908, 1½in (4cm) wide.
£200–240 / €280–340
$320–380 ⚲ DMC

A silver pepperette, London 1895, 2in (5cm) high.
£60–65 / €85–95
$95–105 ⊞ FOX

A silver salt, with blue glass liner, Birmingham 1902, 1in (2.5cm) high.
£60–65 / €85–95
$95–105 ⊞ FOX

A silver crumb brush, by C. & C. Ltd, Birmingham 1905, 7in (18cm) long.
£40–45 / €55–65
$65–75 ⊞ WAC

A silver pincushion, modelled as the liner *Royal George*, Chester 1908, 5in (12.5cm) long.
£220–260 / €310–370
$350–410 ⚲ G(L)

A silver shoe, with gilt interior, London import marks for 1896, 4in (10cm) long.
£170–200 / €240–280
$270–320 ⚲ SWO

A silver salver, by Walker & Hall, with engraved cartouche, Sheffield 1904, 12½in (32cm) diam.
£220–260 / €310–370
$350–410 ⚲ SWO

A silver vesta case, Birmingham 1906, 2in (5cm) high.
£50–55 / €70–80
$80–90 ⊞ EXC

A George V silver-mounted glass inkstand, 5in (12.5cm) wide.
£65–80 / €95–110
$105–125 ⚲ G(L)

A childs' silver rattle, by William Vale & Son, modelled as a teddy bear with two bells, with a mother-of-pearl teether, Birmingham 1912, 3½in (9cm) high.
£110–130 / €155–185
$175–210 ⚒ WW

A silver hatpin stand, modelled as a caddy and two golf clubs, Chester 1913, 3½in (9cm) high.
£300–360 / €430–510
$480–580 ⚒ G(L)

A silver scent bottle, in the form of a hip flask, Birmingham 1919, 2½in (6.5cm) high.
£85–95 / €120–135
$135–150 ⊞ EXC

◄ **A silver sugar caster,** by The Goldsmiths & Silversmiths Co, the pierced lid with a turned finial, London 1931, 7in (18cm) high.
£130–155
€185–220
$210–250 ⚒ BR

A silver toast rack, by Syner & Beddes, Birmingham 1938, 3in (7.5cm) wide.
£55–60 / €80–85
$90–95 ⊞ WAC

◄ **A silver tea strainer,** London 1960, 6in (15cm) wide.
£85–95 / €120–135
$135–150 ⊞ EXC

A silver box, by M. S., Dublin 1949, 2in (5cm) diam.
£100–120 / €145–170
$160–190 ⊞ WAC

Cutlery & Flatware

A silver spoon, the curved stem with a swan's neck and head terminal, corrosion and staining, Roman, excavated in Turkey, probably 4thC, 7½in (19cm) long, 1.3oz.
£1,050–1,250 / €1,500–1,800
$1,700–2,000 ⚒ WW

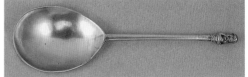

A silver spoon, with a virgin and heart terminal, repaired, 1550–1600, 6½in (16.5cm) long, 1oz.
£260–310 / €370–440
$420–500 ⚒ WW

◄ **A silver apostle spoon,** St Andrew, the gilt figure with a sacred dove, the bowl initialled and repaired by William Corseley, Gloucester, c1660, 7in (18cm) long.
£500–600 / €710–850
$800–960 ⚒ WW

A silver trefid spoon, the flared terminal and stem decorated with shaded roundels, slight repair, five fleur-de-lys marks, 1675, 7½in (19cm) long, 1.25oz.
£330–400 / €470–560
$530–640 ⚒ **WW**

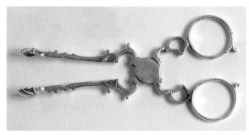

A pair of silver sugar nips, by Henry Plumpton, London 1761, 4½in (11.5cm) long.
£130–145 / €185–210
$210–230 ⊞ **GRe**

A silver soup ladle, by Thomas William Chawner, London, c1770, 12½in (32cm) long.
£250–275 / €350–390
$400–440 ⊞ **FOX**

A silver meat skewer, by William Eley & William Fearn, with a reeded ring handle, 1802, 11¼in (28.5cm) long.
£90–110 / €130–155
$150–175 ⚒ **G(L)**

A set of six silver forks, London 1818, 7in (18cm) long.
£175–195 / €250–280
$280–310 ⊞ **LaF**

A silver laceback trefid spoon, by Robert King, the bowl with a ribbed rattail, London 1680, 7¾in (19.5cm) long, 1.2oz.
£440–520 / €620–740
$700–830 ⚒ **WW**

A silver punch ladle, with a whalebone handle, c1765, 14in (35.5cm) long.
£210–230 / €300–330
$340–370 ⊞ **JAS**

A silver marrow scoop, possibly by James Jones, engraved with a crest, London 1771, 8½in (21.5cm) long, 1.5oz.
£180–210 / €250–300
$290–340 ⚒ **WW**

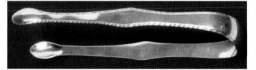

A pair of silver sugar tongs, by F. T., Exeter 1800, 6in (15cm) long.
£35–40 / €50–55
$55–65 ⊞ **WAC**

A silver travelling cutlery set, including knives, spoon, fork and corkscrew, c1810, case 9½in (24cm) wide.
£720–800 / €1,000–1,100
$1,150–1,300 ⊞ **ANGE**

A silver caddy spoon, by Joseph Willmore, Birmingham 1825, 3¼in (8.5cm) long.
£80–90 / €110–125
$130–145 ⊞ **FOX**

◀ **A silver basting spoon,** by Paolo Camilleri, initialled 'SSH', Maltese, 1836, 12in (30.5cm) long, 4.75oz.
£140–170 / €200–240
$230–270 ⚒ **WW**

A pair of silver-plated nutcrackers, with ivory handles, c1840, 6in (15cm) long.
£75–85 / €105–120
$120–135 ⊞ TASV

A pair of silver tablespoons, by John and Henry Lias, London 1841, 9in (23cm) long.
£65–70 / €90–100
$100–110 ⊞ WAC

A silver dessert spoon, with a pierced handle, Exeter 1848, 7in (18cm) long.
£45–50 / €65–70
$75–80 ⊞ PGO

A Victorian silver condiment spoon, Birmingham, 3in (7.5cm) long.
£25–30 / €35–40
$40–50 ⊞ FOX

A Victorian silver-plated Stilton scoop, with an ivory handle, 9in (23cm) long.
£40–45 / €55–65
$65–75 ⊞ TASV

A silver butter knife, with an ivory handle, Sheffield 1900, 7in (18cm) long.
£20–25 / €28–35
$32–40 ⊞ TASV

A silver stuffing spoon, by Henry Lias & Son, London 1862, 12in (30.5cm) long.
£160–175 / €230–250
$250–280 ⊞ GRe

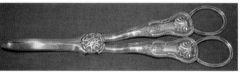

A pair of silver-plated grape scissors, c1870, 7¼in (18.5cm) long.
£55–65 / €80–90
$90–100 ⊞ TASV

A silver pickle fork, with a mother-of-pearl handle, Sheffield 1870, 8in (20.5cm) long.
£40–45 / €55–65
$65–75 ⊞ TASV

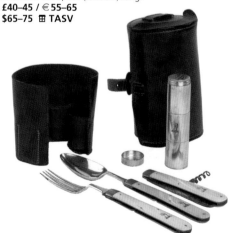

A pair of silver fish servers, with silver ferrules and antler handles, Birmingham 1880, knife 13½in (34.5cm) long.
£85–95 / €120–135
$135–150 ⊞ PGO

◄ **A silver-plated, steel and ivory cutlery and travelling set,** the knife, fork, spoon and corkscrew contained in a roll-up leather pad, each section of the silver-plated condiment tower marked 'Pepper', 'Mustard' and 'Salt', engraved with a dog's head crest, late 19thC, in a leather case 5in (12.5cm) wide.
£130–145 / €185–205
$210–230 ⊞ ChC

A silver jam spoon, Sheffield 1888, 6in (15cm) long.
£45–50 / €65–70
$75–80 ⊞ TASV

A silver bread fork, 1903, 7½in (19cm) long.
£55–60 / €80–85
$90–95 ⊞ FOX

A silver sifter spoon, 1904, 5in (12.5cm) long.
£55–65 / €80–90
$90–105 ⊞ FOX

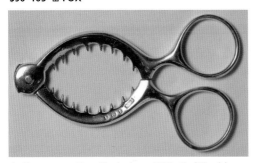

A silver egg cutter, Birmingham 1906, 4in (10cm) long.
£200–225 / €290–320
$320–360 ⊞ BLm

A silver-handled cheese knife, Sheffield 1903, 8½in (21.5cm) long.
£30–35 / €40–50
$50–55 ⊞ TASV

▶ **A set of six picture-backed teaspoons and a pair of sugar tongs,** by T. Bradbury & Sons, Sheffield 1903, 3oz, cased.
£100–120
€145–170
$160–190
⚒ WW

◀ **A silver spoon and fork,** Birmingham 1906, 5½in (14cm) long, cased.
£55–65 / €80–90
$90–105 ⊞ FOX

A silver jam spoon, with engraved decoration, Sheffield 1906, 5½in (14cm) long.
£25–30 / €35–40
$40–50 ⊞ FOX

A silver fruit knife, with a mother-of-pearl handle, Sheffield 1907, open 6in (15cm) long.
£50–60 / €70–85
$80–95 ⊞ TASV

Insurance values

Always insure your valuable collectables for the cost of replacing them with similar items, regardless of the original price paid. Both dealers and auctioneers can provide a valuation service.

▶ **A Sheffield steel carving set,** with ivory handles, c1910, case 15in (38cm) wide.
£15–20 / €20–28
$24–32 ⊞ CCO

A set of six silver coffee spoons,
Birmingham 1916, 3¾in (9.5cm)
long, cased.
£55–65 / €80–90
$90–105 ⊞ FOX

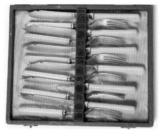

**A set of six silver-plated fish
knives and forks,** with bone handles,
1920s, case 8in (20.5cm) wide.
£24–28 / €34–38
$38–42 ⊞ CCO

**A set of six Art Deco silver-gilt
and enamel coffee spoons,**
Birmingham 1934, 5in (12.5cm) long.
£125–140 / €170–200
$185–220 ⚲ TRM

▶ **A set of six silver-handled
tea knives,** Sheffield 1937,
6½in (16.5cm) long, cased.
£65–75 / €95–105
$105–120 ⊞ FOX

A set of six silver teaspoons,
by Mappin & Webb, Sheffield 1917,
case 7in (18cm) wide.
£80–90 / €115–125
$130–145 ⊞ EXC

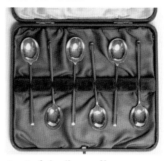

A set of six silver coffee spoons,
Sheffield 1926, 3¾in (9.5cm)
long, cased.
£80–90 / €115–125
$130–145 ⊞ FOX

◀ **An Art Deco
silver-plated
bread fork,**
1930s, 5in
(12.5cm) long.
£22–26
€32–36
$35–42 ⊞ TOP

A set of six nickel-silver teaspoons,
by E. F. Andersson, Scandinavian,
1920s, case 5½in (14cm) square.
£18–22 / €26–30
$30–35 ⊞ CCO

LOCATE THE SOURCE

The source of each illustration
in Miller's can be found by
checking the code letters
below each caption with the
Key to Illustrations, pages
443–451.

**A set of six silver-plated
grapefruit spoons and knife,**
1950s, case 6¾in (17cm) square.
£20–25 / €28–35
$32–40 ⊞ CCO

Metalware

A Georgian copper
funnel, 13in (33cm) high.
£85–95 / €120–135
$135–150 ⊞ TOP

A pair of pewter pint mugs, with twin handles, on
tuck-in feet, hallmarked, early 19thC, 6in (15cm) high.
£95–115 / €135–160
$150–180 ⚒ G(L)

A pair of iron fire tongs, c1880, 24in (61cm) long.
£8–12 / €11–17
$12–18 ⊞ AL

A Victorian brass vesta
case, modelled as an
owl wearing a top hat,
with inset glass eyes,
2in (5cm) high.
£150–180 / €210–250
$240–280 ⚒ G(L)

An iron fireplace shovel, c1890,
27in (68.5cm) long.
£11–15 / €16–20
$18–24 ⊞ AL

A brass reception bell, c1890,
4in (10cm) diam.
£30–35 / €40–50
$50–65 ⊞ AL

A cast-brass paper clip, modelled
as a setter's head, with glass eyes,
late 19thC, 6¾in (17cm) wide.
£160–190 / €230–270
$250–300 ⚒ G(L)

A brass and enamel trinket pot,
c1900, 2½in (6.5cm) diam.
£50–55 / €70–80
$80–90 ⊞ TOP

An iron poker, c1900,
19in (48.5cm) long.
£2–6 / €3–8
$4–10 ⊞ AL

A pair of pewter knife rests, modelled as foxes,
c1900, 4in (10cm) long.
£65–75 / €95–105
$105–120 ⊞ JMC

A pair of pewter knife rests, modelled as dachshunds,
c1900, 3½in (9cm) long.
£25–30 / €35–40
$40–50 ⊞ JMC

An Arts and Crafts copper and enamel charger, the border with applied enamel roundels including a lizard, parrot and flowers, early 20thC, 20½in (52cm) diam.
£300–360 / €430–510
$480–570 ✗ G(L)

A copper and brass bowl, early 20thC, 5in (12.5cm) diam.
£30–35 / €40–50
$50–55 ⊞ TOP

A Tudric pewter bowl, decorated in relief with three owl faces, with glass eyes, early 20thC, 7¼in (18.5cm) diam.
£210–250 / €300–350
$340–400 ✗ G(L)

A Tudric pewter punch bowl, slight damage, marked, early 20thC, 7¼in (18.5cm) high.
£100–120 / €145–170
$160–190 ✗ SWO

◀ **An Art Nouveau Orivit pewter-mounted claret jug,** the fluted glass body with foliate-cast mounts, German, early 20thC, 12¼in (31cm) high.
£300–360
€430–510
$480–570
✗ G(L)

A cold-painted bronze model of a cat, with a wooden leg, offering his hat for donations, Austrian, early 20thC, 2¾in (7cm) high.
£190–230 / €270–320
$310–370 ✗ G(L)

A brass four-letter combination lock, c1910, 1in (2.5cm) wide.
£30–35 / €40–50
$50–55 ⊞ WAB

A cold-painted lead model of a parrot, c1920, 8in (20.5cm) high.
£270–300 / €380–430
$430–480 ⊞ WAA

A brass fire hose nozzle, with a George VI cypher, 1937–52, 9in (23cm) high.
£50–60 / €70–85
$80–95 ⊞ Q&C

Further reading
Miller's Antiques Encyclopedia, Miller's Publications, 2003

◀ **A copper and brass umbrella stand,** modelled as an umbrella, c1950, 30in (76cm) high.
£28–34 / €40–45
$45–50 ✗ SJH

Sixties & Seventies

A Courrèges-style straw hat, with sun visor eyes, Italian, 1960.
£135–150 / €190–210
$210–240 ⊞ LBe

A Bob Dylan poster, by Milton Glaser, 1966, 33 x 22in (83.5 x 56cm).
£220–260 / €310–370
$350–420 ➴ VSP

A set of four interlocking side tables, by Gianfranco Frattini, with reversible black and white tops, c1960, 16in (40.5cm) diam.
£550–650 / €780–920
$880–1,050 ⊞ MARK

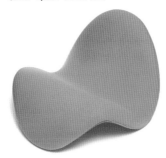

A Pierre Paulin Tongue chair, model 557, 1967.
£550–650 / €780–920
$880–1,050 ⊞ MARK
Pierre Paulin (b1927) was one of France's most successful post-war designers. He created a bold new style of organic seating, inspired by natural forms and using new types of foam and synthetic fabrics to conceal sinuous wood and metal frames. From 1968 to 1972 he helped remodel the public galleries of the Louvre and he was subsequently commissioned by French presidents Pompidou and Mitterand to remodel and finish the Elysée Palace, the presidential residence in Paris. Literally encapsulating the tongue-in-cheek aspect of much '60s design, the tongue chair is one of Paulin's most famous designs.

◄ **A flyer for the musical** *Hair*, 1968, 8½ x 5½in (21.5 x 14cm).
£1–5 / €2–7
$3–8 ⊞ CAST
Hair was the first and most famous musical of the hippy generation. Nudity and songs about sex, drugs and politics created a huge storm, ensuring the success of the show both in New York and London.

A Barker Brothers plate, decorated with Fiesta pattern, c1965, 8¾in (22cm) diam.
£8–12 / €11–17
$12–18 ⊞ HSt

A Human Be-In handbill, *A Gathering of the Tribes,* by Stanley Mouse and Michael Bowen, 1967, 11 x 8½in (28 x 21.5cm).
£220–250 / €310–350
$350–400 ⊞ ASC
This handbill announced the first 'Human Be-In' in Golden Gate Park, and reproduces the richly-decorated Holy Man 'Third-eye' poster, incorporating a photograph by Casey Sonnabend. It lists the main participants including Allen Ginsberg, Timothy Leary, Michael McClure etc. This is one of four colour combinations printed.

A Meakin trio, decorated with Elite Studio pattern, 1960s, plate 7in (18cm) diam.
£14–18 / €20–25
$22–28 ⊞ CHI

A Bouloum stacking lounge chair, designed by Olivier Mourgue, produced by Arconas, American, 1968.
£550–650 / €780–920
$880–1,050 ⊞ MARK
Olivier Mourgue (b1939) was another French designer who produced radical and witty furniture in the 1960s. The Bouloum chaise longue was inspired by the silhouette of one of his friends and called after his childhood nickname. Mourgue's 'Djinn' furniture appeared in Stanley Kubrik's 1968 film *2001: A Space Odyssey.*

A roll of floral wallpaper, 1970, 20in (51cm) wide.
£20–25 / €28–35
$32–40 ⊞ TWI

A Royal Doulton casserole dish, decorated with Seville pattern, 1970s, 7in (18cm) diam.
£45–50 / €65–70
$75–80 ⊞ CHI

A roll of wallpaper, by U.W.P.C., American, 1968, repeat 29 x 27in (73.5 x 68.5cm).
£45–50 / €65–70
$75–80 ⊞ TWI

A Cmielow coffee part-set, comprising six cups and saucers, sugar bowl and coffee pot, 1960s, coffee pot 10in (25.5cm) high.
£55–65 / €80–90
$90–105 ⊞ BET

Tony Blackburn's Chartbuster board game, by ASL Games, 1971, 10 x 14in (25.5 x 35.5cm).
£40–50 / €55–70
$65–80 ⊞ ARo

A stainless steel cruet set, designed by Robert Welch for Old Hall, 1960s, pepper 5in (12.5cm) high.
£30–35 / €40–50
$50–55 ⊞ LUNA

A set of Doulton teaware, decorated in Kaleidoscope pattern, comprising two cups and saucers and one side plate, 1960s, cup 2⅛in (6.5cm) high.
£20–25 / €28–35
$32–40 ⊞ CHI

A pair of snakeskin platform shoes, early 1970s, 4in (10cm) heel.
£135–150 / €190–210
$210–240 ⊞ OH

A set of Arkana moulded plastic dining furniture, comprising a table and six chairs, marked 'Arkana, Bath', 1970s, table 53½in (136cm) diam.
£340–410 / €480–580
$540–650 ➹ SWO

A stainless steel goblet,
by Old Hall, 1970s,
6in (15cm) high.
£14–18 / €20–25
$22–28 ⊞ GRo

**A Pucci maxi-length
skirt and matching
handbag,** 1970s.
£430–480 / €610–680
$690–770 ⊞ Ci

**A Coral plastic alarm
clock,** on a chrome-plated
stand, Japanese, 1970s,
7½in (19cm) high.
£30–35 / €40–50
$50–55 ⊞ GRo

**A plastic handkerchief
ceiling light,** 1970s,
25in (63.5cm) high.
£160–175 / €220–250
$250–280 ⊞ MARK

◀ **A Niba blouse,**
Italian, 1970s.
£60–65 / €85–90
$95–105 ⊞ Ci

**A Roland Klein
stained glass window
dress,** 1970s.
£220–250 / €310–350
$350–400 ⊞ Ci

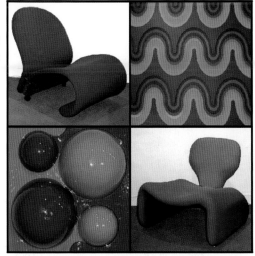

Smoking & Tobacco

An ivory pipe tamper, modelled as a dog, c1730, 2½in (6.5cm) long.
£600–675 / €850–960
$960–1,100 ⊞ RGe

A cast bell metal tobacco jar, with a domed cover, early 19thC, 8in (20.5cm) high.
£50–60 / €70–85
$80–95 ⚒ G(L)

A ram's horn snuff mull, Scottish, c1780, 4in (10cm) wide.
£340–380 / €480–540
$540–610 ⊞ SEA

A horn snuff box, inscribed 'Wm. McGill 1832', 3in (7.5cm) wide.
£320–350 / €450–500
$510–560 ⊞ SEA

A cedar wood snuff box, inlaid with pewter, modelled as a shoe, the hinged cover inlaid with the figure of a woman, late 18thC, 3¾in (9.5cm) wide.
£100–120 / €145–170
$160–190 ⚒ G(L)

A horn snuff mull, modelled as a hoof, with brass mounts, initialled 'C.M.', 1834, 4in (10cm) wide.
£410–450 / €580–640
$650–720 ⊞ SEA

A clay pipe, decorated to one side with a steam locomotive, the other side with a paddle steamer, with roses below, c1850, 4½in (11cm) long.
£65–75 / €90–105
$105–120 ⊞ TML

A horn and silver snuff mull, the lid inset with a citrine, Chester 1886, 3in (7.5cm) wide.
£75–85 / €105–120
$120–135 ⊞ SHa

A clay pipe, decorated with a view of the International Exhibition building, inscribed 'Exhibition 1862', broken, 5¼in (13.5cm) long.
£115–125 / €160–170
$180–200 ⊞ TML

◄ **A brass vesta case,** modelled as a pig, 1890, 2in (5cm) high.
£120–135 / €170–190
$190–210 ⊞ NLS
Vesta matches, produced in 1840 and named after the Roman goddess of the hearth, were made from thick cotton threads dipped in paraffin wax with phosphorous heads that ignited when rubbed. Initially sold in cardboard boxes with sandpaper attached for striking, they easily ignited, hence the need for more durable pocket containers. Vesta cases were produced in a huge variety of styles and materials. Examples in precious metal and rare novelty designs tend to command the highest prices.

A 'Bulkhead' Navy Cut tobacco tin, 1895–1900, 8in (20.5cm) wide.
£220–250 / €310–350
$360–400 ⊞ MURR

A meerschaum pipe, with a wooden stem and amber mouthpiece, Wills Collection label No. M167, 19thC, 13¾in (35cm) long, in original rosewood presentation box.
£105–125 / €150–175
$170–200 ✗ Bri

◄ A brass-mounted porcelain pipe, modelled as a seated cat, with a wood and amber stem, German, 19thC, 8¾in (22cm) long.
£230–270 / €330–380
$370–430 ✗ Bri

A porcelain figural pipe, modelled as a lady with a fan, with a decorative horn stem, European, 19thC, 13¾in (35cm) high.
£500–600
€710–850
$800–960 ✗ Bri

► An inlaid bi-metal nargileh, on a scroll tripod base, Persian, 19thC, 24in (61cm) high.
£400–480
€570–680
$640–770 ✗ Bri

A Doulton Lambeth pipe stand, moulded with masks and foliate swags, the top surmount for a matchbox, the sides with holes for pipes, impressed marks, c1900, 4¾in (12cm) high.
£85–100 / €120–140
$135–160 ✗ L&E

◄ A pine cigar mould, Dutch, c1900, 21in (53.5cm) wide.
£18–22 / €25–30
$28–34 ⊞ Byl

A wood and brass match holder, carved as a Black Forest bear, c1900, 7in (18cm) high.
£170–200 / €240–280
$270–320 ✗ WL

◄ A glass match striker, 1901, 2in (5cm) high.
£150–165 / €210–230
$240–270 ⊞ EXC

A nickel match striker, modelled as a nautical scene, 1900, 7in (18cm) high.
£125–140 / €175–200
$200–225 ⊞ COB

An Asprey & Co silver smoker's compendium, with engine-turned decoration, comprising three graduated boxes for matches, cigarettes and cigars, 1912, largest 6½in (16.5cm) wide.
£1,500–1,800 / €2,100–2,500
$2,400–2,800 ⚒ **G(L)**

A B. D. V. Cigarettes printed advertising cabinet silk, c1917, 19 x 15in (48.5 x 38cm), framed and glazed.
£720–800 / €1,000–1,150
$1,150–1,300 ⊞ **AAA**
Silk advertising flags were given away in each packet of cigarettes and a large cabinet silk poster was given to tobacconists for advertising purposes.

A silver table lighter, by S. W. Smith, modelled as a Roman oil lamp, London 1923, 4in (10cm) high.
£300–325 / €420–460
$470–520 ⊞ **GRe**

A Player's Country Life tobacco tin, 1920s, 4in (10cm) wide.
£35–40 / €50–55
$55–65 ⊞ **WAB**

A Morris's Blue Book Mixed Cigarettes door fingerplate, incorporating a match striker, 1910, 10in (25.5cm) high.
£1,800–2,000
€2,500–2,800
$2,900–3,200 ⊞ **AAA**

A du Maurier Cigarettes advertising showcard, original artwork, 1920s, 10 x 20in (25.5 x 51cm), framed and glazed.
£340–380 / €480–530
$540–600 ⊞ **AAA**
It was common for different studio artists to work on advertising showcards – one would paint the pack, another the horses and yet another would execute the lettering.

◄ **A Player's 'Weights' Cigarettes stonelitho hanging showcard,** by Tom Brown Studios, c1920, 12 x 22in (30.5 x 56cm), framed and glazed.
£1,100–1,250
€1,500–1,800
$1,700–2,000 ⊞ **AAA**

A Murray's Irish Roll poster, 1920s, 25 x 18in (63.5 x 45.5cm).
£220–240 / €310–340
$340–380 ⊞ **Do**

A Royal Doulton Truman's Brown Ale advertising ashtray, 1920s, 6in (15cm) diam.
£65–75 / €90–105
$105–120 ⊞ MURR

A Carreras 'Black Cat' Virginia Cigarettes enamel sign, 1920–30, 36 x 24in (91.5 x 61cm).
£220–250 / €310–350
$350–400 ⊞ AAA

Cross Reference
See Advertising & Packaging (page 19)

A Walters' Cigarettes tin, 1930s, 5in (12.5cm) wide.
£4–8 / €5–11
$6–12 ⊞ RTT

A Dunhill crocodile skin table lighter, 1940s, 4¼in (11cm) high.
£400–450 / €570–640
$640–720 ⊞ OH

◄ A chrome lighter, modelled as an aeroplane, c1960, 6in (15cm) wide.
£130–145 / €180–200
$210–230 ⊞ TOP

A leather and brass cigarette dispenser, modelled as a football, 1935, 5in (12.5cm) diam.
£170–190 / €240–270
$270–300 ⊞ NLS

A Dunhill silver lighter, 1960s, 2in (5cm) high.
£220–250 / €310–350
$350–400 ⊞ OH

Dunhill

Alfred Dunhill Ltd was founded in London in 1893 as a motoring accessories business. In the 1900s, the company expanded into luxury tobacco goods. As cigarette smoking took off in the 1920s and '30s, Dunhill became one of the most famous names in the field, opening shops in Paris, New York and Toronto and expanding into menswear, toiletries and other areas, but it is with smoking accessories that the firm is most notably associated. Dunhill was particularly known for lighters, most famously the Unique lighter, launched in the early 1920s with the slogan 'The lighter that changed public opinion'. Coming in various designs, the Unique could be operated with one hand; its design lessened the risk of petrol evaporation and it rarely needed filling.

An Omega Tissot advertising lighter, 1970s, 5in (12.5cm) high.
£250–280 / €350–400
$400–450 ⊞ TIC

Sport

A brass and glass snooker trophy inkwell, c1870, 7in (18cm) high.
£400–460 / €570–650
$640–740 ⊞ NLS

A set of four lignum vitae bowls, by R. G. Lawrie, 1920–30, boxed, 11in (28cm) square.
£75–85 / €105–120
$120–135 ⊞ AL

Items in the Sport section have been arranged in date order within each sub-section.

A wooden hockey stick, by Northland, 1940, 59in (150cm) long.
£11–15 / €16–20
$18–24 ⊞ TRA

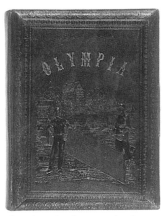

The Olympia photograph album, designed by W. H. S. Thompson, H. Bunnett and others, with illustrations of sporting scenes and musical mechanism, clasp missing, German, c1890, 4°.
£580–700 / €820–990
$930–1,100 ⌁ DW

A white metal Olympic Games medal, minted by Tammaro, 1924, 1¼in (3.5cm) diam.
£95–115 / €135–160
$150–180 ⌁ B(NW)
This medal was awarded to team player Hector Scarone by the Ladies of Montevideo. Scarone was the star of two Uruguay Olympic gold medal winning football teams in 1924 and 1928, in which he contributed with five and three goals respectively. He played his last matches for Uruguay during the inaugural World Cup on home soil in 1930 when his team emerged victorious.

▶ **A plastic sports bag,** 1972, 21in (53.5cm) long.
£30–35 / €40–50
$50–55 ⊞ TWI

A cut-glass curling stone trophy inkwell, with silver mounts and presentation inscription, 1904, 4in (10cm) diam.
£650–750 / €920–1,050
$1,050–1,200 ⊞ MSh

A pair of leather running spikes, with original wooden stretchers, 1930s.
£60–70 / €85–100
$95–110 ⊞ PEZ

A pair of wooden stool ball bats, c1950, 16in (40.5cm) long.
£30–35 / €40–50
$50–55 ⊞ SA
The game of stool ball is more than 500 years old and is the forerunner of the modern game of cricket.

Boxing

Henry Downes Miles, *Pugilistica: being One Hundred and Fourty-four Years of the History of British Boxing,* three volumes, minor damage, 1880, 8°.
£200–240 / €280–340
$320–380 ⚒ RTo

A 'Samson Kina' poster, 1920s, framed, 29 x 20in (73.5 x 51cm).
£320–350 / €450–500
$510–560 ⊞ Do

◀ **A pair of child's cloth boxing gloves,** c1940.
£25–30 / €35–40
$40–50 ⊞ JUN

Muhammed Ali, a signed album page, mounted with a photograph, 1999, 16 x 11½in (40.5 x 29cm).
£75–90 / €110–130
$120–145 ⚒ CO

Cricket

A Bussey Demon Driver cricket bat, 1910, 34in (86.5cm) long.
£90–100 / €125–140
$145–160 ⊞ PEZ

A bronze model of a kangaroo holding a cricket bat, on a chrome base, inscribed 'For the Ashes 1938', 7½in (19cm) high.
£260–310 / €370–440
$420–500 ⚒ TRM

Australia and Britain dominate the market for cricketing memorabilia. Material associated with big names in cricket command the highest prices, one of them being the great Australian cricketer Donald Bradman (1908–2001). At a recent auction of sporting memorabilia, a cricket bat used by Bradman during the 1930s fetched £25,000 / €35,500 / $40,000.

Fishing

'If I might be the judge, God never did make a more calm, quiet, innocent recreation than angling.' Izaak Walton (1593–1683). Fishing is one of the most popular sports across the world, and this certainly spills over into the collectables market. Early equipment can command high prices and recent record-breaking results include £7,600 / €10,800 / $12,150 for a tooled leather fishing creel, made in c1780 by Yorkshire saddlers Atkinson (see Record Breakers page 429).

Vintage fishing books are another sought-after area. First published anonymously in 1653, Izaak Walton's *The Compleat Angler* is arguably the most successful sporting book of all time. With so many different editions having been produced it forms a collecting area in its own right and in 2003 the New York Public Library held a Compleat Angler exhibition to mark 350 years of continuous printing.

Another famous British name in the world of piscatorial antiques is Hardy, leading manufacturers of fishing tackle. In 1872, William Hardy established himself as a gunsmith in Alnwick, Northumberland; the following year he was joined by his brothers and the Hardy

Brothers partnership came into being. The family hobby was fishing and the firm began to produce rods and reels. In 1881, the Hardy Palakona bamboo rod won a gold medal at an exhibition; ten years later the first Hardy Perfect reel was patented. An 1891 reel sold for a record-breaking auction price of £17,000 / €24,150 / $27,200 in 1996. The Perfect was produced in different sizes and materials to suit the various needs of fishermen and, with some modifications, the same basic design is still being manufactured today. Used by generations of Royalty from Prince Albert in the Victorian period to Prince Charles today, Hardy equipment is highly sought after by collectors of antique angling material. Other makers to look out for include Charles Farlow and Samuel Allcock & Co.

Because it was produced for a predominantly wealthy clientele, vintage fishing equipment is often extremely well made – and not just the tackle. Gentlemen liked to preserve their catch in all its glory. From the Victorian period until the 1950s, the leading name in fish taxidermy (a very specialized field) was J. Cooper of London, whose cased fish still command a premium at auction.

Izaak Walton and Charles Cotton, *The Compleat Angler*, second edition by Moses Browne, published by Henry Kent, eight plates, woodcut illustrations, minor repairs, 1759, 12°.
£620–740 / €880–1,050 $990–1,200 ⋏ BBA

A Victorian canvas-covered wood fly tying cabinet, with a lockable front lid and 20 drawers with brass handles, containing feathers, 19in (48.5cm) wide.
£240–290 / €340–410 $380–460 ⋏ MUL

Izaak Walton and Charles Cotton, *The Complete Angler*, first edition by John Hawkins, published by Thomas Hope, 15 engraved plates, 1760, 8°.
£600–700 / €850–1,000 $960–1,100 ⋏ BBA

▶ **Frederic Tolfrey (ed),** *Jones's Guide to Norway, and Salmon-Fisher's Pocket Companion,* published by Longman, eight hand-coloured plates of flies, 1848, 16°.
£5,500–6,500 / €7,800–9,250 $8,800–10,400 ⋏ BBA
This rare publication is the first and most acclaimed British book about fishing in Norway and contains the most exquisitely hand-coloured plates of salmon flies by J. & H. Adlard.

LOCATE THE SOURCE
The source of each illustration in Miller's can be found by checking the code letters below each caption with the Key to Illustrations, pages 443–451.

A Victorian bone fish disgorger, 6in (15cm) long.
£11–15 / €16–20
$18–24 ⊞ AL

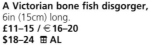

Joseph Crawhall, *The Compleatest Angling Booke That Ever Was Writ,* second edition, one of 100 copies, woodcut and wood-engraved vignettes and illustrations, 1881, 4°.
£360–430 / €510–610
$570–680 ⋟ BBA

A Moscrop Manchester 2¼in brass reel, 1870.
£105–120 / €150–170
$170–190 ⊞ AL

G. Little, *The Angler's Complete Guide and Companion,* published by the author, with 12 hand-coloured plates, c1882, 8°.
£420–500 / €600–710
$670–800 ⋟ BBA
G. Little was the name of a tackle business in Fetter Lane, London, dating back to 1839 under the name Giles Little, who was probably its founder. In the early 1880s it was owned by J. Richardson who, using G. Little as a pen-name, wrote this book.

◄ **A Hardy 2in brass multiplying reel,** with curved crank arm and brass knop, stamped 'Hardy MK IV', late 19thC.
£60–70
€85–100
$95–110 ⋟ G(L)

Piscator, *Handy Guide to the Fishing in the Neighbourhood of Bath,* second edition, original printed wrappers, 1886, 8°.
£300–360 / €420–510
$480–570 ⋟ BBA

A Wells 2in brass reel, with waisted crank arm and ebonite winding knob, late 19thC.
£55–60 / €80–85
$90–95 ⊞ OTB

A Hardy Perfect 3¾in brass reel, with contracted drum, ivory handle and brass foot, c1900.
£1,700–2,000
€2,400–2,850
$2,700–3,200 ⋟ MUL
This is one of the rarest Hardy narrow drum reels, hence its high value.

◄ **A J. Bernard & Son 2½in brass trout fly reel,** c1900.
£60–70 / €85–100
$95–110 ⊞ MINN

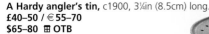

A Hardy angler's tin, c1900, 3¼in (8.5cm) long.
£40–50 / €55–70
$65–80 ⊞ OTB

An eel spear, c1900, 23in (58.5cm) long.
£55–60 / €80–85
$90–95 ⊞ WO

A stuffed and mounted rudd,
by W. F. Homer, in a gilt-lined
bowfronted case, inscribed 'Rudd,
caught in the River Bure by
T. Huskinson, 2nd Aug 1908', 445g.
£400–480 / €570–680
$640–770 ⋏ MUL

▶ **A Hardy Perfect 2⅞in trout fly
reel,** with check mechanism, brass
foot, left-hand threaded drum
locking screw, 1912–17.
£180–200 / €250–280
$290–320 ⊞ OTB

A bait tin, with pierced cover
and wooden handle, c1910,
6in (15cm) high.
£65–75 / €90–105
$105–120 ⊞ YT

A stuffed and mounted trout,
by J. Cooper & Sons, in a gilt-lined
bowfronted case, inscribed 'Caught
by W. Hunt at Stoke-on-Tern, Salop,
June 10th 1916, weight 4lbs', case
26in (66cm) wide.
£1,800–2,100 / €2,550–3,000
$2,900–3,350 ⋏ MUL
Cased fish are perennially popular,
particularly examples created
by J. Cooper, the leading British
taxidermist in the field. The rarest
examples are multiple cased fish
and recent record prices include
£8,900 / €12,650 / $14,250 for a
pair of glass-fronted cabinets by
Cooper containing 15 brown trout
caught by the Earl of Coventry in
1879 during a fly-fishing holiday
in Ireland. Gold lettering on the
case often records the time, place
and details of the catch. Another
dating tip is the coloured
background. Until the late 1920s,
Cooper's interiors were painted
pale blue, but later the firm used
a pale green background.

Items in the Sport section
have been arranged in date
order within each sub-section.

**An Allcock
Collapsing Spoon
lure,** with spring-
loaded wings and
wool treble hook,
c1920, body
1¾in (4.5cm) long.
£20–25
€28–35
$32–40 ⊞ OTB

A 3in wooden reel, c1920.
£15–20 / €20–28
$24–32 ⊞ AL

A folding trout net, with wooden handle and brass fittings, 1920s, 45in (114.5cm) long.
£70–80 / € 100–115
$115–130 ⊞ MINN

A Wheatley trout dry fly box, c1920s, 6in (15cm) wide.
£55–60 / € 80–85
$90–95 ⊞ MINN

A 2¾in brass Malbo reel, c1930.
£35–40 / € 50–55
$55–65 ⊞ AL

A Hardy ebonite Cascapedia 2/0 multiplying fly reel, with ebonite handle in anti-foul rim, Dural spool and block foot, stamped '24', c1931.
£9,500–11,400 / € 13,500–16,200
$15,200–18,250 ⤳ MUL
This is one of the most desirable of Hardy collectable reels.

A Hardy Larmuth brass disgorger, c1930s, 7¼in (18.5cm) long.
£35–40 / € 50–55
$55–65 ⊞ OTB

A Hardy 40lb salmon balance, c1930s, 6¼in (16cm) long.
£35–40 / € 50–55
$55–65 ⊞ OTB

A Hardy steel salmon gaff, c1930s, 17in (43cm) long.
£70–80 / € 100–115
$115–130 ⊞ MINN

A bamboo gaff, c1950.
£11–15 / € 16–20
$18–24 ⊞ AL

A Lesney bread bait press, c1950, in original box, 1½ x 2¾in (4 x 7cm).
£11–15 / € 16–20
$18–24 ⊞ OTB

Football

Football memorabilia is currently performing very strongly. Plenty of good material is arriving on the market because, in collecting terms, it is still a relatively recent subject. Footballing auctions are seeing a high rate of sales, strong prices and rooms packed out with private collectors rather than dealers. Printed materials are one of the strongest performers in the collectable league, including objects such as tickets and programmes which have been making higher and higher prices. Pre-WWII programmes are the most sought after and this year saw a world record auction price paid for a programme for the 1901 cup final between Tottenham Hotspur and Sheffield United (see Record Breakers page 429). World Cup material can attract considerable interest and modern collectables include football shirts, the highest prices reflecting the current celebrity status of the players.

A Pinnacle Cigarettes advertising sign, by Godfrey Phillips, featuring cigarette cards depicting Aston Villa players, 1923–24, 12 x 18in (30.5 x 45.5cm).
£1,100–1,200 / €1,550–1,700
$1,750–1,950 ⊞ MURR

A leather football, 1920s.
£30–35 / €40–50
$50–55 ⊞ MINN

A World Cup ticket, for the opening ceremony and Uruguay v Peru game, with Executive Committee stamp, 1930.
£700–840 / €1,000–1,200
$1,150–1,350 ⚒ B(NW)

A pair of white metal cufflinks, depicting footballers, awarded to Hectore Scarone during the Olympic Games, 1924.
£80–95 / €115–135
$130–150 ⚒ B(NW)

Sir John Langenus, a photograph, 1930, 3¼ x 4¼in (8.5 x 11cm).
£65–75 / €90–105
$105–120 ⚒ B(NW)
John Langenus was the referee for the 1930 World Cup Final.

A Uruguayan team photograph, inscribed 'El Once Glorioso, 1924–1928–1930', 3¼ x 4¼in (8.5 x 11cm).
£100–120 / €140–170
$160–190 ⚒ B(NW)

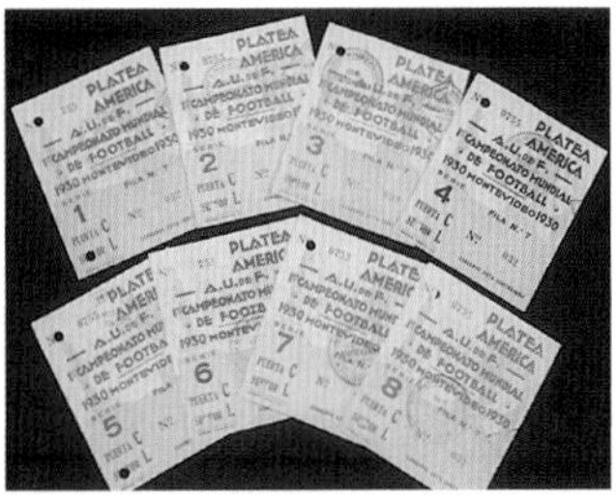

A set of eight World Cup tickets, Platea America Tribune, gate C, No. 755, section 1, seat No. 032, with Executive Committee stamp, 1930.
£4,600–5,500 / €6,550–7,800
$7,350–8,800 ⚒ B(NW)
This is the only known complete set of tickets with the same tribune sector, ticket number and seat number.

◄ **A World Cup ticket,** No. 3, with Executive Committee stamp, 1930.
£820–980 / €1,150–1,400
$1,300–1,550 ⚒ B(NW)

◀ A bronze and enamel World Cup accreditation jacket badge, minted by Stefano Johnson, inscribed 'Consejero de la F.I.F.A.', 1930.
£480–580
€680–820
$770–930
⚒ B(NW)
Only members of FIFA were issued these badges and this is the only known example.

A World Cup Final leather football, Uruguay v Argentina, 1930, with a letter of authenticity.
£10,000–12,000 / €14,200–17,000
$16,000–19,200 ⚒ B(NW)

A spelter figure, in the form of a football player, French, c1930, 12in (30.5cm) high.
£300–350 / €430–500
$480–560 ⚒ PEZ

John Player & Sons, Hints of Association Football, set of 50, 1934.
£35–40 / €50–55
$55–65 ⚒ SOR

A Rugby Town AFC programme, 1949, 5 x 7in (12.5 x 18cm) opened.
£35–40 / €50–55
$55–65 ⚒ MRW

▶ A pair of Tom Finney's autographed leather featherweight football boots, 1950s.
£110–120 / €155–170
$175–190 ⚒ PEZ

A postcard of a football match, 1940s, 3 x 5in (7.5 x 12.5cm).
£45–50 / €65–70
$75–80 ⚒ EE

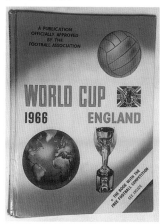

World Cup 1966, 11 x 8in (28 x 20.5cm).
£20–25 / €28–35
$32–40 ⚒ EE

▶ A Weald of Kent Football League medal, 1967, 1¼in (3cm) diam
£13–17 / €19–24
$21–27 ⚒ RTT

An FA Cup winner's 9ct gold and enamel medal, inscribed 'Scottish Football Association, Scottish Cup Winners, 1969–70, J. Forrest', in original case.
£840–1,000 / €1,200–1,400
$1,350–1,600 ⚒ S(O)
James Forrest was born in Glasgow in 1944. Originally signed by Rangers, he transferred to Preston North End in March 1967 and eventually played for Aberdeen where he won a further Scottish Cup medal in 1970.

Goal **magazine,** with Jackie Charlton on the cover, 1970, 11½ x 9in (29 x 23cm).
£1–5 / €2–7
$3–8 ⊞ TWI

◄ **A silver money clip,** decorated with a gold football, 1980s, 2in (5cm) long.
£50–55 / €70–80
$80–90 ⊞ BND

An England No. 7 international jersey, signed by David Beckham and the England squad, together with a letter of authenticity signed by Les Reed, National Coach & Director of Technical Development, Football Association, 2000.
£2,400–2,900 / €3,400–4,100
$3,850–4,650 ↗ S(O)
Mr Reed's letter confirms that this was one of the match shirts issued to David Beckham for the historic last match held at Wembley Stadium against Germany on 7 October 2000. It was donated by the FA to the Bishop's Stortford High School to auction for their sports fund.

A Northern Ireland No. 11 international jersey, signed 'To Terry, Best Wishes, George Best', early 1970s.
£6,250–7,500 / €8,850–10,650
$10,000–12,000 ↗ S(O)

A Scotland No. 8 jersey, signed by Jim Bett and several other Scottish internationals, inscribed 'FIFA World Cup, Italy '90', together with a letter of authenticity signed by Jim Bett.
£350–420 / €500–600
$560–670 ↗ S(O)

An Arsenal FA Cup Final training jersey, worn by Terry Neill, long-sleeved with embroidered inscription 'TN, F.A. Cup Final, Wembley 1978'.
£380–450 / €540–640
$610–720 ↗ S(O)

Nicolas Anelka, a signed colour photograph, c2000, 8 x 10in (20.5 x 25.5cm).
£20–25 / €28–35
$32–40 ⊞ PICC

A France No. 5 international jersey, signed by Zinedine Zidane, c2000, framed and glazed, 34¼ x 30in (87 x 76cm).
£190–230 / €270–320
$300–360 ↗ DW

◄ **A Sunderland replica shirt,** signed by the squad, 2003.
£200–220 / €280–310
$320–350 ⊞ SSL

Golf

Golfing sales have been failing to reach the soaring heights of the 1980s and '90s when a rare feathery golf ball fetched £17,000 / €24,150 / $27,200 at Phillips, and Henry's Rifled Ball (a patented gutta percha example) made a world record £29,900 / €42,450 / $47,850 at Sotheby's. Few great rarities have been coming on to the market and uncertain prices mean that collectors are unlikely to part with their choicest material. Nevertheless, unusual items such as the Caird wry-neck putter, the first of its kind to come to auction, can still do well and the market remains strong for golfing pictures and decorative art objects featuring golfing scenes.

▶ **A J. S. Caird wry-necked putter,** with two strip arms and wide blade, stamped shaft, c1900, 34in (86.5cm) long.
£6,000–7,000
€8,500–10,000
$9,600–11,200 ✗ BGo
Unorthodox putters are much sought after by golf enthusiasts. On this putter the gap between the two arms allows the golfer to see the whole ball. The hosel points in front of the ball rather than at the centre or the striking spot.

A pair of Simplex studded iron sole plates, with adjustable welt clips and leather ankle straps, stamped 'Left' and 'Right', 1890s.
£170–200 / €240–280
$270–320 ✗ BGo

A lofting iron, with smooth face and short thick hosel, c1890.
£90–100 / €125–140
$145–160 ⊞ MSh
A lofting iron is a club designed to hit the ball high into the air. The hosel is the lower extension of an iron club shaft to which the head is fitted.

A Finnigans brass putter, with steel face insert, c1900.
£135–150 / €190–210
$210–240 ⊞ MSh

A brass vesta case, decorated with golf clubs, c1900, 1½in (4cm) high.
£70–85 / €100–120
$115–135 ✗ BGo
Vesta cases were used to contain wooden matches and usually had a rough patch on which they could be struck. Vestas were lightweight and small enough to fit into a waistcoat pocket or hang from the chain of a pocketwatch.

An H. L. Curtis scared-head putter, c1905.
£180–200 / €250–280
$290–320 ⊞ MSh

A silver-mounted pottery match striker, in the form of a golf ball, 1909, 2½in (6.5cm) high.
£145–165 / €210–240
$230–260 ⊞ NLS

Cope Bros & Co, Golfers, set of 50, 1900.
£3,600–4,000 / €5,100–5,700
$5,750–6,400 ⊞ MSh
The first sets of golfing cigarette cards were produced at the turn of the century. Cope's Golfers, issued in 1900 and based on watercolour designs by George Pipeshank, is like a miniature *Who's Who?* of golf, featuring famous players such as Tom Morris alongside such characters as King Charles I wielding a golf club. This rare set is now much sought after by collectors. Beware of modern reprints.

A black and white photograph, featuring the participants of an exhibition match, c1910, 6¼ x 8in (16 x 20.5cm).
£150–180 / €210–250
$240–290 ⋌ BGo

▶ A Mills patent pitching mashie, c1910, 38in (99cm) long.
£155–175
€220–250
$250–280
⊞ MINN
A mashie is an old club equivalent to a five or six iron.

An F. H. Ayres Schenectady Truput putter, c1920.
£200–220 / €280–310
$320–350 ⊞ MSh
The Schenectady was a centre-shafted club.

◀ A golf cocktail set, in a vinyl golf bag, 1970s, 9in (23cm) high.
£20–25 / €28–35
$32–40 ⊞ RTT

A wood and metal Kiddi-Golf crazy golf game, possibly made by Glevum, in a cardboard box, c1930, 10½ x 13in (26.5 x 33cm).
£200–220 / €280–310
$320–350 ⊞ ARo

Souvenir of Carnoustie Golf Course, 1933, 11 x 9in (28 x 23cm), with coloured map.
£500–600 / €710–850
$800–960 ⋌ BGo

◀ A golf cocktail set, *(repeated above)*

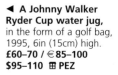

A Table Golf game, with metal golfers and accessories, c1940s, boxed, 8½ x 10in (21.5 x 25.5cm).
£200–220 / €280–310
$320–350 ⊞ ARo

◀ A Johnny Walker Ryder Cup water jug, in the form of a golf bag, 1995, 6in (15cm) high.
£60–70 / €85–100
$95–110 ⊞ PEZ

Horses

A pair of leather and wood stirrup slippers,
Continental, 19thC, 7in (18cm) long.
£50–60 / €70–85
$80–95 ⊞ STS

A ceramic inkwell,
the cover modelled as a
jockey's hat, 1880–90,
4½in (11.5cm) high.
£115–130 / €165–185
$185–210 ⊞ MURR

**A pair of leather and
canvas riding boots,**
with wooden trees, 19thC.
£85–95 / €120–135
$135–150 ⊞ TOP

A cast-iron saddle rack,
c1890, 20in (51cm) long.
£25–30 / €35–40
$40–50 ⊞ AL

▶ **An apprentice piece
leather saddle,** 1920–30,
7in (18cm) high.
£300–330 / €430–470
$480–530 ⋗ RGa

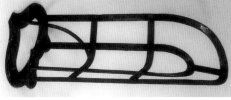

▶ **A pair of ebony and
steel boot pulls,** c1920,
8in (20.5cm) long.
£25–30 / €35–40
$40–50 ⊞ WAB

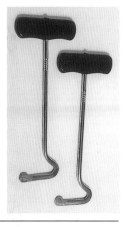

Rugby

▶ **A wooden rugby trophy,** from the
seven-a-side tournament, Bombay, 1945,
3in (7.5cm) high.
£45–50 / €65–70
$75–80 ⊞ PEZ

A glass tumbler,
commemorating the Wales
v All Blacks game, Cardiff,
1905, 4¾in (12cm) high.
£280–340 / €400–480
$450–540 ⋗ DW

A Spalding Touchdown leather rugby ball,
with eight panels, 1930–40, 11in (28cm) long.
£70–80 / €100–115
$115–130 ⊞ PEZ

England's victory in the
2003 Rugby World Cup was
an historic occasion and
memorabilia associated with
it will, no doubt, appear in
future editions of this guide.

Tennis

A silver-plated tennis cruet set, 1900, 5in (12.5cm) wide.
£350–390 / €500–550 $560–620 ⊞ NLS

► **An Amhurst tennis racket,** c1900.
£300–340 / €430–480 $480–540 ⊞ MSh

A tin wind-up musical box, transfer-printed with tennis scenes, c1910, 3in (7.5cm) high.
£65–75 / €90–105 $105–120 ⊞ MURR

A silver bracelet, in the form of linked tennis rackets, 1930, 15in (38cm) long.
£110–125 / €155–175 $175–200 ⊞ NLS

A spelter tennis trophy, 1900–10, 9in (23cm) high.
£220–250 / €310–350 $350–400 ⊞ PEZ

A St Amand plate, decorated with a tennis scene, French, 1920s, 7½in (19cm) diam.
£100–115 / €140–165 $160–185 ⊞ NLS

◄ **A Spalding Top Flite tennis racket,** with open throat, 1930s.
£100–120 / €140–170 $160–190 ⊞ MSh

A Parkstone Film Co poster, *The Art of Tennis and How to Play It*, minor damage, early 20thC, 30 x 20in (76 x 51cm).
£11–15 / €16–20 $18–24 ✗ ONS

An Argus tennis racket, with chequered grip, 1920s.
£110–125 / €155–175 $175–200 ⊞ MSh

◄ **A Terry's tennis racket clip,** 1940s–50s, boxed, 8 x 6in (20.5 x 15cm).
£45–50 / €65–70 $75–80 ⊞ MURR

Teddy Bears & Soft Toys

◀ **A Schuco plush teddy bear powder compact,** with a detachable head and hinged abdomen, c1930, 3½in (9cm) high.
£440–520 / €630–740 $700–830 ⋪ G(L)

A Steiff mohair straw-filled teddy bear, with boot-button eyes, stitched nose, mouth and claws and felt paw pads, slight wear, German, c1909, 8¼in (21cm) high.
£420–500 / €600–710 $670–800 ⋪ B(Kn)

A Farnell plush teddy bear, with shaven snout, hump back and webbed paws, two pads replaced, growler not working, c1920, 15½in (39.5cm) high.
£560–660 / €800–940 $900–1,050 ⋪ G(L)

A Chiltern mohair teddy bear, with glass eyes, stitched nose, mouth and claws and cloth paw pads, some wear, c1930, 14½in (37cm) high.
£750–850 / €1,100–1,200 $1,200–1,350 ⋪ B(Kn)

▶ **A plush teddy bear,** with glass eyes and shaven snout, 1930s, 26in (66cm) high.
£150–180 / €210–250 $240–280 ⋪ G(L)

A Dean's Dismal Desmond Dalmatian, 1930s, 6½in (16.5cm) high.
£150–180 / €210–250 $240–280 ⋪ FHF
Dismal Desmond, the comic strip character created by George Hilderbrandt, was produced by Dean's Rag Book Company in a variety of shapes and sizes. Launched in 1926, Desmond was a huge success, becoming a mascot of the British Cricket team that year as well as for the ladies' changing rooms at Wimbledon. The toy remained in production until WWII and was reintroduced in the 1980s.

A Chiltern musical bear, 1930s, 14in (35.5cm) high.
£220–250 / €310–350 $350–400 ⊞ POLL

▶ **A Pedigree teddy bear,** pads replaced, 1930s, 18in (45.5cm) high.
£220–250 / €310–350 $350–400 ⊞ POLL

A Dean's mohair Scottie dog, 1940,
14in (35.5cm) long.
£45–50 / €65–70
$75–80 ⊞ POLL

A plush Felix the Cat, with velvet eyes and nose, felt mouth and stitched teeth, 1930s, 15¼in (38.5cm) high.
£280–340 / €400–480
$450–540 ⚒ B(WM)
America's most famous cartoon creature before Mickey Mouse, Felix the Cat, was created by animator Otto Messner for film-maker Pat Sullivan and first appeared in the short film *Feline Follies* in 1919. With further films and a syndicated cartoon strip (1923–43), Felix became an international star to rival Charlie Chaplin and Buster Keaton. The Prince of Wales (later Edward VIII) made Felix the mascot of his polo team and he was also Charles Lindberg's mascot on his famous transatlantic flight. Felix inspired a wealth of marketing including soft toys. The English Felix was distinctively skinny with wide-spaced (and slightly disturbing) teeth. The tail served as part of a tripod so that the cat could stand, illustrating the words of his signature tune 'Felix keeps on walking...with his hands behind him'.

A Pedigree dog walker, 1940s, 22in (56cm) high.
£120–130 / €165–185
$190–210 ⊞ POLL

▶ **A panda,** possibly by Dean's, 1940s, 15in (38cm) high.
£220–250
€310–350
$350–400
⊞ POLL

◀ **A Dean's dog,** 1940s, 22in (56cm) long.
£85–95
€120–135
$135–150
⊞ POLL

A poodle nightdress case, 1950, 20in (51cm) long.
£30–35 / €40–50
$50–55 ⊞ POLL

A Steiff goat, German, c1948, 7in (18cm) high.
£45–50 / €65–70
$75–80 ⊞ UD

▶ **A Steiff tiger,** with glass eyes and stitched nose and pads, German, 1950s, 14in (35.5cm) long.
£50–60 / €70–85
$80–95 ⚒ FHF

▶ **A Dean's chimpanzee,** 1950s, 12in (30.5cm) high.
£35–40
€50–55
$55–65 ⊞ UD
Designed by Sylvia Wilgoss, the chimpanzee was one of Dean's most popular toys and was produced from 1955 to 1988.

A Steiff mohair teddy bear, with ear button and plastic eyes, pads worn, German, 1950s, 11in (28cm) high.
**£290–330 / €410–470
$460–530 ⊞ BBe**

A silk plush teddy bear, wearing a vintage dress, 1950s, 27in (68.5cm) high.
**£140–155 / €200–220
$220–250 ⊞ POLL**

A Chiltern Hugmee bear, with squeaker, 1950s, 14in (35.5cm) high.
**£230–260 / €330–370
$370–420 ⊞ POLL**

A Chiltern mohair teddy bear, with glass eyes, 1950s, 17in (43cm) high.
**£320–350 / €450–500
$510–560 ⊞ BBe**

◄ **A Steiff plush kitten,** with glass eyes, German, 1950s, 3½in (9cm) high.
**£50–60
€70–85
$80–95 ✗ FHF**

▶ **A Chad Valley mohair teddy bear,** with glass eyes, Rexine pads and label to side seam, 1950s, 12in (30.5cm) high.
**£170–190 / €240–270
$270–300 ⊞ BBe**

A plush teddy bear, with plastic eyes and growler, 1950s, 25in (63.5cm) high.
£45–50 / €65–70
$75–80 ✗ G(L)

A Merrythought Thumper, 1956–80, 22in (56cm) high.
£115–125 / €160–180
$180–200 ⊞ POLL
Thumper is a character from the Walt Disney film, *Bambi*.

◄ **A Jacko the Monkey** cloth and vinyl soft toy, c1960, 20in (51cm) high.
£15–20 / €20–28
$24–32 ⊞ UD

► **A Pedigree mohair teddy bear,** with plastic eyes and velvet pads, 1960s, 12in (30.5cm) high.
£85–95 / €120–135
$135–150 ⊞ BBe

A felt golly, c1960, 19in (48.5cm) high.
£18–22 / €25–30
$28–34 ⊞ UD

A Wendy Boston synthetic machine-washable bear, with nylon eyes, 1960s, 24in (61cm) high.
£55–60 / €80–85
$90–95 ⊞ BBe
Wendy Boston created the first machine-washable bear in 1954. The bear was unjointed and made from all synthetic materials including nylon fur, nylon screw-locked eyes and plastic foam stuffing that was widely adopted by the toy industry until it was later recognized as a fire risk. Boston advertised the bear on television, showing it being washed and put through a mangle.

A Pedigree Eeyore, 1960s, 8in (20.5cm) high.
£30–35 / €40–50
$50–55 ⊞ POLL
The melancholy donkey from A. A. Milne's Winnie-the-Pooh stories, Eeyore was inspired by the character of Sir Owen Seaman (1861–1936), who was Milne's editor at *Punch* magazine for eight years.

A La Verne & Shirley Kitty cat, American, 1970s, 22in (56cm) high.
£125–140 / €175–200
$200–220 ⊞ SpM

► **A Gordon the Gopher,** c1985, 16in (40.5cm) high.
£18–22 / €25–30
$28–34 ⊞ UD

Sooty

On holiday in Blackpool in 1946, Harry Corbett spent 7s 6d on a bear puppet to amuse his children. An engineer by trade, he was also an amateur magician and he and 'Teddy' got their first TV break on BBC *Talent Night* in 1952. The pair were an instant hit, but Harry was told to make Teddy a bit different – he blackened his nose and eyes and Sooty was born.

Sooty was given his own TV show in 1955 and became one of the last great silent stars. In fact, Harry insured his right finger and thumb for £20,000 / €28,500 / $32,000. The squeaky Sweep joined the team in 1957, and in 1964 came Soo, Sooty's panda girlfriend, although the BBC forbade the pair to touch on screen. Hammers, initially a regular prop, were also banned when a child fan crashed a real hammer on to his father's head because Sooty did it on TV. Water pistols, however, remained a favourite slapstick weapon, and music was provided by Sooty's trademark xylophone.

In 1976, after his father suffered from a heart attack, Matthew Corbett took over as Sooty's right hand man until 1998, when he retired to be replaced by Richard Cadell. Sooty became a cartoon series in 1996 and programmes and stage performances continue today.

For over half a century, generations of children have grown up with Sooty, hence the demand for period material. On 18 November 2003, Bonham's sold a pair of original Sooty and Sweep puppets used by Harry Corbett in what was to be his last TV appearance at Christmas 1975, and which finished with his usual catchphrase: 'Bye bye everybody, bye bye'.

Two Sooty egg cups, the bases modelled as televisions, slight damage, 1950s, 2in (5cm) high.
£20–25 / €28–35
$32–40 ⊞ HYP

Three Sooty ceramic egg cups, 1950s, 2in (5cm) high.
£30–35 / €45–50
$50–55 each ⊞ HYP

A Sooty bear, 1950s, 17in (43cm) high.
£85–95 / €120–135
$135–150 ⊞ TOP

▶ A Sooty Super Xylophone, c1960, 11in (28cm) wide, in original box.
£30–35 / €40–50
$50–55 ⊞ TOP

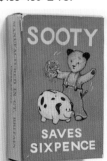

A Sooty card game, 1960, 5 x 3¼in (12.5 x 8.5cm).
£11–15 / €16–20
$18–24 ⊞ HUX

Further reading

Miller's American Insider's Guide to Toys & Games, Miller's Publications, 2002

◀ A set of Sooty, Sweep, Soo and Scampi hand puppets, 1980s, 12in (30.5cm) high.
£25–30 / €35–40
$40–50 ⊞ UD
Scampi is Sooty's cousin.

Telephones

A copper and brass telephone, with Bakelite handset, fully converted, 1920s, 8½in (21.5cm) high.
£165–185 / €230–260
$260–290 ⊞ TASV

A railway telephone, with a mahogany case and original braid lead, fully converted, 1930s, 14½in (37cm) high.
£100–110 / €140–155
$160–170 ⊞ TASV

A Bell Gurder telephone, the metal body containing the bells, 1938–56, 6½in (16.5cm) high.
£80–90 / €115–130
$130–145 ⊞ TL

A 300 series Bakelite telephone, 1940–50, 9in (23cm) wide.
£180–200 / €250–280
$290–320 ⊞ JAZZ
The 300 series telephone was designed by Norwegian artist Jean Heiberg (1884–1976) for the Swedish company L. M. Ericsson. It was manufactured in Europe, the USA and in the UK under license by Siemens. Telephones with cord braid, cheese drawer and call exchange button make higher prices.

▶ **An Ericsson 332 series Bakelite telephone,** 1950s, 6in (15cm) high.
£70–80 / €100–110
$115–130 ⊞ TL

◀ **A Bakelite telephone,** German, 1950s, 7in (18cm) wide.
£350–400 / €500–570
$560–640 ⊞ MARK

A Bell telephone, with a metal body, 1950s, 5½in (14cm) high.
£80–90 / €115–130
$130–145 ⊞ TL
The brass bar at the front hinges upwards to create a carrying handle – thus providing an early version of the portable telephone.

▶ **A Bakelite telephone,** with a 'mother-in-law' listener, French, 1950s, 5½in (14cm) high.
£70–80
€100–110
$115–130 ⊞ TL

A Bell enamel, cast-iron and Bakelite telephone, with a brass carrying handle, fully converted, 1950s, 6in (15cm) wide.
£145–160 / €210–230
$230–260 ⊞ TASV

◀ **A 706L telephone,** fully converted, 1960s, 5in (12.5cm) wide.
£45–50 / €65–70
$75–80 ⊞ TASV

A Bobo telephone, designed by Tecler, Italian, 1970, 8in (20.5cm) wide.
**£115–125 / € 160–180
$180–200 ⊞ LUNA**

A clear Perspex telephone, 1970s, 8in (20.5cm) wide.
**£85–95 / € 120–135
$135–150 ⊞ PLB**

A Winnie-the-Pooh telephone, by The American Telecommunications Corporation, with a plastic body and rubber butterfly, on a *faux* wood base, 1970s, 15in (38cm) high.
**£320–350 / € 450–500
$510–560 ⊞ DHAR**

An Ericsson Ericofon, 1960s, 9in (23cm) high.
**£85–95 / € 120–135
$135–150 ⊞ LUNA**
The Ericofon was the first successful single piece telephone, paving the way towards a cordless future. Originally designed by Ralph Lysell in 1941, it was put into production by Ericsson in 1954. The base incorporates dial and speaker, and all the functions are incorporated into a single lightweight acrylic case. In the USA it was called the Erica and aimed at the housewife market.

A GNT Copenhagen telephone, designed by Henning Andreasen, Danish, 1980, 10in (25.5cm) wide.
**£35–40 / € 50–55
$55–65 ⊞ TL**

▶ **A Mickey Mouse Picnic telephone,** early 1980s, 4in (10cm) high.
**£25–30 / € 35–40
$40–50 ⊞ TL**

A Swatch Two-in-One telephone, late 1980s, 5in (13cm) long.
**£45–50 / € 65–70
$75–80 ⊞ TL**
This was a novel telephone of the 1980s, in which the base was also a telephone, thus allowing a three-way conversation.

▶ **A Darth Vader telephone,** c1990, 11in (28cm) high.
**£65–75 / € 95–105
$105–120 ⊞ LUNA**

A *Star Trek* telephone, comprising a two-piece replica of the *USS Enterprise*, with tone/pulse dialling, redial, mute, ringer features, LED flash and red alert sounder, limited edition, signed, early 1990s, 11¾in (30cm) high.
**£60–70 / € 85–100
$95–110 ⊞ TL**

An Intercity train telephone, with push buttons and flashing lights, early 1990s, 11¾in (30cm) wide.
£11–15 / €16–20
$18–24 ⊞ TL

A Beatles bus telephone, in front of an illuminated billboard featuring the Beatles, Belisha beacon lights up when the telephone rings, early 1990s, 13¾in (35cm) high.
£55–60 / €80–85
$90–95 ⊞ TL

A Betty Boop telephone, the lamppost lights up when the telephone rings, push button dialling, tone/pulse, last number redial and flash, early 1990s, 8in (20.5cm) high.
£35–40 / €50–55
$55–65 ⊞ TL

A *Star Wars* R2D2 telephone, with moving head, lights, sound effects, redial, tone/pulse, early 1990s, 15¾in (40cm) high.
£70–80 / €100–110
$115–130 ⊞ TL

A cat telephone, with tone/pulse, mute and redial, early 1990s, 11¾in (30cm) wide.
£35–40 / €50–55
$55–65 ⊞ TL

A Dalmatian telephone, with barking sound, ringer, redial and tone/pulse, early 1990s, 9¾in (25cm) wide.
£25–30 / €35–40
$40–50 ⊞ TL

▶ **A Hot Lips telephone,** with redial and tone/pulse, early 1990s, 8in (20cm) wide.
£30–35 / €40–50
$50–55 ⊞ TL

◀ **A Snoopy and Woodstock telephone and money box,** with push button dial, electronic ringer, lighted keypad, last number redial and tone/pulse, early 1990s, 4in (10cm) high.
£35–40 / €50–55
$55–65 ⊞ TL

Textiles & Fashion

An appliqué mat, with feltwork cats, American, c1900, 17 x 32in (43 x 81.5cm).
£170–190 / €240–270
$270–300 ⚘ COPA

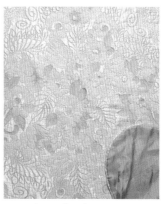

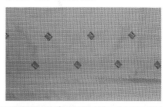

An embossed satin bedspread, 1930.
£160–180 / €230–260
$260–290 ⊞ MARG

A woolwork tapestry, depicting children, dogs, deer, parrots and floral sprays, within a floral border, c1850, 25½ x 25in (64.5 x 63.5cm), in a gilt frame.
£440–530 / €620–750
$700–850 ⚘ RTo

A pair of wool and silk curtain ties, 1950, 38in (96.5cm) long.
£100–120 / €140–170
$160–190 ⊞ JPr

▶ **A length of Hermès silk fabric,** 1960s–70s, 29in (73.5cm) wide.
£6–10 / €8–14
$10–16 ⊞ OH

LOCATE THE SOURCE

The source of each illustration in Miller's can be found by checking the code letters below each caption with the Key to Illustrations, pages 443–451.

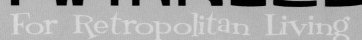

Ladies' Fashion

In recent times, collecting and wearing vintage fashion items has become both increasingly popular and more mainstream. 'We've grown up', says Leslie Verrinder from Tin Tin Collectables at Alfies Antique Market. 'People don't think any more that they have to dress entirely in a period style. Most will mix and match old and new. They're buying vintage to create a great modern look, not because they want to live in the past.'

While pre-1900 clothes can be hard to wear, both because of the fragility and small size of many of the garments, the 20th century offers a huge range of styles to choose from. 'To a certain extent it's like buying modern fashion,' advises Leslie. 'If you are buying to wear, the first rule is to buy what suits you and what you feel good in. Condition is also a factor. Always try things on, check the hems, the seams, underneath the arms, anywhere a garment is likely to become strained or worn.'

From the Edwardian period, Leslie recommends shawls and brocade coats that can easily be slipped over a modern outfit; white lace day dresses for summer wear and beaded evening bags – a good choice for someone who wants to go for a single interesting accessory rather than adopting a whole retro look. Best sellers from the 1920s include beaded flapper dresses which, thanks to their loose, straight-up-and-down line, can still fit the modern figure and look extremely glamorous. 'These are prohibitively expensive to restore, so try to buy in good condition,' recommends Leslie.

'Dresses beaded on cotton voile are more durable than dresses beaded on chiffon, which have to be laid flat. Good examples aren't cheap, but I think that as long as you look after them well they are an investment. A great flapper dress is a classic that will never go out of fashion.' Lamé coats and jackets from the interwar period are another wearable buy, as are velvet pieces. 'In the '20s and '30s they used silk pile velvet which has a lovely sheen to it, much softer and more beautiful than the cotton or viscose pile velvets that came in later.' After WWII, some of the highest prices are reserved for clothes by big designer names such as Dior, Yves St Laurent, Givenchy and Balenciaga.

Whereas Paris set the style in the '50s, in the '60s and '70s, swinging London was the centre of the teenage fashion scene, and labels to look out for include Biba, Mary Quant, Miss Mouse and Ossie Clark. As Leslie warns, however, a big name on the label does not necessarily mean that a garment is worth a fortune. Many designers produced ready-to-wear designs for the department stores, but it is the one-off couture pieces that fetch the highest prices. As well as a maker, provenance can enhance the interest of a garment; for example, a photo of the original owner in her outfit, or any other period documentation, particularly if the owner was a person of some significance. 'As with all collecting, the more you know and learn, the better you'll buy,' concludes Leslie, but the most important thing is to have fun and enjoy wearing the clothes.

◀ **A silk brocade open robe,** with matching petticoat trimmed with furbelows, c1760.
£1,000–1,200
€1,400–1,700
$1,600–1,900
⚱ S(O)

▶ **A Victorian christening gown,** with thistle design, Scottish.
£160–180
€230–260
$260–290
⊞ MARG

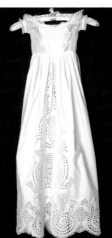

A printed wool shawl, slight damage, late 19thC, 64 x 60in (162.5 x 152.5cm).
£70–80 / €100–115
$110–130 ⊞ DE

A lawn and satin top, with beaded decoration, c1900.
£400–450 / €570–640 $640–720 ⊞ **Ci**

► **An Edwardian cotton voile and lace blouse.**
£50–55 €70–80 $80–90 ⊞ **Ech**

A satin and tulle ball gown, by G. & E. Spitzer, with beaded and embroidered decoration, 1910–12.
£7,000–8,400 €10,000–11,900 $11,300–13,400 ⚬ **S(O)**

An Edwardian lawn and lace child's dress.
£150–170 / €210–240 $240–270 ⊞ **MARG**

◄ **A Fortuny Delphos silk dress,** trimmed with Murano glass beads, with matching stencilled silk belt, belt signed, Italian, early 20thC.
£2,550–3,000 €3,600–4,250 $4,100–4,800 ⚬ **S(O)**

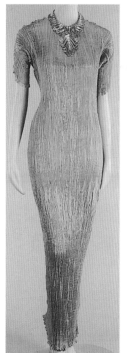

◄ **An Edwardian cotton dress,** with embroidered decoration.
£165–185 / €230–260 $260–290 ⊞ **Ech**

A silk georgette dress, with beaded decoration, French, c1920s.
£1,100–1,250 €1,550–1,750 $1,750–2,000 ⊞ **TIN**

An Edwardian jacquard silk shawl, probably French, 68in (172.5cm) wide.
£180–200 / €250–280 $290–320 ⊞ **VICT**

A silk top, with beaded decoration, 1920.
**£160–180 / €230–260
$260–290** ⊞ Ci

A lamé jacket, 1930s.
**£135–150 / €190–210
$220–240** ⊞ Ci

A chiffon flapper dress,
decorated with bugle beads and embroidery, 1920s.
**£250–280 / €360–400
$400–450** ⊞ Ech

▶ **A silk velvet dress
and jacket,** with beaded decoration, 1930s.
**£145–160 / €210–230
$230–260** ⊞ VICT

**A silk chiffon
dress,** 1930s.
**£220–250 / €310–350
$350–400** ⊞ RER

**A printed crepe-back
satin dress,** 1930.
**£310–350 / €440–500
$500–560** ⊞ TIN

A silk velvet dress, with plastic side-zip, late 1930s.
**£90–100 / €125–140
$145–160** ⊞ VICT

◀ **A lamé and silk
jacket,** 1930s.
**£330–370 / €470–520
$530–590** ⊞ MARG

A cotton sun suit, 1940s.
£65–75 / €90–105
$105–120 ⊞ SpM

A jacket, by W. Hunt, 1940s.
£20–25 / €28–35
$32–40 ⊞ NFR

A two-piece suit, by Joan Griffith, with shell buttons, c1940s.
£50–55 / €70–80
$80–90 ⊞ NFR

Further reading

Miller's Collecting the 1950s, Miller's Publications, 2004

▶ **A velvet evening gown,** by Christian Dior, the matching jacket with detachable sable trim, with matching pair of Delman shoes, French, 1956.
£1,800–2,100
€2,550–3,000
$2,900–3,350 ↗ S(O)
Ex-HRH Princess Lilian of Belgium collection.

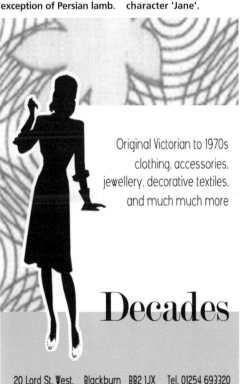

A Persian lamb jacket, by Schiaparelli, with fur trim, 1950.
£310–350 / €440–500
$500–560 ⊞ HIP
Schiaparelli rarely made items out of fur, with the exception of Persian lamb.

A strapless gown, with sequined decoration, 1940s, together with newspaper cuttings and other ephemera.
£460–550 / €650–780
$740–880 ↗ RTo
This gown is reputedly the first stage dress worn by Christabel Leighton-Porter, the artist's model for the *Daily Mirror*'s cartoon character 'Jane'.

HRH Princess Lilian of Belgium

Princess Lilian was a regular client of the great Paris fashion houses in the post-war period. Her daughter, Princess Esmerelda, recalls shopping with her mother. 'On a typical day we would leave Brussels early by car and spend the morning at Christian Dior, Avenue Montaigne. It was like witnessing a ballet with the fitters gyrating around us, laden with tape measures and multicoloured, beaded and embroidered textiles. My mother would try on several designs and discuss the cut or examine a preliminary design sketch. Before returning to Belgium we would go for lunch at the Regent Plaza, often in the company of a fashion designer such as Marc Bohan or Hubert de Givenchy.'

A mink stole, relined, 1950s.
£135–150 / €190–210
$220–240 ⊞ HIP

A jersey, decorated with a poodle, 1950s.
£120–135 / €170–190
$190–220 ⊞ SpM

A cotton skirt, decorated with wine glasses, with bow pockets, 1950s.
£75–85 / €105–120
$120–135 ⊞ SpM

An embroidered organza gown, by Yves St Laurent for Christian Dior, with matching coat and shoes, French, 1959, together with a fashion drawing and photograph of Princess Lilian wearing the gown.
£6,600–7,900
€9,350–11,200
$10,550–12,650 ⚒ S(O)
Ex-HRH Princess Lilian of Belgium collection.

A floral-printed dress, 1950s.
£150–175 / €210–250
$240–280 ⊞ RER

A silk scarf, by Hermès, decorated with equestrian motifs, 1960.
£70–80 / €100–115
$110–125 ⊞ HIP

A brocaded satin formal day dress and jacket, by Yves St Laurent for Christian Dior, the jacket trimmed with mink, French, 1960, together with a matching hat, two fashion designs and a photograph of Princess Lilian wearing the gown.
£960–1,150
€1,350–1,600
$1,550–1,850 ⚒ S(O)
Ex-HRH Princess Lilian of Belgium collection.

A printed organza evening gown, by Marc Bohan for Christian Dior, French, 1961.
£1,650–2,000
€2,350–2,850
$2,650–3,200 ⚒ S(O)
Ex-HRH Princess Lilian of Belgium collection.

A slubbed silk evening gown, by Givenchy, with *faux* jet beaded decoration and ribbon bands, French, 1963.
£1,050–1,250
€1,500–1,800
$1,700–2,000 ⚒ S(O)

A Givenchy silk gown, with a flower-laden tulle over-dress, French, 1965.
£1,850–2,200
€2,600–3,100
$2,950–3,500 ⚒ S(O)

A cotton dress, by Miss Mouse, printed with Martini labels, c1965.
£160–180 / €230–260 $260–290 ⊞ Ci

A printed cotton dress, by Biba, 1970.
£450–500 / €640–710 $720–800 ⊞ RER

A top, by Carlina Barten, with beaded decoration, 1980s.
£75–85 / €105–120 $120–135 ⊞ Ci

A printed chiffon ensemble, by Ossie Clark and Celia Birtwell for Quorom, c1969.
£560–660 / €800–940 $900–1,050 ↗ S(O)
The recent Ossie Clark exhibition at the Victoria & Albert Museum in London has stimulated the value of the late designer's work.

A silk jersey dress, by Jean Muir, early 1970s.
£220–250 / €310–360 $350–400 ⊞ Ci

A hand-embroidered silk shawl, Spanish, 1960s, 40in (101.5cm) square.
£55–65 / €80–90 $90–105 ⊞ HIP

◀ **A velvet evening jacket,** by Yves St Laurent, with diamanté decoration, c1980.
£220–250 / €310–360 $350–400 ⊞ HIP

A cotton dress, by Marimekko, Finnish, 1960s.
£135–150 / €190–210 $220–240 ⊞ RER
Founded in 1951, the Finnish company Marimekko became a leading producer of abstract textiles in the 1960s.

Ladies' Hats

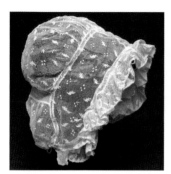

A Victorian child's lace bonnet.
£25–30 / €35–40
$40–50 ⊞ VICT

An Edwardian silk and lace
boudoir cap.
£35–40 / €50–55
$55–65 ⊞ VICT

An Edwardian hat, metallic lace
over a wire structure, decorated
with flowers, American.
£210–230 / €300–330
$330–370 ⊞ RER

A paper Tweeny maid's cap,
in original packaging, 1920s.
£50–55 / €70–80
$80–90 ⊞ LBe

A raffia cloche hat, trimmed with
ribbon, 1920s.
£70–80 / €100–110
$115–130 ⊞ TIN

A straw cloche hat, decorated with
velvet flowers, 1920s.
£70–80 / €100–110
$115–130 ⊞ L&L

A felt hat, American, 1930s.
£20–25 / €28–35
$32–40 ⊞ LBe

A straw hat, with net veil and
artificial flowers, 1940s.
£40–45 / €55–65
$65–75 ⊞ L&L

A straw hat, trimmed with ribbon
and artificial flowers, 1940s.
£40–45 / €55–65
$65–75 ⊞ L&L

A riding hat, by Woodland Bros,
crepe-de-Chine over net with
chiffon and ostrich feather, 1940s.
£100–115 / €140–165
$160–185 ⊞ TIN

Linen & Lace

The word lace comes from the Latin *laqueus,* meaning noose. There are two main types of lace; needle lace, made both by amateurs and professionals, and bobbin lace which is more usually the domain of the professional lace-maker. Both were first produced in 16th-century Italy where magnificent cutwork, drawn threadwork and bobbin laces were created to adorn costume and textiles. Flanders was another main centre of production and, thanks to the business acumen of Flemish merchants, Flemish lace was exported across Europe.

In 17th-century France, Jean-Baptiste Colbert, finance minister to Louis XIV, set up a lace factory at Alençon. He also passed one law forbidding the import of foreign silks and laces, and another stipulating the wearing of uniquely French textiles at court. Other famous French laces include Chantilly and Valenciennes.

In the 18th century, Britain also imposed severe restrictions on the importation of foreign lace, which was being smuggled into the country concealed in everything from loaves of bread to coffins. Main centres of production in the UK included London and Honiton and fine lace was also hand-made in Ireland. In the 19th century, lace was mass-produced by machine and became generally affordable.

A length of cutwork lace, probably Italian, late 16thC, 43in (109cm) long.
£200–230 / €280–330
$320–370 ⊞ **HL**

Two Mechlin lace lappets, Flemish, c1785, 58in (147.5cm) long.
£340–380 / €480–540
$540–610 ⊞ **HL**

A Brussels mixed lace flounce, Belgian, c1850, 104in (264cm) long.
£220–250 / €310–360
$350–400 ⊞ **HL**

► **A muslin whitework shawl,** with bobbin lace edging, c1840, 58 x 85in (147.5 x 216cm).
£135–150
€190–210
$220–240 ⊞ **JuC**

◄ **A Victorian lace wedding veil,** slight damage, 98in (249cm) long.
£160–180
€230–260
$260–290
⊞ **MARG**

► **A Maltese silk lace collar,** late 19thC.
£100–110
€140–155
$160–175
⊞ **VICT**

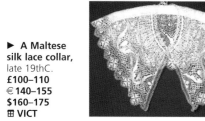

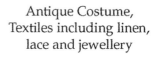

A Honiton lace veil, late 19thC,
35in (89cm) long.
£65–75 / €90–105
$105–120 ⊞ HL

**An Edwardian Brussels
lace handkerchief,** Belgian,
9in (23cm) square.
£11–15 / €16–20
$18–24 ⊞ Ech

A linen cutwork tablecloth,
1920s, 45in (114.5cm) square.
£55–65 / €80–90
$90–105 ⊞ JuC

A linen tea cosy, with crewel-
work decoration, 1920–30,
11in (28cm) high.
£11–15 / €16–20
$18–24 ⊞ HILL

▶ **A Honiton
lace veil,** late
19thC, 79in
(200.5cm) long.
£450–500
€640–710
$720–800 ⊞ HL

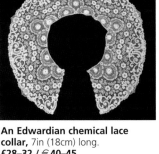

**An Edwardian chemical lace
collar,** 7in (18cm) long.
£28–32 / €40–45
$45–50 ⊞ Ech

A linen cloth, 1920s,
16in (40.5cm) diam.
£10–14 / €14–20
$16–22 ⊞ HILL

A hand-worked linen tablecloth,
1920–30, 45 x 48in (114.5 x 122cm).
£50–55 / €70–80
$80–90 ⊞ HILL

**An Edwardian crocheted
lace collar,** Irish,
23in (58.5cm) long.
£28–32 / €40–45
$45–50 ⊞ Ech

A pair of damask towels, edged
with lace, c1910, 27in (68.5cm) long.
£8–12 / €11–17
$12–18 ⊞ AL

A linen tablecloth, with crocheted
border, 1920s, 30in (76cm) square.
£24–28 / €34–40
$38–45 ⊞ Ech

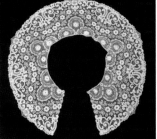

**A hand-embroidered linen
coaster,** 1930s, 6in (15cm) diam.
£2–6 / €3–8
$4–10 ⊞ HILL

Lingerie

A Victorian cotton and lace camisole.
£20–25 / €28–35
$32–40 ⊞ Ech

A boned cotton corset, by W. F. Corset Co, with broderie anglaise edging, c1910.
£80–90 / €115–130
$130–145 ⊞ AFA

A box of Ecstasy Hosiery pure silk stockings, 1940s, 10 x 7in (25.5 x 18cm).
£45–50 / €65–70
$75–80 ⊞ SpM
Some hosiery boxes are sought after by collectors. This box, without its contents, would sell for £20 / €28 / $32.

◄ A crepe and lace nightgown, 1940s.
£15–20 / €20–28
$24–32 ⊞ L&L

► An Extase bra and suspender belt set, French, 1950s.
£85–95 / €120–135
$135–150 ⊞ SpM

A pair of VelvetGrip suspenders, 1940s, 6in (15cm) long.
£1–5 / €2–7
$3–8 ⊞ NFR

A packet of Mary Quant Fancy stockings, 1970s–80s, 8 x 6in (20.5 x 15cm).
£3–7 / €4–9
$5–11 ⊞ RUSS

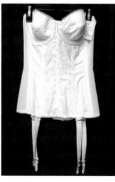

◄ A Lady Marlene corselette, with suspenders, 1950s.
£55–65 / €80–90
$90–105 ⊞ SpM

Men's Fashion

A velvet waistcoat, as worn by Tom Thumb, c1860.
£1,900–2,300
€2,700–3,250
$3,050–3,700 ⚹ MEA

A silver-mounted goat's hair sporran, c1850, 16in (40.5cm) high.
£1,400–1,600
€2,000–2,300
$2,250–2,550 ⊞ BWA

Tom Thumb

General Tom Thumb, the world's most famous miniature man, was born Charles Sherwood Stratton in 1838 in Connecticut. At five months old he was only 25in (63.5cm) tall and grew only another 4in (10cm) in his lifetime. In 1842, Phineas Taylor Barnum persuaded Stratton's mother to allow her son to appear as 'General Tom Thumb' in New York. He was a huge success and people came to visit him in his purpose-built miniature palace.

Tom Thumb spent the rest of his career touring the USA and Europe where he was received by everyone from presidents to royalty. He married Lavinia Warren, a fellow miniature performer who worked in Barnum's museum, and enjoyed a wealthy lifestyle, particularly enjoying food and drink. In 1883 Tom Thumb died of a massive stroke aged 45. He weighed 70lbs (32kg) at the time, which, no doubt, was a contributing factor towards his death.

A silver-mounted leather crossbelt, with Celtic decoration, c1870, 25in (63.5cm) long.
£1,400–1,600
€2,000–2,300
$2,250–2,550 ⊞ BWA

An Edwardian boy's linen suit, with matching tam-o'-shanter.
£50–60 / €70–85
$80–95 ⊞ VICT

◀ **A Victorian silk and cotton waistcoat.**
£100–120 / €140–170
$160–190 ⊞ OH

A tie and handkerchief, American, boxed, 1940s.
£60–70 / €85–100
$95–110 ⊞ CAD

◀ **A doeskin over-coat,** 1930s.
£125–140 / €175–200
$200–220 ⊞ OH

An Edwardian pageboy's silk and velvet suit.
£175–195 / €250–280
$280–310 ⊞ TIN

A hand-made gabardine Western shirt, by Nathan Turk, 1940s.
£240–270 / €340–380
$380–430 ⊞ CAD

A Bancroft knitted pullover, depicting a bowler, 1940s.
£155–175 / €220–250 $250–280 ⊞ CAD

A Tootal rayon scarf, 1950s, 48in (122cm) long.
£8–12 / €11–17 $12–18 ⊞ CCO

A hand-painted tie, depicting skittles, American, 1940s.
£75–85 / €105–120 $120–135 ⊞ CAD

A tie, American, 1940s.
£20–25 / €28–35 $32–40 ⊞ OH

A Daks double-breasted dinner jacket, with peak collar, 1950s.
£75–85 / €105–120 $120–135 ⊞ OH

A Grey Cup gabardine jacket, with Native American decoration, c1955.
£400–450 / €570–640 $640–720 ⊞ CAD

A rayon Hawaiian shirt, Hong Kong, 1960s.
£12–16 / €17–22 $19–26 ⊞ HSt

A Barefoot in Paradise cotton Hawaiian shirt, c1960.
£20–25 / €28–35 $32–40 ⊞ REPS

◄ **A Dege & Skinner cotton and silk smoking jacket,** 1970s.
£145–160 / €210–230 $230–260 ⊞ OH

A printed gabardine jacket, with scenic decoration, c1955.
£75–85 / €105–120 $120–135 ⊞ CAD
Vintage men's fashion in good condition is often more difficult to source than women's outfits because men typically have fewer clothes and tend to wear them longer. American gabardine jackets from this period are very sought after by fans of the '50s style.

◄ **A wool and leather Mickey Mouse bomber jacket,** 1992.
£160–180 €230–260 $260–290 ⊞ COB

A Vivienne Westwood Witches collection wool suit, with horn buttons, c1983.
£800–900 / €1,150–1,300 $1,300–1,450 ⊞ ID

Three Dunhill silk ties, 1980s–90s.
£6–10 / €8–14 $10–16 each ⊞ OH

Men's Hats

Introduced in the late 1700s and inspired by a hat developed for riding, the top hat was worn by men with both day and evening dress throughout the 19th century. Toppers came in various styles, from the tall 'stove pipe' hat to the short squat topper associated with the image of John Bull, the archetypal Englishman. In the USA, Abraham Lincoln popularized the top hat – the example he was wearing on the night of his assassination in 1865 is now preserved at the Smithsonian Institution, Washington, DC.

In 1814, French magician Louis Comte became the first man to pull a rabbit out of a hat, thus launching an enduring connection between the top hat and the stage.

Top hats were made from black beaver felt in the early part of the 19th century, gradually succeeded by black silk plush. Grey top hats were sported during the day; black could be worn day or night. The height of top hats created problems (American financier J. P. Morgan commissioned a limousine with a specially raised roof to allow him to sport his favourite headgear). The first collapsible top hat was invented in 1812 and shortly afterwards, French hat maker Antoine Gibus developed the 'gibus' opera hat (cloth on a metal frame), that could be opened with a single flick of the wrist. Other 19th-century favourites include the bowler hat, which is traditionally associated with the English city gent. Designed by the famous hatters Locke's of St James's, it was manufactured by the Bowler family of Southwark, London, hence its name. In the USA it is known as the Derby.

The Prince of Wales (later Edward VII) popularized the wearing of felt hats such as the homburg, the trilby (named after George du Maurier's eponymous novel) and the fedora, called after V. Sardou's play *Fedora*, first performed in 1881, and a huge hit in the USA. The felt Stetson (the essential headgear of the American cowboy) was developed by John Batterson Stetson, who opened his first Philadelphia factory in 1865. The large waterproof brim was originally designed not just to protect the wearer against the elements, but also to trap water for drinking hence the nickname 'ten gallon hat'.

Vintage hats can be very collectable, particularly top hats made from the traditional silk plush, which is no longer manufactured today. Condition is important to value and size, since many antique hats are too small for today's wearers.

A Victorian opera hat, by Bennett & Co.
£100–110 / €140–155
$160–175 ⊞ TOP

A plush top hat, by A. S. Patey, c1860.
£350–390 / €500–550
$560–620 ⊞ TOP

A silk plush top hat, by G. H. Rhodes, c1900.
£500–550 / €710–780
$800–880 ⊞ OH

A silk top hat, by W. M. Anderson & Sons, 1900–20, with a Henry Heath hat box.
£45–50 / €65–70
$75–80 ⊞ MCa

A bowler hat, by Lincoln Bennett, 20thC.
£50–55 / €70–80
$80–90 ⊞ OH

A top hat, by Dunn & Co, with original hat box, 1930s.
£55–65 / €80–90
$90–105 ⊞ COB

A felt Stetson, in original box, 1940s.
£110–125 / €155–175
$175–200 ⊞ CAD

A silk plush top hat, by Locke's, c1950.
£600–650 / €850–920
$960–1,040 ⊞ OH

Samplers

Samplers are mentioned in wills and inventories dating back as early as the 16th century. Deriving their name from the French word *essamplaire*, they were originally designed to record sewing patterns before printed examples were readily available in books. They also provided a perfect teaching aid and, even once published patterns were commonplace, young girls from every strata of society – from the manor house to the orphanage – sewed samplers.

Samplers were produced on linen and embroidered with wool or silk threads. Coloured silk samplers tend to command the highest prices, particularly when combined with raised work and metal threads, such as gold or silver, which would only have been used by the wealthy. As well as teaching girls sewing techniques, samplers also provided a medium for other forms of learning. They were commonly decorated with the alphabet and numbers, many contain religious or moral verses – Adam and Eve was a favourite pictoral subject – while map samplers provided an extension of geography lessons. Houses are often featured, along with stylized animals, plants and figures; the more interesting the subject matter, the higher the value. While some samplers are very personal, recording family details and even family deaths, others were simply intended as technical sewing exercises such as darning samplers or sampler books, their cloth pages demonstrating examples of different stitches. Samplers are often signed and dated, sometimes the age of the embroiderer is given and occasionally the name of her house or school. Such information gives the piece added interest.

Condition is all important. Moth holes or faded colours will affect value and the edges, where the material has been stretched, should be checked for damage.

A sampler, by Hannah Thorne, worked in silk with alphabet and numerals, dated 1779, 8½ x 8in (21.5 x 20.5cm).
**£260–310 / €370–440
$420–500 ✏ G(L)**

A Georgian needlework map, worked on silk with a map of England and Wales, initialled 'WA', 20in (51cm) high, in a gilt frame.
**£340–410 / €480–580
$540–650 ✏ AH**

> Items in the Textiles & Fashion section have been arranged in date order within each sub-section.

A sampler, c1800, in a wooden frame, 2½in (6.5cm) diam.
**£100–120 / €140–170
$160–190 ⊞ HIS**

◄ **A sampler,** by Maria Spanton, worked with the alphabet and religous verse within a floral border, signed and dated 1806, 13½in (34.5cm) high, framed.
**£450–500 / €640–710
$720–800 ⊞ HIS**

A sampler, worked with the alphabet, numerals and a bird in a tree, American, dated 1807, 13 x 12in (33 x 30.5cm), framed.
**£500–600 / €710–850
$800–960 ✏ COPA**

A pin ball sampler, 1811, 2in (5cm) diam.
£360–400 / €510–570
$580–640 ⊞ HIS

A book of needlework samplers, 1837, 14 x 9in (35.5 x 23cm).
£360–400 / €510–570
$580–640 ⊞ HIS

A sampler, by Charlotte Woods, worked with a verse and Trees of Life and Knowledge of Good and Evil, dated 1845, 12¾in (32.5cm) square.
£200–240 / €280–340
$320–380 ⚒ WilP

◄ A wool sampler, by Florence Mary Mills, worked with the alphabet, dated 1887, 11 x 15in (28 x 38cm), framed.
£270–300 / €380–430
$430–480 ⊞ HIS

A sampler, by Elizabeth Chamberline, depicting a house and animals within a floral border, c1830, 18 x 12in (45.5 x 30.5cm), framed.
£480–570 / €680–810
$770–910 ⚒ BWL

A sampler, by Mary Stockwell, worked with the alphabet and a verse, huntsmen, dogs, birds and flowers, within an acorn border, dated 1843, 15¾ x 13in (40 x 33cm).
£300–360 / €430–510
$480–570 ⚒ EH

A mourning sampler, 1914, 9 x 19in (23 x 48.5cm), framed.
£110–125 / €155–175
$175–200 ⊞ HIS

A sampler, by Emma Fern, worked with numerals, the alphabet and coronets, signed and dated 1831, 15½ x 9½in (39.5 x 24cm).
£135–150 / €190–210
$220–240 ⊞ HIS

A Victorian sampler, by Caroline Campion, worked in silks with a verse, animals and flowers, minor damage, 9 x 8in (23 x 20.5cm), framed.
£150–180 / €210–250
$240–290 ⚒ G(L)

A sampler, by M. M. Morgan, dated 1913, framed and glazed, 27 x 36in (68.5 x 91.5cm).
£260–310 / €370–440
$420–500 ⚒ PF

Shoes

A gentleman's leather shoe, with an iron buckle, c1740.
£1,750–2,100 / €2,500–3,000
$2,800–3,350 ⚲ S(O)

A pair of Lilley & Skinner leather shoes, 1920s, in original box.
£85–95 / €120–135
$135–150 ⊞ TIN

A pair of leather Utility shoes, 1940s.
£90–100 / €125–140
$145–160 ⊞ OH

A pair of suede and leather shoes, retailed by Harrods, 1940s.
£35–40 / €50–55
$55–65 ⊞ CCO

A pair of leather sandals, 1940s, in original box.
£50–55 / €70–80
$80–90 ⊞ NFR

A pair of leather-soled brothel creepers, with original Bakelite shoetrees by Wheatsheaf, 1950s.
£110–120 / €155–170
$175–190 ⊞ OH
Brothel creepers (also known as beetle crushers) had thick, generally crepe, soles. They came into fashion after WWII and were adopted by the Teddy Boys.

A pair of crocodile skin walking shoes, early 1950s.
£35–40 / €50–55
$55–65 ⊞ CCO

Further reading

Miller's Collecting the 1960s, Miller's Publications, 2004

A pair of La Rose Perspex wedge-heeled sandals, American, 1950s.
£85–95 / €120–135
$135–150 ⊞ SpM

A pair of Schiaparelli leopard skin Spring-o-lator sandals, 1950s.
£165–185 / €230–260
$260–290 ⊞ SpM

A pair of leather shoes, with butterfly decoration, American, 1960s.
£50–60 / €70–85
$80–95 ⊞ RER

A pair of Chanel crocodile skin shoes, 1960s.
£80–90 / €115–130
$130–145 ⊞ HIP

A pair of Buffalo platform trainers, 1990s.
£55–65 / €80–90
$90–105 ⊞ MARK

Tools

◀ **An iron tooth chisel,** 18thC, 3in (7.5cm) long.
£400–450
€**570–640**
$640–720 ⊞ **WO**

A walnut adze, with a steel blade, maker's mark of crossed swords and shield, c1780, 12in (30.5cm) long.
£300–350 / €**430–500**
$480–560 ⊞ **MFB**

A string gauge, for violin, viola and cello strings, 19thC, 2½in (6.5cm) long.
£50–55 / €**70–80**
$80–90 ⊞ **WO**

A cabinet-maker's pine tool chest, together with a selection of cabinet-making tools and a set of mahogany-veneered drawers and compartments, 19thC.
£260–310 / €**370–440**
$420–500 🪓 **TRM**

A dovetail saw, with a wooden handle, 19thC, 10in (25.5cm) long.
£80–90 / €**115–130**
$130–145 ⊞ **WO**

Two irons, in the form of a leaf and a flower, with wooden handles, c1860, 9½in (24cm) long.
£150–165 / €**210–240**
$240–270 each ⊞ **MFB**
These irons would have been used in the fashion industry.

A Victorian brass and ebony brace, 14in (35.5cm) long.
£260–290 / €**370–410**
$410–460 ⊞ **WiB**

A gunmetal shoulder plane, with steel sole, 19thC, 14in (35.5cm) long.
£145–160 / €**210–230**
$230–260 ⊞ **WO**

▶ **A Victorian lignum vitae and lead dressing wedge,** with a steel ring, 8in (20.5cm) long.
£14–18 / €**20–26**
$22–30 ⊞ **WiB**

◀ **A wrought-iron button-making tool,** 19thC, 20in (51cm) long.
£65–75
€**90–105**
$105–120 ⊞ **WO**

A Victorian boxwood chamfer plane, 5in (12.5cm) long.
£60–70 / €**85–100**
$95–110 ⊞ **WiB**

A boxwood and brass tailor's rule, by John Rabone & Sons, c1900, 24in (61cm) long.
£25–30 / €35–40
$40–50 ⊞ WO

▶ **A wooden folding measure,** c1910, 24in (61cm) long.
£28–32
€40–45
$45–50 ⊞ YT

◀ **A Norris panel plane,** with beech infill, 20thC, 4in (10cm) long.
£680–750
€970–1,050
$1,100–1,200
⊞ WO

▶ **A Stanley No. 113 compass plane,** 1920s, 10in (25.5cm) long.
£100–120
€140–170
$160–190 ⊞ WO

A thatcher's needle, 20thC, 22in (56cm) long.
£30–35 / €40–50
$50–55 ⊞ WO

A North Brothers Yankee No. 50 drill, with reciprocating rotation, 1930, 15in (38cm) long.
£55–65 / €80–90
$90–105 ⊞ WO

A steel screw gauge, c1910, 10in (25.5cm) long.
£6–10 / €8–14
$10–16 ⊞ GAC

A mahogany mitre square, c1920, 16in (40.5cm) long.
£8–12 / €11–17
$12–18 ⊞ OIA

▶ **A Stanley No. 55 plane,** complete with full set of cutters, 1920s, 12in (30.5cm) long, in original box.
£450–500
€640–710
$720–800 ⊞ WO

Toys

A painted wooden Noah's Ark, with six figures and over 80 painted pairs of animals, birds and insects, German, late 19thC.
£700–840 / €990–1,200
$1,150–1,350 ⚒ B(Kn)

A Roullet & Decamps papier mâché model of a barking bulldog, with glass eyes, hinged jaw, bristle collar with chain to activate bark, worn, French, c1910, 22in (56cm) long.
£420–500 / €600–710
$670–800 ⚒ B(Kn)
Established by Jean Roullet (1832–1907), this Paris company specialized in the manufacture of drawing room automata as well as decorative shop display pieces. Some of their best work was produced in the early 20th century when Roullet's grandson Gaston Decamps (1882–1972) was running the firm. Look for the RD mark when buying one of these toys.

A Cardora Derby Dog Race game, containing six painted hollow-cast lead dogs, c1930, board 11 x 18in (28 x 45.5cm), with box.
£100–120 / €140–170
$160–190 ⊞ ARo

▶ **A Tour du Monde en Vespa game,** with six metal Vespa mascots, French, 1960s, boxed, 9 x 17in (23 x 43cm).
£180–200 / €250–280
$290–320 ⊞ ARo

A painted wooden push-along merry-go-round, early 20thC, 24in (61cm) long.
£45–50 / €65–70
$75–80 ⊞ CHAC

The Magic Box, with mechanism for moving the dancing couple, on a steel base, c1900, 6in (15cm) diam, with box.
£310–350 / €440–500
$500–560 ⊞ YC

◀ **A papier mâché jester marotte,** c1890, 17in (43cm) high.
£200–230 / €280–330
$320–370 ⊞ AUTO
A marotte is a doll's head mounted on a stick or baton which plays music when twirled.

A child's wooden dairy cart, with milk churns, c1930, 17in (43cm) high.
£220–250 / €310–350
$350–400 ⊞ SMI

A Dam Things Establishment troll, 1964, 11in (28cm) high.
£35–40 / €50–55
$55–65 ⊞ UD

A battery-operated Pee Pee Puppy, with remote control, Japanese, 1970s, boxed, 8 x 9in (20.5 x 23cm).
£40–45 / €55–65
$65–75 ⊞ GTM

A hand-held electronic Super Color Screen, with two games, Tarzan and Pirates of the Caribbean, 1982, boxed, 4 x 7in (10 x 18cm).
£115–130 / €165–185
$185–210 ⊞ OW

Three Tomytronic 3-D electronic games, Shark Attack, Thundering Turbo and Sky Attack, 1983, boxed, 8 x 7in (20.5 x 18cm).
£35–40 / €50–55
$55–65 each ⊞ OW

A Nintendo Game & Watch Panorama Screen electronic game, Popeye, 1983, boxed, 5 x 7in (12.5 x 18cm).
£115–130 / €165–185
$185–210 ⊞ OW

A Hasbro Action Force Cobra Water Moccasin, 1984, boxed, 9 x 11in (23 x 28cm).
£65–75 / €95–105
$105–120 ⊞ OW

A Hasbro G. I. Joe Mauler M.B.T. Tank, with driver and battery-operated tank, 1985, boxed, 14 x 13in (35.5 x 33cm).
£110–125 / €155–175
$175–200 ⊞ OW

Aircraft

A Tipp & Co lithographed tinplate clockwork biplane, No. 24, with detachable wings and electric light, c1938, 16¾in (42.5cm) long.
£300–360 / €420–510
$480–570 ⚲ GK

A Dinky Toys diecast Light Tourer, No. 60K, 1945–48, 3in (7.5cm) long.
£110–130 / €155–185
$175–210 ⚲ FHF

◄ **A Techno B17 Flying Fortress,** Danish, 1950s, 6in (15cm) wide.
£45–50 / €65–70
$75–80 ⊞ HAL

► **A Dinky Supertoys Bristol Britannia airliner,** No. 998, finished in Canadian Pacific livery, 1964–65, boxed.
£95–115 / €135–160
$150–180 ⚲ WAL

A Dinky Supertoys Super G Constellation Lockheed, No. 60C, finished in Air France livery, 1950s, boxed.
£75–90 / €105–125
$120–145 ⚲ WAL

Cars & Vehicles

Toys are currently a buoyant collecting area and one of the strongest subjects is diecast vehicles. 'The internet has given a tremendous boost to the hobby, drawing in many more enthusiasts,' explains Glen Chapman from Unique Collections of Greenwich, London, a specialist diecast dealer who has been established for 17 years. As one might expect, the predominantly male market is largely driven by nostalgia as men buy back their favourite boyhood toys. Television- and film-related toys from the 1960s and '70s, for example, are very popular but, warns Glen, condition and details are important to value. 'Take the example of James Bond's Aston Martin DB5, the 261, produced by Corgi in 1965. This was probably the most famous toy of its day. Unboxed and in played-with condition it might sell for £20–25 / €28–35 / $32–40. Perfect and unboxed, maybe £90–100 / €125–140 / $145–160. With the box it might go for £200–400 / €280–570 / $320–910, depending on the condition of the box and car. There was also a bright gold variant and that, boxed, can be worth £800 / €1,150 / $1,300. It's all in the condition and details.' David Nathan from Vectis Auction House agrees. 'If you have two examples of the same car and one is perfect and the other has a few imperfections, the difference in value can be 100–200 per cent.'

Nathan is very optimistic about the state of the market since, over the past seven years, Vectis has seen its business grow tenfold. 'I don't think I can remember interest in diecasts ever being quite so strong, as long as the quality is right,' he claims. For Nathan, Dinky is arguably the market leader. 'They were so successful and so brilliantly named that Dinky has almost become a generic word for toy cars, like Hoover for vacuum cleaners. The Golden Age for collectors of Dinky cars is from the 1930s to the '50s but serious enthusiasts are also collecting examples up to c1978. Dinky produced such a vast range of objects that it would be impossible to collect them all and that is one of the reasons why I think interest will continue to be strong – the variety of items is almost infinite!'

Repeats of classic TV series such as *Thunderbirds* and demand for vintage vehicles have inspired modern reproductions of famous toys but, according to both Chapman and Nathan, rather than damaging the value of period originals, in many instances this has only served to increase demand for the real thing. A more disturbing modern trend is the manufacture of reproduction boxes, which, while unlikely to fool an expert, could trap a beginner. As in all areas, the safest advice is: buy from a reputable vendor, learn about your subject and, where possible, try to buy the best example of an object that you can afford.

A Britains underslung lorry,
No. 1641, with drop-frame trailer, 1938, 10in (25.5cm) long, with box.
£220–250 / €310–350
$350–400 ♣VEC

A Lincoln International plastic mechanised Velam Bubble car,
with gyro motor, late 1950s, 4in (10cm) long, with box.
£60–70 / €85–100
$95–110 ⊞ CBB

◀ **A Tonka Jeep Pamper,** No. 425, 1963, 10¾in (27.5cm) long.
£120–145 / €170–200
$195–230 ♣TQA

A Tonka Dragline crane, No. 514, 1963, 20in (51cm) long.
£65–75 / €90–105
$105–120 ♣TQA
Tonka toys were introduced by the Mound Metalcraft Company established in Mound, Minnesota, in 1946. Initially the firm made gardening equipment until L. E. Streater Co, a local manufacturer, commissioned some steel toys. The first Tonka pick-up truck was produced in 1955. These solid and durable metal toys are particularly popular in America.

A Politoys Fiat 1500 Coupé Siata, No. 502, Italian, 1960s, 4in (10cm) long, with box.
£45–50 / €65–70
$75–80 ⊞ HAL

A Mercury Toys Ferrari Dino, No. 48, Italian, 1960s, 4in (10cm) long, with box.
£45–50 / €65–70
$75–80 ⊞ HAL

A Mercedes Benz 219 Sedan, No. 732, friction drive, from The Automobiles of the World series, Japanese, 1960s, 8in (20.5cm) long, with box.
£130–145 / €185–210
$210–230 ⊞ GTM

A Solido Patton M-47 tank, French, 1960s, 6in (15cm) long, with box.
£45–50 / €65–70
$75–80 ⊞ CBB
Founded in 1932, Solido is the most famous French diecast company. They produced a wide range of vehicles and cannon construction sets before WWII. Early wares could be prone to metal fatigue and are now rare. Today the company are well known for their successful military vehicle range started in 1961.

Further reading

Miller's Toys & Games Antiques Checklist,
Miller's Publications, 2000

◄ **A diecast Moscovich 412 car,** Russian, 1960s, 5in (12.5cm) long.
£15–20
€20–28
$24–32 ⊞ CBB

A Solido Lotus F1, French, 1960s, 4in (10cm) long, with box.
£40–50 / €55–70
$65–80 ⊞ HAL

A Mercury Fiat 2300S Coupé, No. 23, Italian, 1960s, 4in (10cm) long, with box.
£45–50 / €65–70
$75–80 ⊞ HAL

◄ **A diecast Lone Star London bus and fire engine,** 1980, in original box, 9½in (24cm) long.
£30–35 / €40–50
$50–55 ⊞ CBB

Corgi

Corgi Toys were produced by Mettoy Playcraft from 1956. Made in Swansea, South Wales, they were named after a Welsh dog, the favourite breed of the Royal family, and the name was short and snappy like that of their intended rival, Dinky.

Diecast vehicles were of a very high standard and came with many attractive features – plastic windows (Dinky cars had open windows) and from 1959 spring suspension and detailed plastic interiors. The early '60s saw the introduction of 'jewelled' headlights and opening doors and boots. This focus on moving parts and features

made Corgi the natural choice to produce James Bond's gadget-packed Aston Martin DB5 in 1965, one of the most popular toys ever made with sales of nearly three million. A host of other film- and television-related toys followed such as the Batmobile and *The Man from U.N.C.L.E.* car (1966); *The Avengers'* Bentley and Lotus Elan and the *Green Hornet's* Black Beauty (1967); *Chitty Chitty Bang Bang* (1968) and many others, including further Bond cars. In 1970, Corgi introduced their Whizzwheels line to compete with Mattel's hugely successful Hotwheels series.

A Corgi Toys Major Midland Motorway Express coach, No. 112, 1956–62, 5½in (14cm) long, with box.
£80–90 / €115–130
$130–145 ⊞ CBB

A Corgi Toys Karrier Bantam Two-ton lorry, late 1950s, 4in (10cm) long, with box.
£65–75 / €90–105
$105–120 ⊞ HAL

Six Corgi Toys model cars, worn, late 1950s, 4in (10cm) long.
£3–7 / €4–9
$5–11 each ⊞ HAL

A Corgi Toys *Green Hornet* Black Beauty, No. 268, with three missiles and three scanners, 1967, 5½in (14cm) long, in display box.
£130–155 / €185–220
$210–250 ➶ B(WM)

A Corgi Toys James Bond Toyota 2000GT, No. 336, with three missiles, bag of parts missing, 1967, 5in (12.5cm) long, with box.
£140–170 / €200–240
$230–270 ➶ B(WM)

A Corgi Toys E Type Jaguar competition model, No. 312, with driver, Glidamatic spring suspension and plated finish, 1964–68, 4in (10cm) long, with box.
£70–80 / €100–115
$110–125 ⊞ CBB

A Corgi Toys Ford Consul Classic, No. 234, 1960s, 5in (12.5cm) long, with box.
£40–45 / €55–65
$65–75 ⊞ HAL

A Corgi Toys E Type Jaguar, No. 307, 1960s, 4in (10cm) long, with box.
£60–70 / €85–100
$95–110 ⊞ HAL

A Corgi Toys Daktari Gift Set, 1967, boxed, 7½in (19cm) long.
£75–85 / €105–120
$120–135 ⊞ GTM

A Corgi Toys Fiat 2100, No. 232, 1960s, 4in (10cm) long, with box.
£25–30 / €35–40
$40–50 ⊞ HAL

A Corgi Toys Whizzwheels Bond Bug, No. 389, 1970, 3in (7.5cm) long, with box.
£80–90 / €115–130
$130–145 ⊞ HAL

A Corgi Toys Volkswagen Commer van, No. 479, with camera and camera-man, 1960s, 4in (10cm) long, with box.
£90–100 / €125–140
$145–160 ⊞ HAL

◀ A Corgi Toys James Bond Moon Buggy, No. 811, 1972, 6in (15cm) long, with box.
£270–320 / €380–450
$430–510 ⦚ B(WM)

A Corgi Toys Hillman Hunter rally car, No. 302, with kangaroo, late 1960s, 7in (18cm) long, with box.
£100–120 / €140–170
$160–190 ⊞ HAL

A Corgi Toys Hardy Boys Rolls-Royce Silver Ghost, No. 805, c1970, in original box, 8in (20.5cm) long.
£220–250 / €310–360
$350–400 ⊞ UCO

▶ A Corgi Toys Kojak's Buick, No. 290, 1975, boxed, 8in (20.5cm) long.
£110–125
€155–175
$175–200
⊞ GTM

◀ A Corgi Toys Space Shuttle, No. 1364, c1980, boxed, 7in (18cm) long.
£50–55
€70–80
$80–90 ⊞ GTM

▶ A Corgi Toys Spiderman Spiderbike, No. 266, 1984, boxed, 6¼in (16cm) long.
£50–55
€70–80
$80–90 ⊞ GTM

Dinky

Dinky cars first appeared on the market in 1933, created by Frank Hornby, one of Britain's leading toymakers. Designed to complement Hornby train sets, initially they were known as Modelled Miniatures. In 1934, however, the name was changed to Dinky and the pocket-sized diecast vehicles, made in England and France, were extremely successful during the 1930s.

Production ceased during WWII, but with the end of the conflict demand flourished. Pre-war models were reissued and 1947 saw the launch of Dinky Supertoys, the large-sized vehicles that introduced rubber-treaded (as opposed to slick) tyres. The cataloguing of toys also changed. Dinky had used a system of one, two or three digits followed by a letter. In 1954 this was changed to a three digit numeral system with 100s for cars, 200–249 for racing and later sports cars, 250–299 for public service vehicles, 300s for agricultural vehicles, 700s for aircraft and accessories and 900s for Supertoys (replacing their original 500s cataloguing). During the change-over period in the mid-1950s some boxes were printed with both old and new numbers. Dinky has been making good prices in the current market including a recent world record auction price for a post-war Dinky vehicle (see Record Breakers page 428).

A Dinky Toys Esso petrol tanker, 1930s, 4in (10cm) long.
£220–250 / €310–360
$350–400 ⊞ CBB

A Dinky Toys British Salmson sports car, No. 36E, 1947–50, 3¾in (9.5cm) long.
£100–120 / €140–170
$160–190 ➶ FHF

A Dinky Toys Lincoln Zephyr Coupé, late 1940s, 4in (10cm) long.
£135–150 / €190–210
$210–240 ⊞ CBB

A Dinky Toys petrol tank wagon, No. 25D, 1947–48, 4¼in (11cm) long.
£220–260 / €310–370
$350–420 ➶ FHF

A Dinky Supertoys Foden 14-ton tanker, No. 504, first type, late 1940s, 8in (20.5cm) long, with box.
£180–200 / €250–280
$290–320 ⊞ HAL

A Dinky Toys Spratt's Guy Van, No. 917, 1954–56, 5½in (14cm) long, with box.
£310–350 / €440–500
$500–560 ⊞ GTM

A Dinky Toys Talbot-Lago Racing Car, No. 230, 1950s, 4in (10cm) long, with box.
£50–55 / €70–80
$80–90 ⊞ HAL

A Dinky Toys Ford Fordor Sedan, No. 170, 1950s, 4in (10cm) long, with box.
£200–220 / €280–310
$320–350 ⊞ HAL
This is a rare colour combination for this model.

A Dinky Supertoys Coles 20-ton Lorry-Mounted crane, No. 972, 1950s, 10in (25.5cm) long, with box.
£70–80 / €100–115
$110–125 ⊞ HAL

A Dinky Toys Rolls-Royce, worn, 1950s, 6in (15cm) long.
£6–10 / €8–14
$10–16 ⊞ HAL

A Dinky Supertoys Missile Servicing Platform Vehicle, No. 667, 1960–64, 9in (23cm) long, with box.
£150–165 / €210–240
$240–270 ⊞ GTM

A Dinky Toys Camion Amphibie Militaire DUKW, No. 825, 1968, French, 7in (18cm) long, with box.
£130–145 / €185–210
$200–230 ⊞ GTM

◀ **A Dinky Toys Jaguar Mark X,** No. 142, with trunk, 1960s, 4in (10cm) long, with box.
£50–55 / €70–80
$80–90 ⊞ HAL

A Dinky Toys Ford Capri, No. 2162, 1:25 scale, 1970s, 6¾in (17cm) long, with box.
£90–100 / €125–140
$145–160 ⊞ CBB

A Dinky Toys Ford Escort, No. 169, 1970, 4in (10in) long, with box.
£50–55 / €70–80
$80–90 ⊞ HAL

A Dinky Toys London Taxi, 1978, 5in (12.5cm) long, with box.
£20–25 / €28–35
$32–40 ⊞ CBB

▶ **A Dinky Toys Chieftain Tank,** No. 683, late 1970s, 10in (25.5cm) long, with box.
£50–55 / €70–80
$80–90 ⊞ CBB

Guns

A Merit Dan Dare Planet Gun, with three spinning missiles, c1953, boxed, 8 x 12in (20.5 x 30.5cm).
£145–175 / €210–250
$230–280 ⚒ CBP

> Items in the Toys section have been arranged in date order within each sub-section.

A diecast Lone Star Scout Repeater Cap Pistol, 1960s, 7in (18cm) long, with box.
£30–35 / €40–50
$50–55 ⊞ HAL

A Daisy Toy A-Team 12 shot pistol and holster set, 1983, in original packaging, 12 x 7in (30.5 x 18cm).
£35–40 / €50–55
$55–65 ⊞ CTO

Matchbox

School friends Leslie Smith and Rodney Smith (no relation) served together in the Royal Navy during WWII. In 1947 they founded Lesney Products (a combination of their Christian names), and their London-based firm was joined by Jack Odell. Lesney began manufacturing a few cheap toys that were distributed by the Moko agency whose name also appears on the boxes. In 1953 they launched their most famous vehicles, the Matchbox series, inspired by Jack Odell's daughter who was only allowed to take play-things to school that were small enough to fit into a matchbox, hence the name and packaging. These pocket money toys were a huge success. In 1956 Jack Odell was also responsible for introducing the Models of Yesteryear series.

Matchbox cars attract dedicated enthusiasts and have been commanding strong prices. As with all vehicles, however, their worth can rest on the tiniest details such as the colour of a car or the type of its wheels, and condition is always critical to value.

A Matchbox milk float, No. 7, 1954, 2in (5cm) long, with box.
£35–40 / €50–55
$55–65 ⊞ GTM

A Matchbox truck, No. 15, 1955, 2in (5cm) long, with box.
£35–40 / €50–55
$55–65 ⊞ GTM

A Matchbox Austin A50, No. 36, 1950s, 2½in (6.5cm) long, with box.
£25–30 / €35–40
$40–50 ⊞ HAL

◀ **A Lesney Models of Yesteryear London bus,** No. 2, late 1950s, 3¼in (8.5cm) long, with box.
£40–45 / €55–65
$65–75 ⊞ CBB

A Matchbox Ferret Scout car, No. 61, 1950s, 2½in (6.5cm) long, with box.
£12–16 / €17–23
$20–26 ⊞ HAL

▶ **A Lesney Models of Yesteryear steam roller,** No. Y-11, late 1950s, 3¼in (8.5cm) long, with box.
£40–45 / €55–65
$65–75 ⊞ CBB

A Matchbox Volkswagen camper, No. 34, 1960s, 3in (7.5cm) long, with box.
£20–25 / €28–35
$32–40 ⊞ HAL

Model Soldiers & Figures

A Britains South African Mounted Infantry set,
No. 38, minor wear, 1896, boxed, 15in (38cm) long.
£800–950 / €1,150–1,350
$1,300–1,500 ⚹ **VEC**

A Britains First Bengal Cavalry set, No. 46, minor
wear, 1922, boxed, 15in (38cm) long.
£320–380 / €450–540
$510–610 ⚹ **VEC**

A Britains Turkish Cavalry set, No. 71, minor damage,
1922, in Whisstock box, 15in (38cm) long.
£440–530 / €620–750
$700–850 ⚹ **VEC**

A Britains Sudanese Infantry set, No. 116, one mismatch,
minor damage, 1925, boxed, 15in (38cm) long.
£80–95 / €115–135
$125–150 ⚹ **VEC**

A Britains Imperial Yeomanry set, No. 105, 1900,
boxed, 15in (38cm) long.
£700–840 / €1,000–1,200
$1,150–1,350 ⚹ **VEC**

Britains

Britains was established c1860 by William
Britain (1826–1906) in northeast London and,
in the early 1890s, began to specialize in the
manufacture of toy soldiers. Britain's son
William Britain Jnr (1860–1933) is credited with
having invented the hollow casting process
which, applied to the manufacture of toy
soldiers, gave the company a competitive
edge. By 1906 virtually all the toy soldiers in
the Christmas catalogue of the London toy
store Gamages were manufactured by Britains.
   By the 1960s plastic had become the
predominant material of manufacture and in
1966 hollow cast production came to an end.
Throughout the 1960s, '70s and '80s Britains
continued, producing a range of plastic farm
animals and complementary diecast vehicles,
and in the '90s introduced a new range of metal
toy soldiers in the old traditional uniforms.
   In 1997 Britains was purchased by the Ertl
Company, Germany, who are continuing to
develop the range.

A Britains 21st Empress of India's Lancers set,
No. 100, 1925, in Khartoum box, 15in (38cm) long.
£380–450 / €540–640
$610–720 ⚹ **VEC**

◀ **A Britains King's African Rifles set,** No. 225,
1926–41, in Roan box, 15in (38cm) long.
£90–105 / €125–150
$145–170 ⚹ **G(L)**

A Britains Royal Air Force set, No. 240,
1926, in Whisstock box, 15in (38cm) long.
£260–310 / €370–430
$420–500 ✗ VEC

A cast-metal figure of a horse and a cowboy,
1950s, 3½in (9cm) long.
£22–26 / €30–36
$35–40 ⊞ CBB

A Britains Colour Party
of the Scots Guards, No.
2084, 1954, in Roan box.
£110–130 / €155–185
$175–210 ✗ VEC

A Cherilea Toys plastic
military figure, 1950–60,
3in (7.5cm) high.
£1–5 / €2–7
$3–8 ⊞ HAL

▶ A pair of Dinky Hall's
Distemper figures, No. 13,
1930s, 2½in (6.5cm) high,
with box.
£180–210 / €260–300
$290–340 ✗ B(WM)

A Britains painted lead
figure of a milk maid,
1930s, 1in (2.5cm) high.
£3–7 / €4–10
$5–11 ⊞ HAL

◀ A Britains Astro-
Hungarian Infantry of
the Line set, 1930s,
soldier 2½in (6.5cm) high.
£220–260 / €310–370
$350–420 ✗ G(L)

A Britains British Services Display
set, c1939, in Gamages box,
12in (30.5cm) wide.
£1,500–1,800 / €2,150–2,550
$2,400–2,900 ✗ VEC
This rare unlisted set was sold
in Gamages – a famous London
department store.

◀ **A Crescent Toys plastic figure of a Native American,** 1960s, 2½in (6.5cm) high.
£1–5 / €2–7
$3–8 ⊞ HAL
These figures were free gifts with packets of Kellogg's cereals.

A Timpo Toys plastic figure, 1960–80, 3in (7.5cm) high.
£1–5 / €2–7
$3–8 ⊞ HAL

Four Lone Star Metallions diecast figures of famous cowboys and Indians, 1970s, 2in (5cm) high.
£5–9 / €7–14
$8–16 ⊞ HAL

Muffin the Mule

Muffin the Mule was introduced to British television in 1946. First used by puppeteer Ann Hogarth in the 1930s, the hand-carved wooden mule was rescued from retirement by Annette Mills, sister of actor John Mills. She named the mule Muffin and he appeared in her 1946 BBC show *For the Children*. Operated by Ann Hogarth and dancing clumsily on Annette's piano as she played, Muffin became Britain's first television puppet star. By 1950 there was a host of spin-offs including books, records playing the much loved 'We want Muffin' theme tune, puppets and other material. Muffin's last appearance was in 1955, only a few days before Annette Mills' death at the age of only 61.

◀ **Muffin the Mule and his friends,** No. 1, LP record, by Decca, c1948.
£270–300 / €380–420
$430–480 ⊞ MTMC

A Moko Toy Muffin the Mule jigsaw puzzle, No. 3, Muffin's Beach Picnic, 1950s, 8 x 10in (20.5 x 25.5cm).
£310–350 / €440–500
$500–560 ⊞ MTMC

A set of Chad Valley Muffin the Mule picture cubes, with six illustrations of the scenes to be created, c1949, boxed, 6in (15cm) square.
£270–300 / €380–420
$430–480 ⊞ MTMC

An L. F. Booth & Co Muffin the Mule Castime plaster mould modelling set, distributed by Burt Edwards, Hull, 1954, 9½ x 12½in (24 x 32cm).
£310–350 / €440–500
$500–560 ⊞ MTMC

▶ **A Luntoy Muffin the Mule wooden model,** c1954, 8in (20.5cm) high.
£310–350 / €440–500
$500–560 ⊞ MTMC

Pedal Cars

A Steelcraft Highway Patrol police pedal car, restored, American, 1940s, 42in (106.5cm) long.
£900–1,000 / € 1,250–1,400 $1,450–1,600 ⊞ PCCC

A Steelcraft Fire Chief Chrysler pedal car, American, c1941.
£1,100–1,250 / € 1,550–1,800 $1,750–2,000 ⊞ TNS

A painted pedal car, 1940s, 32in (81.5cm) long.
£45–50 / € 65–70 $75–80 ⋟ AMc

A Tri-ang pedal car, c1955, 36in (91.5cm) long.
£150–170 / € 210–240 $240–270 ⊞ JUN

A Mobo Toys tubular steel pedal tipper truck, with lever movement and solid rubber tyres, 1960s, 34in (86.5cm) long.
£65–75 / € 90–105 $105–120 ⊞ PCCC

A pedal fire engine, Model T, with a Briggs & Stratton lawnmower engine, restored, 1960s–70s, 77in (195.5cm) long.
£2,250–2,500 / € 3,200–3,550 $3,600–4,000 ⊞ BAJ

► **A Tri-ang pressed steel pedal tractor,** with working crane and solid rubber tyres, 1960s, 18in (45.5cm) long.
£180–200 € 250–280 $290–320 ⊞ PCCC

◄ **A Tri-ang pressed steel pedal Mercedes Benz,** with chrome fittings and rubber tyres, damage and losses, 1960s–70s, 38in (96.5cm) long.
£65–75 € 90–105 $105–120 ⊞ PCCC

Rocking Horses

◀ **A carved and painted wood rocking horse,** with glass eyes and the remains of a leather harness and saddle, on safety rockers, 1880–1900, 38in (96.5cm) high.
£600–720 / €850–1,000
$960–1,150 ⚒ **FHF**

A rocking horse, with later paint, French, c1890, 38in (96.5cm) wide.
£270–300 / €380–420
$430–480 ⊞ **YT**

A papier mâché hobby horse, with skirt, with wooden base, German, 1940s, 31in (78.5cm) high.
£340–380 / €480–540
$540–600 ⊞ **BAJ**

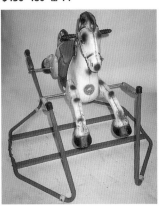

A carved and painted wood rocking horse, on pine safety rockers, 1950s, 41¼in (105cm) high.
£250–300 / €360–430
$400–480 ⚒ **SWO**

▶ **A Mobo Toys steel sprung horse,** 1960s, 36in (91.5cm) long.
£65–75 / €90–105
$105–120 ⊞ **PCCC**

Science Fiction & Television

Thunderbirds, 3D painting set, by J. Rosenthal Toys, 1964, 13 x 16in (33 x 40.5cm).
£50–60 / €70–85
$80–95 ⊞ OW

The Man from U.N.C.L.E., an Illya Kuryakin action figure, by Gilbert, American, 1965, 12in (30.5cm) high, with original box.
£200–220 / €280–310
$320–350 ⊞ HAL

◄ **Thunderbirds**, a cloth hat, 1960s, 10in (25.5cm) wide.
£25–30 / €35–40
$40–50 ⊞ HAL

A Moon McDare, by Gilbert, with accessories, American, 1965, 12in (30.5cm) high.
£100–120 / €140–170
$160–190 ⊞ HAL
In the 1960s many toy companies capitalized on the popularity of the space programme. American firm Gilbert produced Moon McDare. The doll had a range of space accessories and you could also purchase his dog, Space Mutt, who had his own canine astronaut's suit.

Thunderbirds, a plastic Thunderbird 1 pencil sharpener, by Empire, 1960s, 5in (12.5cm) high.
£20–25 / €28–35
$32–40 ⊞ HAL

Thunderbirds, a friction-driven plastic Thunderbird 3, by JR 21 Toys, 1960s, 8in (20.5cm) high.
£50–60 / €70–85
$80–95 ⊞ HAL

Further reading
Sci-Fi & Fantasy Collectibles, Miller's Publications, 2003

◀ **Batman,** a plastic catapult Batjet, No. 5, on original card, 1966, 12in (30.5cm) long.
£45–50 / €65–70
$75–80 ⊞ HAL

Joe 90, Joe's car, No. 102, by Dinky Toys, 1967, 5in (12.5cm) long, with box.
£160–190 / €230–270
$260–300 ⚒ B(WM)

▶ **Dr Who,** a plastic talking model of a Dalek, 1975, 7in (18cm) high, with box.
£120–140 / €170–200
$190–220 ⊞ CBB

Dr Who was premiered on the BBC in November 1963 and the final episode was in December 1989. Video, DVD and endless reruns on cable and satellite television have helped sustain the popularity of this seminal series. Plans are currently afoot to revive Dr Who, which is likely to stimulate the market for collectable products.

Thunderbirds, a friction-driven plastic Thunderbird 2, by JR 21 Toys, 1960s, 10in (25.5cm) long.
£50–60 / €70–85
$80–95 ⊞ HAL

Captain Scarlet, a Destiny Angel figure, by Pedigree, 1970, 6in (15cm) high, with box.
£25–30 / €35–40
$40–50 ⊞ GTM

Dr Who, a press-out book, 1977, 12 x 8in (30.5 x 20.5cm).
£25–30 / €35–40
$40–50 ⊞ WHO

◀ **Dr Who,** a Tom Baker figure, by Denys Fisher for Mego Corp, c1977, 9in (23cm) high.
£40–45 / €55–65
$65–75 ⊞ UD
This figure comes complete with a hat, scarf and sonic screwdriver. The face of the figure is similar to Gambit, the character played by Gareth Hunt in the New Avengers. During production of the figure, the mould for Tom Baker's head was damaged and Gambit's head was substituted.

Dr Who, a War of the Daleks game, by Denys Fisher, with plastic mascots and a moving track, 1970s, boxed, 14 x 18in (35.5 x 45.5cm).
£70–80 / €100–110
$110–125 ⊞ ARo

A bigtrak computer activated vehicle, by MB Electronics, 1979, 10in (25.5cm) high, with box.
£270–300 / €380–420
$430–480 ⊞ OW

▶ **Masters of the Universe,** a plastic Trap Jaw figure, by Mattel, 1982, 5in (12.5cm) high.
£25–30
€35–40
$40–50 ⊞ OW

A *My Little Pony*, Bow Tie, with angled head, 1983, 5in (12.5cm) high.
£1–5 / €2–7
$3–8 ⊞ RAND
This model was also available with a straight head.

A *My Little Pony*, Baby Lemon Drop, 1983, 3in (7.5cm) high.
£25–30 / €35–40
$40–50 ⊞ RAND

Masters of the Universe, an Evil-Lyn figure, by Mattel, 1982, 5in (12.5cm) high.
£75–85 / €105–120
$120–135 ⊞ OW

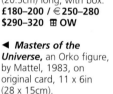

A *Transformers* **Deception Thrust,** by Hasbro, 1985, 8in (20.5cm) long, with box.
£180–200 / €250–280
$290–320 ⊞ OW

Captain Scarlet, a Captain Scarlet figure, by Vivid Imaginations, signed by Francis Matthews, 1994, 4in (10cm) high, on original card.
£180–200 / €250–280
$290–320 ⊞ CoC
Francis Matthews was the voice of Captain Scarlet and has appeared in nearly 50 films.

Space Precinct, a Lieutenant Brogan figure, 1994, 13in (33cm) high, with box.
£11–15 / €16–20
$18–24 ⊞ CTO

◀ *Masters of the Universe,* an Orko figure, by Mattel, 1983, on original card, 11 x 6in (28 x 15cm).
£75–85 / €105–120
$120–135 ⊞ OW

Alien, Hicks and Alien figures, by Kenner for KayBee Toys, American, 1997, 12in (30.5cm) high, with box.
£180–200 / €250–280
$290–320 ⊞ SSF

Alien Resurrection, a Newborn Alien figure, reissue of Hasbro Signature Series, 1997, 7in (18cm) high, with box.
£16–20 / €22–28
$26–32 ⊞ SSF

▶ *Planet of the Apes,* a Gorilla soldier figure, by Hasbro, Signature Series Collector's Edition, 1999, 12in (30.5cm) high, with box.
£25–30 / €35–40
$40–50 ⊞ SSF

A *Living Dead Dolls* **Sheena figure,** by Mezco, 2001, 12in (30.5cm) high, with original box.
£35–40 / €50–55
$55–65 ⊞ NOS

Space Toys & Robots

The word robot derives from the Czechoslovakian word *robota*, meaning forced labour. It was first used to describe the mechanical creatures in Karel Capek's 1921 play R. U. R. (Rossum's Universal Robots). Robots featured in developing science fiction literature – American novelist Isaac Asimov was the first to coin the word robotics in a 1942 short story, and 1950 saw the publication of his first work, I, Robot.

Toy robots and space toys really took off in the 1950s and '60s, coinciding with the development of the space race. Although America was the principal market place, the main centre of production was Japan. The lithographed tinplate toys were produced with friction or wind-up mechanisms and later with batteries. Leading firms include Horikawa, Nomura and Yonezawa. The American company Cragstan imported Japanese toys and sold them under their own label. The 1960s saw plastic robots coming to the fore.

Condition is very important to value since damaged lithographed tinplate is almost impossible to repair. Boxes are also significant both because they can be attractively decorated themselves and for the information they can supply about the maker.

An SY tinplate clockwork spaceman robot, Japanese, c1960, 8in (20.5cm) high.
£145–160 / €210–230
$230–260 ⊞ HAL

An Ideal Toy Corp plastic battery-operated Zeroids robot, American, 1968, 7in (18cm) high, with box.
£90–100 / €125–140
$145–160 ⊞ HAL

A tinplate battery-operated robot, Japanese, 1960s, 11in (28cm) high.
£130–145 / €185–210
$200–230 ⊞ GTM

A tinplate clockwork Emergency Space Rocket, 1960s, 6in (15cm) long, with box.
£75–85 / €105–120
$120–135 ⊞ CBB

◄ **A Cragstan tinplate battery-operated Great Astronaut robot,** American, 1960s, 14in (35.5cm) high.
£560–620 / €800–880
$900–1,000 ⊞ TNS

An ATC tinplate friction-driven Space Ship XZ-7, Japanese, 1960s, 7in (18cm) long, with box.
£50–60 / €70–85
$80–95 ⊞ CBB

A tinplate battery-operated Apollo 11 Eagle Lunar Module, Japanese, 1970s, 10in (25.5cm) high, with box.
£180–200 / €250–280
$290–320 ⊞ GTM

A Calfax battery-operated and AM radio 1-M-1 Starroid robot, Star Command Series, American, 1977, 7½in (19cm) high, with box.
£30–35 / €40–50
$50–55 ⊞ GTM

▶ **A tinplate battery-operated Apollo-Z spaceship,** Japanese, 1970s, 12in (30.5cm) long.
£75–85 / €105–120
$120–135 ⊞ GTM

A Lost in Space robot, 1997, 11in (28cm) high.
£16–20 / €22–28
$26–32 ⊞ SSF
If this robot still had its original box it would be worth double this amount.

Star Trek

Created by Gene Roddenberry (1921–91), *Star Trek* was first shown on NBC in 1966. This was followed by other television series including *Star Trek The Animated Series* in 1973, *Star Trek The Next Generation* in 1987, *Star Trek Deep Space Nine* in 1993, *Star Trek Voyager* in 1995 and *Enterprise* in 2001. A host of films were created along with books, magazines, merchandise and Trekkie conventions, which take place all over the world.

Star Trek, a Mr Scott figure, by Mego, American, 1974, on original card, 9 x 8in (23 x 20.5cm).
£135–150 / €190–210
$210–240 ⊞ OW

Star Trek, Gorn and Cheron figures, by Mego, American, 1974, 8in (20.5cm) high.
£65–75 / €90–105
$105–120 ⊞ OW

◀ **Star Trek,** a Mr Spock action figure, by Mego, American, 1979, 12in (30.5cm) high, with box.
£60–70 / €85–100
$95–110 ⊞ HAL

Star Trek figures

Mego released a second series of classic *Star Trek* figures in 1975. This series consisted of four aliens: Cheron, Gorn, The Keeper and Neptunian. The Cheron half black/half white figure is based on the characters in the classic *Star Trek* episode *Let That Be Your Last Battlefield*. Unfortunately there is a particular strain of bacteria that has an affinity for the dyes used in the plastic, making the figure appear disfigured. The bacteria affects even sealed figures that have never been removed from the original packaging. The black dye from the body often migrates into the costume, which should be half black and half pure white.

When purchasing a carded 8in (20.5cm) Mego figure check for loose pieces. If the legs or arms have come loose, you will hear them rattling in the package. Be aware that an opened package is often worth less than an unopened package containing a figure with loose parts. Always inspect the packaging carefully to see if it has been opened. A reputable dealer will always identify previously opened packages and adjust the price accordingly.

◀ **Star Trek The Next Generation,** a Jean Luc Picard figure, by Playmates, 1992, on original card, 10 x 8in (25.5 x 20.5cm).
£16–20 / €22–28
$26–32 ⊞ OW

Star Trek The Next Generation, a Tricorder electronic game, by Playmates, 1993, boxed, 6 x 10in (15 x 25.5cm).
£70–80 / €100–115
$110–130 ⊞ OW

Star Trek Voyager, Skybox Collector Cards, a boxed set of 98, 1995.
£11–15 / €16–20
$18–24 ⊞ SSF

Star Trek Insurrection, an autograph card, Jonathon Frakes as William T. Riker, 1998.
£135–150 / €190–210
$210–240 ⊞ SSF

Star Trek, a talking Borg figure, by Playmates, Space Talk Series, 1995, 7in (18cm) high, on original card.
£30–35 / €40–50
$50–55 ⊞ SSF

◀ **Star Trek Enterprise,** a mug, 2002, 4in (10cm) high.
£6–10 / €8–14
$10–16 ⊞ CoC

Star Wars

▶ **Star Wars,** Topps bubblegum cards, Series 3, c1977.
£90–100 / €125–140
$145–160 each ⊞ OW

Star Wars, Darth Vader, Snow Trooper and Storm Trooper figures, 1977, 4in (10cm) high.
£6–10 / €8–14
$10–16 each ⊞ SSF

Star Wars, an X-Wing Aces electronic target game, by Kenner, American, 1978, boxed, 26in (66cm) long.
£1,800–2,000 / €2,550–2,850
$2,900–3,200 ⊞ SSF
This toy is extremely rare, hence its high value to dedicated *Star Wars* enthusiasts.

LOCATE THE SOURCE
The source of each illustration in Miller's can be found by checking the code letters below each caption with the Key to Illustrations, pages 443–451.

◀ *Star Wars The Empire Strikes Back,* a Han Solo action figure, by Kenner, American, 1979, on original card, 9 x 6in (23 x 15cm).
£250–300 / €355–425
$400–480 ⊞ OW

May the force be with you! In 1977 a grandmother bought two sets of 20 *Star Wars* action figures. One set she gave to her grandson, the other she put away into a cupboard in case any of his toys got lost or broken. The mint and packaged set remained in the cupboard for 25 years until the grandmother, now in her 80s, contacted Vectis Auction House. The set of 20 figures, which originally cost 49p each, sold for an astonishing **£10,100 / €14,350 / $16,150** including **£1,160 / €1,650 / $1,850** each for Luke Skywalker and Chewbacca.

Star Wars Return of the Jedi, a Princess Leia action figure, by Palitoy, 1983, on a tri-logo card, 9 x 6in (23 x 15cm).
£310–350 / €440–500
$500–560 ⊞ OW

Star Wars Return of the Jedi, a Battle-Damaged Imperial Tie Fighter Vehicle, by Palitoy, 1983, boxed, 11 x 12in (28 x 30.5cm).
£90–100 / €125–140
$145–160 ⊞ OW

Star Wars Return of the Jedi, a sketch book, 1983, 7¾ x 9¾in (19.5 x 25cm).
£10–14 / €14–20
$16–22 ⋗ StDA

Star Wars Return of the Jedi, an Anakin Skywalker action figure, by Palitoy, 1983, 4in (10cm) high, on a tri-logo card.
£145–160 / €200–230
$230–260 ⊞ SSF

▶ *Star Wars Return of the Jedi,* an X-Wing Fighter Vehicle, by Palitoy, 1983, boxed, 13 x 14in (33 x 35.5cm).
£50–60 / €70–85
$80–95 ⊞ OW

Star Wars Return of the Jedi, an Anakin Skywalker action figure, 1984, 4in (10cm) high.
£14–18 / €20–25
$22–28 ⊞ CoC

Star Wars, Collector Series Han Solo and Tauntaun action figures, by Kenner, American, 1997, boxed, 18in (45.5cm) square.
£135–150 / €190–210
$210–240 ⊞ OW

Star Wars Episode 1 – The Phantom Menace, a pod racer propeller, 1999, 8in (20.5cm) diam.
£250–300 / €360–430
$400–480 ⋗ CO

This propeller was part of a pod racer which crashes at the beginning of the film during the pivitol racing scene.

Tinplate

◀ **A Lehmann tinplate clockwork toy,** 'Oh My', German, c1900, 11in (28cm) high.
£580–650 / €820–920 $930–1,050 ⊞ HAL

A Lehmann tinplate clockwork car, with driver, mechanism missing, German, c1907, 6½in (16.5cm) long.
£170–200 / €240–280 $270–320 ✈ GK

A tinplate rocking horse, 1920s, 4in (10cm) long.
£260–290 / €370–410 $420–460 ⊞ RGa

A tinplate windmill, 1920s, 3in (7.5cm) high.
£80–90 / €115–130 $130–145 ⊞ CBB

A Burnett tinplate clockwork parcel van, c1920, 7in (18cm) long.
£630–700 / €900–1,000 $1,000–1,100 ⊞ HAL

▶ **A tinplate clockwork car,** with lady driver, German, c1930, 18in (45.5cm) long.
£450–500 €640–710 $720–800 ⊞ GTM

A Louis Marx tinplate clockwork Dopey toy, American, marked and dated 1938, 9in (23cm) high.
£135–150 / €190–210 $210–240 ⊞ TNS

A velvet-covered clockwork dancing mouse, possibly by Schuco, with key, 1930s, 13in (33cm) high.
£85–100 / €120–140 $135–160 ✈ BR

A Wells tinplate clockwork truck,
with driver, 1930s, 10in (25.5cm) long.
£100–120 / €140–170
$160–190 ⚲ FHF

Toys from German companies, such as Märklin and Bing, or from French companies, can fetch high prices if in good working condition. Lithographed toys from companies such as Ohio Art, Wells-Brimtoy and Marx have a similar look to the German and French companies toys but can be bought for around half the price. Some Japanese toys have the same look and are still very affordable.

A Tipp & Co tinplate clockwork Royal Mail van, German, 1930s, 9in (23cm) long.
£440–490 / €620–700
$700–780 ⊞ CBB

▶ **A tinplate battery-operated Mercedes racing car,** German, 1950s, 10in (25.5cm) long.
£175–195 / €250–280
$280–310 ⊞ GTM

A tinplate clockwork toy,
Japanese, 1930s, 4in (10cm) long.
£45–50 / €65–70
$75–80 ⊞ CBB

◀ **A Tri-ang Minic tinplate clockwork car,** 1930s, 5in (12.5cm) long.
£155–175
€220–250
$250–280
⊞ CBB

A Louis Marx tinplate military tractor and trailer, American, 1940s, 10in (25.5cm) long, with box.
£210–240 / €300–340
$340–380 ⊞ OSF

▶ **A Bandai tinplate battery-operated Cadillac,** Japanese, 1959, 11¾in (30cm) long.
£190–220 / €270–310
$310–350 ⊞ TNS

▶ **A Louis Marx tinplate Coca-Cola truck,** with trolley and 12 plastic Coca-Cola cases, American, c1957, 17in (43cm) long.
£500–560 / €720–800
$810–900 ⊞ TNS

A Tri-ang tinplate horse box,
with horses and chrome fittings, 1950s, 6in (15cm) long.
£135–150 / €190–210
$210–240 ⊞ PCCC

A Tri-ang Minic tinplate clockwork double-decker bus,
1950s, 7¼in (18.5cm) long.
£135–150 / €190–210
$210–240 ⊞ TNS

A tinplate Wyatt Earp paint box,
1950s, 9in (23cm) wide.
£20–25 / €28–35
$32–40 ⊞ HAL

◀ **A Schuco tinplate clockwork Grand Prix Racer,** No. 1070, 1950s, 6¼in (16cm) long, with box.
£45–50 / €65–70
$75–80 ⚒ **TQA**

▶ **A tinplate clockwork clown,** Japanese, late 1950s, 9in (23cm) high.
£260–290 / €370–410
$410–460 ⊞ **CBB**

A Tomy tinplate battery-operated Combat G. I., Japanese, 1960s, 10in (25.5cm) wide.
£175–195 / €250–280
$280–310 ⊞ **GTM**

A Tri-ang Minic tinplate steam roller, 1960, 5½in (14cm) long, with box.
£55–65 / €80–90
$90–105 ⊞ **GTM**

A Chein tinplate Melody Player, decorated with a circus scene, American, 1960s, 7 x 6½in (18 x 16.5cm), with box.
£170–190 / €240–270
$270–300 ⊞ **OSF**
This music box came in other designs such as a Mickey Mouse scene and a woodgrain box decorated with a mythological sylvan scene.

A Chein tinplate mechanical base drummer, American, 1960s, 8¾in (22cm) high, with box.
£170–190 / €240–270
$270–300 ⊞ **OSF**

A tinplate clockwork Winki toy, 1960s, 7in (18cm) high.
£55–65 / €80–90
$90–105 ⊞ **HAL**

A Louis Marx tinplate battery-operated *Flintstones* **Dino the Dinosaur,** American, 1960s, 14in (35.5cm) long.
£260–310 / €370–440
$410–500 ⚒ **VEC**

A tinplate battery-operated Sonicon bus, Japanese, 1960s, 13in (33cm) long.
£50–60 / €70–85
$80–95 ⊞ **HAL**

▶ **A Lehmann mechanical climbing monkey,** Tom, 8in (20.5cm) long.
£115–140 / €165–200
$185–220 ⚒ **FHF**

Trains

A Bassett-Lowke Carette 1 gauge goods van, with repainted roof, 1910–14, 11in (28cm) long.
£210–230 / €300–330
$330–370 ⊞ WOS

A Central Station model, possibly by Märklin, German, c1915, 20½in (52cm) long.
£530–590 / €750–840
$850–950 ⊞ TNS

A Märklin tinplate signal bell, restored, late 1930s, 5in (12.5cm) high.
£20–25 / €28–35
$32–40 ⊞ WOS

◄ **A Hornby 0 gauge tinplate engine shed,** No. E2E, with electric lighting, three rail track, c1936, 19½in (49.5cm) long, with box.
£720–800 / €1,000–1,150
$1,150–1,300 ⊞ MDe
This was the largest accessory made by Hornby. They made two other versions of this size as well as a No. 1 which was half the size. Today this is one of the most sought after accessories of the pre-WWII range and this example is in near mint condition. The clockwork version has a price range of £500–600 / €710–850 / $800–960 and the No. 1 version £400–500 / €570–710 / $640–800.

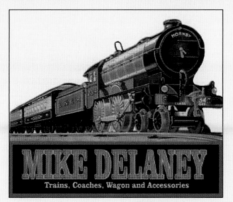

▶ **A Trix Express locomotive,** with three coaches, c1935, locomotive 7in (18cm) long.
£450–500
€640–710
$720–800 ⊞ WOS

A Hornby 0 gauge clockwork locomotive, No. M3, finished in LMS livery, 1930s, 6½in (16.5cm) long, with original box.
£130–155 / €185–220
$210–250 ⚐ FHF

◀ **A Hornby 0 gauge 4–4–0 clockwork locomotive and tender,** finished in LNER livery, 1930s.
£280–330
€400–470
$450–530 ⚐ FHF

Three Hornby 0 gauge wagons, c1945, 6in (15cm) long, with boxes.
£25–30 / €35–40
$40–50 each ⊞ HAL

A Hornby Dublo deltic diesel electric locomotive, No. 3234, 'St Paddy', c1950, 10in (25.5cm) long.
£310–350 / €440–500
$500–560 ⊞ GTM

A Hornby Dublo freight truck, c1952, 3in (7.6cm) long, with box.
£35–40 / €50–55
$55–65 ⊞ CWO

A Hornby Dublo 0–6–2 locomotive, No. 6699, EDL7, slight rust, 1950s, 6in (15cm) long.
£140–170 / €200–240
$230–270 ⚐ VEC

◀ **An 00 gauge locomotive and tender,** 'Duchess of Monrose', First Type with Gloss finish, 1950s, 12in (23cm) long, with boxes.
£90–100 / €135–140
$145–160 ⊞ HAL

A Hornby Dublo locomotive, 'Duchess of Montrose', with three-rail pickup, 1950s, 11½in (29cm) long.
£55–65 / €80–90
$90–105 ⊞ WOS

◀ **A Hornby 0 gauge Cadbury's Chocolates closed wagon,** 1950s, 5in (12.5cm) long.
£200–230
€280–320
$320–370
⊞ WOS

A Hornby Dublo restaurant car, with tin roof, 1950s, 9in (23cm) long, with box.
£16–20 / €22–28
$26–32 HAL

A Hornby 0 gauge tinplate wagon, 1950s, 8in (20.5cm) long, with box.
£30–35 / €40–50
$50–55 WOS

A Hornby Dublo Mobil Oil tank wagon, 1956–57, 4in (10cm) long.
£11–15 / €16–20
$18–24 GTM

◄ **A Tri-ang Dublo locomotive,** No. 41, c1960, 11in (28cm) long.
£30–35 / €40–50
$50–55 HAL

► **A Hornby Dublo 2–8–0 8F locomotive and tender,** No. 2224, minor damage, 1960s, 12in (30.5cm) long, with box, together with instructions, guarantee slip, tube of oil and packing rings.
£140–170 / €200–240
$230–270 VEC

A Louis Marx tinplate clockwork train set, American, 1960, with box.
£75–90 / €105–125
$120–145 GK

A British Rail electric freight engine, possibly Hornby, 1980s, 10in (25.5cm) long.
£18–22 / €26–32
$28–35 ⊞ GTM

A Hornby 0 gauge low sided wagon, No. 50, with Liverpool Cables drum, 1960s, 6in (15cm) long, with box.
£40–45 / €55–65
$65–75 ⊞ GTM

A Tri-ang Hornby train set, 'The Blue Pullman', 1960s, boxed, 15in (38cm) wide.
£75–85 / €105–120
$120–135 ⊞ WOS

▶ **A Gresley 00 gauge 2–6–2 V22 Class Super Smooth Series locomotive and tender,** Bachmann Branch Line, 1990s, 9in (23cm) long.
£40–45 / €55–65
$65–75 ⊞ GTM

Tri-ang Spot-On

Tri-ang Spot-On diecast toys were started by Lines Brothers in 1959. Modelled to 1:42 scale, they were slightly larger than Dinky toys and packed with features. Spot-On toys came with fully-fitted interiors, windows and extremely accurate flexomatic suspension. Electric headlamps were also added c1961. Cars came in a rich variety of colours, and models ranged from the London Routemaster bus in 1963 to haulage vehicles produced 1960–63. Boxed sets of vehicles are rare, since the boxes were fragile and easily damaged. In 1964, Lines Brothers took over Meccano (including Dinky) thus reducing the need to produce the expensive Spot-On products and the Northern Ireland factory was closed in 1967.

A Tri-ang Spot-On crane, No. 117, c1962, 12in (30.5cm) long, with box.
£135–150 / €190–210
$220–240 ⊞ HAL

A Tri-ang Spot-On E.R.F. 68g dropside lorry, No. 109/3, 1960, 8½in (21.5cm) long, with box.
£175–195 / €250–280
$280–310 ⊞ GTM

A Tri-ang Spot-On Humber Super Snipe, No. 306, 1964, 4½in (11.5cm) long, with box.
£75–90 / €105–125
$120–145 ↗ FHF

◀ **A Tri-ang Spot-On United Dairies milk float,** No. 122, c1962, boxed, 6in (15cm) long.
£100–110 / €140–155
$160–175 ⊞ HAL

A Tri-ang Spot-On Mulliner coach, No. 156, 1960s, 11in (28cm) long.
£145–160 / €210–230
$230–260 ⊞ HAL

Treen

A carved wood knitting sheath, 18thC, 11in (28cm) long.
£100–120 / €140–170
$160–190 ⊞ WO

A mahogany priest, c1800, 11in (28cm) long.
£50–60 / €70–85
$80–95 ⊞ SDA
A priest is a small club used by anglers to kill the fish when they have been caught.

A treen snuff box, in the form of a pair of bellows, initialled 'WH' and dated 1863, 4in (10cm) long.
£160–190 / €230–270
$255–305 ➶ Bea(E)

A treen covered inkwell, in the form of a beehive, with applied coloured bees, 19thC, 3½in (9cm) high.
£100–120 / €140–170
$160–190 ➶ DA

A mahogany book press, c1810, 14in (35.5cm) wide.
£380–430 / €540–610
$610–690 ⊞ F&F

A treen snuff box, in the form of a two-headed squatting man, with a hinged cover, 19thC, 3¾in (9.5cm) high.
£480–580 / €680–810
$770–920 ➶ BWL

Cross Reference
See Smoking & Tobacco (pages 340–343)

A fruitwood nutcracker, in the form of a jester, 19thC, 7in (18cm) long.
£160–180 / €230–255
$260–290 ⊞ WAA

A wooden gull-wing knitting sheath, Welsh, c1840, 10in (25.5cm) long.
£340–380 / €485–540
$540–600 ⊞ SEA

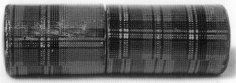

A Tartan ware tube, c1850, 1¾in (4.5cm) long.
£35–40 / €50–55
$55–65 ⊞ VBo

An ivory gavel, carved with a spiral design, c1850, 6in (15cm) long.
£145–160 / €200–220
$230–260 ⊞ LBr

A carved bog oak harp, Irish, c1870, 12in (30.5cm) high.
£520–580 / €740–820
$830–930 ⊞ STA

A Tunbridge ware napkin ring, c1870, 2in (5cm) diam.
£20–25 / €28–35
$32–40 ⊞ MB

A Victorian mahogany miniature chest, the three long graduated drawers with turned knop handles, 9in (23cm) wide.
£75–90 / €110–130
$130–150 ⤳ WL

▶ **An oak desk mallet,** with an inscribed ivory badge, c1911, 28¼in (72cm) high.
£90–100 / €130–140
$145–160 ⊞ MB
This mallet was made with oak from the roof of Glasgow Cathedral.

A carved bog oak candlestick, Irish, 1860s, 9in (23cm) high.
£150–170 / €210–240
$240–270 ⊞ STA

A wooden grain measure, c1880, 6in (15cm) high.
£25–30 / €35–40
$40–50 ⊞ AL

A Tunbridge ware pin tray, depicting Eridge Castle, c1870, 6½in (16.5cm) wide.
£400–460 / €570–640
$640–740 ⊞ PGO

A larch and sycamore basket, Scottish, c1880, 6in (15cm) wide.
£155–175 / €220–250
$250–280 ⊞ MB

A Victorian lignum vitae Masonic gavel, with a carved sandstone head, 10in (25.5cm) long.
£30–35 / €40–50
$50–55 ⊞ WiB

A pair of carved wood napkin rings, in the form of Scottie dogs, Italian, c1920, 4½in (11.5cm) long.
£25–30 / €35–40
$40–50 ⊞ Dall

A carved wood musical box, in the form of a terrier, with glass eyes and a clockwork cylinder movement in the base, Austrian, early 20thC, 7½in (19cm) high.
£950–1,150
€1,400–1,650
$1,500–1,800 ⤳ G(L)

Umbrellas, Parasols & Walking Sticks

Deriving from *ombre* the French word for shade, the umbrella was originally conceived as a sunshade and was an object of religious significance. Umbrellas were used in ancient Egypt and China as a mark of rank and a symbol of protection by the gods and were depicted on Greek vases in portrayals of holy festivals. Although the Romans used umbrellas and parasols for practical purposes, it was not until the late 18th century that they became an essential fashion accoutrement. They remained so until the 1920s, when the vogue for a healthy complexion and a more active life caused ladies to cast aside their parasols along with their corsets, although umbrellas remained a practical and, generally speaking, not very decorative,

accessory. Victorian and Edwardian parasols and umbrellas, however, were highly attractive and reflected changing patterns in dress.

Materials include cotton, silk and lace; flowered textiles and fringing were popular, as was a contrasting lining. Pommels came in various designs and materials including wood, ivory, horn and silver; folding sticks made parasols more convenient to carry. Given their active open-air function, vintage examples have been prone to wear and tear. Textile and silk linings have often perished over the years, and frames can also be damaged. Often the most interesting part of the parasol, as with walking sticks, is the handle, which was produced in a variety of novelty shapes.

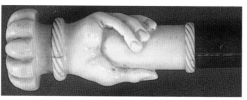

A Victorian parasol, with an ivory handle carved as a hand.
£260–310 / €370–440
$420–500 ⚘ RTo

A Chantilly lace parasol, with an ivory handle and silver fittings, c1850, 22in (56cm) long.
£360–400 / €510–570
$580–640 ⊞ HL

An ivory cane handle, carved as the head of George IV, early 19thC, 2in (5cm) high.
£450–550 / €650–780
$740–880 ⚘ G(L)

A dog correction cane, the handle carved with a dog's head, c1860, 23in (58.5cm) long.
£50–60 / €70–85
$80–95 ⊞ GBr

◀ **A silk carriage parasol,** with an ivory handle, c1860, 25in (63.5cm) long.
£75–85 / €105–120
$120–135 ⊞ CCO

▶ **A bamboo walking cane,** the handle carved with the head of a Turk, with articulated tongue and eyes, mechanism defective, late 19thC, 35in (89cm) long.
£100–120 / €140–170
$160–190 ⚘ G(L)

A silk carriage parasol, 1860, 27in (68.5cm) long.
£75–85 / €105–120
$120–135 ⊞ L&L

A bamboo tippling cane, with a glass drinks container and brass ends, c1880, 36in (91.5cm) long.
£175–195 / €250–275
$280–310 ⊞ GBr

A bamboo umbrella, with an agate handle, c1890, 34in (86.5cm) long.
£70–80 / €100–115
$110–130 ⊞ GBr

A bamboo cane, with an Art Nouveau silver handle in the form of a lily, c1890, 38in (96.5cm) long.
£420–470 / €600–670
$670–750 ⊞ GBr

An Edwardian oak umbrella stand, 28in (71cm) wide.
£160–180 / €230–255
$255–290 ⊞ SAT

An Edwardian hardwood walking stick, the silver handle in the form of a greyhound's head, 35in (89cm) long.
£110–130 / €155–185
$175–210 ⋗ G(L)

A malacca walking stick, with a foliate-embossed silver collar and blue john handle, c1907, 36in (91.5cm) long.
£500–600 / €710–850
$800–960 ⋗ G(L)

A shark-bone cane, with a whale-tooth handle, c1910, 35in (89cm) long.
£85–95 / €120–135
$135–150 ⊞ GBr

An Edwardian ebony cane, the carved ivory handle in the form of a lady, with a silver collar, 35in (89cm) long.
£400–480 / €570–680
$640–770 ⋗ G(L)

An Edwardian oak ...

A walking cane, with a horn handle, c1920, 35in (89cm) long.
£60–70 / €85–100
$95–110 ⊞ GBr

A wooden walking stick, the handle carved with the head of Abraham Lincoln, 1910, 37in (94cm) long.
£260–290 / €370–410
$420–460 ⊞ NLS

A cotton parasol, with floral decoration, 1920, 36in (91.5cm) long.
£40–45 / €55–65
$65–75 ⊞ L&L

An umbrella, by E. Hardy, with a brass handle, Italian, 1950s, 26in (66cm) long.
£35–40 / €50–55
$55–65 ⊞ TWI

Watches

A gilt-copper pair-cased pocket watch, signed 'E. Nilmotini, London', No. 3064, with an enamelled Roman dial and verge movement, 1803.
£120–145 / €170–200
$195–230 🔨 **G(L)**

An 18ct gold open-faced pocket watch, by Peter Martin, Glasgow, No. 12816, with an engine-turned gilt-metal dial, the chain fusee movement with lever escapement, London 1844, 2in (5cm) diam, with a morocco leather case.
£260–310 / €370–410
$420–460 🔨 **BR**

A 9ct gold pocket watch, by J. W. Benson, London, No. J.2859, with subsidiary seconds dial, London 1901, with original case.
£180–220 / €260–310
$290–350 🔨 **DA**

A Rolex 9ct gold wrist-watch, with an enamelled Arabic dial, 1915.
£140–170 / €200–240
$220–270 🔨 **G(L)**

◄ **A diamond wristwatch,** the case and shoulders with single-cut diamonds, c1920.
£300–360 / €430–510
$490–580 🔨 **S(O)**

A Movado silver chronometer watch,
with a shagreen sliding cover, 1930s,
7½in (19cm) wide, open.
£320–380 / € 450–540
$510–610 ↗ TRM

▶ **A diamond-set platinum cocktail watch,**
with an Arabic dial, 1930s.
£100–120 / € 140–170
$160–200 ↗ G(L)

**A Mappin & Webb 9ct gold
pocket watch,** 1930s, with 1920s
gold chain, 12in (30.5cm) long.
£210–240 / € 300–340
$330–380 ⊞ OH

◀ **An Omega silver
pocket watch,** 1930s,
2in (5cm) diam.
£135–150 / € 190–210
$210–240 ⊞ TIC

▶ **An advertising
pocket watch,** 1930s,
7in (18cm) diam.
£165–185 / € 230–260
$270–300 ⊞ TIC

**A silver and enamel
wristwatch,** 1930s,
1in (2.5cm) diam.
£160–180 / € 230–255
$260–290 ⊞ LBe

◀ **A Taylor sterling
silver and gold-plated
watch brooch,** in the form
of a pagoda, American,
1940s, 3in (7.5cm) high.
£220–250 / € 310–350
$350–400 ⊞ RGA

**A Sekonda railway
timepiece,** with a chain,
1940s, 2in (5cm) diam.
£90–100 / € 130–140
$145–160 ⊞ OH

**A Spaceman automatic
wristwatch,** Swiss,
1960s, 1½in (4cm) square.
£160–180 / € 230–260
$255–290 ⊞ ANGE

A Smith's pocket watch, for the visually impaired, with Braille numerals, 1960s, 2in (5cm) diam.
£60–70 / €90–100
$100–110 ⊞ TIC

An Omega Dynamic wristwatch, 1973.
£135–150 / €190–210
$210–240 ⊞ TIC

A Ragen Synchronar stainless steel and plastic solar-powered digital wristwatch, with electronic movement, solar panels, LED display, brick link bracelet, c1975, 16in (40.5cm) long.
£310–370 / €440–520
$500–590 ⚒ S(O)
Ex-John Entwistle collection.

A Heuer Autavia Diver 100 automatic chronograph, with date, c1980.
£720–800 / €1,000–1,150
$1,150–1,300 ⊞ HARP

◄ **Four Pop Swatch wristwatches,** 1980s, 2in (5cm) diam.
£6–10 / €8–14
$10–16 each ⊞ TIC

A Movado purse watch, the silvered dial with subsidiary seconds, in a crocodile skin case, 20thC, 3in (7.5cm) wide.
£120–145 / €170–200
$190–230 ⚒ DMC

A Swatch chrome wristwatch, with a leather strap, 1980s.
£20–25 / €28–35
$32–40 ⊞ TIC

A Rodell-7 Spider wristwatch, the dial with web motif and a spider as the seconds hand, Hong Kong, c1990, 1½in (3.5cm) diam.
£550–650 / €780–920
$880–1,050 ⚒ S(O)
Ex–John Entwistle collection.

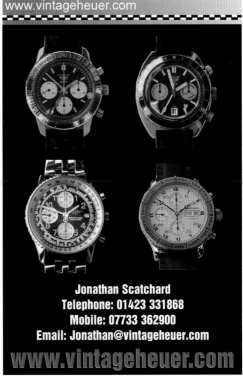

Writing

A Sampson Mordan & Co silver propelling pencil, with machine engraving and banded agate seal, 1830–40, 5in (12.5cm) long.
£70–80 / €100–115
$110–130 ⊞ PPL

A gold-plated propelling pencil, c1850, 3in (7.5cm) long.
£50–60 / €70–85
$80–95 ♪ G(L)

A Victorian Sampson Mordan & Co walnut and brass postal scale, with foliate-engraved brass pans and six brass weights, 8in (20.5cm) wide.
£210–250 / €300–360
$340–400 ♪ G(L)

A Tunbridge ware paper knife, c1870, 8in (20.5cm) long.
£45–50 / €65–70
$75–80 ⊞ MB

A Sampson Mordan & Co ivory slider pencil, set with silver stars, c1880, 2¼in (5.5cm) long.
£60–70 / €85–100
$95–110 ⊞ PPL

A horse hoof inkwell, the hinged brass cover inscribed 'Lady Bird', the name of the horse, c1873, 3in (7.5cm) diam.
£90–100 / €130–140
$145–160 ⊞ MB

A tapestry and leather desk blotter, c1880, 11in (28cm) wide.
£250–280 / €350–400
$400–450 ⊞ LGU

A Mabie Todd & Bard Swan gold-filled fountain pen, with floral, snail and ribbon decoration and engraved inscription, American, 1890s, 5¼in (13.5cm) long.
£340–400 / €480–570
$540–640 ♪ CO
The method of gold-filling is achieved by using heat and pressure to bond a layer of gold alloy to brass or another base metal, then milling it into a sheet or drawing it into a wire. It is much more durable than gold plate and will not flake or peel.

A leather travelling inkwell, 1880, 2½in (6.5cm) high.
£35–40 / €50–55
$55–65 ⊞ HO

▶ Two hand-embroidered pen wipes, French, c1890, 6in (15cm) diam.
£45–50 / €65–70
$75–80 each ⊞ PPL

A silver slider pencil, in the form of a cross, c1890, 2in (5cm) long, on a chain.
£90–100 / €130–140
$145–160 ⊞ PPL

A **Tunbridge ware desk stand,** on bun feet, damaged and repaired, 19thC, 10in (25.5cm) wide.
£190–230 / €270–325
$300–370 ⚲ SWO

A **sterling silver quill knife and eraser,** 19thC, 6in (15cm) long.
£70–80 / €100–110
$110–130 ⊞ PPL
Combination knives and erasers became popular in the mid-19th century. The knife was used for sharpening quill pens and the eraser for scraping the surface of the parchment or paper. An original case or maker's mark will increase the value. Quills were the most common form of writing instrument until the end of the 19th century. Geese were the favourite source for quills and the finest examples were made from the first three flight feathers on each wing. The tips were conditioned by being placed in hot ash. Stationers and booksellers sold cut and uncut quills, although many users preferred to sharpen their own pens.

▶ A **faïence inkstand,** modelled as stacked books, the interior with a pewter inkwell, pounce pot and engraved lining, French, late 19thC, 4½in (11.5cm) wide.
£110–130 / €160–185
$175–210 ⚲ G(L)

A **wooden wagon inkwell,** the two cut-glass bottles with silver collars, c1890, 5in (12.5cm) high.
£540–600 / €770–850
$860–960 ⊞ HAA

A **Black Forest carved wood inkwell and pen tray,** German, 19thC, 4in (10cm) high.
£150–180 / €210–250
$240–280 ⚲ AMB

A **salt-glazed pottery inkwell and quill-holder,** modelled as the head of an ugly woman, slight damage, 19thC, 2½in (6.5cm) high.
£600–720 / €850–1,000
$960–1,150 ⚲ BBR

Five ebony- and ivory-handled quill knives and erasers, 19thC, 6½in (16.5cm) long.
£45–50 / €65–70
$75–80 each ⊞ PPL

A **Mabie Todd & Co Swan silver three-size chatelaine fountain pen,** decorated with snail pattern, with a locking cap, chains and gold gutter nib, American, c1907, 5¼in (13.5cm) long, in a presentation box.
£850–1,000 / €1,200–1,400
$1,350–1,600 ⚲ CO
Three-size chatelaine pens are extremely rare.

A **silver capstan inkwell,** the cover and base with a reeded edge, loaded, Birmingham 1909, 5in (12.5cm) diam.
£160–190 / €230–270
$250–300 ⚲ DA

A **Liverpool Royal Show souvenir pencil,** 1910, 3¼in (8.5cm) long.
£20–25 / €28–35
$32–40 ⊞ Dall

◀ A **silver stamp box,** modelled as a coal scuttle, Birmingham 1910, 1¼in (3cm) high.
£230–270 / €330–380
$370–440 ⚲ G(L)

A Waterman Filigree gold-filled hard rubber fountain pen, decorated with three-leaf pattern filigree, American, 1915–25, 4in (10cm) long.
£80–95 / €115–135
$130–150 ↗ CO

Conway Stewart

Established in east London in 1905, Conway Stewart was one of the pioneers of the lever filling system in which ink was sucked into the sack by using a metal lever in the barrel.

Their designs were aimed mainly at clerical workers and students and were therefore often bright and inventive. During the 1920s and '30s they used the new plastics to create pens in every conceivable colour and in patterns imitating everything from Italian marble to cracked ice. Some of the prettiest were the small pens designed for ladies and known as 'Dinkies', many of which came with a ring in the cap so that they could be worn on a ribbon. The next size up was known as a 'Dandy'.

Conway Stewart pens and pencils from between the wars can be very collectable. With shortages in the ration-bound post-war period the company was forced to use lower grade materials, although some collectable pens were still made. The firm suffered in the 1960s, thanks to the popularity of cartridge pens and the dominance of the Biro, and in 1975 the business was wound up.

A Conway Stewart Dinkie lever-fill fountain pen and pencil, the pen with a ring top, matching Duro-Point No. 2 pencil, nib damaged, late 1920s, 4½in (11.5cm) long, in original box.
£140–170 / €200–240
$230–270 ↗ CO

A brass pencil sharpener,
1930–50, 1in (2.5cm) long.
£11–15 / €16–20
$18–24 ⊞ RUSS

A Conway Stewart Dinkie celluloid lever-fill fountain pen, with marbled pattern case, cap cracked, 1920s, 4½in (11.5cm) long.
£90–110 / €135–160
$150–180 ↗ CO

A Conway Stewart rolled gold pencil, with ball clip, flared crown and black band, 1920s, 5in (12.5cm) long.
£50–60 / €70–85
$80–95 ↗ CO

A Sheaffer gold-plated lever-fill fountain pen, with engraved body, 1920s, 5½in (14cm) long.
£220–260 / €310–370
$350–420 ↗ G(L)

A Parker Duofold Junior button-fill fountain pen, nib replaced, American, c1929, 4½in (11.5cm) long.
£80–95 / €115–135
$135–160 ↗ CO
The classic American-made Parker Duofold was introduced in 1922 and was an immediate success. Originally available in black and red, the design was also produced in smaller sizes, such as this Duofold Junior, and in an adventurous range of colours. Mandarin Yellow was not a great success with the public on the verge of the Depression. The light colour also accentuated any defects, so surviving examples of this pen in good condition are rare.

A Parker Duofold Junior Permanite button-fill fountain pen, c1931, 4¾in (12cm) long, with matching rotary pencil and box.
£100–120 / €140–170
$160–190 ↗ CO

A Pelikan 200 push-button pencil, with simulated lizard skin band, German, 1937–40, 4¾in (12cm) long.
£100–120 / €140–170
$160–190 ↗ CO

A Swan Fyne Poynt 9ct gold pencil, 1930s,
5in (12.5cm) long.
£90–100 / € 130–140
$145–160 ⊞ PPL

A Parker Victory plastic fountain pen, with hatched
marble decoration, c1942, 5¼in (13.5cm) long.
£190–230 / € 270–330
$310–370 ⚹ CO

**A Parker Duofold Senior celluloid button-fill
fountain pen,** with herringbone decoration, c1944,
4¾in (12cm) long.
£320–380 / € 450–540
$510–610 ⚹ CO
**British-made Parkers are popular with collectors.
This herringbone Duofold is particularly desirable
because it is made in an unusual patterned plastic
and was produced for only a limited period.**

A Pelikan 100 piston-fill fountain pen, the celluloid
body with engraved cap bands, German, 1942–44,
4¾in (12cm) long.
£140–170 / € 200–240
$230–270 ⚹ CO

A Sheaffer PFM Mark III snorkel-fill fountain pen,
with rolled-gold trim, c1950, 5in (12.5cm) long.
£100–120 / € 140–170
$160–190 ⊞ PPL

A Pilot lacquer and 18ct gold fountain pen,
decorated with a goldfish by Masaharu Sakamoto,
signed, Japanese, 1960s, 5in (12.5cm) long.
£650–780 / € 920–1,100
$1,050–1,250 ⚹ CO
**Masaharu Sakamoto was born in 1914 and became
a pupil of Tokitaro Nichinan in 1937. He has
designed for Pilot since 1959, and his work has
been awarded many prizes.**

Further reading
*Miller's Pens & Writing Equipment: A Collector's
Guide*, Miller's Publications, 1999

A Yard-o'-Lead 9ct gold pencil, 1968, 5in (12.5cm) long,
in original box.
£125–140 / € 180–200
$200–225 ⊞ PPL

A Parker 65 Flighter polished steel fountain pen, with an extra broad nib, 1960–70, 5¼in (13.5cm) long.
£40–50 / € 55–70
$65–80 ⚹ CO

A Parker 75 enamelled fountain pen, decorated with
garlands of flowers, with gold-filled clip and decoration,
possibly French, 1970s, 5in (12.5cm) long.
£300–360 / € 430–510
$500–600 ⚹ CO

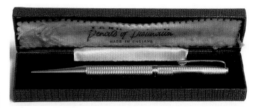

A Montblanc Agatha Christie acrylic fountain pen,
No. 19751/3000, with a silver snake clip set with ruby
eyes and two-colour snake nib, German, 1993,
5in (12.5cm) long, with box.
£400–480 / € 570–680
$640–770 ⚹ CO
**The German company Montblanc created a range of
pens inspired by famous authors. Other examples
include Hemingway (1992), Oscar Wilde (1994),
Voltaire (1995), Alexandre Dumas (1996) and
Dostoyevsky (1997). This pen has a silver trim, but
it was also produced in gold, which is far rarer. It
came in a box shaped like a book and the original
packaging adds to its interest.**

A Parker 51 fountain pen, with a gold-filled Vacumatic
Blue Diamond Fantasy cap, customized with a white-
metal overlay of a winged serpent chasing a winged
nymph, possibly French, 1980s, 5¼in (13.5cm) long.
£170–200 / € 240–280
$270–320 ⚹ CO

Pocket Money Collectables

This section is devoted to collectables at pocket money prices. Collecting doesn't have to cost a fortune – treasures can still be found, and many antique shops and markets have a cheap section where you can find very affordable pieces.

Children are natural collectors and can get a lot of fun turning their attention to antiques and collectables. Young collectors have the advantage of sharp eyes and matchless bargaining power – who can resist knocking a bit off the price for a child? Many who start collecting while young are embarking on an interest that will last for the rest of their lives.

◄ **A glass Hamilton bottle,** c1890, 9½in (24cm) long.
£2–6 / €3–8
$4–10 ⊞ AL

An Aynsley porcelain cup, c1890, 2in (5cm) high.
£1–5 / €2–7
$3–8 ⊞ SER

An iron poker, with a brass handle, c1900, 19in (48.5cm) long.
£2–6 / €3–8
$4–10 ⊞ AL

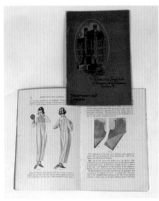

Underwear and Lingerie, Parts 1 and 2 of a set of 50, published by Women's Institute of Domestic Arts & Sciences, American, 1921, 9 x 6in (23 x 15cm).
£1–5 / €2–7
$3–8 each ⊞ MRW

Two *Theatre World* magazines, 1926 and 1937, 11 x 9in (28 x 23cm).
£1–5 / €2–7
$3–8 each ⊞ RTT

Girls' Annual, published by Collins, c1930, 10 x 8in (25.5 x 20.5cm).
£1–5 / €2–7
$3–8 ⊞ TOP

Four aluminium jelly moulds, in the form of rabbits, 1930s, 5in (12.5cm) long.
£1–5 / €2–7
$3–8 ⊞ AL

A pressed glass tray, 1930, 12in (30.5cm) wide.
£1–5 / €2–7
$3–8 ⊞ BAC

◄ **A hand-embroidered linen towel,** 1930s, 18in (45.5cm) long.
£1–5 / €2–7
$3–8 ⊞ HILL

Kensitas, Silk Flowers, two cards from the second series, 1933–34.
£1–5 / €2–7
$3–8 each ⊞ SOR

A dummy pack of Sax cigarettes, 1960s, 3¼ x 2¾in (8.5 x 7cm).
£1–5 / €2–7
$3–8 ⊞ RTT

A hand-painted ceramic vase, possibly German, c1970, 3½in (9cm) high.
£1–5 / €2–7
$3–8 ⊞ CRT

A Rolls Razor, 1940s, with original box.
£2–6 / €3–8
$4–10 ⊞ NFR

Woman's Illustrated magazine, 3 May 1952, 12 x 10in (30.5 x 25.5cm).
£1–5 / €2–7
$3–8 ⊞ FLD

A pair of Elbeo support hose, 1960s, in original packet, 10 x 7½in (25.5 x 19cm).
£2–6 / €3–8
$4–10 ⊞ RTT

A printed silk handkerchief, c1940, 12in (30.5cm) square.
£1–5 / €2–7
$3–8 ⊞ JPr

A Mabel Lucie Attwell Valentine card, c1960.
£1–5 / €2–7
$3–8 ⊞ JMC

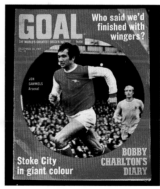

Goal magazine, No. 72, 20 December 1969, 11½ x 9in (29 x 23cm).
£1–5 / €2–7
$3–8 ⊞ TWI

◀ A Teeny Tiny My Little Pony, Baby Rattles, 1990, 2½in (6.5cm) high.
£4–8 / €5–11
$6–12 ⊞ RAND
This is one of the smallest My Little Pony figures to be produced.

Collectables of the Future

A Central Bank of Iraq 250 dinars note, with Saddam Hussein image, 1990.
£6–10 / €8–14
$10–16 ⊞ BAC

A *Harry Potter and the Philosopher's Stone* train set, by Hornby, 2001, box 24in (61cm) wide.
£75–85 / €105–120
$120–135 ⊞ WOS
Pottermania continues. In December 2003 a first edition of *Harry Potter and the Goblet of Fire*, signed and inscribed to J. K. Rowling's father sold at auction for £27,000.

A reheat cameo glass Fish vase, by Jonathan Harris, 2002, 8in (20cm) high.
£390–440 / €550–620
$630–700 ⊞ JHS
The decoration on this vase was achieved by hand-carving through multiple layers of enamel colour and sterling silver leaf.

A Moschino handbag, with original case and labels, 1997, 8in (20.5cm) high.
£220–250 / €310–350
$350–400 ⊞ TIN
The turn of the century has seen a growing obsession with designer handbags, each season bringing its must-have favourites, generally photographed dangling from the arms of celebrities. Handbags are now a well-established collectable.

A Manchester United No. 7 Champions League jersey, David Beckham spare, with embroidered badge and UEFA flash to sleeve, the reverse lettered 'Beckham', 2001–02.
£360–430 / €510–610
$580–690 ➚ S(O)

▶ **A Farewell to Concorde tankard,** depicting Concorde over London, the reverse with Concorde over New York, 2003, 5in (12.5cm) high
£35–40 / €50–55
$55–65 ⊞ PeJ
The sad withdrawal of Concorde in 2003 stimulated an auction of related memorabilia and the production of various collectables commemorating the retirement of one of the most famous aeroplanes of all time.

▶ **A Beck's beer bottle,** with Tracey Emin label, Waiting for a Tidal Wave, 2000, 8½in (21.5cm) high.
£30–35 / €40–50
$50–55 ⊞ PLB
For those who couldn't afford an original Tracey Emin or Damien Hirst, Beck's creative packaging, celebrating 15 years of arts sponsorship, provided an affordable way of acquiring a piece of Brit Art.

A Rugby World Cup Final programme, for the Australia v England match at the Telstra Stadium, Sydney, 22 November 2003, 11 x 8½in (28 x 21.5cm).
£25–30 / €35–40
$40–50 ⊞ RMo

Record Breakers

A tooled leather fishing creel, by Atkinson, with brass fittings, c1780, 13¼in (33.5cm) wide.
£7,600 / €10,800
$12,200 ↗ AGA
This is the most expensive fishing creel ever sold at auction in the UK.

▶ **A salt-glazed stoneware Reform flask,** moulded with soldiers and impressed 'Peace Proclaimed, April 29 1856', the reverse impressed 'War Declared March 28 1854', c1860, 6¾in (17cm) high.
£3,200 / €4,500
$5,100 ↗ BBR
This is a record-breaking price for a Reform flask.

An FA Cup Final programme, Tottenham Hotspur v Sheffield United, 20 April 1901.
£14,400 / €20,500
$23,000 ↗ S(O)
This is the highest price paid at auction across the world for a single football programme.

Beano **comic,** No. 3, Big Eggo Swallows a Ticking Clock, 1938.
£1,800 / €2,500
$2,900 ↗ CBP
This is the highest price paid for a *Beano* No. 3.

Reginald Heade (illus), cover artwork for *Wild Youth* by Paul Reville, signed, 1950s, 22 x 17in (56 x 43cm), framed and glazed.
£1,650 / €2,350
$2,650 ↗ CBP
This is a record-breaking price for a piece of artwork by Reginald Heade.

Cross Reference
See Rock & Pop (pages 309–310)

A Dinky Toys Foden Flat Truck, first type, with chains, c1952, 8in (20.5cm) long, with original blue lift-off box.
£11,750 / €16,700
$19,000 ↗ VEC
This was not a successful toy for Dinky in 1952. The colour was dull and the original price was only just less than the average working wage for a week. The truck only had a six-month production run. This rare and near mint condition example made a world record auction price for a post-WWII Dinky toy.

▶ **A Gibson Explorer guitar,** serial No. 8-4451, 1958, with case.
£95,200 / €135,000
$152,000 ↗ S(O)
This guitar was purchased by John Entwistle in the 1970s and was sold after his death, making a record-breaking price.

The BACA *Winners...*

CATEGORY 1
General Antiques Dealer

UK: NORTH OF M62
Haughey Antiques
Kirkby Stephen, Cumbria

M62 SOUTH, TO M4 / M25
The Country Seat
Huntercombe, Manor Barn,
Henley-on-Thames

LONDON (INSIDE M25)
Gordon Watson
50 Fulham Road, London

SOUTH AND SOUTH-WEST OF ENGLAND
Lennox Cato Antiques
1 The Square, Edenbridge

CATEGORY 2
Specialist Antiques Dealers

FURNITURE
Adams Antiques
Churches Mansion, Hospital Street,
Nantwich

COLLECTABLES
sponsored by
The Girl Can't Help It
Alfies Antique Market, Marylebone,
London

SILVER & PLATE
Sanda Lipton
Elliot House, 28A Devonshire Street,
London

PRINTS
Elizabeth Harvey-Lee
1 West Cottages, Middle Aston Road,
North Aston, Oxfordshire

WATERCOLOUR
Chris Beetles Ltd
10 Ryder Street, St James, London

CERAMICS
Simon Spero
109 Kensington Church Street,
London

GLASS
Mallet & Son (Antiques Ltd)
129 Mount Street, London

JEWELLERY
Joseph H Bonnar
72 Thistle Street, Edinburgh

CATEGORY 3
Auction Houses

UK: NORTH OF M62
Bonhams Auctioneers
17a East Parade, Leeds

M62 SOUTH, TO M4 / M25
Bonhams Auctioneers
Knowle, Solihull

INSIDE M25
Sotheby's Auctions
34–35 New Bond Street, London

SOUTH AND SOUTH-WEST OF ENGLAND
Woolley & Wallis
51–61 Castle Street, Salisbury

CATEGORY 4
Associated Awards

AON AWARD FOR AUCTIONEER OF THE YEAR
sponsored by
David Lay
Penzance Auction Rooms, Alverton,
Penzance

BEST ANTIQUES CENTRE
The Swan at Tetsworth
High Street, Tetsworth, Oxfordshire

ANTIQUES ON THE INTERNET
www.welshantiques.com

BBC HOMES AND ANTIQUES MAGAZINE AWARD FOR BEST ANTIQUES SHOPPING STREET

sponsored by

High Street, Burford, Oxfordshire

ANTIQUES TRADE GAZETTE AWARD FOR IN-HOUSE EXHIBITION
sponsored by Antiques Trade GAZETTE The Antiques Trade Weekly
Christopher Clarke Antiques
"Campaign Furniture"

Directory of Specialists

If you require a valuation for an item it is advisable to check whether the dealer or specialist will carry out this service, and whether there is a charge. Please mention Miller's when making an enquiry. Having found a specialist who will carry out your valuation, it is best to send a description and photograph of the item to them, together with a stamped addressed envelope for the reply. A valuation by telephone is not possible. Most dealers are only too happy to help you with your enquiry, however, they are very busy people and consideration of the above points would be welcomed.

Berkshire
Mostly Boxes, 93 High Street, Eton, Windsor SL4 6AF Tel: 01753 858470
Antique wooden boxes.

Special Auction Services, Kennetholme, Midgham, Reading RG7 5UX
Tel: 0118 971 2949
www.invaluable.com/sas/
Commemoratives, pot lids & Prattware, Fairings, Goss & Crested, Baxter & Le Blond prints. Also toys for the collector.

Buckinghamshire
Yesterday Child Tel/Fax: 01908 583403
djbarrington@btinternet.com
Antique dolls & dolls house miniatures.

Cambridgeshire
Antique Amusement Co, Mill Lane, Swaffham Bulbeck CB5 0NF
Tel/Fax: 01223 813041
Mobile: 07802 666755
mail@aamag.co.uk www.aamag.co.uk
Vintage amusement machines, also auctions of amusement machines, fairground art & other related collectables. Monthly collectors magazine.

Cloisters Antiques, 1A Lynn Road, Ely CB7 4EG Tel: 01353 668558
info@cloistersantiques.co.uk
www.cloistersantiques.co.uk
Writing, stamps, postcards & antiquarian books.

Cheshire
Antique Garden, The Grosvenor Garden Centre, Wrexham Road, Belgrave, Chester CH4 9EB
Tel: 01244 629191/07976 539 990
antigard@btopenworld.com
Original antique garden tools & accessories.

Collector's Corner, PO Box 8, Congleton CW12 4GD
Tel: 01260 270429
dave.popcorner@ukonline.co.uk
Beatles & pop memorabilia.

Dollectable, 53 Lower Bridge Street, Chester CH1 1RS
Tel: 01244 344888/679195
Antique dolls.

M. C. Pottery Tel: 01244 301800
Sales@Moorcroftchester.co.uk
www.Moorcroftchester.co.uk
Moorcroft pottery.

On The Air, The Vintage Technology Centre, The Highway, Hawarden,
(Nr Chester), Deeside CH5 3DN
Tel/Fax: 01244 530300
Mobile: 07778 767734
www.vintageradio.co.uk
Vintage radios.

Specialist Glass Fairs Ltd
Tel: 01260 271975/01260 298042
info@glassfairs.co.uk
www.glassfairs.co.uk
'National Glass Collectors Fair' (Est. 1991). Bi-annual event held on 9th May & 7th November 2004 at The Heritage Motor Centre (Midlands). For more details visit www.glassfairs.co.uk or telephone 01260 271975.

Sweetbriar Gallery Paperweights Ltd, 3 Collinson Court, off Church Street, Frodsham WA6 6PN
Tel: 01928 730064
sales@sweetbriar.co.uk
www.sweetbriar.co.uk
Paperweights.

Charles Tomlinson
Tel/Fax: 01244 318395
charles.tomlinson@lineone.net
www.lineone.net/-charles.tomlinson
Scientific instruments.

Cleveland
Vectis Auctions Ltd, Fleck Way, Thornaby, Stockton-on-Tees TS17 9JZ
Tel: 01642 750616 admin@vectis.co.uk
www.vectis.co.uk
Toy auctions.

Cornwall
Gentry Antiques, Little Green, Polperro PL13 2RF
Tel: 01503 272 361
info@cornishwarecollector.co.uk
www.cornishwarecollector.co.uk
Cornish ware.
Also at Gray's Antique Market Mews, London W1.

Cumbria
Symon Brown Tel: 01900 825505
sheshops123@aol.com
Marbles, solitaire boards.

Devon
The Pen and Pencil Lady
Tel: 01647 231619
penpencilady@aol.com
www.penpencilady.com
Repair service for fountain pens available, please ring for details.
Specialist dealer for pens, pencils,
dip pens & writing equipment from the 19th & 20thC.

Sue Wilde at Wildewear
Tel: 01395 577966
compacts@wildewear.co.uk
www.wildewear.co.uk
Specialists in fashion accessories 1900–50 including beaded & leather bags, purses, hats, powder compacts, buttons & jewellery. Examples from USA, France, Austria, East Germany & UK.

Dorset
Ancient & Gothic, PO Box 5390, Bournemouth BH7 6XR
Tel: 01202 431721
Antiquities.

Books Afloat, 66 Park Street, Weymouth DT4 7DE
Tel: 01305 779774
Books on all subjects, liner & naval memorabilia, shipping company china, ships bells, old postcards, models, paintings.

Dalkeith Auctions Ltd, Dalkeith Hall, Dalkeith Steps, Rear of 81 Old Christchurch Road, Bournemouth BH1 1YL Tel: 01202 292905
how@dalkeith-auctions.co.uk
www.dalkeith-auctions.co.uk
Auctions of postcards, cigarette cards, ephemera & collectors items.

Murrays' Antiques & Collectables
Tel: 01202 309094
Shipping, motoring, railway, cycling items always required. Also advertising related items, eg showcards, enamel signs, tins & packaging & general quality collectables. Anything old & interesting. No valuations given.

Old Button Shop Antiques, Lytchett Minster, Poole BH16 6JF
Tel: 01202 622169
info@oldbuttonshop.fsnet.co.uk
Buttons & collectables.

Essex
Cheffins, 8 Hill Street, Saffron Walden CB10 1JD Tel: 01799 513131
vintage@cheffins.co.uk
www.cheffins.co.uk
Regular auctions of classic cars, motorcycles & automobilia.

Haddon Rocking Horses Ltd, 5 Telford Road, Clacton-on-Sea

CO15 4LP Tel: 01255 424745
millers@haddonrockinghorses.co.uk
www.haddonrockinghorses.co.uk
Rocking horses made & restored.

The Old Telephone Company,
The Old Granary, Battlesbridge
Antiques Centre, Nr Wickford SS11 7RF
Tel: 01245 400601
gp@theoldtelephone.co.uk
www.theoldtelephone.co.uk
Period telephones.

Flintshire
Old Bears 4 U, 45 Chester Close,
Shotton, Deeside CH5 1AX
Tel: 01244 830066
debbie&paul@oldbears4u.co.uk
www.oldbears4u.co.uk
*Buying, selling, repairing & cleaning
old bears.*

Gloucestershire
Bourton Bears Tel: 01451 821466
www.bourtonbears.com
Teddy bears.

Cottage Collectibles, The Top Banana
Antiques Mall, I New Church Street,
Tetbury GL8 4DS Tel: 0871 288 1102
sheila@cottagecollectibles.co.uk
*Open Mon–Sat 10.00am–5.30pm, Sun
1.00pm–5.00pm & by appointment.
English & Continental country antiques
& kitchenalia. Showroom at Eccleshall,
Staffordshire. Open by appointment
only – 01785 850210.*

Gloucester Toy Mart, Ground Floor,
Antique Centre, Severn Road,
Old Docks, Gloucester GL1 2LE
Mobile: 07973 768452
*Buying & selling obsolete toys
& collectables.*

Grimes House Antiques, High Street,
Moreton-in-Marsh GL56 0AT
Tel/Fax: 01608 651029
grimes_house@cix.co.uk
www.grimeshouse.co.uk
www.cranberryglass.co.uk
www.collectglass.com
Cranberry glass.

Keith Harding's World of Mechanical
Music, The Oak House, High Street,
Northleach GL54 3ET
Tel: 01451 860181
keith@mechanicalmusic.co.uk
www.mechanicalmusic.co.uk
Mechanical music & automata.

Jennie Horrocks Tel: 07836 264896
info@artnouveaulighting.co.uk
artnouveaulighting.co.uk
*Also at Top Banana Antiques Mall,
1 New Church St, Tetbury,
Glos GL8 8DS.*

Specialised Postcard Auctions,
25 Gloucester Street, Cirencester
GL7 2DJ Tel: 01285 659057
Sales of early postcards & ephemera.

Telephone Lines Ltd, 304 High Street,
Cheltenham GL50 3JF
Tel: 01242 583699
info@telephonelines.net
www.telephonelines.net
Antique telephones.

Hampshire
Jim Bullock Militaria, PO Box 217,
Romsey SO51 5XL
Tel/Fax: 01794 516455
jim@jimbullockmilitaria.com
www.jimbullockmilitaria.com
*We buy, sell & value war medals,
decorations & militaria.*

Classic Amusements
Tel: 01425 472164
pennyslot@aol.com
www.classicamusements.net
Vintage slot machines.

Cobwebs, 78 Northam Road,
Southampton SO14 0PB
Tel/Fax: 023 8022 7458
www.cobwebs.uk.com
*Ocean liner memorabilia. Also naval
& aviation items.*

Solent Railwayana Auctions,
9 Wildern Close, Locks Heath,
Southampton SO31 7EZ
Tel: 01489 574029
nigel@solentrailwayana.com
www.solentrailwayana.com
Railwayana & transport related auctions.

Tickers, 37 Northam Road,
Southampton SO14 0PD
Tel: 02380 234431
kmonckton@btopenworld.com
Clocks, watches & barometers.

Hertfordshire
Forget-Me-Knot Antiques, Antiques at
Over the Moon, 27 High Street,
St Albans AL3 4EH Tel: 01923 261172
Mobile: 07941 255489
sharpffocus@hotmail.com
Sentimental jewellery.

Isle of Wight
Nostalgia Toy Museum, High Street,
Godshill, Ventnor PO38 3HZ
Tel: 01983 522148
toyman@nostalgiatoys.com
Diecast toys specialist & museum.

Kent
20th Century Marks, 12 Market
Square, Westerham TN16 1AW
Tel: 01959 562221
Mobile: 07831 778992
lambarda@btconnect.com
www.20thcenturymarks.co.uk
Original 20thC design.

Chris Baker Gramophones, All Our
Yesterdays, 3 Cattle Market, Sandwich
CT13 9AE Tel: 01304 614756
cbgramophones@aol.com
www.chrisbakergramophones.com
*Specialist dealer in gramophones
& phonographs.*

Beatcity, PO Box 229, Chatham
ME5 8WA Tel/Fax: 01634 200444
or 07770 650890
Darrenhanks@beatcity.co.uk
www.beatcity.co.uk
Beatles & rock & roll memorabilia.

Candlestick & Bakelite,
PO Box 308, Orpington BR5 1TB
Tel: 020 8467 3743
candlestick.bakelite@mac.com
www.candlestickandbakelite.co.uk
Telephones.

Dragonlee Collectables
Tel: 01622 729502
Noritake.

Stuart Heggie, 14 The Borough,
Northgate, Canterbury CT1 2DR
Tel: 01227 470422
Mobile: 0783 3593344
*Vintage cameras, optical toys &
photographic images.*

J. & M. Collectables Tel: 01580 891657
Mobile: 077135 23573
jandmcollectables@tinyonline.co.uk
*Postcards, crested china, Osborne
(Ivorex) plaques & small collectables
including Doulton, Wade, etc.*

Lambert & Foster, 102 High Street,
Tenterden TN30 6HT
Tel: 01580 762083
tenterden@lambertandfoster.co.uk
www.lambertandfoster.co.uk
Antique auction rooms.

The Old Tackle Box, PO Box 55,
Cranbrook TN17 3ZU
Tel & Fax: 01580 713979
Mobile: 07729 278 293
tackle.box@virgin.net
Old fishing tackle.

Pretty Bizarre, 170 High Street, Deal
CT14 6BQ Tel: 07973 794537
1920s–70s ceramics & collectables.

The Neville Pundole Gallery,
8A & 9 The Friars, Canterbury
CT1 2AS Tel: 01227 453471
neville@pundole.co.uk
www.pundole.co.uk
*Moorcroft & contemporary pottery
& glass.*

Helen Warren, Unit 9, Slaney Place
Farm, Headcorn Road, Staplehurst
TN12 0DT Tel: 01580 895100
conservation@ifwarren.demon.co.uk
www.ifwarren.demon.co.uk
Pottery & porcelain restoration courses.

Wenderton Antiques
Tel: 01227 720295 (by appt only)
*Country antiques including kitchen,
laundry & dairy.*

Woodville Antiques, The Street,
Hamstreet, Ashford TN26 2HG
Tel: 01233 732981
woodvilleantiques@yahoo.co.uk
Tools.

Wot a Racket, 250 Shepherds Lane,
Dartford DA1 2PN Tel: 01322 220619
wot-a-racket@talk21.com
Sporting memorabilia.

Lancashire
Decades, 20 Lord St West, Blackburn
BB2 1JX Tel: 01254 693320
*Original Victorian to 1970s clothing,
accessories, jewellery, decorative
textiles, & more.*

Tracks, PO Box 117, Chorley PR6 0UU
Tel: 01257 269726
sales@tracks.co.uk www.tracks.co.uk
Beatles & pop memorabilia.

Leicestershire
Pooks Books, Fowke Street, Rothley
LE7 7PJ Tel: 0116 237 6222
pooks.motorbooks@virgin.net
Motoring books & automobilia.

Lincolnshire
Junktion, The Old Railway Station,
New Bolingbroke, Boston PE22 7LB
Tel: 01205 480068/480087
Mobile: 07836 345491
*Advertising & packaging, automobilia,
slot machines, pedal cars, etc.*

Skip & Janie Smithson Antiques
Tel & Fax: 01754 810265
Mobile: 07831 399180
smithsonantiques@hotmail.com
Kitchenware.

London
Angling Auctions,
PO Box 2095, W12 8RU
Tel: 020 8749 4175 07785 281349
neil@anglingauctions.demon.co.uk
Angling auctions.

The Antique Dealer,
115 Shaftesbury Avenue,
WC2H 8AD Tel: 020 7420 6684
info@theantiquedealer.co.uk
*Monthly guide to antiques
& collectables.*

Biblion, 1–7 Davies Mews,
W1K 5AB Tel: 020 7629 1374
info@biblion.com
www.biblionmayfair.com
Antiquarian books, maps & prints.

Chelsea Military Antiques,
F4 Antiquarius, 131/141 Kings Road,
Chelsea, SW3 4PW Tel: 020 7352 0308
richard@chelseamilitaria.com
*British campaign medals, 19th & 20thC
Allied & Axis militaria.*

Christie's, 85 Old Brompton Road,
SW7 3LD Tel: 020 7930 6074
info@christies.com www.christies.com
Collectables auctions.

The Collector, Tom Power,
4 Queens Parade Close, Friern Barnet,
N11 3FY Tel: 0845 130 6111 Ext 207
Freephone 1 800 514 8176
collector@globalnet.co.uk
Contemporary collectables including

*Royal Doulton, Beswick, Pen Delfin,
Worcester, Lladro, Border Fine Art,
Wade, Wedgwood, Coalport, Bossons,
Lilliput Lane, David Winter, etc.*

Comic Book Postal Auctions Ltd,
40–42 Osnaburgh Street, NW1 3ND
Tel: 020 7424 0007
comicbook@compuserve.com
www.compalcomics.com
Comic book auctions.

Dix-Noonan-Webb, 16 Bolton Street,
W1J 8BQ Tel: 020 7016 1700
auctions@dnw.co.uk www.dnw.co.uk
*Auctioneers & valuers of orders,
decorations & medals, coins, tokens
& banknotes.*

Liz Farrow T/A Dodo, Stand F071/73,
Alfie's Antique Market, 13–25 Church
Street, NW8 8DT Tel: 020 7706 1545
*Sats Only 9–4pm.
Posters & old advertising.*

GB Military Antiques, Antiquarius
Antiques Centre, 131/141 Kings Road,
Chelsea, SW3 4PW Tel: 020 7351 5357
info@gbmilitaria.com
www.gbmilitaria.com
Military antiques.

Michael German Antiques Ltd,
38B Kensington Church Street,
W8 4BX Tel: 020 7937 2771/020 7937
1776 info@antiquecanes.com
info@antiqueweapons.com
www.antiquecanes.com
Walking canes, arms & armour.

Hayman & Hayman, Antiquarius Stand
K3, 135 Kings Road, SW3 4PW
Tel: 020 7351 6568
Mobile: 07742 987715
georgina@haymanframes.co.uk
*Photograph frames, Limoges boxes &
scent bottles.*

Charles Jeffreys Posters & Graphics,
4 Vardens Road, SW11 1RH
Tel: 020 7978 7976
Mobile: 07836 546150
cjeffreys@cjposters.ision.co.uk
charlie@cjposters.com
www.cjposters.com
*Specialising in selling original, rare
& collectable posters from the
birth of modernism through bauhaus
to the '60s & '70s pop art &
psychedelic culture.*

Francis Joseph Publications,
5 Southbrook Mews, SE12 8LG
Tel: 020 8318 9580
office@francisjoseph.com
www.carltonware.co.uk
Books on 20thC ceramics & glass.

Timothy Millett Ltd Historic Medals and
Works of Art, PO Box 20851,
SE22 0YN Tel: 020 8693 1111
Mobile: 07778 637 898
tim@timothymillett.demon.co.uk
Medals & works of art.

Murray Cards (International) Ltd,
51 Watford Way, Hendon Central,
NW4 3JH Tel: 020 8202 5688
murraycards@ukbusiness.com
www.murraycard.com/
Cigarette & trade cards.

Colin Narbeth & Son Ltd,
20 Cecil Court, Leicester Square,
WC2N 4HE Tel: 020 7379 6975
Colin.Narbeth@btinternet.com
www.colin-narbeth.com
Banknotes, bonds & shares.

Piccypicky.com
Tel: 020 8204 2001/020 8206 2001
www.piccypicky.com
*Artwork, autographs, bubblegum
cards, comics, posters, records & toys.*

Geoffrey Robinson, GO77–78,
GO91–92 (Ground floor) Alfies Antique
Market, 13–25 Church Street,
Marylebone, NW8 8DT
Tel: 020 7723 0449
info@alfiesantiques.com
www.alfiesantiques.com
*Art Deco & post-war lighting, glass, china,
small furniture, mirrors & Art Pottery.*

Rumours, 4 The Mall, Upper Street,
Camden Passage, Islington,
N1 0PD Tel: 020 7704 6549
Mobile: 07836 277274 or 07831 103748
Rumdec@aol.com
Moorcroft pottery.

Tin Tin Collectables, G38–42 Alfies's
Antique Market, 13–25 Church Street,
Marylebone, NW8 8DT
Tel/Fax: 020 7258 1305
leslie@tintincollectables.com
www.tintincollectables.com
*Handbags, Victorian–present day,
decorative evening bags, luggage.*

Twinkled, 1st floor, Old Petrol Station,
11–17 Stockwell Street, Greenwich,
SE10 Tel: 020 84880930/07940471574
info@twinkled.net www.twinkled.net
*Purveyors of fine homeware from the
'50s, '60s & '70s. Open Thurs/Fri
12noon–6pm, Sat & Sun 10am–6pm.*

Vintage Modes, Grays Antique Market,
Mayfair, W1K 5AB
Tel/Fax: 020 7409 0400
www.vintagemodes.co.uk
Vintage fashion.

Vintage & Rare Guitars (London),
6 Denmark Street, WC2H 8LX
Tel: 020 7240 7500
enquiries@vintageandrareguitars.com
www.vintageandrareguitars.com
Guitars.

Nigel Williams Rare Books,
25 Cecil Court, WC2N 4EZ
Tel: 020 7836 7757
nigel@nigelwilliams.com
www.nigelwilliams.com
*Books – first editions, illustrated,
childrens & detective.*

Middlesex
John Ives, 5 Normanhurst Drive,
Twickenham TW1 1NA
Tel: 020 8892 6265
jives@btconnect.com
*Reference books on antiques
& collecting.*

Norfolk
Roger Bradbury Antiques, Church
Street, Coltishall NR12 7DJ
Tel: 01603 737444
*Chinese blue & white porcelain
1690–1820.*

Cat Pottery, 1 Grammar School Road,
North Walsham NR28 9JH
Tel: 01692 402962
Winstanley cats.

Northamptonshire
The Old Brigade,
10A Harborough Road,
Kingsthorpe, Northampton
NN2 7AZ Tel: 01604 719389
theoldbrigade@easynet.co.uk
stewart@theoldbrigade.co.uk
www.theoldbrigade.co.uk
Military antiques.

Nottinghamshire
Helen Martin Tel: 01636 611171
Mobile: 07774 147197
carltonhelen@aol.com
www.carltonware.biz
*Carlton Ware specialist. See me
at Newark & Detling or check
my website.*

Millennium Collectables Ltd,
PO Box 146, Eastwood, Nottingham
NG16 3SP Tel: 01773 769335
mail@millenniumcollectables.co.uk
Limited edition Guinness collectables.

T. Vennett-Smith,
11 Nottingham Road, Gotham
NG11 0HE Tel: 0115 983 0541
info@vennett-smith.com
www.vennett-smith.com
*Ephemera & sporting
memorabilia auctions.*

Oxfordshire
Alvin's Vintage Games & Toys
Tel: 01865 772409
vintage.games@virgin.net
Pelham puppets.

Mike Delaney Tel: 01993 840064
Mobile: 07979 919760
mike@vintagehornby.co.uk
www.vintagehornby.co.uk
*Buying & selling Hornby 'O' gauge &
other vintage toy trains.*

Julian Eade Tel: 01865 300349
Mobile: 07973 542971
*Doulton Lambeth stoneware & signed
Burslem wares.*

Stone Gallery, 93 The High Street,
Burford OX18 4QA
Tel/Fax: 01993 823302

mail@stonegallery.co.uk
www.stonegallery.co.uk
*Specialist dealers in antique & modern
paperweights, gold & silver designer
jewellery & enamel boxes.*

Teddy Bears of Witney, 99 High Street,
Witney OX28 6HY Tel: 01993 702616
or 706616 www.teddybears.co.uk
*Steiff, Merrythought, Deans, Hermann,
artists' bears.*

Pembrokeshire
Arch House Collectables,
St George's Street, Tenby SA70 7JB
Tel: 01834 843246
archhouse@onetel.net.uk
Pen Delfins.

Scotland
Rhod McEwan – Golf Books,
Glengarden, Ballater, Aberdeenshire
AB35 5UB Tel: 013397 55429
teeoff@rhodmcewan.com
www.rhodmcewan.com
Rare & out-of-print golfing books.

Shropshire
Decorative Antiques,
47 Church Street, Bishop's Castle
SY9 5AD Tel: 01588 638851
enquiries@decorative-antiques.co.uk
www.decorative-antiques.co.uk
Decorative objects of the 19th & 20thC.

Mullock & Madeley, The Old Shippon,
Wall-under-Heywood, Nr Church
Stretton SY6 7DS Tel: 01694 771771
auctions@mullockmadeley.co.uk
www.mullockmadeley.co.uk
Sporting auctions.

Somerset
Antique Textiles & Lighting,
34 Belvedere, Lansdown Hill,
Bath BA1 5HR Tel: 01225 310795
antiquetextiles@aol.co.uk
www.antiquetextiles.co.uk
*Antique textiles & a vast selection
of chandeliers & wall lights.*

Bath Antiques Online, Bartlett Street
Antiques Centre, Bartlett Street,
Bath BA1 2QZ Tel: 01225 311061
info@bathantiquesonline.com
www.BathAntiquesOnline.com
Antiques & collectables.

Lynda Brine, Assembly Antiques,
6 Saville Row, Bath BA1 2QP
Tel: 01225 448488
lyndabrine@yahoo.co.uk
www.scentbottlesandsmalls.co.uk
*Perfume bottles.
Open by appointment only.*

Vivienne King of Panache
Tel: 01934 814759
Mobile: 07974 798871
Kingpanache@aol.com
*Specialist dealer in antique perfume
bottles, hatpins, fans, purses, beaded
& petit point bags & other ladies'
accessories & decorative items.*

Philip Knighton, Bush House,
17B South Street, Wellington
TA21 8NR Tel: 01823 661618
philip.knighton@btopenworld.com
*Wireless, gramophones & all
valve equipment.*

The London Cigarette Card Co Ltd,
Sutton Road, Somerton TA11 6QP
Tel: 01458 273452
cards@londoncigcard.co.uk
www.londoncigcard.co.uk
Cigarette & trade cards.

Richard Twort
Tel & Fax: 01934 641900
Mobile: 077 11 939789
*Barographs & all types of
meteorological instruments.*

Vintage & Rare Guitars (Bath),
7–8 Saville Row, Bath BA1 2QP
Tel: 01225 330 888
enquiries@vintageandrareguitars.com
www.vintageandrareguitars.com
Guitars.

Staffordshire
Peggy Davies Ceramics,
Freepost MID 16669,
Stoke-on-Trent ST4 1BJ
Tel: 01782 848002
rhys@kevinfrancis.co.uk
www.kevinfrancis.co.uk
*Ceramics – Limited edition Toby jugs
& figures.*

Keystones, PO Box 387, Stafford
ST16 3FG Tel: 01785 256648
gkey@keystones.demon.co.uk
www.keystones.co.uk
Denby pottery.

Gordon Litherland, 25 Stapenhill Road,
Burton on Trent DE15 9AE
Tel: 01283 567213
pubjugsuk@aol.com
*Bottles, breweriana & pub
jugs, advertising ephemera
& commemoratives.*

The Potteries Antique Centre,
271 Waterloo Road, Cobridge,
Stoke on Trent ST6 3HR
Tel: 01782 201455
sales@potteriesantiquecentre.com
www.potteriesantiquecentre.com
Collectable ceramics.

Suffolk
Jamie Cross, PO Box 73,
Newmarket CB8 8RY
jamiecross@aol.com
www.thirdreichmedals.com
*We buy & sell, value for probate &
insurance British, German & foreign
war medals, badges & decorations.*

W. L. Hoad, 9 St. Peter's Road,
Kirkley, Lowestoft NR33 0LH
Tel: 01502 587758
William@whoad.fsnet.co.uk
www.cigarettecardsplus.com
Cigarette cards.

Suffolk Sci-Fi and Fantasy,
17 Norwich Road, Ipswich
Tel: 01473 400655
Mobile: 07885 298361
mick@suffolksci-fi.com
www.suffolksci-fi.com
Science fiction.

Surrey
British Notes, PO Box 257, Sutton
SM3 9WW Tel: 020 8641 3224
pamwestbritnotes@compuserve.com
www.britishnotes.co.uk
Banking collectables.

eBay (UK) Ltd, PO Box 659,
Richmond upon Thames TW9 1EJ
Tel: 020 8605 3000
ggriffit@ebay.com www.ebay.co.uk
Antiques & collectables online.

The Gooday Gallery, 14 Richmond Hill,
Richmond TW10 6QX
Tel: 020 8940 8652
Mobile: 077101 24540
goodaygallery@aol.com
*Arts & Crafts, Art Deco, Art Nouveau,
Tribal, 1950s & '60s.*

Howard Hope, 19 Weston Park,
Thames Ditton KT7 0HW
Tel: 020 8398 7130
howard_hope@yahoo.co.uk
www.gramophones.uk.com
*Specialising for 30 years in
gramophones, phonographs, anything
related to the history of recorded
sound & other mechanical/musical
items. Dealing by correspondence only,
please no visits – call first. Colour
pictures of any item in stock can be
sent on request by email. Exporting
worldwide. Shipping quotations given
for any machine.*

East Sussex
Tony Horsley, PO Box 3127,
Brighton BN1 5SS
Tel: 01273 550770
*Candle extinguishers, Royal Worcester
& other porcelain.*

Ann Lingard, Ropewalk Antiques,
Rye TN31 7NA Tel: 01797 223486
ann-lingard@ropewalkantiques.
freeserve.co.uk
Antique pine furniture & kitchenware.

Rin Tin Tin, 34 North Road, Brighton
BN1 1YB Tel: 01273 672424
rick@rintintin.freeserve.co.uk
*Original old advertising & promotional
material, magazines, early glamour,
games, toys, plastics & miscellaneous
20thC collectables. Open Mon–Sat
11am–5.30pm.*

Soldiers of Rye, Mint Arcade,
71 The Mint, Rye TN31 7EW
Tel: 01797 225952
rameses@supanet.com
chris@johnbartholomewcards.co.uk
www.rameses.supanet.com

*Military badges, prints, medals,
collectors figurines, dolls'
house miniatures.*

Wallis & Wallis, West Street Auction
Galleries, Lewes BN7 2NJ
Tel: 01273 480208
auctions@wallisandwallis.co.uk
grb@wallisandwallis.co.uk
www.wallisandwallis.co.uk
*Specialist auctioneers of militaria,
arms, armour, coins & medals.
Also diecast & tinplate toys, Teddy
bears, dolls, model railways, toy
soldiers & models.*

West Sussex
Rupert Toovey & Co Ltd,
Spring Gardens, Washington
RH20 3BS Tel: 01903 891955
auctions@rupert-toovey.com
www.rupert-toovey.com
Auctions.

Wales
A.P.E.S. Rocking Horses, 20 Tan-y-Bwich,
Mynydd Llandygai, Bangor, Gwynedd
LL57 4DX Tel: 01248 600773
macphersons@apes-rocking-horses.co.uk
www.apes-rocking-horses.co.uk
Rocking horses.

Jen Jones, Pontbrendu, LLanybydder,
Ceredigion SA40 9UJ Tel: 01570 480610
quilts@jen-jones.com www.jen-jones.com
*Quilt expert dealing mainly in Welsh
quilts & blankets. Between 200 & 300
quilts in stock with a comparable
number of blankets. Looking to buy as
well as sell.*

Warwickshire
Bread & Roses Tel: 01926 817342
Kitchen antiques 1800–1950s.

Chinasearch Ltd., 4 Princes Drive,
Kenilworth CV8 2FD Tel: 01926 512402
info@chinasearch.uk.com
www.chinasearch.uk.com
*Discontinued dinner, tea & collectable
ware bought & sold.*

chrisjamesmedalsandmilitaria.co.uk,
Warwick Antiques Centre,
22–24 High Street, Warwick CV34 4AP
Tel: 01926 495704/07710 274452
user@chrisjames.slv.co.uk
www.medalsandmilitaria.co.uk
*British, German, Japanese & USSR
medals, swords, militaria & aviation
items. For sale & purchased. 'The
International', The National Motorcycle
Museum, Birmingham. The UK's largest
militaria fair. A.M.&.S.E.,
PO Box 194, Warwick.*

West Midlands
Fellows & Sons, Augusta House,
19 Augusta Street, Hockley,
Birmingham B18 6JA
Tel: 0121 212 2131 info@fellows.co.uk
www.fellows.co.uk
Auctioneers & valuers.

Wiltshire
Dominic Winter Book Auctions,
The Old School, Maxwell Street,
Swindon SN1 5DR Tel: 01793 611340
info@dominicwinter.co.uk
www.dominicwinter.co.uk
*Auctions of antiquarian & general
printed books & maps, sports books &
memorabilia, art reference & pictures,
photography & ephemera (including
toys, games & other collectables).*

Yorkshire
Briar's C20th Decorative Arts,
Skipton Antiques & Collectors Centre,
The Old Foundry, Cavendish Street,
Skipton BD23 2AB Tel: 01756 798641
*Art Deco ceramics & furniture,
specialising in Charlotte Rhead pottery.*

The Camera House, Oakworth Hall,
Colne Road, Oakworth, Keighley
BD22 7HZ Tel: 01535 642333
Mobile: 07984 018951
colin@the-camera-house.co.uk
www.the-camera-house.co.uk
*Cameras & photographic equipment
from 1850. Cash purchases, part
exchanges, sales & repairs. National &
International mail order a speciality.
Valuations for probate & insurance.
Online catalogue. Please ring or email
before visiting. Prop C. Cox.*

Country Collector, 11–12 Birdgate,
Pickering YO18 7AL Tel: 01751 477481
www.country-collector.co.uk
*Art Deco ceramics, blue & white,
pottery & porcelain.*

Echoes, 650a Halifax Road, Eastwood,
Todmorden OL14 6DW
Tel: 01706 817505
*Antique costume, textiles including
linen, lace & jewellery.*

Gerard Haley, Hippins Farm, Black
Shawhead, Nr Hebden Bridge HX7 7JG
Tel: 01422 842484
Toy soldiers.

John & Simon Haley, 89 Northgate,
Halifax HX1 1XF
Tel: 01422 822148/360434
toysandbanks@aol.com
Old toys & money boxes.

Harpers Jewellers Ltd, 2/6 Minster Gates,
York YO1 7HL Tel: 01904 632634
harpersyork@btopenworld.com
www.vintage-watches.co.uk
*Vintage & modern wrist &
pocket watches.*

Linen & Lace, Shirley Tomlinson,
Halifax Antiques Centre,
Queens Road/Gibbet Street,
Halifax HX1 4LR
Tel: 01484 540492/01422 366657
*Antique linen, textiles, period costume
& accessories.*

Sheffield Railwayana Auctions,
43 Little Norton Lane, Sheffield S8 8GA

Tel: 0114 274 5085
Mobile: 07860 921519
ian@sheffrail.freeserve.co.uk
www.sheffieldrailwayana.co.uk
Railwayana, posters & models auctions.

www.vintageheuer.com
Jonathan Scatchard Tel: 01423 331868
Mobile: 0773 3362900
jonathan@vintageheuer.com
www.vintageheuer.com
Watches.

East Yorkshire
The Crested China Co, Highfield,
Windmill Hill, Driffield YO25 5YP
Tel: 0870 300 1 300
dt@thecrestedchinacompany.com
www.thecrestedchinacompany.com
Goss & crested china.

South Yorkshire
BBR, Elsecar Heritage Centre, Elsecar,
Nr Barnsley S74 8HJ Tel: 01226 745156
sales@onlinebbr.com
www.onlinebbr.com
*Advertising, breweriana, pot lids,
bottles, Cornish ware, Doulton &
Beswick, etc.*

Republic of Ireland
George Stacpoole, Main Street, Adare,
Co Limerick Tel: 00 353 (0)6139 6409
stacpoole@iol.ie
www.georgestacpooleantiques.com
*Furniture, pottery, ceramics, silver
& prints.*

USA
20th Century Vintage Telephones,
2780 Northbrook Place,
Boulder, Colorado 80304
Tel: 001 44 (303) 442 3304
Vintage telephones.

Antiques & Art, 116 State Street,
Portsmouth NH 03802
Tel: 603-431-3931

The Calico Teddy Tel: 410 366 7011
CalicTeddy@aol.com
www.calicoteddy.com

Henry T. Callan, 162 Quaker Meeting
House Road, East Sandwich MA
02537–1312 Tel: 508-888-5372

Dragonflies Antiques & Decorating
Center, Frank & Cathy Sykes,
New England Events Mgt.,
PO Box 678,
24 Center Street, Wolfeboro,
New Hampshire 03894
Tel: 603 569 0000
Dragonflies@metrocast.net
*Folk Art, mahogany speed boat
models, maps & antiquarian books.*

Du Mouchelles, 409 East Jefferson,
Detroit, Michigan 48226
Tel: 313 963 6255
Auctions.

The Dunlop Collection,
PO Box 6269, Statesville NC 28687

Tel: (704) 871 2626 or
Toll Free Telephone (800) 227 1996
Paperweights.

M. Finkel & Daughter, 936 Pine Street,
Philadelphia, Pennsylvania 19107–6128
Tel: 215 627 7797
mailbox@finkelantiques.com
www.finkelantiques.com
*America's leading antique sampler &
needlework dealer.*

Harbor Bazaar, 5590 Main,
Lexington MI 48450
bazaar@tias.com
www.tias.com/stores/bazaar/

Hunt Auctions, 75 E. Uwchlan Avenue,
Suite 130, Exton, Pennsylvania 19341
Tel: 610 524 0822
info@huntauctions.com
www.huntauctions.com

Randy Inman Auctions Inc,
PO Box 726, Waterville,
Maine 04903–0726
Tel: 207 872 6900
inman@inmanauctions.com
www.inmanauctions.com
*Auctions specialising in advertising,
coin-op, gambling devices, automata,
soda pop, Coca Cola, breweriana,
robots & space toys, C. I. & tin toys,
Disneyana, mechanical music, mechanical
& still banks, quality antiques.*

J's Collectables, 5827 Encinita Avenue,
Temple City CA 91780
Tel: 818 451 0010

Jackson's Auctioneers & Appraisers,
2229 Lincoln Street,
Cedar Falls IA 50613 Tel: 319 277 2256

JMW Gallery, 144 Lincoln Street,
Boston MA02111 Tel: 617 338 9097
www.jmwgallery.com
*American Arts & Crafts, Decorative
Arts, American Art Pottery, Mission
furniture, lighting, color block
prints, metalwork.*

Jo Campbell, Jo's Antiques,
Rt. 1, Box 2390, Mount Pleasant,
Texas Tel: 903 572 3173

Lamps: By The Book, Inc.,
514 14th West Palm Beach,
Florida 33401 Tel: 561 659 1723
booklamps@msn.com
www.lampsbythebook.com
Gift lamps. Also buy leather bound books.

Joyce M. Leiby, PO Box 6048, Lancaster
PA 17607 Tel: (717) 898 9113
joyclei@aol.com

Malchione Antiques & Sporting
Collectibles, 110 Bancroft Road,
Kennett Square PA 19348
Tel: 610 444 3509

Millicent Safro, Tender Buttons,
143 E.62nd Street, New York NY10021
Tel: 212 758 7004
Author of Buttons.

Right to the Moon Alice, Alice and Ron
Lindholm, 240 Cooks Fall Road,
Cooks Fall NY 12776
Tel: 607 498 5750

Mike Roberts, 4416 Foxfire Way,
Fort Worth, Texas 76133
Tel: 817 294 2133

R. O. Schmitt Fine Art, Box 1941, Salem,
New Hampshire 03079
Tel: 603 893 5915
bob@roschmittfinearts.com
www.antiqueclockauction.com
Specialist antique clock auctions.

Skinner Inc, 357 Main Street,
Bolton MA 01740 Tel: 978 779 6241
Auctions.

Skinner Inc, The Heritage On The
Garden, 63 Park Plaza,
Boston MA 02116 Tel: 617 350 5400
Auctions.

Sloan's & Kenyon, 4605 Bradley
Boulevard, Bethesda, Maryland 20815
Tel: 301 634 2330
info@sloansandkenyon.com
www.sloansandkenyon.com
Auctions.

Art Smith Antiques at Wells Union,
Rt. 1, 1755 Post Road,
Wells ME 04090 Tel: 207 646 6996

Sotheby's, 1334 York Avenue at 72nd
St, New York NY 10021 Tel: 212 606
7000 www.sothebys.com
Auctions.

Sotheby's, 9665 Wilshire Boulevard,
Beverly Hills, California 90212
Tel: 310 274 0340 www.sothebys.com
Auctions.

Treadway Gallery, Inc, Treadway
Gallery, Inc 2029 Madison Road,
Cincinnati, Ohio 45208
Tel: 001 513 321 6742
www.treadwaygallery.com
20thC art auctions.

Triple "L" Sports, PO Box 281,
Winthorp, Maine 04364
Tel: 001 207 377 5787 lllsport@att.net
*Winchester collectibles, fishing,
hunting, trapping, knives, primitives,
baseball, football, golf, tennis,
memorabilia & advertising.*

The Unique One, 2802 Centre Street,
Pennsauken NJ 08109
Tel: 001 (609) 663 2554

VintagePostcards.com, 60–C Skiff
Street, Suite 116, Hamden CT 06517
Tel: 001 203 248 6621
quality@VintagePostcards.com
www.VintagePostcards.com

Jo Anne Welsh, PO Box 222, Riverdale
MD 20738 Tel: 001 301 779 6181

Directory of Collectors' Clubs

With new Collectors' Clubs emerging every day this directory is by no means complete. If you wish to be included in next year's directory or if you have a change of details, please inform us by 1 November 2004.

A.C.O.G.B. (Autograph Club of Great Britain) SAE to Mr R. Gregson, 47 Webb Crescent, Dawley, Telford, Shropshire TF4 3DS autographs@acogb.freeserve.co.uk www.acogb.co.uk

American Business Card Club Robin Cleeter, 38 Abbotsbury Road, Morden, Surrey SM4 5LQ

American Toy Emergency Vehicle (ATEV) Club President Jeff Hawkins, 11415 Colfax Road, Glen Allen, Virginia 23060, USA

Antique Wireless Association (AWA) Box E, Breesport, New York 14816, USA

Association of Bottled Beer Collectors 28 Parklands, Kidsgrove, Stoke-on-Trent, Staffordshire ST7 4US Tel: 01782 761048 www.abbc.org.uk www.abbclist.info

Astro Space Stamp Society 21 Exford Close, Weston-Super-Mare BS23 4RE

The Aviation Postcard Club Int & USA Phil Munson, 25 Kerill Avenue, Old Coulsdon, Surrey CR5 1QB Tel: 01737 551 817

Avon Magpies Club Mrs W. A. Fowler, 15 Saunders House, Leith Avenue, Paulsgrove, Portsmouth, Hampshire PO6 4NY Tel: 023 92 380975 wendy@avon4magpies.fsnet.co.uk

B.E.A.R. Collector's Club Linda Hartzfeld, 16901 Covello Street, Van Nuys, California 91406, USA

Badge Collectors' Circle c/o Frank Setchfield, 57 Middleton Place, Loughborough, Leicestershire LE11 2BY www.badgecollectorscircle.co.uk

Barbie Collectors Club of Great Britain Elizabeth Lee, 17 Rosemont Road, Acton, London W3 9LU

The Bead Society of Great Britain Carole Morris (Dr), 1 Casburn Lane, Burwell, Cambridge CB5 0ED Tel/Fax: 01638 742024 www.beadsociety.freeserve.co.uk

Bearly Ours Teddy Club Linda Harris, 54 Berkinshaw Crescent, Don Mills, Ontario M3B 2T2, Canada

The Beatrix Potter Society Charity Reg. No. 281198, 9 Broadfields, Harpenden, Hertfordshire AL5 2HJ Tel: 01582 769755 beatrixpottersociety@tiscali.co.uk www.beatrixpottersociety.org.uk

Belleek Collectors Group (UK) The Hon Chairman Mr Jan Golaszewski, 5 Waterhall Avenue, Chingford, London E4 6NB jangolly@hotmail.com www.belleek.org.uk

The James Bond Collectors Club PO Box 1570, Christchurch, Dorset BH23 4XS solopublishing@firenet.uk.com

British Art Medal Society Philip Attwood, c/o Dept of Coins and Medals, The British Museum, London WC1B 3DG Tel: 01892 613370 pattwood@thebritishmuseum.ac.uk www.bams.org.uk/

The British Beermat Collectors' Society Hon Sec, 69 Dunnington Avenue, Kidderminster, Worcestershire DY10 2YT www.britishbeermats.org.uk

British Button Society Membership Sec Mrs June Baron, Jersey Cottage, Parklands Road, Bower Ashton, Bristol, Gloucestershire BS3 2JR

British Cheque Collectors Society Membership M. P. P.M. Lord, 14 Garsdale Road, Newsome, Huddersfield HD4 6QZ

British Compact Collectors' Society SAE to PO Box 131, Woking, Surrey GU24 9YR www.thebccs.org.uk

British Doll Collectors Club Publisher & Editor Mrs Francis Baird, The Anchorage, Wrotham Road, Culverstone, Meopham, Gravesend, Kent DA13 0QW www.britishdollcollectors.com

British Equine Collectors Forum (Model horses) SAE to BECF Coordinator Mrs Jackie Radwanski, 37 Petwyn Close, Ferndown, Dorset BH22 8BG www.worldofpaul.com/BECF

British Novelty Salt & Pepper Collectors Club Secretary Ray Dodd, Coleshill, Clayton Road, Mold, Flintshire CH7 1SX

British Postmark Society Sec Mrs E. Ethorp, Struanlea, 4 Huagh Road, Dalbeattie, Stewartry of Kirkcudbright DG5 4AR 101,654,3006@compuserve.com http://ourworld.compuserve.com/homepages/Barry-Reynolds

British Teddy Bear Association Sec Penny Shaw-Willett, PO Box 290, Brighton, East Sussex BN2 1DR

The Brooklands Automobilia & Regalia Collectors' Club (B.A.R.C.C.) Hon Sec G. G. Weiner, 4–4a Chapel Terrace Mews, Kemp Town, Brighton, East Sussex BN2 1HU Tel/Fax: 01273 601960 www.barcc.co.uk

Bunnykins Collectors' Club 6 Beckett Way, Lewes, East Sussex BN7 2EB www.bunnykins.collectorsclub.btinternet.co.uk

The Buttonhook Society c/o Chairman Paul Moorehead, 2 Romney Place, Maidstone, Kent ME15 6LE www.antiques-uk.net/aukCClubs/

The Buttonhook Society (USA) c/o Priscilla Stoffel, White Marsh, Box 287, MD 21162–0287, USA Tel: 410 256 5541 buttonhooksociety@tiscali.co.uk www.thebuttonhooksociety.com

Caithness Glass Paperweight Collectors' Society Miss Sam Welsh, Caithness Glass Ltd, Inveralmond, Perth, Scotland PH1 3TZ Tel: 01738 637373 collector@caithnessglass.co.uk www.caithnessglass.co.uk

The Carnival Glass Society (UK) Limited PO Box 14, Hayes, Middlesex UB3 5NU www.carnivalglasssociety.co.uk

The Cartophilic Society of Great Britain Ltd Membership Sec Alan Stevens, 63 Ferndale Road, Church Crookham, Fleet, Hampshire GU52 6LN Tel: 01252 621586 www.csgb.co.uk

Cat Collectables 297 Alcester Road, Hollywood, Birmingham, West Midlands B47 5HJ www.cat-collectables.co.uk

Cigarette Case Collectors' Club 19 Woodhurst North, Raymead Road, Maidenhead, Berkshire SL6 8PH colin.grey1@virgin.net

Cigarette Packet Collectors Club of GB Barry Russell, Talisker, Vines Cross Road, Horam, Heathfield, East Sussex TN21 0HF

The City of London Phonograph and Gramophone Society Ltd Membership Sec D. R. Roberts, 5 The Moorings, 16 Belle Vue Road, Paignton, Devon TQ4 6EA d.robertscolpags@btopenworld.com

The Coca-Cola Collectors Club Membership Dir, PMB 609, 4780 Ashford-Dunwoody Road, Suite A, Atlanta, Georgia 30338, USA

The Cola Club P O Box 293158, Nashville, Tennessee 37229–3158, USA

The Coleco Collectors Club Ann Wilhite 610 W 17th, Freemont NE 68025, USA

Collector's Choice Admail 981, Stoke on Trent, Staffordshire ST12 9JW Tel: 0870 830 8028

The Comic Journal C. J. Publications, c/o 6 Rotherham Road, Catcliffe, Rotherham, South Yorkshire S60 5SW

Commemorative Collectors' Society c/o Steven Jackson, Lumless House, Gainsborough Road, Winthorpe, Newark, Nottinghamshire NG24 2NR Tel: 01636 671377 commemorativecollectorssociety@hotmail.com

Corgi Collector Club c/o Corgi Classics Ltd, Meridian East, Meridian Business Park, Leicester LE19 1RL Tel: 0870 607 1204 susie@collectorsclubs.org.uk www.corgi.co.uk

The Costume Society St Paul's House, Warwick Lane, London EC4P 4BN www.costumesociety.org.uk

Cricket Memorabilia Society Steve Cashmore, 4 Stoke Park Court, Stoke Road, Bishop's Cleeve, Cheltenham, Gloucestershire GL52 8US cms87@btinternet.com www.cms.cricket.org

The Dean's Collectors Club Euro Collectibles, PO Box 370565, 49 NE 39th Street, Miami FL33 137, USA Tel: US toll free 1 800 309 8336 www.deansbears.com

Devon Pottery Collectors Group Mrs Joyce Stonelake, 19 St Margarets Avenue, Torquay, Devon TQ1 4LW Tel: 01803 327277 Virginia.Brisco@care4free.net

Die Cast Car Collectors Club c/o Chairman Jay Olins, PO Box 67226, Los Angeles, California 90067–0266, USA Tel: 1 310 629 7113 jay@diecast.org www.diecast.org

Dinky Toy Club of America c/o Jerry Fralick, 6030 Day Break Circle, Suite A 150/132, Clarksville, Maryland 21029, USA Tel/Fax: 301 854 2217 mrdinky@erols.com www.erols.com/dinkytoy

The Eagle Society Membership Sec Keith Howard, 25a Station Road, Harrow, Middlesex HA1 2UA howard23@fish.co.uk

Egg Cup Collectors' Club of GB Subs Sec Sue Wright, PO Box 39, Llandysul, Wales SA44 5ZD suewright@suecol.freeserve.co.uk www.eggcupworld.co.uk

Embroiderers' Guild Janet Jardine, Apartment 41, Hampton Court Palace, East Molesey, Surrey KT8 9AU Tel: 020 8943 1229 administrator@embroiderersguild.com www.embroiderersguild.com

The English Playing Card Society Sec John Sings, PO Box 29, North Walsham, Norfolk NR28 9NQ Tel: 01692 650496 Secretary@EPCS.org www.wopc.co.uk/epcs

The European Honeypot Collectors' Society John Doyle, The Honeypot, 18 Victoria Road, Chislehurst, Kent BR7 6DF Tel/Fax: 020 8289 7725 johnhoneypot@hotmail.com www.geocities.com/tehcsuk

Festival of Britain Society c/o Martin Packer, 41 Lyall Gardens, Birmingham, West Midlands B45 9YW martin@packer34.freeserve.co.uk www.packer34.freeserve.co.uk

The Followers of Rupert Membership Sec Mrs Shirley Reeves, 31 Whiteley, Windsor, Berkshire SL4 5PJ followersofrupert@hotmail.com www.rupertbear.info

Friends of Blue Ceramic Society Terry Sheppard, 45a Church Road, Bexley Heath, Kent DA7 4DD www.fob.org.uk

The Furniture History Society c/o Dr Brian Austen, 1 Mercedes Cottages, St. John's Road, Haywards Heath, West Sussex RH16 4EH Tel/Fax: 01444 413845 furniturehistorysociety@hotmail.com

Golly Collectors' Club Keith Wilkinson, 18 Hinton Street, Fairfield, Liverpool, Merseyside L6 3AR

Postcard Club of Great Britain c/o Mrs D. Brennan, 34 Harper House, St James Crescent, London SW9 7LW Tel: 020 7771 9404

The Hagen-Renaker Collectors Club Jenny Palmer, 3651 Polish Line Road, Cheboygan, Mitchigan 49721, USA

The Hagen-Renaker Collectors Club (UK) Chris and Derek Evans, 97 Campbell Road, Burton, Christchurch, Dorset BH23 7LY www.priorycollectables.com

Jonathan Harris Studio Glass Ltd Woodland House, 24 Peregrine Way, Apley Castle, Telford, Shropshire TF1 6TH Tel: 01952 246381/588441 jonathan@jhstudioglass.com www.jhstudioglass.com

The Hat Pin Society of Great Britain PO Box 110, Cheadle, Cheshire SK8 1GG www.hatpinsociety.org.uk

Honiton Pottery Collectors' Society Chairman Robin Tinkler, 2 Redyear Cottages, Kennington Road, Ashford, Kent TN24 0TF hpcs@moshpit.cix.co.uk www.hpcs.info

Hornby Collectors Club PO Box 35, Royston, Hertfordshire SG8 5XR www.hornby.co.uk

The Hornby Railway Collectors' Association John Harwood, PO Box 3443, Yeovil, Somerset BA21 4XR

Hornsea Pottery Collectors' and Research Society c/o Peter Tennant, 128 Devonshire Street, Keighley, West Yorkshire BD21 2QJ hornsea@pdtennant.fsnet.co.uk www.hornseacollector.co.uk

Indian Military Historical Society Sec A. N. McClenaghan, 37 Wolsey Close, Southall, Middlesex UB2 4NQ

Inn Sign Society Chairman Mr R. P. Gatrell, Flat 19, Stamford Grange, Dunham Road, Altrincham, Cheshire WA14 4AN

International Bond and Share Society c/o Peter Duppa-Miller, Beechcroft, Combe Hay, Bath, Somerset BA2 7EG

International Bond & Share Society, American Branch Vice President Ted Robinson, PO Box 814, Richboro PA, USA

International Collectors' of Time Association 173 Coleherne Court, Redcliffe Gardens, London SW5 0DX

International Correspondence of Corkscrew Addicts Don MacLean, 4201 Sunflower Drive, Mississauga, Ontario L5L 2L4, Canada

The International Gnome Club Liz Spea, 22841 Kings Ct, Hayward CA 94541–4326, USA

International Map Collectors Society (IMCoS) Sec Yasha Beresiner, 43 Templars Crescent, London N3 3QR 10047.3341@compuserve.com

International Perfume Bottle Association Lynda Brine, Assembly Antique Centre, 6 Saville Row, Bath, Somerset BA1 2QP Tel: 01225 448488 lyndabrine@yahoo.co.uk www.scentbottlesandsmalls.co.uk

International Philatelic Golf Society Sec Ron Spiers, 8025 Saddle Run, Powell OH 43065, USA

International Philatelic Golf Society Sec Dr Eiron, B. E. Morgan, 50 Pine Valley, Cwmavon, Port Talbot SA12 9NF, Wales

International Playing Card Society PR Officer Yasha Beresiner, 43 Templars Crescent, London N3 3QR 100447.3341@compuserve.com

The International Society of Meccanomen Adrian Williams, Bell House, 72a Old High Street, Headington, Oxford OX3 9HW www.dircon.co.uk/meccano/

King George VI Collectors' Society (Philately) 98 Albany, Manor Road, Bournemouth, Dorset BH1 3EW

The Lace Guild The Hollies, 53 Audnam, Stourbridge, West Midlands DY8 4AE

Legend Products International Collector's Club 1 Garden Villas, Wrexham Road, Cefn Y Bedd, Flintshire LL12 9UT Tel/Fax: 01978 760800 sheila@legend-lane.demon.co.uk

Limoges Porcelain Collectors Club The Tannery, Park Stile, Haydon Bridge, Hexham NE47 6BP Tel: 01434 684444 www.limogesboxoffice.co.uk

Lock Collectors' Club Mr Richard Phillips, "Merlewood", The Loan, West Linton, Peebleshire EH46 7HE

The Maling Collectors' Society Sec David Holmes, PO Box 1762, North Shields NE30 4YJ info@maling-pottery.org.uk www.maling-pottery.org.uk

Matchbox International Collectors Association (MICA) of North America c/o Stewart Orr and Kevin McGimpsey, PO Box 28072, Waterloo, Ontario N2L 6J8, Canada

The Matchbox Toys International Collectors' Association Kevin McGimpsey, PO Box 120, Deeside, Flintshire CH5 3HE Tel: 01244 539414 kevin@matchboxclub.com www.matchboxclub.com

Mauchline Ware Collectors Club Sec Mrs Christabelle Davey, PO Box 158, Leeds LS16 5WZ enquiries@mauchlineclub.org www.mauchlineclub.org

Medal Society of Ireland 5 Meadow Vale, Blackrock, Co Dublin, Eire

Memories UK Mabel Lucie Attwell Club Abbey Antiques, 63 Great Whyte, Ramsey, Nr Huntingdon, Cambridgeshire PE26 1HL Tel: 01487 814753

Merrythought International Collector's Club Club Sec Peter Andrews, Ironbridge, Telford, Shropshire TF8 7NJ Tel: 01952 433116 contact@merrythought.co.uk www.merrythought.co.uk

Merrythought International Collector's Club PO Box 577, Oakdale, California 95361, USA

Milk Bottle News Paul & Lisa Luke, 60 Rose Valley Crescent, Stanford-le-Hope, Essex SS17 8EF www.milkbottlenews.org.uk

The Model Railway Club The Hon Sec, Keen House, 4 Calshot Street, London N1 9DA

Moorcroft Collectors' Club W. Moorcroft PLC, Sandbach Road, Burslem, Stoke-on-Trent, Staffordshire ST6 2DQ Tel: 01782 820510 cclub@moorcroft.com www.moorcroft.com

Muffin the Mule Collectors' Club 12 Woodland Close, Woodford Green, Essex IG8 0QH Tel/Fax: 020 8504 4943 adrienne@hasler.gotadsl.co.uk www.Muffin-the-Mule.com

Musical Box Society of Great Britain PO Box 299, Waterbeach, Cambridgeshire CB4 8DT mbsgb@reedman.org.uk www.mbsgb.org.uk

New Baxter Society Membership Secretary, 205 Marshalswick Lane, St Albans, Hertfordshire AL1 4XA Baxter@rpsfamily.demon.co.uk www.rpsfamily.demon.co.uk

Observers Pocket Series Collectors Society (OPSCS) Sec Alan Sledger, 10 Villiers Road, Kenilworth, Warwickshire CV8 2JB Tel: 01926 857047

The Official Betty Boop Fan Club Ms Bobbie West, 10550 Western Avenue #133, Stanton CA 90680–6909, USA BBOOPFANS@aol.com

The Official International Wade Collectors Club Royal Victoria Pottery, Westport Road, Burslem, Stoke on Trent, Staffordshire ST6 4AG www.wade.co.uk/wade

The Old Hall (Stainless Steel Tableware) Collectors' Club Nigel Wiggin, Sandford House, Levedale, Stafford ST18 9AH Tel: 01785 780376 oht@gnwiggin.freeserve.co.uk www.oldhallclub.co.uk

The Old Lawnmower Club c/o Milton Keynes Museum, McConnell Drive, Wolverton, Milton Keynes, Buckinghamshire MK12 5EL Tel: 01327 830675 enquiry@oldlawnmowerclub.co.uk www.oldlawnmowerclub.co.uk

On the Lighter Side (OTLS) PO Box 1733, Quitman TX 75783–1733, USA www.otls.com

Ophthalmic Antiques International Collectors' Club Mr R. M. Ling, 6 Grammar School Road, North Walsham, Norfolk NR28 9JH

Orders and Medals Research Society (OMRS) PO Box 1904, Southam CV47 2ZX Tel: 01295 690009 www.omrs.org.uk

The Oriental Ceramic Society The Sec, 30b Torrington Square, London WC1E 7JL Tel: 020 7636 7985 ocs-london@beeb.net

Paperweight Collectors Circle PO Box 941, Comberton, Cambridgeshire CB3 7GQ Tel: 02476 386172

Pedal Car Collectors' Club (P.C.C.C.) Sec A. P. Gayler, 4/4a Chapel Terrace Mews, Kemp Town, Brighton, East Sussex BN2 1HU Tel/Fax: 01273 601960 www.brmmbrmm.com/pedalcars

Pelham Puppets Collectors Club Sue Valentine, 46 The Grove, Bedford MK40 3JN Tel: 01234 363 336 sue.valentine@ntlworld.com

Pen Delfin "Family Circle" Collectors' Club Cameron Mill, Howsin Street, Burnley, Lancashire BB10 1PP Tel: 01282 432301 boswell@pendelfin.co.uk www.pendelfin.co.uk

The Family Circle of Pen Delfin Susan Beard, 230 Spring Street N.W., Suite 1238, Atlanta, Georgia 30303, USA

The Pewter Society Llananant Farm, Penallt, Monmouth NP25 4AP secretary@pewtersociety.org www.pewtersociety.org

Photographic Collectors Club of Great Britain Membership Office P.C.C.G.B., 5 Buntingford Road, Puckeridge, Ware, Hertfordshire SG11 1RT www.pccgb.org

Pilkington's Lancastrian Pottery Society Wendy Stock, Sullom Side, Barnacre, Garstang, Preston, Lancashire PR3 1GH www.pilkpotsoc.freeserve.co.uk

Poole Pottery Collectors Club Poole Pottery Limited, Sopers Lane, Poole, Dorset BH17 7PP www.poolepottery.com

Postal Order Society Howard Lunn, 1 River View, Gillingham, Dorset SP8 4UB Tel: 01747 821162

The Pot Lid Circle c/o Ian Johnson, Collins House, 32/38 Station Road, Gerrards Cross, Buckinghamshire SL9 8EL Tel: 01753 279001 ian.johnson@bpcollins.co.uk

Royal Doulton International Collectors' Club Royal Doulton, Sir Henry Doulton House, Forge Lane, Stoke-on-Trent, Staffordshire ST1 5NN www.icc@royal-doulton.com

Royal Mail Collectors Club Freepost, NEA1431, Sunderland SR9 9XN www.royalmail.co.uk

The Royal Numismatic Society Hon Sec Andrew Meadows, c/o Department of Coins and Medals, The British Museum, London WC1B 3DG Tel: 020 7323 8577 rns@dircon.co.uk www.rns.dircon.co.uk

The Russian Doll Collectors' Club Gardener's Cottage, Hatchlands, East Clandon, Surrey GU4 7RT www.russiandolls.co.uk

Potteries of Rye Society Membership Sec Barry Buckton, 2 Redyear Cottages, Kennington Road, Ashford, Kent TN24 0TF www.potteries-of-rye-society.co.uk

James Sadler International Collectors Club Customer Services, Churchill China PLC, High Street, Tunstall, Stoke on Trent ST6 5NZ Tel: 01782 577566 diningin@churchillchina.plc.uk www.james-sadler.co.uk

Scientific Instrument Society Reg Charity No. 326733, Executive Officer Wg Cdr G. Bennett, 31 High Street, Stanford in the Vale, Faringdon, Oxfordshire SN7 8LH www.sis.org.uk

Silhouette Collectors' Club c/o Diana Joll, Flat 5, 13 Brunswick Square, Hove, East Sussex BN3 1EH

Smurf Collectors Club International Dept 115 NR, 24 Cabot Road West, Massapeque, New York 11758, USA

Society of Tobacco Jar Collectors (USA) 19 Woodhurst North, Raymead Road, Maidenhead, Berkshire SL6 8PH colin.grey1@virgin.net

The Soviet Collectors Club PO Box 56, Saltburn by the Sea TS12 1YD collect@sovietclub.com www.sovietclub.com

TEAMS Club – The official club for Brooke Bond Card Collectors PO Box 1, Market Harborough, Leicestershire LE16 9HT Tel: 01858 466441 sales@teamsclub.co.uk www.teamsclub.co.uk

The Tool and Trades History Society The Membership Sec, Church Farm, 48 Calne Road, Lyneham, Chippenham, Wiltshire SN15 4PN Tel: 01249 891586 Taths@aol.com

Torquay Pottery Collectors' Society Membership Sec, c/o Torre Abbey, The Kings Drive, Torquay, Devon TQ2 5JX www.torquaypottery.com

Totally Teapots The Novelty Teapot Collectors Club Vince McDonald, Euxton, Chorley, Lancashire PR7 6EY Tel/Fax: 01257 450366 vince@totallyteapots.com www.totallyteapots.com

Train Collectors Society Membership Sec James Day, PO Box 20340, London NW11 6ZE Tel/Fax: 020 8209 1589 tcsinformation@btinternet.com www.traincollectors.org.uk

UK McDonald's & Fast Food Collectors Club c/o Lawrence Yap, 110 Tithelands, Harlow, Essex CM19 5ND bigkidandtoys@ntlworld.com

UK Programme Collectors Club 46 Milton Road, Kirkaldy KY1 1TL, Scotland

United Kingdom Spoon Collectors Club General Sec David Cross, 72 Edinburgh Road, Newmarket, Suffolk CB8 0DQ Tel: 01638 665457 david@ukspoons.fsnet.co.uk

Vintage Model Yacht Group Trevor Smith, 1A Station Avenue, Epsom, Surrey KT19 9UD Tel: 020 8393 1100

The Wade Watch Carole Murdock & Valerie Moody, 8199 Pierson Ct, Arvada CO 80005, USA www.wadewatch.com

The Washington Historical Autograph and Certificate Organization – Whaco! PO Box 2428, Springfield VA 22152–2428, USA

The Writing Equipment Society c/o Sec Mr John S. Daniels, 33 Glanville Road, Hadleigh, Ipswich, Suffolk IP7 5SQ www.wesonline.org.uk

Zippo Click Collectors Club 33 Barbour Street, Bradford PA 16701, USA www.zippoclick.com

Directory of Markets & Centres

Derbyshire

Alfreton Antique Centre, 11 King Street, Alfreton DE55 7AF
Tel: 01773 520781
*30 dealers on 2 floors. Antiques, collectables, furniture,
books, militaria, postcards, silverware. Open 7 days Mon–Sat
10am–4.30pm, Sundays 11am–4.30pm.*

Chappells Antiques Centre, King Street, Bakewell DE45 1DZ
Tel: 01629 812496 ask@chappellsantiquescentre.com
www.chappellsantiques centre.com
*Over 30 dealers inc BADA & LAPADA members. Quality
period furniture, ceramics, silver, plate, metals, treen, clocks,
barometers, books, pictures, maps, prints, textiles,
kitchenalia, lighting, furnishing accessories, scientific,
pharmaceutical and sporting antiques from the 17th–20thC.
Open Mon–Sat 12noon–5pm, Sun 11am–5pm. Closed
Christmas Day, Boxing Day, New Years Day. Please ring
for brochure.*

Heanor Antiques Centre, 1–3 Ilkeston Road,
Heanor DE75 7AE Tel: 01773 531181/762783
sales@heanorantiquescentre.co.uk
www.heanorantiquescentre.co.uk
*Open 7 days 10.30am–4.30pm including Bank Holidays.
Now 200 independent dealers in new 3 storey extension
with stylish cafe.*

Matlock Antiques, Collectables & Riverside Café,
7 Dale Road, Matlock DE4 3LT Tel: 01629 760808
bmatlockantiques@aol.com
www.matlock-antiques-collectable.cwc.net
*Proprietor W. Shirley. Over 70 dealers.
Open every day 10am–5pm.*

Devon

Quay Centre, Topsham, Nr Exeter EX3 0JA
Tel: 01392 874006
office@antiquesontopshamquay.co.uk
www.antiquesontopshamquay.co.uk
*80 dealers on 3 floors. Antiques, collectables and traditional
furnishings. Ample parking. Open 7 days, 10am–5pm.
All major credit cards accepted.*

Gloucestershire

Durham House Antiques Centre, Sheep Street,
Stow-on-the-Wold GL54 1AA Tel: 01451 870404
*30+ dealers. Town and country furniture, metalware, books,
ceramics, kitchenalia, sewing ephemera, silver, jewellery and
samplers. Mon–Sat 10am–5pm, Sunday 11am–5pm. Stow-
on-the-Wold, Cotswold home to over 40 antique shops,
galleries and bookshops.*

Gloucester Antiques Centre, The Historic Docks,
1 Severn Road, Gloucester GL1 2LE Tel: 01452 529716
www.antiques.center.com
Open Mon–Sat 10am–5pm, Sun 1pm–5pm.

Hampshire

Dolphin Quay Antique Centre, Queen Street,
Emsworth PO10 7BU Tel: 01243 379994
*Open 7 days a week (including Bank Holidays) Mon–Sat
10am–5pm, Sun 10am–4pm. Marine, naval antiques,
paintings, watercolours, prints, antique clocks, decorative
arts, furniture, sporting apparel, luggage, specialist period
lighting, conservatory, garden antiques, fine antique/country
furniture, French/antique beds.*

Lymington Antiques Centre, 76 High Street,
Lymington SO41 9AL Tel: 01590 670934
*Open Mon–Fri 10am–5pm, Sat 9am–5pm. 30 dealers,
clocks, watches, silver, glass, jewellery, toys & dolls, books,
furniture, textiles.*

Kent

Castle Antiques, 1 London Road (opposite Library),
Westerham TN16 1BB Tel: 01959 562492
*Open 10am–5pm 7 days. 4 rooms of antiques, small
furniture, collectables, rural bygones, costume, glass, books,
linens, jewellery, chandeliers, cat collectables. Services:
advice, valuations, theatre props, house clearance,
talks on antiques.*

Malthouse Arcade, High Street, Hythe CT21 5BW
Tel: 01303 260103
*Open Fri and Sat Bank holiday Mon 9.30am–5.30pm.
37 Stalls and cafe. Furniture, china and glass, jewellery,
plated brass, picture postcards, framing etc.*

Nightingales, 89–91 High Street, West Wickham BR4 0LS
Tel: 020 8777 0335
*Over 5,000 sq ft of antiques, furniture and collectors
items, including ceramics, glass, silver, furniture and
decorative ware. Open Mon–Sat 10am–5pm (Closed
Suns except December).*

Lancashire

The Antique & Decorative Design Centre,
56 Garstang Road, Preston PR1 1NA
Tel: 01772 882078
info@paulallisonantiques.co.uk
www.paulallisonantiques.co.uk
*Open 7 days a week 10am–5pm. 25,000 sq ft of quality
antiques, objets d'art, clocks, pine, silverware, porcelain,
upholstery, French furniture for the home and garden.*

GB Antiques Centre, Lancaster Leisure Park, (the former
Hornsea Pottery), Wyresdale Road, Lancaster LA1 3LA

Tel: 01524 844734
140 dealers in 40,000 sq ft of space. Porcelain, pottery, Art Deco, glass, books, linen, mahogany, oak and pine furniture. Open 7 days 10am–5pm.

Kingsmill Antique Centre, Queen Street, Harle Syke, Burnley BB10 2HX Tel: 01282 431953
antiques@kingsmill.demon.co.uk
www.kingsmill.demon.co.uk
Dealers, packers and shippers.

Leicestershire

Oxford Street Antique Centre, 16–26 Oxford Street, Leicester LE1 5XU Tel: 0116 255 3006

Lincolnshire

St Martins Antiques Centre, 23a High St, St Martins, Stamford PE9 2LF Tel: 01780 481158
peter@st-martins-antiques.co.uk
www.st-martins-antiques.co.uk

London

Alfie's Antique Market, 13 Church Street, Marylebone NW8 8DT Tel: 020 7723 6066 www.alfiesantiques.com
London's biggest and busiest antique market. Open 10am–6pm Tues–Sat.

Covent Garden Antiques Market, Jubilee Market Hall, Covent Garden WC2 Tel: 020 7240 7405
Visit the famous Covent Garden Antique Market. 150 traders selling jewellery, silver, prints, porcelain, objets d'art and numerous other collectables.

Grays Antique Markets, South Molton Lane W1K 5AB Tel: 020 7629 7034
grays@clara.net www.graysantiques.com
Over 200 specialist antique dealers selling beautiful and unusual antiques & collectables. Open Mon–Fri 10am–6pm.

Northcote Road Antique Market, 155a Northcote Road, Battersea SW11 6QB Tel: 020 7228 6850
www.spectrumsoft.net/nam
Indoor arcade open 7 days, Mon–Sat 10am–6pm, Sun 12noon–5pm. 30 dealers offering a wide variety of antiques & collectables.

Palmers Green Antiques Centre, 472 Green Lanes, Palmers Green N13 5PA Tel: 020 8350 0878
Over 40 dealers. Specialising in furniture, jewellery, clocks, pictures, porcelain, china, glass, silver & plate, metalware, kitchenalia and lighting, etc. Open 6 days a week, Mon–Sat 10am–5.30pm (closed Tues), Sun 11am–5pm, open Bank Holidays. Removals & house clearances, probate valuations undertaken, quality antiques and collectables. All major credit cards accepted.

Norfolk

Tombland Antiques Centre, Augustine Steward House, 14 Tombland, Norwich NR3 1HF
Tel: 01603 761906 or 619129
www.tomblandantiques.co.uk
Open Mon–Sat 10am–5pm. Huge selection on 3 floors. Ideally situated opposite Norwich Cathedral.

Northamptonshire

The Brackley Antique Cellar, Drayman's Walk, Brackley NN13 6BE Tel: 01280 841841
antiquecellar@tesco.net
The largest purpose-built antique centre in the Midlands. Open 7 days 10am–5pm. 30,000 sq ft of floor space, over 100 dealers.

Oxfordshire

Antiques on High, 85 High Street, Oxford OX1 4BG
Tel: 01865 251075
Open 7 days a week 10am–5pm. Sun & Bank Holidays 11am–5pm. 35 friendly dealers with a wide range of quality stock.

Scotland

Scottish Antique and Arts Centre, Carse of Cambus, Doune, Perthshire FK16 6HD Tel: 01786 841203
sales@scottish-antiques.com www.scottish-antiques.com
Over 100 dealers. Huge gift & collectors sections. Victorian & Edwardian furniture. Open 7 days 10am–5pm.

Scottish Antique Centre, Abernyte PH14 9SJ Tel: 01828 686401
sales@scottish-antiques.com www.scottish-antiques.com
Over 100 dealers. Huge gift & collectors sections. Victorian & Edwardian furniture. Open 7days 10am–5pm.

Shropshire

Stretton Antiques Market, Sandford Avenue, Church Stretton SY6 6BH Tel: 01694 723718
60 dealers under one roof.

Surrey

Maltings Monthly Market, Bridge Square, Farnham GU9 7QR Tel: 01252 726234 info@farnhammaltings.com
www.farnhammaltings.com
9.30am–4.00pm first Sat of the month.

East Sussex

The Brighton Lanes Antique Centre, 12 Meeting House Lane, Brighton BN1 1HB Tel: 01273 823121
peter@brightonlanes-antiquecentre.co.uk
www.brightonlanes-antiquecentre.co.uk
A spacious centre in the heart of the historic lanes with a fine selection of furniture, silver, jewellery, glass, porcelain, clocks, pens, watches, lighting and decorative items. Open daily 10am–5.30pm, Sun 12noon–4pm. Loading bay/parking – Lanes car park.

Tyne & Wear

The Antique Centre, 2nd floor, 142 Northumberland Street, Newcastle-upon-Tyne NE1 7DQ Tel: 0191 232 9832
time-antiques@btinternet.com

Wales

Offa's Dyke Antique Centre, 4 High Street, Knighton, Powys LD7 1AT Tel: 01547 528635/520145
14 dealers. Ceramics, 18th & 19thC earthenware, stoneware and porcelain, early 20thC industrial and studio pottery. Reference books on ceramics and general antiques. Good antique drinking glasses. Country antiques and bygones. 19th and 20thC paintings and drawings. Antiquities. General antiques and collectables.

The Works Antiques Centre, Station Road, Llandeilo, Carmarthenshire SA19 6NH Tel: 01558 823964
theworks@storeyj.clara.co.uk www.works-antiques.co.uk
Open Tues–Sat 10am–6pm, Sun 10am–5pm. Open Bank Holiday Mondays. 5,000 sq ft 60 dealers. Ample parking. Free tea and coffee.

Warwickshire

Stratford Antiques Centre, 59–60 Ely Street, Stratford-upon-Avon CV37 6LN Tel: 01789 204180
Come and visit Stratford-upon-Avon. A one stop collectors experience with 2 floors and courtyard full of shops. Open 7 days a week from 10am–5pm.

West Midlands

Birmingham Antique Centre, 1407 Pershore Road, Stirchley, Birmingham B30 2JR Tel: 0121 459 4587
bhamantiquecent@aol.com
www.birminghamantiquecentre.co.uk
Open 7 days, Mon–Sat 9am–5pm, Sun 10am–4pm. Cabinets available to rent.

Wiltshire

Upstairs Downstairs, 40 Market Place, Devizes SN10 1JG Tel: 01380 730266 or 07974 074220
devizesantiques@amserve.com
Open Mon–Sat 9.30am–4.30pm, Sun 9.30am–3pm, closed Wed. Antiques & collectables centre on 4 floors with 30 traders.

Worcestershire

Worcester Antiques Centre, Reindeer Court, Mealcheapen Street, Worcester WR1 4DF Tel: 01905 610680
WorcsAntiques@aol.com
Porcelain & pottery, furniture, silver & dining room accessories, jewellery, period watches & clocks, scientific instrumentation, Arts & Crafts, Nouveau, Deco, antique boxes & treen, books, ephemera, militaria & kitchenalia with full restoration & repair services on all of the above.

Yorkshire

St Nicholas Antique Shops, 35 St Nicholas Cliff, Scarborough YO11 2ES Tel: 01723 365221
sales@collectors.demon.co.uk www.collectors.demon.co.uk
International dealers in stamps, postcards, silver, gold, medals, cigarette cards, cap badges, militaria, jewellery, commemorative ware, furniture, clocks, watches and many more collectables.

York Antiques Centre, 1a Lendal, York YO1 8AA Tel: 01904 641445

USA

Alhambra Antiques Center, 3640 Coral Way, Coral Cables, Florida Tel: 305 446 1688
4 antiques dealers that sell high quality decorative pieces from Europe.

Antique Center I, II, III at Historic Savage Mill, Savage, Maryland Tel: 410 880 0918 or 301 369 4650
antiquec@aol.com
225 plus select quality dealers representing 15 states. Open every day plus 3 evenings – Sun–Wed 9.30am–6pm, Thurs, Fri and Sat 9.30am–9pm. Closed Christmas, Easter and Thanksgiving days. Open New Year's Day 12 noon–5pm.

Antique Village, North of Richmond, Virginia, on Historic US 301, 4 miles North of 1–295 Tel: 804 746 8914
Mon, Tues, Thurs, Fri 10am–5pm, Sat 10am–6pm, Sun 12 noon–6pm, closed Wed. 50 dealers specialising in Art Pottery, country & primitives, Civil War artifacts, paper memorabilia, African art, toys, advertising, occupied Japan, tobacco tins, glassware, china, holiday collectibles, jewellery, postcards.

Antiques at Colony Mill Marketplace, 222 West Street, Keene, New Hampshire 03431 Tel: (603) 358 6343
Open Mon–Sat 10am–9pm, Sun 11am–6pm. Over 200 booths. Period to country furniture, paintings and prints, Art Pottery, glass, china, silver, jewellery, toys, dolls, quilts, etc.

The Coffman's Antiques Markets, at Jennifer House Commons, Stockbridge Road, Route 7, PO Box 592, Great Barrington MA 01230 Tel: (413) 528 9282/9602
www.coffmansantiques.com

Fern Eldridge & Friends, 800 First NH Turnpike (Rte. 4), Northwood, New Hampshire 03261 Tel: 603 942 5602/8131
FernEldridgeAndFriends@NHantiqueAlley.com
30 dealers on 2 levels. Shipping available in USA. Open 10am–5pm daily. Closed major holidays, please call ahead.

Goodlettsville Antique Mall, 213 N. Main St, Germantown, Tennessee Tel: 615 859 7002

The Hayloft Antique Center, 1190 First NH Turnpike (Rte. 4), Northwood, New Hampshire 03261 Tel: 603 942 5153
TheHayloftAntiqueCenter@NHantiqueAlley.com
Over 150 dealers offering Estate jewelry, sterling silver, rare books, glass, porcelain, pottery, art, primitives, furniture, toys, ephemera, linens, military, sporting collectibles and much more. Open 10am–5pm daily. Closed major holidays, please call ahead.

Hermitage Antique Mall, 4144–B Lebanon Road, Hermitage, Tennessee Tel: 615 883 5789

Madison Antique Mall, 320 Gallatin Rd, S. Nashville, Tennessee Tel: 615 865 4677
18th and 19thC English antiques and objets d'art.

Michiana Antique Mall, 2423 S. 11th Street, Niles, Michigan 49120 www.michianaantiquemall.com
Open 7 days, 10am–6pm.

Morningside Antiques, 6443 Biscayne Blvd., Miami, Florida Tel: 305 751 2828
The city's newest antiques market specialising in English, French and American furniture and collectibles in a mall setting with many different vendors.

Nashville Wedgewood Station Antique Mall, 657 Wedgewood Ave., Nashville, Tennessee Tel: 615 259 0939

Parker-French Antique Center, 1182 First NH Turnpike (Rt. 4), Northwood, New Hampshire 03261 Tel: 603 942 8852
ParkerFrenchAntiqueCenter@NHantiqueAlley.com
135 antique dealers all on one level offering a good mix of sterling silver, jewelry, glassware, pottery, early primitives. No crafts, reproductions or new items. Open 10am–5pm daily. Closed major holidays, please call ahead.

Quechee Gorge Antiques & Collectibles Center, Located in Quechee Gorge Village Tel: 1 800 438 5565
450 dealers. Open all year, 7 days a week. Depression glass, ephemera, tools, toys, collectibles, Deco, primitives, prints, silver and fine china.

Showcase Antique Center, PO Box 1122, Sturbridge MA 01566 Tel: 508 347 7190
www.showcaseantiques.com
Open Mon, Wed, Thurs, 10am–5pm, Fri, Sat 10am–5pm, Sun 12 noon–5pm, closed Tues. 170 dealers.

Tennessee Antique Mall, 654 Wedgewood Ave., Nashville, Tennessee Tel: 615 259 4077

Key to Illustrations

Each illustration and descriptive caption is accompanied by a letter code. By referring to the following list of Auctioneers (denoted by ⚹), Dealers (⊞) and Clubs (§), the source of any item may be immediately determined. Inclusion in this edition in no way constitutes or implies a contract or binding offer on the part of any of our contributors to supply or sell the goods illustrated, or similar articles, at the prices stated. Advertisers in this year's directory are denoted by (†).

If you require a valuation for an item, it is advisable to check whether the dealer or specialist will carry out this service and if there is a charge. Please mention Miller's when making an enquiry. Having found a specialist who will carry out your valuation it is best to send a photograph and description of the item to the specialist together with a stamped addressed envelope for the reply. A valuation by telephone is not possible. Most dealers are only too happy to help you with your enquiry; however, they are very busy people and consideration of the above points would be welcomed.

A&O ⊞ Ancient & Oriental Ltd Tel: 01664 812044 alex@antiquities.co.uk

AAA ⊞ Ad-Age Antique Advertising Tel: 01622 670595

ABBC § Association of Bottled Beer Collectors, 28 Parklands, Kidsgrove, Stoke-on-Trent, Staffordshire ST7 4US Tel: 01782 761048 www.abbc.org.uk www.abbclist.info

ABCM ⊞ A. B. Coins & Medals, 23–25 'Old' Northam Road, Southampton, Hampshire SO14 Tel: 02380 233393 Mob: 07759 655739/ 07770 671832

ADD ⊞ Addyman Books, 39 Lion Street, Hay-on-Wye, Herefordshire HR3 5AD Tel: 01497 821136

AEL ⊞ Argyll Etkin Ltd, 1–9 Hills Place, Oxford Circus, London W1F 7SA Tel: 020 7437 7800 philatelists@argyll-etkin.com

AFA ⊞ Alex Fane, Somerset

AFD ⊞ Afford Decorative Arts Tel: 01827 330042 Mob: 07831 114909 affordecarts@fsmail.net

AGA ⚹† Angling Auctions, PO Box 2095, London W12 8RU Tel: 020 8749 4175 or 07785 281349 neil@anglingauctions.demon.co.uk

AH ⚹ Andrew Hartley, Victoria Hall Salerooms, Little Lane, Ilkley, Yorkshire LS29 8EA Tel: 01943 816363 info@andrewhartleyfinearts.co.uk www.andrewhartleyfinearts.co.uk

AL ⊞† Ann Lingard, Ropewalk Antiques, Rye, East Sussex TN31 7NA Tel: 01797 223486 ann-lingard@ropewalkantiques.freeserve.co.uk

AMB ⚹ Ambrose, Ambrose House, Old Station Road, Loughton, Essex IG10 4PE Tel: 020 8502 3951

AMc ⊞† Antique Amusement Co, Mill Lane, Swaffham Bulbeck, Cambridgeshire CB5 0NF Tel: 01223 813041 Mob: 07802 666755 mail@aamag.co.uk www.aamag.co.uk

AMH ⊞ Amherst Antiques, Monomark House, 27 Old Gloucester Street, London WC1N 3XX Tel: 01892 725552 Mob: 07850 350212 amherstantiques@monomark.co.uk

AMR ⊞ Amron Antiques Tel: 01782 566895

ANG ⊞† Ancient & Gothic, PO Box 5390, Bournemouth, Dorset BH7 6XR Tel: 01202 431721

ANGE ⊞ Angelo Tel: 01753 864657

ANO ⊞ Art Nouveau Originals Tel: 01733 244717 Mob: 07774 718 096 cathy@artnouveauoriginals.com

APC ⊞ Antique Photographic Company Ltd Tel: 01949 842192 alpaco47@aol.com

ARo ⊞† Alvin's Vintage Games & Toys Tel: 01865 772409 vintage.games@virgin.net

ARP ⊞ Arundel Photographica, The Arundel Antiques Centre, 51 High Street, Arundel, West Sussex BN18 9AJ Tel: 01903 882749

ASA ⊞ A. S. Antique Galleries, 26 Broad Street, Pendleton, Salford, Greater Manchester M6 5BY Tel: 0161 737 5938 Mob: 07836 368230 as@sternshine.demon.co.uk

ASC ⊞ Andrew Sclanders, 32 St Paul's View, 15 Amwell Street, London EC1R 1UP Tel: 020 7278 5034 sclanders@beatbooks.com www.beatbooks.com

ASP ⊞ Aspidistra Antiques, 51 High Street, Finedon, Wellingborough, Northamptonshire NN9 9JN Tel: 01933 680196 Mob: 07768 071948 info@aspidistra-antiques.com www.aspidistra.antiques.com

ATK ⊞ J. & V. R. Atkins Tel: 01952 810594 Mob: 07808 747151

AUTO ⊞ Automatomania, M13 Grays Mews, 58 Davies Street, London W1K 5LP Tel: 020 7495 5259 Mob: 07790 719097 magic@automatomania.com www.automatomania.com

AVT ⊞ Alexander von Tutschek Tel: 01225 465532 vontutschek@onetel.net.uk

B ⚹ Bonhams, 101 New Bond Street, London W1S 1SR Tel: 020 7629 6602/7468 8233 www.bonhams.com

B(Kn) ⚹ Bonhams, Montpelier Street, Knightsbridge, London SW7 1HH Tel: 020 7393 3900 www.bonhams.com

B(NW) ⚹ Bonhams, New House, 150 Christleton Road, Chester CH3 5TD Tel: 01244 313936 www.bonhams.com

B(O) ⚹ Bonhams, 39 Park End Street, Oxford OX1 1JD Tel: 01865 723524 www.bonhams.com

B(SF) ⚹ Bonhams, 500 Sutter Street, Union Square, San Francisco, California 94102, USA Tel: +1 415 391 4000 www.bonhams.com

B(WM) ⚹ Bonhams, The Old House, Station Road, Knowle, Solihull, West Midlands B93 0HT Tel: 01564 776151 www.bonhams.com

B&R ⊞† Bread & Roses Tel: 01926 817342

BAC ⊞† The Brackley Antique Cellar, Drayman's Walk, Brackley, Northamptonshire NN13 6BE Tel: 01280 841841 antiquecellar@tesco.net

BAJ ⊞ Beaulieu Autojumble

BAL ⊞ A. H. Baldwin & Sons Ltd, Numismatists, 11 Adelphi Terrace, London WC2N 6BJ Tel: 020 7930 6879

BARCC § The Brooklands Automobilia & Regalia Collectors' Club (B.A.R.C.C.), Hon Sec G. G. Weiner, 4–4a Chapel Terrace Mews, Kemp Town, Brighton, East Sussex BN2 1HU Tel: 01273 601960 www.barcc.co.uk

BAu ⚹ Bloomington Auction Gallery, 300 East Grove St, Bloomington, Illinois 61701, USA Tel: 00 1 309 828 5533 joyluke@aol.com www.joyluke.com

BAY ⊞ George Bayntun, Manvers Street, Bath, Somerset BA1 1JW Tel: 01225 466000 EBayntun@aol.com

BB(L) ➤ Bonhams & Butterfields, 7601 Sunset Boulevard, Los Angeles CA 90046, USA Tel: 00 1 323 850 7500

BB(S) ➤ Bonhams & Butterfields, 220 San Bruno Avenue, San Francisco CA 94103, USA Tel: 00 1 415 861 7500

BBA ➤ Bloomsbury Book Auctions, 3 & 4 Hardwick Street, Off Rosebery Avenue, London EC1R 4RY Tel: 020 7833 2636/7 & 020 7923 6940 info@bloomsbury-book-auct.com www.bloomsbury-book-auct.com

BBe ⊞† Bourton Bears Tel: 01451 821466 www.bourtonbears.com

BBR ➤† BBR, Elsecar Heritage Centre, Elsecar, Nr Barnsley, S. Yorkshire S74 8HJ Tel: 01226 745156 sales@onlinebbr.com www.onlinebbr.com

BD ⊞ Banana Dance Ltd, 16 The Mall, Camden Passage, 359 Upper St, Islington, London N1 0PD Tel: 020 8699 7728 Mob: 07976 296987 jonathan@bananadance.com www.bananadance.com

BDA ⊞ Briar's C20th Decorative Arts, Skipton Antiques & Collectors Centre, The Old Foundry, Cavendish Street, Skipton, Yorkshire BD23 2AB Tel: 01756 798641

Bea(E) ➤ Bearnes, St Edmund's Court, Okehampton Street, Exeter, Devon EX4 1DU Tel: 01392 207000 enquiries@bearnes.co.uk www.bearnes.co.uk

Beb ⊞ Bebes et Jouets, c/o Post Office, Edinburgh EH7 6HW, Scotland Tel: 0131 332 5650 Mob: 0771 4374995 bebesetjouets@u.genie.co.uk www.you.genie.co.uk/bebesetjouets

BERN ➤ Bernaerts, Verlatstraat 18–22, 2000 Antwerpen/Anvers, Belgium Tel: +32 (0)3 248 19 21 edmond.bernaerts@ping.be www.auction-bernaerts.com

BET ⊞ Beth, GO 43–44, Alfie's Antique Market, 13–25 Church Street, Marylebone, London NW8 8DT Tel: 020 7723 5613 or 0777 613 6003

BEV ⊞ Beverley, 30 Church Street, Marylebone, London NW8 8EP Tel: 020 7262 1576 Mob: 07776 136003

BGO ➤ Bob Gowland International Golf Auctions, The Stables, Claim Farm, Manley Road, Frodsham, Cheshire WA6 6HT Tel: 01928 740668 bob@internationalgolfauctions.com www.internationalgolfauctions.com

BIB ⊞† Biblion, 1–7 Davies Mews, London W1K 5AB Tel: 020 7629 1374 info@biblion.com www.biblionmayfair.com

BIG ➤ Bigwood Auctioneers Ltd, The Old School, Tiddington, Stratford-upon-Avon, Warwickshire CV37 7AW Tel: 01789 269415

BiR ⊞ Bill Robson Tel: 01434 270206

BLm ⊞ Lyn Bloom & Jeffrey Neal, Vault 27, The London Silver Vaults, Chancery Lane, London WC2A 1QS Tel: 020 7242 6189 Mob: 07768 533055 bloomvault@aol.com www.bloomvault.com

BND ⊞ Brian Barnfield, Bourbon Hanby Antiques Centre, 151 Sydney Street, Chelsea, London SW3 6NT Tel: 020 7565 0002

BNO ⊞ Beanos, Middle Street, Croydon, London CR0 1RE Tel: 020 8680 1202 enquiries@beanos.co.uk www.beanos.co.uk

BOB ⊞ Bob's Collectables Tel: 01277 650834

BR ➤ Bracketts, The Auction Hall, The Pantiles, Tunbridge Wells, Kent TN2 5QL Tel: 01892 544500 sales@bfaa.co.uk www.bfaa.co.uk

BRG ⊞ Brandler Galleries, 1 Coptfold Road, Brentwood, Essex CM14 4BN Tel: 01277 222269 john@brandler-galleries.com www.brandler-galleries.com

Bri ➤ Bristol Auction Rooms, St John's Place, Apsley Road, Clifton, Bristol, Gloucestershire BS8 2ST Tel: 0117 973 7201 www.bristolauctionrooms.co.uk

BrL ⊞ The Brighton Lanes Antique Centre, 12 Meeting House Lane, Brighton, East Sussex BN1 1HB Tel: 01273 823121 Mob: 07785 564337 peter@brightonlanes-antiquecentre.co.uk www.brightonlanes-antiquecentre.co.uk

BSA ⊞ Bartlett Street Antique Centre, 5–10 Bartlett Street, Bath, Somerset BA1 2QZ Tel: 01225 466689 info@antiques-centre.co.uk www.antiques-centre.co.uk

BTC ⊞† Beatcity, PO Box 229, Chatham, Kent ME5 8WA Tel: 01634 200444 or 07770 650890 Darrenhanks@beatcity.co.uk www.beatcity.co.uk

BWA ⊞ Bow Well Antiques, 103 West Bow, Edinburgh EH1 2JP, Scotland Tel: 0131 225 3335 murdoch.mcleod@virgin.net

BWL ➤ Brightwells Ltd, The Fine Art Saleroom, Ryelands Road, Leominster, Herefordshire HR6 8NZ Tel: 01568 611122 fineart@brightwells.com www.brightwells.com

ByI ⊞ Bygones of Ireland Ltd, Lodge Road, Westport, Co Mayo, Republic of Ireland Tel: 00 353 98 26132/25701 bygones@anu.ie www.bygones-of-ireland.com

C&W ⊞ Carroll & Walker Tel: 01877 385618

CAD ⊞ Cad Van Swankster, Alfie's Antique Market, 13–25 Church Street, Marylebone, London NW8 8DT Tel: 020 7724 8984

CaH ⊞ The Camera House, Oakworth Hall, Colne Road, Oakworth, Keighley, Yorkshire BD22 7HZ Tel: 01535 642333 Mob: 07984 018951 colin@the-camera-house.co.uk www.the-camera-house.co.uk

CAL ⊞ Cedar Antiques Ltd, High Street, Hartley Wintney, Hampshire RG27 8NY Tel: 01252 843222 or 01189 326628

CARS ⊞ C.A.R.S. (Classic Automobilia & Regalia Specialists), 4–4a Chapel Terrace Mews, Kemp Town, Brighton, East Sussex BN2 1HU Tel: 01273 60 1960 cars@kemptown-brighton.freeserve.co.uk www.brmmbrmm.com/barc www.brmmbrmm.com/pedalcars www.brooklandsbadges.com www.brooklands-automobilia-regalia-collectors-club.co.uk www.carsofbrighton.co.uk

Cas ⊞ Castle Antiques www.castle-antiques.com

CAST ⊞ Castaside, FO13 Alfie's Antique Market, 13–25 Church Street, Marylebone, London NW8 8DT Tel: 020 7723 7686 post@ealfies.com

CAu ➤ The Cotswold Auction Company Ltd, inc Short Graham & Co and Hobbs and Chambers Fine Arts, The Coach House, Swan Yard, 9–13 West Market Place, Cirencester, Gloucestershire GL7 2NH Tel: 01285 642420 info@cotswoldauction.co.uk www.cotswoldauction.co.uk

CBB ⊞ Colin Baddiel, Gray's Mews, 1–7 Davies Mews, London W1Y 1AR Tel: 020 7408 1239/ 020 8452 7243

CBGR ⊞† Chris Baker Gramophones, All Our Yesterdays, 3 Cattle Market, Sandwich, Kent CT13 9AE Tel: 01304 614756 cbgramophones@aol.com www.chrisbakergramophones.com

CBP ⚒ Comic Book Postal Auctions Ltd, 40–42 Osnaburgh Street, London NW1 3ND Tel: 020 7424 0007 comicbook@compuserve.com www.compalcomics.com

CCC ⊞† The Crested China Co, Highfield, Windmill Hill, Driffield, East Yorkshire YO25 5YP Tel: 0870 300 1 300 dt@thecrestedchinacompany.com www.thecrestedchinacompany.com

CCH ⊞ Collectors Choice, PO Box 99, Guildford, Surrey GU1 1GA Tel: 01483 576655 louise@collectors-choice.net www.collectors-choice.net

CCO ⊞ Collectable Costume, Showroom South, Gloucester Antiques Centre, 1 Severn Road, Gloucester GL1 2LE Tel: 01989 562188 Mob: 07980 623926

CCs ⊞ Coco's Corner, Unit 4, Cirencester Antique Centre, Cirencester, Gloucestershire Tel: 01452 556 308 cocos-corner@blueyonder.co.uk

CEMB ⊞ Christina Bishop Kitchenware 1890s–1960s By appointment only Tel: 020 7221 4688

CHAC ⊞ Church Hill Antiques Centre, 6 Station Street, Lewes, East Sussex BN7 2DA Tel: 01273 474 842 churchhilllewes@aol.com www.church-hill-antiques.co.uk

ChC ⊞ Christopher Clarke (Antiques) Ltd, The Fosse Way, Stow-on-the-Wold, Gloucestershire GL54 1JS Tel: 01451 830476 cclarkeantiques@aol.com www.campaignfurniture.com

CHI ⊞† Chinasearch Ltd, 4 Princes Drive, Kenilworth, Warwickshire CV8 2FD Tel: 01926 512402 info@chinasearch.uk.com www.chinasearch.uk.com

ChM ⊞ Chelsea Military Antiques, F4 Antiquarius, 131/141 Kings Road, Chelsea, London SW3 4PW Tel: 020 7352 0308 richard@chelseamilitaria.com

Ci ⊞ Circa, 8 Fulham High Road, London SW6 Tel: 020 7736 5038

CNM ⊞ Caroline Nevill Miniatures, 22A Broad Street, Bath, Somerset BA1 5LN Tel: 01225 443091 www.carolinenevillminiatures.co.uk

CO ⚒ Cooper Owen, 10 Denmark Street, London WC2H 8LS Tel: 020 7240 4132 www.CooperOwen.com

COB ⊞† Cobwebs, 78 Northam Road, Southampton, Hampshire SO14 0PB Tel: 023 8022 7458 www.cobwebs.uk.com

CoC ⊞ Comic Connections, 4a Parsons Street, Banbury, Oxfordshire OX16 5LW Tel: 01295 268989 comicman@freenetname.co.uk

CoCo ⊞ Country Collector, 11–12 Birdgate, Pickering, Yorkshire YO18 7AL Tel: 01751 477481 www.country-collector.co.uk

COPA ⚒ Copake Auction, Inc, PO Box H, Copake NY 12516, USA Tel: 518 329 1142 info@copakeauction.com www.copakeauction.com

CP ⊞† Cat Pottery, 1 Grammar School Road, North Walsham, Norfolk NR28 9JH Tel: 01692 402962

CRIS ⊞ Cristobal, 26 Church Street, London NW8 8EP Tel: 020 7724 7230 Mob: 07956 388194

CRT ⊞ Cancer Research, High Street, Tenterden, Kent

CS ⊞ Christopher Sykes, The Old Parsonage, Woburn, Milton Keynes, Bedfordshire MK17 9QM Tel: 01525 290259 www.sykes-corkscrews.co.uk

CTO ⊞† Collector's Corner, PO Box 8, Congleton, Cheshire CW12 4GD Tel: 01260 270429 dave.popcorner@ukonline.co.uk

CUF ⊞ The Cufflink Shop, Stand G2 Antiquarius, 137 Kings Road, London SW3 4PW Tel: 020 7352 8201 Mob: 0771 538 1175

CuS ⊞ Curious Science, 319 Lillie Road, Fulham, London SW6 7LL Tel: 020 7610 1175 Mob: 07956 834094 curiousscience@medical-antiques.com

CWO ⊞ www.collectorsworld.net, PO Box 4922, Bournemouth, Dorset BH1 3WD Tel: 01202 555223 info@collectorsworld.biz www.collectorsworld.net www.collectorsworld.biz

DA ⚒ Dee, Atkinson & Harrison, The Exchange Saleroom, Driffield, East Yorkshire YO25 6LD Tel: 01377 253151 exchange@dee-atkinson-harrison.co.uk www.dahauctions.com

DAL ⚒† Dalkeith Auctions Ltd, Dalkeith Hall, Dalkeith Steps, Rear of 81 Old Christchurch Road, Bournemouth, Dorset BH1 1YL Tel: 01202 292905 how@dalkeith-auctions.co.uk www.dalkeith-auctions.co.uk

Dall ⊞ P&R Dallimore Antique Collectibles Tel: 01242 820119 rdalli5760@aol.com

DAN ⊞ Andrew Dando, 34 Market Street, Bradford-on-Avon, Wiltshire BA15 1LL Tel: 01225 865444 andrew@andrewdando.co.uk www.andrewdando.co.uk

DE ⊞† Decades, 20 Lord St West, Blackburn, Lancashire BB2 1JX Tel: 01254 693320

DgC ⊞ Dragonlee Collectables Tel: 01622 729502

DHA ⊞ Durham House Antiques Centre, Sheep Street, Stow-on-the-Wold, Gloucestershire GL54 1AA Tel: 01451 870404

DHAR ⊞ Dave Hardman Antiques, West Street, Witheridge, Devon EX16 8AA Tel: 01884860273 Mob: 0797973 7126 dave@hardmanantiques.freeserve.co.uk

DMC ⚒ Diamond Mills & Co, 117 Hamilton Road, Felixstowe, Suffolk IP11 7BL Tel: 01394 282281

DN ⚒ Dreweatt Neate, Donnington Priory, Donnington, Newbury, Berkshire RG14 2JE Tel: 01635 553553 fineart@dreweatt-neate.co.uk www.auctions.dreweatt-neate.co.uk

DNW ⚒† Dix-Noonan-Webb, 16 Bolton Street, London W1J 8BQ Tel: 020 7016 1700 auctions@dnw.co.uk www.dnw.co.uk

Do ⊞ Liz Farrow t/a Dodo, Stand F071/73, Alfie's Antique Market, 13–25 Church Street, London NW8 8DT Tel: 020 7706 1545

DPC § Devon Pottery Collectors Group, Mrs Joyce Stonelake, 19 St Margarets Avenue, Torquay, Devon TQ1 4LW Tel: 01803 327277 Virginia.Brisco@care4free.net

DSG ⊞ Market Street Gallery Ltd t/a Delf Stream Gallery, Bournemouth, Dorset Tel: 07974 926137 oastman@aol.com www.delfstreamgallery.com

DuM ⚒ Du Mouchelles, 409 East Jefferson, Detroit, Michigan 48226, USA Tel: 313 963 6255

DW ⚒† Dominic Winter Book Auctions, The Old School, Maxwell Street, Swindon, Wiltshire SN1 5DR Tel: 01793 611340 info@dominicwinter.co.uk www.dominicwinter.co.uk

E ⚒ Ewbank Auctioneers, Burnt Common Auction Rooms, London Road, Send, Woking, Surrey GU23 7LN Tel: 01483 223101 antiques@ewbankauctions.co.uk www.ewbankauctions.co.uk

EAL ⊞ The Exeter Antique Lighting Co, Cellar 15, The Quay, Exeter, Devon EX2 4AP Tel: 01392 490848 Mob: 07702 969438 www.antiquelightingcompany.com

Ech ⊞† Echoes, 650a Halifax Road, Eastwood, Todmorden, Yorkshire OL14 6DW Tel: 01706 817505

EE ⊞ Empire Exchange, 1 Newton Street, Piccadilly, Greater Manchester Tel: 0161 2364445

EH ⚒ Edgar Horns, 46–50 South Street, Eastbourne, East Sussex BN21 4XB Tel: 01323 410419 sales@edgarhorns.com www.edgarhorns.com

ES ⊞ Ernest R. Sampson, 33 West End, Redruth, Cornwall TR15 2SA Tel: 01209 212536

ETO ⊞ Eric Tombs, 62a West Street, Dorking, Surrey RH4 1BS Tel: 01306 743661 ertombs@aol.com www.dorkingantiques.com

EV ⊞ Marlene Evans, Headrow Antiques Centre, Headrow Centre, Leeds, Yorkshire Tel: 0113 245 5344

EXC ⊞ Excalibur Antiques, Taunton Antique Centre, 27–29 Silver Street Taunton Somerset TA1 3DH Tel: 01823 289327/07774 627409 pauldwright@btinternet.com www.excaliburantiques.com

F&C ⚒ Finan & Co, The Square, Mere, Wiltshire BA12 6DJ Tel: 01747 861411 post@finanandco.co.uk www.finanandco.co.uk

F&F ⊞ Fenwick & Fenwick, 88–90 High Street, Broadway, Worcestershire WR12 7AJ Tel: 01386 853227/841724

FHF ⚒† Fellows & Sons, Augusta House, 19 Augusta Street, Hockley, Birmingham, West Midlands B18 6JA Tel: 0121 212 2131 info@fellows.co.uk www.fellows.co.uk

FLD ⊞ Flying Duck, 320/322 Creek Road, Greenwich, London SE10 9SW Tel: 020 8858 1964 Mob: 07831 273303

FMN ⊞† Forget-Me-Knot Antiques, Antiques at Over the Moon, 27 High Street, St Albans, Hertfordshire AL3 4EH Tel: 01923 261172 Mob: 07941 255489 sharpffocus@hotmail.com

FOX ⊞ Fox Cottage Antiques, Digbeth Street, Stow-on-the-Wold, Gloucestershire GL54 1BN Tel: 01451 870307

G ⚒ Gorringes Auction Galleries, Terminus Road, Bexhill-on-Sea, East Sussex TN39 3LR Tel: 01424 212994 bexhill@gorringes.co.uk www.gorringes.co.uk

G(L) ⚒ Gorringes inc Julian Dawson, 15 North Street, Lewes, East Sussex BN7 2PD Tel: 01273 478221 auctions@gorringes.co.uk www.gorringes.co.uk

G&CC ⊞† Goss & Crested China Centre & Museum, inc Milestone Publications, 62 Murray Road, Horndean, Hampshire PO8 9JL Tel: (023) 9259 7440 info@gosschinaclub.demon.co.uk www.gosscrestedchina.co.uk

GAC ⊞ Gloucester Antiques Centre, The Historic Docks, 1 Severn Road, Gloucester GL1 2LE Tel: 01452 529716 www.antiques.center.com

GBM ⊞† GB Military Antiques, Antiquarius Antiques Centre, 131/141 Kings Road, Chelsea, London SW3 4PW Tel: 020 7351 5357 info@gbmilitaria.com www.gbmilitaria.com

GBr ⊞ Geoffrey Breeze Antiques, Top Banana Antiques Mall, 1 New Street, Tetbury, Gloucestershire GL8 8OS Tel: 01225 466499 antiques@geoffreybreeze.co.uk

GGv ⊞ G. G. van Schagen Antiquair Tel: 0031 229 275692 Mob: 06 51 393975 g.schagen@wxs.nl

GK ⚒ Auction Team Koln, Postfach 50 11 19, 50971 Koln, Germany Tel: 00 49 0221 38 70 49 auction@breker.com

GLB ⊞ Glebe Antiques, Scottish Antique Centre, Doune FK16 6HG, Scotland Tel: 01259 214559 Mob: 07050 234577 RRGlebe@aol.com

GM ⊞† Philip Knighton, Bush House, 17B South Street, Wellington, Somerset TA21 8NR Tel: 01823 661618 philip.knighton@btopenworld.com

GRe ⊞ Greystoke Antiques, 4 Swan Yard, (off Cheap Street), Sherborne, Dorset DT9 3AX Tel: 01935 812833

GRI ⊞† Grimes House Antiques, High Street, Moreton-in-Marsh, Gloucestershire GL56 0AT Tel: 01608 651029 grimes_house@cix.co.uk www.grimeshouse.co.uk www.collectglass.com www.cranberryglass.co.uk

GRo ⊞ Geoffrey Robinson, GO77–78, GO91–92 (Ground floor), Alfie's Antique Market, 13–25 Church Street, Marylebone, London NW8 8DT Tel: 020 7723 0449 info@alfiesantiques.com www.alfiesantiques.com

GTM ⊞ Gloucester Toy Mart, Ground Floor, Antique Centre, Severn Road, Old Docks, Gloucester GL1 2LE Mob: 07973 768452

H&G ⊞ Hope & Glory, 131A Kensington Church Street, London W8 7LP Tel: 020 7727 8424

H&H ⚒ H & H Classic Auctions Ltd, Whitegate Farm, Hatton Lane, Hatton, Warrington, Cheshire WA4 4BZ Tel: 01925 730630 www.classic-auctions.co.uk

HAA ⊞ Hampton Antiques, The Crown Arcade, 119 Portobello Road, London W11 2DY Tel: 01604 863979 Mob: 07779 654879 info@hamptonantiques.co.uk www.hamptonantiques.co.uk

HaG ⊞ Harington Glass, 2–3 Queen Street, Bath, Somerset BA1 1HE Tel: 01225 482179

HaH ⊞ Hayman & Hayman, Antiquarius Stand K3, 135 Kings Road, London SW3 4PW Tel: 020 7351 6568 Mob: 07742 987715 georgina@haymanframes.co.uk

HAK ⊞ Paul Haskell Tel: 01634 891796 Mob: 07774 781160 www.antiqueslotmachines.inuk.com

HAL ⊞† John & Simon Haley, 89 Northgate, Halifax, Yorkshire HX1 1XF Tel: 01422 822148/360434 toysandbanks@aol.com

HaR ⊞ Mr A. Harris Tel: 020 8906 8151 Mob: 079 56 146083

HarC ⊞ Hardy's Collectables Tel: 07970 613077 www.poolepotteryjohn.com

HARP ⊞† Harpers Jewellers Ltd, 2/6 Minster Gates, York YO1 7HL Tel: 01904 632634 harpersyork@btopenworld.com www.vintage-watches.co.uk

HAYS ⚒ Hays & Associates, Inc, 120 South Spring Street, Louisville, Kentucky 40206, USA Tel: 502 584 4297 www.haysauction.com

HEG ⊞† Stuart Heggie, 14 The Borough, Northgate, Canterbury, Kent CT1 2DR Tel: 01227 470422 Mob: 0783 3593344

HEL ⊞ Helios Gallery, 292 Westbourne Grove, London W11 2PS Tel: 077 11 955 997 heliosgallery@btinternet.com www.heliosgallery.com

HiA ⊞ Rupert Hitchcox Antiques, Warpsgrove, Nr Chalgrove, Oxford OX44 7RW Tel: 01865 890241 www.ruperthitchcoxantiques.co.uk

HILL ⊞ Hillhaven Antique Linen & Lace Tel: 0121 358 4320

HIP ⊞† Hilary Proctor, Vintage Modes, Shop 6 Admiral Vernon Antiques Market, 141–151 Portobello Road, London W11 2DY Tel: 07956 876428 hproctor@antiquehandbags.fsnet.co.uk

HIS ⊞ Erna Hiscock & John Shepherd, Chelsea Galleries, 69 Portobello Road, London W11 Tel: 01233 661407 Mob: 0771 562 7273

HL ⊞ Honiton Lace Shop, 44 High Street, Honiton, Devon EX14 1PJ Tel: 01404 42416 shop@honitonlace.com www.honitonlace.com

HO ⊞ Houghton Antiques Tel: 01480 461887 Mob: 07803 716842

HOR § Hornsea Pottery Collectors' and Research Society, c/o Peter Tennant, 128 Devonshire Street, Keighley, West Yorkshire BD21 2QJ hornsea@pdtennant.fsnet.co.uk www.hornseacollector.co.uk

HPCS § Honiton Pottery Collectors' Society, Robin Tinkler (Chairman), 2 Redyear Cottages, Kennington Road, Ashford, Kent TN24 0TF hpcs@moshpit.cix.co.uk www.hpcs.info

HRQ ⊞ Harlequin Antiques, 79–81 Mansfield Road, Daybrook, Nottingham NG5 6BH Tel: 0115 967 4590 sales@antiquepine.net www.antiquepine.net

HSt ⊞ High Street Antiques, 39 High Street, Hastings, East Sussex TN34 3ER Tel: 01424 460068

HTE ⊞ Heritage, 6 Market Place, Woodstock, Oxfordshire OX20 1TA Tel: 01993 811332 or 0870 4440678 Mob: 07831 850544 dealers@atheritage.co.uk www.atheritage.co.uk

HUM ⊞ Humbleyard Fine Art, Unit 32 Admiral Vernon Arcade, Portobello Road, London W11 2DY Tel: 01362 637793 Mob: 07836 349416

HUN ⊞ The Country Seat, Huntercombe Manor Barn, Henley-on-Thames, Oxfordshire RG9 5RY Tel: 01491 641349 wclegg@thecountryseat.com www.thecountryseat.com

HUX ⊞ David Huxtable, Sat at: Portobello Road, Basement Stall 11/12, 288 Westbourne Grove, London W11 Tel: 07710 132200 david@huxtins.com

HYP ⊞ Hyperion Collectables

ID ⊞ Identity, 100 Basement Flat, Finsborough Road, London SW10 9ED Tel: 020 7244 9509

J&J ⊞ J & J's, Paragon Antiquities Antiques & Collectors Market, 3 Bladud Buildings, The Paragon, Bath, Somerset BA1 5LS Tel: 01225 463715

J&S ⊞ J. R. & S. J. Symes of Bristol Tel: 0117 9501074

JAd ⚒ James Adam & Sons, 26 St Stephen's Green, Dublin 2, Republic of Ireland Tel: 00 3531 676 0261

JAM ⊞ Jam Jar Tel: 078896 17593

JAS ⊞ Jasmin Cameron, Antiquarius, 131–141 King's Road, London SW3 4PW Tel: 020 7351 4154 Mob: 077 74 871257 jasmin.cameron@mail.com

JAY ⊞ Jaycee Bee Antiques

JAZZ ⊞ Jazz Art Deco Tel: 07721 032277 jazzartdeco@btinternet.com www.jazzartdeco.com

JBB ⊞ Jessie's Button Box, Bartlett Street Antique Centre, Bath, Somerset BA1 5DY Tel: 0117 929 9065

JBL ⊞ Judi Bland Antiques Tel: 01276 857576 or 01536 724145

JBM ⊞ Jim Bullock Militaria, PO Box 217, Romsey, Hampshire SO51 5XL Tel: 01794 516455 jim@jimbullockmilitaria.com www.jimbullockmilitaria.com

JDJ ⚒ James D. Julia, Inc, PO Box 830, Rte 201 Skowhegan Road, Fairfield ME 04937, USA Tel: 207 453 7125 jjulia@juliaauctions.com www.juliaauctions.com

JHa ⊞ Jeanette Hayhurst Fine Glass, 32a Kensington Church Street, London W8 4HA Tel: 020 7938 1539

JHo ⊞ Jonathan Horne, 66 Kensington Church Street, London W8 4BY Tel: 020 7221 5658 JH@jonathanhorne.co.uk www.jonathanhorne.co.uk

JHS § Jonathan Harris Studio Glass Ltd, Woodland House, 24 Peregrine Way, Apley Castle, Telford, Shropshire TF1 6TH Tel: 01952 246381/588441 jonathan@jhstudioglass.com www.jhstudioglass.com

JMC ⊞ J & M Collectables Tel: 01580 891657 Mob: 077135 23573 jandmcollectables@tinyonline.co.uk

JMM ⊞ JMM Collectibles Ltd, Scottish Antiques & Arts Centre, Abernyte, Perthshire, Scotland PH14 9SL Tel: 01828 686 401 Mob: 07734 543323 jmmiddlemiss@freeuk.com

JOA ⊞ Joan Gale Antiques Dealer, Tombland Antiques Centre, 14 Tombland, Norwich, Norfolk NR3 1HF Tel: 01603 619129 joan.gale@ukgateway.net

JOL ⊞ Kaizen International Ltd, 88 The High Street, Rochester, Kent ME1 1JT Tel: 01634 814132

JON ⊞ Jonkers, 24 Hart Street, Henley on Thames, Oxfordshire RG9 2AU Tel: 01491 576427 bromlea.jonkers@bjbooks.co.uk www.bjbooks.co.uk

JPr ⊞† Antique Textiles & Lighting, Joanna Proops, 34 Belvedere, Lansdown Hill, Bath, Somerset BA1 5HR Tel: 01225 310795 antiquetextiles@aol.co.uk www.antiquetextiles.co.uk

JTS ⊞ June & Tony Stone Fine Antique Boxes, PO Box 106, Peacehaven, East Sussex BN10 8AU Tel: 01273 579333 rachel@boxes.co.uk www.boxes.co.uk

JuC ⊞ Julia Craig, Bartlett Street Antiques Centre, 5–10 Bartlett Street, Bath, Somerset BA1 2QZ Tel: 01225 448202/310457 Mob: 07771 786846

JUJ ⊞ Just Jewellery

JUN ⊞† Junktion, The Old Railway Station, New Bolingbroke, Boston, Lincolnshire PE22 7LB Tel: 01205 480068/480087 Mob: 07836 345491

KA ⊞ Kingston Antiques Centre, 29–31 London Road, Kingston-upon-Thames, Surrey KT2 6ND Tel: 020 8549 2004/3839 enquiries@kingstonantiquescentre.co.uk www.kingstonantiquescentre.co.uk

KES ⊞† Keystones, PO Box 387, Stafford ST16 3FG Tel: 01785 256648 gkey@keystones.demon.co.uk www.keystones.co.uk

KEY ⊞ Key Antiques of Chipping Norton, 11 Horsefair, Chipping Norton, Oxfordshire OX7 5AL Tel: 01608 644992 info@keyantiques.com www.keyantiques.com

KMG ⊞ Karen Michelle Guido, Karen Michelle Antique Tiles, PO Box 62, Blairsville PA 15717, USA Tel: (724) 459 6669 Karen@antiquetiles.com www.antiquetiles.com

L&E ⚒ Locke & England, 18 Guy Street, Leamington Spa, Warwickshire CV32 4RT Tel: 01926 889100 www.auctions-online.com/locke

L&L ⊞† Linen & Lace, Shirley Tomlinson, Halifax Antiques Centre, Queens Road/Gibbet Street, Halifax, Yorkshire HX1 4LR Tel: 01484 540492/01422 366657

LaF ⊞ La Femme Tel: 07971 844279 jewels@joancorder.freeserve.co.uk

LBe ⊞ Linda Bee Art Deco, Stand L18–21, Grays Antique Market, 1–7 Davies Mews, London W1Y 1AR Tel: 020 7629 5921

LBr ⊞ Lynda Brine, Assembly Antiques, 6 Saville Row, Bath, Somerset BA1 2QP Tel: 01225 448488 lyndabrine@yahoo.co.uk www.scentbottlesandsmalls.co.uk

LCC ⊞† The London Cigarette Card Co Ltd, Sutton Road, Somerton, Somerset TA11 6QP Tel: 01458 273452 cards@londoncigcard.co.uk www.londoncigcard.co.uk

LCM ⚒ Galeria Louis C. Morton, GLC A7073L IYS, Monte Athos 179, Col Lomas de Chapultepec CP11000, Mexico Tel: 52 5520 5005 glmorton@prodigy.net.mx www.lmorton.com

LENA ⊞ Lena Baldock, Mint Arcade, 71 The Mint, Rye, East Sussex TN31 7EW Tel: 01797 225952

LGU ⊞ Linda Gumb, Stand 123, Grays Antique Market, 58 Davies Street, London W1K 5LP Tel: 020 7629 2544 linda@lindagumb.com

LU ⊞ Lucia Collectables, Stalls 57–58 Admiral Vernon Antique Arcade, Portobello Road (open Sat), London Tel: 01793 790607 sallie_ead@lycos.com

LUNA ⊞ Luna, 23 George Street, Nottingham NG1 3BH Tel: 0115 924 3267 info@luna-online.co.uk www.luna-online.co.uk

MARG ⊞† Margaret Williamson, Vintage Modes, Grays Antique Market, 1–7 Davies Mews, Mayfair, London W1K 5AB Tel: 020 740 90 400 chelsealace@aol.com www.vintagemodes.co.uk

MARK ⊞† 20th Century Marks, 12 Market Square, Westerham, Kent TN16 1AW Tel: 01959 562221 Mob: 07831 778992 lambarda@btconnect.com www.20thcenturymarks.co.uk

MB ⊞† Mostly Boxes, 93 High Street, Eton, Windsor, Berkshire SL4 6AF Tel: 01753 858470

MCa ⊞ Mia Cartwright Tel: 07956 440260 mia.cartwright@virgin.net

MCC ⊞ M. C. Chapman Antiques, Bell Hill, Finedon, Northamptonshire NN9 5NB Tel: 01933 681260

McD § UK McDonald's & Fast Food Collectors Club, c/o Lawrence Yap, 110 Tithelands, Harlow, Essex CM19 5ND bigkidandtoys@ntlworld.com

MCL ⊞† Millennium Collectables Ltd, PO Box 146, Eastwood, Nottingham NG16 3SP Tel: 01773 769335 mail@millenniumcollectables.co.uk

McP ⊞ R & G McPherson Antiques, 40 Kensington Church Street, London W8 4BX Tel: 020 7937 0812 Mob: 07768 432 630 rmcpherson@orientalceramics.com www.orientalceramics.com

MDe ⊞† Mike Delaney Tel: 01993 840064 Mob: 07979 919760 mike@vintagehornby.co.uk www.vintagehornby.co.uk

MDL ⊞ Michael D Long Ltd, 96–98 Derby Road, Nottingham NG1 5FB Tel: 0115 941 3307 sales@michaeldlong.com www.michaeldlong.com

MEA ⚒ Mealy's, Chatsworth Street, Castle Comer, Co Kilkenny, Republic of Ireland Tel: 56 41229 www.mealys.com

MEM § Memories UK Mabel Lucie Attwell Club, Abbey Antiques, 63 Great Whyte, Ramsey, Nr Huntingdon, Cambridgeshire PE26 1HL Tel: 01487 814753

MFB ⊞ Manor Farm Barn Antiques Tel: 01296 658941 Mob: 07720 286607 mfbn@btinternet.com btwebworld.com/mfbantiques

MGC ⊞ Midlands Goss & Commemoratives, The Old Cornmarket Antiques Centre, 70 Market Place, Warwick CV34 4SO Tel: 01926 419119

MINN ⊞ Geoffrey T. Minnis, Hastings Antique Centre, 59–61 Norman Road, St Leonards-on-Sea, East Sussex TN38 0EG Tel: 01424 428561

ML ⊞ Memory Lane, Bartlett Street Antiques Centre, 5/10 Bartlett Street, Bath, Somerset BA1 2QZ Tel: 01225 466689/310457

MLL ⊞ Millers Antiques Ltd, Netherbrook House, 86 Christchurch Road, Ringwood, Hampshire BH24 1DR Tel: 01425 472062 mail@millers-antiques.co.uk www.millers-antiques.co.uk

Mo ⊞ Mr Moore

MPC ⊞† M C Pottery Tel: 01244 301800 Sales@Moorcroftchester.co.uk www.Moorcroftchester.co.uk

MRW ⊞ Malcolm Welch Antiques, Wild Jebbett, Pudding Bag Lane, Thurlaston, Nr Rugby, Warwickshire CV23 9JZ Tel: 01788 810 616 www.rb33.co.uk

MSB ⊞ Marilynn and Sheila Brass, PO Box 380503, Cambridge MA 02238–0503, USA Tel: 617 491 6064

MSh ⊞ Manfred Schotten, 109 High Street, Burford, Oxfordshire OX18 4RG Tel: 01993 822302 www.antiques@£schotten.com

MTMC § Muffin the Mule Collectors' Club, 12 Woodland Close, Woodford Green, Essex IG8 0QH Tel: 020 8504 4943 adrienne@hasler.gotadsl.co.uk www.Muffin-the-Mule.com

MUL ⚒† Mullock & Madeley, The Old Shippon, Wall-under-Heywood, Nr Church Stretton, Shropshire SY6 7DS Tel: 01694 771771 auctions@mullockmadeley.co.uk www.mullockmadeley.co.uk

MUR ⊞† Murray Cards (International) Ltd, 51 Watford Way, Hendon Central, London NW4 3JH Tel: 020 8202 5688 murraycards@ukbusiness.com www.murraycard.com/

MURR ⊞ Murrays' Antiques & Collectables Tel: 01202 309094

NAR ⊞ Colin Narbeth & Son Ltd, 20 Cecil Court, Leicester Square, London WC2N 4HE Tel: 020 7379 6975 Colin.Narbeth@btinternet.com www.colin-narbeth.com

NBL ⊞ N. Bloom & Son (1912) Ltd, 12 Piccadilly Arcade, London SW1Y 6NH Tel: 020 7629 5060 nbloom@nbloom.com www.nbloom.com

NEG ⊞ C. Negrillo Antiques, Antiquarius P1/P2/P3, 135 Kings Road, London SW3 4PW Tel: 020 7349 0038 Mob: 07778 336 781 negrilloc@aol.com

NFR ⊞ The 40's Room, Unit 40 Rugeley Antiques Centre, Main Road, Brereton, Rugeley, Staffordshire WS15 1DX Tel: 01889 577166 info@cc41homefrontdisplays.co.uk

NLS ⊞ Lenson-Smith, 153 Portobello Road, London W11 2DY Tel: 020 8340 8767 Mob: 07774 196932

NOS ⊞ Nostalgia and Comics, 14–16 Smallbrook Queensway, City Centre, Birmingham, West Midlands B5 4EN Tel: 0121 643 0143

NW ⊞ Nigel Williams Rare Books, 25 Cecil Court, London WC2N 4EZ Tel: 020 7836 7757 nigel@nigelwilliams.com www.nigelwilliams.com

OH ⊞ Old Hat, 66 Fulham High Road, London SW6 3LQ Tel: 020 7610 6558

OIA ⊞ The Old Ironmongers Antiques Centre, 5 Burford Street, Lechlade, Gloucestershire GL7 3AP Tel: 01367 252397

OLA ⊞ Olliff's Architectural Antiques, 19–21 Lower Redland Road, Redland, Bristol, Gloucestershire BS6 6TB Tel: 0117 923 9232 marcus@olliffs.com www.olliffs.com

OLD ⊞ Oldnautibits, PO Box 67, Langport, Somerset TA10 9WJ Tel: 01458 241816 geoff.pringle@oldnautibits.com www.oldnautibits.com

ONS ⚒ Onslow's Auctions Ltd, The Coach House, Manor Road, Stourpaine, Dorset DT8 8TQ Tel: 01258 488838

OPB ⊞ Olde Port Bookshop, 18 State Street, Newburyport, Massachusetts 01950, USA Tel: 978 462 0100 Oldeport@ttlc.net

ORI ⊞ Origin 101, Gateway Arcade, Islington High Street, London N1 Tel: 07769 686146/ 07747 758852 david@origin101.co.uk www.naturalmodern.com www.origin101.co.uk

OSF ⊞ Olde Scissors Factory Antiques, 107 Avenue L, Matamoras PA 18336, USA Tel: 570 491 2707 toyfolks@warwick.net

OTA ⊞† On The Air, The Vintage Technology Centre, The Highway Hawarden, (Nr Chester), Deeside CH5 3DN Tel: 01244 530300 Mob: 07778 767734 www.vintageradio.co.uk

OTB ⊞† The Old Tackle Box, PO Box 55, Cranbrook, Kent TN17 3ZU Tel: 01580 713979 Mob: 07729 278 293 tackle.box@virgin.net

OW ⊞ Offworld, 142 Market Halls, Arndale Center, Luton, Bedfordshire LU1 2TP Tel: 01582 736256 off_world@btconnect.com

PaA ⊞ Pastorale Antiques, 15 Malling Street, Lewes, East Sussex BN7 2RA Tel: 01273 473259 or 01435 863044 pastorale@btinternet.com

PCC § Paperweight Collectors Circle, PO Box 941, Comberton, Cambridgeshire CB3 7GQ Tel: 02476 386172

PCCC § Pedal Car Collectors' Club (P.C.C.C.), Sec A. P. Gayler, 4/4a Chapel Terrace Mews, Kemp Town, Brighton, East Sussex BN2 1HU Tel: 01273 601960 www.brmmbrmm.com/pedalcars

PeJ ⊞ Peter Jones, Dept 1128, 22 Westgate, Wakefield, Yorkshire WF1 1LB Tel: 01924 362510 www.peterjoneschina.com

Penn ⊞ Penny Fair Antiques Tel: 07860 825456

PEZ ⊞ Alan Pezaro, 62a West Street, Dorking, Surrey RH4 1BS Tel: 01306 743661

PF ⚒ Peter Francis, Curiosity Sale Room, 19 King Street, Carmarthen SA31 1BH, Wales Tel: 01267 233456 Peterfrancis@valuers.fsnet.co.uk www.peterfrancis.co.uk

PFK ⚒ Penrith Farmers' & Kidd's plc, Skirsgill Salerooms, Penrith, Cumbria CA11 0DN Tel: 01768 890781 penrith.farmers@virgin.net www.penrithfarmers.co.uk

PGO ⊞ Pamela Goodwin, 11 The Pantiles, Royal Tunbridge Wells, Kent TN2 5TD Tel: 01892 618200 mail@goodwinantiques.co.uk www.goodwinantiques.co.uk

PIC ⊞ David & Susan Pickles Tel: 01282 707673/ 07976 236983

PICC ⊞† Piccypicky.com Tel: 020 8204 2001/ 020 8206 2001 www.piccypicky.com

PIL ⊞ Pilgrim Antique Centre, 7 West Street, Dorking, Surrey RH4 Tel: 01306 875028

PLB ⊞ Planet Bazaar, 149 Drummond Street, London NW1 2PB Tel: 020 7387 8326 Mob: 07956 326301 info@planetbazaar.co.uk www.planetbazaar.co.uk

POL ⊞ Politico Book Shop, 8 Artillery Row, London SW1 Tel: 020 7828 0010

POLL ⊞ Pollyanna, 34 High Street, Arundel, West Sussex BN18 9AB Tel: 01903 885198 Mob: 07949 903457

PPH ⊞ Period Picnic Hampers Tel: 0115 937 2934

PPL ⊞ The Pen and Pencil Lady Tel: 01647 231619 penpencilady@aol.com www.penpencilady.com

PrB ⊞† Pretty Bizarre, 170 High Street, Deal, Kent CT14 6BQ Tel: 07973 794537

PSA ⊞ Pantiles Spa Antiques, 4, 5, 6 Union House, The Pantiles, Tunbridge Wells, Kent TN4 8HE Tel: 01892 541377 Mob: 07711 283655 psa.wells@btinternet.com www.antiques-tun-wells-kent.co.uk

PTh ⊞ Antique Clocks by Patrick Thomas, 62a West Street, Dorking, Surrey RH4 1BS Tel: 01306 743661 clockman@fsmail.net

Q&C ⊞ Q & C Militaria, 22 Suffolk Road, Cheltenham, Gloucestershire GL50 2AQ Tel: 01242 519815 Mob: 07778 613977 www.qcmilitaria.com john@qc-militaria.freeserve.co.uk

QW ⊞ Quiet Woman Antiques Centre, Southcombe, Chipping Norton, Oxfordshire OX7 5QH Tel: 01608 646262

RAND ⊞ Becky Randall, 36 Highfield Road, Wilmslow, Buckinghamshire MK18 3DU Tel: 07979 848440

RBA ⊞† Roger Bradbury Antiques, Church Street, Coltishall, Norfolk NR12 7DJ Tel: 01603 737444

RCo ⊞ Royal Commemorative China Tel: 020 8863 0625 royalcommemorative@hotmail.com

REG No longer trading

REPS ⊞ Repsycho, 85 Gloucester Road, Bishopston, Bristol BS7 8AS Tel: 0117 9830007

RER ⊞† Red Roses, Vintage modes, Shops 57 & 58, Admiral Vernon Antiques Markets, 141–149 Portobello Road, London W11 2DY Tel: 01793 790 607 Mob: 07778 803 876 sallie_ead@lycos.com

RET ⊞ Retro-Spective Tel: 07989 984659 fineart692hotmail.com

RGa ⊞ Richard Gardner Antiques, Swanhouse, Market Square, Petworth, West Sussex GU28 0AN Tel: 01798 343411

RGA ⊞ Richard Gibbon, Shop 4, 34/34a Islington Green, London N1 8DU Tel: 020 7354 2852 Mob: 07958 674447 neljeweluk@aol.com

RGe ⊞ Rupert Gentle Antiques, The Manor House, Milton Lilbourne, Nr Pewsey, Wiltshire SN9 5LQ Tel: 01672 563344

RH ⊞ Rick Hubbard Art Deco, 3 Tee Court, Bell Street, Romsey, Hampshire SO51 8GY Tel: 01794 513133 Mob: 07767 267607 rick@rickhubbard-artdeco.co.uk www.rickhubbard-artdeco.co.uk

RMo ⊞ Rugby Memories, 2 Chalkshire Cottages, Chalkshire Road, Butlers Cross, Buckinghamshire HP17 0TW sales@rugbymemories.com www.rugbymemories.com

RTo 🔨 Rupert Toovey & Co Ltd, Spring Gardens, Washington, West Sussex RH20 3BS Tel: 01903 891955 auctions@rupert-toovey.com www.rupert-toovey.com

RTT ⊞ Rin Tin Tin, 34 North Road, Brighton, East Sussex BN1 1YB Tel: 01273 672424 rick@rintintin.freeserve.co.uk

RTW ⊞† Richard Twort Tel: 01934 641900 Mob: 077 11 939789

RUSK ⊞ Ruskin Decorative Arts, 5 Talbot Court, Stow-on-the-Wold, Cheltenham, Gloucestershire GL54 1DP Tel: 01451 832254 william.anne@ruskindecarts.co.uk

RUSS ⊞ Russells Tel: 023 8061 6664

RW ⊞ Robin Wareham

RWA ⊞ Ray Walker Antiques, Burton Arcade, 296 Westbourne Grove, London W11 2PS Tel: 020 8464 7981 rw.antiques@btinternet.com

S(O) 🔨 Sotheby's Olympia, Hammersmith Road, London W14 8UX Tel: 020 7293 5555 www.sothebys.com

S&D ⊞ S&D Postcards, Bartlett Street Antique Centre, 5–10 Bartlett Street, Bath, Somerset BA1 2QZ winstampok@netscapeonline.co.uk

SA ⊞ Sporting Antiques Tel: 01480 463891 john.lambden@virgin.net

SAAC ⊞ Scottish Antique and Arts Centre, Carse of Cambus, Doune, Perthshire, Scotland FK16 6HD Tel: 01786 841203

SaB ⊞ Sara Bernstein Antique Dolls & Bears, Englishtown, New Jersey 07726, USA Tel: 732 536 4101 santiqbebe@aol.com www.sarabernsteindolls.com

SaH ⊞ Sally Hawkins Tel: 01636 636666 sallytiles@aol.com

SAS 🔨† Special Auction Services, Kennetholme, Midgham, Reading, Berkshire RG7 5UX Tel: 0118 971 2949 www.invaluable.com/sas/

SAT ⊞ The Swan at Tetsworth, High Street, Tetsworth, Nr Thame, Oxfordshire OX9 7AB Tel: 01844 281777 antiques@theswan.co.uk www.theswan.co.uk

SBL ⊞ Twentieth Century Style Tel: 01822 614831

SDA ⊞ Stephanie Davison Antiques, Bakewell Antiques Centre, King Street, Bakewell, Derbyshire DE45 1DZ Tel: 01629 812496 Mob: 07771 564 993 bacc@chappells-antiques.co.uk www.chappells-antiques.co.uk

SDP ⊞ Stage Door Prints, 9 Cecil Court, London WC2N 4EZ Tel: 020 7240 1683

SEA ⊞ Mark Seabrook Antiques, PO Box 396, Huntingdon, Cambridgeshire PE28 0ZA Tel: 01480 861935 Mob: 07770 721931 enquiries@markseabrook.com www.markseabrook.com

SER ⊞ Serendipity, 125 High Street, Deal, Kent CT14 6BB Tel: 01304 369165/01304 366536 dipityantiques@aol.com

SHa ⊞ Shapiro & Co, Stand 380, Gray's Antique Market, 58 Davies Street, London W1K 5LP Tel: 020 7491 2710

SJH 🔨 S. J. Hales, 87 Fore Street, Bovey Tracey, Devon TQ13 9AB Tel: 01626 836684

SMI ⊞† Skip & Janie Smithson Antiques Tel: 01754 810265 Mob: 07831 399180 smithsonantiques@hotmail.com

SOR ⊞ Soldiers of Rye, Mint Arcade, 71 The Mint, Rye, East Sussex TN31 7EW Tel: 01797 225952 rameses@supanet.com chris@johnbartholomewcards.co.uk www.rameses.supanet.com

SPA ⊞ Sporting Antiques, 10 Union Square, The Pantiles, Tunbridge Wells, Kent TN4 8HE Tel: 01892 522661

SPE ⊞ Sylvie Spectrum, Stand 372, Grays Market, 58 Davies Street, London W1Y 2LB Tel: 020 7629 3501

SpM ⊞ Sparkle Moore, The Girl Can't Help It!, Alfie's Antique Market, G100 & G116 Ground Floor, 13–25 Church Street, Marylebone, London NW8 8DT Tel: 020 7724 8984 Mob: 07958 515614 sparkle.moore@virgin.net www.sparklemoore.com

SRA 🔨† Sheffield Railwayana Auctions, 43 Little Norton Lane, Sheffield, Yorkshire S8 8GA Tel: 0114 274 5085 Mob: 07860 921519 ian@sheffrail.freeserve.co.uk www.sheffieldrailwayana.co.uk

SSF ⊞ Suffolk Sci-Fi and Fantasy, 17 Norwich Road, Ipswich, Suffolk Tel: 01473 400655 Mob: 07885 298361 mick@suffolksci-fi.com www.suffolksci-fi.com

SSL ⊞ Star Signings Ltd, The Burbeque Gallery, 16a New Quebec Street, London W1H 7DG Tel: 020 7723 8498 starsignings@btconnect.com

SSM ⊞ Sue Scott Motoring Memorabilia Tel: 01525 372757

STA ⊞ George Stacpoole, Main Street, Adare, Co Limerick, Republic of Ireland Tel: 00 353 (0) 6139 6409 stacpoole@iol.ie www.georgestacpooleantiques.com

StC ⊞ Carlton Factory Shop, Carlton Works, Copeland Street, Stoke-on-Trent, Staffordshire ST4 1PU Tel: 01782 410504

StDA 🔨 St. David's Auctions, Mill Road Trading Estate, Barnstaple, North Devon EX31 1JH Tel: 01271 343123 info@stdavidsauctions.co.uk www.stdavidsauctions.co.uk

STS ⊞ Shaw to Shore Tel: 07970 178636

SUW ⊞ Sue Wilde at Wildewear Tel: 01395 577966 compacts@wildewear.co.uk www.wildewear.co.uk

SWB ⊞† Sweetbriar Gallery Paperweights Ltd, 3 Collinson Court, off Church Street, Frodsham, Cheshire WA6 6PN Tel: 01928 730064 sales@sweetbriar.co.uk www.sweetbriar.co.uk

SWN ⊞ Swan Antiques, Stone Street, Cranbrook, Kent TN17 3HF Tel: 01580 712720

SWO 🔨 Sworders, 14 Cambridge Road, Stansted Mountfitchet, Essex CM24 8BZ Tel: 01279 817778 www.sworder.co.uk

T&D ⊞ Toys & Dolls, 367 Fore Street, Edmonton, London N9 0NR Tel: 020 8807 3301

TAC ⊞ Tenterden Antiques Centre, 66–66A High Street, Tenterden, Kent TN30 6AU Tel: 01580 765655/765885

TASV ⊞ Tenterden Antiques & Silver Vaults, 66 High Street, Tenterden, Kent TN30 6AU Tel: 01580 765885

TB ⊞ Millicent Safro, Tender Buttons, 143 E.62nd Street, New York NY10021, USA Tel: 212 758 7004 Author of BUTTONS

TDG ⊞ The Design Gallery 1850–1950, 5 The Green, Westerham, Kent TN16 1AS Tel: 01959 561234 Mob: 07974 322858 sales@thedesigngallery.uk.com www.thedesigngallery.uk.com

TH ⊞† Tony Horsley, PO Box 3127, Brighton, East Sussex BN1 5SS Tel: 01273 550770

TIC ⊞† Tickers, 37 Northam Road, Southampton, Hampshire SO14 0PD Tel: 02380 234431 kmonckton@btopenworld.com

TIN ⊞† Tin Tin Collectables, G38–42 Alfie's Antique Market, 13–25 Church Street, Marylebone, London NW8 8DT Tel: 020 7258 1305 leslie@tintincollectables.com www.tintincollectables.com

TL ⊞† Telephone Lines Ltd, 304 High Street, Cheltenham, Gloucestershire GL50 3JF Tel: 01242 583699 info@telephonelines.net www.telephonelines.net

TMA 🔨 Tring Market Auctions, The Market Premises, Brook Street, Tring, Hertfordshire HP23 5EF Tel: 01442 826446 sales@tringmarketauctions.co.uk www.tringmarketauctions.co.uk

TMa ⊞ Tin Man Tel: 01480 463891 john.lambden@virgin.net

TML ⊞ Timothy Millett Ltd, Historic Medals and Works of Art, PO Box 20851, London SE22 0YN Tel: 020 8693 1111 Mob: 07778 637 898 tim@timothymillett.demon.co.uk

TNS ⊞ Toy's N Such Toy's – Antiques & Collectables, 437 Dawson Street, Sault Sainte Marie MI 49783–2119, USA Tel: 906 635 0356

TOP ⊞ The Top Banana Antiques Mall, 1 New Church Street, Tetbury, Gloucestershire GL8 4DS Tel: 0871 288 1102 info@topbananaantiques.com www.topbananaantiques.com

TOT ⊞ Totem, 168 Stoke Newington, Church Street, London N16 0JL Tel: 020 7275 0234 sales@totemrecords.com www.totemrecords.com

TQA 🔨 TreasureQuest Auction Galleries, Inc, 2581 Jupiter Park Drive, Suite E 9 Jupiter, Florida 33458, USA Tel: 561 741 0777 www.tqag.com

TRA ⊞ Tramps, 8 Market Place, Tuxford, Newark, Nottinghamshire NG22 0LL Tel: 01777 872 543 info@trampsuk.com

TRM 🔨 Thomson, Roddick & Medcalf Ltd, 60 Whitesands, Dumfries DG1 2RS, Scotland Tel: 01387 255366 www.thomsonroddick.com

TWI ⊞† Twinkled, 1st floor, Old Petrol Station, 11–17 Stockwell Street, Greenwich, London SE10 Tel: 020 84880930/07940471574 info@twinkled.net www.twinkled.net

TWO ⊞ Two P'S Tel: 01252 647965 Mob: 07710 277726 twops@ntlworld.com

UCO ⊞ Unique Collections, 52 Greenwich Church Street, London SE10 9BL Tel: 020 8305 0867 glen@uniquecollections.co.uk www.uniquecollections.co.uk

UD ⊞† Upstairs Downstairs, 40 Market Place, Devizes, Wiltshire SN10 1JG Tel: 01380 730266 or 07974 074220 devizesantiques@amserve.com

VB ⊞ Variety Box, 16 Chapel Place, Tunbridge Wells, Kent TN1 1YQ Tel: 01892 531868

VBo ⊞ Vernon Bowden Tel: 01202 763806

VEC 🔨† Vectis Auctions Ltd, Fleck Way, Thornaby, Stockton-on-Tees, Cleveland TS17 9JZ Tel: 01642 750616 admin@vectis.co.uk www.vectis.co.uk

VICT ⊞† June Victor, Vintage Modes, S041–43, Alfie's Antique Market, 13–25 Church Street, London NW8 8DT Tel: 020 7723 6066 Mob: 07740 704723

VK ⊞† Vivienne King of Panache Tel: 01934 814759 Mob: 07974 798871 Kingpanache@aol.com

VS 🔨†T. Vennett-Smith, 11 Nottingham Road, Gotham, Nottinghamshire NG11 0HE Tel: 0115 983 0541 info@vennett-smith.com www.vennett-smith.com

VSP 🔨 Van Sabben Poster Auctions, PO Box 2065, 1620 EB Hoorn, The Netherlands Tel: 31 229 268203 uboersma@sabbenposterauctions.nl www.vsabbenposterauctions.nl

WAA ⊞ Woburn Abbey Antiques Centre, Woburn, Bedfordshire MK17 9WA Tel: 01525 290350 antiques@woburnabbey.co.uk

WAB ⊞ Warboys Antiques Tel: 01480 463891 john.lambden@virgin.net

WAC ⊞ Worcester Antiques Centre, Reindeer Court, Mealcheapen Street, Worcester WR1 4DF Tel: 01905 610680 WorcsAntiques@aol.com

WAL 🔨†Wallis & Wallis, West Street Auction Galleries, Lewes, East Sussex BN7 2NJ Tel: 01273 480208 auctions@wallisandwallis.co.uk www.wallisandwallis.co.uk

WAm ⊞ Williams Amusements Ltd, Bluebird House, Povey Cross Road, Horley, Surrey RH6 0AG Tel: 01293 782222 Mob: 07970 736486 adrian@williams-amusements.co.uk www.williams-amusements.co.uk

WeA ⊞ Wenderton Antiques Tel: 01227 720295 (by appointment only)

WHO ⊞ The Who Shop International Ltd, 4 Station Parade, High Street North, East Ham, London E6 1JD Tel: 020 8471 2356 Mob: 07977 430948 whoshop@hilly.com www.thewhoshop.com

WiB ⊞ Wish Barn Antiques, Wish Street, Rye, East Sussex TN31 7DA Tel: 01797 226797

WilP 🔨 W&H Peacock, 26 Newnham Street, Bedford MK40 3JR Tel: 01234 266366

WL 🔨 Wintertons Ltd, Lichfield Auction Centre, Fradley Park, Lichfield, Staffordshire WS13 8NF Tel: 01543 263256 enquiries@wintertons.co.uk www.wintertons.co.uk

WO ⊞ Woodville Antiques, The Street, Hamstreet, Ashford, Kent TN26 2HG Tel: 01233 732981 woodvilleantiques@yahoo.co.uk

WOS ⊞ Wheels of Steel, Grays Antique Market, Stand A12–13, Unit B10 Basement, 1–7 Davies Mews, London W1Y 2LP Tel: 020 7629 2813

WP ⊞† British Notes, PO Box 257, Sutton, Surrey SM3 9WW Tel: 020 8641 3224 pamwestbritnotes@compuserve.com www.britishnotes.co.uk

WRe ⊞ Walcot Reclamations, 108 Walcot Street, Bath, Somerset BA1 5BG Tel: 01225 444404

WW 🔨 Woolley & Wallis, Salisbury Salerooms, 51–61 Castle Street, Salisbury, Wiltshire SP1 3SU Tel: 01722 424500/411854 mail@salisbury.w-w.co.uk www.w-w.co.uk

YC ⊞† Yesterday Child Tel: 01908 583403 djbarrington@btinternet.com

YR ⊞ Yorkshire Relics of Haworth, 11 Main Street, Haworth, Yorkshire BD22 8DA Tel: 01535 642218 Mob: 07971 701278

YT ⊞ Yew Tree Antiques, Woburn Abbey Antiques Centre, Woburn, Bedfordshire MK17 9WA Tel: 01525 872514

Index to Advertisers

Index

Bold numbers refer to information and pointer boxes